LEARNING RESOURCES CTR/NEW ENGLAND TECH

3 0147 1000 9769

W9-CZB-700

NEW ENGLAND INSTITUTE
OF TECHNOLOGY
LEARNING RESOURCES CENTER

CENTURY

YALE UNIVERSITY PRESS   NEW HAVEN AND LONDON

THE ☆ ☆ ☆ ☆

AMERICAN

CENTURY

The Rise and Decline of the

United States as a World Power

DONALD W. WHITE

-99   # 3265106

Copyright © 1996 by Donald W. White.
All rights reserved.
This book may not be reproduced, in whole or in part, including illustrations, in any form (beyond that copying permitted by Sections 107 and 108 of the U.S. Copyright Law and except by reviewers for the public press), without written permission from the publishers.

Excerpts from "Colloquy for the States" and "America Was Promises," from *Collected Poems, 1917–1982* by Archibald MacLeish. Copyright © 1985 by The Estate of Archibald MacLeish. Reprinted by permission of Houghton Mifflin Co. All rights reserved.

Excerpts from "Iron Horse," from *Collected Poems, 1947–1980* by Allen Ginsberg. Copyright © 1966 by Allen Ginsberg. Reprinted by permission of HarperCollins Publishers, Inc., and Penguin Books Ltd.

Excerpts from "America," from *Collected Poems, 1947–1980* by Allen Ginsberg. Copyright © 1956, 1959 by Allen Ginsberg. Copyright renewed. Reprinted by permission of HarperCollins Publishers, Inc., and Penguin Books Ltd.

Set in Times Roman and CgTowerCd type by The Composing Room of Michigan, Inc.
Printed in the United States of America by Book Crafters, Inc., Chelsea, Michigan.

Library of Congress Cataloging-in-Publication Data
White, Donald Wallace.
The American century: The rise and decline of the United States as a world power / Donald W. White.
p.   cm.
Includes bibliographical references (p.) and index.
ISBN 0-300-05721-0 (cloth: alk. paper)
       0-300-07878-1 (pbk.: alk. paper)
1. United States—Foreign relations—1945–1989.   2. United States—Politics and government—1945–1989.   I. Title.
E744.W538   1996
327.73—dc20   95-506
                        CIP

A catalogue record for this book is available from the British Library.

The paper in this book meets the guidelines for permanence and durability of the Committee on Production Guidelines for Book Longevity of the Council on Library Resources.

10   9   8   7   6   5   4   3   2

To my mother and father,
and to my students

CONTENTS

PREFACE

The origins of this study lie in the experience and education of a post–World War II youth. When I was a boy, I learned in school from textbooks depicting skyscrapers, wheat fields, mile-long factories, oil derricks, and the other symbols of prosperity, supported by the statistics of industrial production and standard of living. They called America an affluent society and the most powerful of world powers. America had its faults—racial segregation and pockets of poverty—but, the textbooks implied, these failings could be overcome by men and women of good will using the resources at their command. When I traveled by railroad from a suburban home in the northern New Jersey hills to New York City, I passed from streams and fields to factories with smoking stacks, power-generating plants, and great fuel tanks, over multilevel engineering feats combining tunnels and tressels, and beneath the soaring New Jersey Turnpike, until beyond a tunnel, there appeared the skyline of New York City dominated by the spire of the Empire State Building. Crossing the Hudson River by ferry, I saw in the harbor ocean liners and freighters entering or departing with commerce of the world's greatest port. I wondered why.

Why did America—as one book declared at the time—have the greatest national industrial output on earth; the largest merchant marine at sea; the largest number of transport and commercial airplanes in the sky; an agricultural plant capable of contributing to feeding hungry peoples; the greatest national production of steel, petroleum, cotton, and other vital products; vast holdings of monetary gold and silver; the most powerful navy that had ever sailed the five oceans; and the biggest and hardest-hitting air force the world had ever known? I was never satisfied with the lists of these assets that sufficed for the explanations in textbooks. The answers were not that easy. It was not just because of America's talents, and it was not just because other centers of power in a war-weary world had fallen on hard times. The significance of an elusive mixture of elements was uncertain to me.

When I went to college, I began to direct my studies toward understanding how nations had achieved exceptional world positions. But by the time I had written a prospective senior thesis on the theories of history to which were attributed the rise and expansion of nations, I had to adjust my thinking to new realities—to deal with the decline of power.

After another America was taking form in the 1960s and early 1970s—its society divided by protests and its military mired in the jungles of Vietnam—as I entered graduate school, I faced new questions. Why was the nation being torn from within? Why was its prowess in trade lessening? Why was its massive military power ineffectual?

The answers in the textbooks, once unsatisfying, were now worthless. I had mastered statistics and geopolitical theories—the levels of steel production and computer chip output, the rate of capital investment, and the first principles of Mackinder, Spengler, and Toynbee. My readings on the cold war had revealed the lack of a generally recognized context in which to study the logic of American internal dynamics during the post–World War II period. The traditional accounts of the cold war, uncritical of government policy, were oblivious to dangers, and the revisionist interpretations, rooted in economic or Marxist theory, lacked awareness of the benefits of national strength. Neither argument addressed the fundamental issues of rise and decline.

My goal was to understand how this world I knew had come to be, its virtues and faults, because I also wanted to know what had gone wrong. I sought a means of organizing economic, social, cultural, and political attitudes within the context of America's place in the world. To accomplish this study, I read for a period of years all I could of the great bulk of primary source material, traveled across reaches of the country, interviewed those who had lived through events, and immersed myself in the period's popular culture of film, music, television, and radio. For whatever limitations the study has, I alone am responsible.

A work of many years and vast scope would not have been accomplished without the generous help of many people. First, I am indebted to Paul Baker, a professor, colleague, and friend for many years. He was my dissertation adviser, when many of the ideas of this book were taking shape, and I want to express my deepest thanks for all he has done since he allowed me to embark on a study of unusually broad scope. His unselfish and honest guidance then and since, his warmth of encouragement, and patient dedication to fair-minded thought were invaluable. I also want to thank the members of my dissertation committee. I am especially grateful to Irwin Unger for impressing on me the need for clarity of thought and for his constructive suggestions on careful writing. David Reimers challenged me to ask significant questions in examining the validity of my ideas and methods. I also thank Albert Romasco and Vincent Carosso for their help and inspiration. Marilyn Young, the chair of the New York University History Department, read with insight parts of various drafts. I thank too Thomas Bender, Carl Prince, David Hicks, Frederick Schult, and Michael Lutzker.

I am indebted to some leading historians of international affairs. At a critical point Akira Iriye encouraged me to proceed with this larger study after he had read one of my journal articles presenting the arguments of part 1 of this book. John Lewis Gaddis offered an exceptionally insightful evaluation of the opening chapters. From McGeorge Bundy I gained a sense of the political world, apart from the world of ideas and intellect to which scholars retreat. My years of work assisting him in his massive study of the political decision-makers of nuclear weapons taught me a great deal about the constraints under which government officials are compelled to operate. His encouragment of my project, which necessarily departs from certain policies he participated in making as national security adviser to Presidents Kennedy and Johnson, is a measure of his generous and open-minded spirit, and his rigorous evaluations of some early drafts still leave me in awe of one of the most brilliant individuals I have known.

I also wish to note the great assistance rendered by the librarians and archivists of the many institutions I visited in the course of my research. I have spent countless days over many seasons at the New York Public Library on Forty-second Street, where the excitement of doing primary source research, often in dusty, dated periodicals and ancient books, unfortunately now crumbling, first took hold while I was researching my senior college thesis. I have returned again and again to use the library's unique collections up to the final efforts of checking this book's citations. The librarians at the Elmer Holmes Bobst Library of New York University have also extended innumerable courtesies and unflagging aid, particularly in the reference room, the social science division, the microform center, and the Avery Fisher Media Center. To archivists, I am most grateful: at the National Archives and the Library of Congress in Washington, D.C.; at the Franklin D. Roosevelt Library, Hyde Park, N.Y.; at the Harry S. Truman Library, Independence, Mo.; at the Dwight D. Eisenhower Library, Abilene, Kan.; at the Time, Inc., Archives, New York City; at Columbia University Library, New York City; at Yale University Library, New Haven, Conn.; and at Princeton University Library, Princeton, N.J. I especially appreciate the help of Edward Reese at the Military Archives Division of the National Archives, and of David Haight at the Dwight D. Eisenhower Library.

Supporting my research was a generous grant from the National Endowment for the Humanities. The funds helped to provide a block of time so essential to productive scholarship. I am also appreciative for postdoctoral research funds from the History Department at New York University.

Formative chapters of the book originally appeared in several journals, and I wish to thank their editors and editorial readers for their valuable comments, especially Michael Hogan of *Diplomatic History,* Norris Hundley of *Pacific Historical Review,* Jerry Bentley of *Journal of World History,* and Robin Higham of *Journal of the West.* Jack Hopper brought his editing skill and fresh perspective to a draft of the completed book manuscript.

I don't know how to thank properly my students, graduate and undergraduate. Colloquia and seminar classes on foreign policy and culture offered uplifting discussion and beneficial critique of parts of the manuscript. Some outstanding graduate students read extended sections of the book at various stages: David Cowen, Saverio Giovacchini, Peter Braunstein, Renqiu Yu, James Eber, and David Gluck. This book is truly for my students. When I was finishing the manuscript for publication, they successfully nominated me for an Outstanding Teaching Award of the College of Arts and Science at New York University. I have firmly believed that scholarly research and excellent teaching are not at odds but are interdependent, and that teachers may learn from the questions and insights of students as much as students may learn from the knowledge and wisdom of teachers. At least, I recall the influence a few teachers had on me in public school and college: Ruth Ann Wichelman, who in a sixth-grade classroom first opened up to me the wonders of world history and comparative geography through maps and original outlines; James Nicholas and William Gilliam, who in high school expanded this knowledge of America and the world; and in college Alban Hoopes, who revealed in his masterful lectures on diplomatic history both the irony in history and the joy of learning it.

The association with Yale University Press has been long and fruitful. My editor, Charles Grench, has offered enthusiastic support and valued friendly advice at every stage of the publication process. Otto Bohlmann was instrumental in meticulously cutting a manuscript that was considerably longer than the final version. My thanks too to the anonymous outside readers, who made thoughtful suggestions. To those who helped in many ways but whom I neglect to mention, I express my apologies.

My brother, Richard White, a former professor of English, read extended versions of the manuscript, offering suggestions to improve the literary quality. My grandmother, Mrs. Donald Wallace, granted me permission to spend weeks over several summers writing at her cottage at Cranberry Lake, N.J. My mother and my father were most generous and supportive over this enduring effort.

PROLOGUE

Throughout history, civilizations have arisen and reached outward beyond their borders. From their heartlands and capital cities have stretched trade connections of vast complexity, elaborate networks of social institutions, widespread communications systems, and far-flung garrisons. Their peoples have possessed worldviews of their origins, destiny, and roles. For Romans, the worldview was a Pax Romana embodied in a divine Caesar; for Arabs, it was Islam; for Englishmen, it was the imperialism of the "White Man's Burden"; for Soviet Russia, it was Marxist communism. The language, law, religion, politics, and technology of these societies influenced lands far beyond the home territories even after once powerful empires had crumbled or disappeared.

The growth, flourishing, and decline of the world roles of civilizations is a fundamental problem of history, often involving the effects of such forces as climate, geography, and resources on the character of societies. The worldviews conceived of various dynamic factors in the creation and demise of the roles, including the expanses of territory making up homelands and empires; the size, youth, and vitality of populations; the technological versatility and wealth of economic systems; and the morale and outlook of the people at various times and in various places.

As the United States rose to power, flourished, and began to decline in the world, Americans, like peoples of earlier nations, expressed views of their world role at each stage. They weighed the destiny that had created their role of extraordinary range and involvement. They projected the manifestations of that role in trade, aid, culture, diplomacy, and war; and they deliberated, perplexed, over the eventual crumbling of that world role.

This book studies the ways Americans placed their nation into the mainstream of world history. It looks at the nation in the world through the eyes of contemporaries and, by exploring their writings and records, evaluates their impressions against the totality of events with which they dealt. Their thoughts and experiences raise questions of nations and societies: What were the origins of a new world role? Why did that role develop, and then eventually enter crisis and decline? What objectives did Americans seek in the world? What was successful in foreign policy, what failed, and why?

1

Theories of the United States in the World

In American history several explanations of the national experience in the world have recurred. One theory holds that environmental forces shaped the nation's place in the world. The Americans who expanded their land from one ocean to another often accounted for their part in the world by their geographical habitat and climate. In the 1840s the publisher John L. O'Sullivan declared that the Manifest Destiny of Americans was "to overspread the continent allotted by Providence for the free development of our yearly multiplying millions." Along the passage of their expansion, whether in Texas, California, or Oregon, O'Sullivan believed, Americans would spread the virtues of commerce and develop resources. The idea of territorial forces captured the attention of the press and Congress, where Rep. Robert Winthrop of Massachusetts saw the "right of our manifest destiny" opening a "new chapter in the law of nations."[1]

Later in the nineteenth century, the theory that territory and its continuous settlement and expansion explained American power and outlook on the world received serious historical treatment by Frederick Jackson Turner, a professor of history at the University of Wisconsin and later at Harvard. Delivering his famous address in 1893 entitled "The Significance of the Frontier in American History," Turner declared that in the nation's westward advance, the frontier—which he never precisely defined but measured by the decennial federal census and described as the meeting point of "savagery and civilization"—had forged a new society. The expanse of territory, he argued, had supplied that society with resources—timber, precious metals, grain, cotton, and livestock—to achieve powerful nationhood. More than that, concurring with O'Sullivan, Turner believed that the frontier had shaped the people's worldview of "manifest destiny." He was certain that obscured in the American forests would be found "the meaning of America in world history."[2]

Turner determined that frontier influences impelled the United States to move beyond its continental borders. As open land in North America disappeared, the country expanded abroad, taking colonies, developing trade, and exerting power. "For nearly three centuries the dominant fact in American life has been expansion," Turner wrote in the mid-1890s. "That these energies of expansion will no longer operate would be a rash prediction." After the Spanish-American War in 1898 appeared to confirm his forecast, the historian did not find it strange for the nation to be involved in colonization far removed from contiguous continental territory. Turner saw American overseas expansion as a revolution in world politics. The nation had not only struck down the empire that had discovered the New World but had also laid the foundation for an empire of its own, stretching from Puerto Rico to the Philippines to the Isthmian Canal.[3]

The repercussions of the frontier experience in forming a world role, however, are uncertain. The great European powers, England, France, and the Netherlands, which had not known frontier growth like that in America, led the world in expansion by taking colonies on every continent. Russia, Canada, and Brazil had vast territories, multitudinous resources, and diversified climates, but their environmental similarities were not matched by similarities in either power or outlook. Finally, we must return to Turner's question about the influence of the frontier once the land was filled. Turner felt that as attractive and dynamic as the natural environment was, the dense forests had been burned and plowed, the open plains had been fenced off by private hands, and the settlement of the frontier as the nation's consuming activity was at an end. The ways a terminate pioneering experience could alter an entire society's part in the world had not been demonstrated.[4]

Another theory attempted to explain the American part in the world by the nature of the people, their inherent character. This theory relied on the historical development that North America had been populated mainly by immigrants from Europe, early on from the British Isles and northern countries and then, after the 1880s until about the first decade of the twentieth century, from southern and eastern regions. Toward the end of the nineteenth century the United States was becoming a world power, ranked with the great Western European nations, raising questions concerning why the United States and Europe possessed the capability to extend Western influence over the globe.

In 1859 the English naturalist Charles Darwin published his *On the Origin of the Species,* proposing the hypothesis that natural selection had favored the higher forms of life over the lesser. The work created a great stir not only among scientists but also among other intellectuals, who applied the biological principle of evolution to people and nations. The success of a people's industry, social order, and colonies, they proclaimed, was the result of the survival of the fittest. Such ideas may sound quaint to the modern ear, or dangerous after the institutions of racial segregation and the extremes of Nazi Germany's racial aggrandizement; however, Darwin himself proposed that the reason one nation rose, became more powerful, and spread more widely than another, was natural selection. That progress depended on an increase in population in addition to a people's intellectual and moral faculties. Darwin further expressed a sentiment about America's place in the world. "There is apparently much truth in the belief that the wonderful progress of the United States, as well as the character of the people, are the results of natural selection; the more energetic, restless, and courageous men from all parts of Europe having emigrated during the last ten or twelve generations to that great country, and having there succeeded best. . . . All other series of events—as that which resulted in the culture of mind in Greece, and that which resulted in the empire of Rome—only appear to have purpose and value when viewed in connection with, or rather as subsidiary to . . . the great stream of Anglo-Saxon emigration to the west."[5]

Chief among the adherents to Darwin's theory as a social philosophy was the English philosopher Herbert Spencer, who, like Darwin, found the basis of national power in both the biological struggle for survival and the competition for the highest intelligence, energy, bravery, and patriotism. American Social Darwinists assimilated these ideas, implying that Americans had to seize whatever sphere of the earth they could. They had to behave aggressively to build an empire. They needed to extend their business and trade into the world's markets. They were required to build a modern steam-driven navy and to obtain coaling stations in foreign harbors. They were compelled to enter a missionary struggle for the hearts of people. Expansion appeared as a necessity determined by scientific law.[6]

One of the first to seek a correlation between race and America's world affairs was the Harvard-trained historian and philosopher John Fiske. "The day is at hand when four-fifths of the human race will trace its pedigree to English forefathers," he wrote, "as four-fifths of the white people in the United States trace their pedigree to-day." For John W. Burgess, a professor at Columbia University who after study in Germany organized Columbia's graduate work in politics, the theories of natural science were applicable to colonial policy. His findings: the "highest talent for political organization" had been "exhibited by the Aryan nations," and of all the Aryans, "the Teuton really dominates the world by his superior political genius." Josiah Strong, a Congregational minister from the Midwest, wrote in his bestselling *Our Country* that the Anglo-Saxon race, which was not only to be the most populous race in the world but was already producing the "highest civilization," was to find its great seat of power in North America. Strong predicted, "If I read not amiss, this powerful race will move down upon Mexico, down upon Central and South America, out upon the islands of the sea, over upon Africa and beyond. And can any one doubt that the result of this competition of races will be the 'survival of the fittest'?"[7]

As they had done with doctrines of Manifest Destiny, influential government figures asserted that race was a reality that determined a nation's role. Leading these politicians, whose ranks included Secretary of State John Hay and Senators Albert T. Beveridge and Henry Cabot Lodge, was President Theodore Roosevelt. Once a student of Professor Burgess, Roosevelt believed that the nation required a colonial policy. In *The Winning of the West,* published in 1889, Roosevelt wrote that for three centuries "the spread of the English-speaking peoples over the world's waste spaces has been not only the most striking feature in the world's history, but also the event of all others most far-reaching in its effects and its importance." On the train with his Rough Riders to their departure point for Cuba to fight the Spanish in 1898, Roosevelt read Edmond Demolins's *Anglo-Saxon Superiority,* which maintained that the English-speaking peoples were superior to Continental Europeans. Roosevelt agreed, confidently extending that superiority to "American 'militarism.'"[8]

These themes reappeared in the later "scientific" histories of Madison Grant and Lothrop Stoddard. Grant, a chairman of the New York Zoological Society, and Stoddard, a scholar who had been exposed to theories of racial capabilities at Harvard, argued that race, not environment, climate, or soil, was the moving force of history. The relationship was primeval. "Would you understand what is happening in the world, why nations act as they do, what their relations are to America, and what our policy should be toward them?" Stoddard asked in the *Saturday Evening Post* in 1924. To understand world politics, he argued, required recognition of the physical characteristics of peoples and other "racial factors."[9]

The implication was that because a particular race had conquered much of the world, it was inherently superior. But nowhere did this "scientific" approach to history prove the relationship between race and world affairs. No proof existed that the color of one's skin related to intelligence or creativity, or that collectively one race was better adapted than another to the development of cultures or world powers. Temporary advancement of one people in science or industry did not imply a natural superiority, because these fields of endeavor could be learned, imitated, and improved. Critics of Social Darwinism pointed out that race theories were consciously or unconsciously used to justify discrimination at home or colonial exploitation abroad. A number of Social Darwinists became anti-imperialists too. Theodore Roosevelt in time regretted his empire-building racial ideas, discovering in them about 1910 "an element of unconscious and rather pathetic humor in the simplicity of half a century ago." A confessed desire of the later race theorists was to save the traditional make-up of American stock by restricting immigration, fearing "a menace to the very existence of our race." This was personal prejudice, not scientific observation. Theories that race determined a nation's role in the world were fallacious and absurd.[10]

A third theory expressed the view that the nation's world role was the product of the economy and power of production. The enormous growth of industry since the Industrial Revolution had deeply influenced observers of the changes in manufacturing, transportation, and communication. As industrial technique came into being in England in the eighteenth century and then spread to other countries, the Scottish political economist Adam Smith wrote his seminal study *The Wealth of Nations,* which posed as a major question why some nations were richer than others and why some grew poorer, for Smith related wealth to a nation's success in trade, arms, and building colonial empires. He found the answer in laissez-faire capitalism, the skill and initiative of a nation's workers to produce. Observing America not as a nation but as a colony when he wrote in 1776, Smith recognized that "there are no colonies of which the progress has been more rapid than that of the English in North America." This development he attributed to two main causes: plenty of good land and the liberty of the people to manage their own affairs their own way.[11]

As industrialization grew through the middle of the nineteenth century, the German philosopher Karl Marx, spending hours in the British Museum reading and writing, arrived at a theory of economy diametrically opposed to that of Adam Smith. But Marx shared with Smith a belief that economic dynamics accounted for the rise and fall of nations in history. The capitalist struggle for economic advantage, Marx admitted, had originally caused the rise of modern states and explained the nineteenth-century imperialist thrust of the European powers. The United States, Marx wrote in *Das Kapital* in 1867, though an independent nation, was, because of its economic ties, "still only a Colony of Europe." But America was industrializing as effectively as Europe, and after the 1917 Bolshevik Revolution set up the Soviet state, Vladimir Lenin adapted the Marxist thesis to the developments of the twentieth century. Since the Spanish-

American War, Lenin noted, the United States had been developing as a power, younger and stronger than any in Europe, and was building its own economic monopoly by organizing large cartels and underselling other nations' goods.[12]

In the period of Progressive reform early in the twentieth century, historians analyzed foreign relations with an emphasis on economic as well as on political motives and forces. Among the American historians to make this case, Charles Beard was foremost. A Progressive rather than a Marxist, Beard nevertheless agreed with the Marxists in stressing the importance of economics in driving politics and world affairs. Beard fundamentally altered the writing of American history in 1913 with *An Economic Interpretation of the Constitution of the United States,* which attributed the legacy of the founding fathers not to disinterested enlightenment but to self-interest. Beard extended his theories to affirm an economic basis for the rise and fall of nations. "Whatever the formulas for the ownership and use of property," he wrote, "the state— despotic or democratic—must secure for itself an economic underwriting sufficient to sustain it or it will in fact wither away, as many states and empires have in the past." Politics "must have an economic basis or perish." Even the military, because of its enormous demand for materials, was more than ever before dependent on economic production. "With economics left out of account," Beard declared, "political science cannot rise much above the level of astrology."[13]

Beard believed that the system of production provided more than elemental power. It was the source of the national outlook abroad. In *The Idea of National Interest,* published in 1934, Beard located a pivot of national motivation in commercial expansion. He stated his theory fearlessly: "The Government is not now and never has been an independent engine operating in a vacuum under its own momentum"; rather, it had ties to a profit economy by the common ideas and connections among people in influential positions. Men in government could not escape a philosophy of private advancement inherent in an economy characterized by intense competition for advantage, for raw materials, and for markets. "In short, domestic politics and economics enter into foreign policy and influence its course."[14]

But Beard never did come to grips with what he himself called "the problem of great history, in which all economic, political, military, and other events take place." Inevitably, by the 1940s he had come to realize the central problem of historiography and philosophy: "the origin, nature, dynamics, and capacities of human beings in relation to one another and their environment." He believed that the human mind could not grasp original causes or the dynamics of civilization in the flow of personalities and events, functioning independently in particular ways and places. Even to say "economics comes first and determines politics" was an arbitrary act of will, Beard admitted, and such a formula was "untenable in view of relevant historical knowledge."

Beard had frankly demolished his own economic thesis more effectively than most of his critics had. He had been a victim of his immersion in the overwhelming industrial thinking and capitalistic business ethic of his day, and he came out of his years of study ready to give "political man" and "military man" an important place alongside "economic man."[15]

Mythic Explanations

The theses about the social forces of land, people, and economy were expressed and taught as scientifically acceptable principles to explain the phenomenon of the rise and decline of nations—that is, as explanations of reality. But the actions of a people are not capable of prediction; hence they cannot be reduced to science. In attempting to explain American development, Manifest Destiny, Social Darwinism, and Economic Determinism were myths rather than laws of human conduct. Each myth represented a significant reality of its day—Manifest Destiny echoed the open expanse of a vast frontier; Social Darwinism, European immigration to the New World amid the expansion of Western civilization; and Economic Determinism, the increasing industrialization of economic production. But none of these myths completely comprehended the dynamic of national activity in the world.[16]

The theories had value as myths. Myths are imaginative traditions about the nature, history, and prospects of a society. Myths are not simply stories. They are part of the fabric of a society's life, experience, and beliefs, justifying institutions, customs, and values. Leaders and intellectuals used these myths to interpret the course of events of their experience, to tell the saga of a people or nation, supporting their sense of unity, purpose, confidence, and pride. These explanatory myths—Manifest Destiny, Social Darwinism, and Economic Determinism—embodied symbolic conceptions that were ambiguous enough to have different meanings to different people. Their functional nature was to mediate disagreements, sometimes inconsistently, and to express the general attitudes of the people of a society.[17]

The myths provide a beginning in the search for a dynamic of world affairs, for they unfolded a varied range of explanations. The mythic worldview conceptions enable us to see the problem of a society's development in the world not as determined by environment, inherent characteristics, or economics, but as a process involving many forces.[18]

Though scholars have done much research on foreign confrontations, little has been written about the underlying conceptions. The orthodox view—that the United States was time and again forced to confront aggressive enemy states—does not take into account the domestic forces that shaped America's world role. It does not explain that role any more than Japan's attack on Pearl Harbor or the Soviet occupation of Eastern Europe explains the entirety of American involvement in World War II or the cold war. In attempting to understand the forces behind foreign policy within the country, the usual recourse has been to the economic theories of Charles Beard and the New Left revisionists. They argued that domestic economic conditions essentially determined the main foreign thrust as the search for markets or the protection of them.

This intellectual development does not account for the complexity of factors that shape a nation's outlook. Both the orthodox and revisionist interpretations were themselves phenomena of the cold war experience and must be studied as parts of the history of the country's myths and thought.[19]

New Myths: The American Century and the Century of the Common Man

When Arnold J. Toynbee, the English historian of civilization, was concluding in the early 1950s his monumental ten-volume *A Study of History,* which had occupied him since the 1920s, he described alternative mythic conceptions representing American social thought concerning humankind following World War II. The influence of North America on Western civilization, according to Toynbee, would depend on whether the twentieth century came to be described as the "American Century" or the "Century of the Common Man." In spite of the brevity of these "two competing 'slogans,'" Toynbee wrote, they brought out the essence of the issue of the establishment and maintenance of a world order.[20]

One of the first new myths offered was the "American Century." On the eve of American entry into World War II, Henry Luce, the publisher of the magazines *Time* and *Life,* proposed this conception of American leadership as a preeminent power. Luce's ideas took form in speeches in scattered cities across the nation, and he made them widely known in an editorial in *Life* in February 1941 and later that year in a small book. The twentieth century, Luce affirmed, was to be "The American Century. . . . It is [ours] not only in the sense that we happen to live in it but ours also because it is America's first century as a dominant power in the world."[21]

A second myth, the "Century of the Common Man," was conceived by Henry Wallace, the vice president of the United States during Franklin Roosevelt's wartime term as president. He envisioned an egalitarian society of common men and women of all nations seeking common interests. On May 8, 1942, Wallace delivered a speech to the Free World Association, in which he said that "the century on which we are entering—the century which will come out of this war—can be and must be the century of the common man," with farmers and workers seeking their own freedom, education, and equal opportunities. The speech was reprinted in newspapers, magazines, and his 1943 book, *The Century of the Common Man.*[22]

Presidents, senators and representatives, philosophers, historians, political scientists, economists, anthropologists, theologians, and journalists discussed the conceptions of the American Century and the Century of the Common Man, making them collective representations, rather than the work of single minds. Like the earlier myths, the American Century and the Century of the Common Man were imaginative traditions about the nature, history, and prospects of the society in the world. They connoted many things to different people across the political spectrum, embracing ideas that helped to define the subsequent orthodox and revisionist interpretations. Among the wartime intellectual spokespersons lauding the American Century for offering peace and stability were the columnist Dorothy Thompson and the playwright Robert Sherwood. Liberals and leftists, including Norman Thomas, the leader of the Socialist Party, and Freda Kirchwey, the editor of the *Nation,* attacked the American Century as imperialistic and Hitler-like. Charles Beard and the anthropologist Margaret Mead discussed it as a significant choice for the nation's future. Reinhold Niebuhr, the theologian, was concerned about the pride inherent in the American Century's "Messianic" presumptions. On the floor of the House of Representatives, Martin J. Kennedy, a Democratic congressman from New York, introduced a resolution to institute a "Committee to Preserve and Propagate Democracy," which he stated was inspired by Luce's article, and he addressed the House on the subject of the American Century.[23]

After the war, posing the question whether this was "The American Century," Saul K. Padover, a historian and assistant secretary of the interior during the New Deal, recorded that the "great historic event of our time" was "the emergence of the United States as *the* super-power on the globe." The father of power politics, Hans J. Morgenthau, writing his classic treatise *Politics among Nations,* noted "the conception of the 'American Century,' a world dominion based upon American power," and the American Century was discussed in Council on Foreign Relations publications as reminiscent of Manifest Destiny. The Republican senators Ralph Flanders and Robert Taft endorsed the American Century as a basis for policymaking. And President Harry Truman was on record that "this is America's century," adding that it should "be more than that. We want it to be humanity's century."[24]

President Roosevelt praised Wallace for the Century of the Common Man speech, and after publication of the book he wrote Wallace that he was "delighted" with it, though he did not endorse specific proposals. Conservative critics and liberal supporters debated the value of the Century of the Common Man. Dorothy Thompson praised Wallace's conception no less than Luce's; the vice president had made the "first statement from a high American personality giving this war a real sense." The commentator Raymond Gram Swing wrote in *PM* that the speech "should be read by all Americans" because Wallace had given voice to their aspirations. Maj. George Fielding Eliot, a military news analyst, called it "the greatest speech on this war which has been delivered by any public man of the United Nations since the conflict began." Excerpts of the speech became parts of editorials, sermons, radio discussions, movies—including Frank Capra's documentary *Why We Fight*—and even comic books. Neither conception remained solely with elite thinkers. They became widespread as polls revealed that Americans, nationwide, were thinking about the postwar visions of the American Century and the Century of the Common Man.[25]

What, then, can these two myths of a world role tell us in their original texts? Certain common themes emerge. They reveal fear of foreign threats. The myths agree on the danger to American society of totalitarian states. Luce's first point was that Japan and Germany threatened the United States and its way of life. If Britain, the last of the great Western democracies of Europe to hold out, should falter soon, Luce foresaw in early 1941, a Japanese attack in the South Seas could force Americans to withdraw to Hawaii to "wait." Wallace perceived the threat to American society to be from a totalitarian "slave world." The demagogues were superhuman, defying "God Himself" and turning "Satan . . . loose upon the world." The totalitarians were propagating doctrines that one race was inherently superior to another, and their system degraded the people mentally and politically.[26]

But the myths do not rely exclusively on foreign threats to explain national policy. They deal most tellingly with the nature of the society itself. For Luce, the United States had the capability to create a world order because of American commerce, culture, and prestige. But the American people had not yet recognized their power, so Luce wanted Americans "to accept wholeheartedly our duty and our opportunity as the most power-ful and vital nation in the world and in consequence to exert upon the world the full impact of our influence, for such purposes as we see fit and by such means as we see fit." The United States had to fill the role occupied by previous great powers, which Luce cited as the Roman Empire, the Roman Catholic Church, Genghis Khan, the Ottoman Turks, the Chinese emperors, and nineteenth-century England.[27]

In Wallace's view, Americans shared with other peoples the interest of world order because of a democratic tradition. For 150 years the common men and women had been waging a "Great Revolution of the people." After the American Revolution of 1775, the people had fought in the French Revolution of 1792, the Latin American revolutions of the early 1800s, the German revolution of 1848, and the Russian Revolution of 1917. Some of these struggles, Wallace believed, had gone to excess, but the people, espe-cially those in the United States and Western Europe, had steadily made progress in democratic freedoms and efficient industry. Countries elsewhere had begun to develop in the past twenty years as popular education became widespread.[28]

The myths magnified the confrontation between the United States and the total-itarian states to mammoth proportions. The problems of war and dictatorship in an age of revolution, Luce said, were global. He urged Americans to assume world leadership and believed that "most men living" wanted the twentieth century to be "to a signifi-cant degree an American Century." Wallace believed that the struggle would be tremendous—a "fight to the death between the free world and the slave world." But the common men and women would rise up: "if the rights of the common man are attacked, it unleashes the ferocity of a she-bear who has lost her cub." The United States should contribute its might to the effort because "when the rights of the American people are transgressed, as those rights have been transgressed, the American people will fight with a relentless fury which will drive the ancient Teutonic gods back cowering into their caves." But the common people of many nations would have to act to create a new postwar world.[29]

Certain overriding themes from these myths may provide insight into the origin of the American role. The United States rejected a tradition of aloofness from the world under the threat from totalitarian states. To meet this threat, the United States planned to provide other nations the benefits of its wealth, technology, culture, and aid. The role of the United States would be worldwide, but its exact character was not made entirely clear.

How was the United States to act? In these myths we see alternative visions of the nation in the postwar era—one as a preeminent power, another as a participant in an egalitarian international society. The first was essentially an ethnocentric view, while the second strove to be cosmopolitan. When Wallace described his "Century of the Common Man," he explicitly took the American Century as a point of departure. "Some have spoken of the 'American Century.' I say that . . . out of this war . . . must [come] the century of the common man."[30]

The differences between the myths stemmed from domestic circumstances. Luce believed in the virtue of American business and capitalistic free enterprise and wanted the United States to lead in the world economy. The desirability of profits for Americans was evident. He also had a sincere belief that other people wanted what American industry could offer, because trade carried with it the possibilities of "enormous human progress." Wallace, by contrast, aware of the abuses of capitalism, opposed unregulated free enterprise and international cartels. He criticized German cartels along with those "that serve American greed," and he proposed that they be placed under international control.[31]

But economic policies alone do not account for the differences between the myths. Both Luce and Wallace agreed about the necessity of expanding trade. By eliminating restrictive tariffs, they believed, the enlargement of American markets would benefit workers at home as well as bring technology and goods to other peoples.[32]

The myths represented the humanitarian benefits of aid. Luce proposed that America be the "Good Samaritan of the entire world." It was "the manifest duty of this country to undertake to feed all the people of the world who as a result of this worldwide collapse of civilization are hungry and destitute." For every dollar Americans spent on armaments, Luce wanted them to spend at least a dime to feed the hungry and poor abroad. Farmers could be encouraged to produce greater harvests and "a humanitarian army of Americans" would dispense the food free of charge. Aid was an important goal for Wallace, but only as a temporary measure. Industrial nations should help the young nations get started on the path to industrialization, and he cautioned against any sort of economic imperialism. By learning modern science, the world's people would get enough to eat. The process of gaining a better standard of living had to originate not merely in the United States or England but also in India, China, and Latin America.[33]

The myths also expressed strong ideas regarding the exchange of culture. Luce wanted America to send out through the world its engineering, science, medicine, movies, aircraft, road-building expertise, and education, which would be welcomed by other peoples. He expected ships and planes of America and its allies to go to any region they pleased. Wallace too had grand ideas about sharing information and technology, but he stressed the need for global contributions. India, China, and Latin America had significant parts to play. With American help the common people would set about to build their own industries, so that their children could "eventually pay to the world community all that they have received." Wallace emphasized that technology could be learned by any people and that in the long run there would be no backward peoples. As Indians, Chinese, and Latin Americans became productive mechanics, their standards of living would double and triple.[34]

Regarding the world's political future, the myths expressed disapproval of the old colonial regimes holding peoples in subjugation. Empires went against the egalitarian and democratic American orientation. In his own eyes, Luce had been a consistent critic of British and European imperialism. Freedom, equality of opportunity, and self-reliance, he stated, were characteristic of the American experience, and justice, truth, and charity were ideals inherited from Western civilization. "It now becomes our time to be the powerhouse from which the ideals spread throughout the world and do their mysterious work of lifting the life of mankind from the level of the beasts to what the Psalmist called a little lower than the angels." Wallace spoke out against imperialism and for the emancipation of colonies. "Perhaps it will be America's opportunity to suggest the freedoms and duties by which the common man must live." He stressed, "No nation will have the God-given right to exploit other nations. . . . We ourselves in the United States are no more a master race than the Nazis."[35]

The distinctions between the American Century and the Century of the Common Man are evident. In economic enterprise the American Century held that the job be done directly by American businessmen, and to a lesser extent by diplomatic and governmental institutions. The Century of the Common Man expressed the view that the development of other people had to be their own—with American help, certainly, but not with Americans taking charge. In the exchange of culture, the American Century represented the United States as a generator disseminating its way of life. The Century of the Common Man put forth the hope that each people better its own culture through an international sharing of arts and customs. For the American Century, what was realistic was in the American interest. For the Century of the Common Man, what was realistic was in the common interest of the world's peoples, because policies pursued by the United States that were not also in the interests of others would meet resistance. The American Century sought trade, cultural exchange, and negotiation with friendly nations. The Century of the Common Man sought these relations with all countries regardless of their form of government or economic system, in the firm conviction that the American example would speak for itself.

These myths, which represented the rise of the United States and its manifestations in trade, aid, culture, and alliances, did not foresee exact events or entail notions of decline. They did provide a means to organize thinking about divergent approaches to the world—of national preeminence, and of an international egalitarian society of nations—over the course of America's role in the world.

The Method of Study

The study of social myth has lacked coherent method. Some historians treat ideas as abstractions without regard for social life. Other historians emphasize the social function of thought. A whole study requires recognition that experience shapes the mind, as the mind directs action. Thinkers produce creative thought, but not entirely alone. Communities shape individual thought through discourse that is in turn shaped by events, historic and present. Moreover, thought may lead to social action and influence events.

This work explores the development of myth for the interwoven relationship between thought and experience. It re-creates the conceptions of the mind, where myth takes form, and relates them to the external world and to social action. By examining contemporary explanations for a national role in the world, we may analyze them for significance as to how a people have become aware of themselves, with an identity in history and a place among the world's peoples. We may organize the discourse among political leaders, economists, sociologists, and theologians of diverse groups who helped create the mythic explanations and those who disapproved. We may weigh their perceptions against the world with which the contemporaries dealt, against historical events, and observe tensions between conceptions and the external world. This work suggests conclusions about the consequences of actions that follow myth.

Attempting to trace myths held by the American people is difficult, since no standard measurements are available. Votes cast in presidential elections are of little use, for elections involve many issues, not one. Congressional votes are centered on limited proposals rather than on overall attitudes. But if myths cannot be conveniently quantified, the substantive materials available for study are so vast that their sheer magnitude threatens to overwhelm the historian. The sources can be made manageable through selection.

Considerable material of importance to this study is available in magazines addressed to general audiences and accessible through periodical indexes. Of course, readers do not always approve of what they read. Yet the magazines with the largest circulation would not have been so widely read if their points of view had been too far removed from those of their readers. To attempt to capture this mainstream view, this study deals in part with articles from general-circulation periodicals across the country and supplements them with lesser journals for disparate opinions.

Public opinion polls, which began to adopt scientifically selected and weighted sampling methods in the 1940s, provide some valuable data on popular perceptions unavailable in earlier years. Though polls may not consistently reveal general attitudes with accuracy or represent more than responses of members of select groups, they offer guidelines as direct evidence left behind by the usually "inarticulate" people of the time.

The speeches delivered by politicians in Congress and on the campaign trail reveal the popularity of national issues. The *Congressional Record,* a report of the speeches and statements made on the floor of Congress, along with other material inserted by members, was published daily during legislative sessions. In addition, senators and representatives frequently published books or articles.

The declarations of the presidents to the American people and foreign governments carried the authority of the only spokesmen and leaders elected to represent the nation as a whole. Their *Public Papers* are supplemented by memoirs, autobiographies, and campaign literature, as well as unpublished papers in the presidential libraries.

The works of secretaries of state are instructive on issues of foreign affairs. When presidents have relied heavily on special assistants, as Franklin Roosevelt did with Harry Hopkins and Richard Nixon did with his national security adviser, Henry Kissinger, the papers and memoirs of these officials are additional source materials.

Intellectuals and opinion leaders voiced their points of view of the American role in the world. Essayists, editors, journalists, historians, college professors, politicians, and other thinkers in economics, sociology, and philosophy became advocates or critics. Those in this study were selected, first, because they were among the most significant writers in their fields, and, second, because they related their disciplines to world affairs.

This study is not limited to the written word. It also samples the popular culture of photography, recorded music, film, radio, and television. Documentary films and tapes of radio and television news programs supply evidence of events and the lives of people, and fictional motion pictures and television shows illustrate beliefs and values of the people.

This study is not a history of the foreign policy crises of the cold war. Rather, it concerns the rise, flourishing, and decline of a world role, evaluating contemporaries' explanations of such things as geography, resources, and character of the people during each of these stages. Mythic conceptions do not deliver the truth; they do provide hypotheses that may help us get nearer to the truth. Our task is to reexamine this course of history as a quest, to find the right points of interest and to give them expression.

The rise of the United States to preeminent power and the spread of American economic, cultural, foreign-aid, and political institutions are among the extraordinary occurrences of world history. At the close of the cold war, in a period of the decline of the superpowers and a diffusion of power, an examination of the successes and dilemmas of America's past relationship to the world may be instructive in comprehending what lies ahead.

PART I

The

Origins

of

a

World

Role

☆ ☆ ☆ ☆

1

The

Frontiers

At mid-twentieth century, when the second great world war ended, the United States enjoyed wealth and prosperity unknown in foreign lands and rose to a summit of power. The interests and influence of Americans extended far from home. Their commerce was carried by merchant ships and aircraft to distant cities. The dollar was the standard of international finance and the credits of American banks flowed everywhere. Food, clothing, movies, machines, and science made the American name known throughout the world. The people shared their fortune by distributing charitable aid abroad in quantities without precedent. As after earlier wars in their history, their citizen-soldiers were disbanded and sent home. Yet the government pledged to defend friendly states and kept units of its undefeated army in strategic outposts, sea power that patrolled the oceans, and an air force that guarded the sky. It was a time of general peace and faraway local conflicts; no third world war erupted. The United States kept an order favorable to its allies and demonstrated its art of trade and ways of culture and modern living to aged societies.

The frontiers of American interest that came to gird the world began with the first colonial settlements huddled along the Atlantic coast. At independence in 1783, the United States took possession of forest and lake lands westward to the Mississippi River. In 1803 it expanded across the Great Plains of the Louisiana Territory as far as the Rocky Mountains. In 1819 it gained the Florida peninsula. The flatlands of Texas were incorporated into the Union in 1846, as were the forests of Oregon. At the conclusion of the war with Mexico in 1848, the United States won the southwestern desert regions, the Rocky Mountains, and the western coastal slopes all the way to the Pacific Ocean, leaving only minor adjustments, such as the wedge-shaped Gadsden Purchase in the Southwest, to fill out its linear boundaries.

Through treaties, commitments, and unilateral declarations, the United States made allies with far-flung countries in areas where the interests of American trade, philanthropy, culture, and security were often greater than those of any other power, and the boundaries of some distant lands became the frontiers of these interests. These foreign affiliations first covered the Western Hemisphere. As early as 1823 President James Monroe proclaimed influence over both North and South America by opposing European control or meddling. Here the frontiers stood, for the most part, until around the end of the nineteenth century, when in a burst of expansive energy the United States consolidated its hemispheric interests by taking colonies in the West Indies: Puerto Rico, occupied by troops in the Spanish-American War in 1898, and the Virgin Islands, purchased from Denmark in World War I. The Panama Canal Zone came under the jurisdiction of the United States in 1903. To the west the United States extended its possessions deep into the Pacific Ocean, from Alaska, owned since 1867, to the Hawaiian islands and the Philippines in 1898. To connect the American mainland with the Far East, the United States quickly gained as outposts the islands of Guam and Samoa.

At the turn of the century, the area Americans had committed themselves to defend covered the Western Hemisphere and far beyond: on the Atlantic side, from Greenland to Brazil to Tierra del Fuego at the southern tip of South America; and on the Pacific side, across the world's largest ocean from Alaska to the Philippines. This area of security, Walter Lippmann calculated in 1943, comprised nearly 40 percent of the land surface of the earth. There it remained until World War II.

The outer reach of American interest grew into distant zones once dominated by the empires of the Old World. The frontiers were never precisely defined, though they could be seen in the country's overseas wars and the visible remnants of its military bases, airstrips, and patrol roads. Other evidence of the frontiers was invisible: trade, cultural diffusion, and diplomatic commitments. After World War I, American interest in Britain, France, and Germany dwelled more on the export of products and investment than on political order or military force. Early in World War II, President Franklin Roosevelt denied reports that he had said the American frontier ran along the Rhine River. But he made no secret of his belief that American interests lay along the German border, for he feared that if the lands adjacent to the Rhine, which flowed through the industrial heart of Western Europe, came under the domination of a hostile totalitarian power, American trade and security would be weakened. The Western Hemisphere would be a besieged island.

After victory in the European war, the United States quickly established occupation bases in Germany, and its frontier of interest penetrated deep into Europe. In March 1946, former Prime Minister Winston Churchill, accompanied by President Harry Truman, delivered a speech at Westminster College in Fulton, Missouri, that defined the new area within which the United States was obliged to assert its power. This area came up against regions held by Soviet Russia, which had brought down a communist "iron curtain" running from the Baltic Sea across the Eurasian plain to the Adriatic.

A year later Truman in effect extended this frontier of interest from the Adriatic across the Balkan peninsula, beyond the straits of the Dardanelles linking Europe with Asia, nearly to the edge of the Caucasus Mountains. American financial grants supported the borderlands of Greece and Turkey, and credits and aid flowed throughout Western Europe, even to the British Empire, so recently the major world power. In the

Atlantic, where Europeans had once dominated exploration and trade, the American merchant marine and navy had become triumphant.

In the Pacific, a defensive perimeter drawn up in January 1950 by Secretary of State Dean Acheson established a line of security running from near the tip of Alaska, southwest along the Aleutian Islands, across the sea to the islands of Japan, along the chain of the Ryukyu Islands, the largest of which was Okinawa, to the Philippines. The commitments to the East were at first not so strong, nor so well defined, as those to Europe. As an ally in the war against Japan, China had received American backing until its 1949 revolution made it a communist cohort of the Soviet Union. China then fell from favor, while the former enemy, Japan, under occupation for years by the American army, became a friend. Taiwan was not included behind this original perimeter, and it was uncertain for a time whether the lower part of Korea, south of China, was behind the line or a no-man's-land. But within the year of Acheson's expansion of the frontiers of American protection, the line fell across Korea, and American forces rushed to defend a front in the south against communist Koreans invading from the north. Far to the south lay the island continent of Australia, which, despite its distance, maintained close ties with America.

These frontiers of influence were strengthened with the formation of a military alliance system in Western Europe in 1949 and in eastern Asia in the early 1950s. But the frontiers on opposite sides of the world did not yet connect. To complete the circle, the United States gained allies in the 1950s among the nations of southern Asia, where political frontiers or perimeters were intermittently broken or lacked firmness. The line of influence extended through Southeast Asia, including South Vietnam, Laos, and Cambodia. It continued along the northern boundaries of divided Pakistan, Iran, and Turkey, though India and Burma declared neutrality after gaining independence from Great Britain. The frontier was buttressed by rugged natural barriers that ran the length of the Himalaya range from the Khyber Pass, past the gates of India, to the southern shores of the Caspian Sea, around the great deserts above the Persian Gulf, to, once again, the Caucasus, the Dardanelles, and Europe.

Such was the state of the frontiers of American interest as they developed from World War II into the 1950s. They were not the borders of an empire that held territory under a single sovereign authority. The United States was a republic and its principal means of establishing influence were aid, commerce, and diplomacy, though it came to offer protection against belligerents. It assumed the role of a primary power for which no other could substitute. Along the frontiers of this defensive area, the Americans confronted a revolutionary and mighty adversary, the Russians, and their massive nation with adjacent satellites.[1]

To the allied states along this frontier, the promise of American aid and defense reached, and from those lands this influence was never to retreat under coercion of aggressors. On the European frontier the American pledge had no foreseeable end: "continuous," declared the treaty that united under American protection the Western

European empires of Britain, France, the Netherlands, Belgium, and Denmark. In the Pacific, to the Philippines, and later to Australia and New Zealand, the American commitments would remain in force "indefinitely." As for Japan, no change in its deference to the United States for its defense or to America's exclusive right to bases could take place without American consultation. In Southeast Asia, too, the Americans promised not to yield, and again the term "indefinitely" applied. American treaties were open to review by sovereign nations, but those commitments implied, no less than respect for the sovereignty of the allies, that the Americans intended never to surrender a foot of territory to aggressor nations. The Americans had never lost a war; the United States would not retreat. Where the strategic frontier lay at its farthest extent, in Southeast Asia, President Dwight Eisenhower compared the borderland to "a leaky dike, and with leaky dikes it's sometimes better to put a finger in than to let the whole structure be washed away."[2]

It is these dimensions of space and time that provide a context in which the trade, cultural exchange, and battles fought in defense of American influence took place. Let us now continue not by reciting these events but rather by seeking to explain how and why a seaboard nation swelled into a world state. What are the origins of America's world role?

The Problem of the Rise to World Power

Americans at midcentury dealt with the glories and problems of power as the people of every preceding age had done, but their global power was distinguished by its magnitude. As World War II was drawing to a close, in late 1944 President Roosevelt reflected, "At the end of this war this country will have the greatest material power of any Nation in the world. It will be a clean, shining America." He attributed America's rise to an expanding economy of peaceful production, richer than any other in skilled workers, and advanced in engineering, farming, business, and technological know-how.[3]

Government officials envisioned the same exceptional rise to power. Explanations of it varied, however. Harry Hopkins, an intimate adviser to the president, agreed. "We will emerge from this war the richest and most powerful people in the world." The United States alone, of all the great powers, would possess lands unscarred, a people well nourished, and a breadbasket filled to overflowing. "We will have the largest navy and merchant fleet on the seven seas, more airplanes than any other nation. Already a technological people before the war, we will find ourselves, as the result of our work in munitions factories, with the largest army of skilled workers in history. Our industrial production capacity, vaster than the combined capacity of our Allies, will be sufficient, once converted to the uses of peace, to fill consumer needs at home and, at the same time, to supply . . . heavy goods . . . for rehabilitation abroad. Our raw materials and natural resources . . . will be sufficient, with wise stewardship, to last for generations.

But, above all, we will emerge with our democratic institutions intact, a people free to shape our destiny as we see fit."[4]

Soon after succeeding to the presidency, Truman made an even more ambitious claim for America's rise. "We tell ourselves that we have emerged from this war," he remarked in a radio address in August 1945, "the most powerful nation in the world—the most powerful nation, perhaps, in all history. That is true, but not in the sense some of us believe it to be true." The war had shown Truman that the United States had tremendous material resources, skilled workers, managers, able generals, and a brave people capable of bearing arms. "The new thing—the thing which we had not known—the thing we have learned now and should never forget, is this: that a society of self-governing men is more powerful, more enduring, more creative than any other kind of society, however disciplined, however centralized."[5]

Campaigning for the presidency in his own right in 1948, Truman barnstormed the country to convey to citizens the world-changing importance of their power. He hammered away at this theme from the back platform of the presidential train and in big-city convention halls and stadiums:

Salem, Oregon, June 11: "This is the greatest Nation on earth, I think. The greatest Nation in history, let's put it that way. We have done things that no other nation in the history of the world has done."

Trenton, Missouri, September 18: "this country will continue for another thousand years as the greatest country in the world."

Dayton, Ohio, October 11: "Now, this great Republic—the greatest in history, the greatest that the sun has ever shone upon—is charged with leadership in the world for the welfare of the whole world as well as our own welfare."[6]

Not only political leaders but also editors, columnists, and writers proclaimed America's extraordinary rise. In early 1941 Henry Luce had decided to throw the weight of his publishing empire behind an effort to explain the emergence of the United States as a dominant power. Neil MacNeil, an editor of the *New York Times,* stating in 1944 that for a time "the United States must remain the most powerful of world powers," listed American assets in a particular order: the "most powerful navy that has ever sailed the five oceans"; the "biggest and hardest hitting air force that the world has ever known"; the greatest national industrial output on earth; the largest merchant marine at sea; the largest number of transport and commercial airplanes in the sky; an agricultural plant capable of feeding Americans and contributing more than any other to feeding hungry peoples; the "greatest national production of steel, petroleum, cotton and other vital products"; a domain located in the Western Hemisphere; and vast holdings of monetary gold and silver. Writing in *Reader's Digest,* Harry Scherman, a popular journalist, called America simply "the most powerful nation in history."[7]

Government policy analysts examined in secret the status of national power. Following a request in 1948 by Secretary of Defense James Forrestal for a study of "the proportion of our resources which should be devoted to military purposes," the National Security Council produced a series of reports. The most comprehensive consideration of America's possession of "superior overall power," the document numbered NSC 68, which Truman approved in 1950, cited as vital components "a unique degree of unity" in society, "the capability of the American economy," and "military strength," including atomic armaments. The NSC subsequently sent a report to President Eisenhower, advising again that the American position as the "leader of the free world" was sustained by a "strong military posture," a "sound, strong and growing economy," and a high "morale and free institutions," to which were added "sufficient atomic weapons and effective means of delivery." The implication of the national security papers, even those of different administrations, was that to maintain superiority over the Soviet Union, the United States had to develop its assets to their maximum potential.[8]

These ideas were not entirely new. Leaders had been assessing America's rise in the world from the beginning of the Republic. In 1780 John Adams told the French foreign minister, comte de Vergennes, that the "United States of America are a great and powerful people, whatever European statesmen may think of them." The country, Adams asserted, had unbounded possibilities for the future because of its enormous territorial expanse, embracing rich soil, mild climate, and incalculably plentiful natural resources, and because of the American people, rapidly expanding in numbers, and their production of agricultural goods for trade abroad.[9]

Yet only in the late nineteenth century did the nation become widely recognized as a world power. William McKinley was the first modern president to claim that American power was the greatest in the world. In 1892, before assuming office, he quoted from an article written fourteen years earlier by the British statesman William Gladstone in the *North American Review*. England and America, Gladstone said, were then "the two strongest nations in the world, but there can hardly be a doubt as between the America and the England of the future that the daughter, at some no very distant time, whether fairer or less fair, will be unquestionably yet stronger than the mother." To McKinley that "no very distant time" suddenly arrived in the early 1890s. "America," he said, "'whether fairer or less fair'—certainly freer—is now 'stronger than the mother.'" America had become the strongest nation in the world because "her power lies in a free and intelligent and progressive people," as well as in a strong, expanding economy and in social well-being. The Spanish-American War, a quick triumph resulting in the acquisition of an overseas empire in the Caribbean and the Pacific, dramatically confirmed for McKinley America's rise to world-power status.[10]

Victory in World War I revealed the enormous strength and potential of the industrialized continental nation. At the close of the conflict, President Woodrow Wilson stated that the United States was "a nation as powerful as any in the world," yet it alone had achieved "the primacy of the world." If America joined the League of Nations, Wilson declared, the country would be "partners" with the other powers. But, he added, "let me predict we will be the senior partner. The financial leadership will be ours. The industrial primacy will be ours. The commercial advantage will be ours. The other countries of the world are looking to us for leadership and direction." Through the "growth of our power," Wilson said, "we have become a determining factor in the history of mankind." Industry and capital continued to grow through the 1920s, and so did the nation's economic prowess. Advances in education, science, invention, efficiency, and production were among the factors that led Herbert Hoover to claim that America had attained a "position of transcendent power."[11]

The attributes contemporaries accorded to this progress in each period were largely unanalyzed. They made lists of divergent factors—material and psychological, human and technological, peaceful and military—but these lists did not adequately distinguish one item from another. Enumerations did not indicate what was a significant development and what was not. We seek some structure of thought and analysis in an effort to understand why the United States became capable of exercising world influence.

The Analysis of Power

An extensive attempt to comprehend the rise and decline of nations came in a new school in international politics that emerged around the theory of power politics. Under the impetus of world war, political scientists and strategists developed this theory in the 1930s and made it popular in the 1940s, believing that it was the only realistic way to see the world; hence their common name, "realists." They were direct about pursuing the national interest: a nation that abandoned self-preservation as the chief motive of its policy risked its very survival.[12]

One of the ablest of the early realists was Nicholas John Spykman, a political scientist at Yale, who stressed in 1942 that all civilized life rested "in the last instance on power." Without power, he believed, no social progress was possible. Mechanical power—the ability to move mass—was the product of technology, and political power—the ability to move people—put technology at the service of society.[13]

Spykman was baffled as to why power had a "bad name." He argued that Americans were wrong to condemn power as connoting evil, because power was only a means to an end. Sometimes the end was worthy, and in any case people were pursuing power with whole-hearted devotion. In ladies' sewing circles, he gathered, no less than in struggles between nations, power was a fact of life. A sound and practical foreign policy, Spykman stressed, should be designed "in terms of the realities of international relations, in terms of power politics." Already supposed to be in possession of unquestioned hegemony over a large part of the New World, the United States, Spykman predicted, should be expected in the post–World War II era to exercise its power in all parts of the world in pursuit of its interests.[14]

A year before the close of the war, William T. R. Fox, a research associate at the Yale Institute of International Studies, gave currency to the idea of a new status to which the United States had risen: that of superpower. He began his book by talking about squirrels and elephants. He was quick to explain that the Soviet Union and the Dominican Republic were not both elephants, nor were they both squirrels; and he wanted to make clear that "we are not fighting to make them both squirrels." For Fox, the elephants mattered most in keeping the postwar peace. Differences in power would continue to exist among nations, he said, and the problems of the world would not be solved by endeavors to create a world of "no-power politics." Fox, like Spykman, insisted that power itself was ethically neutral. He urged Americans to recognize that power was a basic feature of political life and that it made "the most enormous difference in whose hands predominant power rests." After the war, he predicted, the United States would be rated as greater than a regional power restricted to a single area. As a superpower, it would have interests and influence from the East to the West. " 'Great power plus great mobility of power' describes the super-power," he claimed.[15]

The political scientist Hans J. Morgenthau did more than any other figure to establish the realist interpretation of international affairs. In 1948 he published his classic treatise *Politics among Nations: The Struggle for Power and Peace,* which argued that struggle for power was the essence of international affairs. Born in Germany in 1904, Morgenthau fled to Switzerland to escape Hitler and in 1937 emigrated to the United States, where he found the study of international affairs disorganized. While teaching at Brooklyn College, later at the University of Kansas and, beginning in 1943—the year he became a citizen—at the University of Chicago, he criticized the writing in his field by historians and international lawyers as overly legalistic and idealistic. Morgenthau brought from the Old World a pessimism about man's nature and the state of the world, while his scholarly work led him to believe that objective truths about politics could be discovered by human reason. His wealth of knowledge enabled him to lecture to his classes on world politics without a text; one of his students took a stenographic transcript of what he said, which became the draft of his book.[16]

Morgenthau directly related his power theories to the observation that "the United States is at the moment of this writing the most powerful nation on earth." He was intrigued with the problems and rivalries this power created. "International politics," he wrote, "like all politics, is a struggle for power." Power was more than brutal force, it was the central aim of national interest. He proposed that the pursuit of power was the source of state behavior. No matter what the ultimate aims of nations, whether freedom, security, or prosperity, their immediate goal was power. Power was the means to national ends. Political power meant "man's control over the minds and actions of other men." It followed that power was also "a psychological relationship between those who exercise it and those over whom it is exercised," enabling some people to control the actions of others through orders, threats, persuasion, or a combination of these. Since he had traced the struggle for power back through history, he believed the contest for power must be ever-present.[17]

Morgenthau, impatient with moral sentiment or wishful idealism, believed that the pursuit of power was not necessarily immoral. "To act successfully," he wrote in *Scientific Man vs. Power Politics* in 1946, " . . . is political wisdom. To know with despair that the political act is inevitably evil, and to act nevertheless, is moral courage. To choose among several expedient actions the least evil one is moral judgment. In the combination of political wisdom, moral courage, and moral judgment, man reconciles his political nature with his moral destiny."[18]

The chief opponents of the realists were the humanitarian moralists who saw the world from a different, ethical perspective. Of a longstanding tradition in the nineteenth century, the moralists included philosophers and writers who attributed America's rising world influence not to external force but to the internal example of a society. They opposed the power politics and imperialism of Europe. One of the early, clearsighted moralists was Albert Gallatin, who wrote "The Mission of the United States" at the time of the Mexican War. "Your mission was, to be a model for all other governments" and "to apply all your faculties to the gradual improvement of your own institutions" and, "by your example, to exert a moral influence most beneficial to mankind at large. Instead of this, an appeal has been made to your worst passions; to cupidity, to the thirst of unjust aggrandizement by brutal force; to the love of military fame and of false glory." Aware that the world powers of the past had been empires and monarchies, the moralists argued that the United States should not act imperially in emulation of them but rather show the way to reform by exhibiting the success of its democratic society. Morgenthau pointed to John C. Calhoun and William Graham Sumner as worthy representatives of this world perspective, the latter writing during the Spanish-American War that "expansionism and imperialism are at war with the best traditions, principles, and interests of the American people."[19]

The realists responded that in the past the moralists could afford to advocate that their nation be small and inconsequential but virtuous. After all, they had lived on a continent insulated from the outside. But their legacy threatened to damage the national interest, which required growing world involvement. Even when leaders made decisions for "realistic" actions, the realists contended, they had been perverted by irrelevant moralistic justifications. A case in point was President McKinley's defense of colonizing the Philippines: after prayer in the wee hours of the morning, he revealed, he had heard the voice of God tell him to annex the islands.[20]

Of all the spokesmen of the moralistic point of view, Woodrow Wilson was the most eloquent and his thought the most far-reaching. His conviction, well founded in nineteenth-century liberal thought and the ethical standards of Christian and Calvinistic theology, was that democracy and constitutional government would temper the maneuvers of the big powers. "It is a very perilous thing," he said in an address in Mobile, Alabama, in October 1913, "to determine the foreign policy of a nation in the terms of material interest. It not only is unfair to those with whom you are dealing, but it is degrading as regards your own actions. . . . We dare not turn from the principle that morality and not expediency is the thing that must guide us."[21]

The realists countered that however much Wilson had wanted to "make the world safe for democracy," he had relied on the American army to achieve his ends. Wilson had fully recognized the historical implications of America's economic rise. But he wanted to help shape the peace at Versailles on the moral principles of democracy. After his return in 1919, he declared in Los Angeles: "The day we have left behind us . . . was a day of balances of power. It was a day of 'every nation take care of itself or make a partnership with some other nation or group of nations to hold the peace of the world steady or to dominate the weaker portions of the world.' Those were the days of alliances. This project of the League of Nations is a great process of disentanglement." The league was supposed to be a democratic organization of the world's nations, America's contribution to a general world order.[22]

Congress, however, rejected the Treaty of Versailles. When Sen. Henry Cabot Lodge introduced a series of reservations restricting the league's jurisdiction, Wilson, fearing the destruction of the democratic intent of the league, refused to accept them. In the end, the moral example of democratic aspiration in isolation at home failed to reconcile foreign nationalistic demands voiced around the world. The league, which had no other power than that of its member states, was helpless to prevent Japanese expansion in Manchuria and China, Italy's conquest of Ethiopia, and Hitler's repudiation of the Versailles settlement.

These crises threw American thought about the world in turmoil, and World War II gave impetus to the intellectual tradition of the realists. After the war Morgenthau's *Politics among Nations* became probably the most influential textbook of its time, read by specialists and students for the framework it offered in the field of world affairs. By mid-century the preoccupation with power politics and the struggle for political and military power had largely replaced the economic doctrines that Lenin and Charles Beard had expounded as the basis of world affairs in earlier days.

Realism entered the plane of government and diplomacy. Influential among the realists who applied theory to policy was George Kennan, a student of history, diplomat, policy analyst, and expert on Soviet affairs. Kennan believed that the most serious fault of American policy was what he called the "legalistic-moralistic approach to international problems." That approach he labeled idealistic, for it projected the common concepts of American law and politics into international relations—as in the Hague conferences on disarmament, the Kellogg Pact to make war illegal, and the League of Nations. Remarkably, Kennan asserted that realism would free foreign affairs from concepts of right and wrong, and correct the "assumption that state behavior is a fit subject for moral judgment. . . . It is a curious thing, but it is true, that the legalistic approach to world affairs, rooted as it unquestionably is in a desire to do away with war and violence, makes violence more enduring, more terrible, and more destructive to political stability than did the older motives of national interest." Kennan pleaded in the early 1950s for the realism of power politics—or, as he wrote, for whatever "is realistic in concept, and founded in an endeavor to see both ourselves and others as we really are." In his cabled dispatches from Moscow to the State Department, Kennan urged—as strongly as in his later writings, including *Realities of American Foreign Policy*—that relations with Russia be placed entirely on a "realistic and matter-of-fact basis," guided not by morality or altruism, but by the strengths and weaknesses of nations.[23]

The nation's rise in the world, from the perspective of the realists, rested on power and its elements, which included geography, natural resources, population, industrial development, military ability, and national morale. The balance of power enabled the United States in the mid-twentieth century to pursue interests in remote regions of the earth through trade, cultural activity, and war. Opposed as it was to moralism, realism nevertheless reflected not merely a concern for fact or reality but also a regard for elemental power as force and influence. Realism was a way of looking at the world, comprehended as power politics. For our purposes, power is defined as the qualities or properties that make possible the national exertion of influence or force in the world. Power, in this sense, means essentially capability rather than actual force or influence, though we may find that the ways influence was exerted might indeed eventually enhance or weaken the power that supported it.

Our attempt to understand the origins of America's world role turns now to the themes of the elements and balance of power. We will first examine the various reasons for the balance of power that contemporaries set forth according to their rational beliefs about the world. Our work, as the study progresses, is to analyze these explanations and to weigh them for significance against the world with which contemporaries dealt.

2

A

Circuit

of

the World

The American realist view of the world in the mid-twentieth century focused on the steep decline of the empires of Western Europe and on the aged European world order that appeared to be crumbling around the North American continent. In the past thousand years, the European nations, clustered on a peninsular extremity thrusting outward from the Ural Mountains into the Atlantic Ocean, had gained the strength to defend their continent against invaders and to expand their influence. European civilization had grown beyond the several other civilizations on earth, none of which had been more terribly powerful than another. But as Joseph Marion Jones, a member of the State Department staff, wrote of the European order in the late 1940s, "An era, a power system, that had lasted hundreds of years, that had not been perfect but had brought a degree of balanced order out of chaos, had ended."[1]

Understanding the origins of the American world role depends on observations of the United States in relation to other nations. Fundamentally, these observations recognized the relativity of power. American influence reached only insofar as it was not resisted by other powers. The balance of power from the end of World War II to the early 1950s allowed for the far-reaching frontiers of American influence, and to measure this distribution of power, we should explore Americans' perceptions of foreign lands and people. These perceptions can then be weighed against events, facts, and statistics. We begin a circuit of the world, a world that was war-weary and war-weakened, from the heartland of Europe.[2]

The European World

About 1500 European enterprise had come alive and made Europe a citadel of power. The Europeans won command of the oceans and settled the New World. Even as Europe was expanding, in 1662 it faced a massive invasion by Ottoman Turks, who pushed westward with the goals of capturing Vienna and colonizing lands all the way to the Rhine. The invasion did not succeed. The Hapsburg monarchy's army, reinforced by troops from as far away as the France of Louis XIV, held the eastern defenses. After 1683, when the Europeans began a counteroffensive against the Turks, the continent was free of foreign threats from the east and Europe became the master of its own political fortunes. It and America remained free of such threats until 1941, when the Japanese attacked Pearl Harbor, a colonial base of the former European colony.

The date realists usually ascribed to the foundation of the European world order of the nineteenth century was 1815, when representatives of Austria, Prussia, and Great Britain met at the Congress of Vienna to decide Napoleon's fate. In the era of general peace that followed across the continent, Europeans turned outward to colonize remote lands. From the capitals of the mother countries, they administered a political realm of unparalleled extent. Europe became the center of an expanding world economic system, which exploited resources and developed markets elsewhere. The empires spread authority over others, while keeping international conflict limited in scope. Gunboats, firearms, and cannon caused alarm among native peoples, at least until they came to acquire these weapons for their own use.[3]

From the realist perspective, Europe seemed to dominate the world until the twentieth century. In World War I, the Austro-Hungarian, German, Ottoman, and Russian empires all collapsed, but the victorious Western European powers actually expanded their overseas empires. At the end of the war the land area dominated by Europe stood at its greatest extent, but the imperial domains tottered as forces of nationalism began to be exerted in the colonies. Torn apart again by World War II, Europe lost the ability even to defend itself against invading armies. Dean Acheson, who became secretary of state in 1949, compared the task of replacing the European world order to the labors described in the first chapter of Genesis. Then the world had to be created out of chaos; the new challenge was "to create half a world, a free half, out of the same material without blowing the whole to pieces in the process." Acheson added, "Only slowly did it dawn on us that the whole world structure and order that we had inherited from the nineteenth century was gone."[4]

"The age of Europe has passed," Eric Fischer, a scholar of geography and history who had fled Austria in 1938 when it was absorbed by the Nazis, declared in a wartime book. "Europe can never regain the position it maintained during the last two centuries." Hajo Holborn confirmed this historical perspective in *The Political Collapse of Europe,* published after the war. Born in Berlin, Holborn went to the United States in 1934 and became a professor at Yale. He contended that the end of the old world order should have been apparent in 1919, when the Europeans had toppled their own ancient empires on the continent, and Britain and France had been severely weakened. In Holborn's view, the United States had determined the allied victory over the central powers, and President Wilson had played a leading role in the peace settlement. Nevertheless, American policy had suffered from the illusion that the Europe of old would revive. Implicit in his argument was that America might earlier have been a transcendent power, but, instead, on the eve of World War II it shared great-power status with Germany, Japan, Italy, Britain, France, and the Soviet Union.[5]

By the end of World War II, some American realists believed that no great power remained in Europe. William T. R. Fox, who located no superpower on the Continent, wrote that the "transition from the old, world-dominating Europe to the new 'problem Europe' is a central fact in the international politics of our time." Of course, others argued that Europe was not dying: It continued to have nearly four hundred million people, a great accumulation of skills and talents, a stimulating climate, and considerable resources of minerals and forest. But Holborn and Acheson were among those troubled that the European war had been decided by the participation of two great powers which they characterized as non-European—the Soviet Union, straddling Eurasia, and the United States. The "collapse of the traditional European system became an irrevocable fact," argued Holborn. The " 'historic Europe' " was "dead and beyond resurrection."[6]

Great Britain warranted special regard in the passing order. A foggy green island of rippling fields broken by stone fences, and the city of London with its Parliament standing by the Thames, was how American realists and Anglophiles alike pictured Britain, mixing sentimentality with awe at the contributions it had once made to keep the peace. Britain was an ancient democracy and the first nation to master modern parliamentary government. Britain was also the nation that had begun the Industrial Revolution and led the world in economic development. The small island had become the world's wealthiest nation.[7]

It was hard for writers in *Foreign Affairs* to believe that a short time before Great Britain had been an enormous force in the world. The English people had built the most extended empire that had ever existed. With its mighty navy, Britain controlled the sea lanes around its island and the oceans beyond. The nation held strong bases at Gibraltar, Malta, Suez, Aden, Singapore, and Capetown. The British had spread over the world's unorganized areas—Canada, India, Australia, South Africa—and added colonies in all parts of the world until the empire ultimately embraced one-quarter of the earth's land surface. British merchant vessels dominated the world's commerce. The pound sterling was accepted as the common world currency. The imperial pagentry and spectacle of the late nineteenth-century jubilees celebrating the reign of Queen Victoria were symbolic of the empire's worldwide prestige and influence.[8]

The conclusion seemed inescapable during and after the war that, standing by herself, Great Britain no longer fulfilled the functions of a great power. Nor could it be expected to regain that capacity. War-ravaged London, witnessed by Americans, revealed the vulnerability of Britain at the heart of the empire. Standing on the chimney-covered rooftops of the city, and walking out into the streets amid the muffled thunder of nighttime onslaughts, the correspondent Edward R. Murrow reported to Americans on the radio: "The damage to small dwellings has been severe. Not all the German bombs hit the docks—and poor people live near those docks. Entire streets are uninhabitable." He described the bombs, the fires, the blasted buildings, the craters, and the windows blown out over a wide area. He reported the British people in constant fear of invasion: "Britain is in mortal danger."[9]

In the days when Britain had made a stand virtually alone against a totalitarian power that dominated Europe only twenty miles away across the English Channel, the

American ambassador to the Court of St. James, John Gilbert Winant, saw "the fatigue and the monotony, the sight of the injured and the dead, the pathetic exposure of the interiors of smashed homes, broken rooms with maybe a picture still hanging on the walls and torn curtains still up at the windows." He reflected on the early Sunday morning bombings that destroyed the House of Commons chamber and also smashed the altar of Westminster Abbey. To him, these two strikes symbolized the objectives of the Nazi dictator and pagan against the shared American and British values of democracy and worship. The costs of that common fight impressed Secretary of State James Byrnes, who surveyed the damage to London at war's end. Fearing that it would take fifteen years to repair the buildings, he came away "deeply moved by the patience and the courage of the British people."[10]

Yet the war merely hastened a decline that had long been under way. The British economy was in a crisis so severe as to shake the foundations of British power. Britain was still the world's second-largest trader after the United States, but while it continued to import food and raw material, its capacity to produce goods competitively had been reduced, and more than half of the British merchant marine had been destroyed. The British trade deficit mounted. Even before the war Britain had been liquidating small portions of overseas investments to balance its international account. To pay for its military effort, Britain had exhausted the wealth it had accumulated during decades of foreign commerce. The former banker of the world had huge external debts that made its international economic position desperate. In 1949 the exchange rate of the pound sterling was drastically cut from $4.03 to $2.80. In 1947 the Joint Chiefs of Staff had put Britain first on a list of nations essential to American security that needed American assistance. Although the United States responded with loans and aid, in 1953 a joint study group of the Council on Foreign Relations in New York and the Royal Institute of International Affairs in London described Britain as a country in continual decline, growing poorer while the United States grew richer.[11]

Britain's once dominant navy had become too costly. Whereas the United States had in the previous century depended for its protection on the Royal Navy, now the fate of Britain and its possessions depended, according to American naval analysts, "almost completely" on the protection of American sea and air power. The only way naval strategists could conceive of Britain remaining a first-rate naval nation was for the English-speaking countries on the opposite sides of the Atlantic to form "a coalition of sea power as formidable, as stable, and as useful in the future as British sea power was in the period following the Napoleonic wars."[12]

Nothing exposed the British Empire's downfall so starkly as the loss of India, the earth's largest colony, parts of which Britain had held since the 1700s. India's independence in 1947, the result of a nonviolent revolt led by Mahatma Gandhi, was something British Tories had sworn never to grant. "We mean to hold our own," Churchill claimed in 1942, and according to American press reports, the boast that he had not become the king's First Minister to preside over the liquidation of the empire was tied up in the very essence of British power. Britain only slowly came to be reconciled to the loss of empire, for without colonies, how would it be distinguishable from Sweden or Belgium or Poland? At a party given by the British viceroy in India on July 4, 1942, a British general asked an American visitor, "But could a free India defend itself?" "Can a free England?" the American replied.[13]

Within two years after the war, Britain had withdrawn from Burma, Egypt, Palestine, and most of the Middle East. The motherland anticipated maintaining ties with its former dominions in a weak Commonwealth of Nations and holding onto colonies in Africa and scattered islands in every sea. But the dreams of empire clashed with the aspirations for independence among captive peoples. In 1950 the chargé d'affaires at the American embassy in London described for the secretary of state the British leaders caught up in "fighting a last-stand battle for survival as a world power." They were "trying simultaneously to maintain their Commonwealth and Empire and military commitments, balance their trade, modernize their industry, balance their budget, fight off inflation, and prevent a fall in their standard of living." The sun was setting on an empire on which the sun was never to set.[14]

Americans who crossed into Europe west of the Rhine witnessed the tremendous dislocation of France and the Low Countries. A war correspondent reported that one town in Normandy, caught in the resistance to the American D day invasion, "was not rubble. It was dust." Millions were close to starvation. They lacked clothing, housing, and tools. Industry was nearly at a standstill and production in France, Belgium, and the Netherlands had dropped to less than 20 percent of what it had been before the war. Steel production had fallen even more startlingly. Crop production in 1945 fell to less than 60 percent of the prewar total. The transport system was nearly paralyzed. In the Netherlands, the ports of Amsterdam and Rotterdam suffered severe damage, and the merchant marine lost 40 percent of its tonnage.[15]

The Rhine valley, a land of bountiful resources, vineyards on terraced hills, and great forests, as well as heavy industrial centers, was left "a desolate land of rubbish piles." A soldier in the Army Air Corps, flying low over the valley after the war, the shadow of his B-17 hurtling over the land below, saw the destruction that had been carried into Germany. "Aachen lay bleaching in the sun like bones on a desert." He looked straight down onto topless buildings. "Only skeletal walls were standing, enclosing ruin. They were gaunt frames surrounding mouldy nothingness. It looked what it was, a city of the dead . . . . Mannheim existed no more"; it was "tossed dirt." A shaken comrade looked below and wondered, "Where do the people live?"[16]

The European winter of late 1945 and early 1946 was severe, but it was snows and winter winds of 1947 that drove home the point of war ruin. Toward the end of January, blizzards and frigid storms blowing out of northern Siberia blanketed European skies and for three weeks swirled over the Continent. In Berlin people froze and starved. In France, Holland, and Belgium, they shivered in a fuel shortage. Coal barges were trapped in ice-locked canals and rivers. Firewood was scarce. Snow lay even on the gondolas of Venice and the palms of Nice. Snow gales swept the English Channel, paralyzing England's industry, cutting off villages, stopping trains, and flickering the lights of homes. One winter did not change the balance of power, but the weather, reported *Newsweek,* had dealt the island nation a blow "more severe than anything the German Air Force was able to inflict on Churchill's Britain."[17]

After Germany surrendered in the spring of 1945, Americans entering that former power saw around them in the streets, narrowed by fragments of ruins, mounds of rubble that had once been buildings. "Wherever we looked we saw desolation," reported Gen. Lucius Clay, the American military governor of the occupying forces in Berlin. The people appeared weak and intimidated, without hope. "It was like a city of the dead." "Dead bodies still remained in canals and lakes and were being dug out from under bomb debris. It was a common sight to see a headstone of wood on top of a mound of debris with flowers placed at its foot." The American diplomat Robert Murphy recorded that the "odor of death was everywhere." Berliners were in a "dazed condition," roaming around the shattered city or living in "cave-like ruins." "In the center of the town GIs could walk for blocks and see no living thing, hear nothing but the stillness of death, smell nothing but the stench of death," reported *Life* of Berlin. Those who were alive "had dull eyes. Their clothes were unkempt. The old men were unshaven. There were no young German men in the city." Of Berlin's prewar population of 4,250,000, less than half remained. In the Reichschancellery palace, where Adolf Hitler had made his last stand, crystal chandeliers had fallen to the floor, the marble-pillared halls had collapsed, and the führer's underground bunker had been torn into. Touring the ruins, President Truman moralized, "That's what happens . . . when a man overreaches himself," and in his private diary he confided, "Never did I see a more sorrowful sight, nor witness retribution to the nth degree."[18]

This was the end of a great power, the most centrally located, the most populous, and the most highly industrialized of Europe, a power whose Nazi leaders, in President Roosevelt's estimation, had been "unrestrained seekers of world conquest and permanent world domination." Realists did not fear Nazi production, large as it was, as much as military conquest. Before the war Germany had been the most important producer of steel in Europe, larger than Britain and Russia, but it produced less than a fourth as much as the United States. As John Kenneth Galbraith, an economist serving as a director of the U.S. Strategic Bombing Survey, later discovered, even in 1941, when Germany had been at war two years and the United States had scarcely begun to arm, the United States was outproducing Germany in tanks and aircraft. Nevertheless, the Third Reich insatiably invaded one nation after another until it occupied the Rhineland, Austria, Czechoslovakia, Poland, Denmark, Norway, the Netherlands, Belgium, Luxembourg, and France. German forces assaulted Britain by air, moved into the Balkans, and invaded the Soviet Union, reaching the outskirts of Moscow. In the autumn of 1942, at its greatest expanse, Hitler's Germany dominated lands from the coast of the Atlantic to the Eurasian plains, and across a large area of North Africa. It had plans to take the Suez Canal and roll into the Middle East.[19]

After Germany's unconditional surrender, the Allies' first essential task was to destroy its war machine. An early plan by Secretary of the Treasury Henry Morgenthau called for Germany to be restored to an agrarian countryside. In a memorandum to Roosevelt in September 1944, Morgenthau proposed that, as part of the "complete demilitarization of Germany in the shortest possible period of time after surrender," the heart of German industrial power in the Ruhr be totally wiped out or removed from German control. At the Quebec Conference that month, the president approved the plan, as did Churchill, but Roosevelt's advisers at the State and War departments opposed it. Secretary of State Cordell Hull called it blind vengeance that would effectively wreck the Continental economy. Roosevelt later rejected the plan, but other harsh measures were carried out, demonstrating the almost total control the United States exercised in its zone of occupation.[20]

The Joint Chiefs of Staff ordered General Clay to dissolve the Nazi party and annul Nazi laws. The German armed forces were to be disbanded and any citizens suspected as dangerous to American objectives were to be arrested. The production of war equipment was to be prohibited and excessively powerful cartels broken up. The publication of newspapers and the operation of radio stations, theaters, and telephones were to be controlled. No German parades were to be permitted.[21]

In July 1945 Truman flew into the heart of the defeated country for a conference at Potsdam with the leaders of Great Britain and the Soviet Union to decide the fate of Germany. In the city where the Prussian kings had created the German military, the president passed freely, protected by a garrison of American forces. When he reviewed the principal armored division, its tanks, cleaned and lubricated, their guns pointing to the front, lining the highway between Potsdam and Berlin, the victorious legions stood at attention before the president. "It was an impressive demonstration of American military power," recalled General Clay.

At the American headquarters in Berlin on July 20, President Truman attended the raising of the national flag, the same banner that had flown over the Capitol on December 7, 1941, and had been raised in Rome after the conquest of Italy. The president took position in front of the flagstaff, and as the band played "The Star-Spangled Banner," the flag rose to the top of the mast. The president stated his conviction that the United States had "conclusively proven that a free people can successfully look after the affairs of the world." At the conference the leaders proceeded to organize the dividing of Germany and its overall administration by military representatives in an Allied Control Council.[22]

The Americans established their authority at a court in Nuremberg in 1945 and 1946. The chief American member of the unprecedented tribunal, Robert Jackson, justified the trials of German war criminals by explaining that the United States, as an occupying force in concert with the Allies, had to mete out justice. The need for judgment, he had reported to the president, required that the United States be prepared, if the victorious powers did not agree, to conduct an inquiry on its own. "The wrongs which we seek to condemn and punish have been so calculated, so malignant and so devastating," he said in his opening statement to the court, "that civilization cannot tolerate their being ignored because it cannot survive their being repeated." The evidence for the magnitude of these crimes included the Nazi scheme for dominating the world and the motion pictures of concentration camps.[23]

Some hostility remained among soldiers who had lost close comrades, but in September 1946, when Secretary of State Byrnes came to Stuttgart, he began to soften the punitive tone of military occupation. The Germans required assistance in rebuilding, Byrnes determined, and the American people wanted "to help the German people to win their way back to an honorable place among the free and peace-loving nations of the world." He insisted that Germans learn the fundamentals of democracy as Americans had striven to build it, in which power had to originate with the people and be subject to their control. Leaders would come to office through popular elections; political parties would be democratic, the right of individuals preserved by law. After four years in Germany, the occupiers felt their fundamental objectives had been accomplished and were ready to support the writing of a constitution to set up the Federal Republic of Germany.[24]

West Germany became an independent democracy in 1949 but remained virtually defenseless. The American forces stayed to protect it. The withdrawal of these forces, Secretary of State Acheson said in a policy statement, depended no longer on the elimination of indigenous Nazis but on the Soviet Union agreeing to end its control of economic and political life in the eastern regions of Germany.[25]

A few Americans observed the desolation in Eastern Europe. In Poland the correspondent John Hersey saw the remains of the capital in 1945: "Warsaw is the worst urban scar in the world. Warsaw was destroyed systematically, street by street, alley by alley, house by house. Nothing is left except a mockery of architecture." Warsaw had lost 68 percent of its dwellings, and some eight million Poles, many from the capital, were eventually forced into mass migrations. While moving through the city's remains, Hersey heard three shots, fired by a soldier destroying an army horse that had slipped and broken its leg. Within two minutes the hot carcass had been slashed open for food by twenty-five people using pen knives and their bare hands. "God, my God, God," repeated a Polish colonel accompanying him.[26]

Vienna was "a morose, hungry city," stripped of its past glory as an imperial center of the Hapsburg Empire. Approximately 70 percent of the city's center had been destroyed by bombs. The Viennese queued up for bread rations, reported *Life,* and gathered sticks from the Vienna Woods against the coming winter. The Hungarian capital of Budapest too was badly damaged. All the bridges over the Danube were demolished, and the 860-room palace of Franz Josef was reduced to empty walls and desolate piles of stone and plaster mixed with the remnants of tapestries, portraits, statuary, and dishes. "The streets were in total darkness. The odor of death was strong in the summer air."[27]

The Developing Regions

American views of the world took in areas far beyond Europe, where the old Continental empires, weakened at home, began, like Britain, to dismantle their possessions around the world. The French grudgingly began to grasp the resistance to their empire in Africa and in Indo-China. The Dutch were slow to surrender rule of the East Indies, as were the Portugese and the Belgians of their colonial possessions. These developing regions, then known as underdeveloped or backward, stretching mainly across the lower half of the globe from South America to Africa and the Pacific, were throwing off European dominance, but they were not yet centers of power.

Prevailing American perceptions of the world Europe had once dominated came from travelers, who described not the power of cohesive nation-states but the lure of romantic, exotic places. An article in *National Geographic Magazine* entitled "Yank Meets Native" showed soldiers overseas reacting to native societies seemingly bypassed by modernity. The soldiers noted ancient and strange customs that seemed to hold back development: tree worship and witchcraft in New Guinea, snake charmers and barefoot men running over coal fires in India, and bloodletting in Africa.[28]

Africa, the second-largest continent, with an area three times that of Europe, was, according to the geographer of the State Department, called the "Dark Continent," for it was the last vast domain to be explored and exploited by Europeans. American impressions of African mystery and strangeness were sketched in a 1946 *National Geographic* article on Saõ Tomé, the "Chocolate Island," an ancient Portugese possession off the west African coast. A white man, waiting for American travelers at the pier, ordered a black man standing behind him to "get some boys to carry the gentlemen's luggage." The white man warned the Americans that so long as they stayed on the island, they "must never, at the risk of losing caste, perform any labor more strenuous than pulling up a chair for a lady." Surrounding them were the scenes of colonialism: the governor's palace near the harbor, native men carrying aboard ocean-going ships bundles of wood on their heads, and women turning over layers of cocoa beans with "back-breaking labor" to ensure even drying in the sun.[29]

National Geographic writers traced the history of inland Africa from the nineteenth-century arrival of white explorers, beginning with the missionary David Livingstone. The climactic event was the coming of Cecil Rhodes, who founded the British colony of Rhodesia and dreamed of a chain of British possessions from the Cape of Good Hope to the Mediterranean. Then came the settlers from the colonial powers, who divided up Africa around the first decade of the twentieth century. Only in the 1930s were the boundaries established on maps as they existed through the 1940s. Late in seeking imperial conquest, Italy in 1935 invaded Ethiopia, the only large African country that had not been colonized. The spectre of world war and the destruction of houses, schools, and bridges lingered there until the Italians retreated in 1941, though the German desert campaigns raged across the northern Sahara until the later years of the war.[30]

European rule of these seemingly easily controlled peoples wrought what one American called "White Magic in the Belgian Congo." In the East African bush, the same observer contrasted British colonials, using bulldozers to clear acres of tangled thornbush for peanut fields, with ocher-smeared Wagogo tribesmen leaning on their spears. The sight of black bicyclists on the streets encouraged hope that their advancement was possible, and European influence was "still young." The American writer made only fleeting mention of a mob "gone berserk" that burned shops and stoned cars, including his own. The enduring scenes, it seemed in the 1950s, were of midget Pygmies, giant dancing seven-foot Watusies, and once warlike, now pacified Zulus in wild jungles, where elephants, giraffes, hippopotamuses, zebras, and antelopes wandered; this contrasted with neat rubber, coffee, and tea plantations and English gardens cut out of the bush.[31]

Articles on southern Africa underscored another American interest in the continent: its mineral resources. The region at large contained a wealth of cobalt, manganese, and copper, and the Union of South Africa was a major source of the world's diamonds and gold. The country's white population of a little more than two million, mostly of English and Dutch descent, living in bustling cities with skyscrapers, like Cape Town and Johannesburg, was upheld for its organization of technically advanced mines, the deepest on earth. The eight million blacks received lesser attention as workers in the mines, dancers of wild dances, or bicycle riders carrying bundles as large as dining room tables on their heads. Scant mention was made of racial discrimination; the natives, it was said, were granted employment and were being taught to govern themselves. The preoccupation of the American government in World War II was the uranium in the Shinkolobwe Mine in the Belgian Congo. The mine had been the major source of uranium ore shipped to the United States for its atomic bombs, but in the interest of secrecy its name disappeared from maps of the continent. About half of the earth's known uranium ore lay there.[32]

Asia

The ravages of global war reached far beyond Africa and Europe. In Asia, Japan was vanquished. The war had already shaken a complacent American view of Japan, described by a popular magazine as a "doll-house country of miniature gardens and paper dwellings, peopled by polite little men and women." Japan had built steel mills, chemical works, and automobile plants with astonishing speed, expanding its economy nearly twofold from 1930 to 1939, while the economy of the United States stagnated in depression. Japan's empire extended from the mid-Pacific across Asia to Burma, leading realists to fear that the distance between the German and Japanese armies might be closed early in the war and totalitarian world domination thus realized. When a Japanese submarine shelled an oil refinery near Santa Barbara on the California coast in February 1942, Americans worried that the Imperial Navy might attack the mainland.[33]

Japan, however, never ranked close to the United States as a power. A *Fortune* study in 1944 judged that Japan was "not much" of an industrial nation; it had "not made the major league," and it was "more closely challenged by the Dominion of Canada than the U.S. is challenged by Japan." It had succeeded in exporting sneakers, flashlights, ashtrays, and golf balls, and making cheap goods rather than developing heavy, sophisticated industry. It lacked the capabilty to match the U.S. production of merchant ships and munitions. Japan's troubles steadily worsened as the American navy and army advanced across the Pacific, cutting the main islands off from their supply of raw materials. By the summer of 1945 the Japanese economy had ground to a halt and the country was close to complete collapse.[34]

The U.S. Air Force carried the war to Japan. B-29s fire-bombed Tokyo, leaving many more buildings destroyed than standing. The city, an American soldier later recorded, resembled a "graveyard," its chimneys rising like tombstones over the site of a "vast cremation." In a final blow the United States dropped the first atomic bombs used in warfare on Hiroshima and Nagasaki. Over one-third of Hiroshima's population was killed and another third seriously injured. "A mass flight from the city took place," reported the United States survey of the attack. "All utilities and transportation services were disrupted. . . . Trolley cars, trucks, and railroad rolling stock suffered extensive damage. . . . The electric power transmission and distribution system was wrecked. . . . Industry in the center of the city was effectively wiped out." Stark as the official description was, it did not begin to express the impact of the explosion, the rain of fire, and the shower of radiation. A Japanese-American soldier, who went to Hiroshima to find the section of the city where his ancestors had lived and died, saw in the early light of a December 1945 day "the ruins of the city were dark against the sky . . . . Hiroshima makes one feel as though everything and everyone had given up trying altogether."[35]

The capitulation marking the end of the Japanese empire, presided over by Gen. Douglas MacArthur, the supreme Allied commander in the Pacific, took place on board the battleship *Missouri* in Tokyo Bay, amid the greatest fleet in the world. Above the proceedings waved the very flag that had flown at previous ceremonies in Berlin and Rome. Another flag, tattered, with thirty-one stars, was hung on one of the turrets of the battleship—the flag of the infant American republic, which Commodore Perry had brought with him to the same bay almost a hundred years before. "The deck was crowded with the apostles of the American genius—the technicians," reported a staff correspondent of *Time,* Theodore H. White. "The ship itself was the apotheosis of all American skills, from the cobweb of radar at the foretop above to the gray slabs of armor, carefully compounded of secret and mysterious alloys, below. It was an American show. . . . This victory had been an American victory, one achieved by an overwhelming weight of metal, guns, and superior technique, which had crushed Japan utterly and completely."[36]

MacArthur, who earlier in humiliating retreat from the Philippines had sworn to return to the islands and had pushed on to the capital of Japan in triumph, recorded his own impressions of the momentous victory: "Was the day beclouded by mists and trailing clouds? Were there lone trees cresting Tokyo's shores against the moving sky? Were there voices of waters falling far up within some wild ravine racing into the bay? Were there nearby fields where bees were buzzing? I cannot remember, but this I do— the all-embracing pride I felt in my country's monumental victory. Its future seemed to gleam as though seen through the optimistic gates of youth. I told myself, the tide of world affairs may ebb and flow, old empires may die, new nations be born; alliances may arise, thrive, wither and vanish—but in its effort to build economic growth and prosperity, an atmosphere of hope and freedom, a community of strength and unity of purpose, a lasting peace of justice, my own beloved country now leads the world."[37]

The basic document of occupation plans, jointly agreed on at the Potsdam Conference, mandated the permanent elimination of the Japanese warlords. Despite protests from both the Soviets and the British, the United States insisted on administering Japan alone. The highest law came no longer from the palace of the divine emperor Hirohito, but from MacArthur's offices in an insurance company building. In perhaps the greatest single administrative enterprise the United States had undertaken outside its borders, costing several billions of dollars, Americans assumed what one attached to the Supreme Commander's headquarters called the "primary responsibility for the government, the economic life, and the re-education of some eighty million Japanese."[38]

The aim of the occupying forces was not merely to hold territory but to create fundamental social change. The Americans did not know what to expect on landing, except that they faced a difficult task to reform a people who, humbled in defeat, were thought by MacArthur's expert on Japanese affairs, Col. Sidney Mashbir, to be on the verge of hysteria and under such emotional stress that they might forsake civilized behavior and go on illogical rampages of rape, torture, and murder. In a charter approved by the president, the U.S. government laid out the basic objectives for MacArthur: "to foster conditions which will give the greatest possible assurance that Japan will not again become a menace to the peace and security of the world and will permit her eventual admission as a responsible and peaceful member of the family of nations." The limits of Japanese sovereignty were to be not an Asiatic empire but four home islands and a few minor islands. Militarism and ultranationalism in any form were to be abolished. Japan was to be disarmed and demilitarized, with continuing American control over its capacity to make war. Liberal principles of democratic self-government were to be encouraged. Japan was to be brought out of its feudal and authoritarian tendencies. In September 1945 the emperor, in formal tuxedo, paid homage to MacArthur, in his army fatigues, at the U.S. Embassy, and on New Year's Day 1946 Hirohito disavowed his divinity. The following year the Americans wrote a new Japanese constitution, vesting sovereignty in the people. Forever outlawed was any Japanese military establishment.[39]

The Japanese economy was in chaos, dependent on the United States for foodstuffs and raw materials. There were those who feared the economy could never fully recover because Japan was a "have-not" nation, incapable of self-sufficiency, the main islands having been stripped of colonial resources and markets. American GIs mocked Japanese industrial products. The "frail" Datsun was a "midget car" that threatened to fall apart on starting. Americans sold to Japan over five times what Japan sold Americans, and the United States had to supply the aid to make up the enormous difference in Japan's trade deficit. In 1949 the United States provided Japan with imports worth about $468 million and in return received only about $82 million in Japanese exports.[40]

Still, Japanese dependence on American aid had remarkably transformed the defeated nation. MacArthur proclaimed that "Japan could not rearm for modern war within a century," and press accounts told of sweeping away autocratic rule by a warrior god and installing a democratic government based on the will of the people as expressed in free elections. But Theodore White, who knew the Far East from his years of reporting, warned that there was no indication at the moment of victory on the *Missouri*, or in the days of exuberance after it, that America understood the war it had been fighting in the Pacific. He fixed his attention on China.[41]

There were storms on the Asian horizon. The Far East revolved around China, torn by conflict. When Japan had invaded the mainland with ease in the early 1930s, realist experts did not classify China as a leading power. During the war, as China kept up its resistance, Roosevelt accorded it a first rank, and at Cairo he met as a nominal equal with the Nationalist leader Chiang Kai-shek and Churchill. With Japan defeated, China was the only Asiatic power to which the U.S. government might entrust the maintenance of security in the western Pacific. But the extent of Chinese power was open to question: "Will postwar China possess real military strength capable of being employed outside her borders against a well-equipped opponent? Or will postwar China present a picture of military weakness, based on a poverty-stricken agrarian economy and on primitive forms of government and social organization?" The usual conclusion: "China presents a picture of both 'bigness' and weakness."[42]

China was the world's most populous nation. No reliable modern census had ever been taken, but an unofficial estimate by an American professor was 474 million people, or about one-third of humankind. In these people was China's greatest strength, its population exceeded only possibly and temporarily by that of the entire British Empire at its height right after the war. Compared to the American population, though, the number of Chinese was excessive for their means of production, and the rate of population increase was high. Even learned and friendly observers took for granted that Chinese ways were inherently unsuited to democracy and industrialization. "More than any other mature non-Western state," wrote one American historian, "China has seemed inadaptable to the conditions of modern life."[43]

Poverty and malnutrition were rampant. Theodore White observed the terrible want in the village streets of China, "the desperate struggle of all Chinese to live, to scratch up enough for an existence above the line of misery." He described the famine in Honan: "There were corpses on the road. A girl no more than seventeen, slim and pretty, lay on the damp earth, her lips blue with death; her eyes were open, and the rain fell on them. People chipped at bark, pounded it by the roadside for food; vendors sold leaves at a dollar a bundle. . . . Ghostlike men were skimming the stagnant pools to eat the green slime of the waters."[44]

Images in American books and magazines depicted the green Shantung plain in springtime, soaring mountains mirrored in the water of rice fields, and the moon shining over the silver Chialing River twisting through the grassy Chungking hills. Thirty-five hundred years old, China seemed locked in a medieval past and barely a modern unified nation. Since the nineteenth century, the European powers had taken Chinese seaports and divided the land into spheres of influence for trade. Westerners, including Americans, enjoyed extraterritoriality—exemption from the laws of China—a privilege usually reserved for diplomats. Except for the long conflict with Japan, China had lost every war against foreign powers in the past century. The masses had been wearied by the Sino-Japanese war. After plunder by the Japanese, Shanghai was left, according to one postwar American traveler, "a sick city."[45]

Nevertheless, looking to China's future, the Nobel Prize–winning novelist Pearl Buck, reared by missionary parents in China, believed the country was leaping into a new world position. The old image of China was passing, she wrote: "Only a few years ago as a human lifetime goes, I remember China being called the Sleeping Dragon. They used to say, 'China will never wake up.'" But now the people were building a modern federal democracy, industry would develop after the war, and travel was possible by bus, train, and plane. Buck thought that China's evolution into a modern state had been achieved without the bloody revolution that Russia had endured. She looked on Chiang Kai-shek as a great leader of "high moral worth," a "legend to the people."[46]

But the age-old cleavages in China's social order deepened and cracked in the clash between Chiang's Nationalist and Mao Zedong's Communist forces. Shortly after World War II, the Communists controlled vast regions of the country. For White this was the biggest story in the Far East, bigger by far than the victory over Japan: "America's war had cut blindly across the course of the greatest revolution in the history of mankind, the revolution of Asia." A report in the *New York Times* revealed in 1947 how Americans were being drawn into the Chinese revolution. They were part of two foreign zones of influence. The "American zone" included American bases in the Pacific, Nationalist China, American-occupied Japan, and southern Korea. The other zone, communist in orientation, appeared to the reporter to be directed from the Soviet Union—Soviet Siberia, Sakhalin, the Kuriles, northern Korea, Dairen, Port Arthur, Outer Mongolia, and Manchuria.[47]

Some Americans who saw China firsthand looked on the revolution as a reaction against the corruption that haunted the Chinese government. Henry Wallace was convinced of the need for "fundamental reforms," but Chiang was more interested "in fighting the communists" than in coming to grips with the problem of feudal landlords who exploited them. White's dismal wartime dispatches to *Time* about Chinese corruption were rewritten in New York to present a rosy outlook, reflecting in part Henry Luce's hopes for his adopted land. White repeated his charges in his 1946 book on

China, but the review of it in *Time* questioned his judgment that the government was frequently indifferent to the welfare of its people in ways that resembled fascist cruelty; China's problems, argued *Time,* were not all Chiang's fault. Yet corruption was only part of the picture. An internal State Department memorandum characterized a multitude of Chinese plagues: "(1) an implacable population pressure, which is likely to result in (2) a general standard of living around and below the subsistence level, which in turn will tend to cause (3) popular unrest, (4) economic backwardness, (5) cultural lag, and (6) an uncontrolled crude birth rate." By 1949 Mao and the Communists had won the country and Chiang fled to Taiwan.[48]

Another revolution was taking place largely unnoticed. On September 2, 1945, the same day that MacArthur saw the Japanese surrender and the emperor ordered his subjects to obey the general's commands, Ho Chi Minh, the leader of the Viet Minh, declared the independence of the Democratic Republic of Vietnam. But Americans celebrating Victory Day in the Far East did not take heed. The guerrilla warfare faced by the French, who returned to rule their colony, indicated to Americans who saw brief reports in the press not so much the power of the rebels as the decline of the French and of the colonial system.[49]

The Union of Soviet Socialist Republics

The fundamental alteration in the international distribution of power, precipitated by the European world system's decline, exaggerated the already significant might of the Union of Soviet Socialist Republics. In 1950 a top-secret national security policy report to President Truman related the rise of Soviet power to the collapse in World War I of five empires, the Ottoman, Austro-Hungarian, German, Italian, and Japanese. "For several centuries it had proved impossible for any one nation to gain such preponderant strength that a coalition of other nations could not in time face it with greater strength"; no "state was able to achieve hegemony." The report continued with the "defeat of Germany and Japan and the decline of the British and French Empires" in World War II. That left the Soviet Union as the one nation in both Europe and Asia to rival effectively the United States in power.[50]

The power of the Soviet Union, emerging from chaos after the 1917 revolution, had grown, but an accurate assessment was difficult for American observers to make. In June 1941, when the tremendous German war machine, which had already defeated the nations of Western Europe, turned its tanks to the east and attacked the Soviet Union, the chance of the Soviets repelling this invasion seemed small to War Department intelligence officers. They advised Secretary of War Henry Stimson that the campaign would last only one to three months. The press, too, predicted Soviet collapse. "In Russia Hitler will find more men to conquer and more territory to cover than in any previous campaign," declared the editors of the *New York Times*. The "quality of the strategists and the equipment" encountered by Hitler would be inferior to what he had already met in the West, and he would be able to achieve his main military objectives "within a few weeks." The Soviet army retreated, fighting as it fell back. Even when the Russians stopped the German forces at the Battle of Stalingrad and defeated them in 1943, the prospect of the Soviet Union actually reversing its defeats remained "gloomy." Mighty Soviet counterattacks over an eight-hundred-mile front in 1944 finally convinced disbelieving Americans. With the Germans fallen into panic, a *New York Times* editorial reevaluated the paper's earlier position. "The European-Asiatic colossus has come not only into strength but into a supreme confidence in her strength." Some observers desired Russia "to be strong enough to insure an Allied victory but not quite as strong as she actually is." In the end the Allies could not "have it both ways."[51]

The Soviet nation, which had proven its power against invasion, had strength rooted in the land. The country encompassed a vast sweep of territory over the greatest land mass in the world, across two continents, nearly half-way around the earth. Only the scattered British Empire had a greater extent. "Its land area is greater than the surface of the moon," began a 1945 piece on the Soviet Union in the *New Yorker*, "and its forests would more than cover the United States. . . . Russia's coastline is longer than the circumference of the earth at the equator. . . . The Yakut Republic, which is just one section of one of the states making up the U.S.S.R., is as big as all non-Russian Europe. . . . During the four centuries preceding this one, Russia increased its territory at a rate that averaged fifty square miles a day." The country was potentially rich in the natural resources of forests, oil, iron ore, coal, gold, minerals, and timber, even if poor transportation had left them largely undeveloped. The Soviets produced only one-sixth as much oil as the Americans in the 1940s, but their oil wealth, potentially the largest of any country, was still hidden in the earth. Among the independent nations at the end of World War II, the USSR had a population second in size only to China's.[52]

These sources of power, the land and the people, could readily be agreed upon by watchers of the Soviet Union, but the country had suffered a loss of some twenty million dead, and millions more were maimed or wounded. Soviet cities were in ruins. The nation lost 1,710 towns, more than 70,000 villages, and 6,000,000 houses; 31,850 industrial plants; and 98,000 collective farms. Foreigners were allowed to observe little of the direct destruction of war, but what they saw was disturbing. When Eisenhower flew into Russia in 1945, he "did not see a house standing between the western borders of the country and the area around Moscow." Ambassador W. Averell Harriman found Stalingrad "a desert of broken brick and rubble, the survivors huddling in cellars or tar-paper shanties." Margaret Bourke-White, the *Life* photographer, saw a battlefield that "looked like the end of the world. . . . As far as the eye could reach was wasteland, pitted with shell holes, channeled with trenches, littered with the remains of war which had swept in concentrated fury back and forth across it." One town she came across near the front was "reduced to a collection of skeleton fingers, pointed toward the sky."[53]

Since the late 1930s the Soviet Union had ranked in industrial production second only to the United States. From far behind it had surpassed France, Britain, and Germany in quick succession. But the potential of Russian industry remained questionable.

"Need We Fear Russia's Economic Strength?" was the question heard again and again. Near the war's end, after Russian industry had been wiped out in the western regions, the Soviets were producing less than two-thirds as much steel as in 1938, little more than half the pig-iron and coal, and smaller amounts of iron ore and manganese. Of the country's sixty-six thousand miles of railroad track, which was merely a fourth of the American rail system, half had been destroyed. Some large plants suspended production when they were moved in their entirety from war-endangered regions to safety deep within Soviet territory. Wendell Willkie reported seeing a factory that had been "picked up bodily from its foundations in Moscow" and put back in operation more than a thousand miles away with some thirty thousand workers. This feat, which showed him what the Soviets could accomplish with time and patience, was costly and rare.[54]

In the summer of 1944 Eric Johnston, a leading businessman and the president of the U.S. Chamber of Commerce, observed Soviet factories at work during a six-week trip. He saw nothing in any industrial center to convince him that the Russian output per person was more than roughly 25 to 50 percent of that in most American factories. Trudging through a factory making planes for the Soviet air force, W. L. White, the journalist accompanying Johnston, noted that even though the factory was equipped with "the best American machine tools," it was unlit and dirty and seemed "to lack proper organization." In the plant that made one of two automobile models in all the Soviet Union—which looked rather like "a 1935 model Buick sedan with the difference that it is a sloppy engineering job"—the journalist found "no smooth-running assembly line but a series of linked bottlenecks and connected piles."[55]

The Soviet standard of living was abysmal. Moscow's monotonous rows of apartments were "like the architecture of an institution." The people were suffering—"the crowd is almost as poorly fed as it is poorly dressed." It did not matter that the Soviets were hard-working, White recorded; they produced so little that their living standard was less than that of the American jobless on work relief. He told one Russian, "I wouldn't expect you to believe that your standard of living here is less than was that of our poorest on WPA." He found most of the people in milk lines holding American-made tin cans to carry the milk home in.[56]

Shortly after the war, the Soviets claimed to be making rapid economic advances: industrial output in 1950 was 73 percent higher than in 1940. Their sweeping assertions concerned realist strategists, who feared the growing economic strength of the Soviet Union, particularly in heavy industry. Actually, production of petroleum, copper, iron, and steel lagged far behind that of the United States. Production of consumer goods like cloth and shoes was less than half that of the United States. The automobile industry was "in the infancy stage." Taken as a whole, the size of the Soviet economy was not much more than one-third that of the United States. A study in the early 1950s concluded that the "relative economic weakness" of the Soviet economy stood out, "rather than economic strength."[57]

Little had apparently changed for the Soviet citizen after the war. "My first impression was one of general grayness," wrote the American ambassador Walter Bedell Smith, who came to Moscow in 1946. The buildings were in an advanced state of disrepair and the "entire city looked mildewed." The Soviet economy might be rising slightly, observed Smith, but only by dragging down that of Germany and Eastern Europe. The standard of living for the entire region was being "lowered, not raised," as Soviet production concentrated on the heavy industries of steel and machinery instead of consumer goods. A Soviet citizen had to work 14 hours and 5 minutes for one pound of coffee, the American 22 minutes; the Soviet, 104 hours and 30 minutes for a pair of shoes, the American, 7 hours and 15 minutes.[58]

The Soviets maintained an imposing military, technically somewhat backward, but formidable in manpower. To Hanson Baldwin, the military affairs expert, the Russian forces resembled "none of the ordered chaos of Western armies on the move but rather the terrible surge of the hordes of Genghis Khan—cavalry, tanks, busses, carriages, mules, oxen, cows driven along for meat and milk, soldiers, women, camp followers, all joined in inexorable mass movement." Although not an efficient army, it was effective. Wendell Willkie had observed in war that, despite the scarcity of food, fuel, clothing, and medicine, "no Russian talked of quitting." The Soviets' ferocity in defending their homeland may have been fired by a confident mission to protect and spread communism, although, as W. L. White explained, the Russians were fighting for something more important than ideology. They fought "in the name of Holy Mother Russia."[59]

The Soviets were limited in the materiel they could mobilize for the military, but Soviet secrecy made it difficult to know exactly how strong the postwar military was. A *Foreign Affairs* analysis of Soviet defense expenditures revealed that the military was demobilizing, with outlays in real terms in 1947 only 40 percent of those of 1944. While the Soviet forces probably shrank from over 11 million members at their 1945 peak to around 2.8 million in 1948, many estimates in both government and the press at that time placed the figure over 4 million. In either case, the Soviet armed forces were second in size only to the Chinese. During the Soviet demobilization, *U.S. News and World Report* declared, "Russia, at this stage, is the world's No. 1 military power. Russia's armies and air forces are in a position to pour across Europe and into Asia almost at will." But Chief of Staff Dwight Eisenhower was confident that the Soviets were not planning for war. He assured Truman and the Joint Chiefs of Staff, "I don't believe the Reds want a war. What can they gain now by armed conflict?" They had taken about all they could assimilate, he reasoned. In addition, the Soviets lacked a strategic air force and a navy, and their army could not launch an offensive to defeat American forces in Europe.[60]

The Soviet Union was a power because of its people, resources, territorial extent, and fervent nationalism, George Kennan pointed out in a 1946 telegram to the secretary of state, but he did not believe that the country's desire to enhance its power through intensive industrialization and military development necessarily meant that it was bent on outright conquest. Yet Soviet strength was sufficient to hold the Eastern European regions over which Soviet armies had run in the last days of the war. So in place of the old world order there arose two alignments, one centered in the United States and the other in the Soviet Union.[61]

An American news correspondent in Europe, Howard K. Smith, standing on the levee of the Elbe River as the war drew to a close, looked across at "the New Russia" on the other bank not a hundred yards distant: "Not since the medieval end of the *Völkerwanderung* had an outsider pitched his tents so deep in Europe, and I confess to feeling an involuntary resentment at the intrusion," he recorded. "Then a stranger thought struck me: namely, that it was *I* who stood on the German Elbe—not a neutral visitor from Mars, but a taxpaying citizen of the U.S.A., without passport or visa, five thousand miles from home. With me on the levee were fifty more Americans, behind us ten thousand more, and linked to us across half the width of Europe a hundred divisions more. It was going to be a long time before Europe got over this, too." A glance at the map led Smith to a startling conclusion: the nation that had expanded most since the outbreak of World War II had not been the USSR but the United States. "The farthest of Russia's new areas of dominance are 600 miles from her borders. The farthest of America's are 7,000 miles."[62]

The picture of the world after its greatest war was one of vast and terrible dislocations. The war had torn the laborers, farmers, and businessmen from the tasks that had made the world work. It had wrecked the foundations of the old world order, with its historic traditions, politics, social institutions, and commerce.

The United States, spared this devastation, began to influence areas of the world that had been part of the old order. Among the new centers of self-imposed American responsibility were the potentially strongest Asiatic power, Japan, and the potentially strongest European nation, Germany, each having lately dominated nearly a continental area by itself. The liberated countries, and most of America's allies as well, were in the process of reconstruction under predominantly American influence. The task of cleaning up rubble, restoring ways of life, and building the world anew was herculean.

But the general weaknesses that hindered war-torn and developing nations did not in the end make America strong. One did not necessarily lead to the other, though it is obvious that American strength, its relative strength in a particular piece of time, had been magnified by a power vacuum in areas of the world where other nations had once been dominant. Still, external weakness did not create internal strength, for otherwise why did other large countries distant from the destruction of war, such as Australia, Brazil, India, or Canada, not become great powers? We must explore further, turning our attention to the properties of the nation itself.

3

The

Elemental

Forces

To understand the origins of the American world role requires that we look closely for dynamism within the nation. The search includes a broad view of the environment and qualities of the society. Geographers, demographers, scientists, economists, and military leaders put forth various explanations. They cited elements of power: the continental size of the United States; the plentiful endowments of resources; the demographic characteristics of the population; the advancement of science; the dimensions of economic production; and the force of the military. Our task is to understand what was new or unique about America that set it on its mid-century course in the world, comparing its elements with those in the nation's past and with those of other countries.

Geography

A search for the power base of the world role begins with the elemental forces of nature, resting in the geography of the land and the sea. In a time of global war the realists examined geographic distances, topography, and climate through the study of geopolitics, which defined the power of a nation by the spaces it controlled.

The early realist Nicholas John Spykman pioneered in charting the country's geopolitical place in the world by publishing *America's Strategy in World Politics* in 1942. Spykman began with the proposition that states "make the preservation and improvement of their power position a primary objective of their foreign policy." Therefore, the United States had to "develop a grand strategy for both war and peace based on the implications of its geographic location in the world." His idea that the natural power of the United States had prepared it for an enlarged part in the world received wide acclaim in the press, and *Time* gave Spykman credit for writing with "the colossal calm of the new fatalism in which geography is destiny." In the same year as Spykman's study, Robert Strausz-Hupé's *Geopolitics* stated the case: "Geopolitics is concerned with power-politics."[1]

American geopolitical interest was new but not original; it revived germane writings of European geographers. At the turn of the century in England, Halford J. Mackinder had theorized that the geographic spaces of Eurasia fashioned the great world empires of history. In a paper delivered to the Royal Geographical Society in London in 1904, he argued that the Eurasian heartland, which he defined roughly as the interior region from the Arctic coast to the central deserts and from the Baltic to the Black Sea, was the pivot for exercising authority in the world's land areas. He grouped the other land areas around the heartland in crescents, the first encompassing Europe, the next the British Isles, and the farthest, North and South America. World War II convinced Mackinder of Eurasia's strategic importance. Writing in *Foreign Affairs* in 1943, he recognized that the United States now rivaled the British Empire as a world power, but he held to his theory that whichever country occupied the Eurasian heartland was the greatest land power of the globe. The Germans became especially intrigued by geopolitics, reformulating Mackinder's treatise as a science of national expansion. Karl Haushofer, a German army officer and later professor, wrote of the "demoniac beauty of geopolitics." In his books and the monthly journal he edited, *Zeitschrift für Geopolitik,* he devised Nazi strategies to dominate lands to the east.[2]

Americans' interest in geopolitical theory grew as they sought to understand the enemy in war. Maj. George Fielding Eliot warned that Americans had better learn from geopolitical strategy before it was too late, since Hitler came closer to world domination than any other dictator or emperor. Geopolitics also became a respectable basis for designing postwar power relationships. In 1942 a Columbia University geographer, George T. Renner, envisioned a postwar division of Europe that reduced some forty nations to nine major powers. He not only kept their overseas empires intact but went so far as to grant Germany the Congo and Japan islands far into the Pacific, leading critics to charge that such a peace would amount to an overwhelming victory for the country's enemies. Despite this false start, geopolitics remained in vogue after the war as a way to map out national interests.[3]

Geopolitical theory focused on strategic location. Great oceans separated America from Europe and Asia, although technological revolutions in travel and communication had eroded the country's isolation. Reversing Mackinder's vision, American geopoliticians placed America not on the world's fringes but at its pivot. The United States had become a metropolitan center, situated between the two great population regions of Western Europe and Eastern Asia, and geopoliticians asserted that world maps centered on Europe misrepresented the power status of nations. The line marking the middle of the world map—zero degrees longitude—drawn through Greenwich, England, at the heart of the British Empire, demonstrated an outdated worldview of European primacy. North America was no longer a mere satellite, for the United States had become a commercial hub, using the oceans as highways both east and west. It also served as an arsenal and base for mobilizing forces in wars across either ocean.

Reflecting on America's world situation, Spykman saw a need for new maps. "Such a radical alteration in the distribution of power in the world" as the rise of the United States, Spykman observed, "was an adequate basis for the introduction of world maps adapted to the task of telling more accurately the story of world relationships." A map with the United States in the center, he posited, would give a clear picture of its actual world position in regard to both Europe and the Far East. Suddenly, in the 1940s, it appeared to Neil MacNeil of the *New York Times* that geographically the United States had come to sit "in the very center of the civilized world."[4]

Geopolitical strategy also emphasized the enormous land mass of the United States—close to three million square miles, over 6 percent of the land of the earth. There was space in America for a growing people, thriving farms, and expanding industry, and the hinterland defied conquest by any invading army. "Is space power?" asked Robert Strausz-Hupé. The history of World War II convinced him that it was. He drew the lesson: None of the small nations had been able to repel an Axis invasion; the largest nations survived.[5]

Colonies added several hundred thousand square miles to the government's officially compiled gross land area. At the turn of the century the organization of territory, administered directly from Washington, had been the standard measure of power for statesmen who thought colonial expansion realistic and necessary for the nation to rank with the empires of Europe. The United States kept its hold on outlying territories, the largest by far being Alaska, followed by the Philippines. After the Japanese invaded the Philippines and Guam early in World War II, the U.S. Army and Navy fought to retake the lost colonies.[6]

During the war the United States set the groundwork for an elaborate network of bases. In 1940 the government acquired from Great Britain naval and air bases in Newfoundland and on the islands of Bermuda, the Bahamas, Jamaica, St. Lucia, Trinidad, and Antigua, and in British Guiana. Securing these bases, President Roosevelt stated, was "the most important action in the reinforcement of our national defense that has been taken since the Louisiana Purchase." The bases abroad were not only to defend the continent but also to project power quickly and effectively against an enemy anywhere around the globe. As President Truman declared emphatically in 1945, "we are going to maintain the military bases necessary for the complete protection of our interests of world peace. Bases which our military experts deem to be essential for our protection, and which are not now in our possession, we will acquire." The United States took fortifications on Okinawa, and shortly after the war American bases went up in Iceland, Greenland, the Azores, Saudi Arabia, and North Africa.[7]

For a brief period after the war the United States, with the acquisition of Pacific islands once part of the Japanese empire, reached its greatest overseas territorial expanse. But even at this extent, the United States including its possessions was far smaller than the British and French empires, and on balance it soon lost far more territory than it had taken in war. The Philippines gained independence on July 4, 1946, subtracting 115,000 square miles from the aggregate gross area of the United States. The country was setting free its empire, not amassing one. But so was Britain, overtaxed by its overseas responsibilities, soon to dismantle the greatest empire of all in a vain effort to regain its waning vitality in world affairs. A large imperial domain was an antiquarian foundation of power, though the need for bases remained a strategic preoccupation.[8]

The danger of atomic attack led geopoliticians, at least temporarily, to see value in America's continental territory. They fashioned elaborate plans to reduce the vulnerability of cities and industrial complexes. "Even atomic bombs meet their master in the invincibility of space," wrote the strategist Ralph E. Lapp. If spacious new cities were built, new factories set apart from one another, and people dispersed into adjacent suburbs or broad areas of untouched country, they might be safe. To combat a hydrogen bomb attack, Lapp proposed a plan for Washington, D.C.: the Pentagon should be cleaned out and used only for "dead records," the Senate should be moved from the Capitol to nearby Alexandria, Virginia, and the House of Representatives removed to Bethesda, Maryland. But the costs involved were prohibitive, and the numbers and magnitude of atomic weapons rapidly confounded these outlandish schemes.[9]

No explanation of the world role that ignored geography fully comprehended it. But other nations stretched across continents or lay in temperate climates, in strategic locations, or across trade routes. The United States was less than half the size of the Soviet Union. Australia occupied a whole continent. The areas of China, Canada, and Brazil were larger. With the exception of the Soviet Union, these nations were isolated from European conflicts. Canada and Brazil were New World nations with similar opportunities for development. Moreover, Britain had been a great power in the nineteenth century on a little island off the coast of a continental land mass. There was no consistent correlation between the country's size and location and its power.

Natural Resources

The United States had enough natural resources to meet the bulk of its own needs with more to spare. In the words of the geopolitians Harold and Margaret Sprout, "no other large country has so generally favorable a natural environment." The eastern forests and fields provided timber, furs, and crops; the plains of the Midwest produced food and clothing fiber; the meadowlands of the northern lake country supplied dairy products; the Western prairies and pastures offered beef, milk, pork, and lamb; and the deposits of the Rocky Mountain West yielded iron, copper, lead, zinc, and gold.[10]

The statistics were dramatic. Americans harvested one-third of the grain and half of the cotton grown on earth. The United States was the world's largest producer of iron ore, copper, gypsum, phosphates, zinc, salt, and lead. It produced substantial amounts of gold and platinum, and more silver than any other nation. It ranked first in the production of petroleum and had supplied more oil than the rest of the world together. It refined 60 percent of the world's oil and produced 90 percent of the natural gas. The United States was the earth's largest producer of coal, and its deposits of uranium became a source of future power with the splitting of the atom.[11]

In metals, the United States produced as much as the combined output of Canada, the Soviet Union, and Chile; in fuel minerals, as much as the Soviet Union, Germany, Britain, Venezuela, Japan, France, Poland, Iran, the Netherlands, India, Burma, Belgium, and Luxembourg. U.S. production of all minerals was about four times larger than that of the Soviet Union, the second largest producer, and was larger than the combined ouput of the Soviet Union, Germany, Britain, Canada, Venezuela, France, and Japan.[12]

Projections of reserves, too, were impressive. The estimated life of the coal fields in the Appalachian Mountains and the West had been fixed at 5,000 years. Iron ore in the Lake Superior region, extracted at the wartime rate of 90 million tons a year, a rate that seemed unlikely to continue in peacetime, would run for 50 years; low-grade ore would no doubt remain for an additional 250 years. Copper reserves could hold out 30 years, and zinc, 25 years. Potash would last for centuries. Water power was perpetual, and forests and the soil of farms, with proper care, would last forever.[13]

Americans had at hand the materials to build factories, highways, railroads, ships, and planes. Geopoliticians pointed out that Americans enjoyed the advantage of not having to buy excessive resources abroad. Furthermore, since American production of coal, copper, iron ore, sulphur, and phosphates exceeded consumption, the United States sold surpluses to foreign buyers. To wage war, the nation easily expanded production, furnishing 80 percent of the petroleum used to win World War I and as much as 95 percent of the aviation gasoline used in World War II.[14]

Conservationists revealed that certain reserves—tin, nickel, and oil—were growing low, but this was not a dire prospect in the 1940s. Low-grade minerals remained in the earth, available for use as research scientists uncovered ways to tap them efficiently. Imports supplemented resources in short supply, and materials critical in the event of future war could be stockpiled. The advice of the Joint Chiefs of Staff was to keep on hand a five-year supply of all the materials received from outside the Western Hemisphere. That would keep industry free of imports.[15]

Oil was a prime strategic resource. In 1944, Secretary of the Interior Harold Ickes feared that the American supply of oil would eventually dry up—by his reckoning, proven reserves at current consumption rates equaled only fourteen years' supply. He recommended that the life of irreplaceable American fields be prolonged by developing foreign sources, the most promising of which was the Saudi Arabian oil field, perhaps the world's richest. But just then it did not seem that America needed Middle East oil. In Texas alone *Fortune* counted a hundred thousand wells, and some twelve hundred new wildcat wells were being drilled every year. Saudi Arabia had a total of thirty-three wells—three of which failed to produce oil. Yet in the postwar years oil was no longer taken from the ground inside America or off-shore on the continental shelf and in the Gulf of Mexico as fast as consumers demanded it.

Negotiations to secure foreign oil were not alone with the Middle Eastern monarchs but mainly with the British government. Between them, the United States and

Britain controlled approximately 80 percent of the world's oil, and the two governments divided up the Middle East into spheres. An American corporation, the Arabian
American Oil Company, owned in equal shares by Standard Oil of California and the
Texas Company, possessed exclusive rights to the bonanza of Saudi oil, and for the time
being the British retained rights in Iran. J. Howard Pew of Sun Oil, stating that an
Anglo-American agreement on oil could be "a first step in what might be a carefully
laid plan for a superstate cartel," reflected an easy optimism that a far-spread United
States oil industry would transport oil from producing to consuming areas with relative
economy.[16]

Foreign sources of uranium preoccupied the government beginning only in the
1940s, during work on construction of the atomic bomb. The head of the Manhattan
Project, Leslie Groves, had the notion that if the United States gained worldwide
control of uranium ore, it would thwart attempts by any other power to challenge its
lead in atomic weaponry. The most productive uranium mines were in the Belgian
Congo, and the American ambassador in Britain, Winant, requested a secret agreement
with the Belgians, whose government-in-exile in London administered the African
colony. He sought a monopoly of uranium but did not object to an arrangement allowing Britain alone to share access to the supply. In September 1944 the United States
obtained what it wanted—first refusal to purchase the Congo uranium. These diplomatic maneuvers to control world supply soon proved futile when uranium deposits
were found in other lands.[17]

A bountiful physical environment contributed massively to making America a
resource capital of the world, but not because the land had more resources than other
countries. Once Britain had made great advances as a world power with few domestic
natural resources besides coal. At the other extreme, the Soviet Union had substantially
failed to tap reserves of resources that were probably larger than those of any nation.
Land and resources were without value until they were used. When Secretary Ickes
computed for the first time in 1944 the total value of American assets—arriving at the
imponderable figure of $12,023,000,000,000—he concluded that natural resources
meant little without the ingenuity and the genius of the people, who were both the
creators and the inheritors of this wealth.[18]

Population

Approaching the problem of the world role through demography, Joseph Davis stated
in *Foreign Affairs* in 1950, "Our most basic resource is our people. Both numbers and
quality are important." America's population, which in the late 1940s stood at 145
million—6 percent of humankind—led a director of the U.S. Bureau of the Census,
Philip M. Hauser, to make a direct association between spectacular population growth
and the development of the United States into "a large, primarily urban, industrialized

world power." The growth had been fueled by a stream of 40 million immigrants from the Old World, constituting the largest migration in all recorded history.[19]

Not only population size but continuing growth was vital. In the early 1940s Hauser had predicted that with a slowing of growth "the relative position of the United States from the standpoint of the demography of the world will become increasingly less important." A smaller portion of the world's population might adversely "affect the position of the United States as a world power." But despite the terrible losses of war, the increase in the 1940s, nearly 20 million, turned out to be the largest on record. Both the absolute increase and the percentage increase were more than double those of the 1930s. So in 1950 Joseph Davis projected that the "strength of this nation 30–50 years hence promises to be far greater than had seemed likely." The recent growth was less from immigration, which had been restricted by law in 1924, than from natural increase. The baby boom that began in 1945, as soldiers returned from duty abroad, married, and resumed their domestic lives, continued into the 1950s.[20]

The more populous a country, the larger the industrial plant it could furnish and the greater the number of battalions it could muster. America's youth translated into a large pool of potential laborers or soldiers. The median age of the population was thirty in 1950, and demographers figured that when the children of the baby boom reached maturity, a new high tide of births could be expected to sustain growth in the 1960s or 1970s. Overpopulation or its debilitating effects of starvation and depleted resources were not feared because Americans had room to grow and to improve the quality of their life. They lived about fifty to a square mile, far more sparsely than in Europe or China. They constantly shifted from farms to cities and from region to region to take advantage of the opportunities of industrialization. By 1950, nearly 60 percent of the population lived in industrial urban areas.[21]

The value that Americans placed on education to improve the condition of the next generation increased their proficiency in the know-how of a productive manufacturing society. Only 3 percent of the population was illiterate in 1948; no other nation of comparable size had a literacy rate so high. By statistical standards, the levels of education were rising, and education was carried further for more young people than in any other country. By one count, the number of students at American colleges and universities was as large as in all the rest of the Western world.[22]

It is doubtful that America could have reached its world position with a population the size of Australia's or Canada's. On the other hand, the American population did not rank with those of China, India, or the Soviet Union, and when it had exceeded the population of Great Britain during the nineteenth century, the United States did not suddenly achieve the stature of Britain in world affairs. In addition, the American population was not increasing as quickly as those of Latin American and Asian countries, which were often more youthful as well. Still, the American levels of education in technical skills were unmatched in other nations, which leads us to another element of power.

Technology

Technology, the expertise to harness the forces of nature, had brought forth inventions of steam and steel, transportation, and mass communication. For some observers these were the secrets of power both to build and to destroy. In 1943, Ralph Turner, a professor at Yale, argued that the possession of technology made for a unique economy of effort: "Today mere numbers of men, or the possession of raw materials, or the holding of strategic positions is not the essential source of power. Only those nations having scientists, engineers, and skilled workers who are masters of the knowledge and the skills required for devising and operating intricate machines and chemical processes can adequately equip armed forces. Armed forces are now the cutting edges of a vast social machine organized to achieve the maximum power which contemporary technology makes it possible to produce." After the war, the physicist Arthur H. Compton asserted in 1945, America would have to depend on science to maintain its world position. The United States, he added, had recently taken "a leading place in searching out nature's secrets."[23]

Exemplifying technological prowess in World War II, American soldiers had built and run railroads on five continents and laid pipelines that together stretched nearly halfway around the world. U.S. Navy engineers had built modern seaports out of the reefs of Pacific islands and a pier at Naples out of the superstructure of a ship the Germans had overturned to block the harbor. A Twentieth Century Fund study claimed that the ancient pyramids of Egypt, erected by untold toil over decades, could be built anew in a matter of weeks or months by a few battalions of Seabees with power-driven equipment. After all, by one calculation, the output of a single day's electricity by Consolidated Edison plants in New York City was enough to do the work of three million harnessed horses or ten times as many laboring men.[24]

One explanation for this technological creativity was the nurturing of it by a free, open society. Albert Einstein, who had conceptualized his revolutionary theory of relativity in Europe but fled to America after the Nazis took power, believed that freedom of speech and thought encouraged scientific imagination: "Making allowances for human imperfections, I do feel that in America the most valuable thing in life is possible, the development of the individual and his creative powers . . . . Here, for generations, men have never been under the humiliating necessity of unquestioning obedience. Here human dignity has been developed to such a point that it would be impossible for people to endure life under a system in which the individual is only a slave of the State and has no voice in his government and no decision on his own way of life."[25]

Yankee ingenuity put abstract scientific ideas into practice, producing a historical record of inventiveness in the cotton gin, the telegraph, the sewing machine, the telephone, the phonograph, and the electric light. "While Europe was refining her science," Arthur Compton said, "we were applying our knowledge to the every-day jobs of making agricultural machinery, electric lights and transcontinental railroads."

The work of lone experimenters was supplemented by research organizations in industrial laboratories, university facilities, and government projects.[26]

A standard measure of a people's inventiveness, the number of patents issued by the government had risen steadily from 12,137 in 1870 to 42,238 in 1940. Choice inventions of the 1930s and 1940s were air conditioning, plastics, synthetic rubber, artificial fibers, television, helicopters, and gasoline produced from coal. Although few scientific inventions originated during the war—the number of patents fell temporarily by nearly half—some military efforts had peaceful adaptations in the magnetic wire recorder, photoprinting, microfilm, diesel engines, plywood, aluminum, and atomic energy. After the war, the number of patents rose again, to 43,040 in 1950, and technology had a discernible impact on consumer and other peaceful products with electronic computers and transistors.[27]

Technology takes us on a next step in our quest. Inventions and scientific discoveries had a strong bearing on international relations. Steel, steam, and electrical output were factors in the calculations for ranking powers, and aviation and mass communications had their impact on trade, spheres of influence, and diplomatic procedure. Technology alone, though, was not the decisive element. It had to be controlled and applied for certain ends. Technology contributed to power insofar as it enhanced a nation's industrial and material strength.

Economic Production

With a new sophistication, economists analyzed economic production as a dynamic element of power that had more impact on the world role than the space of a nation or the size of its population or armies. "Differences among nations in levels and rates of change in productivity," the economist John W. Kendrick wrote, played "a crucial role in the competition among nations" and were fundamental to their survival and advancement. National power therefore increased with the total production of goods and services. When Dean Acheson considered the different bases of power—"political, economic, and military"—he concluded that the most essential was "industrial productivity." Patriotic speeches and economic analyses developed the image of a powerful, productive America. The United States is now "the greatest single economic force on earth," stated Department of Commerce economists in the late 1940s, "and the kind of foreign economic policy we follow now and in the next few years will inevitably determine in large measure the policies to be followed by the rest of the world."[28]

The United States had long taken an ever-increasing proportion of the world marketplace. By the late nineteenth century the American economy had become an industrialized power of the first rank. In 1870 it accounted for 23.3 percent of the world's industrial production. In 1880 the United States surpassed Great Britain as the world's largest industrial producer, creating 28.6 percent of the world total. By the eve of World War I, in 1913, the figure stood at 35.8 percent, and in the boom of the 1920s it reached 42.2 percent. The Great Depression of the 1930s brought a retrenchment, but the energetic growth in the wartime economy more than offset the loss.[29]

Immediately after World War II until about 1950, the economy peaked at about 50 percent of the total production of goods and services of the entire earth, measured in gross national product. Even if this measure of GNP by contemporaries was approximate, the American achievement was unprecedented in the modern world, since the early Industrial Revolution in Britain. No other nation produced close to half of what the United States did.[30]

Economists sought to explain this productive advantage as something more than the result of the enormous war destruction inflicted on competing industrial nations of Europe and Asia. They alluded to Adam Smith's *The Wealth of Nations,* which had set forth the factors of production as land, labor, and capital. Shepard B. Clough's *The American Way: The Economic Basis of Our Civilization* encapsulated in 1953 the factors of a vast land stored with abundant natural resources; a highly advanced technology; saving and investment on a large scale for new firms and equipment; and a labor force possessed of characteristics of growth and incentives to increase their material lot.[31]

Theoretically, an increase in any one of these factors would increase production, and contemporary economic analyses showed that they all had increased, though some existed in exceptional abundance over the period since the United States became an industrial nation in the late nineteenth century. As for the amount of land and quantities of resources, the country's continental boundaries had not changed significantly since the aftermath of the Mexican War. The population had increased more than the land area—threefold, from 40 million in 1870 to 150 million in 1950—and the labor force had grown proportionately. In the same period the total stock of capital had increased far more than the population—twenty times, from $45 billion to over $895 billion. New technology usually required capital, and technological development, as measured by the increase in horsepower of equipment in manufacturing industries, had increased at a similarly high rate—fifteenfold. Based on these comparisons of growth in these factors of production, a critical way of generating the productivity of a modern, industrial economy was the devotion of capital resources to the development of technology.[32]

The accelerating growth of the American economy—over forty times from 1870 to 1950—nevertheless warranted recognition of factors that were not part of the traditional equation of production. The education of the populace in the skills of new ways of work, the pursuit of research to increase knowledge, the organization of business administration, and the spirit of enterprise all served to increase efficiency. These new factors were difficult to quantify because they could be variously classified as the quality of labor, as investment in what economists called human capital, or as technological development. By postwar qualitative or quantitative measures of these new factors, however, the United States excelled in their development or led the world. Production increased as the people applied their skills and their capital to new techniques, equipment, and facilities.[33]

Vast production provided opportunities that were unavailable to other nations. The chairman of the War Production Board in 1945 reported that even with the rationing and shortages of war, "the American consumer and his family remained by far the best-fed, best-housed, and best-clothed civilians in the world." Millions found jobs. Their paychecks rose. Their savings increased. In 1944 the president scaled down his estimate of the Depression that one-third of the nation was in poverty, but he stated that he could not be content "no matter how high that general standard of living may be," if "some fraction" of the people was "ill-fed, ill-clothed, ill-housed, and insecure." Farm families in the Appalachians and on the plains remained in hardship, and slum dwellers, mainly blacks, had a hard time getting by inside big cities.[34]

Postwar affluence was evident in the abundance of consumer goods and the opening of vast suburban housing tracts. "August 14, 1945, marked not only the war's end but the beginning of the greatest peacetime industrial boom in the world's history," was *Fortune*'s forecast for the economy. The United States "cannot avoid the most wonderful times in world history." In 1949 the per capita income in the United States was $1,453. The next highest incomes were found in Canada, New Zealand, and Switzerland, in the $800–900 range. Sweden and the United Kingdom were at the $700–800 level. No others exceeded $700—half as high as in the United States. In the Soviet Union, per capita income was estimated at $308, and in China, $27. Another measure of American plenty was the amount of nourishment taken by the people. In 1949 the average daily consumption of Americans was 3,186 calories, higher than anywhere else in the world. Consumption in England was near 2,700 calories, while in Algeria, the Philippines, Japan, and India, it was below 1,800.[35]

By about 1950 Americans had, per capita and in total, more automobiles, more telephones, more radios, more vacuum cleaners, more electric lights, more movie theaters, and more hospitals than the people in any other country. Americans could buy up to six times as much clothing and shoes as non-Americans. They saved more money each year than the citizens of most other nations earned. Americans owned 70 percent of the world's automobiles, operated 35 percent of the railroads, and 83 percent of the civilian aircraft. They had 50 percent of the world's telephones and listened to 45 percent of the radios. All of this resulted from their amazing productivity, which allowed Americans the shortest work week in the world.[36]

Even after the wants of the population had been satisfied, the American economy was of such proportions that politicians and economists expected it to defray the immense costs of exercising influence abroad without difficulty. A small part of the national surplus lay stockpiled in the nation's treasure. The government held over 60 percent of the world's monetary gold, over twenty-four billion dollars' worth in 1949. In addition, vast national production offered the opportunity to divert labor and resources from civilian consumption toward national defense or other overriding purposes. The surplus private and government-held wealth backed investment and grants to foreign nations. The United States was able to aid foreign allies with dollars, foodstuffs, technology, and services. It could build war machines, construct foreign bases, and pay expeditionary forces.[37]

World War II dramatically demonstrated what the American economy could produce when necessary. In a short time automobile plants converted to tank production, and shipyards and aircraft factories turned out warships and bombers. The huge war program had succeeded "largely by increasing total production," the Department of Commerce reported in 1945. "It was superimposed upon the aggregate flow of goods and services to civilians rather than displacing the latter." As the momentum of war production grew, new laborers, including women, joined the effort. Large modern plants went up, the largest in the world being the new Ford Willow Run plant near Detroit for production of heavy bombers, the B-24s. By 1945 unemployment had nearly vanished, and millions were in the military service. America had achieved a miracle of production; the gross national product had doubled, from less than $100 billion in 1940 to over $200 billion by 1945.[38]

The steel industry was symbolic of industrial might. Mills topped by row after row of stacks of belching smoke and lapping fire produced more steel than all of America's enemies and allies together. While steel capacity had increased a mere 17 percent by the end of the war, the increase alone was more than the Japanese empire ever produced in war, and nearly a third as much as Germany. *Fortune* granted the United States "a large margin of superiority" in the ability to produce about as much steel in a year as Germany could in three, or Japan in eight.[39]

When President Roosevelt asked the nation's manufacturers in 1940 to turn out 50,000 aircraft a year, they balked, questioning their ability to procure supplies and machine tools. In the mid-1930s the industry had produced a little more than 1,000 planes a year. In 1944, Roosevelt announced the rise in aircraft production: it had reached his expectation, and doubled it. He remembered gleefully "the most awful howl all over the country—couldn't be done—just couldn't be done. Well . . . we are keeping on going—keeping on making records." "American labor and management have turned out airplanes at the rate of 109,000 a year; tanks—57,000 a year; combat vessels—573 a year; landing vessels, to get the troops ashore—31,000 a year; cargo ships—19 million tons a year . . . ; and small arms ammunition—oh, I can't understand it, I don't believe you can either—23 billion rounds a year."[40]

The defense budget had risen from a little over $1 billion a year in 1940 to a wartime peak of over $81 billion in 1945. After the war, defense budgets were kept in the $13–14 billion range because of concerns that heavy expenditures might have serious economic consequences. In planning for postwar production, the Joint Chiefs of Staff had initially believed that the public would fail to accept the use of economic resources to maintain "overwhelmingly strong" forces in peacetime. Prosperity soon encouraged confidence among national security analysts that the economy could easily afford a massive military and that the public could be brought around to accept it. "The capability of the American economy," stated NSC 68, "to support a build-up of economic and military strength at home and to assist a build-up abroad is limited not, as in the case of the Soviet Union, so much by the ability to produce as by the decision on the proper allocation resources to this and other purposes." Expenditures on the military would not jeopardize economic production, but might enhance it. Early in the 1950s the national security analyses of the business-minded Eisenhower administration did not question this assumption.[41]

The exceptional ability of the American economy to support the military was expressed in a comparative study by the Council on Foreign Relations and the Royal Institute of International Affairs in 1953. The study reasoned that the British economy, which once had supported the world's largest navy and forces overseas, could not keep up: British military expenditures had become too costly and were expected to reduce the standard of living of the British people. The American economy, on the contrary, should be exempt from this overtaxation of its resources; "because of the American economy's enormous capacity to expand," expenditures on the military might actually raise "the standard of living of the American people . . . somewhat."[42]

Wealth afforded the wherewithal for the nation to create and maintain a world role, but the exceptional nature of this element of power was not new in the postwar period. After World War I American industrial production was over 40 percent of the world's total—a level approaching the post–World War II mark. The people, apart from visionary national leaders, had created a strong world power without primarily having that end in mind. They worked in pursuit of livelihoods and produced a self-sufficient nation whose development was eminently domestic. The purposes for which wealth was used were also important. The volume of production alone was not an accurate measurement of the magnitude of power, for wealth could be employed for private purposes. Production served to make choices about its uses possible.

Military Preparedness

After the world's two most devastating wars, realists frequently equated military force with national power. The military stood as the final recourse in international affairs, when peaceful efforts had failed. In 1945 the United States had the world's largest navy, the most far-reaching air force, the best-equipped army, and the monopoly of a weapon of enormous destructivity. The 1950 report on national security policy stated, "The United States now possesses the greatest military potential of any single nation in the world." The word *potential* was important in this analysis: the United States could quickly mobilize at levels unmatched by any other nation, and already its armed forces were stronger than ever before in peacetime.[43]

This military power was new in the American experience. In the summer of 1939, when Hitler's army invaded Poland, Dwight Eisenhower was distressed that the Polish army, which was crushed, far surpassed the United States Army in numbers and pieces of equipment. The American army's strength at home was less than 130,000 soldiers, with an additional 45,300 soldiers abroad, from Panama to Corregidor.[44]

By 1945 the United States Army had grown to over 8.2 million. More than 12 million military personnel were on active duty in all the services, outstripping the armed forces of the Soviet Union, according to U.S. and Soviet figures, as well as those of Britain, though probably not those of China. The Americans were better outfitted than any other military in the world. Moreover, George C. Marshall, the army chief of staff, granted this "great citizen army" qualities unknown to mercenaries or professional soldiers. As he told a graduating class of Trinity College, the soldiers would fight with more than their bodies, hands, and weapons. They would fight "with their souls in the job to do." He called it "the morale of omnipotence."[45]

A striking index of the increase in military power was the growth of the navy. In 1942–1943 the United States Navy for the first time in history surpassed the British Navy, both in tonnage and in number of vessels. The United States Navy had nearly equaled the British Navy in World War I, and as a result of the Washington Conference in the 1920s it had achieved legal parity with the British. In 1940 it embarked on a program to become the greatest sea power on earth. What followed was new. No longer did the United States Navy bear comparison merely with a single navy, even the British. "This nation at the end of 1944," Under Secretary of the Navy Forrestal predicted, "will have naval power and accompanying air power . . . to match the naval forces of the rest of the world." On January 1, 1946, the United States Navy had by official count 70,579 vessels, including battleships and cruisers, but also patrol boats and landing craft, comprising 13,828,000 tons. Forrestal was not content. He wanted to maintain after the war the margin of superiority that the United States had gained.[46]

On Navy Day, October 27, 1945, as an armada lay at anchor in New York City, President Harry Truman made a speech from a stand in Central Park to a throng of about a million that crowded the area to its farthest limits and to a radio audience across the country. On the recent day of victory over Japan, the president stated, "ours was a seapower never before equalled in the history of the world." *Time* pictured the event: "It was Navy Day for the greatest Navy of the world in the greatest city in the world." "Seven Miles of Sea Power Reviewed by the President," was a headline in the *New York Times,* which described the "world's mightiest fleet in all its glory." On that autumn day as cumulus clouds rolled by and the wind blew, Truman viewed battlewagons, cruisers, aircraft carriers, submarines, and submarine chasers, which stretched from 60th Street to Spuyten Duyvil, hearing twenty-one-gun salutes all along the way.[47]

The entire United States Air Force of 1939 had consisted of about 1,175 planes, far fewer than either Germany's or Britain's, and had grown to 72,726 planes in 1945. In addition, there were nearly 40,000 planes in the navy. This force, the mightiest in the world, played a major part in the aerial destruction of Hamburg, Dresden, Cologne, and other German cities. The U.S. Strategic Bombing Survey deemed Allied air power "decisive" in Western Europe and critical to the success of the invasion. It had "brought the economy which sustained the enemy's armed forces to virtual collapse" and "brought home to the German people the full impact of modern war." Some of the survey's members dissented from this popular view. John Kenneth Galbraith, who had inspected German factories, found evidence that German production had actually increased even under the heavy bombing, and he pressed the argument with perplexed Air Force officers: "The aircraft, manpower and bombs used in the campaign had cost the American economy far more in output than they had cost Germany." How, then, did the United States prevail? Galbraith's answer: because, "our economy being much larger, we could afford it."[48]

With the return of peace, the armed forces underwent a rapid demobilization that reached what Eisenhower called "the proportions of hysteria." The army, navy, and air force were slashed to 1.5 million members. The remaining ground forces numbered half those of Britain and possibly about one-third those of the Soviet Union. Eisenhower and Marshall opposed the mass discharge as disarmament, and they urged compulsory military service in peacetime to keep the nation strong: "A weakling, particularly a rich and opulent weakling, seeking peaceable solution of a difficulty, is likely to invite contempt," Eisenhower counseled; "but the same plea from the strong is listened to most respectfully." In 1948 a peacetime draft, a radical departure in the life of the nation, was begun, inducting several hundred thousand young men into the armed services each year for two years of active duty.[49]

In his Navy Day speech Truman had pledged that even after demobilization, the United States would remain the "greatest naval power on earth." In 1947 the American tonnage of 3,800,000 was still well over half the world total. Further cuts brought the force down to 2,844 ships in 1950, including the reserve mothball fleet. Both the navy and the air force, which was down to 18,370 planes in 1951, began to rebuild during the Korean War. Strategists and scientists had also dreamt of future aerial forces: "Aircraft, manned or pilotless," would "move with speeds far beyond the velocity of sound" and "unmanned devices" would "transport means of destruction to targets at distances up to several thousands of miles."[50]

What transformed the entire nature of military strategy was the atomic bomb. "It is a harnessing of the basic power of the universe," Truman declared in August 1945, announcing that a B-29 superfortress had dropped the first atomic bomb used in war. "The force from which the sun draws its power has been loosed against those who brought war to the Far East." The heat, blast, and radiation fall-out of one bomb destroyed the city of Hiroshima on August 6, and a second bomb was dropped on Nagasaki three days later. The writer John Hersey found that the survivors he interviewed had at first no conception of what had hit them, and "even if they had known the truth, most of them were too busy or too weary or too badly hurt to care that they were the objects of the first great experiment in the use of atomic power, which (as the voices on the short wave shouted) no country except the United States, with its industrial know-how, its willingness to throw two billion gold dollars into an important wartime gamble, could possibly have developed." On the radio President Truman had threatened "a rain of ruin from the air, the like of which has never been seen on this earth," and the Japanese government decided to surrender the day after the second bombing, on August 10.[51]

The bomb was the last great blow of the war, but the political value of atomic weapons was questioned even at the beginning. Secretary of War Stimson, who was directly responsible to the President for the administration of the bomb's development and use, argued that without the bomb a massive invasion would have been necessary to defeat Japan. He believed that a bloody fight might have been "expected to cost over a million casualties" to American forces. Stimson's estimate, the most authoritative in the postwar years, was nonetheless exaggerated beyond secret War Department figures in 1945. Before the first bomb fell, the war had been brought to the shores and skies of Japan by the American navy and air force. "The Hiroshima and Nagasaki atomic bombs did not defeat Japan," stated the U.S. Strategic Bombing Survey; the bombs shortened the war by perhaps a few weeks: "Based on a detailed investigation of all the facts and supported by the testimony of the surviving Japanese leaders involved, it is the Survey's opinion that certainly prior to 31 December 1945, and in all probability prior to 1 November 1945, Japan would have surrendered even if the atomic bombs had not been dropped, even if Russia had not entered the war, and even if no invasion had been planned or contemplated."[52]

Even disregarding the conventional capabilities of the navy, army, and air force, the increase in American military power because of the atomic bomb was inestimable. Truman received the news of the bomb's explosion while with members of the crew of the *Augusta* on his return from the Potsdam conference: "This is the greatest thing in history," he said to a group of sailors. Because of the bomb, he felt a sense of pride bordering on hubris. He was not alone. The military strategist Arnold Wolfers described it too: "this country occupies a unique position among the nations—one, in fact, that has no parallel in history. If this country, due to its naval and air superiority, enjoyed an unusual degree of immunity from attack even before the atomic bomb was invented, the solitary possession of this all-powerful weapon has put the cities and production centers of the entire world, including the mighty Soviet Union, at the mercy of our peaceful intentions. There may never have been a time when all other great powers were so dependent upon the attitude of one major country."[53]

That no other nation then had the bomb gave outward credibility to this opinion. Both Germany and Japan had mounted programs to apply nuclear fission to wartime uses as energy or explosives, and the fear that Germany might be the first to build a bomb had spurred the American effort; Einstein had expressed these fears to Roosevelt. But neither old enemy at war's end was close to assembling atomic bombs. German science atrophied because of its complacency, its control by Hitler, and its loss to exile of some of the country's greatest physicists. In Japan, five cyclotrons that had been devoted primarily to basic atomic research and could not be used to make bombs were destroyed by occupation forces. As for the Allies, Great Britain and Canada had cooperated in building the bomb but had left its actual construction to the United States. Because of the complex technology, industrial production, and expense needed to construct an atomic bomb, other nations could not attain the same results as quickly as

the United States. "Whether any nation—we are excluding Great Britain and Canada—
could achieve such an intensive program is a matter of serious doubt," reported the
State Department panel on the problem of atomic energy headed by David Lilienthal
and Dean Acheson. Although this view may have deserved skepticism because the
science that had produced the bombs was worldwide, a fact that the Acheson-Lilienthal
report also emphasized, it was widely recognized that some years would pass before
other powers could be expected to discover the so-called secret of the bomb and begin
production.[54]

Estimates by scientific advisers of five years or more for another power to produce
a bomb were not uncommon, but as I. I. Rabi later put it, these estimates tended to be
extended indefinitely: "If you had asked anybody in 1944 or 1945 when the Russians
would have it, it would have been 5 years. But every year that went by you kept on
saying 5 years." Government predictions, based on intelligence estimates, were inaccu-
rate. In July 1949 Secretary of State Acheson told a meeting of senators and congressmen that "the Soviets might have a bomb by mid-1951 and, in three or four years' time
thereafter, a fairly serious quantity." In the event, the American monopoly of the bomb
ended before autumn of that year, 1949. Even after the Soviet Union exploded the
bomb, some of the old way of thinking lingered. Truman had his doubts that the Soviets
were ever equal to the accomplishment. In 1953, following his departure from Washington, he stated, "I am not convinced the Russians have achieved the know-how to put
the complicated mechanism together."[55]

It was realized immediately on inspecting the damage in Japan that a war with
atomic bombs would be immeasurably more destructive and terrible than any the world
had known. Truman's initial reaction was tempered by his realization of "the tragic
significance of the atomic bomb." General Eisenhower's revulsion against this new
weapon was extraordinarily immediate. When Secretary of War Stimson informed him
of its existence in 1945, Eisenhower remembered "a feeling of depression" coming
over him, and he expressed the hope that "we would never have to use such a thing
against any enemy" because he "disliked seeing the United States take the lead in
introducing into war something as horrible and destructive as this new weapon."[56]

Thus the possession of the bomb posed the problem of how the bomb could be used
for practical purposes in war. As early as 1946, the strategist Bernard Brodie set forth
certain lasting propositions about what he called the "absolute weapon": the power of
the bomb was such that any city in the world could be effectively destroyed—ten
bombs comparable to the one used on Nagasaki would eliminate New York; no adequate defense existed; missiles carrying bombs would be unable to be stopped; and,
what was marvelously perceptive, superiority in the number of bombs did not in itself
guarantee strategic superiority. In the five years after the invention of the atomic bomb,
the number of nuclear warheads in the stockpile grew slowly. In 1945 the stockpile had
only two weapons, both of which were dropped on Japan. In 1946 no atomic bombs
were ready for delivery and components were on hand to assemble probably no more

than nine. In 1947 the stockpile had thirteen weapons, and in 1948 it had fifty. The United States was depending on the deterrent effect of the know-how to make the bomb, rather than on the possession of a large stockpile.[57]

In the years of the American monopoly, after dropping the two bombs on Japan, the United States did not explode another in anger on the territory of an adversary. Its use was considered. The National Security Council inaugurated discussion of this problem in NSC 30 in 1948, concluding that "in the event of hostilities, the National Military Establishment must be ready to utilize promptly and effectively all appropriate means available, including atomic weapons." These weapons, according to NSC 162/2, at the beginning of the Eisenhower administration, should be considered for use as conventional weapons, though the President's approval of this document did not mean that he would relinquish his control of them. Accordingly, the use of the bomb was envisioned in plans for war against the Soviet Union. But the final decision was never made.[58]

Despite the unparalleled potential of destructive force, the idea that power was consistently, if not exclusively, lodged in the military was not accurate. After World War II the United States, by demobilizing its army, navy, and air force, enhanced its power more by its skilled population's industrial production than by its actual military force. The demobilization resembled that at the end of World War I, when the United States rapidly disbanded forces and had the potential, if it had continued its naval build-up, to possess the greatest fleet in the world. Even during the years of the American atomic bomb monopoly, the United States had no more than a handful of the weapons in its stockpile. Moreover, superior numbers of soldiers and arms alone did not necessarily ensure supremacy. The outcome of combat was also determined by the intangibles of morale. Advances in the technology of efficient weapons, particularly the atomic bomb, would not necessarily guarantee the success of national endeavors. After the Soviet Union developed atomic weapons in 1949 and built the means for their delivery several years later, the military usefulness of these weapons was further placed in doubt. The nation that launched an attack faced retaliation. The destruction on both sides might be so great that the ultimate reason for the existence of atomic weapons would be to deter their ever being used. We must look further for the sources of the world role.

4

The

Legitimacy

of Power

The origin of the American role in the world was dependent not only on material elements but also on intangibles. The evaluations we have made of the material factors of geography, resources, population, technology, production, and military potential are multifaceted and complex. The capacity among the people for a world outlook is even less susceptible to precise analysis.

National Character

A few realist thinkers contested the very existence of a national character because of the difficulty of establishing widely acceptable generalizations about an entire people. National character was nevertheless a quality that they did not disregard. Secretary of State Dean Acheson once considered it vital: "When I speak of the 'character' of a population," he wrote, "I am thinking of what Milton had in mind when he said, 'Citizens, it is no small matter what manner of men ye are!' Indeed, it is not a small matter at all. It is an essential matter." Character comprised "everything that enables a people to act together with vigor and decisiveness, and—as de Tocqueville put it—'to persevere in a great design.'" The conception behind national character was that national communities with common territory, economy, language, and culture shared certain qualities of character that occurred more frequently in one nation than in another.[1]

For a long time national character had been studied by travelers and traders, usually from foreign places, who appraised the country from an outsider's point of view. Their analyses were in the tradition of Alexis de Tocqueville, whose nineteenth-century descriptions of American society attracted Americans to his insights a century later. Modern-day visitors examined how Americans differed from other nationals to explain the power Americans had built up on their continent.[2]

D. W. Brogan, a British commentator and professor at Cambridge, published in 1944 *The American Character,* which he intended as "a personal book" of his impressions of Americans. "All over the United States," Brogan discovered in his travels, "there was the same life, conditioned by the same history, by an experience in which the outside world grew more and more remote, backward, barbarous, and—so it was thought—relatively weak." He looked at this "American civilization"—in "God's Country," he called it—of advertisements, gadgets, radio programs, movies, medicines, and solutions to human woes, and of highways, concrete roads navigated by new-model cars, and great trains. Brogan saw the strength of this civilization from within. The few foreign-make cars were lost among the Buicks, Chevrolets, and Fords, and the air was full of American-built passenger planes. Brogan lauded the American way of life, its mechanization, colossal business enterprise, experimental zeal, and disregard of formalities. There was immense power, too, seen in the military and the mobilization of "more men in the air over Berlin than Washington had Americans under him at Valley Forge or at Yorktown." The United States had come to press "with unconscious weight and power" on a world that would not leave it alone.[3]

Another Englishman, Alistair Cooke, who began delivering radio broadcasts from the United States to Britain in 1937 and later became a naturalized citizen, collected his impressions in *One Man's America* in 1952. Well traveled across the country from New England to the Rockies, he presented "what is most characteristic, about the people and landscape of the United States": Americans were proud, "self-reliant" and "reckless," and they were a people of "technical genius." Cooke accentuated favorable characteristics and their value to the national power. The assumption that Americans had "grown soft" from their labor-saving gadgets was unproved in his experience, for the Americans who were "most devoted to convertible automobiles and glass-enclosed showers made no complaint on this score when they ripped up Japanese jungles for airfields or waded ashore at Okinawa."[4]

Though the English were the most prolific in writing about American character, other nationals joined them. Father R. L. Bruckberger, a French Roman Catholic priest, wrote in his journal upon arriving in New York for the first time about his qualification for seeking out the national character: "This is . . . adventure starting from zero . . . . Ignorance can be a privilege . . . . I have decided to look, to listen, and to learn America, as if I had never even heard of it." After eight years of life among Americans, travel coast to coast, and research, Bruckberger used his perspective to write in 1959 his *Image of America*. He believed that the American nation had characteristics well suited to engaging the rest of the world. "A great hope for the world lies in the élan which I feel in this nation's response to the appeal of a universal vocation, and the immense capacity for fidelity to that vocation once it is given." What struck Bruckberger was that "Americans are so proud of their superlatives in nature and industry as the Pharaohs could conceivably have been of the pyramids. They are right . . . . The results are here: America has many of the best physicists, the best chemists, the best civil engineers, the best doctors, in the world." He did not claim the same for achievements in theology and philosophy, but he did believe that the United States would "no longer retreat in defense of the freedom of the world."[5]

Noting that the character of the people had reached maturity of age with World War II, cultural historians explored another approach to national character. They sought to describe the traits of the people in thought and conduct over time. They posed again the question asked by the Revolutionary-era poet and naturalist Hector St. John de Crève-coeur: "What then is the American, this new man?" In this effort, Henry Steele Commager assigned character a central role in the nation's power, declaring that "a people's character is, in the last analysis, the most important thing about them—more important by far than statistics of armies and navies, of production or of shipping or of finance. For material things cannot in themselves achieve any thing . . . . What is, in the end, of decisive importance are the intangible factors that we call character."

Commager and other historians analyzed diverse historical forces that had forged the new men and women who had built modern America. They had come from foreign nations seeking to escape oppression or to improve their material condition. In settling the vast North American continent, they transformed their old ways to become uniquely American: restless, enterprising, wealthy, optimistic, egalitarian, and free, characteristics that they represented abroad. The American "took for granted that his was the most favored of all countries, the happiest and most virtuous of all societies, and, though less sure of progress, was still confident that the best was yet to be." His "genius" was "inventive, experimental, and practical." He remained "careless, good natured, casual, generous, and extravagant." He had "developed his own art and literature and claimed a native music, while his motion pictures had conquered the world." Americans ultimately had "achieved such power as no other modern nation had ever known," wrote Commager, but he continued to see a dichotomy: "would that passion for peace which Henry Adams had named the chief trait in their character triumph over the temptation to establish a Pax Americana by force?"[6]

Moving beyond the traditional impressionistic observations of random travelers' accounts and historical studies, anthropologists applied scientific research to national character as a contribution to the World War II effort. Margaret Mead, who had been examining the native cultures of Samoa and Bali since the 1920s, turned homeward to study the culture of her native land. In her 1942 book *And Keep Your Powder Dry,* she pioneered examination into "the strengths and weaknesses of the American character—the psychological equipment with which we can win the war." "To win we must take accurate inventory—not only of our copper and our aluminum, of the number of skilled mechanics and potential fliers with good eyesight—but of our American character." "What then is this American character," she asked, "this expression of American institutions and of American attitudes which is embodied in every American . . . ?" Her discovery: "We believe that the strength of those who are reared to freedom is greater than the strength of those reared in an authoritarian state." But, not coming to any final conclusions in her wartime effort, she continued her examination in the late 1940s. She sought to develop scientific methodology for the study, and she called for field studies within complex modern states, involving methodical cooperation with historians and members of other disciplines working in various cultures.[7]

Expressing a debt to Mead, Geoffrey Gorer, a Briton, adapted anthropological technique to analyzing his knowledge of the United States based on extended visits and considerable travel over ten years. Finding Americans to be collectively different from any other people, he selected the American characteristics that he thought contributed to world power: "The bounty of nature, the fortunes of war, and the drive and know-how of individuals have made the United States already the richest country in the world and potentially the strongest; if to these qualities are added general civic responsibility and political farsightedness its power and influence will be incalculable." In their attitudes toward the rest of the world, Gorer thought, Americans tended to believe that "full Americanism and full humanity are equated."[8]

An innovation of American sociology further contributed to "scientific" study of national character. Beginning in the 1940s, poll data were collected on national stereotypes from the populace at large, thus shifting emphasis away from scholars and scientists. These data revealed that Americans most frequently described their own countrymen as peace-loving, generous, intelligent, progressive, hard-working, and brave. In several countries data were collected from peoples on their impressions, and among the adjectives chosen most frequently to describe Americans were practical, progressive, hard-working, and generous.[9]

The travelers, historians, cultural anthropologists, and social scientists, while not always in agreement, frequently concurred in their findings. The sources of national power, they found more often than not, lay in the characteristics that Americans had evidenced in their daily lives, developed through centuries of experience in the New World. Generally, Americans were seen as competitive and hard-working, habits acquired from the early settlers and pioneers who had felled forests and broken prairies to create farms and towns. Mechanically proficient, Americans had excelled in devising, improving, and repairing tools and implements. Mobile geographically, they sought to achieve a higher standard of living. Because Americans had been preoccupied in building their own country, they traditionally had few ambitions beyond their own borders. Pursuing a free and independent course, they were said to prefer hard-headed compromise and international arbitration in their dealings with other nations, despite wars and conflicts in their past. They were considered pragmatic in their international policies, such as Dollar Diplomacy, but also had an idealistic side, as reflected in Woodrow Wilson's declaration of war address against Germany in 1917. Americans continued to favor an antimilitarist posture until the beginning of World War II, shunning the wasteful maintenance of a large army and navy. But once war broke out, they had not hesitated to bring to bear their traits of individual initiative, improvisation, and technical skill. If other peoples had been engaged in grand schemes and misguided ideologies, Americans had the capability to set out to achieve practical goals and succeed.

These characteristics were capable of change and adaptation. Henry Steele Commager investigated this phenomenon. World War II did not test the American character as it did the British, French, and German characters, he observed, but it "did dramatize that character and, as it were, recapitulate it." What was significant was that "the greatest crisis of modern history found American public opinion sensitive to the moral issues involved, that this war united Americans as had no previous war, that it was fought for what seemed unselfish ends, and that Americans generally supported a just peace and a postwar program of unparalleled generosity." He believed that the war reinforced most of those traits distinguished as peculiarly American, rather than changed them:

> It confirmed Americans in their optimism, their self-confidence, and their sense of superiority, for it ended, after all, in the greatest of victories and one for which they could claim a major part of the credit. They had bet on material power, on machinery and science, on organization and the assembly line, on a citizen army and a democratic system of government—and they had won. They had been sure that America was the best and happiest of nations, and what they had seen overseas had strengthened this conviction . . . . They were used to material comforts, and their government supplied them with such comforts as no other armies knew; they took the envy of less fortunate peoples and soldiers as a proper tribute and gave generously of their surplus. They were, most of them, honorable, brave, and idealistic; the war did not force them to abandon honor for treachery, soldiers fought as bravely at Bataan or Okinawa or Bastogne as their forefathers had at Bunker Hill or Gettysburg or the Argonne, and idealism remained not only an individual characteristic but an official policy.[10]

Yet, as Commager saw the matter, the war may have affected some American traits.

> Probably Americans overseas were broadened by their experience with other peoples and civilizations, and some assuredly learned that superiority in plumbing did not necessarily mean superiority in all the amenities of life or in moral qualities. Cultural isolationism dissolved, along with economic, political, and military, and the average American of 1950 probably knew more about European society, literature, and politics than had his father or his grandfather. Certainly Americans emerged from the war less self-centered and more conscious of the economic interdependence of all nations and of their responsibilities for the maintenance of sound international economy. The military came to occupy a larger place in the American scene than ever before and to exercise an unprecedented influence on the formulation of political policy . . . . No previous American war had discovered such a breakdown of personal integrity, such looting and destructiveness, such sexual promiscuity. It at once exacerbated race relations and advanced racial equality: the total effect was to bring the whole issue of race out into the open, to expose the gap between the pretense of equality and the reality of inequality, and to force the government to take some action toward bridging that gap. Finally the achievements and responsibilities of the war seemed to have brought, along with a sense of power,

bewilderment and confusion. Americans knew that theirs had become the most powerful nation on the globe, but they were, for the most part, embarrassed rather than exalted by their position and their power.[11]

Analyses like Commager's were full of insights into the Americans, but quite contradictory characteristics could be identified in the past. Americans had been both inward- and outward-looking; pragmatic and idealistic; militaristic and pacific; proud of and embarrassed by power. National character study might reveal certain definitive traits, but it emphasized generalizations concerning a diverse people over a long period without explaining which traits predominated at any particular time.

Morale

The morale or spirit of a people, like character, was an imprecise element, and the realists, who preferred the concrete and clearly observable, often eliminated it from calculations of power. Morale meant the will of a people to choose and follow a certain way. It determined the degree to which people devoted their energy and imagination to agriculture, industry, or foreign relations in war or peace. Its measurement was often as public opinion. The journalist Walter Lippmann once complained that in "undertaking to explain our foreign policy in terms of our public opinion I would be offering to explain one mystery in terms of another." But it was clear to Gabriel Almond, who wrote a classic analysis of public opinion and foreign policy in 1950, that within a single decade, the 1940s, the American people had been torn from "the privacy of civilian pursuits and thrust into a position of world leadership." Never "perhaps in history has a people risen to such power in so short a time." Their potential was extraordinary. "The most powerful nation in the world today is the United States," declared the diplomatic historian Thomas A. Bailey in 1948, "and consequently the most powerful body of public opinion in existence is formed by the American people."[12]

American participation in the war against Germany and Japan turned nearly every expression of opinion—the statements of leaders, the stories of newspapers and magazines, and broadcasts on the radio—toward the promotion of public cohesion. President Roosevelt used the means of persuasion at his disposal to attract the people's support for his war policy. "Our strength," he said, "is measured not only in terms of the might of our armaments. It is measured not only in terms of the horsepower of our machines." The "true measure of our strength" lay imbedded in a democratic social system: "For you can build ships and tanks and planes and guns galore; but they will not be enough. You must place behind them an invincible faith in the institutions which they have been built to defend." Believing that the war had shown how interdependent were the "groups and sections of the population of America," he discouraged "bickerings, self-seeking partisanship, stoppages of work, inflation, business as usual, politics as usual, luxury as usual."[13]

The newsreel, poster, and press image was of a people marching together, shoulder to shoulder, as they faced adversaries abroad. In his 1942 bestseller, *Prelude to Victory,* James Reston, a *New York Times* reporter, charged that it was a disservice for Americans to think as Republicans or Democrats, labor or capital, farmers or managers, left wing or right wing. "We must, therefore, fight as the people of the United States of America." Reston urged the press to take the lead in unifying the people. Editors in every little town should assist in the education of the local men and women who necessarily played a part in America's international responsibilities. Americans "cannot win this war," Reston wrote, "until it ceases to be a struggle for personal aims and material things and becomes a national crusade for America and the American Dream."[14]

Failure to agree on foreign policy would be dangerous, was Walter Lippmann's warning. Lippmann, highly influential through his newspaper columns, published in 1944 *U.S. Foreign Policy: Shield of the Republic.* The best-selling work argued that divisions among the people about the conduct of foreign relations would damage the nation's interest. "Our failure now to form a national policy," he exhorted, "will, though we defeat our enemies, leave us dangerously exposed to deadly conflict at home and to unmanageable perils from abroad."[15]

Those promoting consensus were working toward one essential goal: the nation's involvement in the world. They usually framed the discussion by opposing isolationism. The term had implied abstaining from permanent alliances and from formal foreign commercial, aid, and cultural commitments. It began to be used about 1900 after the Spanish-American War and was used in 1914 about American intervention in the world war. The word was highly charged with emotion in the 1930s debates over entry into World War II. The claim of isolationism actually concealed a history of territorial expansion, growing foreign trade, international agreements, and involvement in major wars. But it did represent a deep mood of the American people until the 1940s not to intervene in world affairs.[16]

"We have learned," Roosevelt said in his fourth inaugural address, "that we cannot live alone, at peace . . . that we must live as men and not as ostriches." We "shall not repeat the tragic errors of ostrich isolationism," he also said. Whether on the left, right, or center, there was little argument. Wendell Willkie, the Republican who had campaigned for the presidency against Roosevelt in 1940, repeatedly assailed the isolationist stand. The liberal vice president Henry Wallace said early in 1941, "We of the United States can no more evade shouldering our responsibility than a boy of eighteen can avoid becoming a man by wearing short pants. The word 'isolation' means short pants for a grown-up United States." The conservative senator Robert Taft denied that a desire "to withdraw entirely from any interest in world affairs" had ever existed as a policy, but he acknowledged that postwar conditions would be sufficiently different to "require a departure from our traditional policy." Henry Luce put it this way: It was time for Americans to realize "the moral and practical bankruptcy of any and all forms of isolation." Walter Lippmann also charged that isolationist policy was in "bankruptcy" and suggested substituting for the term "isolation," "insolvency."[17]

The great sea change in opinion began sweeping the country on December 7, 1941, with the sudden and unexpected attack on Hawaii, leaving Pearl Harbor in ruins and smoke, and ships of the Pacific fleet flaming wrecks. The next day at the Capitol, the president came to deliver his six-and-a-half-minute message decrying the infamy. Roosevelt's ovation was reportedly unmatched in his years as chief executive, and when he said that Americans must always remember the sneak attack of the Japanese, the audience stood and cheered. At the close he looked up and smiled and waved his hand. In Congress there was no debate over the president's words, only speeches by a few members declaring unity for war. The vote for entry into World War II was 82 to 0 in the Senate and 388 to 1 in the House, contrasting sharply to the divided vote over American entry into World War I.[18]

Images of Pearl Harbor burned into the memories of the leaders and the citizens but were only the beginning in the formation of new opinion among those who had once been staunch isolationists. Striking and symbolic was the change in attitude of Henry Cabot Lodge, Jr., the grandson and namesake of the senator who had worked to keep the United States out of the League of Nations. The younger Lodge remembered long evenings spent in front of the fire of a high-ceilinged library talking alone with his grandfather about the league. The grandfather, a "beloved counselor and friend," the younger man recalled, influenced his choice of the Republican party and his isolationist affiliation. Lodge remained an isolationist after his election to the Senate in 1936 until Pearl Harbor, when he vehemently rejected isolation, becoming a captain in the Army Reserve and seeing combat with the tank units in North Africa. While in service, he was reelected to the Senate in 1942, but when the War Department decreed that incumbents of Congress must choose between the legislature or the armed forces, Lodge chose the army.[19]

The most influential shift from isolationism within the government came from another senator, Arthur Vandenberg, a Republican from Michigan, who had led the opposition party's criticism of Democratic foreign policy until the war. The Sunday of the Pearl Harbor attack, he was at home pasting clippings in his scrapbook record of his battle against President Roosevelt's interventionist steps. That afternoon, he reflected years later, "ended isolationism for any realist." Vandenberg's change of heart gained notoriety because of his position as the chairman of the Foreign Relations Committee. On January 10, 1945, Vandenberg made a major statement to the Senate declaring isolationism dead; it was no longer feasible in the light of modern warfare. He was for a "realistic unity" that would end the war in victory and "best validate" the national "aspirations" and "dreams" for afterward.[20]

After Pearl Harbor, Herbert Hoover and Alfred Landon, Republican leaders who had both been defeated in election by Roosevelt, rallied to the president's side and urged Congress, before it had voted, to make the decision for war. Hoover freely admitted that the war had changed his attitude toward American world involvement. In his 1942 book of peace plans, written with Hugh Gibson, *The Problems of Lasting Peace,* he opposed isolationism as a postwar policy and, like Taft, denied that it had ever fully existed. While defending his own policies of cooperation with the League of Nations, not membership in it, and reduction of armament through international conferences, he was clear that from this point on America had to cooperate with the Old World powers.[21]

The foremost isolationist group, the America First Committee, urged "all those who have subscribed to its principles to give support to the war effort," and the isolationist movement collapsed. Having proclaimed the "America First" doctrine since the 1930s, Charles Lindbergh changed his mind. For the aviator whose solo flight across the Atlantic had narrowed the gap between Europe and America in 1927, his thought about the world finally caught up with the technological breakthrough he had engineered. December 7 found Lindbergh in doubt about where the Japanese had attacked. He might have expected a move on the Philippines. "But Pearl Harbor! How did the Japs get close enough, and where is our Navy?" The next day, with the hard news confirmed and after a walk on the beach near his home on Martha's Vineyard, he determined, "I can see nothing to do under these circumstances except to fight." A few days later he volunteered to serve his country. The War Department and U.S. Army Air Corps turned him down because of his prior isolationist expressions, but as a consultant on aircraft to the military, he flew fifty missions against the Japanese, and in one dog fight he came close to death. The "issue between so-called interventionists and isolationists is past except from an academic standpoint," Lindbergh stated in November 1945. "We fought the war together and we face the future together as Americans."[22]

The press brought home the hardening of opinion after Pearl Harbor. Beginning the morning of the war declaration, the *New York Times* editorialists called for congressional "unanimity which will speak for a united nation." On December 9, after Congress had "thundered" its answer to the "madmen of Japan": "Gone is every sign of partisanship in the Capitol of the United States. Gone is every trace of hesitancy and indecision. There are no party lines today in Congress. There are no blocks, no cliques, no factions. . . . From every section of the country, from every walk of life, come pledges of support for the Administration." An editorial after the November elections of 1942 lauded the recognition that "isolationism, as an issue, is dead." The paper singled out Henry Wallace for his foresight in the stand against isolationism, for as early as ten years before, "when the trend of American opinion ran so strongly in the direction of political and economic isolation," he had pointed out "in clear and vigorous language, the limitations and the disadvantages of such a policy."[23]

That the mass of people supported the government was the impression of the leaders and the media. After the Japanese attack, President Roosevelt declared that "the Union was never more closely knit together." In its issue on Pearl Harbor, *Time* went so far as to report that "the war came as a great relief . . . . Japanese bombs had finally brought national unity to the U.S."[24]

Polls supported these impressionistic descriptions of unity, above all that the public had rejected isolationism before the end of World War II. Since Pearl Harbor, pollsters repeatedly asked the public, "Which of these two things do you think the

United States should try to do when the war is over—stay out of world affairs as much as we can, or take an active part in world affairs?" Never fewer than two-thirds of Americans favored taking an active part. In December 1941, 58 percent of the public wanted the United States to play a larger part in world affairs, rather than a smaller part or about the same part as it did before the war. By June 1943, the number voting for a larger part had increased to over three-quarters of the American public.

In the formation of this overwhelming majority, no class and no region differed from the national view. Even in the Midwest, the bastion of 1930s isolationism, well over two-thirds of the people favored the United States taking an active part in postwar world affairs. In the early summer of 1943, in New England 81 percent favored the United States taking an active part; on the West coast, 80 percent; in the mountain states, 79 percent; in the west-central states, 78 percent; in the South, 76 percent; in the middle Atlantic states, 76 percent. Economic classes showed solidarity in a majority view. The less well-off were not as adamant as the well-to-do, but the poor as well as the rich favored an active American role in the world. Political parties likewise agreed.

Even when pollsters tried to persuade people to abandon their anti-isolationist stance, the people remained unyielding. One survey during 1942 challenged those who favored taking an active part in world affairs: "Have you ever considered the possibility that we might have to keep up a large army, navy, and air force at great expense to help police the world if we want to take an active part in world affairs? Do you think this expense would be justified?" They were also asked, "If our trade with other countries after the war gets us involved in entangling alliances and power politics, as Europe always has been, would you still think it would be best to take an active part in world affairs?" The results: 93 percent still wanted to take an active part, regardless of the expense of an international police force, and 61 percent wanted international cooperation, despite the danger of entangling alliances.

Further confirmation of the end of isolation was the people's preference for postwar planning to begin right away in wartime. In the summer of 1943, 59 percent were in favor of planning the peace immediately, rather than waiting.[25]

So by the end of the war, amid the exaltation and relief, there was a commitment that the United States enter into the postwar world. And in the news of the day, August 14, 1945, were the stirrings of creativity that the United States would participate in the crisis of reconstruction, not because of the imminent aggression of any other power, but because the United States was ready to play a full part in the world. Truman came out on the north portico of the White House and, looking to the gathering crowd, congratulated the celebrants on their victory and urged them to remain involved in world affairs: "This is the day we have all been looking for since Dec. 7, 1941. . . . This is the day when we can start on our real task of implementation of free government in the world where we are faced with the greatest task we've ever been faced with. The emergency is as great as it was on Dec. 7, 1941."[26]

In New York, hundreds of thousands gathered and roared in joy after the victory message—"Official—Truman announces Japanese surrender"—flashed around the moving electric sign on the Times Tower at 7:03 P.M. Times Square was jammed. The police estimated the crowd at two million and proclaimed it an all-time record. The headline of the *Times* was "All City 'Lets Go.'" "Restraint was thrown to the winds." The *Herald Tribune* called the city "a roaring, writhing spectacle of elation," for those in the crowds tossed hats and flags into the air, and out of the windows of offices and hotels came streams of paper and confetti. Half a million people were still there at 3 A.M., and the celebration continued for two days.[27]

But even amid all the noise and celebration, the daily papers, like the president, connected the thought of victory with the call for postwar world involvement: "Never was the power and leadership of the United States more dramatically illustrated than by the spontaneous selection of President Truman as spokesman for all the nations fighting Japan," began a *Times* editorial after surrender. China, Great Britain, the Netherlands, India, and Australia had all fought against Japan, the editors recognized. "But it was the spectacular development of American power on land, on the sea and in the air that proved the decisive factor. . . . America's dominant part remains unchallenged." The day after next, the paper turned from Asia toward Europe to reinforce its position: the end of the European-dominated world presented "a special challenge to the United States, which stands before the world today not only as the mightiest of all nations but also as the principal representative of democracy . . . . We have already turned our backs upon the isolationism born of the last war"; America was now "jointly responsible for everything that happens anywhere in the world." In all this discussion, Russia was mentioned only in passing, as the dominant land power. But the implication was clear: America would remain a great power, even with the achievement of "a cordial understanding between Russia and the United States."[28]

Life covered the victory celebrations across the nation: the "biggest spree in U.S. history," it called the release of pent-up emotions that had been building for three years, eight months, and seven days, since Sunday, December 7, 1941. But beyond the cacophony of church chimes, air-raid sirens, honking horns, and shouting around the Chicago Loop, at the White House gates, on Hollywood Boulevard, and in New York's Times Square, the *Life* editorial proclaimed the meaning of America's victory. It was in America's world position: "During the war many Americans . . . learned for the first time about power politics and America's place as a nation in the world power equation. That place has grown so far and fast during the war that, as Mr. Churchill said last week, 'the U.S. at this minute stands at the summit of the world.'" Whether the war would be worthwhile was a judgment "still to be passed, and it is entirely up to us which it shall be." The story in *Time* conveyed the same theme: "The job of world politics, which the U.S. would now have to play to the hilt, would not be easy." The problems that required American attention included internal strife in China and hunger and unrest in Europe; Russia was not mentioned.[29]

The liberal *New Republic* cautioned its readers not to let the immense relief of victory make them aloof from world affairs. Americans had to be active in the world to prevent the conditions from persisting that had allowed the totalitarians power before the war. "We have not established forever a citadel of joy and peace against the assault of a barbarous invader. We have simply won the chance to do better in the future than we have done in the past." Again, Russia was not discussed in this context; the problems were of reconstruction: "The struggles and toils of arriving at a decent civilization are still ahead. Something of this feeling tempers jubilation at the prospect of victory."[30]

The end to the overarching tradition of isolationism by war's end forced the creation of another outlook. While isolationism had inferred separation from the world, internationalism meant involvement in it, in the pursuance of alliances and of economic, foreign-aid, and cultural commitments. Like "isolationism," the term "internationalism" was used loosely, as a precept to hold the people together. The rationale to maintain popular support was revolutionary: In a country once fully consumed with its everyday domestic needs, President Truman told his countrymen in a September 1946 news conference, the "foreign policy of this country is the most important question confronting us today."[31]

The charge of Harry Truman in May 1948—"Political issues ought to end at the water's edge"—was exactly the same that his erstwhile opponents Vandenberg and Lodge used to defend their support of the other party's policy. Their conception of the government's free hand in making foreign policy was taken for granted in secret official reports. NSC 68 found "expressions of national consensus in our society are soundly and solidly based." "The full power which resides within the American people will be evoked only through the traditional democratic process." That process required the government to lead the people by providing information on world affairs "so that an intelligent popular opinion may be formed. Having achieved a comprehension of the issues now confronting this Republic, it will then be possible for the American people and the American Government to arrive at a consensus. Out of this common view will develop a determination of the national will and a solid resolute expression of that will."[32]

The increasing preoccupation of American foreign policy with an expansive Soviet Union and its conception of a world order based on communism served not to initiate but to confirm the American unity over international involvement. Those who had converted to internationalism usually came subsequently to approve, though some only reluctantly, of the clash of the two world orders. On his return from the war in Europe, Lodge campaigned for the Senate again, this time calling the United States a superstate with responsibility to do all in its power to act internationally. The "bipartisan approach must be continued," he maintained in 1947, and the principal foreign policy concerned reconstruction rather than fighting communism, he held in 1948, though he nevertheless criticized communism. Senator Vandenberg defended his unflagging internationally minded postwar leadership in the Senate on the need for America to maintain a "maximum authority against those who would divide and conquer us and the free world." Even then he remembered the attack on Pearl Harbor, not some hostile action by Soviet communists, as the cause of his conversion to internationalism.[33]

In the 1949 work *The Vital Center,* the Harvard historian Arthur Schlesinger, Jr., analyzed the unprecedented large body of opinion that he believed supported international policy. The "interventionist-isolationist" debate was over, he declared, and Americans were thinking in global terms. "History has thrust a world destiny on the United States." Schlesinger warned that Americans had to defend the broad center against both fascists on the right and communists on the left, and he singled out the leftists and communists both within and without the country as the greatest threat. "The center is vital; the center must hold," he concluded, and because of it the United States was "in the great world to stay."[34]

In 1952 the presidential election verified the essential consensus for internationalism. For the first time in twenty years, a Democratic candidate had been defeated by a Republican, and the shared goal stated by both sides was to maintain the underlying consensus of foreign policy, not on every issue, but on the necessity for the United States to maintain a leading world role. President-elect Eisenhower and President Truman exchanged telegrams that went further than usual postelection congratulations and greetings. On November 5 Truman's message to Eisenhower stressed "the international dangers and problems that confront this country and the whole free world" and suggested that the two men meet soon at the White House to make "clear to all the world that this nation is united." Eisenhower agreed the next day, saying "I share your hope that we may present to the world an American unity in basic issues." The expressions of unity and world involvement marked a revolution in thought completed by the 1950s.[35]

Analysis of the Elements

Now we have come to the significant new element in the transformation in America's part in the world. In the development of its land, the size of its population, and the production of its economy, the United States was a mature nation in the late nineteenth century. These elements worked together to create a world power. But the physical properties of power existed before the nation took an active role in the world. The United States had been drawn into the major conflicts of the European world empires, beginning with the American Revolution amid the struggles between England and France, and continuing with the War of 1812 and the Napoleonic Wars. But for most of the nineteenth century, even following the Spanish-American War, when the United States acquired an overseas empire, the prevailing moods of the people toward foreign affairs were indifference and innocence. With few exceptions, the United States had been protected from world politics by the European balance-of-power system. The United States eventually entered World War I and emerged from it with the world's most productive economy, an energetic population of immigrant peoples, and a navy equal to the best. Yet again the nation rejected the role of a great power. The United States turned down membership in the League of Nations and, while the European system was breaking down, sought an illusive separation and normalcy.

Even reserves of material power were of limited significance in creating a world
role if the people and their leaders were not prepared to use them to influence international affairs. At the end of World War II, as after World War I, the American land mass
was vast, the large population was growing, the American industrial plant was producing by far the greatest percentage of world output, and the navy, air force, and army had
the potential to be equal or superior to all others in size and effectiveness. These
material elements were roughly comparable in their extraordinary magnitude at the end
of both world wars. Not until World War II did public discussion about keeping the
nation out of foreign affairs finally subside.

The emergence of the world role of the United States in the twentieth century
depended on the will of the people. The conversion to an international outlook among
the leaders of government and society became accepted by the mass of people of
different occupations, home towns, political parties, religions, ethnic groups, and races,
who, though divided by their separate interests, adopted unifying concepts to bring
them together in a collective worldview.

This mass of people and leaders drawn together in a general ideological harmony
of opinion and belief we shall call the "consensus." The consensus was defined not by
full agreement on policies of the American world role, but rather by broad agreement on
issues, expressed as unqualified enthusiasm or mere readiness to tolerate. The consensus generally shared the conviction that isolationism was at an end and that internationalism had replaced it, that the United States would become a full participant and use
its extraordinary power—political, economic, and cultural—to influence the relations
of the world.

The will of the people brought to bear the other elements of a world power. Once at
war with Japan and Germany, and on into the postwar period, the people supported the
reorientation of the nation's resources, manpower, technology, and production to interests far beyond the continental domain. Accepting geopolitical thinking, the largest
number in a wartime poll believed that the United States should acquire military bases
but refrain from annexing new territory. To mobilize labor for war-directed industries,
65 percent of Americans polled favored the government drafting persons to fill those
jobs. Postwar polls showed strong public support not only for compulsory military
service for young men but also for the requirement that all citizens up to age sixty-five
register with draft boards for defense work if needed. Nearly two-thirds of the people in
1948 and 1949 supported an enlarged army, navy, and air force, and a majority was
willing to pay higher taxes to support the nation's strength. Although the wartime
development of the atomic bomb had been secret, right after it became public knowledge in August 1945, a Gallup poll found that the overwhelming majority of citizens—
85 percent—approved the use of the bomb on Hiroshima and Nagasaki. More than
two-thirds were ready for the United States to use atomic weapons again, before any
other nation used them first on the United States. In the early 1950s the public favored
development of the hydrogen bomb by nearly four to one.[36]

What were the chances of the new consensus enduring? In the decade that followed the formation of consensus, the leaders did not doubt the obligation of the United States to be involved in the world, but some viewed the democratic process as poorly organized to direct foreign actions. One critic who came to downgrade public opinion as a molding force in foreign policy was Walter Lippmann. In *Essays in the Public Philosophy,* published in 1955, he looked back longingly to the nineteenth century, when a strong government had acted decisively without the constraints of mass opinion. In contrast, modern democratic government vacillated in decisions of war and peace. The reactions of the people were, for Lippmann, almost always negative: Public opinion would block preparing for war in time of peace because the people disapproved of raising taxes. It would oppose intervening in a conflict because that might provoke war. It would avoid withdrawing from a conflict because the adversary should not be appeased. "The unhappy truth is that the prevailing public opinion has been destructively wrong at the critical junctures."[37]

Lippmann's naysaying was not popular among a people whose will was supposed to be supreme. Henry Wriston, the president of the Council on Foreign Relations from 1951 to 1964, refused to believe that the people were not intelligently aware of international issues. "Never before in history, at no other place in the world, has a government of continental size, actively controlled by public opinion, faced issues either in scale and scope or in difficulty and complexity such as now confront the United States." But the temperament of the people determined the career of the nation in the world: "In the United States foreign policy is the expression of the will of the people." They did not have to be instructed in the day-to-day tactics of diplomacy, but if a president or secretary of state seemed too belligerent or too passive, or functioned in a way to irritate the public, he would come under pressure to alter his tactics. The people as a whole could be counted on to determine the nation's fundamental objectives, Wriston affirmed. "There is now a general consensus that we are caught up in the great tide of world events . . . . There is general agreement that we are in the world, and must play a great, if not a decisive, role. This is a tremendous gain, for it means that there is no such studied attempt to retreat from reality as occurred after the first World War. No one in a place of effective leadership has recently spoken of 'normalcy' as though it were possible to undo, or at least forget, a part of history that was dramatically costly in life and treasure."[38]

So through national democratic traditions that the moralists had once praised was wrought, perhaps ironically, the change the realists so favored: the emergence of the new world role. In a democratic society of free and vigorous discussion, a common point of view on international issues emerged among the people and the leaders. Both liberals and conservatives professed an end to isolationism, and both sides wanted the United States to assume the new role. At a time of victory when old enemies had been defeated and close allies had not yet turned into enemies, their expectations for America's world involvement prevailed over current fears of some foreign menace.

The general consensus over internationalism posited no alternative to a new relationship between American society and other societies around the globe. The exact nature of this involvement was still in doubt in the early postwar years when the United States began to confront the Soviet Union. Then the argument was not over isolationism and internationalism but over what form of internationalism the country should pursue. Would the preeminent nation be cosmopolitan or ethnocentric?

Legitimacy: The Reservoir of Good Will

There remains another dimension of power for us to consider. To convert these domestic elements into power, the nation had to establish an interrelationship with those over whom or on whose behalf the power was exerted. Other nations had to accept and confirm American power and objectives sufficiently to be guided by the lead of the United States.

After World War II, Americans, who earlier had expanded across the continent and went on to take colonial possessions, eschewed military coercion to annex territory to their domain. Rather, they expected to base their exercise of world power on longstanding expressions of mutual consent among nations. The symbols of authority were there, the great economy and strong military, and they might become effective tools in confronting an enemy. But for the most part, the ascendancy of American power was to rest not on violence but on respect, loyalty, and common interests. The extent to which these qualities were valued determined the extent to which the use of power was justified. These qualities would determine the legitimacy of the American role.[39]

Amid the destruction of World War II, the nations of the Western world looked to the United States for leadership. This was the determination of American policymakers and travelers who visited other nations. In the fall of 1942 Wendell Willkie, President Roosevelt's personal emissary, circled the globe in a four-engine bomber on a trip to the Middle East, Russia, and China. On his return from a 31,000-mile sojourn that took forty-nine days, he reported his impressions in a nationwide radio address and set forth his internationalist views in *One World*.[40]

All around the world Willkie encountered millions of people he felt held in common one particular idea that had tremendous significance for Americans. It was the "mixture of respect and hope with which the world looks to this country."

> Whether I was talking to a resident of Belém or Natal in Brazil, or one toting his burden on his head in Nigeria, or a prime minister or a king in Egypt, or a veiled woman in ancient Bagdad, or a shah or a weaver of carpets in legendary Persia, now known as Iran, or a follower of Ataturk in those streets of Ankara which look so like the streets of our Middle Western cities, or to a strong-limbed, resolute factory worker in Russia, or to Stalin himself, or the enchanting wife of the great Generalissimo of China, or a Chinese soldier at the front, or a fur-capped hunter on the edge of the trackless forests of Siberia—whether I was talking to any of these people, or to any others, I found that they all have one common bond, and that is their deep friendship for the United States.

They, each and every one, turn to the United States with a friendliness that is often akin to genuine affection. I came home certain of one clear and significant fact: that there exists in the world today a gigantic reservoir of good will towards us, the American people.

Willkie claimed the friendship of Stalin and some peoples that would soon be in doubt, but as Willkie saw it, the existence of this reservoir was "the biggest political fact of our time."[41]

Pearl S. Buck, the novelist who was reared by missionary parents in China, described in 1948 why she believed America was the world's hope at war's end. "All the world's peoples—not the politicians and the militarists and the big money-makers, but the peoples—were looking to the United States. They . . . were looking for a statement for humanity . . . . Our Constitution and the Bill of Rights were known around the world. Men hidden in caves and villages in countries ridden by tyrants memorized these documents in order to strengthen their own spirits." This confidence was the basis of considerable power: "We could have had our way with them, provided it was a way that would engage the highest in human spirit. By the power of our moral attractiveness we could have cowed even the nationalism of Soviet Russia and the crassness of communism. But we were so ignorant that we did not know our own power."[42]

Disgruntled critics of the country who had once fled abroad and returned to America found themselves feeling hope for their estranged land. The writer Henry Miller, after spending years in Europe, wrote in 1945, "We had the good-will of the world. We had no desire to take over the world and run it," and he made a connection between this good will and national power. "We have been forced to take a hand in the running of the world; we have been forced to share our treasures; we have been forced to make enemies and to fight them. In doing these things we have also been forced to take stock of ourselves. We have been obliged to ask ourselves whether we are a force for good or for evil. That we are a force we know."[43]

However romantic or sentimental, these reports connote an important concept of legitimacy—that the interests of both the nation exercising power and the nation accepting it must be upheld. American power employed to uphold the self-determination of peoples would be an irresistible force.

The other world powers deemed American material power to be predominant. In 1947 the *Economist* of London issued a report circulated widely by Americans as verification: "In any comparison of the potential resources of the Great Powers, the United States, even before Hitler's War, far outstripped every other nation in the world in material strength, in scale of industrialisation, in weight of resources, in standards of living, by every index of output and consumption. And the war, which all but doubled the American national income while it either ruined or severely weakened every other Great Power, has enormously increased the scale upon which the United States now towers above its fellows. Like mice in the cage of an elephant, they follow with apprehension the movements of the mammoth. What chance would they stand if it were to begin to throw its weight about, they who are in some danger even if it only decides to sit down?"[44]

Yet even to the vanquished, America held out hope, engendered not simply by the power of its battleships and weapons. In a report officially rendered to the Japanese emperor and read approvingly by General MacArthur, a Japanese diplomat recorded his feelings toward America at the surrender ceremonies aboard the *Missouri*. "I raised a question whether it would have been possible for us, had we been victorious, to embrace the vanquished with a similar magnanimity. Clearly it would have been different. . . . Indeed, a distance inexpressible by numbers separates us—America from Japan. After all, we were not beaten on the battlefield by dint of superior arms. We were defeated in the spiritual contest by virtue of a nobler idea. The real issue was moral—beyond all the powers of algebra to compute."[45]

In the Soviet Union, too, the United States was apparently the object of particular interest. When General Eisenhower visited Moscow after the fighting stopped in 1945, Joseph Stalin honored the American visitor by requesting his company on top of Lenin's tomb to view a great parade in Red Square. As far as anyone at the American Embassy knew, no other foreigner had ever been invited to set foot on that hallowed ground. For five hours the two men stood together while the show passed, and as Eisenhower recalled, Stalin "evinced great interest in the industrial, scientific, educational, and social achievements of America. He repeated several times that it was necessary for Russia to remain friends with the United States. Speaking through the interpreter, he said in effect: 'There are many ways in which we need American help. It is our great task to raise the standards of living of the Russian people, which have been seriously damaged by the war. We must learn all about your scientific achievements in agriculture. Likewise, we must get your technicians to help us in our engineering and construction problems, and we want to know more about mass production methods in factories. We know that we are behind in these things and we know that you can help us.'" This was not the only time Stalin had uttered praise, however fleeting, about America. At the Teheran Conference with Churchill and Roosevelt, Stalin proposed a toast that the president regarded as a moving tribute: "I want to tell you, from the Russian point of view, what the President and the United States have done to win the war." Without American production of the machines of war dispatched to Russia through Lend-Lease, "we would lose this war."[46]

Soviet foreign minister V. M. Molotov once referred to the 1946 *World Almanac* to describe American power with admiration or awe. In that book he found the figures that the "mere increase in the national income of the U.S.A. during the war years was equal to its total national income in 1938. . . . We know that the United States made a very great effort in this war, in defence of its own interests and of our common aims, for which we are all very grateful to the United States." He continued to regard the United States as a uniquely wealthy nation that had escaped the grave material damage and ruin of other combatants: "We are glad that this did not happen to our ally, although we ourselves have had to go through trying times, the consequences of which will take us long years to heal."[47]

In Poland, where the Nazis had been driven out by the Soviet army in 1945, the people accorded General Eisenhower a hero's welcome as he walked out of his hotel in Warsaw. Spontaneous cries of *Niech zyje!*—"Long life to you!"—arose from a crowd of several hundred who had suddenly assembled when word of his arrival had spread. Eisenhower edged his way through the crowd without any police or military protection, and the American ambassador, Arthur Bliss Lane, contrasted Eisenhower's friendly reception with that of the Soviet marshals, who a few days before, even in the gardens of the Polish president's palace, had flanked themselves with armed guards.[48]

Around the globe this good will was evident in the pictures, films, and news stories of the soldiers liberating Rome, Paris, and thousands of small towns and villages in occupied or oppressed lands, where cheering people turned out along the roads and waved. After the resistance ended in the outskirts of Rome and the soldiers entered by the Appian Way, crowds of Italians, some of them singing, some laughing or crying, surged out of the houses and up the streets. An old lady with white hair ran up and kissed a tank. A girl stuck a rose behind an infantryman's ear. The men drank wine out of bottles they passed around. In Paris the Americans paraded down the Champs Elysées from the Arc de Triomphe. One soldier said, "As long as I live I don't guess I'll ever see a parade like that. . . . We were marching 24 abreast . . . and we had a helluva time trying to march, because the whole street was jammed with people laughing and yelling and crying and singing. They were throwing flowers at us and bringing us big bottles of wine."

The Philippines was a colony, but even here, at least temporarily, some people welcomed the return of the overlords as liberators. At the outskirts of Manila, American soldiers reached a bridge that had been blown up by the Japanese and began to ford the river, when local Filipinos met the Yanks with greetings of "Victoree." The group pitched in and helped the men build the rafts to ford the river. When fighting resumed, a soldier warned a civilian that he had put himself at risk. He answered, "We have waited so long for your to come—and with the Japanese it was not easy. We would gladly die for you now that you are here."[49]

The sources of American legitimacy were in its industrial development and in its democratic institutions of self-determination. The interest in these institutions was keen even in some remote—and ironic—places in 1945, places that had no traditions of industrialism or democracy. When Ho Chi Minh proclaimed the independence of Vietnam from French rule on September 2, 1945, he used the words "We hold these truths to be self-evident. That all men are created equal"—from the American Declaration of Independence. During celebrations in Hanoi later that day, U.S. Army officers stood on the reviewing stand with the Vietnamese leaders, and a Vietnamese band played the "Star-Spangled Banner." One leader spoke of Vietnam's "particularly intimate relations" with the Americans, "a pleasant duty," he noted "to dwell upon."[50]

Numerous such reports require some qualification. There was friction with some wartime allies: with the Soviet Union over the burgeoning cold war, with Britain and France over their attempts to hold on to empire, and with developing nations over their neutrality. But public opinion polls in foreign nations, apart from the Soviet Union and its sphere of influence, where such polls were not allowed, supported the general impression in many lands of considerable good will—good will surpassing that expressed toward any other great power. The first full-scale polling of public opinion in ten countries, conducted in early 1948 by Elmo Roper for *Time* magazine, surveyed Great Britain, France, Italy, Sweden, Switzerland, Germany, Brazil, Mexico, and Canada, as well as the United States. When asked where they would like to live if they had to leave their own country, people usually named the United States. It was the first choice among the Swiss, Italians, Swedes, Canadians, Mexicans, and Brazilians. The French placed the United States second, after Switzerland, and only the British made the United States a distant fifth choice, after some Commonwealth dominions.[51]

The people of foreign nations also tended to put the United States at the top when asked which country offered not only businessmen the best chance for success but also workers the best chance to earn a good living and farmers the best chance to make enough to live comfortably. In Sweden, Germany, Mexico, and Brazil, the only countries outside the United States where these questions were asked, the Swedes alone thought their country was the best place for the worker and the farmer, with the United States in second place, but they granted that the United States was the best place for the businessman.[52]

An international study, sponsored by the United Nations Educational, Scientific and Cultural Organization, similarly investigated different peoples' perceptions of each other. Begun in 1947 and published in 1953, the UNESCO study tended to reflect a strong friendliness by the world's peoples toward the United States. A majority of the peoples polled felt "most friendly" toward Americans. The nationalities so inclined included the Australians, British, Germans (in the British Zone of Occupation), Italians, Mexicans, Dutch, and Norwegians. Only the French among the eight foreign nationalities surveyed did not feel most friendly toward Americans.[53]

At the outset of the world role, the United States, the bulk of the evidence indicates, had convinced much of the world that its legitimacy abroad did not lie in puppets or satellites but in friends and allies who supported it because they wanted to. The hope was that America's world role was not ethnocentric but cosmopolitan, that is, one of openness and magnanimity. Because of the democratic, egalitarian traditions of the republic, it could with unique agility demonstrate a respect for world opinion. In its power, and with confidence in it, the United States could afford to be patient in its reluctance to use the force and coercion of past imperial powers and instead regard a diversity of the conditions, interests, and policies of friends and allies, which would in turn enhance the American position in the world. So long as other peoples perceived American power as a positive force, they would agree to its use.

Thus the world role originated as postwar analysts evaluated various elements that gave rise to the power that supported it. The difficulty analysts had stemmed from the remarkable superiority of so many of America's assets. Taken together, the analyses emphasizing single factors point toward an important realization: No single element of power could be regarded in every instance as more or less important than any other. Each was dependent on the other. The material elements provided by geography, resources, population, technology, production, and the military could not further American influence without the determination of Americans to use power and the readiness of other nations to accept its use. Conversely, without material power, arguments for the willingness to use it would be moot. The new element, never before asserted in the American experience, or at least not sustained for an era of American history, was the will of the people and leaders that their nation pursue worldwide interests. There was a unique combination of elements at a particular period of time, when an old power system was in collapse.

In following the precepts of realpolitik, realist analysts tended to overstress the easily accountable material elements, particularly defense. The moral components of power were less perfectly understood and often taken for granted. Material support for the post–World War II world role came from within American society and from the early consensus conception of postwar internationalism. Before World War II the United States had invested its energy, capital, and enterprise in developing its land, in expanding its skilled labor force, and in promoting science and technology, and had created a dynamic economy, which enabled it to be the first nation in innovation. Then, by acting according to democratic tradition, the new consensus of leaders and people determined after World War II to direct their national creativity and energy to opportunities abroad—increased involvement in world trade, grants of foreign aid, and the exchange of culture, fads, and customs. As for the military, America had generally assigned it a low profile and after World War II reduced its armed forces, until a military buildup began in the Korean War.

Still, in creating the early legitimacy of the world role, the peaceful manifestations of a productive way of life in the service of commerce and aid, which stood in stark contrast to the militarism and imperialism associated with the European powers, had been remarkable, nearly irresistible. The fundamental nature of American power then lay less in the weight of material force than in the dynamism of the society and what its internationalism could offer the world. What mattered as much as elements of power were the ways—ethnocentric and cosmopolitan—in which that power might be used. Power was, after all, a dynamic and transforming force.

PART II

The

Growth

of

a

World

Role

☆ ☆ ☆ ☆

5

The

Pressure

from

Abroad

The world role of the United States, of uncommon scope and vision by the time of the Japanese surrender, was as yet uncertain in its form. The historian Eric Goldman named the years of the world role's unfolding, after V-J Day, the Crucial Decade, a "frightening, heartening" time when "it was next to impossible to discuss domestic problems coherently without having the points become entangled in foreign affairs." Throughout the decade the question lingered: "Could the United States pull off the new world role it was assuming?"[1]

Once the world role was born, why did it develop and expand? Why did it not end? The United States did not assume a full global role after the Spanish-American War, and it shunned involvement after World War I. The maturation of consensus thought, as national leaders urged the people to maintain the internationalism inherent in the activity of World War II, must be addressed, for it accepted world involvement. But to what extent? What was its nature: ethnocentric or cosmopolitan? And how would it last?

We may search for clues to the ways the world role developed in the center of the consensus that held together after the war. Consensus ideas may contribute to an explanation of development, as they did of origins. We have established the unity of public opinion concerning internationalism, but the nature of that internationalism has yet to be resolved. The myths that held this society together in its relations with the rest of the world told of mass fears and national loyalties. Our starting point is the part that the external threat played in shaping unity.

The Soviet Union and Communism

The threat of Soviet Russia governed so great an extent of American policy that anticommunism became a rubric to sustain American initiatives in the period of confrontation known as the cold war. A 1948 House of Representatives Foreign Affairs Committee report on the schemes of communism was sweeping: "the foreign policy of the United States has increasingly found that communism is a factor in every problem or situation." Communism invariably assumed "top priority for the attention of all concerned with the foreign affairs of the United States." The consensus carried forward from World War II into the postwar era unity on opposition to totalitarianism, whether fascist or communist. Was this the reason for the new worldview of the United States?[2]

Early frustrations in dealing with the Soviets came forth in Secretary of State Marshall's speech in Chicago in November 1947. Marshall looked back to the end of World War II, when peace had seemed possible: "I think it was a fact that the people of the United States had as high a regard, or I might better put it, appreciation, for the Soviet people and their sacrifices, and for the Soviet Army and its leaders, as they held for any other people in the world. But today, only two years later, we are charged with a definite hostility toward the Soviet Union and its people, which constitutes a complete change in our attitude since the summer of 1945." "What," Marshall asked, "produced this tremendous change in our national feeling and attitude?" As he saw it, since the termination of hostilities "the Soviet Government has consistently followed a course which was bound to arouse the resentment of our people."[3]

Fear and suspicion of Russia had existed as long ago as the imperial regime of the czar. When the Russian Revolution of March 1917 overthrew the monarchy, the United States was one of the first nations to recognize the new democracy, but the good feelings faltered in November after a second revolution set up the Bolshevik government. The United States broke off ties and steadfastly refused to recognize the Soviet Union until November 1933. The hope of President Roosevelt's restoration of relations faded rapidly when Stalin consolidated his dictatorial power by purging his rivals. Relations worsened in 1939 when Stalin and Hitler signed a nonaggression pact. The two dictatorships, driven by their divergent ideologies of nazism and communism, presented a totalitarian bloc that stretched from the center of Europe on the Rhine to the Pacific Ocean, a territory that geopoliticians declared controlled the heartland of Eurasia. The *New York Times* editors offered slight consolation: at last "the anti-democratic systems are on one side and the democracies on the other." The Soviet Union's invasion of Finland substantially added to this conviction. Roosevelt denounced the aggression: the Soviet Union "has allied itself with another dictatorship, and it has invaded a neighbor so infinitesimally small that it could do no conceivable possible harm to the Soviet Union."[4]

World War II reversed the course of strained relations again, when Hitler attacked his professed ally, Russia. Even as the two giants warred against each other, it remained difficult for some observers to distinguish between their totalitarian systems. Sen. Harry Truman said, "If we see that Germany is winning we ought to help Russia and if Russia is winning we ought to help Germany and that way let them kill as many as possible, although I don't want to see Hitler victorious under any circumstances." Once fervent critics of the Soviet Union were nonetheless sympathetic to the communist regime. As the Soviets met Hitler's attack with an unbending fight, the *New York Times* wrote that "never during the past quarter of a century, has Russia stood so high in the respect and admiration of the free nations." *Time* magazine put the Russian resistance to the German thrust into the Ukraine in terms Americans could understand: Philadelphia taken and with it Independence Hall; industrial New England captured; Rhode Island and its naval base at Newport isolated; New York, Boston, and Washington, D.C., besieged. The Mississippi might be reached by the enemy before winter.[5]

To combat the common enemy, the United States and the Soviet Union forged an alliance after the United States entered the war in 1941. The war did not necessarily lessen the American fear of communism, but it did change attitudes toward Russia. Roosevelt praised the Soviet contribution to the cause: "Put it in terms of dead Germans and smashed tanks," he told a press conference in 1942. The Soviet Union, though it might have spread its ideology through the Comintern, was not bent on military conquest: "I think the Russians are perfectly friendly," he said; "they aren't trying to gobble up all the rest of Europe or the world." They might even be capable of evolution to more democratic ways. Roosevelt cited Article 124 of the "Constitution of Russia," whose provisions he specified as "Freedom of conscience, freedom of religion. Freedom equally to use propaganda against religion, which is essentially what is the rule in this country, only we don't put it quite the same way." The president believed that through his personal diplomacy he could cooperate with Stalin after the war. "I 'got along fine' with Marshal Stalin," Roosevelt told the nation in a radio fireside chat after the Teheran Conference. "I believe that we are going to get along very well with him and the Russian people—very well indeed."[6]

With cooperation in war, the image of the Soviet Union improved among its close observers. In 1941 Joseph E. Davies, the ambassador to the Soviet Union in 1937 and 1938, published memoirs of his Russian experiences in *Mission to Moscow*. Davies found the Soviets trying to build their own egalitarian society based on ethical principles, which, Davies believed, were in theory not far removed from Christianity and the brotherhood of man. He liked the Soviet leaders for their "honest convictions and integrity of purposes." Stalin, he said, was a simple man; a "child would like to sit in his lap and a dog would sidle up to him." Davies's respect and affection for the people—for their qualities of imagination and idealism reflected in their literature, music, and art— led to his conviction that the Soviets posed no threat, nor were they out to spread revolution around the world. To deal with the Soviets, Davies recommended that Americans adopt "the simple approach of assuming that what they say, they mean; that they are honest in their beliefs, speak the truth and keep their promises." His story was adapted into a 1943 feature film by Warner Brothers; Davies himself introduced the film.[7]

On his 1942 goodwill mission around the world, Wendell Willkie brought from his Russian travels a message of warm relations in *One World*. He had the strong impression that the Soviet government was working to improve the life of the people. He too admired Stalin's simple, candid style, and he believed that it was "possible for Russia and America, perhaps the most powerful countries in the world, to work together for the economic welfare and the peace of the world." At least, he added, "there is nothing I ever wanted more to believe." After Willkie's reports of what he had seen and learned, American distrust of Russia, recorded in the opinion polls, fell to its lowest point.[8]

Roosevelt sent Vice President Wallace to the Soviet regions of Asia, as well as to China, in 1944. Wallace, like Willkie, saw the Russians wanting most to develop their own country, much as Americans had done on their frontier. "Soviet Asia, in American terms, may be called the wild West of Russia," he wrote. Just as Americans after the Civil War developed the West, so the Soviets after this war would build cities in Siberia. Like the United States, the Soviet Union would in turn become a principal power in the Pacific. On his return he gave a nationally broadcast speech in Seattle, disclosing that the leaders of Soviet Asia were "eager for the most friendly relationship" with the United States.[9]

At home scholars assumed a positive view toward Russia. Russian history was depicted as earnest and peaceful. Foster Rhea Dulles, a diplomatic historian at Ohio State University, stressed the near total absence of conflict between Russia and the United States since Catherine the Great. The United States had taken up arms against every other major power, France in naval warfare in the 1790s, England in the War of 1812, and Germany, Italy, and Japan in twentieth-century wars. Despite "friction" between the two nations near the end of World War I, the "peoples of Russia and America have fought together as allies; never as declared enemies." It was difficult for the historian to explain the one exception, the American invasion of Russian soil in World War I. Dulles was apologetic. President Wilson had agonized over the decision to send in American troops—it was against his better judgment. The nominal reason was to keep stores of war supplies out of the hands of the Germans, but, Dulles admitted, the lack of American fondness for communism was another reason for the intervention. The policy toward Russia in 1918 and 1919 "could hardly be reconciled with the democratic principles we professed, or with our declared intention to allow the Russian people to settle their own internal problems." To Dulles, the struggle against Hitler was not a passing phase but revived a long, historic Soviet-American friendship. He projected an enduring peace between the two allies.[10]

Regardless of its past, the modern Soviet Union by virtue of its own egalitarian life and industrial strides appeared to current observers to be emulating the United States. Ralph Barton Perry, a philosopher at Harvard, assumed that Soviet policy was steadily swerving "away from a strict and narrow Marxian ideology in the direction of ideas that we can call, in very broad terms, democratic." Stalin's government had begun to encourage what Perry called "the philosophy of opportunity," a new conviction among the Soviet people that they had a chance "to rise to positions of power and of leadership," an idea that had "certainly never been emphasized elsewhere" so much as in the United States.[11]

Life presented a special issue on Russia in March 1943. It described Lenin as perhaps "the greatest man of modern times." The Russians, it stated, were "one hell of a people," who to "a remarkable degree . . . look like Americans, dress like Americans and think like Americans." The NKVD was "a national police similar to the FBI." The editorial added that Americans should "not get too excited" that the Russians lived "under a system of tight state-controlled information. . . . If the Soviet leaders tell us that the control of information was necessary to get this job done, we can afford to take their word for it for the time being." The magazine stated, "Clearly it is up to both the U.S.S.R. and the U.S. to seek a broader and more enlightened base for their future relationship."[12]

The new attitude appeared even at the annual congress of the Daughters of the American Revolution in 1942. "Stalin is a university graduate and a man of great studies," said Mrs. Tryphosa Duncan Bates-Batcheller, amid a reaction described as an obbligato of gasps from the audience. "He is a man, who, when he sees a great mistake, admits it and corrects it. Today in Russia, Communism is practically non-existent."[13]

As early as October 1941 American opinion professed that the United States should work with Russia, even provide it with aid to defeat Hitler. In four months those who favored helping the Soviet Union swelled from 73.3 percent to 84.3 percent of the population. By 1943 the public was ready to support a permanent postwar military alliance between the United States and Russia, so each would come to the other's defense if attacked. Opinion vacillated, but Americans in 1945 expected to "get along better" with the Soviets in the future than they had in the past. In the spring of 1945 the largest group of Americans said they had "nothing to fear" from Russia after the war. But among those who were suspicious of Russia, what they feared was the Soviet political system—communism. That fear may have lessened, but it never entirely disappeared.[14]

Not all comments were cordial. William Henry Chamberlin, Moscow correspondent for the *Christian Science Monitor,* questioned attempts "to soft-pedal any criticism of Stalin and his régime." The argument that sturdy Soviet resistance of the Nazis automatically refuted the negative features of communist dictatorship was groundless. Chamberlin warned Americans to be on guard: "Until and unless its system of government is drastically changed it can never be the ideological partner of a free America." The Soviets were allies because they were fighting American enemies. William L. White's *Report on the Russians,* the result of a six-week trip to Russia, found that the Russians did not yet trust the outside world and were suspicious even of allies, as White was of them. He urged American caution: "there is no guarantee that they will not stumble into policies which might provoke another war which nobody wants, least of all themselves."[15]

Anticommunism

The conflicting attitudes toward Russia in the middle and late 1940s never eroded the consensus over internationalism, but they did have a good deal to do with how that internationalism would develop. One point of view stemmed from the favorable wartime opinion of Russia—that the two nations had more in common than fighting the same enemy. This view fitted into a cosmopolitan outlook that downplayed the Soviet Union as a threat, seeing it behaving like a traditional great power within the international system. Even those close to Roosevelt did not know how his friendly opinion of the Soviet Union might have changed after the war. He surely did not know himself. In a note to Churchill in the last hours before his death, the president stated that there should be understanding and firmness. "I would minimize the general Soviet problem," he cabled. "We must be firm, however, and our course thus far is correct." But how much understanding and how much firmness?[16]

In the crucial early postwar years, each of those close to Roosevelt maintained an intention to pursue the dead president's policies. Believing that Roosevelt's understanding attitude toward the Russians should prevail, Henry Wallace, who had become secretary of commerce in Roosevelt's fourth term, was critical of so-called enemies of peace who had tried to stir up trouble between the United States and the Soviet Union. "We must offset their poison by following the policies of Roosevelt in cultivating the friendship of Russia in peace as well as in war." Wallace continued to believe that the Soviet people were not naturally aggressive or fanatical about spreading communism. Rather, they had valid and ancient concerns for their security, especially along the border with Poland, through which the Germans had invaded their homeland twice in a generation. Wallace believed that Americans should take the lead to foster mutual understanding with the Soviet people. He was critical when the United States stopped further financial credits at the close of hostilities, and he encouraged American commerce to improve the economies of both nations. Wallace, in sum, favored a policy that would shift the emphasis from a suspicious hostility to a tolerant rivalry between the two political and economic systems. He fully expected the American system to be the more successful. He advocated seeking friendship with Russia: "I know this is the intention of President Truman. I am also satisfied that it is the will of the vast majority of the American people." In 1952 Wallace stated straight out his belief that "if Roosevelt had remained alive and in *good health* the whole course of history would have been changed."[17]

The second point of view, by contrast, saw the Soviet Union as a revolutionary state committed to ideological warfare and driven to dominate the world. According to this perspective, the Soviet Union was a monumental danger to the United States and its world role. Even Eleanor Roosevelt, who had served the president as his "eyes and ears" throughout the nation, writing in her newspaper column in 1948, expressed doubts about working with the Soviets: "I do not think we have always been wise or tactful in our approach to the Government of the U.S.S.R., but basically we have been the ones to make the constructive offers and they have been the ones to refuse."[18]

The fundamental differences between the two powers during World War II—the division of Germany between them, and the right of the peoples of eastern Europe to choose their own government—had not altered. There was a change in mood. In a meeting with Soviet foreign minister V. M. Molotov, Truman, not much more than a week after succeeding Roosevelt as president, bluntly attacked the Soviet presence in Poland. He wanted it clearly understood: American friendship with Russia could not be a one-way street.

"I have never been talked to like that in my life," Molotov said. Truman told him, "Carry out your agreements and you won't get talked to like that."[19]

Truman himself was conscious of his own quick temperament and inexperience in Russian affairs. Writing Eleanor Roosevelt in 1947 that while his only effort had been to carry out the wishes of the late president, he confided, in looking over Roosevelt's correspondence with Stalin, "I don't see how he continued as patiently as he did with developments as they were then progressing, but he didn't let his personal feelings enter into his international commitments and the country is certainly lucky that that was the case." One of the close advisers to both presidents on Soviet affairs, Averell Harriman, who had been in the room with Molotov and Truman during their encounter, subsequently expressed his displeasure that "Truman went at it so hard": "his behavior gave Molotov an excuse to tell Stalin that the Roosevelt policy was being abandoned. I regretted that Truman gave him the opportunity."[20]

Relations deteriorated in 1946, when Stalin's government prodded Turkey to share the defense of its straits into the Black Sea, delayed withdrawal of Soviet troops from northern Iran beyond the deadline it had set, and fastened communist rule on Poland, eastern Germany, and Romania. That March Truman appeared with Churchill in Fulton, Missouri, when the former prime minister warned that an "iron curtain" had fallen across Europe.

Having lived in the Soviet Union for ten months, the Russian correspondent of the *New York Times,* Brooks Atkinson, reported on his return home in 1946, "we have to abandon the familiar concepts of friendship" with the Soviet Union and should prepare for conflict. Although Atkinson had found the Russian people admirable, hardworking, and practical, as far as he knew, they supported the Soviet totalitarian government and believed in it. The best Atkinson could hope for was "an armed peace." The Soviet leaders were vicious in their treatment of political prisoners, some ten to fifteen million of them having been jailed or exiled. Fearful and insecure, Stalin was probably the "most heavily guarded person in the world." In this "abnormal climate," it seemed to Atkinson, "group aberrations" abounded and "the most conspicuous and also the most irritating abnormality in Soviet leadership" was a collective "paranoia." The leaders imagined themselves "surrounded." By Atkinson's reasoning, the United States should confirm their suspicion: it had to apply its power to confine Russia. Upon leaving the Soviet Union, he reflected, "It is a pity, perhaps it will be a tragedy, that as a nation we have to live with the Russian nation in an atmosphere of bitterness and tension. But we have to. There is no other way."[21]

Life, which reprinted Atkinson's articles, commissioned John Foster Dulles to write two long articles on Soviet foreign policy in 1946. A statesman of stature, he had accompanied his grandfather to the Second Peace Conference at the Hague in 1907 and had served with the American delegation at Versailles in 1919. Dulles made his point sharply: the Soviets were out to impose a "Pax Sovietica" on the world and Americans had to stop it. For one who had helped prepare the United Nations Charter, his warning that the two countries were headed toward confrontation was foreboding. The differences with the Soviets were unsolvable so long as Soviet leaders sought to force into existence totalitarian regimes under their control throughout the world.[22]

The view that the Soviet Union could not be trusted and had to be confronted received official support in early 1947, when Truman proposed that nations of the world choose between two "alternative ways of life": "One way of life is based upon the will of the majority, and is distinguished by free institutions, representative government, free elections, guarantees of individual liberty, freedom of speech and religion, and freedom from political oppression. The second way of life is based upon the will of a minority forcibly imposed upon the majority. It relies upon terror and oppression, a controlled press and radio, fixed elections, and the suppression of personal freedoms." Truman did not then name this other way of life as communism—he spoke instead of totalitarianism—but by June 1948 he was roundly denouncing "communism" as "a challenge to everything we believe in."[23]

An intellectual catalyst to the policy of opposition to the Soviet Union was the American Foreign Service officer George Kennan. One of a small group of American diplomats with extensive experience in Moscow, he was a scholar who wrote with a sense of history and public philosophy and wrote of realpolitik with literary passion. Kennan addressed the "intricate," "delicate," and "strange" issues confronting American postwar policy in a long telegram from Moscow in February 1946: the "Kremlin's neurotic view of world affairs" and its "increase of military and police power" had committed the Soviet Union to the fanatical belief that "no permanent *modus vivendi*" was possible with the United States. After returning home, Kennan studied at the National War College and became head of the policy-planning staff of the State Department. He gained influence within the department, and he made his ideas public in the famous article "The Sources of Soviet Conduct," written for *Foreign Affairs* in 1947 under the pseudonym Mr. "X." To Kennan's knowledge, the Soviet leaders were belligerent, secretive, and suspicious because they were struggling to achieve power in the Kremlin. They justified dictatorial power at home by foreign threats, but Soviet conduct was the result not so much of foreign antagonism as of the need to suppress domestic opposition. The enemy Americans faced was not the Soviet people; on the contrary, they were the victims of the dictatorship's forceful prohibitions and police actions. The enemy was the leadership, the dictators. For Kennan, that explained why the Soviet Union was uncooperative, and why the United States had to check Soviet hostility and combativeness.[24]

As the leaders were making up their minds about what to think of the Soviet Union and were unclear about the exact threat—Kennan himself later claimed in his memoirs that he had not been as careful and precise as he should have been—the American people were confused. In 1946 a majority of Americans criticized their government for not telling them enough about what was "going on" between Russia and the United States, and they further criticized the newspapers for making Russia look worse than it really was. In September of that year, when asked whether Russia or America was entirely to blame for their problems, or whether both countries were responsible, 74 percent of Americans said both countries; only 17 percent said one country. Americans were willing to accept living in peace with Russia, even if that country was under the communist system. Americans tended to believe that the primary purpose of the Soviet Union was to build a strong socialist state, rather than to spread communism throughout Europe or the rest of the world.[25]

The confusion represented in large part feelings, formed mainly by the leaders, rather than facts. So the polls found. Americans as a whole lacked facts about Russia. The polls estimated toward the end of the war that seventy million Americans did not know that relatively few people in Russia were members of the Communist party or that the Russians themselves produced most of the war materials used by their army. In answering pollsters' questions, Americans were far more likely to answer "Don't Know" about Russian topics than about a wide range of other issues. Strikingly, the people who were most confident that Russia would cooperate were also the best informed about Russia. The more a person knew about the Soviets, the more confident the individual was likely to be that the United States and the Soviet Union would have good relations.[26]

But, as a public opinion study in mid-1947 confirmed, the lack of information shadowed American perceptions: "The most menacing aspect is that we, as a people, are at the mercy of anyone who claims to know about Russia. We have no adequate standards of judgment by which to assess the statements which constantly assail us." The study blamed the barrier to learning on Soviet secrecy and also faulted the distortions of both American promoters and attackers of the Soviet Union. The "contentions of one 'expert' are vigorously contradicted by his rivals. The would-be learner is baffled. What is he to think? Whom can he believe?" The "ordinary citizen" was likely to become "the easy prey of propagandists and pressure groups, both Communist and anti-Communist."[27]

Even while in his post in the Moscow embassy, George Kennan had realized this problem. "We must see that our public is educated to realities of Russian situation," he cabled home in 1946. He could not "over-emphasize" the importance of his plea. The press could not do the job alone. The main responsibility belonged to government, which was most experienced and best informed. The people would be far less susceptible to "hysterical anti-Sovietism" if they understood the situation.[28]

The lines were being drawn in the American stance toward Russia between those who wanted cooperation and those who favored confrontation, and most people were listening to the leaders in government who did not trust the Soviet Union. In September 1946 pollsters asked the public about the clash over Soviet policy between Truman's secretary of state, James F. Byrnes, and his secretary of commerce, Wallace. The administration's firmness with Russia, which the public understood to be telling the Soviets "just where they stand," were manifestly at odds with Wallace's ideas, perceived as going "easy with Russia" and trying "to see Russia's viewpoint." Asked which policy should be followed, the public answered overwhelmingly: 78 percent favored the Truman-Byrnes position, while only 16 percent backed Wallace's. Of those polled in 1946, 62 percent said that their feelings toward Russia were less friendly than they had been a year before.[29]

The Fears

What did the leaders and people fear? Americans had opposed monarchy in the early years of the Republic and fascism in World War II, but neither aroused the anxiety that communism did.

One attitude was that communism threatened the wealth accumulated by capitalism, which Americans had amassed beyond all precedent. Communism was a threat to the pocketbook. This fear of redistributing wealth was one not readily associated with other forms of totalitarianism. In July 1940 polls discovered that the people feared communism more than fascism—even after Nazi armies had moved throughout Europe. Communists were characterized as poor, ignorant have-nots who wanted more. The key issue, the study determined, seemed to be property rights; the communists coveted a rising standard of living dependent on common ownership of property. W. L. White argued with a Russian woman over how much better things would be for her people if they adopted a free economy like that in America. The woman replied with a personal statement of communist theory: "my dress may not be so good as an American dress, but at least I know that no other Russian woman has a better dress!" White answered: "your system is founded only on jealousy. In America many people have better clothes than I and live in finer houses. But I am not so jealous that I would pull down a system which gives me good things just because it gives someone else something better. . . . Here, there are more differences between rich and poor than in America."[30]

American visitors did not find that the Soviet redistribution of wealth had necessarily guaranteed economic equality. A new Soviet aristocracy, evidenced by the gulf between the officers and men in the Red Army, was replacing the one overthrown in the revolution. In 1943 Cyrus Sulzberger of the *New York Times* reported from Moscow that officers were accorded excessive special privileges. Orderlies were assigned to attend to the personal affairs of all officers from the rank of platoon commander upward, a privilege explained officially as czarist policy, going back to Peter the Great. To enhance the officers' already privileged living standards, Brooks Atkinson noted in 1945, increased food rations granted them much more of a much greater variety of foods than Soviet workers. Benefits taken from the fighting men to give to the generals had the taint of inequality.[31]

Taking from the wealthy to give to the state was not the only American fear. The rich might be supposed most angered by communism, as if in a personal way; but the people most inclined to trust Russia were in the upper, not the lower, income groups. Among those who trusted Russia least were workers, both skilled and unskilled. The ones who had the most to lose to a communist redistribution of wealth were the most disposed to cooperation with Russia. Those who had the most to gain in a system of free opportunity were least disposed to the restraints that communism put on individual initiative and free enterprise. These sentiments made light of the ideology of Russian sympathies for the ranks of labor and of Marxist class solidarity.[32]

In a larger view, communism, by theory, threatened individualism, the political, social, and spiritual freedom that Americans enjoyed. Capitalism had its foundation in a society that permitted each individual to acquire property according to his or her abilities and encouraged freedom in thought and life. When a poll asked in 1945 what the United States had most to fear from Russia, the largest concern of the people was of the political ideas of communism as a form of government. Wendell Willkie questioned a young Soviet production superintendent in a large factory: Why didn't he feel the urge to invest his money, as Willkie had as a young businessman, so that it would bring in a return? Didn't he ever aspire to own his own plant? The worker brushed these questions off as "mere capitalistic talk." But Willkie pressed him to a larger issue: "How can you ever have political freedom and economic freedom where the state owns everything?" The worker replied in a "seemingly endless rush" of theories, but, Willkie said, he had "no answers beyond the Marxian ones in which he was so well grounded, and to that basic question, Marxism gives no answer."[33]

The Soviet Union had been named a federation of republics, but in the words of George Kennan, the government ruled "a police regime par excellence." The agencies of the state that Ambassador Walter Bedell Smith encountered had "complete supervision of every phase of national life." Citizens participated in a "political puppet show" in which they could vote, but only for one candidate selected by the sole political party. An election allowing choice was unknown to Soviet citizens. In *The Great Challenge,* Louis Fischer, who had been writing about Soviet Russia since his first trip there over thirty years before, told of his son, a captain stationed in an American base in the Ukraine, trying to explain to Soviet officers the purpose of the balloting conducted in the armed forces in the presidential election of 1944. "I don't understand," said a Red Army lieutenant. "You mean that Roosevelt is a Democrat, and he has been President for several years, and there are still Republicans in the American Army?"[34]

Neither could Stalin fathom the peaceful change of power in a democracy. When he met Eric Johnston in a three-hour meeting in 1944, Stalin asked his guest about the politics in that year's forthcoming elections. Johnston explained to Stalin that his perspective was different from that of Roosevelt's Democrats because he was a member of the opposition party. "I am a Republican," he said. "You're a Republican," Stalin said incredulously. He looked at Johnston in confusion and conferred with Molotov. "So you're a Republican," he mused. "We don't see many. You must be about the first I have met." Johnston reminded Stalin that he knew Wendell Willkie. Stalin "just couldn't understand how a Democratic President had let a Republican loose to run around the world representing the United States even unofficially," Johnston reflected. "Perhaps he wondered how I got a passport."[35]

Soviet individuals were restricted in their freedom of movement. So were foreign travelers, diplomats, and journalists. Most were confined to Moscow, and this restraint on "freedom as individual human beings" was what Ambassador Smith called their "greatest complaint against the Soviet Government." The "strictest kind of segregation" divided the foreigners from Soviet citizens. "We were completely cut off from the great bulk of the Russian people by constant police surveillance, by propaganda and by the fear of punishment."[36]

George Kennan felt stifled by Soviet restrictions. He was fascinated by the great land of Russia but distressed that he was not free to explore it. He would stroll through Moscow and visit parks in the evenings, but he had to sneak off on random weekend jaunts to mingle with the ordinary people in the countryside. As it was, he was sure the Soviets thought he might be spying, even during the days of the wartime alliance. On one innocent Sunday expedition in July 1944, he encountered no harassment but felt alienation. He took the city subway to connect with a suburban train, which was so crowded that he could find only a step outside on which to ride, and he held on until he arrived at a station. Atop a knoll near a church, he sketched for an hour or two. Later he talked anonymously to a soldier on crutches, and to a woman in a white dress who showed him inside her old, damp brick house, which used to belong to an aristocrat. He felt he could never reveal his identity to people he met casually, because he feared they might be embarrassed or blamed for talking with him. Only years later, when he was ambassador in Moscow, did the authoritarian insistence on the isolation of diplomats weigh more heavily on him. He lamented Soviet suspicion. "We were sincerely moved by the sufferings of the Russian people as well as by the heroism and patience they were showing in the face of wartime adversity," he wrote. "We wished them nothing but well. It was doubly hard, in these circumstances, to find ourselves treated as though we were the bearers of some species of the plague."[37]

Travel restrictions extended to foreigners who wished to enter the country. The correspondent Howard K. Smith found it much more difficult to get a visa to enter Russia after the war than before it. Arthur Schlesinger, Jr., blamed the Soviet Union for closing its borders to members of his generation, those too young to recall the revolution in 1917. Cut off from Russian life, they had images not of Soviet youth joyfully building the subway or doing mass calisthenics but of millions doomed to forced labor and mass starvation.[38]

The lack of freedom in communist Russia was further manifested in censorship of the press, an impediment that disturbed the journalist W. L. White. A communist demanded of him why the press in America was critical of the Soviet Union. "America was a free country," White replied, "and therefore had a free press. And while most Americans supported both President Roosevelt and Russia, all of us would fight anyone who tried to stop criticism of them." The state's restrictions on individuals were most graphically illustrated to White when he was talking to a female Tass correspondent during a factory inspection tour. An NKVD plainclothes agent grabbed her by the elbow and lectured her. White attempted to resume his talk with her, but she would neither answer nor look at him. White was outraged. He decided "to stop this foolishness." He collared the agent, who refused to give a satisfactory answer. White said, "if he came to America, he would find that nobody would be detailed to go around scaring people he tried to talk to. One of the reasons we were able to get things done was because we didn't have any army of able-bodied men tied up to spy on our Allies."[39]

White's companion, Eric Johnston, took his criticism of press censorship directly to Stalin. Johnston insisted that the American correspondents in Moscow, representing hundreds of newspapers with millions of readers, could "keep the American people better informed if given proper assistance and allowed to travel more freely." The correspondents had not been allowed to go see the new Soviet industrial sites in the Urals, where Johnston was soon to head. "That's why I would like to ask permission to take four correspondents with me to the Urals."

"Why not?" asked Stalin.

"Does that mean I can take them?"

"Of course it does."

Johnston thanked him, saying, "But I don't know whether Mr. Molotov will approve. You see, his office has not yet granted my request." Molotov quickly said, "I always approve of Marshal Stalin's decisions."

The dictator grinned. "Mr. Johnston, you really didn't expect Mr. Molotov to disagree with me, did you?" This incident convinced Johnston of Stalin's dictatorial control over the press.[40]

Censorship reached beyond matters of national security to information on Soviet society and to official statistics that did not point up a favorable trend. Margaret Bourke-White, a photographer for *Life,* and the only foreign photojournalist allowed in Moscow when German bombs started falling, found that even a photograph of her own hotel had to be arranged, complete with escorts. When the press was invited to see a German scouting plane that had been forced down in the country, she was told she needed a permit to photograph it. "But a German plane that has been brought down by Soviet pilots!" she protested. "Surely you will want pictures of that published in America!" Told that Soviet photographers would take the pictures, she burst out: "Americans know that Russians are masters of stage effects! Whenever they see Soviet pictures of wrecked German planes, our people will believe that these alleged Fascist planes are built of papier-mâché." Finally, she was allowed to take her pictures.[41]

General Eisenhower talked at length about the press with Gen. Gugori Zhukov, who complained about an American author's false statement that Zhukov was shorter by two or three inches than his wife. Zhukov was also angry that an American magazine had published an unflattering likeness of Stalin that had hung in Berlin nightclubs. "If a picture of you like this one should appear in a Russian magazine, I would see that the magazine ceased operations at once. It would be eliminated. What are you going to do?" Eisenhower's attempt to describe the free press of America made no impression whatsoever. The marshal merely repeated, "If you are Russia's friend you will do something about it."[42]

Soviet schools and libraries, Americans feared, were agencies of state-approved information. Yet Wendell Willkie once told Stalin that the Soviet schools and libraries he had seen seemed effective, adding, "if you continue to educate the Russian people, Mr. Stalin, the first thing you know you'll educate yourself out of a job." Stalin merely laughed hard at this.[43]

Creativity in the arts and letters was stifled in the opinion of Brooks Atkinson, who before becoming the head of the *Times* Moscow bureau had been the paper's drama critic in New York. Through censorship and restrictions, the Soviet Union had cut itself off from intellectual and cultural association with the rest of the world, so that Soviet culture had become "colorless and conventional." The "general level of theatre, art and music" was "low," sculpting took the form of statues and portraits of Lenin and Stalin in front of public buildings, and literature read like propaganda. Atkinson tried to be fair: "Soviet art contains just as much hokum and bathos as ours, without producing occasional works of originality that compensate for the failures." He placed the blame squarely on the totalitarian control of the individual artist.[44]

Freedom of religion, too, was threatened. At a time in 1946 when 96 percent of Americans affirmed a belief in God, they also asserted that the communists did not believe in Christianity and that the people in Russia were not free to worship as they pleased. Kennan found that the Russian Orthodox church was never allowed to operate outside a few run-down buildings. Other edifices had been converted to antireligious museums. Churches were not able to publicize their services, so the people would congregate at meetings announced by word of mouth. Still they had to face religious rejection in silence.[45]

The Soviets were ignorant of the outside world. An "unsolved mystery," cabled Kennan from Moscow, was "who, if anyone, in this great land"—including Stalin—received "accurate and unbiased information" about the outside world. In an atmosphere of "oriental secretiveness and conspiracy" that pervaded the government, the possibilities for distorting or poisoning sources of information were "infinite." The Soviet fear, Kennan suggested, was the same fear as on the American side. While Americans had little knowledge of the Soviets, the Soviets had little information about Americans.[46]

The fear that intensified the others was that communism was expansionist. Without this fear Americans might have tolerated a power with a strange ideology. The United States had not dreaded Russia before it became a communist state, nor had it been unduly preoccupied with communism abroad before the Soviet Union was recognized as a great power. Marxism had long called for international union of workers, but Americans had avoided direct, large-scale confrontation with the Soviet Union through its early years as a struggling entity. Americans were not afraid of communism alone, but of its new force in the world.

By 1945 the Soviet army had driven into Eastern and central Europe, and it was not ready to relinquish its hold, creating a new territorial line across Europe that roughly followed the points where the Allied armies met. The Soviet Union held half of

Germany. It controlled Latvia, Lithuania, and Estonia. It established satellite states in Poland, Yugoslavia, Albania, Hungary, Bulgaria, Romania, and Czechoslovakia. It posed threats to the next line of states, Italy, Greece, Finland, the Scandinavian countries, and Korea. It conducted espionage in Canada, Britain, and the United States. "No nation ever held such extensive sway over Europe," reported Howard K. Smith—forgetting Napoleonic France—after Russia had in effect annexed the entirety of Eastern Europe. Soviet army garrisons on the outskirts of Hamburg, once the greatest continental port, were "not a long cannon shot from the Western seas," and the Soviets were as near to London as Denmark or Switzerland. This strategic reorientation of space had a historical dimension across time, considered by Hajo Holborn: Not only was Weimar, where German literature had flourished 150 years before, under Soviet control but also Eisenach, where in Wartburg castle Martin Luther had translated the Bible into German in 1521 and 1522. Russia had penetrated into the heart of European civilization. From the Elbe River and the Adriatic Sea on the west, stated a government report, the "Soviet world" extended to Manchuria on the east and included one-fifth of the earth's land surface. Communism had expanded so far so fast that the interests of Soviet leaders seemed to former Secretary of State Byrnes unlimited and directed toward the whole of international society: "If we regard Europe as the tinderbox of possible world conflagration, we must look upon Asia as a great smoldering fire."[47]

Initially, it was difficult for Americans to understand why attempts at cooperation with the Soviet Union had failed to halt the spread of communism. The American government had apparently been willing at the close of hostilities to accept a Soviet sphere of influence in eastern Europe. In 1944 Sumner Welles, who had served as under secretary of state, concurred in the Soviet right to "a regional system of Eastern Europe, composed of co-operative and well-disposed independent governments among the countries adjacent to Russia"—just as the United States had been "justified in promoting an inter-American system of the twenty-one sovereign American republics of the Western Hemisphere."[48]

Polls in the United States expressed fear that Russia would try to install communist governments in Europe. In 1943 the public expected Russia to want more territory than it had before the war, mainly in the borderland countries of Eastern Europe, above all Poland; but the majority of Americans did not think that Russia should have this territory. American sympathies lay with the Poles, but the understanding remained that Russia wanted to hold adjacent lands "to count on them in case of attack." The major problem was what to do: "do you think the United States and the other Allied countries should try to stop her" from taking those lands? The issue was unresolved. Yes—39 percent; no—38 percent. By the summer of 1946, 54 percent of the people thought Russia wanted to spread the communist way of life. The concern among the people was less about Russia's internal affairs—the lack of democracy, free enterprise, and freedom of religion under communism—than about Russian foreign relations. So long as Russians kept communism to themselves, they could live according to their own ways and government, even if communism was opposed to what Americans were accustomed to. But the spread of communism beyond Soviet borders, leading to the possibility of war, was the great fear.[49]

In his first interview with Stalin in 1946, Ambassador Walter Bedell Smith put the question, "What does the Soviet Union want, and how far is Russia going to go?" Stalin spoke at length about Soviet interests but did not answer the question to Smith's satisfaction, and Smith repeated it, insisting it was "uppermost in the minds of all the American people: 'How far is Russia going to go?'" Looking directly at Smith, Stalin replied, "We're not going much further." But Smith did not pin Stalin down, and his annoyance at the uncertainty of the danger grew: "The foreigner who sees police state regimentation at close range might be able to regret it in a detached and impersonal way, return with relief and renewed confidence to his own democratic system, imperfect though it might be, and leave the whole thing for time and evolution, were it not for the sinister implications involved in a political religion that preaches hatred of all other political systems. It is this facet of communism that shocks Americans most." Back in America, the polls reflected these fears. Of all nations—even more than England or France, which still held world empires—Russia was, to the American public, "imperialistic."[50]

Traveling into the Soviet realm, Howard K. Smith gathered evidence of the dangers of the spread of Soviet communism. Smith was the last Westerner to use Czech radio facilities to make a radio broadcast in the midst of a communist coup, just as a few years earlier he had been the last American correspondent to leave Nazi Germany. Before flying out of Prague, he had walked the city's icy streets for five days in February 1948 witnessing the communists close down newspapers, stage large demonstrations, and send armed workers to pressure the government. Not long before, Smith had tried to keep an open mind about Soviet incursions. On a Sunday in the summer of 1947, during a drive through a Hungarian farming district, he stopped to talk to perhaps a dozen fathers of peasant families, sunning themselves in the town square and complaining of the high prices for goods and of the government's decree forcing them to pay costly taxes in commodities. "They had apparently not heard of the restrictions on free speech," Smith quipped. But there could be no true democracy under foreign domination, and that same summer, when the Czech foreign minister, Jan Masaryk, invited Smith to the palace in Prague for a drink and a talk, he poured out his feelings to the reporter. "If only," he said, "it were possible to cut the planet into two parts and let them drift apart in space; that would solve the problem." Smith asked which side Masaryk would be on. "Czechoslovakia does not lie between East and West," he replied. "It lies between Russia and Germany. I would have no choice. I would go East. But it would kill me!" Days after the coup Masaryk was dead—according to official accounts by suicide, though the exact circumstances were unclear—and the Czechs realized they could no longer speak their minds or choose their rulers by free vote.[51]

This shadowy view of communism was enlarged. The National Security Council considered a report in 1948 that stated: "The ultimate objective of Soviet-directed world communism is the domination of the world." "Stalin has come close to achieving what Hitler attempted in vain." The NSC repeated the theme again and again in its secret memos. "Soviet leaders hold that the Soviet communist party is the militant vanguard of the world proletariat in its rise to political power, and that the USSR, base of the world communist movement, will not be safe until the non-communist nations have been so reduced in strength and numbers that the communist influence is dominant throughout the world." Dean Acheson wrote of "Communism as an aggressive factor in world conquest." In 1950 Truman graphically described the design of "the evil forces of communism to reach out and dominate the world," an opinion that may have been growing in him for some time; as he remembered in his memoirs, when in 1945 Stalin did not want to internationalize the Black Sea straits and the Danube, the "Russians were planning world conquest." The danger to John Foster Dulles in 1950 was of "a great power—Russia—under the control of a despotic group fanatical in their acceptance of a creed that teaches world domination and that would deny those personal freedoms which constitute our most cherished political and religious heritage." President Eisenhower perceived it all as "the Soviet conspiracy to achieve world domination." Again Americans were haunted by the specter of totalitarian world conquest, something they had so recently fought to end in World War II.[52]

Taking this expansive goal to its conclusion, the communists, according to Dean Acheson, had picked "out our country as the principal target of their attack," forcing the two nations into direct confrontation. The policymakers concluded that "the hostile designs and formidable power of the USSR" formed the "gravest threat to the security of the United States" and to its own world role. "The political, economic, and psychological warfare which the USSR is now waging," said the NSC, had dangerous potential for weakening the relative world position of the United States and "disrupting its traditional institutions by means short of war, unless sufficient resistance is encountered in the policies of this and other non-communist countries."[53]

The ultimate fear of cold war, felt in the councils of the NSC, was that it might quickly turn hot: "the USSR has engaged the United States in a struggle for power . . . in which our national security is at stake and from which we cannot withdraw short of eventual national suicide." World domination could come "by subversion, and by legal and illegal political and economic measures," but might ultimately come by war.[54]

The Extremes: Henry Wallace vs. Joseph McCarthy

Henry Wallace was among the dwindling few who continued to believe through the late 1940s and the beginning of the 1950s that the fears of Soviet threats were exaggerated. However much he disapproved of the Soviet dictatorship, communism should not be begrudged the Soviets. He discouraged talk about ideology and anticommunism. Instead he focused on Soviet industrial development and the possibilities for cooperation in diplomacy and commerce.[55]

Wallace did not see communism as a direct threat to the United States, its capitalism, or its individualism. He had encountered the NKVD secret police on his Siberian trip, noting that the Soviet people treated these "old soldiers" with respect, but he did not think the people were submissive. Some of Wallace's colleagues objected to being led about by the NKVD on conducted tours, but Wallace found ways to test the "stiff and formal" relationship. Leaving a guest house unannounced late one afternoon, Wallace headed toward a radio tower on a hill, scrambling through a wicket fence that barred the way. Soon the Russians were following him, but Wallace saw no reason to obey their shouts to turn back.

Wallace even heard expressions of a freedom of speech of sorts. On a Sunday afternoon, seeing local people working in the roadside fields, he brought his motorcade to a stop and encouraged everyone with him to help. After he had been digging for a while, an old woman came over to him. She did not know who he was, and she did not inquire, but she did criticize the local officials in a vigorous "tongue-lashing." "Bureaucrats!" she snapped.

Wallace did not fear Soviet expansion, either by invasion beyond a sphere of neighboring countries or by subversion within the United States. The Soviets had their hands full in developing the frontier regions of their large nation. The people of Siberia were not "whipped into submission." The "only whip driving them is the necessity to master a vast new land. In the past all of Russia, not just the miserable convicts in Siberia, was beaten time and again, as Stalin has never ceased saying, by its economic and political backwardness, by being fifty years behind the times. The need to catch up with the advanced industrial nations is the force behind the great stirring movement among all the peoples of today's Soviet Asia. Awareness of that need is what makes them work so hard."[56]

Wallace's beliefs attracted many supporters among those who yearned for cooperation between Americans and the Soviets, but by 1944 they also aroused many opponents even among his fellow Democrats. He did not campaign for renomination for vice president, and Roosevelt, while expressing personal affection for Wallace, dumped him to increase the chances of his election to a fourth term. Wallace's subsequent hard campaigning for Roosevelt nevertheless gained him a place in his cabinet as secretary of commerce. After Truman asked Wallace to stay on, Wallace expressed his convictions concerning the Soviets in private to the new president, but his public speeches and statements offering an alternative to the administration's foreign policy created a furor in the government and eventually forced his resignation from the cabinet in September 1946.

The confrontation between the two American views toward the Soviets came out clearly after the war, in the exchanges between Wallace and congressmen in hearings before the House Committee on Foreign Affairs in 1948 and 1949. The differences between Wallace on the one hand and Truman and lawmakers of both parties on the other were by then substantial. One issue was whether it was communism or Russia that worried Americans—a competitive ideology, or a combative power.

Mr. [Lawrence H.] Smith. The philosophy . . . is that communism is a real threat to the world. President Truman said we are going to stop it wherever there is a call for help; we are going to rush to their assistance. . . .

Mr. Wallace. I think it is really Russia as such even more than communism. Russia happens to have the communistic way of life, but I do not think the Communist Party would cause us to spend so many billions of dollars every year were it not for Russia.

There was disagreement about whether the Soviet Union was seeking expansion beyond its borders.

Mr. Smith. We were told that . . . the Communists would take over Europe. You do not agree with that?

Mr. Wallace. . . . . Hungry people reach out in desperation for very strong measures and usually totalitarian measures of some kind or another are there. However, with the situation as it now is, I do not see the danger of communism in western Europe. Let us put it this way: I do not see the danger of Russia taking over western Europe. The Communist regime might come into power in one place or another but I do not see how it would satisfy the needs of the people very well if they were exceedingly short of goods.

So too there was conflict over whether the Soviet Union was a threat to the United States.

Mr. [John Davis] Lodge. What country do you consider presents the greatest threat to peace?

Mr. Wallace. I would say it is the condition which exists between the United States and Russia. I would not undertake to assess which one is contributing most to the threat.

Mr. Lodge. Would you say we are contributing as much to the threat as Russia?

Mr. Wallace. It is impossible to say.[57]

Out of office, Wallace made a final stand for his beliefs. In 1948 he ran for the presidency as the candidate of the new leftist Progressive party. He blamed the Truman administration for worsening cold war tensions and polled over a million votes, but this respectable total for a third party was a mere fraction of nearly fifty million cast. He was clearly outside the mainstream of the popular vote. Wallace had striven to lead the nation to take another way, but he had stretched the American capacity for self-examination. He failed to redirect consensus thought or to create a new consensus, and his failure left the consensus of anticommunism unchallenged.

The shocks of Soviet expansion resulted in a wave of domestic anticommunist hysteria. Chief among the politicians, most of them on the right, who exploited the growing fears and sought to extend the consensus to accept the notion of an all-pervasive threat, was the junior Republican senator from Wisconsin after 1947, Joseph

R. McCarthy. McCarthy emphasized a monstrous communist menace that threatened the nation directly from within, even more surely than the Soviets confronted it from without. To McCarthy, at the end of World War II the United States was physically the strongest nation on earth, and potentially the most powerful, intellectually and morally. That no nation rivaled its power led him to certain suppositions. The United States could have had the "honor of being a beacon in the desert of destruction, a shining living proof that civilization was not yet ready to destroy itself." Unfortunately, he lamented, the United States had "failed miserably and tragically to arise to the opportunity." Most striking was the loss of millions to communism since 1945, especially after the Chinese revolution. By his count the 180 million people within the Soviet orbit in 1945 had increased to 800 million by 1950. The Soviet Union had also acquired technical secrets and the blueprints to make atomic bombs.

What was the reason for the Soviet advances? "The reason why we find ourselves in a position of impotency," McCarthy stated in a speech at Wheeling, West Virginia, in 1950, "is not because our only powerful potential enemy has sent men to invade our shores, but rather because of the traitorous actions of those who have been treated so well by this Nation. It has not been the less fortunate or members of minority groups who have been selling this Nation out, but rather those who have had all the benefits that the wealthiest nation on earth has had to offer—the finest homes, the finest college education, and the finest jobs in Government we can give. This is glaringly true in the State Department." McCarthy charged publicly that there were card-carrying communists in the State Department. He cited varying numbers, usually between 51 and 205.[58]

A nation so powerful could only have been betrayed from within, McCarthy declared, by communists and those easily misled by them. The main targets of the witch hunt he launched were Dean Acheson and George Marshall. He criticized Marshall's record as furthering communism: his desire for a second front early in World War II would have given the Mediterranean basin away to the communists; his apparent acquiescence in the Soviet army's entry into Berlin before the other Allies had allowed their domination of eastern Europe; his failed trip to China in 1945 had sold out Chiang Kai-shek and appeased the communists. Acheson, Marshall's "faithful friend," was likewise serving "the interests of nations other than his own." And "President Truman is in the custody of Marshall and Acheson." "He is their captive." "This must be the product of a great conspiracy, a conspiracy on a scale so immense as to dwarf any previous such venture in the history of man."[59]

Truman's response to McCarthy was cold and angry. He blasted the senator in a news conference; there was "not a word of truth" in the charges. Truman had a totally different view of the communist threat. The tyrannical force of communism, he elaborated, was from a central source, the Soviet Union, wherein lay its military and economic strength. The greatest danger did not come from a handful of communists in the United States, "a noisy but small and universally despised group," but rather from "Communist imperialism abroad." Truman later explained that when he had instituted a loyalty program in 1947, out of 2.2 million employees, some 205 left of their own accord. "Does anybody remember those figures exactly?" he asked. "It's a very small figure . . . . An infinitesimal part of 1 percent."[60]

Those less zealous and more moderate than McCarthy supported the sentiment of anticommunism—there was little objection to fighting communism; indeed, that was a major source of his popularity. He carried on his crusade in 1954, as chairman of the Senate permanent investigations subcommittee. In hearings that received wide attention on television, he accused Secretary of the Army Robert T. Stevens of attempting to cover up evidence of communist espionage. But growing numbers rejected McCarthy's insinuations and unsubstantiated charges.

To accuse the nation's leaders of disloyalty or treason would be to place them outside the existing consensus. If these radical accusations had been widely believed, McCarthy would have broken apart the national solidarity. The anxieties aroused by this threat to consensus precipitated McCarthy's fall. In 1954 Eisenhower denounced McCarthy as one who had tried to set himself above the laws of the land, and the Senate voted to censure McCarthy for his conduct. He died in 1957, a broken, lonely man.

McCarthy's challenge to the consensus had checked the development of his own attempts at a mass movement. But his emphasis on anticommunism was widely accepted among the consensus, and his game of calling people strong or soft on communism could be played even by those within the consensus he was attacking. President Truman, campaigning for Adlai Stevenson in 1952, refuted Republican claims that he had been soft on communism. He cited a statement Eisenhower had made before a congressional committee in 1945: "There is no one thing that guides the policy of Russia more today than to keep friendship with the United States." The Republican nominee, then commanding general in Europe, Truman declared, "was in close contact with the Russians. His advice carried great weight and it therefore did a great deal of harm."[61]

So the consensus over anticommunism in the late 1940s was broadly defined by President Truman and his advisers in government—that Soviet communism as an aggressive, expansive force had to be confronted—and the polls showed that the people came to support that attitude. The anticommunist strictures took formal shape in the famous secret NSC document, numbered 68 in 1950 and approved by the president. The Soviet Union was after world "hegemony": it was "animated by a new fanatic faith" and sought to impose "its absolute authority over the rest of the world." The Soviet designs were the subversion and domination of the United States, "the principal center of power in the non-Soviet world and the bulwark of opposition to Soviet expansion." The Soviets threatened the American world role and the very national destiny, the "destruction not only of this Republic but of civilization itself." The "mischief" the Soviets were planning might be "a global war" or a campaign "for limited objectives." In any event, the Soviet Union was "developing the military capacity to support its design for world domination."[62]

Henry Stimson's Clue

Anticommunism was a facile way to hold together the consensus. The anticommunist foreign policy consensus held a relatively straightforward, sincere, but singleminded view of the world: the Soviet Union and its satellite countries were a monolithic enemy seeking to expand and take over parts of the free world as well as nations that sought to remain nonaligned. The hope that the communist and noncommunist parts of the world might be able to live together without war limited anticommunism, but only slightly. Criticism by liberals and the left of the consensus, as led by Henry Wallace, challenged the excesses of anticommunism. So despite a measure of dissension, the differences over the propensity to anticommunism were relatively minor compared with earlier divisions over isolationism and internationalism, and the differences over anticommunism took place without challenging belief in internationalism. Internationalism had drawn America into the world; anticommunism helped make the world seem understandable. The consensus envisioned an open yet restricted rivalry with the Soviet Union to be fought with the economic, propagandistic, and political resources of the nation. No one wanted recourse to weapons, but anticommunism threatened war.

Still, anticommunism was not a sufficient basis for the development of the American role in the world. By defining communism and determining the need to oppose it, anticommunist thinkers were also brought face to face with the predetermined beliefs of their own society. Opposition to communism presupposed habits and a manner of living that shaped perceptions of the rest of the world. Striving to stop the spread of communism was one side of the problem. But what had aroused the United States as a world state? What were the ideas and conceptions of the people of their own country in relation to the rest of the world?

One wise statesman, Henry Stimson, who had served in government for much of his life, including tenures as secretary of state in the Hoover administration and as secretary of war in World War II, came to believe that the problem of American internationalism lay not so much abroad as at home. Here was Stimson's clue: America could not be an island to itself; its life was bound up with that of other peoples. "No private program and no public policy, in any sector of our national life, can now escape from the compelling fact that if it is not framed with reference to the world, it is framed with perfect futility. This would be true . . . if all the land eastward from Poland to the Pacific were under water." What mattered was not so much the fear of communism as the capability to help other people help themselves. The "essential question is one which we should have to answer if there were not a Communist alive. Can we make freedom and prosperity real in the present world? If we can, Communism is no threat. If not, with or without Communism, our own civilization would ultimately fail."[63]

With the internal dimension of foreign policy, we enter an area seldom explored— the elusive connection between the home society and life abroad. We continue our exploration beginning with the mythic expressions of the American consensus about the national experience and its relation to the world.

6

The

Formulation

from

the Past

Returning to New York at the end of the European war, the war correspondent and writer Max Lerner left a bustling Hudson River pier, and even as he took to the street and looked for a taxi, he pondered the country's new relationship to the world. It was an early spring afternoon and there was a sultry, germinal feeling in the air. He liked being back. The only shock he felt was seeing the crowds of prosperous-looking people on the streets. America, he sensed, was like nowhere else. There were no ruins, no shabby, strained look, no dead. "Only sunlight streaming on millions of people—America in the sunlight." It was the same sunlight that was streaming on the rest of the earth—on battlefields, ruined cities, and sea lanes scattered with wreckage. But, he thought, "only in America do you have the feeling that the sun is not ironic."

As Lerner roamed through the city, a citadel of wealth and confidence, he reflected on the diversity of America, and in a remarkable essay he touched on themes of history and society that were to recur in American intellectual life over the next years. "This is where the soldiers come from. This is America," he wrote, "passionate for freedom and riddled with unfreedoms, generous and insular together, far-roaming yet deep-rooted, rich beyond the dreams of men yet fearful lest its men will not have jobs. All that massed power of tanks and guns and men and supplies that I saw in Germany—this is what backs it up. All that mixture I saw in the American soldiers of confusion and simplicity, geniality and roughness—this is where it comes from." He was struck by the sheer paradox of America. It had wealth but spent its riches on comforts, while millions of people all over the world starved and wore ragged clothes. America was the symbol of immense and unified power yet remained in essence a collection of small towns. America was trying painfully to build a culture, and in doing so it was reaching out to other lands to discover what other societies had thought and wrought.

Back in his home and soon in his study, Lerner took from the shelves a book about a young man growing up in the ancient Roman world. Like America, he thought, Rome had produced a glittering culture to which everyone was drawn, built on its riches, fame, and power. He recalled a conversation he had had in Paris with a young Englishman. "We English are Greece," the man had said. That comment

111

made Lerner think what had happened to Rome: how it had flung its armies over the world, built cities everywhere, fashioned administrative structures, developed codes of law, but had never created great tragedy or philosophy; and how it had finally grown fearful of barbarians and disintegrated before their vigor. He was not sure he liked the Englishman's historical parallel.

Then the correspondent thought of the wounded servicemen with whom he had come back on the ship, and he worried no longer. "I shall never forget the cry that arose from them as they stood on their crutches at the portholes, ready to greet New York and its haven. 'See the old lady with the torch,' they said, and the sentence was echoed by hundreds of throats. Nobody but an American would think of calling his national symbol of liberty 'the old lady with the torch.' " The boys had yearned to get home. The more they had seen of the world, the more of a jungle it seemed to them. They might not be able to escape this world, but, in trying to make sense of it, they could hold on to the ideas of home when everything else in the world seemed to be reeling.[1]

Here in Lerner's chronicle was a pattern of the domestic forces that played a part in America's subsequent world role: a sense of historical destiny, a feeling for the national homeland, and a pride in economic efficiency and an affluent, egalitarian society. The national response to external crises was based on more than anticommunism. It was based also on the traditions and values of the society and on the organization of its political, economic, and social system. The consensus of leaders and people had formed not only over external crisis but also over a satisfactory society within. The consensus had favored a role as a world leader, even as the Soviet Union was held in some regard as an ally.

Let us examine the central opinions and ideas regarding domestic society that accompanied the development of America's international role. The search for its meaning was urgently pursued by historians, economists, sociologists, and theologians. What were their prominent theories at this pivotal time? To what extent were the theories ethnocentric or cosmopolitan in their analyses of precedents for American contacts with other nations? It is to the theories of the past that we turn first.

Historical Tradition

In his famous *Foreign Affairs* essay on the sources of Soviet behavior, George Kennan made a statement that revealed a source of America's own new world role after World War II: America would be most successful if it could create "among the peoples of the world generally the impression of a country which knows what it wants" by measuring up "to its own best traditions." Americans, said the policy analyst, would then be "accepting the responsibilities of moral and political leadership that history plainly intended them to bear." Kennan, in proposing the principle of containment of the Soviet Union, was taking for granted suppositions about America's place not only in space but also in time. We have examined the spaces occupied by American influence—the alliance system that reached globally and the network of strategic bases. But what can we learn of the historical traditions of America as a world power in the long sweep of time?[2]

The historical record of ideas and institutions yielded a shared national memory, the forms and symbols of a national heritage. Historians shaped this heritage. Standing at the summit of the mid-twentieth century, they searched for a usable past consistent with the rise of American internationalism. Their histories typically ended with declarations that America was the greatest nation in the world and the embodiment of democracy, freedom, and technological progress. A central purpose of history in this era was to trace the events, perhaps not obvious to contemporaries, that had led to America's world involvement. The content of histories devoted to world affairs increased, and they were filled with sections entitled "America Becomes a World Leader" or "The Responsibilities of World Power." The themes of the historic challenges, rewards, and responsibilities that power presented to the citizens were repeated in speeches on the stump and in newspaper columns and editorials.[3]

External Theory: The Westward Course of Empire

An early theory prominent after World War II explained American internationalism as the result of an external force: the movement of the center of Western civilization across the Atlantic from a declining Europe to the United States. This theory derived from the perception of a westward course of empire, apparently originating in Asia, moving through Europe for thousands of years, and coming to rest in the New World. The idea was not new. Visionary nineteenth-century intellectuals, including Brooks Adams, John Fiske, and Josiah Strong, represented it as a scientific law of history. University seminars, taught by a new breed of professional historians schooled in the German method of education, such as Herbert Baxter Adams at Johns Hopkins, talked about a germ theory in which the genesis of American national institutions was in the Old World. By around the turn of the twentieth century, when the United States won an empire in the Spanish-American War, Woodrow Wilson, who held a doctorate after studying history and government at Johns Hopkins, had pictured as nearly complete "civilization's 'journey with the sun.'" Theodore Roosevelt, who became president of the American Historical Association in 1912, traced this journey from Egypt to Babylonia, Carthage, Greece, Rome, Venice and Genoa, Spain, Portugal, France, Holland, and England, ending finally in America.[4]

It was this classical history that historians taught to the nation's future leaders, whether at elite academies or in rural schoolhouses. The boy Franklin Roosevelt, who had the advantages of the best schooling, private tutors at home and Groton School in the late 1890s, learned that man's material and spiritual progress had advanced in westward steps. Years later, he remembered the instruction by his Groton headmaster, the Reverend Endicott Peabody, of the stages: the triumphs of Rome, the renaissance of Europe, and then the American Revolution, which marked a new epoch. About a grade behind Roosevelt, in the distant Missouri public schools, Harry Truman learned the same history. Seeking to understand the development of the United States as part of his "total education," Truman stated that he had "read the standard histories of ancient Egypt, the Mesopotamian cultures, Greece and Rome," supplemented by exploits of Genghis Khan and the stories of Oriental civilizations, and topped off by the "accounts of the development of every modern country, and particularly the history of America." Like Truman, young Dwight Eisenhower, who lived on the edge of the plains of Kansas, read about ancient Egypt, Assyria, Persia, Greece, Rome, and later the British and French. He dreamt of the conquerors and battles of these empires, and he recalled reading accounts of them instead of doing his chores and homework.[5]

Evidence for the westward course of empire was provided by the newly proclaimed emergence of the United States as a first-class world power during the formative years of the nation's future leaders. The seminal event was the Spanish-American War, in which the United States took possession of an empire of islands in the Atlantic and Pacific. At Groton, sixteen-year-old Franklin Roosevelt, a fifth cousin of Theodore Roosevelt, the Rough Rider soon to charge up San Juan Hill in Cuba, was excited by the war; he and two other boys planned to escape from school in a pieman's cart to enlist, but just then he came down with scarlet fever. Franklin Roosevelt's future secretary of state, Cordell Hull, raising his own company, served in the war and later credited the conflict with giving him a glimpse of the wider problems of international relationships that "would face the Republic from then on." When Dwight Eisenhower, seven years old, heard about the war, he thought of the outside world creeping into Abilene, Kansas. The future supreme Allied commander could never forget the glee of his uncle, Abraham Lincoln Eisenhower, when the news arrived of Dewey's May Day victory over the Spanish fleet at Manila Bay.[6]

Only in retrospect was the confirmation of America's growing power in World War I fully grasped by these future leaders. Serving on the European front, Truman reminisced about barely escaping barrages of enemy fire, but he did not recognize the war's importance in world politics until after the event. Eisenhower was commanding a tank training center in San Antonio; the war ended before he could be sent overseas. Walter Lippmann recalled that as a boy he had been greatly excited by the sinking of the battleship *Maine* and by Dewey's victory, and from his "grandfather who hated Prussia" he had acquired the conviction that "wherever the American flag was planted, there tyranny must disappear." But he confessed that not until World War II did he become aware of the "revolutionary consequences of the Spanish-American War."[7]

During and after World War II, with the collapse of the European-dominated world system, the study of the transfer of world power was revived. In 1947 Brooks Adams's nearly fifty-year-old book, *America's Economic Supremacy,* was rediscovered as an explanation of the current world situation and reprinted. Writing in 1900, Adams had traced the steady westward march of seats of empire from China and India, through to Chaldea and Assyria, Phoenicia, Carthage, Rome, and Britain; then, perceiving that England was in decline, he saw the far-reaching consequences of the enormous growth of American economic power. That set the stage for a supreme America and the emergence of only two great powers. Foretelling the decline of the world's dominant empire and the rise of the United States, to be rivaled perhaps only by Russia, was a revolutionary conception in 1900, but it had become commonplace by midcentury. "If Adams had written last year, for publication this year," wrote Marquis W. Childs, "he would have had to alter scarcely anything to relate his views to the world of today."[8]

Historians continued to use the same epic story of international affairs when they wrote about events in Europe that antedated the exploration and settlement of the New World. In his 1947 work *Westward Expansion: A History of the American Frontier,* Ray Allen Billington, a professor at Northwestern University, observed that the "settlement of the American continent" was no less than "the last stage in a mighty movement of peoples that began in the twelfth century," when feudal Europe pushed back the barbarian hordes that threatened the city of Rome. Billington recalled the opening passages of Theodore Roosevelt's four-volume *The Winning of the West,* published between 1889 and 1896, which spoke of "great Teutonic wanderings" westward across Europe to Germany, France, Holland, and finally England. American history to Billington and Roosevelt was not an isolated episode but a climactic development following the colonization efforts of Western European nations.[9]

The comparison of the United States to earlier empires inevitably aroused the question whether the United States, a republic, born in a war of independence against British imperial rule, was indeed an empire. Carl Becker made thoughtful comparison of the United States to earlier empires, from Babylon and Rome to Spain and Britain, and he concluded: "We do not commonly speak of the United States empire. Why not? I do not know. Since the United States has acquired Alaska, Puerto Rico, the Hawaiian Islands and the Philippines, and has thereby acquired what Walter Lippmann calls political 'commitments' extending over half the globe, it has, by every common test, the right to be recognized as an empire, as one of the great imperial powers." Neither Becker nor most contemporaries implied that the United States was seeking to extend imperial authority over conquered territory or was terribly exploitive in its imposition of power, but rather that it possessed power great enough to rival or surpass that of past empires. Because the United States had taken on worldwide political, economic, and cultural enterprises, historians continued to compare it to an empire even after the Philippines became an independent nation in 1946 and Alaska and Hawaii became states of the Union in the 1950s.[10]

The idea of the United States after World War II as the latest achievement in a sequence of mighty world movements proved appealing. The "wheel of destiny has turned," declared Sen. Ralph Flanders in a series of lectures at Harvard in 1950. "In the long succession of principalities and powers, the blooming and withering of cultures in our Western world, Greece succeeded the valleys of the Nile and the Euphrates; Rome succeeded Greece and Western Europe succeeded Rome. In Western Europe, France succeeded Spain and England succeeded France. Now the revolving wheel has come to a momentary pause, and the destinies of the world, fortunately or unfortunately, are placed in our surprised, reluctant, and untrained hands." It was as if an external force had thrust power on America, which had little recourse about its new station.[11]

President Truman conceived of the world history that produced America as cyclical, because of the rhythm of the rise and fall of empires, and cumulative, since events that seemed to be new "might have existed in almost identical form at various times during the past six thousand years." But the circumstances of America's rise to power, mused Truman, were unprecedented. "From Darius I's Persia, Alexander's Greece, Hadrian's Rome, Victoria's Britain," he said, "no nation or group of nations has had our responsibilities." The United States, as Truman saw it, had surpassed the achievements of earlier empires, since history, despite setbacks, was "a story of improvement" from Hammurabi, Rameses, Rome, the Renaissance, to the present. To Truman power balances shifted more rapidly in modern times than in ancient. In the short period since 1789, the United States had become "the greatest and most powerful nation in the world." "It seems almost incredible," he marveled. "It took Rome more than a thousand years to arrive at that situation."[12]

The selection of the powers and empires preceding America was often arbitrary, and sometimes not in a strictly westward course, but certain dominant empires were usually included sequentially in these analyses. Rome, the great empire of antiquity that stretched from the isle of Britain to Persia, and Great Britain, at its height the largest global empire, were the standards of comparison. Lippmann singled these two empires out in 1939: what Rome was to the ancient world, what Britain was to the last century, "America is to be to the world of tomorrow." The past generation had already witnessed what he took to be "one of the greatest events in the history of mankind"—the movement across the Atlantic of the controlling power in Western civilization. The next American generations, Lippmann was certain, would see, whether they wanted it or not, their nation as the geographic and economic center of the Occident.[13]

Implicit in the theory that the seat of power had moved across time to America was the belief that history had culminated in the present. By calling the twentieth century the "American Century," Henry Luce meant to compare the United States to the dominant powers of the past. He cited the Roman Empire and nineteenth-century England, and he mixed in the Vatican, Genghis Khan, the Ottoman Turks, and the Chinese emperors. Great power, according to Luce, made it impossible for the United States to avoid making the present century the "American Century," any more than earlier empires had escaped power in their eras of ascendancy.[14]

Luce, who had studied history, including a year at Oxford, was not without some support from scholars. When Saul K. Padover, a historian and former assistant secretary of the interior, asked in 1947 if this was the "American Century," he replied that nothing like the dimensions of American power had been seen on earth since Rome. In the early 1950s in a historical inquiry into power politics, Frederick L. Schuman asserted that the twentieth century was the "American Century": "From time to time in the course of human events a single community . . . has come to dominate most of mankind and to build thereby some facsimile of world government. Such was the destiny of Persia in the sixth century B.C., of Macedonia in the fourth century B.C., of Rome later, and subsequently of Islam, the Mongols, and the Muscovites. In our own century such a community has once more emerged." That community, the United States, he called "a supercolossus of technology and productivity" that might "have been expected long since to 'rule the world.'"[15]

According to the same theory of the westward course, the United States was heir to institutions and principles that established the content of American internationalism. The germ theory of Herbert Baxter Adams had led the way in professing that the seeds of American democracy originated in the sunless forests of Germany, crossed the North Sea to England, and then the Atlantic Ocean to New England. But this theory had fallen from favor with the coming of Turner's frontier study and was not revived during and after the struggle against Nazi Germany. The theme of America's inheritance now emphasized the Judeo-Christian legacy, which upheld the importance of the individual and of morality in governing human relations. This legacy, transmitted from the ancient Middle East through Greece, Rome, and Western Europe, was the basis of democratic life. "In World War II and in the years immediately following it Americans, with the aid of their allies," wrote the intellectual historian at Yale, Ralph H. Gabriel, "had preserved for the time being the principles of human freedom and dignity whose formulation had been the greatest consummation of Western civilization." Neither the colonial era nor the American Revolution had marked the beginning of American political ideas. As Clinton Rossiter told readers of his *Seedtime of the Republic,* "our political faith" stems "back through the colonial past almost to the beginning of Western political thought."[16]

This historical tradition helped to define an American world role in the face of regressive Old World governments under communism and fascism. While Europe was being torn apart by war against fascism, President Roosevelt delineated the democratic heritage from the beginning of human history to Greece, where the philosophy of democracy was articulated; to Rome, which extended throughout much of the then known world a strange mixture of laws, military conquest, and personal dictatorship; to the British Isles, which "led the world in spreading the gospel of democracy among peoples, great and small"; and, finally, to America, where, he said, there began a "new order." In the "scheme of civilization from which ours descends," he continued, "I suppose that we can recognize that in approximately 2,500 years there have been only a very few 'new orders' in the development of human living." Vice President Wallace summarized the course of social justice through the religions of Western civilization from the "prophets of the Old Testament," to the beliefs of Christianity, to the last phase—the "complete and powerful political expression" that was "our nation . . . formed as a Federal Union a century and a half ago." As for Soviet Russia, President Truman found it lacking this Western moral tradition, which he followed from ancient Israel and the Sermon on the Mount. He added for worthy mention the moral principles of Egypt, Mesopotamia, Greece, and Rome.[17]

The exact origins of these democratic traditions were obscure. Robert Sherwood, the writer, editor, playwright of *Abe Lincoln in Illinois,* and recipient of Pulitzer Prizes in 1936, 1939, and 1941, stretched his imagination as far back as anyone. "The story began," he wrote of the heritage of freedom for which America fought in World War II, "probably, in the primordial jungle, when the first ape man first managed to straighten up and stand on his own two feet." Since he admitted not knowing that for certain, Sherwood also looked to the Book of Genesis, which expressed the belief that man was created in God's image, a conception that gave dignity and virtue to the individual. Moving through recorded history, he mentioned the people of Israel leaving Egypt, Athens in the Golden Age of Pericles, the birth of Christ, the Magna Carta, the Declaration of Independence—all as prelude to America's postwar world role.[18]

In this tradition of Western democracy, Great Britain had been the most important home, recognized not only for its worldwide empire but also for its ancient parliament. Secretary of State Hull thought that the final achievement of a five-hundred-year struggle for Anglo-Saxon liberty was attained in the Declaration of Independence, the Bill of Rights, and Jefferson's first inaugural address. In a talk to foreign service officers, Hull expressed an almost sentimental view of English liberties: "I sometimes think that I would have given all the wealth of this great Hemisphere—and I am no more patriotic than any of you folk—if I could have been one of that little band that went out to the field of Runnymede in 1215 and extracted from King John that wonderful collection of human liberties known as Magna Carta. After liberty had been banished from the world for a thousand years," the English "took the first step back toward human freedom," which "finally culminated in our own country in the Revolution and the structure of our free government."[19]

Thus, according to the theory of the westward course, American internationalism developed as world power and civilization settled in North America, to remain there in the future, for there were no new worlds to conquer. Beyond was the Orient, and its day seemed past and its tradition in decay. The United States would use its power to influence other lands and bring renewal through advanced technological and democratic civilization.

Universal Theory: Arnold Toynbee

A few American historians made connections between world history and American internationalism that broke out of the confining theory of a westward sweep of empire. In 1942 the American Historical Association planned a wartime meeting on the quest for political unity in world history. The organizers believed this question was perhaps the greatest of the twentieth century, which was witnessing "the most sweeping and penetrating" change of the last four hundred years. Although the meeting was canceled at the request of the Office of Defense Transportation, some papers were subsequently published. A "universalist" approach to history was difficult "to formulate clearly and fairly," Robert Palmer admitted in his essay, but it had to be attempted. The essays as a whole, however, were eclectic and they made no pretense of covering the subject logically or completely. Qunicy Wright's piece reverted to the position that the precedents for world unity were the Pax Romana and Pax Britannica. The editor of the volume predicted without equivocation that the future would be determined chiefly by Britain and the United States, not Russia, because of their worldwide interests. In 1948 Crane Brinton of Harvard made a subsequent attempt in a slim book, *From Many One,* to comprehend the process of world political integration. He believed that the field of study was still inadequately cultivated, and even as he introduced his own attempt as "elementary, perhaps even naïve," he traced "international" relations from the heyday of the Nile and Euphrates valleys through the Roman and British empires, leaving aside the experience of China and India and other lands "for lack of competence."[20]

Among the most serious in their labors were the American contributors to the post–World War II plans for an objective, universal history of mankind by the United Nations Educational, Scientific and Cultural Organization (UNESCO). Beginning with proposals in the late 1940s and authorized by the international agency to proceed in 1950, American historians, together with their counterparts around the world, hoped to remove from their study the judgment that any one nation was invariably right in its actions or superior in its advancement. In the optimistic, cosmopolitan spirit of the United Nations, these historians sought to explain American international involvement not as a pinnacle of history toward which the thrust of the past had been tending, but as part of a universal process of history. Yet American historians took a dim view of the collective historical enterprise by international committees that glossed over the differences among nations.[21]

Greater inspiration for a universal history came from the epic *A Study of History* by the English historian Arnold Toynbee. Toynbee's work, structured like philosophy and written with poetic color, was a comparative investigation of global civilizations. The first six volumes of the study, which began appearing in the 1930s and were published in the United States in 1947 in abridged form, running 589 pages, explored the birth, growth, decay, and death of twenty-six world civilizations. The edition remained for weeks on American best-seller lists, transforming Toynbee into a popular sage who traveled on lecture tours across the country. *Life* devoted a major article to Toynbee's work, and what seemed a Toynbee "cult" prompted Max Lerner to charge mischievously: "It is not Toynbee's fault that he has been made part of Henry Luce's gallery of secular saints and been canonized in both *Time* and *Life* and his writings treated as if they were a Koran of the American Century." The interest of Americans in Toynbee's breadth of historical knowledge peaked as they sought a guide to a world whose moral and intellectual outlines they had only begun to glimpse. Some attempted to discover from his "laws" of history the origins and future of American international involvement. Toynbee's own assessment of his work's popularity was that "America was entering the main stream of history and Americans wanted to know more about it."[22]

In 1947 Toynbee observed that a key to the understanding the present lay in the superpower status of the United States. Because of its overwhelming superiority in industrial production and its monopoly of the knowledge about the atom bomb, the

United States, he wrote in *Foreign Affairs,* was "impregnable against military attack by the Soviet Union." In addition, he recognized, the country's large population expanded by the influx of European immigrants, natural resources spread across a vast territory comparable to all of Europe excluding Russia, and position as the greatest creditor nation had long put Europe in America's shadow.[23]

Toynbee's visit to the United States early in 1947 persuaded him that Americans were realizing that the British Empire was in disintegration. In place of the empire a huge political vacuum would be left, and into it the United States might find itself constrained to move to forestall the Soviet Union. He found that Americans, while trying to grasp the global implications of such change, were abandoning their traditional denunciation of British imperialism. They had discovered "the convenience, for them, of the British Empire's existence just at the moment when, as they see it, the British Empire is being liquidated." They were becoming conscious of services performed by the empire, for so long taken for granted.[24]

In Toynbee's view, the United States had no immediate rivals. It was so much stronger than the Soviet Union that, short of attempting to wrench from the Soviet grasp some country already under its control, the United States could "assert her own protectorate over any country she chooses in the no-man's-land between the Soviet Union and herself." The United States was in the position of being able to exercise worldwide influence. In a lecture at Columbia University in 1948, Toynbee drew a parallel between British efforts to seek a balance of power with France and Russia, and the confrontation between the United States and the Soviet Union. He suggested "a provisional partition of the world into a Russian and an American sphere by agreements between the two."[25]

Despite its vast power, the United States in Toynbee's scheme was not the pinnacle of empire but merely a small unit of Western civilization. If one were "to try to understand the history of the United States by itself, it would be unintelligible," he wrote in *Harper's* in 1947. It was impossible to understand the American institutions of federal government, democracy, industrialism, monogamy, and Christianity without looking beyond the United States to Western Europe. To "make American history and institutions intelligible for practical purposes, you need not look beyond Western Europe into Eastern Europe or the Islamic World, nor behind the origins of our Western European civilization to the decline and fall of the Graeco-Roman civilization. These limits of time and space give us the intelligible unit of social life of which the United States or Great Britain or France or Holland is a part: call it Western Christendom, Western Civilization, Western Society, the Western World."

Toynbee's broad conception took in more than the current impression among American historians that their country was in a special historical position of power, and too all-encompassing for a school of American historians to follow. The United States, he pointed out, although not more than 150 years old, might not last much longer as a separate entity: "States are apt to have short lives and sudden deaths." The "Western Civilization of which you and I are members," Toynbee observed, "may be alive centuries after the United Kingdom and the United States have disappeared from the political map of the world like their late contemporaries, the Republic of Venice and the Dual Monarchy of Austria-Hungary." Toynbee's assertions sparked rebuttals, one of them in the late 1950s, when Lerner debated him over whether the United States qualified as a separate civilization. To Lerner America was exceptional and unique.[26]

Toynbee especially aroused the ire of American historians engaged in specialized studies. These scholars as a whole shared Charles Beard's doubts, broached in his review of the first three volumes of *A Study of History,* that very different civilizations were comparable. They wondered whether civilizations had parallel developments or were philosophically compatible. They criticized his efforts to visualize history as global. They objected to a view of history that seemed oversimplified and subjective, and agreed with Franklin L. Baumer of Yale, who called *A Study of History* "anything but history." Toynbee's application of his theories to the United States came under particularly sharp criticism. Noted Brinton: "The love of symbols and metaphors, the constant use of comparisons so odious to most of us, the claims to omniscience his themes seem to impose . . . , the very British piety that makes even his good manners seem a form of patronizing—all this and much else we find irritating." Even Luce fell out with Toynbee over the assertion that the United States was simply a peripheral part of European civilization. "I regard America as a special dispensation—under Providence," Luce declared. Toynbee had urged Americans to view their past a little less parochially and to see their internationalism in light of the historical experiences of civilizations around the globe. But Toynbee's approach was a road not taken; it would have little immediate impact on the writing of American history.[27]

Internal Theory: The Consensus School

As Toynbee quickly learned, postwar American historians tended to conceive of their country's internationalism as unique, possessing qualities that set it apart from that of previous empires. Power had not been thrust on Americans by external circumstance; they had had something to do with it. The inhabitants had not simply nurtured the civilization they had inherited but transformed it into something different on their own continent. Placing America's emergence at the center of history, these historians saw the vast wealth of a once virgin continent and the development of a vigorous civilization. The often-repeated theme of American history, here stated by the Harvard historian Oscar Handlin, was that the "people of the thirteen British colonies became a nation. The United States spread from a narrow line of settlement along the Atlantic across the continent to the Pacific. From a weak band of states, it became a great power, disposing enormous might throughout the world." President Truman robustly rephrased this academic conception: "we started out with 13 Colonies and about 3 million people. Now we have 48 States and 148 million people, and a worldwide interest in the peace of the whole world. We have grown from the newest and smallest nation in the world to the greatest nation in the history of the world."[28]

Historical scholarship isolated the features that made the United States historically separate and distinct from other lands. Ralph H. Gabriel, Richard Hofstadter, Daniel Boorstin, and Louis Hartz, among a host of others, explored these features and formed a loose group of scholars referred to as the consensus school of historiography. They built in large part on Turner's thesis that the American people had formed on the frontiers of their territory unique and striking national characteristics. These historians also added to the tradition of Perry Miller, who had cultivated the field of American studies at Harvard in the 1930s. They did not agree on all things, but they did proceed in their separate works to emphasize what they believed the progressive historians had overlooked—behind the disputes that had racked the United States throughout its history, Americans had united in broad ideological agreement on the merits of their national life. Conflicts between special interests—landed enterprises and industrial capital, large and small property, and liberal and conservative political thought—all took place within a generally accepted American way. Whatever their divisions, Americans held to the central faith of American political ideology. Put another way by Henry Steele Commager, historians ceased debunking the past, instead recreating it sympathetically, even affectionately.[29]

The consensus historians emphasized an exceptional development that had culminated in the nation's present success, a success that was taken fully for granted, to explain its world role. America, they contended, had achieved a society more open, an economy more vigorous, and a government more free than anywhere else primarily through the force of its domestic circumstances. Hofstadter was among the first to assume the consensus position. American society was unique and superior, he thought in 1948, because it was practical. Observing that in "material power and productivity the United States has been a flourishing success," Hofstadter could find the precondition of successful development in the unifying ideas of Americans. Working societies, he commented, had "a kind of mute organic consistency" among their people, not destructive dissension. A distinctive historical development was a main theme shared by Boorstin in his explanation of national success. He emphasized, with Hofstadter, the practicality of the American experience. As Boorstin wrote, America "had something to teach all men: not by precept but by example, not by what it said but by how it lived." In *The Genius of American Politics,* Boorstin hypothesized, "The genius of American democracy comes not from any special virtue of the American people but from the unprecedented opportunities of this continent and from a peculiar and unrepeatable combination of historical circumstances." Boorstin, who had gained a perspective on American uniqueness from his experiences as a Rhodes Scholar at Oxford and as a lecturer in American history at the University of Rome, argued, "in a word, that American democracy is unique. It possesses a 'genius' all its own."[30]

The historical viewpoint was not that the United States as a unique nation lacked a claim to international leadership, because the rest of the world would be alien and incomprehensible. On the contrary, unique American characteristics were to serve as guides to exercising globally a unique role, spreading modern technology and democracy. Arthur Schlesinger, Jr., of Harvard pointed up the importance of his research on democracy in the age of Andrew Jackson by offering the lesson of his study to the post–World War II era. If democracy was to prevail after the world crisis, he wrote in his Pulitzer Prize–winning book, Americans needed to seek its distinct meaning in the record of their past. He did not know how the United States would move to meet its external postwar perplexities, and his lessons for the present were vague. But he was certain that the nation would meet current crises as it had met earlier ones, even though the new crises were of world dimensions.[31]

America's advent as an international power was to be the culmination of its past, stated Louis Hartz of Harvard, and would also serve to shatter American "provincialism": if America was the "fulfillment of liberalism, do not people everywhere rely upon it for the retention of what is best in that tradition?" Hartz explained that the American experiment was in the tradition of liberal philosophers, prominently John Locke, whose ideas had been transformed by the founding fathers. That liberal tradition Hartz called a "storybook truth" about American history: that the settlers of America had fled from the feudalism of the Old World. Escape from the feudal tradition, in Hartz's analysis, not only affirmed America's uniqueness but also had tremendous consequences for America as a world power. Indeed, Hartz argued, America's world position demanded the study of American uniqueness. The "payoff" of the American experience, he expounded, was its world power, after an insularity that had excelled that of any other power, including Britain. Given the totalitarian nature of Russian socialism, "the hope for a free world surely lies in the power for transcending itself inherent in American liberalism." In Hartz's call for transcendence, there were ambiguities, for how could the United States attain a new level of consciousness about the world if, as he had striven to show in his work, the uniqueness of the American tradition did not inspire the confidence that it could? Still, that uniqueness did not keep him from hoping that something in the American past, perhaps its fundamental respect for the individual or its philosophy of democracy, could lead it to proper action as a world power.[32]

Confronted by the philosophies and crusades of fascism and communism, Americans, Boorstin believed, had to find instruction for their world involvement in a "wholesome conservatism of the past." While Hartz was emphasizing liberalism, Boorstin, in lauding conservatism, was closing the circle of the wide spectrum of consensus over internationalism. They were really not so far apart. Hartz found precedents for America's world role in the liberal tradition of the founding fathers, and Boorstin, who saw precedents in the same founding fathers, wanted to conserve their philosophies in exercising world power: "Through no special virtue or effort of our own, we may be peculiarly fitted for the role which we are called on to play." But the American attitude to this role could survive only so long as it preserved a "sense for the uniqueness of the American experience." "The science of uniqueness is the study of history, and our feeling for the uniqueness of our culture will be proportionate to our knowledge of our past." At the beginning of his three-volume *The Americans,* Boorstin quoted John

Winthrop's words to the early Puritan colonists: "Wee shall be as a Citty upon a Hill, the eies of all people are uppon us." For Boorstin, "No one writing after the fact, three hundred years later, could better have expressed the American sense of destiny."[33]

The consensus historians tended to support each other in their common endeavor of seeking to understand their nation's past as a guide to the world. In a review, Arthur Schlesinger, who published *The Vital Center* in 1949, found merit in Hofstadter's "important and refreshing" *American Political Tradition*. Although Schlesinger wondered why Hofstadter had not added to the American shared belief in property rights, individualism, and competition, ideas such as God, home, and mother, he agreed with Hofstadter's consensus viewpoint; "it serves as a valuable corrective for any who would suppose that American history has been a series of profound and convulsive conflicts." And it was the new condition of interaction with the world that made this view current: "The crisis in the middle of the twentieth century may lead us in principle to talk broadly about the great unities of our past." Henry Nash Smith described the revised 1956 edition of Ralph H. Gabriel's *Course of American Democratic Thought* as a book of "established importance." In comparing the new edition with the old, Smith found the author "somewhat more disposed than he was in 1940 to claim universal validity for the moral content of the American democratic faith."[34]

Commentators and leaders found support for American internationalism in a whole range of American developments. If "we comprehend our destiny," said Lippmann of the post–World War II world, "we shall become equal to it. . . . For America is now called to do what the founders and the pioneers always believed was the American task: to make the New World a place where the ancient faith can flourish anew, and its eternal promise at last be redeemed." Franklin Roosevelt with others could benignly choose any number of precedents—from the Pilgrims landing in America, the founding fathers fighting the American Revolution, the pioneers forcing their way through frontier wilderness, Lincoln preserving the nation in the Civil War—to support international involvement. As for the American Revolution, its goals were "so unlimited" that Roosevelt called them "the primary objectives of the entire civilized world." Truman was fond of parallels between the American past and present, and at the closing session of the United Nations Conference in San Francisco in June 1945, he compared the framing of the U.S. Constitution to that of the U.N. charter. He hoped for "an international bill of rights" similar to the one attached to the American Constitution. Later, when he no longer held the United Nations in such high esteem and was calling for the formation of the North Atlantic Treaty Organization, Truman was asked for parallels in American history to the situation he faced in the world. His response: "Jefferson's decision to wipe out the Barbary pirates caused almost as much denunciation as my decision to implement the Atlantic Treaty—so conditions do not change." Truman's application of the American frontier experience to the world took some liberties with Turner's frontier thesis and the census report of 1890: "Some people believe that the American frontier vanished forever when the 48th State came into the Union. That is nonsense. . . . This Nation has never stopped growing in wealth and strength." As

Henry Bamford Parkes noted, "All the earlier history of the American people, at least when superficially considered, seemed to have prepared them for such a role" of world leadership. He was careful to use the word *superficially*.[35]

At the zenith of American power, then, historians offered several explanations for the development of internationalism. One theory emphasized external forces and traced America's world involvement through a series of past Western empires; another emphasized exceptional internal development. Each theory suggested the need for a new world role, and none told the whole story. They competed for attention. The external theory was popular during and after World War II, for it drew on the long-established tradition of the westward course of empire, but the theory that eventually gained the largest following and the most authority in the late 1940s and 1950s stressed the domestic determinants of America's emergence as a preeminent world power. The theory of universal history, aside from the rush of interest in Toynbee, was largely rejected and remained undeveloped in America.

The internal and the external theories shared certain distinctions that reflected the historical character of American internationalism. The evidence for either theory provided confidence for the future based largely on the successes of the past. This use of the past was essentially a "Whig" view of history—what Herbert Butterfield had described as the tendency of British historians of the nineteenth century and after to study the successes of the British Empire from the viewpoint of the victorious English Whigs: to emphasize past progress and to produce a story that ratifies, if not glorifies, the present. At the height of the British Empire, English histories ended with uncanny similarity to mid-twentieth century American histories. The career of England, the story ran, was of too much importance to the history of the human race to be handled in a partisan spirit; consensus about its success was evident. The theme of lecturers like Sir John Seeley, writers such as Rudyard Kipling, and statesmen, notably Joseph Chamberlain, was that the growth of the empire was the result of the unique pluck and daring of England. The British Empire, scattered all over the globe and owning half of the ocean commerce of the world, lay in all zones and bore all products. The only comparison was with the Roman Empire, the Mongolian empire being usually forgotten.

The theories of the westward course of empire and the uniqueness of American history both overlooked the contrary trends of human history and tended toward the ethnocentric, not the truly international. The westward-course theory did not conceive of global civilizations in their entirety but only a few of them, usually chosen at random. Native societies in Africa, Asia, and Latin America, some of them once seats of great empires themselves, were ignored by historians except in the context of the exploration and colonization efforts of Europeans. In the same way, consensus historians risked projecting the domestic experience of one great power, even unintentionally, onto that of other cultures. Moreover, the exact meanings of the nation's past to foreign relations were not always clear. Did the westward movement of the American frontier condition Americans for a world role, as Turner had proposed as early as the 1890s, or was the frontier a restraining and insulating experience on an American world role? Henry

Nash Smith wrote that the myth of the western frontier as a garden "will be recognized as the core of what we call isolationism," while Charles Sanford argued to the contrary that the sense of an Eden of the West resulted in "a world mission of regeneration," "the great underlying postulate of American foreign policy." The argument could be pressed either way. These variants of the theory of internal forces shaping internationalism were essentially American attempts to comprehend their own sense of national identity in the world. As with the external western-course theory, they failed to take full account of the desires, interests, and life of other cultures.[36]

Neither the external nor the internal theory of American internationalism admitted the possibility of retreat from preeminent power. Historians tended to overlook the prospect of American decline in the years after World War II because their studies of the past convinced them that, while the previously great empires had collapsed, the story of America remained one of growth. Only a few Marxists maintained a dogmatic belief that capitalist societies were condemned, but their views lacked objectivity. The enormous power and vitality of the United States belied any warnings of decline.[37]

Eisenhower's philosophy of history was more subtle than Truman's, usually avoiding exaggerated parallels between the United States and earlier empires. Once the supreme Allied commander in World War II, he realized that history was written by victors rather than the vanquished, and that social and economic forces played a significant part. History "is not made merely by big names or by startling actions, but also by the slow progress of millions and millions of people." Toward the end of his second term, Eisenhower warned of the threats that had corrupted previous empires. "Since time began, opulence has too often paved for a nation the way to depravity and ultimate destruction," he declared in an address at the National Automobile Show Industry Dinner in Detroit in 1960. "The ancient civilizations of Egypt, Greece, Rome and more recently the splendid court of Louis XV fell thus, each having developed a false sense of values and its people having lost their sense of national destiny. This could be a threat to the United States."[38]

American loyalties to the past were insufficient to sustain the contemporary consensus without devotion to what presently existed. The postwar generation's vantage point was different from that of earlier generations or of those that followed. Its history was in some degree contemporary history, with its own particular vision of America, offering the first glimpse of a golden age of power and prosperity. Further study of the meaning of the past might have impressed on historians that the course of world history was not about to come to an end with American preeminence in 1945 or 1950. The comparative study of the history of societies, sorely neglected, might have led to an internationalism broader in scope than historians had then developed. The idea of the progress of one nation in history might have continued, as it encountered and accommodated views of people among diverse nations around the globe.

7

The

View

from

the Present

When the war was over and the soldiers had left Guadalcanal, North Africa, Normandy, Iwo Jima, Okinawa, and lesser-known battlefields around the world, they returned to rediscover their land—to the fields where they had played as children, the forests of hemlock and fern, the cornfields and pastures of briar, the hills that rose and fell in an undulating rhythm, and the dirt roads at the crest of a hill, where the blue green of the countryside reached the sky; and to the small-town main streets and the city tenements and skyscrapers. They returned to the Appalachians, Plains, and Rockies, and to Massachusetts, Kansas, New Jersey, New York, and the rest of the states. They wanted to be home, like the veterans of any war, and they sought refuge in their land. Their fathers had come back from World War I and many had found their sanctuary in the land. But this time their sons could not escape the outside world. The refuge of tranquil forests, plains, mountains, and lake country had become an enormous arsenal and an industrial powerhouse.

The land had long been used to explain the elemental forces of a nation's power. But the American landscape was more than the source of such supplies as logs, stone, minerals, and waterpower. There was a deep sense about the land all around—the forest, the flashing stream, the sun and soil, the wind and rain and snow. After all, it was widely believed that the land held the people together, and that the bond between the people and the land was connected to feelings of nationality. The people's feelings for the land corresponded to their preference for their home, their own language, and their customs. A consensus notion was that from the land the people derived an outlook on the world. They connected to a country marked by continental variation in climate and geography, and by human achievements —tall buildings, big dams, large cities. In the late 1940s this landscape gave confidence for large undertakings.

Consider the feelings of one citizen-soldier returning from Europe, where he had observed the war for *National Geographic Magazine,* as he disembarked from a troop ship with his comrades. To his eyes, conditioned for years to the shorter distances and smaller dimensions of Europe, the lavish scale of America made this country seem mightily magnified. Boarding a train heading west with his fellow soldiers, he found a place in a railroad car, large in proportion to the petite ones of Britain and France. The haunting

127

train whistle blasts were wholly different from the peeps of Europe's locomotives, and he looked out on passing trains that gave him the sense of the sweeping geography of the land. The names on the boxcars spoke to him with a strange, thrilling eloquence: "Great Northern, Union Pacific, Pennsylvania, Grand Canyon, Rio Grande, Santa Fe"—names suggesting home and open spaces, where one could wander and look up at the clouds, and perhaps "do a little fishing."

As the train chugged through the outlying towns, the riders felt the expectancy of traveling home. "Things are surely different here," the soldiers thought. "All morning it had been dawning on them how rich was the land in which they lived." The train sped past woods and fields and highways: "That's no autobahn, but a good old U.S. express highway," said one. "We've had 'em since Hitler was a peanut politician trying to get himself elected dogcatcher." They saw new construction completed during the war, new industrial plants, additions to old ones, and housing for workers. Past the train windows raced the pulse-quickening parade of Americana: diner lunchrooms, shoe-shine parlors, baseball diamonds, handsome schools in the poorest towns. Now and then a billboard blotted out a green view. Some soldiers leafed through newspapers—not the thin, four- to six-page papers of European cities but thick ones, full of comics and advertisements. "These thronging advertisements bespoke a standard of living fabulously high compared with the mere subsistence level of life in belt-tightened Britain." When they got to telephones, the men were amazed at the speed with which their calls were completed.

"How lucky we are!" the soldier on the train thought, as he mused on America's resources—"forests of oil wells in the great Southwest, oceans of wheat rippling in the sun of the Plains, countless cattle lowing on the western ranges, cotton ripening in the Deep South, mountains of metal on the Great Lakes and in the Rockies, giant dams wringing power from surging rivers, industrial plants turning out marvels of mechanics and chemistry." He thought of resources of another kind, too—"human resources, compounded of the fusion of men and women of every origin and yielding the energy, ingenuity, and 'know-how' to harness and use the inanimate resources of the land." What did the soldier think? "Deep inside him the soldier was thankful—not smug, but humble, and fully conscious that all this was only by grace of God." He hoped that in setting right the wrongs of the world "Uncle Sam would acquit himself as well and as wisely as he and his nephews and nieces had done in helping to win the war."[1]

Or take another example, of Secretary of State Dean Acheson, returning home to Middletown, Connecticut, in April 1950 and reminiscing about his bond with his early surroundings. It was not only the strongest of ties, he believed; it had become more important than ever in an age when human problems were on a scale wider than ever before. He remembered his house on Broad Street, the church down the way, and the harness shop on Main Street, as well as the post office, where the customers and passersby stopped to talk about the topics of the day. Without these fixed points of the land of one's youth, Acheson reflected, "we would have nothing to hold onto." The neighborhood and the community, as Americans knew and recollected them, were the sources to which they had to return for reasons to sustain their world efforts. Across America he had seen many hometowns. Not all were alike in their traditions and views, but he did not think it necessary that they should be, because America accepted and reconciled its diversity. The "experience of growing up in any American community, from Connecticut to California," Acheson believed, constituted "the indelible stamp of nationality." It was what made the people American. He rejoiced that "the real elements of our immense strength" were to be found "at the foundations of our society, in the homes and the shaded streets of many tens of thousands of quiet and decent and God-fearing American communities."[2]

At the height of America's power, what was the consensus view of national self-image? The connection between the bustling domestic landscape and the acceptance of the country's international role was common to works of travel and description, to literature and poetry, and to pictorial records.

Travelers' Accounts

The magic of the land remained a theme of modern American life, as it had since the early settlements. Immense virgin spaces and a frontier to conquer were parts of that theme. The mixed feelings of admiration, fear, and wonder at the vastness of the American land emerged from Jacques Barzun's writings about his travels. In 1954 Barzun completed *God's Country and Mine,* a forthright celebration of America, which began:

> The way to see America is from a lower berth about two in the morning. You've just left a station—it was the jerk of pulling out that woke you—and you raise the curtain a bit between thumb and forefinger to look out. You are in the middle of Kansas or Arizona, in the middle of the space where the freight cars spend the night and the men drink coffee out of cans. Then comes the signal tower, some bushes, a few shacks and—nothing. You see the last blue switch-light on the next track, and beyond is America—dark and grassy, or sandy, or rocky—and no one there. Nothing but the irrational universe with you in the center trying to reason it out. It's only ten, fifteen minutes since you've left a thriving town but life has already been swallowed up in that ocean of matter which is and will remain as wild as it was made.
>
> Come daylight, the fear vanishes but not the awe or the secret pleasure. It is a perpetual refreshment of the soul to see that the country is so large, so indifferent to the uses we have put it to. . . . It is good that in this place at least there is more of just plain territory per square mile than anywhere else in the civilized world.

This was not a landscape of retreat but one of awe, inspiration, and vigor. Barzun, an influential intellectual and professor of history at Columbia University, was not entirely uncritical of America. He found fault with the standardization of the American assembly-line, the materialistic consumption of national wealth, and the banality of advertising. But Barzun was certain that the United States was God's country. The land had a largeness like nowhere else on earth. "Anywhere in the world we hold our breath at monuments of beauty and unexpectedness. But we cannot hold our breath for the hundred miles of endlessly renewed beauty in the Feather River Canyon. . . . Any stretch before us makes us stare and hold our breath again." The people had built a landscape of cities of equally prodigious scale: "New York is a sky line, the most stupendous, unbelievable manmade spectacle since the hanging gardens of Babylon."

Barzun, a naturalized citizen born in France, saw that America had moved past European accomplishments. To begin with, Americans had built what he called "a complete Europe"—Swedes came together with Armenians, Germans with French, English with Italians, and so on. These groups did not always live in harmony, Barzun admitted; in many towns that had two sides of the railroad tracks, the poor and ethnic groups faced discrimination. "But at what a rate these distinctions disappear! In Europe a thousand years of war, pogroms and massacres settle nothing. Here two generations of common schooling, intermarriage, ward politics, and labor unions create social peace." America was the modern nation, and Barzun wondered whether it was "possible that modern civilization is something new, incommensurable with the old, just like the character of the American adventure itself." The book concluded: "we scarcely need Emerson's gentle reminder and advice: 'The ear loves names of foreign and classic topography. But here we are, and if we tarry a little, we may come to learn that here is best.'"[3]

The themes of bigness and diversity recurred in an outpouring of books celebrating the American land. In 1947 John Gunther published *Inside U.S.A.,* a massive, encyclopedic work of a thousand pages of his impressions of the United States based on his travels. In the seven years since 1940, he had visited all forty-eight states and all the cities of more than two hundred thousand people, as well as numerous small towns. He had talked with politicians, business people, and representatives of different religious and racial groups. Gunther had a unique perspective: he had spent years traveling through distant parts of the world, and he had previously written *Inside Europe, Inside Asia,* and *Inside Latin America.*

He structured *Inside U.S.A.* geographically. Beginning in California, he moved from Montana to Utah, from Massachusetts to New York, and from Georgia to Texas. Like a newsreel camera, he recorded what he saw, without taking time for deep analysis or historical constructs. He was showing an America of the present without roots, a restless, shifting, fast-changing America. He was quick to point out where North Dakota was different from South Dakota and Oregon from Washington. He did not attempt to draw comprehensive connections between the law, labor, religion, and art that he saw in the different states and sections. He did picture airports unfolding in many places, great factories and mills going up, rivers being tamed by giant dams, coal mined in huge quantities, invention creating new products. The pride in bigness and the self-confidence of wealth he encountered all over, particularly in growing cities such as Fort Worth, Dallas, Seattle, and Tacoma. When his American odyssey was over, Gunther pondered how American power and responsibility in the world mirrored the bigness of the American landscape:

> Here, then, is this enormous abstract something known as "the United States," spread before us. Here, in the first gaunt years of the Atomic Age, lies a country, a continental mass, more favored by man and nature than any other in history, now for the first time attempting with somewhat faltering steps to justify its new station as a mature world power. Here, beyond anything else on the whole earth, is a country blessed by an ideal geography and almost perfect natural frontiers, by incalculable bulk and wealth and variety and vitality, by a unique and indeed unexampled heritage in democratic ideas and principles— and a country deliberately founded on a good idea.

"What are we going to do with it?" he asked, as he considered some American superlatives. The United States was the first nation in the world in production of coal, petroleum, steel, electric energy, copper, cotton, lumber, and multitudinous other industrial and agricultural materials; but, in contrast, he found, "its political stamina and wit leave something to be desired." It contained four-fifths of the world's automobiles and one-half of its telephones; but "not quite so overwhelming a proportion of its moral character or most interesting ideas." The "United States is, we like to think, the greatest republic, the greatest democracy, and the greatest nation in the world. It is also one of the few great nations with no national planning agency. The United States is statistically the richest country in the world. It is also a country with no national unemployment or health insurance." As far as its energy, enterprise, and power could take it, Gunther seemed to be saying, America was equipped for the duty of captaining the world. How far those attributes would carry the nation without a magnanimous character he left as another problem.[4]

The Literary Landscape

The same themes also appeared in literature. Starting in the early 1950s, Ben Lucien Burman's accounts of his American travels, collected in the book *It's a Big Country*, described the wide land and an American outlook. Burman, a veteran severely wounded in France in World War I and a war correspondent in North Africa in World War II, returned after both wars to write about America. The narrative began as the author prepared to leave home, a town in Kentucky. "It's a big country," said an old man who had built a fire near a shabby trailer on a riverbank and cooked his noonday meal. Across a railroad bridge, freight engines rumbled, pulling coal cars, tank cars, and flatcars loaded with lumber. On the river a large towboat pulled barges from Pittsburgh to New Orleans.

"It's a big country," the author agreed, and he left on his own travels to the hills of the Ozarks, the marshes of Louisiana, the bush country of the West, the Florida Everglades, and Cape Hatteras. When he returned, he sought out the old man one warm summer afternoon on the same riverbank. The old man, preparing to leave for the West, for Seattle and San Francisco, said, in the language of American names and places that sounded a little like that of the poet Walt Whitman:

> I want to see them Bad Lands they say look like you was on the moon out in
> South Dakota and them geysers that squirt hot water in your face out in Wyo-
> ming. I want to see that big salt lake where you can't sink out in Utah and them
> big cactus and them Gila monsters spit their poison at you out in Arizona. I
> want to see the Golden Gate and them fancy houses where the picture stars live
> in California. I want to look at them Apache Indians and them big canyons
> where you can't see the bottom and the big dams and all them trees turned to
> stone. I want to go on them glaciers where it's so cold the antifreeze for your
> auto comes out of the can in a solid chunk, all frozen. I want to watch them fel-
> lows driving them twenty-mule teams out of Death Valley where it's so hot it
> ain't rained since nobody can remember. . . . I tell you if a fellow could live
> five hundred years he wouldn't see half the things in the United States or know
> nothing about the people. 'Cause it's sure a big country.[5]

It was a big planet, too, and Americans could no longer escape the world. In World War I soldiers had straggled home from Europe, and their expatriation and return had been a theme of the novels of Ernest Hemingway and John Dos Passos, both of them ambulance drivers in World War I. In the 1920s both writers had traveled widely around Europe and Dos Passos had gone to Russia. World War II aroused a new mood in Dos Passos. While becoming more interested in America, he ceased thinking it would retreat into its old isolation. He had turned against his earlier infatuation with communism; his increasing interest was in power rather than in economics.

Dos Passos studied a panoramic view of America in wartime and in the postwar years. He aimed to learn about the country by writing travel narratives; his storytelling was based on factual information, on the people he had met and the places he had seen. He traveled from Washington, D.C., to Spokane, Washington, to Mobile, Alabama. He set out in the northeastern winter snows, went to the greening South in spring, and worked his way to the Pacific West by fall, ending up in the cold rain and mists of the San Francisco coast. He talked to administrators and senators in Washington, whose bureaucracy often frustrated him, but his affection was for the working people. He was uplifted by their optimism and their ability. In *State of the Nation* in 1944, he spliced together vignettes and character sketches as if he were what he called in an early novel a camera eye. His impression was clear: America was its land and its people. There were ship builders from Maine, an Alabama bus driver, Texas migrant workers, a Washington streetcar checker, striking Pennsylvania coal miners, farmers from Ohio to North

Dakota, and Army and Navy servicemen from all over. For Dos Passos, landscape merged with people, and perhaps never more so than when he was up on a snowy Michigan hill late at night in a cottage in an apple orchard, where "way out of town, in the middle of the winter cold there wasn't a sound. There was that feeling you sometimes get in the Middle West that you are alone on the American continent, that there's nothing but the American continent in the whole world."

America's growing place in the world was founded on America at home, observed Dos Passos. The secret of America's victory in war had been its immense production on the farm and in the factory, while experiencing minimal dislocation from its normal habits of life. "We have got to develop as clear notions about the shape of our country and what we want it to become" as the eighteenth-century founding fathers had of their America. "Any military victories we win abroad will be based upon this initial victory at home." The stakes seemed even higher after the war.[6]

Dos Passos's next book of reportage, *The Prospect before Us,* published in 1950, drew on his wartime experiences in England and on his travels in 1948 through Colombia, Brazil, and Chile. This work was the vehicle for his own political slant on America's place in the world, delivered by a character named "Mr. Lecturer." Again Dos Passos noted the good fortune of the American economy and the standard of life. And again he found beauty in the land and the people. "Green and immense, undulating in low smooth swells to the horizon the cornbelt landscape swings past the windows of the empty club car," he wrote of one train trip.

Dos Passos was a critic, but a loving critic. "The prospect before us," he wrote, "is one of mighty effort against great odds but it is not all black. It is impossible to travel back and forth across this continent without seeing here and there the beginnings of a better balanced society." America was at a new beginning. He saw no limits to the initiative of individuals and the productivity of agriculture and manufacturing. "There are only rare moments in history when a community of men finds itself in the position to choose alternatives. We are in that position. For a very few short years we will be able to make the choice between a stratified autocratic society more or less on the Russian model and the self-governing Republic which is our heritage." The country showed the alternative to Russian autocracy: "our society has the best chance any society ever had to mitigate the domination of man by men," and it could achieve this by working in "the service of the underlying proposition upon which the Republic was founded." To get a notion of the penalty for failure, all anyone had to do was to visit the ruins of Berlin or to imagine the lives of people in Prague or Bucharest or Moscow. No nation could stand still.[7]

The American land was also the province of poets. Emerson and Thoreau reveled in it. Whitman had a strong feeling for the land, as did Carl Sandburg in more recent days. Archibald MacLeish wrote again and again of the landscape of America. In "America Was Promises" he declared:

The promises were Man's: the land was his—
Man endowed by his Creator:
Earnest in love: perfectible by reason:
Just and perceiving justice: his natural nature
Clear and sweet at the source as springs in trees are.

During the war, while MacLeish was serving as director of the Office of Facts and Figures and as assistant secretary of state, his voice regarding the American landscape came into its own with a wartime colloquy, composed of fragments of characteristic speech of various parts of the country. He represented the different sounds of speaking in areas like central Illinois, rural Maine, and the range of Texas. The lines sing out the praise of a new people whose different qualities of life had developed according to the opportunities of the land. For example, he brought the heartland alive:

Have they seen our towns, says Kansas: seen our wheat:
Seen our flatcars in the Rocky Mountains:
Seen our four-lane highways: seen our planes
Silver over the Alleghenies the Lakes
The big timber the tall corn the horses—
Silver over the snow-line: over the surf?
Have they seen our farms? says Kansas: and who plowed them?
Have they seen our towns? says Kansas: and who planned
    them?[8]

Despite regional differences, the people were together in the fight against enemies "east of the Rhine."

MacLeish spelled out his poetry in his essays. The image that Americans held of themselves was changing in dimension. Until recently that image had been not much different from Jefferson's—a clean, small landscape with its isolated, pleasant farms, its horizons clear of the smoke of cities, its air still, its frontiers protected by ocean and wilderness. Now there was a new image. MacLeish saw a "new American dream of the new America"—the industrial nation of the huge machines, the limitless earth, the vast and skillful population, the mountains of copper and iron, the research laboratories, the mile-long plants, the tremendous dams. The statistics of production were well known. Still MacLeish asked, "What are they *for,* these plants and products, these statistics?" "What is the ideal landscape of this new America? What are we trying to become, to bring about?" The future was America's to make, he believed. He took care to avoid the criticisms of Henry Luce's American future by explaining that America's future was not to master or exploit. "And yet it is our future. It is ours to shape," not only because America had many planes or ships or rich industrial resources, but "because we have the power as a people to conceive so great a future as mankind must now conceive"— because of the imagination of the people.[9]

The Photographic Record

Piles of books filled with photographs supplemented the written record in capturing the landscape and daily living of the people. Lately Americans who had become more conscious of their land were reading books about American regions, rivers, lakes, and other celebrations of valleys, mountains, monuments, districts, cities, and inhabitants. No one could see the entire country, but the editors of one glossy picture magazine hoped to help satisfy the interest to know it better by putting out *Look at America,* a series that glorified the nature and the bounty. The *Look* staff and photographers worked for more than a year to compile the first volume in 1946. It was designed not merely to rediscover the nation to which the soldiers who had been fighting abroad were returning, but to place that landscape in a global perspective: "having achieved the conquest and development of a continent, America today holds world leadership in its grasp," stated the introduction. "And, as if for the first time, the nation gropes toward the spiritual, seeking a way of life it can pass on to others."

The early Americans had patterned their civilization on that of Western Europe, mainly Britain. "But what a difference!" exclaimed the editors. "The western European was the leader of the world for centuries and has imposed his pattern well-nigh universally. However, he became the product of an ancient, exhausted, fatigued and cynical civilization. If the first settlers in America thought of the country as a larger, more spacious and perhaps superior Europe, they did not reckon with the land itself. . . . Out of the western European, transplanted to a new world, a new man was forged: the American." The different meanings of the word *frontier* itself were illuminating. To citizens of the Old World, the editors wrote, frontier called up "striped sentry boxes, soldiers, police, immigration and customs inspectors who might speak another language." It reminded Europeans that, across the barrier, lay the cities and towns of another country. To the American, the frontier meant "the edge of his own civilization, with beyond it the wilderness, the unknown—pregnant with possibilities, full of opportunity."

"Symbols of pre-eminence are everywhere at hand to help the traveler understand America." The book considered the significance of the skyscrapers of New York in typifying "the bigness, the ascendancy of America." Its skyline was one of the wonders of the world. This busy city-state, its news agencies, radio networks, and entertainment industry centralized in its towers, was a focal point for ideas. The merchant ships from all over the world, riding at anchor, and the sleek liners tied to the piers were symbols of the enormous trade and exchange between America and the world across the Atlantic. In Washington, D.C., the colonnaded monuments and stately Greek buildings lining the avenues and squares signified the American democratic government, which was perhaps "better able than any other to stimulate, guide, control and above all integrate the economy of a powerful nation." The coal mines, the long stretches of deep woods, the giant dams, the fertile fields of the prairies, the oil wells, and the iron mines recalled the great holdings of natural resources, larger than any other in the world. "Taken symbolically, almost everything the traveler sees can in some way be related to one or more of the factors establishing America's pre-eminence: the pioneer spirit of enterprise; the vast extent of the national domain; a geographical orientation favoring interchange with Europe; a varied, propitious climate; fertility of soil; staggering richness in major raw materials; the tools of production; the means of distribution; a great progressive population of diverse backgrounds and capabilities; widespread educational facilities; a stable, relatively efficient democratic government; an accumulation of capital." *Look* published a series of books on each region, with snapshots and portraits covering the states—a Maine fisherman mending his net, a Navajo weaver, or a Wall Street businessmen at noon.[10]

National Geographic, integrating the American landscape with the world, published photographs of battle-torn Europe that contrasted sharply with those of American scenes—increasingly in full color. In May 1945, after the fall of Germany, readers saw in "Nebraska, the Cornhusker State," the cattle ranches and the well-kept farms for the production of corn. That summer readers looked at the Potomac, the river that flowed through the green Virginia hills and cut through the nation's capital. The month Japan surrendered, August, the magazine featured Wyoming, high up on the windswept Continental Divide, with its "infinite stretches" of range, empty except for grazing cattle. In the first month of peace, there was Boston, where New England met the sea, and its houses with widow's walks, steepled churches, ships, and rocky coastline. In the three years or so after the war there were articles covering areas from Cape Cod—depicted through its seaside cottages, wharfs, and lighthouses—to California's Great Central Valley, compared to the Nile, "except that this American valley is much bigger"; and from Aroostook County, Maine—"Source of Potatoes"—to Louisiana, the delta of the Mississippi; and also in between from the deserts and poppy-filled meadowlands of Arizona to the plains and hills of South Dakota. One clearly saw further images of America in the illustrated periodical advertisements for railroads, airlines, heavy industries, or vacation resorts.[11]

With skill and grace, Margaret Bourke-White, one of the most important photographers for the picture magazine *Life,* turned her camera on America. On the strength of her images of American steel mills incandescent with molten metal and of the inner workings of mechanized factories, Bourke-White had been hired by Henry Luce to illustrate stories about American industry in *Fortune* in 1929. In 1936 her photograph of a giant concrete dam under construction in the Columbia River Basin was the first cover for *Life,* a magazine designed by Luce to depict and celebrate America. In the early 1940s Bourke-White collaborated on *Say, Is This the U.S.A.* with her husband, Erskine Caldwell, a writer known for his earthy novels *God's Little Acre* and *Tobacco Road.* Their book opened to the Kansas heartland in frigid winter, a freight train pulling into a yard next to tall grain silos. Other pages showed the drug- and liquor-store fronts of a small-town main street in South Carolina, and machines weaving cloth in a Lowell, Massachusetts, factory.[12]

Bourke-White traveled to Europe and Russia, and after World War II drew her abroad to photograph the fighting and ruins, she was again attracted home to photograph the mist lifting off the Connecticut River as the morning sun warmed the fields, and to capture the dry, flat southwestern farms plowed in snakelike contour patterns to protect them against the wind. In a 1950s photographic story, "A Helicopter View of the U.S.A.," she became one of the first photographers to use a helicopter successfully, showing a perspective lower than that of an airplane and higher than a rooftop: the Statue of Liberty's face and crown, the mass of bathers at Coney Island, an oceanliner docking amid a swirl of currents and tugboat wakes in New York Harbor, and sailboats cruising San Francisco Bay in the shadow of the Golden Gate Bridge.[13]

Hollywood Images

Hollywood films too projected an image of America, from the stark New England town seen in Orson Welles's *The Stranger* to the sprawling, brightly lit metropolis of *The Naked City*. The West, where stories of confident American heroes unfolded, was portrayed in *Across the Wide Missouri, Red River, Colorado Territory, Montana, Along the Great Divide,* and *High Sierra*. Scenes of innocence—of a virgin environment unencumbered by corruption and isolated from other places—contrasted with those of civilization, where individuals dreamt of affluence and power. *Giant,* directed by George Stevens, was an epic film that made Texas the sprawling backdrop to the twentieth-century saga of a wealthy family, the Benedicts, who owned one of the biggest ranches, Reata, totaling over a half-million acres. On the red-brown grazing land, the Benedicts raised cattle numbering in the tens of thousands. Later the scenes of unbroken prairie were filled with oil wells—first one or two derricks, then a dozen, then hundreds, with potential revenues for the one ranch of a billion dollars a year.[14]

The Best Years of Our Lives opened with the cross-country flight of three homeward-bound, war-weary servicemen in the belly of a B-17 bomber, from which they saw the whole expanse of America. After arriving at their hometown's new airport, they saw from a taxi a stream of images of postwar America—the ballpark, a hot rod, a bus stop, a hot dog stand, a five-and-dime store, a used-car lot, a steak house, a bar, apartment buildings, and suburban homes. Film crews dispatched by the director, William Wyler, shot these scenes on location in Cincinnati because of its typical American town appearance envisioned by Robert Sherwood in his script. The wide-screen camera in *North by Northwest,* directed by Alfred Hitchcock, followed Cary Grant playing a Madison Avenue business executive as he was chased two thousand miles across the country by spies, from the glistening modern Manhattan skyscrapers, the United Nations headquarters, and Grand Central Station, to the sleek Twentieth Century Limited long-distance train, to the open sky and cornfields of the Great Plains. The triumphant finale takes place at the national monument of Mt. Rushmore. This America is marked by modern stone-and-glass architecture, aerodynamic airplanes, and late-model Ford and Lincoln cars.[15]

Even as American forces were demobilizing after the war, John Wayne's 1949 portrayal of a tough marine top sergeant leading his men into island battle, in *Sands of Iwo Jima,* signaled a change in the Hollywood representation of the American hero. A celebrated prewar hero was Jimmy Stewart as the young Senator Jefferson Smith fighting defiantly yet nonviolently for his ideals against special privilege and corruption in Frank Capra's *Mr. Smith Goes to Washington,* which was showing in Paris in protest of the Nazis who had invaded the city and shut the film down. After the war John Wayne's different sort of hero, the swaggering Sergeant John Stryker, was the kind he played again and again in his later films. Jimmy Stewart also underwent a transformation, gaining a new persona as a cold warrior who returned to active Air Force duty to pilot a U.S. bomber in *Strategic Air Command.* He matured into a John Wayne character and having lost his innocence was not sensitive and idealistic but rugged and hard.

America lacked a long experience of world power, so in Hollywood's sagas of past empire, a conspicuous change came about in big epics, from *Gone with the Wind* in 1939, covering vistas of the windswept South against red skies, to the new historical sagas of dominion. A series of spectaculars depicted the stages of the "westward course of empire," from Egypt to Macedonia to Rome—*Samson and Delilah* in 1949, followed by *Quo Vadis?* and *David and Bathsheba* in 1951, *The Robe* in 1953, *The Egyptian* in 1954, and two of the biggest and most successful epics, *The Ten Commandments* in 1956 and *Ben-Hur* in 1959. To these movies of ancient empires were added films about the expansion of the British Empire, like *Lawrence of Arabia* in 1962. These revivals of the glories of the past were extravagant products that only American capital, technical innovations of Cinerama and Cinemascope, and cinematic expertise could then produce. The movies often ended with lavish scenes of destruction: Gaza crumbled in *Samson and Delilah;* Rome burned in *Quo Vadis?;* Jerusalem suffered a wild storm in *Ben-Hur.* The British left the Middle East to turmoil in *Lawrence of Arabia.* If these epics implied that America emerged from the pitfalls of isolation, they did not resolve the danger of the excess of the empire.[16]

In the Metro-Goldwyn-Mayer film *It's a Big Country,* a cast of the studio's top stars enacted a series of vignettes of life in America. The first segment set the theme of the movie: James Whitmore, riding on a transcontinental train with William Powell, observed breezily that the United States was a great country. Just which country did he mean, Powell asked. To what instant in the country's changing life did he refer? And to what part of America—the political America of the Declaration of Independence, the Congress, and political parties; or the historical America of the Pilgrims, the western pioneers, and the Civil War; or the America that was part of the world community from World War I to World War II? Whitmore was stumped. In the stories that followed, Ethel Barrymore played an elderly Irish woman in Boston who, missed by the census takers, wanted to be included in the national census before she died. Gary Cooper uttered an ironic discourse on the modesty of Texas. A newsreel montage showed the accomplishments of negroes in the military, sports, law, government, religion, and international affairs, and a comedy segment represented the value of tolerance in ethnic rivalries between Greek and Hungarian immigrant groups. In another episode a young Jewish veteran of the Korean War calls on the mother of a lost comrade and helps her overcome her anti-Semitism. The camera swept past bustling cities, waving fields of grain, oil dericks for as far as the eye could see, while a deep-voiced narrator intoned, "Yes, it's a big, wonderful country. Proud of its past. Strong in its present. Confident in its future. A country determined and strong. Strong because of its people and its resources." The film was full of lines like, "What a country! . . . The greatest country in the world. Sure we got our problems. But we'll lick 'em. . . . I'm just a guy who loves America." Or, "America! The conscience. The heart. The will." The film was uneven, some episodes pointless, and, said the reviewer Bosley Crowther, the whole was "not modest or subtle in the way it professes a passion and devotion for the good old U.S.A."; but at the end, Crowther was in the spirit: "It's a big country, all right."[17]

Critical Views

Not that there were no troubles in paradise. At least some critics were not quite so glowing in their descriptions of the American landscape. In his 1945 book *The Air-Conditioned Nightmare,* Henry Miller, returning from Europe by ship, came on deck to catch his first glimpse of the Boston shoreline and was "immediately disappointed" and "saddened." It was a wintry day and a gale was blowing. The American coast looked bleak and uninviting. Continuing along the coast to New York, Miller saw bridges, railroad tracks, warehouses, factories, and wharves. "It was like following in the wake of a demented giant who had sown the earth with crazy dreams." "It was a vast jumbled waste created by pre-human or sub-human monsters in a delirium of greed." "It was a bad beginning." The sight of New York, its harbor, bridges, and skyscrapers, did nothing to eradicate his first impressions at Boston. "Sailing around the Battery from one river to the other, gliding close to shore, night coming on, the streets dotted with scurrying insects, I felt as I had always felt about New York—that it is the most horrible place on God's earth. No matter how many times I escape I am brought back, like a runaway slave, each time detesting it, loathing it, more and more."

Mingling with his countrymen again, Miller sensed a chauvinism had set in. "Aren't you glad to be back in the good old U.S.A.?" was the usual greeting. "No place like America, *what?*" To this he felt he was expected to say, "You betcha!" But he was disappointed. "America," he reflected, "is made up, as we all know, of people who ran away from . . . ugly situations" in Europe. "America is the land par excellence of expatriates and escapists, *renegades,* to use a strong word." "A new world is not made simply by trying to forget the old. A new world is made with a new spirit, with new values. Our world may have begun that way, but to-day it is caricatural. Our world is a world of *things.* It is made up of comforts and luxuries, or else the desire for them." "What have we to offer the world beside the superabundant loot which we recklessly plunder from the earth under the maniacal delusion that this insane activity represents progress and enlightenment? The land of opportunity has become the land of senseless sweat and struggle."

In New York, a Hungarian friend led Miller to the window and asked him to sit down. "Look at that view!" the Hungarian said. "Isn't it magnificent?" Miller looked out on the Hudson River and saw a great bridge twinkling with moving lights. "I knew what he felt when looking out upon that scene; I knew that for him it represented the future, the world which his children would inherit. For him it was a world of promise." But Miller knew that behind the lights there were faults. "To me it was a world I knew only too well, a world that made me infinitely sad."

Having made his way through the Holland Tunnel, Miller found his own America, and he continued his writings in a second volume in 1947. "America is full of places. Empty places. And all these empty places are crowded. Just jammed with empty souls. All at loose ends, all seeking diversion." The country had "the greatest advantages" and "so little to show" for them. "With the proper will we in America could, almost overnight, supply the whole world with everything it needs. We don't need the support of any country. Everything exists here in superabundance—I mean the physical activity. As for our potential, no man can estimate it." But Miller was not at all sure it would be realized.[18]

George Kennan was chagrined at his rediscovery of America in the early 1950s on his return from Russia and Europe. Drawn to the beauty of nature, he was especially close to a patch of farmland he held in the rich river country of Pennsylvania, where he could stand on the high rises of his fields on a summer's day and see the shadowy northern outrunners of the Blue Ridge Mountains. But he was not always happy about what man had made of nature. He took a trip by train across half the continent in 1950. On a Sunday in February he woke up early; he "raised the curtain . . . and looked out," but his reactions were more reserved than Barzun's: "We were crossing a river. It was just the beginning of a Sabbath dawn. The half-light reflected itself in the oily scum of the water, left in kindly obscurity a desolation of factories and cinder-yards and railroad tracks along the shore, but caught and held, in its baleful gleam, the cold mute slabs of skyscrapers overhead. It was the business district of some industrial city: what city I did not know, nor did it matter." It occurred to him that in the chill light the dreams of the city were disturbed; the dawn exposed its "neon signs, its eroticism, and its intoxication."

Kennan was repulsed by the dirt, desolation, and ugliness of the large midwestern cities. He wandered around them feeling estranged. Even the language of the children playing in the streets felt unfamiliar to him. In 1952 Kennan complained that "our country bristles with imperfections," including racism, graft, slums, juvenile deliquency, decline of community, inflation, mass-media culture, deterioration of the soil, and lack of spiritual purpose. He felt a deep pessimism, even causing him to doubt "whether America's problems were really soluble at all by operation of the liberal-democratic and free-enterprise institutions traditional to our country." Miller and Kennan wrote with force and passion, but they bucked the national view of their land.[19]

The generally colorful and exciting view of the American scene was the setting for America's new relationship with the world. Many of the principal authors and photographers had seen other parts of the world; they were pleased to return home and seek a haven from turmoil. But at the same time they could not find refuge in an isolated land, as they had after the earlier world war. Americans had taken up the habit of internationalism, of looking beyond the horizon, and thus were less concerned with boundaries, which were limits, than with frontiers. The greater world was wide open to opportunity. It could be built anew. The requirements were human energy and determination, characteristics like those the immigrants had applied to American lands. There was also diversity, and the consensus among the people and leaders was that America uniquely demonstrated how people from every continent could come together to avoid bloodly conflict and to build a society of affluence.

American perceptions, nonetheless, also revealed limits in outlook. The creative thought of Americans about the outer world was often narrowly bound by ethnocentric ideas about their own land. Their presuppositions about the reasons for American success to be found in the national landscape were not necessarily applicable to wider regions. The message Americans offered other peoples arose from the benefits of their own landscape. This was internationalism, to be sure, but, stemming from domestic life, it could never be objective.

Although beliefs about the domestic landscape might not be translatable in policies to foreign situations, landscape was crucial in representing American thought about the world. It is necessary to look closely at the components of this modern environment—the booming economy, thriving society, and spiritual beliefs. A few individuals created theories of economic, social, and religious developments that gained wide appeal, and we should examine them for their international implications.

8

The

Consensus

Theories

Postwar American thought was absorbed with consensus theories. Not only historians, looking for unity in the past, and travelers and poets, seeking unity in the modern landscape, but also sociologists, political scientists, and intellectuals in a range of fields examined what constituted consensus in a democracy and how it held together in support of national activity. In 1947, the president of the American Sociological Society, Louis Wirth, addressed its annual meeting: "I regard the study of consensus as the central task of sociology, which is to understand the behavior of men in so far as that behavior is influenced by group life." His fellow sociologists took up the subject of consensus as a process of social interaction and communication.[1]

The study became popular and interdisciplinary. In political science, scholars emphasized the relationship of consensus to government policies; national will was seen to be founded on a broad-based consensus. Robert A. Dahl considered these ideas fundamental to his field. "Prior to politics, beneath it, enveloping it, restricting it, conditioning it, is the underlying consensus on policy that usually exists in the society among a predominant portion of the politically active members." He believed that consensus did not rule out disputes over policy alternatives, but winnowed debate down to that within the broad area of agreement in a democracy. The sociologist Seymour Martin Lipset stated simply, "without consensus . . . there can be no democracy." By the end of the 1950s the sociologist Theodore Newcomb had written, "No one . . . needs to be persuaded that some manner and degree of interpersonal consensus is a necessary condition for social organization."[2]

Scholars in many fields shifted emphasis from conflict in a pluralistic society, how conflicts arise among groups of different interests, to cooperation, how agreement takes place among the people as a whole. Consensus was everywhere promoted, but its definition was imprecise. The shades of meaning of consensus, beyond the common usage of the word as a synonym for agreement, were seldom explored. There was the problem of who made up the consensus. Was agreement required among an entire electorate or only those actively participating in public affairs?[3] There was the problem of what were the binding ideas of consensus. Was belief in shared values required or merely agreement over the procedures of government?[4] There was also the question of how extensive the agreement of consensus had to be. Did consensus require a majority of people, and if so, half or three-quarters of them, and how many people were required to form consensus—two or more?[5]

The study of consensus was a self-conscious search for the mythic conceptions of the people and their leaders to explain their worldview, practices, and beliefs. While scholars provided explanations of consensus, leaders favored conditions to promote it. According to opinion polls, at least a majority, and usually more, of the people agreed on the central concepts of the national world role: isolationism was at an end and increased world involvement was necessary. Similarly, consensus was based on a state of mind, not necessarily on existing individual conditions, for the consensus of internationalism cut across factors of economic class, political party, and geographical region. Consensus could be formed by a process of social conditioning or education because though an abstract state of mind, it was a quantity measurable in the opinion polls.[6]

Consensus theory provides a means to investigate the developing thought over America's world role. We turn to the crucial points of discussion by leading exponents in various fields, in economics, sociology, and religion.

Economic Thought: David Potter and John Kenneth Galbraith

The discipline of economics extended notions of prosperity to include internationalism abroad. Instead of the Great Depression that had diminished the country in the 1930s returning, the surge of prosperity of World War II continued nearly unabated. After a mild recession in 1953 and 1954, the GNP stood at $364 billion, and it kept growing until it topped $500 billion in 1960. Personal income almost doubled. Unemployment reached the lowest peacetime percentage since the booming 1920s, as low as 2.9 percent and hovering around 4 percent. Investment climbed. The inflation rate was negligible. The suburbs became home for millions of Americans, who rapidly acquired the trappings of the richest nation in the world. In 1946, some 8,000 homes had television sets; by 1960, there were 45,750,000 sets. Automobile models came in styles featuring tailfins and chrome radiators. In 1956 the government launched the largest domestic program in the history of the country, the interstate highway system, linking all the major cities.[7]

Americans sought meaning in this wealth by identifying themselves as a "people of plenty" and an "affluent society." "People of plenty" was the phrase of David Potter, a member of the faculty of Yale beginning in 1942, who devoted his early studies to the development of the West and post-Civil War Reconstruction, and began exploring the phenomenon of abundance in the United States. Potter compiled the statistics that confirmed the immense national differential between the United States and other countries in per capita income, wages per hour, and average daily consumption of calories. Potter attributed this prosperity not to the country's bountiful resources, essential though they were, but to the initiative, enterprise, and vigor of the people. As evidence for human enterprise, he noted that between 1820 and 1930 Americans had increased fortyfold the supply of energy per capita. Moreover, 71.8 percent of the American working population had been farmers in 1820; by 1950, the 11.6 percent of the working population who were farmers fed the entire country, leaving more to share with others. The increase in the American standard of living, Potter concluded, was achieved not merely by accepting nature's gifts but by applying improved technology, the organization of a complex economy, and hard toil.[8]

Potter did not confine his study to domestic prosperity. Because of its uniqueness among nations, this plenty had enormous implications for American international relations. Potter took issue with America's traditional message abroad: to exemplify and even to propagate democratic institutions. He believed that this mission, however noble, had a limited application. Since the Declaration of Independence, prospects for democracy's ascendancy in the world had not been realized, beginning with the French Revolution of 1789, which had turned to the guillotine and terror. Revolts against despotism had unfortunately tended to grow despotic: the Greek revolt and Latin American wars for independence in the 1820s, the Cuban struggle for freedom before the Spanish-American War, the establishment of a republic in China in 1912, and World War I's crusade "to make the world safe for democracy." Even in World War II Franklin Roosevelt's goals of the Atlantic Charter and the Four Freedoms had proved illusory, and ironic when applied to the wartime Soviet ally.[9]

According to Potter, what America had to offer other peoples—and what they looked to America for—was the secret of abundance: "We supposed that our revelation was 'democracy revolutionizing the world.' " Rather, Potter stressed, the United States had displayed better than any other nation "the variety and magic of the new abundance," and it had done "more than any other to disseminate the belief that this abundance may actually be placed within the grasp of ordinary men and women." That did not mean preaching the virtues of capitalism, as a theory. "We have talked so much about 'free enterprise' as if we just meant laissez faire economics." He wanted Americans to show the actual means by which they had achieved unsurpassed wealth. What Americans had to do, Potter proposed, was to combine abundance with democracy in an international program.[10]

The economist John Kenneth Galbraith was, like Potter, in the mainstream of thinking about the problem of abundance and its meaning for a world role. His characterization of America as the "affluent society" was commonly accepted by economists and the public alike. But Galbraith was something of a liberal maverick who reveled in criticizing the generally accepted, highly predictable ideas, which he called "conventional wisdom."[11]

For Galbraith, it was no sin for America to be rich. Ever since the end of World War II, the United States economy had been setting new records in production, employment, and income, and Galbraith wanted to figure out why. In 1952 he opened his book *American Capitalism* by comparing the American economy to a bumblebee: According to aerodynamic principles, the bumblebee could not fly; its wing load was too great. But the bumblebee did fly, despite the theories of Isaac Newton and Orville Wright. So too the American economy worked, defying the theories of economists, and in the years since World War II it had worked "quite brilliantly."[12]

Galbraith shook up the usual thinking about prosperity, and he did so as an outsider. A Canadian by birth, he took a doctorate at the University of California in 1934 and taught at Harvard and Princeton on his specialty, the economics of agriculture. Early in World War II, he was in charge of price control in the Office of Price Administration. Galbraith was competent in price theory, but, trained as a writer for *Fortune,* he sought to communicate his theories to laymen in books written in a lively style with little scholarly apparatus. He was a popular economic philosopher, but, omitting technical terms, he was suspect to academic colleagues.[13]

Production was what the American economy was capable of, Galbraith wrote, pleased that a generous endowment in physical resources and a high development of intellectual resources spurred on this production. Galbraith's complaint was that the United States, which had produced few innovators in economic theory, had turned abroad for its theory; a Briton, Adam Smith, still had the last word. But since about the turn of the twentieth century the American economy had gradually ceased to operate according to the classical capitalist forces of supply and demand, and after the Depression of the 1930s and World War II, no economist could argue that the American economy possibly conformed to the old model.[14]

Galbraith argued that Americans had to understand anew their own system before advising other peoples what to do. He had an answer to the dilemma that in achieving prosperity Americans had failed to meet the requirements for a capitalist economy: his concept of countervailing power—what he had at first wanted to call "countervailence," until he decided coining a new word might be less understandable. Countervailing power was an economic force equivalent to political checks and balances in which one group counterbalanced another. Thus, for example, the Goodyear Tire & Rubber Company counterbalanced the chain store; the Great Atlantic & Pacific Tea Company counterbalanced its suppliers. Above all, since the domestic revolution in the 1930s and the 1940s, when the government took great responsibility for social well-being, the government counterbalanced business. Galbraith surmised that "economic power is held in check by the countervailing power of those who are subject to it. The first begets the second." Prosperous buyers and sellers developed together. Because of countervailing power, America did not have to be competitive in the classic sense to be capable of surviving—and, more, prospering like no other nation.[15]

The advantages of wealth, Galbraith proceeded, required new attitudes, because nearly all nations throughout history had been poor. Only in the last few generations, in regions populated by Europeans, had peoples experienced wealth. The United States especially had known "great and quite unprecedented affluence." Obviously, he wrote in *The Affluent Society,* Americans were not poverty-stricken, seeking subsistence. They were driven to need not by hunger but by advertising. Still, affluence had created new problems. There was great disparity between private riches and public want. Few seemed to worry, because the GNP was rising, as were retail sales, personal income, and productivity. The people had plenty of food and television sets, and the amenities of entertainment, transportation, and plumbing that not even the very rich could dream of a century before. But Galbraith argued that the nation could do a good deal more in the public sector by providing education, police protection, parks, sanitation, and transportation.[16]

Galbraith extended his theories to foreign policy, having gained a perspective on it when in 1945, as a director of the U.S. Strategic Bombing Survey, he had studied the effects of war on enemy economies. While he found that the German economy could never have supplied a winning army because its controlled business had been badly run, Galbraith observed, Americans had presented an image of themselves to strangers as a "lone island of youthful confidence and self-assurance in a world that is either searching for a debilitating security or has taken refuge in an all-embracing authoritarianism. Uniquely, we are sure of the quality and durability of our economic institutions." The success of American foreign policy in the 1940s was not the result of the wisdom of government or of the policies of any party, although Galbraith did not dismiss them. The reason for the success was that "foreign policy in these years mirrored the domestic revolution." Foreign policy became identified with masses and not classes. It reflected concern not for a privileged few in governments but for the people of other countries; "our domestic policy and our foreign policy are cut from the same piece." But, taking his domestic thesis into the international area, he did not believe it was simply free enterprise that Americans had to offer other peoples.[17]

These views Galbraith applied to India, a developing land with which he became infatuated after traveling there in the late 1950s and to which he later returned as ambassador of the United States. He had heard Americans urge the Indians to modernize by turning to free enterprise. But the irony Galbraith found was that while the different levels of government in the United States disposed of about 20 percent of total production, in India, government disposed of not over 10 percent. By this test, he concluded, the economy of the United States was "subject to a far greater degree of public guidance and direction than that of India." Of course, Galbraith pointed out, military outlays were a sizable portion of American production, but American agriculture was more tightly controlled by the state than Indian farming, and wages, hours, and conditions of labor were much more tightly regulated in the United States than in India.[18]

The answer for socialist India was not the Western capitalism Americans preached any more than it was Soviet communism, Galbraith argued. Both these systems had failed to make contact with the Indian experience. The economic policy of rugged individualism and rigorous competition that Americans commonly exported conflicted with their own government's intervention in the economy with social security, farm subsidies, and resource development. Galbraith complained, "Men who wouldn't think of taking this medicine themselves unhesitatingly prescribe it for foreigners." India needed economic development, not capitalism, Galbraith emphasized, echoing Potter's

constructs. Until recent times capitalist enterprise in India had been enforced by imperial control; it bore the stigma of colonialism. But he was persuaded that the lessons of
the experience of developed lands were "not revealed in any comprehensive doctrine or
theory and that this is equally the case with Western capitalism and Soviet Communism."[19]

Galbraith's critique of economics was searching but not angry. On the contrary, it
contributed to a general view of American prosperity and the uses of that prosperity in
the world. Galbraith and Potter respected the affluence of which they wrote, for the
benefits it gave Americans and offered other peoples. As it happened, Potter praised
The Affluent Society as more than a treatise on the difficulty of avoiding depressions and
inflation in the present society of 1958; Potter ranked it as a work that should contribute
in the long run to reshaping basic American goals. The two theorists of prosperity
remained thinkers within the consensus; they helped to make consensus, stimulating it
and its internationalism. While Americans offered other peoples their economic
methods and institutions, Potter and Galbraith believed that American productivity
offered something else, apart from capitalism: the way to modern development,
growth, welfare, and prosperity was a can-do approach that other nations could take by
following the example of technological innovation and production for the masses.[20]

Sociology: David Riesman and C. Wright Mills

Sociologists, too, made connections between American life and the nation's internationalism. There were growing numbers of young Americans, and David Riesman's
The Lonely Crowd, published in 1950, expressed the restlessness of a dynamic, changing people. More and more Americans were moving to suburbs and working in offices
rather than on assembly lines, trends captured by C. Wright Mills' *White Collar: The
American Middle Classes,* which came out in 1951, and by William H. Whyte's study of
growing bureaucracies, *The Organization Man,* which appeared in 1956. The attitude
above all others that typified Americans at home and abroad was a new outward look;
the people had become, in Riesman's phrase, "other-directed."[21]

David Riesman, along with Reuel Denney and Nathan Glazer, analyzed the new
attractions of world power for the American people, assuming that the change in the
attitude toward internationalism began with a change in the character of the American
people. In the past Americans had been a people Riesman knew as "inner-directed,"
driven by strong individualist ideals and expectations of achievement instilled early in
their lives by local authority and parents. Increasingly the people had become "other-
directed," their character shaped by contemporaries and peers. Open ambition, aggression, and competition were no longer so deeply valued. The new way implied affability,
blandness, and a sensitivity to the opinion of the group. Differences should be mini-
mized.[22]

Riesman, born in Philadelphia in 1909, graduated from Harvard and became a lawyer. During World War II he was a deputy assistant district attorney in New York City. But in 1946, attracted to the study of society more than to the technicalities of law, he began teaching at the University of Chicago. He first began to research the lives of teenagers, along with their interests in music, reading, and movies. In the late 1940s, as director of a project at Yale on the American character and apathy, he pursued his major work. It was broadly conceived. Riesman plotted the stages of development through which societies, like the individuals who constituted them, had passed. The first stage was tradition-directed. It was based on an economy of agriculture, hunting and fishing, and mining, and typical of India. The second stage of social development was inner-directed. It was based on an economy of manufacturing, and represented by the Soviet Union. The third stage was other-directed, based on an economy of trade, communications, and services, and epitomized by the United States.[23]

Riesman saw the United States as "big and rich." At the forefront of national development, it had reached a point at which wealth had become plentiful enough to permit a rapid accumulation of capital—and it was shifting from an age of production to an age of consumption. Societies of the past had once surpassed others to reach the top stage, currently held by the United States, among them Imperial Canton, Athens, Alexandria, and Rome. Britain was presently at this stage. Increasingly, as the United States had matured in power, it had become sensitive to world problems and responded by setting national goals.[24]

Many Americans, not merely specialists, Riesman observed, had become accustomed to looking outward, or—in some other Riesman phrases—thinking in "world-political" and "cross-cultural" terms. This outward look Riesman attributed to his theory of the other-directed character type. The prevalence of other-directed thinking had led to the public's desire to be well-informed on events in other nations and had contributed to the rapid change of opinion toward the Soviet Union from wartime ally to postwar enemy. Not merely Russian moves but also impulses within American society determined attitudes toward Russia. Riesman's evidence from polling data indicated that better educated and middle-class opinion toward Russia had swung much more widely than lower-class opinion. So the middle class, caught up in politics and susceptible to the mass media, was capable of readily adapting to an attitude of "violent hostility" toward Russia. Politics, indeed, served other-directed people "chiefly as a means for group conformity." They had to have acceptable opinions and engage in politics in acceptable ways. They were creatures of consensus.[25]

An other-directed outlook also favored the vogue of realism in world politics found wanting by earlier moralizers, who had advocated "world-brotherhood idealisms." In the nineteenth century, Riesman explained, journalistic treatments of international politics drew on parochial slogans of "national honor"—as in the blowing up of the *Maine*. Since then the mass media generally appeared to "discuss world politics in terms of strategic, including propaganda, considerations." The public was often asked to support a policy because that support, "in a kind of self-manipulative balancing act, will influence public opinion; such arguments can only be made because of the heightened understanding, in an era increasingly dependent on other-direction, of psychological forces in politics."[26]

The current widespread talk Riesman had heard about "our 'way of life,' " he went on, might remind some people of discussions of national honor. The change, he contended, was not merely one of phrasing. "National honor" bespoke the "various internal xenophobias of the nineteenth century," and what it demanded of the national enemy was quite specific. "Our way of life," on the other hand, took in a much broader consensual range of opinion, and it had "many more psychological connotations; it is fairly specific in domestic content but highly unspecific in foreign policy demand. 'National honor' sometimes strait-jacketed our foreign policy in moralizing beyond our power resources or power readiness. As against this, 'our way of life' gives almost no moral guidance to foreign policy, which seems, therefore, to be left to *Realpolitik*. Only seems to be, however. For just as the phrase 'national honor' calls to mind a Victorian form of hypocrisy, so the phrase 'our way of life' reminds us that the other-directed man conceals from himself as well as from others such morality as he possesses by taking refuge in seemingly expediential considerations."[27]

Together these changes revealed that American society was looking outward as in no previous period, but underneath the outer satisfaction and celebration, not all was well. As the top nation, the United States was on a lonely precipice, and solitary and exposed, it felt threatened, according to Riesman, by the pressure of population and expansion of nations undergoing transitional growth. The Soviet Union, and even more the huge oriental countries, were still in this phase of high-growth potential. Riesman theorized that international tensions helped to preserve in the most advanced nations the inner-directed character types that had been appropriate in the earlier era of growth.[28]

Concerned like Riesman with the new social forces that shaped the American world role was C. Wright Mills. From a perspective to the left of Riesman, he described the sociology of power and its influence on American internationalism. From the late 1940s through the 1950s he produced major studies of three groups that he inevitably applied to American foreign policy. The first group was labor leaders, about which he wrote *The New Men of Power* in 1948. Labor leaders, who had led the bottom mass of society, Mills thought had been growing in influence. "Now, in the middle of the twentieth century, their movement involves one-third of the American people, the power of the world is one-half American, and democracy everywhere is unsafe and in retreat." His next comment about America's role in the world was revealing of one who had high expectations for it, but who in a short time would become agitated and bitterly critical of it: "What the U.S. does, or fails to do, may be the key to what will happen in the world. What the labor leader does, or fails to do, may be the key to what will happen in the U.S."[29]

Born in Texas and educated at the University of Wisconsin, Mills became a highly regarded professor of sociology at Columbia University. He was prolific, conducting research for the government, corporations, and labor unions, lecturing in Europe, and producing books that were both scholarly and popular. He was an inspiring teacher, and he was known to ride a motorcycle around the Columbia campus. While acknowledging a debt to Marx, Mills fully recognized the cohesion of the national consensus. He believed that neither the progressive sentiment of the early 1900s nor Marxist flirtations of the 1930s enabled Americans to comprehend the modern condition of prosperous postwar society.[30]

But Mills did not remain satisfied with the explanation that labor may reform the American role in the world once he noted another group arising in American society: the white-collar worker. He wrote *White Collar,* on the managers, salaried professionals, salespeople, and office workers who had come to make up well over half of the middle class. The white-collar workers, who claimed a level of prestige lacking in blue collar jobs, had increased in numbers with the productivity of manufacturing and the accompanying affluence. Mills marveled at the continuing boom of real income, severely broken only by the depression of the 1930s. The people experiencing this increasing material contentment, Mills admitted, were not likely to develop economic resentments that would tear their political institutions apart, as had plagued Europe.[31]

World War II underscored the influence of the white collar. While men fought all over the world, women filled in for men on the homefront, laborers worked hard and long and bought war bonds, and the people together believed in America and in its cause, Mills noted the formation of bureaucracies administered by white-collar workers, who were efficient but alienated from their product: "Some sort of numbness seemed to prohibit any awareness of the magnitude and depth of what was happening," Mills wrote. People "sat in the movies between production shifts, watching with aloofness and even visible indifference, as children were 'saturation bombed' in the narrow cellars of European cities. Man had become an object; and in so far as those for whom he was an object felt about the spectacle at all, they felt powerless, in the grip of larger forces, having no part in these affairs that lay beyond their immediate areas of daily demand and gratification. It was a time of somnambulance." Mills's sense of the irony of the glory of great wealth and power, and the danger of their being wasted and misspent, was growing.[32]

In the late 1950s he wrote his most ambitious and controversial study, *The Power Elite,* describing the military officers, business executives, and politicians who ruled the big corporations, ran the machinery of state, and directed the military establishment. The power elite completed the climb of Mills's study up the ladder of American society; the elite represented the "higher circles." The power of the elite had increased enormously. The economy, once distributed among small producers, had become dominated by two or three hundred corporations. The political order, once divided among the several states, had become a centralized, executive establishment. The military, once a lean militia, had become the largest and most costly part of government. Mills argued that the warlords, the corporation chieftains, and the political directorate cooperated through interlocking institutions.[33]

The repercussions of this power elite were international. No ruling class anywhere in the world could "contain that of the United States when industrialized violence came to decide history." Mills followed the growth of state power from Caesar's Rome to Napoleon's France, Lenin's Russia, and Hitler's Germany, culminating in the power of the American elite. He pointed to the fate of Germany and Japan in the two world wars, and to that "of Britain herself and her model ruling class, as New York became the inevitable economic, and Washington the inevitable political capital of the western capitalist world." Chief among the decisions of the elite, Mills wrote, was the dropping of atomic bombs over Japan: the decisions were made in secret, the people never consulted. The development of American power—military, administrative, and psychic—in the middle years of the twentieth century had made of the United States "an epochal pivot" in history.[34]

By the late 1950s Mills had taken a direct interest in foreign affairs. He believed that the history of modern society could be understood as the progressive enlargement and centralization of the means of power since feudal societies. The climax of this centralization, Mills saw, was the modern industrial nation-state represented by the United States and the Soviet Union, however much their ideologies of capitalism and communism differed. He ranked the United States as a supernation. Its military was seemingly absolute; its economic system was autarchic; its political influence was increasing around the globe; and its bureaucracy extended worldwide. And Mills related the centralization of international power to the three broad groups that he had distinguished within American society. The bottom mass of laborers and the middle levels of white-collar workers increasingly fell in line with a power elite whose power probably exceeded "that of any small group of men in world history, the Soviet elite possibly excepted." "In the American white-collar and professional hierarchies . . . we now witness the rise of the cheerful robot, of the technological idiot, of the crackpot realist. All these types embody a common ethos: rationality without reason. The fate of these types and of this ethos, what is done about them and what they do—that is the real, even the ultimate, showdown on 'socialism' and on 'capitalism' in our time."[35]

The consensus saw the Americans as a powerful, outward looking, other-directed people, and Mills did not argue with Riesman on this account. Mills neither argued with American success, nor questioned that Americans were a people of plenty. How could literate Americans in the postwar world, who had traveled and lived in other nations and had seen the fact of national differences, think otherwise? he asked. But, even after reading Potter's book in 1955, Mills questioned if a bounteous new man was all that the American should be known for. Mills became more and more disgruntled with consensus thinking, contending that sociologists should not be merely disinterested observers but assert their social responsibility. He was met with resistance by the consensus. *Time* recommended that *The Power Elite* be read—it was too important, even if full of "half truths," to be ignored—but "the average U.S. reader is apt to emerge from this nightmare-shored-by-platitudes wondering how, with such irresponsible interlocking monsters running the country, things manage to go so well and so many people stay happy, decent and prosperous." By the time of his sudden death of a heart attack in 1962, short of his forty-sixth birthday, Mills had angrily all but rejected the consensus and gained a following of young radicals who sought fundamental change.[36]

Theological Thought: Reinhold Niebuhr and Paul Tillich

It was an age of religious revival. New churches and synagogues sprang up, and the numbers of worshipers grew. Evangelists led by Billy Graham held outdoor crusades for mass audiences in stadiums across the country. Televised sermons by the Catholic bishop, Fulton J. Sheen, rivaled in the ratings one of the most popular shows starring the comedian, Milton Berle. The Protestant clergyman Norman Vincent Peale wrote *The Power of Positive Thinking,* urging Americans to overcome feelings of limitation and despair in part by considering the greatness of their country, a land of opportunity. Dwight Eisenhower began his administration with prayer. As the new president raised his hand from the two Bibles on which he had just sworn and began his inaugural speech, he led the nation, saying: "Almighty God . . . .May cooperation be permitted and be the mutual aim of those who, under the concepts of our Constitution, hold to differing political faiths; so that all may work for the good of our beloved country and Thy glory. Amen." The president appointed one of the country's most prominent Protestant laymen, John Foster Dulles, as secretary of state, and together they regularly opened cabinet meetings with prayer.[37]

The revival fostered religious expressions of new involvement and brotherhood in international affairs. Among theologians, Reinhold Niebuhr was at the forefront of religious discussion of the moral issues raised by American world power. Niebuhr upheld the reality of power in the modern world. He was a critic of traditional idealism and moral illusion; he was in short a realist. The ancient doctrine of original sin convinced him that permanent felicity was not possible and that human motives and choices inevitably mixed good and bad. The divine might be absolute and pure, but on earth humans must deal with the imperfect, the corrupt, and the unsatisfactory. Niebuhr did not think that declarations and treaties made much difference in world affairs. Power had to oppose power, whether in American politics, in economics, or in world affairs. The use of power was a way of restraining a universal predisposition to sin through pride, illusion, and greed.[38]

Writing *Christianity and Power Politics* early in World War II, Niebuhr assailed American churches for their pacifist stance toward totalitarian tyranny. He focused on Nazi tyranny, but his advocacy of a new world role for America based on religious principles continued to apply after the war. By disavowing the responsibilities of power, Niebuhr argued, the nation invoked far worse guilt than whatever guilt came from wielding power. "The Christian Church of America," he said, "has never been upon a lower level of spiritual insight and moral sensitivity than in this tragic age of world conflict . . . .If modern churches were to symbolize their true faith they would take the crucifix from their altars and substitute the three little monkeys who counsel men to 'speak no evil, hear no evil, see no evil.'" American Christianity simply had to face up to overcoming international anarchy if it was to survive as a civilization.[39]

Niebuhr, born in the backcountry Missouri town of Wright City, became a Protestant pastor in Detroit in 1915. *Does Civilization Need Religion?*, published in 1927, was the first of his many works on Christian ethics and realism. The following year he became a professor at Union Theological Seminary in New York City. His reputation grew during the 1930s, as he applied ethics to American foreign affairs. His stand against isolationism marked a personal transformation. He had been a socialist with Marxist leanings, after his exposure to the workings of the automobile industry in Detroit. In the 1930s he broke with the Socialist party over its noninterventionist platforms on foreign policy. Niebuhr had also been a pacifist. Even though he had felt revulsion against World War I, he persuaded pacifist Christians to support the war against Hitler.[40]

In isolation, Niebuhr believed, Americans had denied their responsibilities to their fellow human beings in peril. American Christians had reasoned that if Europe was evil, Americans would remain unaffected by refusing to become involved in its affairs. Niebuhr countered that tyranny in Europe would be morally intolerable and would challenge American interests. Neutrality could be maintained "only at the price of accentuating every vice in American character," particularly Pharisaism and self-righteousness. Christian "patriotic isolationists" were trying to "throttle every impulse of sympathy and every sense of common responsibility which might establish a common humanity among us rather than a unique guiltlessness." The result was the depreciation of the Christian idea of love into a lovelessness that had cut itself off from a suffering world. Neutrality policy, then, was "not only bad morals but bad politics."[41]

Following World War II, Niebuhr was heartened by the acceptance Americans had of their power and by the abandonment of their moral complacency. "Our own nation," he wrote in the late 1940s, "has achieved a degree of power in the contemporary world community which dwarfs the dominions of the empires of the past." Its power had achieved hegemony in the western world. "Though it cannot be said that we carry the royal purple of our authority with complete ease, we have not done too badly in sensing the scope of our responsibilities and in learning to discharge new duties." Because Niebuhr believed that no powerful nation in history had ever been more reluctant to acknowledge its world position than the United States, he did not at first worry that his country possessed the moral flaw of a strong lust for power. Still, he did fear that the more Americans indulged in an uncritical reverence for the supposed virtue of their society, the more odious they made it in the eyes of the world and the more they were in danger of destroying their authority, without which their economic and military strength would wane. Americans were in danger of undermining the reality of their power by their uncritical pride in it.[42]

While Niebuhr pointed out that Americans had lapses in virtue, they were, he believed, preserving a system of freedom that communists threatened. He could not countenance the state control sought by Marxist communism. He saw the whole world suffering from the evil malignancy of communism, which was attempting to establish a power monopoly. It was a vast injustice, despite its pretensions of innocence. Marxist utopian illusions of self-righteousness, economic determinism, and dogmatism exhibited the problems of communist secular society. The opening paragraph of Niebuhr's book, *The Irony of American History,* in 1952 came to grips with his views of American power and communism: "Everybody understands the obvious meaning of the world struggle in which we are engaged. We are defending freedom against tyranny." Americans had to continue to use their inordinately great power for the good of mankind. The most powerful of the democratic nations, he argued, should use its power in the service of justice, which could be achieved largely by responding to world public opinion.[43]

The irony Niebuhr saw was that the more powerful Americans became, the less secure they felt. There was the irony of scientific progress in an age of mass slaughter and possible atomic war. There was the irony of the prosperity of the United States amid global poverty and instability. The danger was that the irony of American history would be the same as the irony he found in communism: lofty pretensions of justice threatened to give way to demonic behavior. This irony was central to Niebuhr's feelings about original sin; ideal aspiration was undone by human nature. The liberal realistic world that opposed communism, Niebuhr wrote, was filled with milder forms of the same pretensions. Fortunately, these abuses had not resulted in the same evils as communism, partly because American political institutions contained safeguards against the selfish abuse of power, which had been insisted on by Calvinist fathers. Niebuhr referred to the "accents in our constitution which spell out the warning of John Cotton: 'Let all the world give mortall man no greater power than they are content they shall use, for use it they will.'" In the end God was the judge of nations and of their history.[44]

To Niebuhr's colleague at Union Theological Seminary, Paul Tillich, who had fled Europe after suffering Nazi oppression, America held out a hope that was well founded in his theology of brotherhood. Tillich's thought about world affairs changed as he left behind the war-troubled old world where he had worked and lived for forty-seven years. The coming and outbreak of World War II and the tremendous problems of postwar reconstruction had forced on him "a larger participation in practical politics" than he had ever intended. In New York, where he adjusted to an unknown culture in a new country, on a new continent, he reflected that he learned from American theology a sense of realism relating moral idealism to activism in the world. He hoped his understanding of the "world-historical situation" had become more "realistic."[45]

Tillich feared onset of disillusion after World War II, but there was a hope in a world organized on the principle of responsibility for others: "the point I want to make above all—and the one I think religion must make today in this country—is that America, if she takes responsibility for the present world catastrophe, must take it completely and with the full knowledge of what it means. It does not mean defending America against the dictators, it does not mean defeating Hitler, it does not mean conquering Germany a second time: it means accepting her share of responsibility for the future structure of Europe and consequently for the whole world. Whatever happens during the later years of the war, any victory will be won on the physical and moral ruins of Europe. It would be a cynical opportunism if America helped to augment those ruins without being ready and able to build something radically new on them. If this country will not look beyond the day of victory, that day will become the birthday of another defeat of all human values and noble aims. The word that religion has to speak to this nation and to all those who fight with her is the grave question: Are you willing, are you able, to take upon you the full weight of the task before you? If not, keep away from it; do not follow the cause of an easy opportunism."[46]

The intellectual consensus, the ideas of which gave construction to common attitudes of people and leaders in their generally accepted vision of historic traditions, landscape features, economic prosperity, social institutions, and moral values, presented America as a successful society, proud of its might and progress. Not even those who were most critical of the domestic dimensions of internationalism doubted American affluence and world power. The very conceptions of the consensus thinkers exuded the confidence of this society—"a big country," "people of plenty," "affluent society," "other-direction," "white collar," and "power elite." They thought of the society as unique and measured its accomplishments against those of other countries, from the size of its gross national product to the customs of its national character. In the United States of the late 1940s and the 1950s, troubles were subordinated to world responsibility, and while room existed for argument, even agitation, there was little confrontation. Even if the authors of these theories did not collectively favor specific international policies—they were all not without criticism of American ways, finding fault with a failure to promote global prosperity, to restrain power, or to be less arrogant—they did agree on domestic developments behind American involvement in the world. Neither Mills, probably the most radical of the prominent intellectuals, nor Galbraith, in his attacks on conventional wisdom, nor Niebuhr, skeptical of pride in power denied American dynamism or the desirability of basing the country's international role on its national experience.

The content of this consensus domestic thought moved directly, consciously, and explicitly to international affairs. In history, this thought reflected a sense of destiny that the past had reached a climax in the present. In the landscape, it was a grand view of bigness and diversity. In economics, it was a vision of wealth through technological expertise and productivity. In sociology, it was the other-direction idea that the social problems that had been solved in America could be solved abroad. In religion, it was the theology of brotherhood that the United States must be involved in the ways of the world. Americans had rethought their national identity as an international state. By these theories, many Americans believed the rest of the world aspired to affluence, diversity, and cooperation. The idea of these theories was to implement peace, self-determination, economic development, social welfare, democratic government, and spiritual freedom.

The domestic content of the consensus clashed with the fears of the Soviet communist threat. But it explained the perception of that threat. The fears of communism were of an economy that took wealth from the prosperous and successful; of a closed, totalitarian society, inward-looking and mistrustful of even well-meaning foreigners to the extreme of paranoia; and of an atheistic morality that denied the existence of God and the ethical Judeo-Christian individualistic traditions of Western society. These strange and ominous characteristics of communist Russia were diametrically opposed to the characteristics of modern America. After the war the paramount fear was of Soviet expansion—the pursuit of "world domination," as Truman and Eisenhower and many others called it. This final fear raised hostility toward the Soviet Union to an unprecedented pitch.

Was the American consensus offensive or defensive? Did it center on national exertion or on fear of foreign threats? In 1954 President Eisenhower addressed these disparate motivations in a speech broadcast on radio and television. He began with the fundamental fact of American power. "Now, as we first take a look at the strength of America, you and I know that it is the most productive nation on earth, that we are richer, by any standard of comparison, than is any other nation in the world. We know that we have great military strength—economic—intellectual." He called particular attention to "spiritual strength," for without spiritual strength "everything else goes by the board." All in all, he added, "this total strength of America is one of those things we call—and the world calls—unbelievable."

Then Eisenhower continued with the fears. "Now why, then, with all this strength, should we be worried at times about what the world is doing to us?" Americans saw threats coming at them "from all angles—internal and external." They were concerned about the communists in the Kremlin, about nuclear weapons, about the loss of friends abroad to communist dictatorship, about communist penetration of America, and about the possibility of a depression. Underlying all these dangers, Eisenhower said, was the "threat that we have from without, the great threat imposed upon us by aggressive communism, the atheistic doctrine that believes in statism as against our conception of the dignity of man, his equality before the law—that is the struggle of the ages." The answer: "We can stand up and hold up our heads and say: America is the greatest force that God has ever allowed to exist on His footstool. As such it is up to us to lead this world to a peaceful and secure existence." So we can discount neither the threat nor the assertion in the development of the American world role.[47]

Still, the United States was ready to be a dominant power regardless of the Soviet threat. "Even if there were no Soviet Union," said NSC 68, echoing the earlier thought by Henry Stimson, "we would face the great problem of the free society, accentuated many fold in this industrial age, of reconciling order, security, the need for participation, with the requirements of freedom. We would face the fact that in a shrinking world the absence of order among nations is becoming less and less tolerable." The threat by the Kremlin did not create this imperative; it added urgency to it. The United States tried to overcome its insecurity by enhancing its power.[48]

The problem was less over whether the world role was offensive or defensive than whether it was ethnocentric or cosmopolitan. The course of action was still malleable, and the manifestations of a world role able to be directed between an ethnocentric internationalism and cosmopolitan internationalism. But the risks of ethnocentricism to a lasting world role are already evident. Thought about internationalism was in danger of being ethnocentric, too often narrowly limited by ideas drawn from domestic history, economy, society, and religion.

The major thinkers had laid the groundwork for the consensus that lasted over time, but the harmony of consensus had to depend on agreement about the decisions that emerged from disagreements, on acceptance of the way things were, and on the common belief that the people, having followed their leaders this far, would follow them anywhere. Consensus depended on continued economic prosperity, social cohesion, and moral action. If these failed, the consensus stood to fail.

The consensus values, in turn, were crucial to the development of the American world role and determined whether it was to be cosmopolitan or ethnocentric. Yet while Americans came together in agreement on their general national mission, they did not always see eye to eye on the immediate objectives of particular policies, about how that mission should be carried out.

PART III

The

Manifestations

of

a

World

Role

☆ ☆ ☆ ☆

9

Economic

Enterprise

The spread of the American world order is one of the extraordinary occurrences of world history in the rapidity of its organization and in the scope of its contact with nearly every society on earth. The United States, unlike Britain or the European world empires, did not carry a global imperial burden of the past or act on the compulsion of maintaining shifting colonial positions on every continent by limiting the sovereignty of subject peoples. The United States had no need to defend an accumulation of special privileges or to demand tribute even from conquered enemies. The world role of its creation offered assets of innovation, practicality, and modernity.

From the late 1940s to the 1960s, the exercise of American influence brought to world affairs the main consensus ideas of economic abundance, philanthropy and social welfare, egalitarianism and technological advance, federalism and democracy. Let us examine how the uncommon unanimity of cultural values, traditions, ideals, and myths constituted the native environment for specific international policies and institutions. In which cases did these manifestations transcend ethnocentric tendencies, and to what extent were they cosmopolitan? Americans pursued their interests through policies and institutions that might serve other peoples as well as themselves, but revolutionary transformations of other societies might not take place as expected. Why did the United States succeed in spreading its influence? When did it fail?

"Made in America"

Wherever they journeyed, Americans saw the earth's economic development from the perspective of their own spectacular growth. From the plane carrying the businessman Eric Johnston across the Soviet border in 1944, the passengers peered out the window onto the dense green lower slopes of foothills and the streams. "Look, Bill!" one shouted to the journalist W. L. White. "What an opportunity for dams!" Their response to undeveloped territory, some of it left by local people almost as it had always been, was one of possibility and expectation of improvement. Crossing over the Soviet Union, the reporter observed that the settlements were small, reminding him of America's crossroads towns of a half-century or more before, in the 1880s or 1890s, except that the roofs were thatched. Fascinating to him was the dearth of connected paved highways. He could make out wagon tracks leading from the villages to the fields, and sometimes faint trails from town to town, but not one strip of clean, flowing concrete or blacktop. Looking through the plexiglass window at five thousand feet, the reporter surmised that modern life had little affected the Russians: "all this might have been here in the middle ages," White wrote. Not until he approached the ruins of Stalingrad and later, near the outskirts of Moscow, an electric power line running from horizon to horizon, did he see landmarks that he was sure had been built since 1917.[1]

In lands at nearly every stage of development, Americans in the decade after World War II found a scarcity of modern products, except for their own omnipresent manufacturers, services, and conveyances. Four-engine, propeller-driven Constellations of the American Overseas Airline brought New World observers in and out of Europe. On the streets of London and Paris they saw huge American automobiles. On the German autobahns, Americans in Chevrolets and Plymouths sped along in the absence of Volkswagens. In European homes Americans found Scotch Tape and Pyrex heat-resistant glassware for cooking. Coca-Cola signs were spotted in at least nine different languages from Oslo to Casablanca.[2]

In Ethiopia, American travelers flew from Addis Ababa to Diredawa on board a plane of the government-owned Ethiopian Air Lines, managed and operated by America's Trans World Airlines. A Pan American Airways Constellation landed Americans in Léopoldville, in the Belgian Congo, on a route deep within the African tropics. While traveling through South Africa in the 1950s, the daughter of Alexander Graham Bell picked up a newspaper in Port Elizabeth and read an article headlined "Thanks to Mr. Bell," about the installation of the city's new automatic phone exchange. Most private cars, trucks, and taxis observed in the Belgian Congo in the 1950s were American-made. American passengers rode over the Outeniqua Mountains in South Africa in an American car assembled in that country. Plymouths crossed the Sinai desert in hours, whereas it took days on camelback. A party of American explorers drove a 1956 Chevrolet station wagon over the dirt roads of Southwest Asia from Pakistan through Iran and Iraq to Turkey. Heavy American ten-wheel trucks passed over Iranian mountain routes. An American visitor two miles underground in a South African mine watched American cutting machines break up thick seams of coal and divide the lumps to be shuttled by cars toward the surface.[3]

In wartime Russia W. L. White observed an aircraft factory making wings of aluminum stamped "Alcoa" and noticed American jeeps with instructions in Russian stenciled in Detroit. Margaret Bourke-White saw that the automobile carrying Stalin to the Kremlin was a large, black Packard. Henry Wallace was surprised to find Pillsbury flour from Minneapolis in a Siberian warehouse and miners wearing United States Rubber boots at a gold mine in Kolyma. He saw an American-built icebreaker, Studebaker trucks, machine tools of American make in an aircraft factory, American wheels installed on Russian locomotives, and a Bucyrus Erie electric shovel shipped from the United States.[4]

Americans reveled in finding their goods abroad, the signs of their work and prestige. *Foreign Affairs* compared America's diffusion of commercial culture with that of ancient Egypt, Greece, and Rome, though the ancient traders had never scattered the knowledge of new goods, new metals, and new industrial arts over the entire globe. No longer did goods flow primarily from Europe to the rest of the world. The upshot was "Today, in the minds of millions of the white, brown, red, black, and yellow races they bear one label: *Made in America*."[5]

Few disputed that this economic colossus would affect world consumption and production. Going so far as to state that American international economic policy was perhaps of greater importance to two billion people living abroad than to 140 million Americans, Harvard's Seymour Harris contended, "It is largely true that as goes the American economy so goes the world." "World security and world peace," said Alvin Hansen, a wartime adviser to the Federal Reserve Board, "depend in a very fundamental sense upon how good a job we do in managing our own economy." America's immediate interest in the world economy was to prevent the recurrence of the Great Depression, which had followed the American economic boom of the 1920s and rapidly affected Europe, hitting Germany and Great Britain and then spreading worldwide. Secretary of Commerce W. Averell Harriman told a meeting of the U.S. Chamber of Commerce in 1947 that the "first requirement in meeting our responsibilities to the world . . . is to maintain the productivity and health of our own economy," for the United States was "the only nation" equipped to provide a good life for its own people and at the same time help other peoples of the world.[6]

But the international consequences of America's prosperity had repercussions far beyond relatively short-term monetary factors and business cycles. Americans foresaw an influence that would help other peoples develop as they encountered modernity. This proposition was David Potter's: America's "export of goods and gadgets, of cheap, machine-produced grain and magic-working medicines, which opened new vistas to the human mind," made Americans instigators of social change worldwide. If Americans were unique in initiating production expertise, they were not unique in possessing the potential assets to realize the application of technological skill. Thus Americans were in a position to affirm to the world: "although we are in many respects set apart by our natural plenty, in many other respects we are qualified to show other countries the path that may lead them to a plenty like our own."[7]

To meet the demands of domestic prosperity and the task of the development of the world economy, Americans had to reconcile tensions between the two. The extent to which they harmonized their domestic and international concerns would determine the success of the economic dimension of their world role. They had three main instruments at their command in this work: trade, capital investment, and currency.

The World's Workshop: Trade

A great sea change in world commerce had occurred. In the nineteenth century, when Europe was the world's workshop, turning out products for all regions, America was dependent on Europe's goods. Americans chronically received more in imports than they gave in exports until the 1870s, when the United States, adding manufactured goods and machinery to its foreign sales of cotton, meat, and grain, began to export more than it imported. By World War I the United States rivaled Britain as the greatest trading nation in the world; in World War II it became by far the largest. The "United States is of paramount importance to world trade," wrote J. M. Letiche. Moreover, the annual excess of exports over imports was the greatest in history. Yet the exchange of goods and services across national borders, of vast importance to the world economy, represented only a small portion of the American national income, averaging less than 10 percent.[8]

At its peak in 1947, world demand for American goods, services, and raw materials was the cause of some amazement to Americans and of mixed appreciation and apprehension to foreigners. In 1947 America's exports amounted to credits of more than $14 billion, while its imports tallied debits of some $5 billion. The economist Robert Heilbroner discovered to his surprise that in the first quarter of 1947 alone Americans shipped abroad $4.9 billion worth of goods—almost as much as in the entire boom year of 1929. In the first half of 1947 Americans exported nearly double the amount for all of 1939.[9]

Foreign purchases of food were up eight times from before the war, and of raw materials, up four times. The world demanded American manufactures—automobiles, trucks, busses, factory machinery, electrical apparatuses, office appliances, steel goods, and agricultural equipment—in quantities nearly doubled from 1939. Not only necessities were sold. Sales of nylons, rayons, and synthetic textiles, soap and toilet articles, and cigarettes were many times prewar levels.

Every part of the world bought more from America than it had before the war. By 1947 orders had doubled to Britain, tripled to Canada, quadrupled to Asia, and quintupled to Europe. It was not just the war-ridden, impoverished areas that sought imports. Latin American nations, many of which had benefited from trade during the war, began to spend their accumulated dollars on American consumer goods, and their purchases increased eightfold. Exports to Africa were up 500 percent. In world terms, the United States was shipping a third of all exports.[10]

With scarcities worldwide, countries devastated by war required the goods and services to rebuild, and people everywhere wanted the products of American mass production for mass consumption—automobiles, refrigerators, televisions, radios, and Hollywood movies. The "whole world is hungry for American goods," said the economist John Condliffe. "Every one would like to have the opportunity of riding in American automobiles, of drinking American fruit juices, and of possessing electric refrigerators and other conveniences of life."[11]

Most analysts expected this unprecedented trade surplus to continue. According to Hansen, "We are always selling to foreigners more than they are able to pay for." No other way could be seen for the future by Roosevelt's secretary of the treasury, Henry Morgenthau, who stated in congressional testimony that even though the United States was already "the largest exporting nation in the world," after the war "we will have even more reason for exporting and importing, for expanding trade."[12]

Businessmen prepared to meet rising demand abroad. Reviving the dream of trade with China, Henry Luce looked to the day when Asian commerce would be worth from four to ten billion dollars a year. In 1946 he told a meeting of businessmen: "I urge each and every one of you to participate actively in overseas business. If you are not regularly engaged in it, find some way to give part of your time to it." As secretary of commerce, Wallace also pressed producers to expand trade, whether in the northern Pacific and eastern Asia or in Latin America. Since the United States had kept up a larger foreign trade with the 12 million people of Canada than with all 140 million people of Latin America, he saw "an abundance of new frontiers of opportunity for our factories and for our industrial and scientific know-how."[13]

In World War II a majority of the public had strongly favored expanding trade as much as possible with other countries, rejecting the Depression-era wisdom that the nation should focus on domestic development. "Should the U.S. try to develop its own industries to the point where it does not have to buy any products from foreign countries?" was a question asked in a 1939 poll and again in the middle of World War II. The number who wanted the United States to trade more than doubled and became a majority. Toward the end of the war, 76 percent wanted to sell more goods to foreigners and 68 percent were ready to buy more products from other countries.[14]

The principal theory for the continued growth of American foreign commerce was free trade, which carried with it the belief that it yielded higher real income for the participants. When Britain had reigned as the world's great trader in the early nineteenth century, British economists had based the theoretical case for free trade on Adam Smith's argument that the division of labor among nations leads to efficiency and high levels of production. The United States, in contradiction to this theory, had raised a tariff in 1789 and maintained a high wall through most of the nineteenth and early twentieth centuries. Tariffs increased in the 1920s, culminating with the Hawley-Smoot tariff of 1930, the highest in American history, but eventually the country adapted to classical free trade thought.

The new argument was that the rest of the world would buy American goods if the United States lowered its duties. The exports would be large if other countries could earn dollar exchange. "In other words," Sumner Slichter wrote, "we can help the world equip itself with American machines, tools, radios, and automobiles by raising our standard of living, by making it easier for Cuba and the West Indies to sell us winter vegetables, pineapples and other fruits, for Australia, the Near East and South Africa to sell us wool, for France and Italy to sell us wines, for Britain to sell us worsteds and china, and so on." Since the 1920s most countries had experienced difficulty earning enough dollars to meet their demand for American goods, and recent technological developments, the substitutes for silk and wool, and synthetic rubber, had only aggravated the problem. Hence "it is more necessary than ever that the United States reduce artificial barriers on imports."[15]

Old arguments for protection nonetheless resurfaced in the 1940s in pockets across the country. The need to protect home industries was one argument. The propagation of a new synthetic rubber industry in World War II was important enough that six in ten Americans were willing to pay higher postwar prices for synthetic rubber than for cheap foreign natural rubber. Another point favoring restricted trade was protection of industrial jobs. If European workers could make shoes more cheaply than Americans, 46 percent of the Americans polled rejected the suggestion that they change jobs, while 32 percent gave their support. A further argument favored blocking goods from countries with a standard of living below that of the United States. Considering that the "cheap labor" of Europe could make various products for much less than American workmen, 68 percent of Americans voted to keep these foreign goods out of the country.[16]

But the new economic thought found these old arguments wanting. Because tariffs had peaked with the onset of the Depression in the 1930s, they did not keep money in the country, raise wages, help special-interest groups without harming everyone, or raise much revenue for the government. By 1932 the total value of American and world trade had plummeted by more than half; wages fell, and workers were thrown out of work.

The government had been impelled to free trade principles largely by the efforts of Secretary of State Cordell Hull. Since the early 1930s he had contended that the United States should reverse its high-tariff policy. Sponsored by Hull, the Trade Agreements Act of 1934 authorized the president to negotiate reciprocal agreements by granting low tariff rates to other nations in return for similar reductions from them. Under the authority of the act, Hull negotiated for the president twenty-two agreements before World War II, including ones with Britain, France, Canada, the Latin American countries, and eventually Soviet Russia. Hull's continuous, patient labors Alvin Hansen called "Herculean," and the agreements proved sufficiently satisfactory that the act was renewed in 1937 and extended for another three years in 1940.[17]

Above all the other reasons supporting free trade, America was no longer a young country of infant industries struggling to get started under protection. It was a highly industrialized, efficient producer that Hull believed should set the example of free trade. The secretary lashed out at tariffs as the "most virulent expression" of self-centered nationalism in the economic field. Trade barriers increased foreign tensions, fomenting dictatorship and war. He wanted to establish among the nations a "circle of mutual benefit."[18]

The Atlantic Charter supported free trade in 1941, as did lend-lease provisions, which participating countries pledged to abide by. The extent to which the United States could get the doctrine of free trade accepted by other nations through bilateral agreements, Hull believed, would determine its own prosperity and peace. Hull testified before congressional committees in 1943 that the nations entering into the cooperative economic agreements were "peace-loving," and Congress voted to extend the Trade Agreements Act for two years. Although that period was less than the three years he had asked for, Roosevelt signed the legislation. When the president died in April 1945, Hull was composing a letter to Congress on trade agreements, due to expire again.[19]

Hull pleaded for a nonpartisan consensus on trade agreements, and both liberal and conservative politicians spoke out for freeing international trade from constraints. Vice President Henry Wallace and Hull were often at odds, but Wallace was no less equivocal about the need for low tariffs than Hull had been. As early as 1942 Wallace foresaw that America's trade surplus would be far greater than ever before. "We can be decently human and really hardheaded if we exchange our postwar surplus for goods, for peace and for improving the standard of living of so-called backward peoples." Not unlike Hull, he was convinced that economic warfare caused by tariffs of the 1920s, the severest being the Hawley-Smoot tariff, was the first step toward war.[20]

Businessmen too generally welcomed free trade. *Fortune* was a strong advocate of it, and so was Henry Luce. Together they urged businessmen to favor comprehensive reciprocal tariff cuts, which placed the interest of the nation above the concern of any particular industry. They did not fear competition or the penetration of American markets by foreigners. On the contrary, businessmen could apply their production and marketing skills to expand sales abroad. That would bring in profits and increase national prosperity, production, and income by providing employment for workers, who would in turn spend their income on the products of other American companies and raise the standard of living. American citizens stood to live better if they did not spend excessive amounts on imports. The argument for free trade was that it would also be mutually profitable to peoples across the globe because it allowed everyone to produce and sell goods and thereby to raise their standards of living.[21]

Economists who promoted free trade often thought that the government had not gone far enough in lowering tariffs. John Kenneth Galbraith believed that America should show the way unilaterally, regardless of the action of other nations. If the country wanted other nations to lower tariffs, it had to lower its own even more than Hull's reciprocal agreements had done. And it could afford to do so. Admitting in 1949 that the United States was "no longer a high tariff country," Galbraith argued that the Hull program, which had served so well, was now "obsolete." Tariff bargaining had little point when the problem of other countries was not that they wished to forego American products but that they found themselves impelled to buy more than they could afford. The appropriate course was "to abandon the shadowboxing of tariff bargaining and to make unilateral reductions in our own tariff."[22]

Along with liberal economic theorists, businessmen, and political leaders, public opinion came around to a thoroughgoing reduction of postwar tariffs. Asked whether Congress should renew the trade agreements program, as Secretary of State Hull had requested in the spring of 1945, 75 percent of Americans polled thought so. Moreover,

57 percent approved arranging even further tariff reductions in the United States and other countries. Both Democrats and Republicans were in favor of these reductions. Similar opinions, regardless of region or occupation, prevailed nationwide through the 1950s.[23]

American producers seemed to have all the advantages. How would other peoples benefit from free trade? The experience of American businessmen trading with Europe provided the answer: they had to do business in countries with different tariffs and numerous currencies, which obstructed trade not only with Americans but among the European nations themselves. In contrast, the model of an open marketplace among nations was the duty-free American continental market. The virtues of an open system were self-evident to W. Averell Harriman, who was an experienced international banker. He vividly recalled asking some European bankers and industrialists at a meeting of the International Chamber of Commerce in Paris in 1927 why, while Europe was in a period of stagnation and high unemployment, the United States was prosperous with expanding production. The European businessmen unanimously agreed that the primary reason was that Americans had opened up a continent of free trade, whereas Europeans had restricted trade among their various countries. Harriman asked them why they did not break down these barriers. They replied that this was impossible unless the European countries could arrange mutual security arrangements. That appeared a most unlikely prospect in 1927, but Harriman had hope for free trade after World War II. The Reciprocal Trade Agreements remained in force through the postwar period, and the United States and its trading partners did lower trade barriers dramatically from their peak in the early 1930s.[24]

Chosen Instruments: Ships and Planes

Prominent symbols of overseas activity in trade were the enterprising transportation companies and their ocean liners and aircraft carrying cargo and passengers. Prestige would accrue to the nation sending near and far the largest fleet, flying its national flag in the ports of Hankow, Papeete, Valparaiso, and Zanzibar. "Our goal is to have the best ships in the world and as many of them as any other nation," declared Admiral Emory S. Land, chairman of the Maritime Commission. "We must plan, too, that those ships shall carry a sufficient portion of world trade to restore the United States to a maritime position befitting a nation of her status."[25]

America's advances in merchant ships had long kept pace with growing foreign trade, and for a time in the mid-nineteenth century the United States had claimed shipbuilding leadership with the Yankee clippers, the speediest vessels of their day. In World War I the need for American ships to carry goods abroad made the United States second only to Britain in the tonnage of its merchant marine. Then in World War II a productive drive turned out enormous quantities of ships. At war's end the U.S. fleet, including ships that Americans continued to own after their lend-lease transfer to allies, accounted for half the world's total. These ships formed "the greatest merchant fleet in history," declared Frederick E. Hasler, the president of the New York State Chamber of Commerce.[26]

In the summer of 1952 the biggest, fastest, and most luxurious ship ever built in the United States was launched. It was named the *United States*, and although it was only the third-largest passenger ship in the world, behind the British liners *Queen Elizabeth* and *Queen Mary*, it was the fastest ever designed. "For the first time in many decades we are playing again in the major league of the North Atlantic," said Vice Admiral Edward Cochrane, chairman of the Federal Maritime Board. There was no excuse—no war or depression—for American ships not to meet the competition, and what European country could afford to construct a competitor? The federal government had subsidized the ship's construction and operating costs, as it had with other vessels, to maintain a healthy American-flag merchant fleet. President Truman declared his conviction of "the importance of such a fleet for reasons of national defense and our international commerce. The SS *United States* admirably serves both of these purposes."[27]

This was a superliner—a marvel of technology, designed by the naval architect William Gibbs, who had developed the mass-production methods of building liberty ships in World War II. The ship had watertight compartments with automatic doors that aimed at "unsinkability." The boasts were not small: "No single torpedo could sink her as one did the Lusitania. She could survive a collision like that which sank the ill-fated Titanic." To keep the ship fireproof, no wood was on the ship, except in the pianos and butchers' chopping blocks. Walls, doors, decks, and chairs were of aluminum, and the paint was fire resistant. The ship was almost completely air-conditioned. The design of the ship allowed for its rapid conversion from a liner carrying nearly two thousand passengers in comfort to a transport vessel carrying fourteen thousand troops. For this reason the ship's top speed, said to be as fast as a destroyer's, as well as details of its construction, were guarded secrets.[28]

To travelers crossing the Atlantic, the *United States* would look as modern and prodigious as any ship in the world. Its two giant stacks, the largest ever built, had fins to sweep the ship's exhaust away from the sun decks below. The hull was black and the superstructure white, topped by the stacks of red, white, and blue. The SS *United States* was built and run by United States Lines: "There is a very American cut to it," said a writer in the *New York Times Magazine*, "in the springing jut of the prow and in the easy modernity of the furnishing. There is great mass in its lines, but no bulkiness. From the outside it seems far too big an object to move at all, much less at better than thirty knots, but deep inside is a seething power plant that will handle that speed with ease. It is in many ways a ship to pop the eyeballs."[29]

When the *United States* set out on July 3, 1952, to race east across the Atlantic from New York, cutting through the white-flecked waves, it was chasing the previous Atlantic record of three days, twenty hours, and forty-two minutes, set in 1938 by the *Queen Mary*. The last time the Americans had led the world was in 1852, when the *Pacific* had crossed the Atlantic in over nine days. As the *United States* streaked past Bishop Rock off the coast of England near dawn, with a windstorm and heavy rain driving against the ship, the passengers celebrated with champagne, and the ship's band struck up the "Star Spangled Banner." The old record fell, with a time of three days, ten hours, and forty minutes. The new ship's skipper, Commodore Harry Manning, said, "I feel like a pitcher who has pitched a no-hit game." Chief Engineer William Kaiser said, "I believe the new records will stand for good," because of the ship's power held in reserve. As the *United States* crossed the path of the *Queen Mary* at sea, the British ship lowered her colors in courtesy. Setting another record on its return to America, the ship reentered New York harbor on a hot morning in July as the sun rose in a red haze veiling the skyscrapers. Fire boats sent up towering geysers as the ship moved past the Statue of Liberty, and ships blew horns. The thousands of spectators were astonished at the paint pealing from the black hull—a result of wave friction while the ship averaged over thirty-eight knots through the ocean. The *United States* was a symbol of a prodigious merchant marine: more merchant vessels flew the United States flag than any other into the 1950s.[30]

Yet the old ways of travel were rapidly being transformed. For the first time, in 1943, most passengers coming to or departing from the United States journeyed not by sea but by air. And the flag carriers of their choice, whether by sea or by air, were American.[31]

In the generation after 1903, the year the Wright brothers attached a motor to a glider, a succession of advances in the technology of flight had enabled the United States to begin a global airline. In 1927, when the United States had no overseas service at all, Juan Trippe merged three airlines into what became Pan American Airways, starting a route from Key West to Cuba. Three years later, Pan American was already the world's largest airline. Pan American opened routes to Puerto Rico and the Panama Canal Zone, and by the early 1930s it was flying deep into South America.

The airline conquered first the Pacific, instead of the Atlantic, after the lagging British had refused to grant landing rights to an American company until they were ready with their own overseas airline. Pan American put into service the most advanced craft for rapid speed over long distances: giant flying boats, the Clippers, named after the fast sailing ships Americans had once navigated to China and around the globe. The Clippers, landing at the airline's facilities on Midway, Wake, and Guam, brought American service to Manila in 1935, to Hong Kong in 1937, and to Singapore in 1941. In 1939 Pan American began transatlantic passenger service. By World War II Pan American's routes crisscrossed the globe. It was the only American overseas airline, and under Juan Trippe's leadership it became synonymous with the nation's aeronautical prestige and influence.[32]

Trippe envisioned a postwar American world airline greater than any in existence, including his own. "While we invented the airplane, and while we are today the greatest military air power in the world, we alone among the trading nations have no official policy to guide our overseas air transport effort in the Air Age. What shall we do?" he asked. "Shall we have ten or fifteen separate American airlines each competing with the other as well as with powerful foreign monopolies?" He wanted American enterprise to compete on even terms with the great foreign-flag air transport monopolies of Britain, Germany, France, Italy, Japan, the Netherlands, and Canada.[33]

After the war Trans World Airlines and Northwest Airlines mounted competition, but Trippe conceived of Pan American as the closest the United States had to a "chosen instrument," a giant national company approved by the government. He proposed to Congress that all American international air transportation in the postwar world be "united in a single enterprise, privately owned but under Government regulation." Consolidation of "all American-flag overseas and foreign air transportation operations into a single American company" would "best serve our national interests," he believed. Since Pan American had been the only American-flag airline in the prewar decades, he thought that all operations could be consolidated into it, or into a new supercompany. Although Congress never designated Pan American the nation's chosen instrument, the company continued to expand through its own resources, and after the defeat of Japan Pan American opened a route to Tokyo.[34]

In June 1947 Pan American, using the sleek Lockheed Constellation, began round-the-world flights. The first trip of 25,003 miles from New York to New York took thirteen days, which the daily press calculated to be one-sixth of the eighty days allowed by Jules Verne for a global voyage in the nineteenth century. Leaving New York, the plane, with Trippe aboard, landed at Gander, Newfoundland; Shannon, Ireland; London, Istanbul, Calcutta, Bangkok, Manila, Shanghai, Tokyo, Guam, Wake Island, Honolulu, San Francisco, and Chicago, its four powerful motors propelling the craft over oceans and continents. At ceremonies along the way, the travelers met Prime Minister Clement Attlee in London, Generalissimo Chiang Kai-shek in Shanghai, and General Douglas MacArthur in Tokyo. Back in New York Trippe was the first to step off the plane, and he spoke of the significance of the flight and the part played in it by American enterprise.[35]

The aeronautical breakthrough of the commercial jet plane came in the 1950s, above all with the Boeing 707. In October 1958 a Pan American jet soared off from New York across the Atlantic to bring American service to Europe, though bad weather forced the diversion of the flight from its scheduled destination of Paris to Brussels. Just a few weeks earlier the British had opened the first transatlantic jet service with its Comet, and a rivalry with the Americans developed. In November the American jet beat the British jet into New York from London by eleven minutes—even though the American plane had taken off thirty-six minutes after the British plane—and the headlines in New York the next day congratulated the winner: "707 Jet Outruns the Comet at Sea."[36]

Pan American, which grew into the most extensive global airline, carried the flag conspicuously on the side of its planes, and the Pan American logotype was omnipresent in the world's major capitals. The Pan American name became identified with the prestige and influence of the nation, in concert with the other overseas airlines and the merchant marine.

Banker to the World: Credit

Exports were not the only tools with which the United States influenced the world economy. Because American industry had developed capital resources far beyond those anywhere else in the world, the United States, the world's largest creditor nation, had the reputation of banker to the world. Only the United States had the capital that could be drawn on to revive the weakened industrial nations and to finance technological development in advancing areas. "The United States is the richest country in the world," Paul Samuelson said in 1948. "Also, it is the pace-setter in technological progress, and increasingly in setting fashions of standards of life. It is natural for the poor to want to borrow from the rich."[37]

This excess of capital had only become available in the twentieth century. From the Revolutionary War until 1914 Americans had lacked capital. The British had led the Europeans in heavy investment in the new nation, financing canals and cotton plantations, making it possible for Americans to pay for their imports, while aiding their capacity to produce. The inflowing foreign capital continued through the nineteenth century, underwriting railroads, steel mills, and agricultural machinery, though the significance of foreign investment as a proportion of total capital formation dwindled after the 1830s.

When the flow of international capital reversed in 1914, the United States became for the first time a creditor, and during World War I, all at once, it became the world's greatest. As the United States expanded its exports, it accumulated capital. Private citizens made loans to the warring Allied powers, which were selling their investments in America, and the government lent money to Britain and France for war materials.

Investment of capital resources abroad reached new dimensions after World War II. American business stood to gain from overseas investment by taking profits. Resources were waiting for development abroad, and people wanted to work even at low wages. In the late 1940s and the 1950s, *Changing Times* proclaimed that the opportunities for businessmen were unlimited, if only they applied their know-how. What they needed to provide was the capital and technology to get the industries started and the factories built.[38]

In return for an increased flow of investment, foreign industries could generate sales by more than enough for repayment. As Herbert Feis reasoned, the "investment we make partly out of a sense of duty *could* also bring us substantial economic advantage," but he balanced out the advantages for foreigners as well. "Our power to provide capital *could* provide a basis for economic improvement everywhere in which the more reasonable and constructive impulses of man could flourish; it *could* serve to lessen internal disputes, soften trade rivalries, reduce the need for exclusive economic bargains, and foster friendship among nations."[39]

The practical question usually asked by economists was not whether the United States should provide capital, but how it would provide all that was needed, particularly in places where it was most needed. Concerned about the sufficiency of foreign investment, John Kenneth Galbraith envisioned the United States performing the role of Britain in the nineteenth century, building things anew as Britons had once built railroads in, and for, other countries. This investment for local development was the kind that countries sought, Galbraith believed, but the United States had no tradition of general overseas investing apart from a spree in the 1920s. Nearly all the funds had been either to develop raw materials for the American market, such as oil, or to establish outlets to supplement the home market for manufactured goods.[40]

Expanded investment offered a significant contribution to world production and trade, potentially to benefit all involved. "The job is to participate in a worldwide capital expansion of a sort that will link our industries, our finances and our markets directly with every other country in the world," Henry Luce said. Luce found an American model in Westinghouse Electric International, which was negotiating deals to build factories in Mexico and China, and brought Chinese and Mexicans to America to learn how to run them. Westinghouse management did not fear, Luce gathered, that this investment was going to put the company out of the Chinese and Mexican waffle-iron and light-bulb markets, and certainly not out of the market for generators and high-technology equipment. Instead, this was to be the start of a mutually profitable association. The name "Westinghouse," Luce stated, had "gone into those countries to stay."[41]

No part of the globe had to lack industrial efficiency. China, which was much in Luce's mind as his adopted nation and regarded by Henry Wallace as a rising land after his wartime trip there, was certain, both men believed, to increase its material welfare through science and technology. The Chinese wanted a higher standard of living and would get it. With modern railroads and transportation the people would solve a basic fault in their agriculture—famine in one province while surpluses piled up in another. Hydroelectric plants and machinery—as well as the technical skill to go with the goods—were the tools to lift their living standards. In India, Nehru, who had read Galbraith's *The Affluent Society,* told the author, then serving as ambassador in New Delhi, that he did not care for the economic and social system described in the book, a system spoiled by congested highways and opulent gadgets. Galbraith, something of the critic at home, was less so abroad. With a wisp of the ironic, he felt that he had helped Nehru "find a hitherto unrevealed virtue in the uncomplicated poverty over which he presided." Yet Galbraith remained convinced that Indians could better their condition through an influx of technology and capital.[42]

And in Russia, even if the Soviets found capitalism abhorrent, they looked to American wealth and technical skill before all others. In 1944 Eric Johnston found Stalin more interested in hearing about American industry than about the Soviet factories Johnson had visited. "Undoubtedly American industry is more interesting," Stalin interjected. "Many of the large plants in the Soviet Union have been constructed with American help or with the benefit of American experience." Johnston agreed that he had seen American machines, techniques, and assembly lines in Soviet industry, but the Soviets still had a lot to learn: "In your terrifically congested cities people stand in long queues waiting in line to buy food. It is a waste of human energy that you can ill afford. You need better distribution to make for better efficiency. You have called in American production engineers. What you now need is American technical advice on distribution. A few experts from our chain stores who—"

"What's a chain store?" Stalin interrupted.

Johnston explained. "But," Stalin said, "in order to distribute, there must be something to distribute." Johnston's answer to that problem was for the Soviets to increase production of consumer goods, but to this suggestion he noticed Stalin shifting in his chair and even thought he heard a sigh, so he quickly changed the subject.

Stalin, after regaining his composure, told Johnston of his dream: to increase steel production. "We are going to double the size of our railroads; build bridges; use it for rehabilitation and reconstruction."

"In all of this program," Johnston wondered, "will you need American technical assistance, as well as heavy equipment?"

"Of course," Stalin answered. "We will need both. Soviet engineers have learned how to build good plants, but we will still need technical help."[43]

But to what extent did foreigners welcome American capital investment? Johnston had at first taken for granted that the Soviets did, yet Marxist theory had considered capital investment a tool of European imperialism and associated it with the exploitation of dependent peoples. Johnston was confronted by these charges on a trip he made to South America in the 1940s. President Getúlio Vargas of Brazil told him bluntly that South American nations intended to get rid of "imperialistic Capitalism." How would Americans like it in Washington, D.C., "if the utilities were totally owned and operated by foreigners," just as the utility companies in Rio de Janeiro were owned by foreign capital? Johnston replied that Americans would not like it. But he added that American transcontinental railroads had originally been financed in part by foreign capital. Eventually Americans were able to buy out the foreign stockholders. "That's what we're going to do down here," Vargas pointed out. Johnston noted that shares in the light and power company in Rio, owned by Americans and other foreign interests, were for the first time being sold to Brazilians. Private Brazilian ownership was to Johnston better than government nationalization, as had happened when the Argentinian government took over the railways and the telephone and telegraph companies owned by British and American interests. Investment in partnership with other peoples was not "Yankee imperialism" or "dollar diplomacy," Johnston declared. "It's a good-neighbor policy with more than talk to it."[44]

Capital nevertheless moved abroad in enormous quantities. As American private investment soared from $19 billion in 1950 to $49 billion in 1960, American corporations and businesses built plants and set up and ran newspapers, radio stations, hot-dog stands, advertising agencies, handicraft shops, cement factories, weaving shops, trucking depots, boating businesses, tourist services, farms, economic advisory services, engineering outfits, laundries, and hundreds of other enterprises. Giant international corporations such as GM, Ford, RCA, Mobil, Time-Life, and MGM opened factories and offices abroad and sold their goods locally. Exports had been the mainstay of the nation's foreign transactions, and though they continued to grow through the 1950s and 1960s, they were becoming less and less important in relation to the returns on foreign capital investment.[45]

As investment reached $81 billion in 1965, businessmen faced charges of economic invasion not only of developing countries but also of the developed nations of Europe: the sheer amount of capital investment and the prodigious size of American firms put them on the verge of taking over the European economy as a subsidiary of the American. George C. McGhee, a former businessmen and ambassador to West Germany, defended this investment. "American business in Germany is German business," he declared in an address at Düsseldorf. "It operates under German laws; pays German taxes; provides work for thousands of Germans; purchases goods and services giving work to other German business and industry; and—last but not least—makes a major contribution to Germany's overall exports." So, for McGhee, these "foreign connections can and do operate for the good of all concerned." Fears of foreign investment overwhelming Germany were unjustified, he told his listeners. How could Germany not benefit from American investment capital as well as from technical knowledge and managerial skill?[46]

"Compass of Enterprise": International Firms

Fortune pointed to the opening and expansion of international firms and plants as Americans were "doing good—by making money." Corporate enterprises like Esso, Westinghouse, and Sears, became symbols of America's economic dynamism.[47]

The Standard Oil Company of New Jersey, known as Esso, was by far the largest American overseas oil trader. Through affiliates in Europe and North Africa—selling one-fourth of all petroleum products marketed in the countries where it operated, more than any other company—Esso embarked on a global modernization strategy. In 1950, while Esso was completing its reconstruction of war-damaged plants and service stations, it planned to invest $150 million of capital to expand its refineries in England and France and to build a refinery in Antwerp, and it sought to meet the rising European demand by increasing production in the Middle East.

Esso's way of doing business abroad was lean and efficient, as it was at home. Since the 1890s Esso had been acquiring control or ownership of one European oil company after another. It operated plants, distributed petroleum in tank-cars and barges, and ran curbside pumps and filling stations all over the Continent. After World War II Esso's marketing coordinators in New York were also sounding a new motto, "Sales Security through Lower Costs." The managers began to take steps to teach its distributors how to boost sales and to cut the number of service stations, eliminating the need to supply places along narrow or steep roads, beyond light bridges, or in areas of scattered population.

Along with the economy program, Esso promoted aggressive merchandizing methods similar to those in the American market. The affiliates set up salesmanship courses to teach dealers to clean the motorists' windshields, check tires and oil, and give maps and road advice. In Germany, Esso customer service included providing beer or coffee in waiting rooms. If Britain's petrol dealers did little to increase sales through antiquated service customs, the results of Esso's marketing education in the Low Countries sometimes astonished even Esso officials from New York: When an Esso expert drove up to a darkened Belgian station late at night and rang for service, a neon sign promptly flashed him the message *"J'arrive"* (I'm coming).

Esso also prospered through another efficient American way of business: plowing back profits for future profits. Esso devoted more than twice the $160 million it earned after dividends to step up production and expand the capabilities of its refineries, tankers, and pipelines. The company aimed to continue reaping the substantial profits it had made since the 1930s from the sale of foreign oil.[48]

Westinghouse International, like Esso, had plans for overseas expansion. It offered for export some three hundred thousand products—the total line of electrical appliances and equipment turned out in its American plants. The company sold entire power plants and industrial facilities to customers around the world. Several packaged plants went to Russia during the days of lend-lease, and technical equipment was provided for a cement plant in Chile, for a Cuban sugar mill, and for a chain of Turkish airfields.

But Westinghouse took an interest in direct, expansive activity. It did not buy factories all over the world, as General Electric and General Motors had done, but instead licensed foreign manufacturers to use its inventions and processes, and it helped them lay out their own plants and train their technicians. By offering licenses, management had reevaluated the decision taken after World War I to liquidate most of its foreign investments. Westinghouse had a worldview: in the office of President William E. Knox were autographed portraits of national leaders of very different outlooks, including Nehru, Churchill, and Franco. It did business in 123 nations and territories, though not with the Soviet Union and its satellites.

With its exports and licenses, Westinghouse was consciously teaching its skills abroad, and at the main works in East Pittsburgh foreign engineers gathered information for the use of licensees. At the East Pittsburgh Westinghouse graduate engineering school, foreign students also worked alongside American college graduates. The faculty figured that the foreigners would "stay impressed by Westinghouse for a long time": In one long aisle of the home plant, a foreign student might see "in various stages of construction, more generating capacity than his whole country possesses." The foreign licensees employed a hundred thousand people worldwide, slightly more than the parent company itself, and together they produced a considerable percentage of the world's total electrical capacity. Among the European licensees were the English Electric Co., Belgium's largest electrical manufacturer, and a major French supplier. Through these firms Westinghouse technology was routed to Africa and other colonial regions. The assistant general manager of the company believed that the "backward areas" of the world needed managerial talent even worse than dollars.

The chief uncertainty about Westinghouse's future was the extent to which Europe would recover. Europe was not competing well and Japan seemed like a long shot. Westinghouse salesmen believed "the facilities behind them in Pittsburgh and the other plants are so strong—from the viewpoint of product quality as well as delivery dates— that the company can take business away from foreign firms that may underbid it." Management had no fear of the rest of the world catching up with Westinghouse International in technology, because the company was crediting its royalties and fees against the vast sums spent on research. The attitude was one of can-do. President Knox was known to buzz for his assistant general manager, as he glanced at the big map of the world on the wall, and say, "You know, Bob, it just occurred to me . . . ."[49]

The wide selection of goods offered by Sears, Roebuck represented abundance. David Potter had reported Franklin Roosevelt's assertion that, if he could place one American book in the hands of every Russian, the volume of his choice would be a Sears catalogue. Sears was shut out of markets in Russia, but in a postwar push abroad it opened them up in Cuba, Mexico, and Venezuela. In 1949 Sears expanded into Rio de Janeiro and Saõ Paulo. Company managers conceived of Sears as Brazil's first department store, marketing a full range of goods for the home, kitchen, garage, workshop, and garden. Even though Brazil had the equivalent of a five-and-dime chain, Sears was revolutionary in offering one-stop shopping.

Consumer goods from the United States enabled the Sears outlets in Brazil to set sales records. Shoppers flocked to the stores until the Brazilian government, trying to beat the mounting dollar shortage, put a virtual embargo on American imports. So Sears buyers tried to get products—from scissors and needles to nails and knives—locally. But they found that the quantity of Brazilian goods was insufficient, quality was not up to American standards, and prices were nearly prohibitive.

Sears recognized the need to give technical advice to Brazilian suppliers. It set about teaching them the virtues of mechanization and the benefits of imported equipment and efficient factory-floor practice in assembly lines. The company taught suppliers not to overstock raw materials and understock inventory of goods, but it had trouble overcoming old customs. One manufacturer gave his price for a thousand lots of a dozen clothespins, and when later asked the unit cost of ten thousand lots, he gave a higher price, because, he explained, expanded production would involve him in more work, and if the item was going to be so popular, he reasoned, why not charge the public more for it?

Sears revolutionized sales in Brazil. Full-page advertisements in newspapers were becoming frequent, their design imitative of the Sears format. Stores were preparing to build escalators, install air-conditioning, and provide one-day truck delivery service, counter displays, and money-back policies. Instead of customers having to deal with a succession of salesclerks, cashiers, and package wrappers, they would get their wrapped packages instantly when they paid their cash.

No one at Sears voiced fears of Brazilian competition, because the imitators of American goods were few and the work difficult to match in its sophistication. Although, with only two stores, Sears could not hope to have exclusive rights to merchandise for long, the company was plowing back profits. Brazil had no means to export the items it produced and had no foreign distributors.

In all, Sears was doing more than making money. Sears declared its own revolution in Brazil, and *Fortune* noted: "To say that it will make the U.S. popular would be silly." The United States was "already popular" in Brazil. But Sears could "advance the standing of U.S. business, including capital goods and semifinished mass-production items with which Brazil will not compete in the foreseeable future." Beyond that, it was anybody's guess.[50]

The World Money: Currency

The predominant position of the American economy led to its currency becoming the standard of international payments. Economists ascribed a key importance to the dollar because of the huge demand for American products in a widespread trading area. The dollar was strong because it was the currency of the world's greatest producer and exporter. It was also strong because it was backed by stockpiles of gold. By the end of World War II the United States had accumulated $21 billion in gold, about 60 percent of the world's supply, stockpiling much of it in the vaults of Fort Knox in Kentucky. By dint of these financial resources, peoples all over the world actually accepted the dollar as a better holding than gold.[51]

The dollar had taken the place of the previous world standard, the British pound sterling. In the nineteenth century, when London was the world's leading financial center, the pound's prestige caused France, the United States, Germany, and Japan eventually to adopt the gold standard. Britain maintained the gold standard until 1914, and in the 1920s the United States began to participate in the regulation of a new gold standard. After the stock market crash in 1929 and the onset of the Depression, the Bank of England ceased conversion of pounds into gold in 1931 and the pound became a floating currency. Country after country followed suit and abandoned the gold standard. Finally, the United States did too.

The World War II fear of German expansion caused gold to flow into the United States, supporting the dollar's ascension to the standard world currency by 1940. After the war the difference between what foreigners could earn in dollars and what they needed to buy in dollars became known as the "dollar problem," "dollar shortage," or "dollar gap." America was so enormously rich and bought so little abroad that America's customers could not earn enough dollars for their needs, and they were depleting their dollar holdings. Economists could measure the dollar gap in billions of dollars— about $11.5 billion in 1947 and $2.2 billion in 1950—but it also had its human costs. Foreigners were spending their dwindling foreign exchange and gold reserves to buy food, raw materials, and various goods that the United States produced in record quantities. Paul Samuelson wrote: "The great and universal 'dollar shortage,' . . . is the financial counterpart of the great need in Europe for food, fertilizer and capital equipment that only America can provide."[52]

For the economist C. P. Kindleberger, the dollar shortage reflected the comparatively strong economic position of American productive capacity: "At basis the explanation for the chronic world shortage of dollars is to be found in the technical superiority of the United States in the production of many goods necessary to a high modern standard of living." The United States "had large and fairly balanced natural resources, relatively modern and efficient capital equipment, a comparatively small population in relation to natural resources and capital equipment, but a large domestic market for the output of its own mass-production industries."[53]

The American position was so strong that American economists began to consider that their nation might be emancipated completely from worry about spending too much abroad, whether on luxury items, travel, or foreign aid. "Theoretically, of course, the world's payments system could adjust itself to any level of dollar outflow, but in practice these adjustments are sluggish and difficult in a world of managed economies," stated Raymond Mikesell, who advised the State Department. "It is quite possible, therefore, that a world system of multilateral payments may require a continually expanding flow of dollars to the rest of the world." *Newsweek* entitled a column "Dollar Shortage Forever," and *United States News* observed that "a turnabout is years away for most areas, and may never occur on a very large scale."[54]

It did not at first seem to Americans as a whole that their success in trade, investment, and currency posed a threat to that very success, but American exports would grow only so long as foreign countries could afford them. What foreigners received they had to pay for by drawing on their cash or assets, and their capital was running out. In 1947 Britain faced bankruptcy, as it was depleting its own overseas capital and had spent nearly all of a $3.75 billion loan; Holland had been selling its American securities; and France had nearly exhausted its gold reserves. Canada and Latin America were accumulating massive deficits. The United States was failing to replenish the world's wealth. It was like a poker game. When "one player gets all the chips, the game breaks up," Robert Heilbroner thought. "It would be a gloomy prospect to feel that our export-import trade balance would never even out; that we must go on forever facing an incipient export collapse and bailing it out with fruitless loans." Galbraith worried that "drastic steps" might be necessary to close the dollar gap. What could be done to spread dollars abroad?[55]

Americans might import more, sending from what John Condliffe called "the largest and most influential sector of the world economy" a large and steady supply of dollars to foreign producers. But Americans were reluctant to import. They did not need or want foreign goods. Self-sufficiency had been an American virtue, hearkening back to life on the frontier and the Puritan work ethic. Besides, the products that bore the imprint "Made in America" had the reputation of top quality for low price. In comparison, foreign goods were commonly of inferior quality and overpriced. "Importing unfortunately has the odious connotation of coolie labor and sweatshop goods," explained Heilbroner.[56]

Faced with this resistance, the government began to coax Americans to buy foreign goods. President Truman told American consumers that the "way to keep our economy on an even keel and keep it expanding is to encourage and help the development of the rest of the world. There will come a time when many of the things we need we will have to get from outside of the United States." Those needs, Truman quickly added, were the kinds of raw materials an advanced nation required. It was a classic formulation—a great metropolis taking in the resources of the hinterlands in exchange for modern manufactured goods or currency reserves. Americans might have to "go to Labrador and to Liberia to get the ore necessary to keep our steel plants running," to Bolivia and Malaya for tin, and to Indonesia for rubber. Give other peoples a proper return for the things we need, Truman determined, so that we can keep our own great production program going. "We can expand only if the world expands."[57]

Like Truman, President Eisenhower encouraged imports of raw materials for industry—tin for canning food, columbite and cobalt in the manufacture of alloys, and manganese for steel. These imports were "effectively strengthening our friends in the world at large—strengthening them not only to fortify their own economies . . . but also to buy from us what we must sell to the world." The president believed that domestic production had been spurred on by goods paid for in friendly countries: half a million refrigerators and home-type freezers, more than $250 million worth of machine tools and agricultural machinery, and more than a quarter of the total production of lubricating oil. "Now, these facts and figures affect every American, no matter who he is: all who work on our farms, all who labor in our industries. They can signify for our whole economy the difference between productive profit and paralyzing loss."[58]

The government pleaded the case for things foreign. The State Department informed Americans that they should be willing to accept the foreign goods they needed, mainly raw materials to keep factories and assembly lines running. To make its point, a State Department pamphlet—the publication of which made front-page coverage of the *New York Times*—told the story of the fictional Johnsons, an "average American family" of four, and the trials they would face in an America cut off from imported goods. Their mounting troubles began when Jim Johnson lost his job at the steel mill because it had been unable to get metals for mixing the iron ore. His mood worsened when he had to give up smoking, because cigarettes made wholly of American tobacco tasted flat. At breakfast Jim's coffee and his wife's tea were missing. The children wanted bananas, but none could be found. The television set could not be repaired because the tubes had been made of imported metals. The telephone was gone—forty-eight imports had made it possible—so Jim could not phone the drugstore for a medical prescription. He had to walk to the drugstore because gasoline was expensive and the car was growing old. And so on. The United States, the report added, needed foreign

materials to keep radar and other electronic equipment essential to defense in operation.[59]

The exhortations to increase imports were aimed at returning equilibrium to the
world economy by distributing dollars. Americans realized this principle. Of a sample
polled during World War II, 65 percent agreed that the "best way to make sure of
prosperity in this country after the war is to make sure that other countries are in a
position to buy goods from us. . . . There just can't be prosperity in one country for long
unless all countries are prosperous." In 1944, 68 percent were in favor of the United
States buying more products from other countries. Again the usual assumption was that
Americans would spend their rising levels of income on raw materials, quantities of oil,
copper, and high-grade bauxite. They might perhaps buy increased loads of foreign
coffee, sugar, hides, and furs. Or they might be attracted to exotic luxuries—English
clay for tennis courts, Florentine leather, alabaster, and gift-shop items. These were
indulgences, however, that most Americans were not then interested in. They usually
sought what was practical and productive—the resources to fuel their factories.[60]

Even as individuals accepted some foreign goods, their purchases were not large-
scale, nor were they expected to be any time soon. American companies found it far
easier to sell their goods in distant countries than to sell foreign goods at home. In 1944
Westinghouse planned to go into the importing business and shortly after the war put its
considerable managerial skills and capital resources into selling Italian silk, Danish
silverware, Mexican whisk brooms, and Argentinian alligator handbags. Although
successful in selling its electrical equipment abroad, Westinghouse took heavy losses
on these foreign handicrafts in the United States. Seeking imports that could be sold at a
profit, the company after 1947 obtained industrial raw materials to feed American
industry—chrome from Turkey and South America, manganese and mica from India,
and tungsten from Australia. Not until 1949 did the Westinghouse import division make
money.[61]

Before the world ran out of dollars, the United States had to send dollars abroad,
and it contrived to do so through increased trade and flow of capital investment—and,
as we shall see, foreign aid and grants. But an equilibrium had not been achieved.
Stronger measures than these were contemplated.

The International Trade Organization

The United States adopted a new outlook on international efforts to regulate world
currency, investment, and trade. This outlook derived from the view that the domestic
economy was inextricably connected with the world economy. The Depression had
important consequences for this realization of postwar American economic thought
concerning the continuation of Hull trade agreements and the movement of capital to
borrowing nations. But these accommodations were bilateral, and problems of trade
restriction, capital needs, and currency regulation were clearly multilateral, calling for

solutions among many nations. World prosperity, Alvin Hansen stated, depended in no small measure on two American actions: (a) the achievement of full employment within the United States, and (b) the active, wholehearted cooperation of the United States in the development of international economic organizations designed to ensure a new world order.[62]

The conception of United States participation in international organizations was a great leap for economists because they acknowledged the failure of any one nation to regulate unilaterally the world economy. It was the United States government, despite its considerable power to pursue unilateral interests, that invited representatives of the leading nations to work out procedures of international economic cooperation.

At Bretton Woods in New Hampshire's White Mountains in July 1944, these representatives presented their positions. The Americans and the British each had earlier prepared plans for the postwar economic world order, and the British sent their best minds to the United States to present their ideas of an international central bank. John Maynard Keynes was the author of the British plan, and Harry D. White of the Treasury Department readied the American position. But the power of the American economy held sway over the sophistication of technical experts. As John Williams wrote in *Foreign Affairs* in 1944, the pressing problem of the postwar world was the need for nations to lend and to borrow, and the United States was the great creditor. He considered the United States to be in a far stronger position than Britain had been prior to 1914, when it had held a central role in trade and the pound sterling was the world currency. Not only was the United States an industrial nation, like Britain, but it had an agricultural base, and though England had been a creditor on income account, it had a deficit in its balance of merchandise trade. The United States had both a favorable balance of trade and was collecting interest on its capital exports.[63]

The Americans made some concessions to their wartime partners, but mainly the American plan prevailed. The Bretton Woods representatives recognized the dollar as the linchpin of a new international monetary system. They in effect replaced the gold standard with a system based on the dollar, by setting up a reserve supply of money in the International Monetary Fund, which the nations could draw on to maintain stable rates between different moneys.

The Bretton Woods Conference also devised international procedures for the movement of capital. Despite the growth in American private foreign investment, economists feared it was insufficient to meet the worldwide demands for capital, and some entrepreneurs, remembering the rapid expansion of overseas investment in the 1920s and its subsequent contraction, were anxious about foreign bonds and stocks. What it meant to be the world's largest creditor hit home with the onset of the Depression: when Americans stopped lending abroad, international trade fell apart; debts were defaulted worldwide.

To encourage investment in countries that needed the influx of capital, the representatives at Bretton Woods established the International Bank for Reconstruction and Development, known as the World Bank. "The chief purpose of the Bank," as the chairman of the American delegation, Secretary of the Treasury Henry Morgenthau, stated near the end of the conference, was "to guarantee private loans made through the usual investment channels." Only when private capital was "not available on reasonable terms" would the bank supplement it by providing finance for productive purposes out of its own resources.[64]

America would wield influence commensurate with its financial resources in the World Bank, which became the world's largest multilateral aid organization. The United States contributed about a third of the bank's capital to provide long-term loans for development of industry and natural resources. Other member nations contributed their share. This was the way of international cooperation of which Alvin Hansen approved. The logic was simple: "The Bretton Woods Plans are international in scope. As such they are superior to bilateral arrangements," which were threatened by economic nationalism and isolationism, rival economic blocs, and international friction.[65]

Still, American proposals, resources, and influence held sway at Bretton Woods. " 'As America goes, so goes the world' may be an exaggeration," Henry Morgenthau admitted. "But it is a pardonable exaggeration in a world made one by time and fate, in which America's strength and potentialities are perhaps more clearly realized by the rest of the world than by the American people itself." So, when Roosevelt urged Congress to adopt the Bretton Woods agreements in February 1945, he used words that he had first used nine years earlier in a period of catastrophic depression: "This generation has a rendezvous with destiny."[66]

The United States aimed further to organize free trade on a global scale. The State Department pamphlet *Proposals for Expansion of World Trade and Employment*, prepared late in 1945 as the formal American plan for the world's trade, offered countries a choice of struggling against each other "for wealth and power" or working "together for security and mutual advantage." The stakes were the improvement of living standards everywhere, which the United States sought to achieve through freedom in trade. Although the reciprocal trade agreements were extended in 1945, the new proposals represented a great reorientation of Secretary Hull's bilateral reciprocal program: the free trade program would transcend itself to become multilateral.[67]

Following these proposals, Americans took a leading role in developing a charter for world trade drafted at the international conferences on trade in London in 1946 and refined in Geneva in 1947. The General Agreement on Tariffs and Trade was signed in Geneva in October 1947 by twenty-three countries, which among them accounted for four-fifths of world trade. On the same day, the United States, Britain, France, Belgium, the Netherlands, and five other countries accepted a protocol bringing the agreement into force on January 1, 1948. Support for the agreement was forthcoming from the American people. Of those who had heard of it, 63 percent were in favor.[68]

The GATT, as it was called, prompted nations to conform to a uniform policy of nondiscrimination and reduced tariffs. But its creation was preliminary to a final American proposal to be concluded at Havana in 1948: the formation of a new body to regulate world trade, the International Trade Organization.[69]

The rationale for an ITO began with the belief that it would simply not be enough to hold occasional international conferences on commercial policy. A continuous institution "always . . . on the job" was essential to Alvin Hansen's hope for world trade. Critics in the State Department dismissed any declaration of "broad generalities, without definite rules, without specific commitments, and without provisions for implementation," and President Truman stated that the formation of the ITO was necessary to complete the work that had been begun in the interim GATT and "to achieve the objectives of the Atlantic Charter."[70]

The ITO would interpret and administer the GATT and give its principles authority. The ITO would collect information, make analyses, promote international agreements, and render technical assistance to governments. It would facilitate consultations and sponsor negotiations between member states. Most important, it would settle disputes. As the American charter proposed for the ITO, it would be the final authority for trade matters: If a member complained of unfair treatment in trade, it could bring the case before the Executive Board for arbitration. The board might officially sanction corrective action by releasing the complaining member from any of its trade obligations. It would judge which nations overprotected their markets, whether by high tariffs or by other means, including government restrictions or quotas on imports, and which nations were entitled to some protection. The objectivity of the ITO stood to end the bickering and resentment among nations that put up trade barriers.[71]

The ITO was also to complete the work of Bretton Woods by cooperating closely with the International Monetary Fund and the World Bank. Through comprehensive action in the areas of currency, capital, and trade, Hansen said, the international trade authority would promote "an optimum international division of labor based upon the utmost development of resources both human and material throughout the world." As Claire Wilcox, another ITO supporter, explained, the trade organization was the missing link, "designed to take its place beside the . . . Bank, and the Fund among the specialized agencies of the United Nations." The ITO was what Dean Acheson called the "capstone" of the economic structure that America had been trying to erect.[72]

The ITO would be a cooperative organization. Believing that unilateral pursuit would "not work; it leads to disaster," Norman Burns, an adviser to the Office of International Trade Policy, expected the ITO to benefit countries that were not so dynamic in world trade as the United States and had difficulty competing. Since the "chief balance-of-payment problem" was argued to be "the world shortage of dollars resulting from the overwhelming demand of other countries for products obtainable only in the United States," the poor countries could use quotas to favor imports from countries that had adequate supplies of foreign exchange.[73]

But the United States, by virtue of its economic power, would have certain privileges. Its voice would be the strongest and the most consistently heeded because it had the most to teach about successful economic development and it would have permanent representation on a governing board. The American "position of world leadership" would make "its actual influence in ITO far greater than its single vote might indicate," the State Department assured Americans.[74]

The ITO was the ultimate effort to extend domestic free trade policy into the international arena. "We look forward to the day when the differences between doing business abroad and doing business at home will be much less than at present," Acheson said. He hoped that, as within America, currencies abroad would be kept stable, trade and travel would be opened up, and investment risk would be reasonable. Just "as every State in our union recognizes that the immeasurable advantages of membership in our Federal system far outweigh the occasional defeats which it suffers in the Congress, so nearly every delegation at Habana saw that the loss involved in the concessions it had to make was eclipsed by the great gains of the charter as a whole."[75]

American action would show the way to international organization: this was the final State Department rationale, and the United States had put its prestige behind it. "The United States has become the economic giant of the world. What this country does, affects the lives, thoughts, and hopes of the Italian factory worker using American cotton to make cloth, of the English city dweller consuming American meat, of the Congo copper miner selling metal to America, of the Australian wheat farmer competing with us in world markets. . . . Our example will largely determine whether other countries adopt" the organization. So rejection of it by the United States would weaken its "leadership in the international economic sphere."[76]

But this argument by the government was soon contradicted by its action: the United States in the end rejected the ITO, and it did so on the grounds that it would not sacrifice any prerogative of its preeminence. Acheson did not blame the Soviets for the failure of these efforts at international cooperation. Even after relations between the United States and the Soviet Union had turned sour, he still pressed for passage of the ITO in 1949. This move was up to the United States. Several Western governments endorsed the proposals, as did many other countries in regions that were both economically backward and advanced; creditors and debtors; producers of manufactured goods and providers of raw materials; countries that had deficits in their balance of payments and others that had surpluses. But in 1950 the Truman administration firmly decided not to seek congressional approval of the charter. The whole organization was rejected, not because of communism but because of a failure among the allies to agree. The ITO was dead.[77]

To this point there was consensus; beyond it, on the issue of international economic organizations, the consensus was under strain. Henry Wallace, who had opposed unregulated free enterprise and cartels at home, looked to international organizations as the proper way to regulate excesses in trade and investment abroad, whether American, British, or German. When Wallace had proposed in 1943 to President Roosevelt that a United Nations Organization "be set up *now*," a specific function of it was to be formulation of "world-wide policies regarding international cartels, so as to prevent these 'private governments' from thwarting the true peace aims of the common peoples of the world."[78]

But American businessmen who opposed government control of buying and selling at home also opposed it abroad. They countenanced the control of investment and currency, again as they did at home, but not of trade and private business. In 1949 *Fortune* called the ITO "worthless," and its charter an "extremely disappointing document" and a "wretched compromise." The *Fortune* editors did not want weaker governments to set trade policy in the ITO, thereby discriminating against U.S. products, nor did they want the debtor nations to control the ITO. They wanted instead an American trade policy directed from America, without compromise.[79]

Rejecting an organized cooperative approach, *Fortune* presented a vision of unilateral glory. The ITO would even fail to satisfy anyone who thought that "the U.S. is powerful and rich enough to afford some generosity and courage in its foreign economic policy." American policy would be more enlightened, even more idealistic, *Fortune* contended, than a world policy. The American government was not only powerful enough to protect the interests of its own businessmen but was also the only one "in any position to befriend the neglected rights of foreign individuals as well." The United States would model its world market not on a universal dream but on the example of the old British Empire. "In the whole history of the world, there has been only one market that could be termed a world market. It was the market created and sustained by British free trade, and it lasted about seventy years (1846–1914). This market was made not by consultation and agreement among the nations, but by the bold unilateral action of one strong nation; the others, most of them indifferent or hostile to capitalism, went along because it paid, and became more or less capitalist as a result. If we wish a world market, we must start making it ourselves."[80]

Of course, it was taken for granted that the economic preeminence of the United States in these manufactured goods was permanent, for no one could foresee a day when the United States might be weak in trade or a debtor. But would the United States be better off in the event its power declined?

The rejection of an international organization to oversee world trade did not shake American interest in the expansion of free trade. President Truman reaffirmed his faith in the reciprocal agreements, President Eisenhower called for them to be strengthened, and Congress repeatedly extended them into the 1960s. Even when foreign industry began to penetrate a few American markets in the 1950s, and a dozen American industries complained of imports that threatened their own production, free trade remained strongly in vogue. In 1952 President Truman turned down higher tariffs on Swiss watches, and Eisenhower subsequently rejected them on scissors and shears from Germany and Italy. No action was contemplated against "cheap" woolen gloves and mittens from Hong Kong and Japan. After all, these countries were buying more from America than America was from them. If "we wish to sell abroad we must buy abroad," Eisenhower declared. It was a decision, said Luce's *Time,* that pitted the interests of industries that sought protection against "the nation's overriding interest in freer trade."[81]

Even without an administrative body, the free trade principles of the GATT continued to have the full support of the American government: No trade discrimination of any kind should be allowed. The most-favored-nation provision was to be upheld. Customs unions and free trade associations would be legitimate means of trade regulation, provided those arrangements did not discriminate against third countries. The principles of agreement included various qualifications. Nations might be exempted from free trade provisions because of balance-of-payments disequilibrium; serious damage to domestic production; the requirements of economic development; the need to protect raw materials; and the interests of national security.

So the overall result of the GATT was that after World War II tariff barriers and currency restrictions among nations were diminished. But the allowance for exemptions, without a means to pass judgment on offenders, would permit two nations in a trade dispute to claim they were upholding the GATT. One could charge that the other had denied its access to markets and present a case according to the GATT's principles; the other nation could claim in turn that it had the right to protective measures according to the GATT's exemptions. In consequence, different nations, depending on their own economic circumstances and on their political and military ambitions, preferred varying mixtures of restriction and freedom. Because of the inability to take corrective action, disputes endangered the future equilibrium of the trading system.

The long-term performance of economic programs helped to stimulate a general postwar prosperity and stability. Relatively free multilateral trade, toward which the United States took the lead by reducing tariffs, contributed to the boosting of national income of trading countries. The magnitude of the capital provided to other countries by private entrepreneurs, government, or international agencies supported the postwar recovery of industrial economies and the development of new nations. In addition, during the period of the great strength of the American dollar from the 1940s through the 1950s, exchange rates of the world currencies, which were pegged to the dollar, remained relatively stable. Only occasional fundamental irregularities in the balance of payments of troubled countries caused their currencies to be revalued.

Americans as a whole lived better because they received profits from their sales and investments abroad, which added to their wealth and allowed them to increase imports of goods and luxuries from abroad. Other peoples were not as a whole worse off for having to buy and borrow from Americans, not when the capital provided borrowers with the opportunity to build up their domestic production, which created more wealth than had to be sent to American lenders in interest and dividends and might allow prospective local buyers ultimately to purchase the companies. Development depended above all on each country's resources, labor, and technology, and many peoples who received what Americans provided used it to advantage. During the period that America made available more funds and goods than any other lender and trader, West Germany turned recovery into a miracle of development. Throughout Western Europe, in the Netherlands, France, Italy, Greece, and Austria, similar phenomena occurred.

Japan embarked on an advance hardly ever before equaled in history. Taiwan and Korea raced forward. Around the world, whether in Brazil or Mexico, countries found paths to sustained growth.

Americans with incomes far above the subsistence level raised expectations of developing peoples to deal with problems once considered normal conditions of life—floods, famines, and sickness. Yet the record of American enterprise was mixed when locals had the sensation of being reduced to the rank of economic colonials. The Europeans, along with the Latin Americans and peoples of developing countries, resented their debts when the strict motivation of foreign business was to make profits without reinvestment locally or consideration of the social consequences of development. Investments might take years to be paid off, or might not be paid off at all.

How could the abuses have been avoided? One way would have been for the United States to have acted concertedly through the international organizations it had been instrumental in setting up but had backed away from or neglected to utilize fully. The nation failed to support the International Trade Organization, and its support for the World Bank and the International Monetary Fund was limited relative to the extent of developmental needs. While international organizations would have helped protect others from the abuses of unilateral penetration of trading goods and investment, the organizations would also have helped to protect the United States from foreign abuses by rising trading nations—though this was seldom thought of in those days when America's world role was at high tide—in the event the economic system faltered.

The last word was that American economic activity helped to teach other peoples. The American lesson was that by utilizing technology and taking advantage of investment and assuming a can-do attitude, they could rise above poverty and achieve comforts. Countries seeking modernization could imitate American ways, but not necessarily as Americans might have desired that development to take place. Other peoples could borrow capital and technology to create new enterprises and learn how to make their own steel and manufactured goods with new methods using their own managerial and organizational prescriptions. Institutions and services—corporate structures, agricultural services, and government bureaucracies—were not necessarily transferable to other cultures.

The benefits of the American example were open to observation by friend and foe alike, who were ready to choose and adapt what they wanted to their own social imperatives. These peoples might engage labor and management to work cooperatively, rather than competitively, or involve novel mixtures of private initiative and state planning in economic development. In the long-term future, these peoples forged their development and prosperity.

10

Foreign

Aid

Foreign aid was a new way for a powerful state to deal with the world's nations. Past empires had conquered weak states to demand tribute and increase their wealth. In victory, Soviet Russia extracted materiel from Germany and the Eastern European states that its armies occupied. The Soviets demanded reparations, carried off equipment from still-standing factories, and confiscated food supplies. Even in friendly Manchuria, the Soviets plundered Chinese allies and removed steel mills. The way of American aid was different.[1]

The conception of foreign aid stemmed directly from a unique position of wealth. Whereas by the end of World War II the world economy's machinery of production and distribution had broken down, America's great industrial plant provided the United States with a surplus of wealth. A prerogative of the world's greatest creditor nation was to demand that reparations and debts be paid, but the likelihood of receipt was poor if exports and investment did not by themselves repair the breakdown. The United States was the only country with sufficient resources to share them with many nations.

But foreign aid was not the result only of this condition of wealth. Distribution of foreign aid followed the measure of charity that the rich Americans had given to the poor at home. Since the Gilded Age, philanthropic industrialists like Andrew Carnegie, John D. Rockefeller, and Henry Ford felt a self-proclaimed duty—a gospel of wealth, Carnegie called it—to give to the poor. These rich men distributed millions from their fortunes to feed the needy and to build libraries and medical schools. They set up private philanthropic organizations, the largest of which after World War II was the Ford Foundation. The rich had not been forced to give their wealth away, but they established a tradition of businesslike giving of aid. In like manner, the American nation was responsible to give to poor nations.

Corporations and the government itself, which had taken on the responsibility of contributing to domestic welfare since the New Deal, had a social purpose to help peoples around the globe in their development. Recalling that businessmen had declared themselves in favor of the social planning of the National Recovery Act of 1933, the historian Richard Hofstadter drew a connection with world aid: "Just as the Chamber of Commerce's NRA idea had been clothed in the language of the liberal social planners and had brought gains to the most hard-ridden sections of the working class, so a new American conquest of world markets might well go forth under the banner of international welfare work." Foreign aid by the government seemed "characteristic" of American life.[2]

Both liberals and conservatives believed in the humanitarian benefits of international aid. Virtually no one dissented. Aid represented an American consensus. Ordinarily conservative businessmen, consumed by the adventure of foreign expansion, driven by patriotism, or convinced that business enterprise could put the world right, joined with liberals, who saw the aid spreading America's New Deal internationally. They looked to more than the need to keep the United States exporting by bridging the dollar gap. Henry Luce proposed that America be the "Good Samaritan" of the world. "It is the manifest duty of this country to undertake to feed all the people of the world who as a result of this worldwide collapse of civilization are hungry and destitute." For every dollar Americans spent on armaments, Luce wanted Americans to spend at least a dime in a gigantic effort to feed the poor abroad. Farmers would be encouraged to produce greater harvests and "a humanitarian army of Americans" would distribute the food free of charge.[3]

Like Luce, the liberals who agreed with Henry Wallace wanted Americans to go all out for aid. Wallace became notorious for a remark he supposedly made that milk for Hottentots was an American war aim. He clarified his position after the columnist Arthur Krock charged that Wallace wanted the United States to be spendthrift. Puzzled by this commentary, Wallace wrote to Krock, "I do not now and never have had in mind that the United States would over a long period of time play the role of Santa Claus to the rest of the world." But he strongly believed that Americans had a responsibility to help developing countries increase agricultural efficiency and, later, industrialization. The "charity angle of this work," he insisted, should be "tapered off" as quickly as possible and be replaced by a permanent policy of self-help.[4]

Wallace was an advocate for the application abroad of some of the New Deal social welfare programs. Having once recommended an ever-normal granary to weather bad times in America, he urged establishment of international granaries to ease world food shortages. He also supported an international investment corporation to assist development. He backed off when it came to the United States building Tennessee Valley Authorities in other parts of the globe. Other nations should create TVA-like projects of their own. "There ought to be a TVA on the Danube, another on the Ganges, another on the Ob, and another on the Parana." Americans could give technical advice and even sell at low cost the modern machinery needed to build the dams.[5]

Consensus existed over the propriety of foreign aid. But foreign aid would come in many forms—financial aid in currency or credits, goods or technology, or military weaponry. It could be granted through government agencies or distributed through international organizations. The theory of aid could easily be reduced to simple economic terms or be raised to a moral plane.

The economics of aid were straightforward: America had the resources to apply toward avoiding another Great Depression and also to improve the standard of living of poor countries. John Kenneth Galbraith analyzed assistance as a free flow of goods to Europe, "where the standard of living necessary for decency and conventional comfort—a standard which must be met if men are not to search for desperate solutions—is higher than can be supplied from the resources of that community." America would provide the food, fuel, and other necessities of life, as well as steel, industrial equipment, farm machinery, and other capital goods to repair war damage and depleted plant.[6]

The moral dimension of aid raised questions: What were the motives behind this aid? Was it given out of ideals or self-interest? Should aid be given openly to needy people, whether or not democratic, of whatever form of government? Should it be given to exert pressure on other societies? These dilemmas complicated the problem of aid giving. David Potter, for one, favored the spread of America's abundance by means that would not cut it off from "actual moral leadership." But the very transfer of wealth "placed American generosity—much of which is both genuine and unselfish—under the curse of chronic envy."[7]

Reinhold Niebuhr, for another, questioned America's motives: whether aid was for moral or nonmoral reasons, to help others or to work the national will on them. Americans moved "inconsistently from policies which would overcome animosities toward us by the offer of economic assistance to policies which would destroy resistance by the use of pure military might." Niebuhr was baffled. "We expect Asians to be grateful to us for such assistance as we have given them; and are hurt when we discover that Asians envy, rather than admire, our prosperity and regard us as imperialistic when we are 'by definition' a non-imperialistic nation."[8]

"A Matter of Enlightened Self-Interest": From Lend-Lease to UNRRA

America began giving aid early in World War II through lend-lease agreements, devised by President Roosevelt. While the United States was still neutral in the early 1940s, the president proposed to grant or lease equipment to any nation whose defense he deemed vital to the defense of the United States. Roosevelt's original description of lend-lease as the loan of a garden hose to a neighbor whose house had caught fire was symbolic of the absence of demand for repayment. He so designed this aid as to avoid the debt obligations that had led to distrust and economic dislocations after World War I. The Lend-Lease Act, by which Congress authorized this precedent in 1941, did not decree that the goods shipped to other countries be paid for.[9]

In all the theaters of conflict—England, Egypt, China, Russia, Europe, New Guinea, India, North Africa—observers of lend-lease saw the contribution of nearly $50 billion put to use, consisting of an extraordinary array of materiel—guns, tanks, planes, ships, food, steel, copper, machine tools. New ports were constructed on the Red Sea and the Persian Gulf, a railroad in Iran, a naval base in Northern Ireland, and a highway and railroad through Burma to China. The American ambassador in Great Britain, evaluating the impact of lend-lease there, asserted that its "tools for defense" enabled the British, who received the largest quantities of lend-lease aid of any people, to prevail against greater numbers, better armed, though the force of Russia and the United States was needed to "finish the job."[10]

Surveying the influx of lend-lease to the Soviet Union, the destination for nearly one-third of all the aid, a reporter for *National Geographic* surmised that without these commodities and armaments, "victory would have been delayed and conceivably might have been lost altogether." The Soviets received 420,000 field telephones and wanted 62,000 miles of field telephone lines a month; they got considerably more—ultimately more than a million miles of lines, enough to go around the earth fifty times. The United States supplied the Soviets with nearly 14,000 aircraft, including fighters, bombers, trainers, cargo planes, observation planes, and flying boats. The jeep became "as well known in Russia as it is in the United States." Under lend-lease the United States sent everything needed to run railroads—tons of rails, wheels, axles, and rolling stock; 1,825 steam locomotives; 10,000 flatcars; 1,000 dump cars; 100 tank cars; and 70 diesel-electric locomotives. Entire factories were exported, among them a tire plant, an aluminum rolling mill, and two pipe mills. In addition, Americans sent 4 million tons of food, including sugar, butter, and margarine. Nearly half of the exports under lend-lease consisted of munitions and army equipment, from 7,000 tanks to 15 million pairs of army boots, but the Soviets also got ships, medical supplies, bridges, paint, plastics, rubber, paper, photographic materials, fish nets, and buttons.[11]

The administrator of lend-lease, Edward Stettinius, the former chairman of the board of U.S. Steel, drew a lesson from this war experience. By pooling their resources, the Allies achieved victory. Stettinius believed that the United States should continue this collaboration. Subsequently secretary of state in 1944 and 1945 and later the American representative to the United Nations, he questioned, "What have we to fear?" The United States should not fear the power of Britain and the declining European empires. "We shall have by far the greatest industrial power, immense material resources, a country undamaged by the enemy, businessmen who can stand up to businessmen anywhere in the world, and a new and intimate knowledge of other peoples and other lands gained by the millions of our men who have gone abroad." Nor should the United States fear communist Russia. "Why should we? Is our faith so weak in our own form of Government and in what free enterprise regulated in the interests of democracy has done and will continue to do for the United States?"[12]

The public valued the benefits of lend-lease, while realizing that the loans would not be repaid. Opinion had changed since money had been lent in World War I, and as late as August 1938 only 9 percent of those polled favored cancelation of the unpaid allied debts. Although three-quarters thought the World War II lend-lease funds should be paid back, only about a third expected they would be. Americans did not want to cause their allies hardship. If forcing payment threatened a depression in England, even many of those who insisted on compensation in principle changed their views and would forgo collections.[13]

At the war's end the authority for lend-lease deliveries ceased and, except for material already in movement, the shipments ground to a halt. Lend-lease, though, was not the only aid program Americans funded. In 1943 the United States helped organize the United Nations Relief and Rehabilitation Administration. UNRRA's purpose was collective: to bring together the world's nations to aid poor and undernourished peoples. "All of the United Nations agree to cooperate and share in the work of U.N.R.R.A.—each Nation according to its own individual resources," Franklin Roosevelt proclaimed at its inception. The work confronting UNRRA was "not only humane and charitable" but also "a clear matter of enlightened self-interest." The sufferings of people could be relieved "only if we utilize the production of *all* the world to balance the want of *all* the world," Roosevelt said. "Why not? We Nations have common objectives." UNRRA's prime emphasis—filling needs for food, clothing, fuel, and medicines—Roosevelt called a first bold step toward the "practicable, workable realization of a thing called freedom from want," one of his Four Freedoms.[14]

Vice President Wallace favored the internationalist and humanitarian objectives of UNRRA and directed the U.S. Bureau of Economic Warfare to develop reconstruction plans for countries torn apart by war. These plans soon became part of UNRRA's work. Wallace believed, as did Roosevelt, that the bulk of international responsibility after the war would fall on UNRRA. Though maintaining that in the long run nations had to follow "the principle of self-help" and rely on their own efforts to raise living standards, Wallace believed that strong nations like the United States had to provide through UNRRA guidance and substantial financial support. He did not suggest that the United States should receive in return a disproportionate influence in UNRRA, which had to be multilateral and cooperative.[15]

The American people overwhelmingly supported the principles governing UNRRA. They were ready to help the hungry and sick. By one poll, more than 90 percent approved of continuing food rationing if necessary to feed countries hard hit by war. Feelings were strong. "After the war, do you think we should or should not plan to help other nations get on their feet by sending them money and materials?" the American people were asked: 73 percent favored aid. Businessmen who looked at the war-ravaged countries as marketplaces to be reconstructed were ready to provide the aid. But not just venture capitalists wanted to make this national investment: 86 percent of executives supported aiding with money and materials, as did 70 percent of the factory workers and 75 percent of the farmers, once staunch isolationists. By these responses, morality clearly entered into the public's opinion, though 40 percent of those polled thought it was not necessarily America's "*moral* responsibility" to ensure that other nations were well fed.[16]

Self-interest was also evident in public opinion. When people were asked whether aid in reconstruction would help Americans prosper or would diminish their standard of living, 59 percent saw prosperity as an outcome of their aid and only 22 percent thought that their living standard would decline. Americans were ready to send food (96 percent of the people), medical supplies (84 percent), and clothing (81 percent), as well as machinery, building materials, and household furnishings. The people were prepared to pay higher taxes in this effort. A majority of Americans wanted to help reconstruct even the enemy countries. Reported Jerome Bruner in his 1944 study of public opinion, "The spirit of UNRRA suits the American temper."[17]

Before the end of the war, UNRRA had supplied large-scale immediate human needs of food, clothing, fuel, and medicine. South Africa contributed coal; India, peanut oil and jute; Australia and New Zealand, raw wool and food; Brazil, livestock; and among small nations, the Dominican Republic supplied corn, and Cuba, sugar. But the United States was by far the principal supplier among UNRRA's forty-eight nations, contributing three-fourths of the total aid.

As soon as victory made rehabilitation possible, in early 1946, UNRRA sent quantities of agricultural supplies, including seeds, fertilizers, livestock, and farm tools, to devastated countries. It provided industrial equipment, such as spare parts for machinery in mines and factories, fuel, locomotives, railway cars, trucks, and barges, as well as technical personnel.[18]

The Americans who headed the organization—beginning with Herbert Lehman in 1943, followed by Fiorello H. La Guardia, the former mayor of New York—made an effort to rise above the interests of any one nation. "This is an international organization," La Guardia declared in a fiery speech accepting the position in 1946. "And . . . I am responsible to this organization," a responsibility that required him to speak frankly and critically to any country that did not respond sufficiently. He began with his own countrymen. "The American people are kindly; they wouldn't want to see mass suffering," but whatever sacrifices they made were little in comparison to the hardship of other peoples. His point was that nations had to unite "to preserve life, to build, not to kill, not to destroy." La Guardia found no precedent for UNRRA in international law. But there was humanitarian precedent for it "in the old scripture, in the new scripture, to love our neighbor, to aid the needy. That is not original. It just hasn't been carried out."[19]

In mid-summer 1946, La Guardia left on a tour to Warsaw, Belgrade, Rome, Athens, and Munich. Truman bade him farewell in Washington, after joining with him in a radio appeal from the White House in support of UNRRA's efforts, renewing the pledge he had made since 1945: to do "all that is reasonably possible to alleviate the suffering of our war-torn allies" through UNRRA. He pleaded with Americans not to withdraw their support, because this service was America's obligation to the Allies after their sacrifice in keeping the enemy "from bringing his military might to bear upon our own shores." UNRRA was the "chosen instrument" of the world's nations, the "first of the international organizations to operate in the post-war period," and the one that the United States had originally sponsored. La Guardia's international quest had broad support—from *United States News,* pleased that La Guardia would "dramatize the perilous European food storage" with his "flair for the dramatic," to the *New Republic,* which described La Guardia as unwilting: "He will raise hell, heaven and earth to fulfill UNRRA's commitments."[20]

But while La Guardia was abroad in July, the United States government took an emphatic line against UNRRA's future. "The gravy train is going round for the last time," Under Secretary of State William L. Clayton said publicly. "End of UNRRA Is Sought by Agency's Big Backers" was the front-page headline of the *New York Times.* Right away, there was a public division of thought over this move. *United States News* leaned away from an international organization, because it thought the Soviet Union had been uncooperative. Ships dispatched to Odessa to take on the wheat and barley promised for France had found no stockpiles there, although small quantities were trickling in. On the other hand, the *New Republic* could see no alternative to cooperative measures: "Millions of the same people that UNRRA food helped save this year face starvation during Europe's bleak winter unless international arrangements are worked out." The magazine condemned the idea of direct American administration, since "bilateral action would encourage the development of economic blocs."[21]

For one thing, UNRRA was criticized for not bringing about recovery. As a welfare program it had helped tide over those in need, but its rehabilitation efforts had not corrected the serious dislocations of the war. Looking at the plight of the Italians, Eugene Rostow argued that UNRRA would "do nothing" to alleviate the crisis in Italy. "Fifty million for children, mothers, and refugees does not begin to measure Italian needs." He saw "no end to the process of relief."[22]

UNRRA was also criticized for mismanagement. Reports reached home that shipments from UNRRA to Greece ended up in the hands of black-market profiteers, who turned over the goods to wealthy people and restaurants, despite UNRRA's pleas that 75 percent of Greek children were malnourished. Tons of American textiles sent through UNRRA lay piled in warehouses. The Greek government feared the increased supply would lower prices for domestic textiles. UNRRA could force no change as an international agency, because Greece was a sovereign entity. One senator was convinced that the U.S. Army would do a better job of supplying food and rehabilitation goods than UNRRA could do.[23]

Finally, the American government did not want its resources squandered without its approval as to where its funds were going. Under Secretary Clayton argued that UNRRA should end and should not be resurrected. Canada, Argentina, Brazil, Australia, New Zealand, and South Africa could all help Europe, but "we must avoid getting into another UNRRA. *The United States must run this show.*"[24]

The decision about what would replace UNRRA was made before the end of 1946. The United States would insist on carrying out any relief undertakings on its own. Secretary of State Byrnes left no doubt: "whatever the United States does in the way of relief should be done by the United States unilaterally"; "we want to give that aid as the

United States and not as a member of an international organization having a committee composed of other Governments determining the allotment of what relief is given by the United States." The United States had to replace UNRRA.[25]

By 1947 President Truman had given up on international aid agencies, recommending on February 21 that "this relief assistance be given directly rather than through an international organization, and that our contribution be administered under United States control." He explained that the United States was "keeping with our traditions of immediate and whole-hearted response to human need," standing "in the forefront of those who have checked the forces of starvation, disease, suffering and chaos." On January 1, 1947, the activities of the Health Division of UNRRA were transferred to the nascent World Health Organization. In February UNRRA's agricultural activities were moved to the Food and Agriculture Organization. On June 30 UNRRA's responsibility for displaced persons passed to the International Refugee Organization.[26]

As the deadline for UNRRA's demise approached, neither the problems of recovery nor the role of the United States ceased. Confidence that Europe would recover on its own had disappeared. On February 3 the *New York Times* published a lengthy survey of the need of other countries for food. "End of UNRRA a Blow," read the front-page headline. "With famine already on the march in China and the food supply in Britain more limited than it was during the U-boat campaign, Europe and Asia are paying the price for the most destructive war in history. . . . The end of the UNRRA presages particularly hard times." In France wheat planted in the autumn was destroyed in the January cold. Italian farmers were not sending supplies to the markets. Poland, Hungary, Greece, Austria, and Yugoslavia were still in desperate condition. Underfed, freezing people threatened to undermine governments and tear apart economies. The voting strength of French and Italian communists rose to about one-third of the total. General strikes threatened to break out.[27]

Through 1946 and into early 1947, President Truman prodded American measures to relieve the world food shortage apart from UNRRA. Informing the public that "a food crisis has developed which may prove to be the worst in modern times," he appealed to "the conscience of the American people." He called on them repeatedly to conserve food, particularly bread. They could cut down on their selection of meats, cheese, evaporated milk, and ice cream to save lives in lands that did not have even the bare necessities. "America cannot remain healthy and happy in the same world where millions of human beings are starving. A sound world order can never be built upon a foundation of human misery."[28]

By the close of June 1947, UNRRA had completed spending the resources it had available and made a final accounting. It had shipped a total of 23,405,978 tons with a value of $2,768,373,000. Some 44 percent of the shipments were foodstuffs, 22 percent industrial equipment, 15 percent clothing, and 11 percent agricultural supplies. Americans had not been passive in the face of the danger. Already, in total, Americans had given away $9 billion through outright grants since the war had ended to meet a series of emergencies as they arose. These measures were only a beginning.

The Truman Doctrine

The United States embarked on a new course of direct action to provide aid to other peoples. On March 12 President Truman declared his intention to stop the communist inroads in Greece and Turkey. The United States would support peoples resisting subjugation by armed minorities or outside pressure, but he insisted that American "help should be primarily through economic and financial aid which is essential to economic stability and orderly political processes." Congress approved his request for $400 million to aid Greece and Turkey. But was Truman's initial proposal enough to meet the problems of Europe? Was it the right kind of aid? And was it given in the right way?[29]

There was consensus over giving aid to Greece and Turkey, over America acting as a service institution—over whether, but not immediately over how, aid would be given. Therein lay strains in the consensus. In a quick and angry rebuttal on a radio broadcast on March 13, Henry Wallace asked, "If aid to the people of the world is our objective, why did the President and the Congress allow the United Nations Relief and Rehabilitation Administration to die?" He went on to question the amount of the grants and their purpose: "Why are we doing so little to help the million displaced persons without homes in Europe? Why are we speaking of only $400,000,000 when the need is far greater?" As an alternative to Truman's doctrine, Wallace wanted increased amounts of the aid to Greece and Eastern Europe administered internationally through an organization like UNRRA. And he wanted assurance that American funds would be used for the welfare of the Greek people.[30]

La Guardia, who had headed UNRRA until its liquidation, attacked the unilateral plan. He could not understand why his recommendation for an International Control Board for Food Relief was not preferred to President Truman's plan for direct action. In a series of radio broadcasts, La Guardia argued that most of the $400 million the government planned to spend would not go for food. "It will go to bolster, to strengthen, to equip, to train the Armies of Greece and Turkey." Because America was "so mighty and rich," he took for granted that "the American people want to give help to Greece, or any other country that is hungry. . . . There are two ways of doing it. I'm in favor of doing it in the Christ-like way. Let us take our bread in baskets to the hungry people and hand it out kindly, with love, and understanding. The other way, the proposed way, is to fork the bread out at the point of bayonet. 'Do it our way if you want to eat our bread.' That is not the American way." La Guardia contradicted those who claimed that the United Nations organization was unable to provide proper aid. It was "not prepared today," he declared, "because the United States Government, the United States Delegation to the United Nations, did not permit them to be prepared." Under his plan "all nations" would participate in helping Greece and the other nations in need of food, but "it was the United States that opposed this plan. There were 48 nations in favor of it. It was the United States that said: 'Don't do it; we'll do it alone.'" "The plan that I offered to the United Nations, which was acceptable to all countries except the United

States—my own country—would have made the present military intervention unnecessary. . . . Relief would have been under international control with all countries participating." La Guardia continued to attack the unilateral program until he fell ill and
died in September 1947.[31]

In Europe that summer of 1947 there was praise for UNRRA and disappointment
at its end. Arriving in Rome in June, about two weeks after UNRRA closed up shop,
Thomas Bailey, who had been commissioned by the National War College in Washington to inspect conditions in Europe, noted in his diary "the dismay of many Italians"
plagued by the inflation of their currency. It had risen to nearly fifty times the prewar
level, and the budget deficit was roughly 600 billion lire (when he calculated the lira's
worth to be about one-third of an American cent). A former UNRRA official remarked
to Bailey that UNRRA, "with Uncle Sam carrying the heavy end of the financial log,
had operated rather intelligently, more so than the Americans were then doing under
their substitute relief efforts."[32]

Howard K. Smith had a reporter's eye on UNRRA in action around Europe, and he
could not comprehend why it was discontinued. He argued that it was perverse to scoff
at UNRRA, given its record: UNRRA had directly halted mass starvation in half a
dozen European countries and had indirectly prevented epidemics, upheavals, and
perhaps a rash of local wars. UNRRA was probably "the most perfect expression" of a
new international attitude. "It is a highly important key to the Cold War that with
UNRRA—that is, aid with no strings tied, internationally administered—American
observers were for the first time allowed free run inside Soviet Russia." He could not
resist the thought that if this spirit had continued, "the walls around Russia might in
time have been lowered." But UNRRA had been "killed—by America—before its
work was done." When America turned to give aid unilaterally, Smith thought, one
"suspicious question hovered over it from the outset. If its aim was not to foster
American imperialism but to benefit the world, why was the pattern of the administration of UNRRA not followed . . . ? Quite clearly, the Russians must have surmised, the
aim is to keep its administration in American hands for American ends."[33]

Congressmen, columnists, editorial writers, and radio commentators generally
agreed on the necessity for more aid to more countries, but they differed over the
auspices through which the aid would be given. Support shifted to Truman's position.
The day after the President's speech Walter Lippmann argued that there were were
plenty of practical and humanitarian reasons for the United States to intervene in the
Middle East, even if not through the United Nations. On March 13 the *New York Times*
dropped its earlier expression of hope that aid would be distributed through international auspices to communist nations, for Truman's aid was "to be spent under American supervision" to stabilize the Middle East. The newsmagazines—*Time, Newsweek,
United States News*—continued the build-up of expectations that the United States
would be able to assume responsibility for aiding Europe. On March 23 Herbert Hoover
released a report on economic conditions in Germany and Austria urging that Europe be
revived or American taxpayers would face an ever-increasing burden. "To persist in the

present policies will create, sooner or later, a cesspool of unemployment or pauper labor in the center of Europe which is bound to infect her neighbors."[34]

On April 5 Lippmann wrote a consequential column describing Europe on the verge of collapse. None of the leading nations of Europe—Great Britain, France, Italy, and Germany—was recovering from the war or had any reasonable prospect of recovery through its own means. He was adamant that he was not exaggerating Europe's plight but emphasizing what the responsible men he knew said when they did not have to keep up appearances in public. The decline of Britain was most stark in its consequences, despite the British government's attempt to prop up its people's morale by claiming that the British had the situation in hand. Lippmann countered that the "economic collapse of Britain—if it is not dealt with thoroughly before it occurs—will spread economic dislocation and have political repercussions throughout all the regions of the world which are within the sterling area." Lippmann suggested that the British could no more get out of this economic crisis without American assistance than they could have won the war. "The truth is that political and economic measures on a scale which no responsible statesman has yet ventured to hint at will be needed in the next year or so." To prevent the crisis that would otherwise engulf Europe and spread chaos throughout the world, "no less than the equivalent of a revival of lend-lease" was required.[35]

Public backing for increased direct action continued to grow on all sides of the political spectrum. The *New Republic* noted that the coming of spring "could do little now to soften the hunger and hardship that were still commonplace." But neither had American aid to date ended the suffering. *United States News* summed up a new sense of American obligation: "Putting World on Its Feet: America's New Responsibility." The thrust of these discussions for more aid was reported by James Reston in the *New York Times* on May 25: It was not enough to aid one or two countries, "lending now to Britain, then to France, then to Italy. . . . Europe cannot recover by shoring up, one at a time, the various national economies." The *Times* editors lent their full support. By now they had accepted that the end of UNRRA and Truman's direct approach meant American funds should "not be used for the support of Communist-dominated governments." But however it was distributed, the "future of the world" depended on "continued American generosity." The time had come "to go ahead, with Russia if possible, without her if necessary."[36]

Thomas Bailey was aghast at the ruins that still remained two years after the end of hostilities. In London he saw the "heavily damaged" tower of the Houses of Parliament and the "soot-blacked St. Paul's Cathedral." Wooden screens had been erected between buildings to conceal the wreckage that had yet to be cleared. Live bombs were still being dug out. Wild flowers bloomed in the rubble.

But it was in Germany where the worst destruction remained, two years after General Clay had entered Berlin. Bailey found ruins in the city that "fully lived up to its billing as the biggest rubble heap in the world." The dead still lay beneath the piles of broken brick and twisted steel, "all of which served as macabre gravestones." Occasionally he saw a wooden cross on a pile of debris, sometimes with a few scattered flowers on top. It was like "a nightmare." He walked through the remains of Hitler's once-palatial Reichschancellery, picking up mimeographed documents as souvenirs, hardly believing that after all that time they would be lying there.

The ruins were merely symbolic of the human suffering. Bailey witnessed poverty and hunger everywhere "in this city of the dead." He learned that a German had killed for food a dog belonging to an employee of the American military government. A worker's monthly salary was 300 marks, enough for one pound of butter. American cigarettes served as something of a currency, and Bailey could barely believe that twelve cartons of cigarettes, which cost $9.40 in American money, could be converted into 15,400 marks, or about $700. The people looked gaunt and hungry, the old ones gray-faced, and the small children undernourished. What was America to do?[37]

The government renewed consideration of aid, where it should go, and why. On May 12, 1947, the Joint Chiefs of Staff produced a novel enterprise: a list of countries ranked according to their *"importance to the national security of the United States and the urgency of their need, in combination."* They recognized two purposes of aid: the humanitarian need of other nations and the national interests of the United States. In their thinking, the "mere giving of assistance" would not necessarily enhance the national security, and the United States could not give aid to "all countries in the world." So it should provide aid to "firm friends" in areas of strategic importance that in the event of war would enhance the nation's security. The "primary rule" governing assistance, according to the Joint Chiefs, was the exclusion of the Soviet Union and every country under its control, regardless of the need of their peoples. Since the area of primary strategic importance "in the event of ideological warfare" covered Western Europe, including Great Britain, that was where most of America's aid should go. The final list of nations that the Joint Chiefs decided on in the order of their importance was Great Britain, France, Germany, Italy, Greece, Turkey, Austria, Japan, Belgium, the Netherlands, Latin American countries, Spain, Korea, China, the Philippines, and Canada.[38]

On May 23, 1947, George Kennan and the Policy Planning Staff of the State Department took a different point of view. American security was not directly at stake; the welfare of other nations was. American aid should aim "to combat not communism, but the economic maladjustment which makes European society vulnerable to exploitation by any and all totalitarian movements and which Russian communism is now exploiting." The Truman Doctrine had resulted in misconceptions about the purpose of aid. The effort to restore sound economic conditions in other countries should not be only a by-product of a defensive reaction to communism, but an interest of Americans even "if there were no communist menace."[39]

Even as the government argued over motive, it was clear that something had to be done beyond anything earlier contemplated. Under Secretary Clayton, after conferring with European leaders about the steady deterioration of their countries, wrote to Dean Acheson that there was need for massive aid. On May 27, 1947, the analysts in government realized that they had "grossly underestimated the destruction of the European economy by the war." They had understood the physical destruction but not the effects of economic dislocation. The political crises denoted "grave economic distress." Millions of people in the cities were "slowly starving" and the modern system of division of labor had "almost broken down."

America had to meet the needs, according to Clayton's analysis, because they had to be met and no one else could meet them. "Our resources and our productive capacity are ample to provide all the help necessary." All that was needed was for Americans to redistribute their surpluses from "our enormous production." A "strong spiritual appeal" to Americans to sacrifice a little and "to draw in their own belts" would save the Europeans from chaos and starvation and preserve the Western heritage.[40]

The Marshall Plan: European Recovery

In Europe the hard winter of 1947 turned to a hot summer. From early spring rainless, scorching days had followed one another. Crops upon which Europe depended failed. By now the government had decided: the human misery, physical wreckage, and communist menace required bold action.

On June 5, 1947, Secretary of State George C. Marshall proposed a massive program to aid Europe. That morning, in Cambridge, Massachusetts, Marshall received an honorary degree of Doctor of Laws at the Harvard commencement, where he shunned the ceremonial cap and gown and wore instead a plain civilian suit with a blue tie. In an address to the alumni in the afternoon, he spoke in a simple and frank manner of the plight and long suffering of the peoples of devastated Europe, and in a clear, businesslike way of what Americans should do. He depicted again the loss of life and the devastation. Beyond the visible destruction he noted the dislocation of the entire structure of the European economy: machinery broken down; banks, insurance companies, and shipping institutions eliminated; confidence in national currencies shaken; food production diminished. Governments were exhausting their foreign credits to procure necessities from abroad.

The American role in helping the Europeans out of their predicament was, for Marshall, crucial: "Europe's requirements for the next three or four years of foreign food and other essential products—principally from America—are so much greater than her present ability to pay that she must have substantial additional help." The alternative, Marshall suggested, was grave "economic, social, and political deterioration."[41]

Marshall outlined many fundamental principles of American foreign aid that continued to influence giving during the postwar period. The institution of foreign aid combined charitable, fiscal, social, political, and military motives into a view of the world: "Aside from the demoralizing effect on the world at large and the possibilities of disturbances arising as a result of the desperation of the people concerned, the consequences to the economy of the United States should be apparent to all. It is logical that the United States should do whatever it is able to do to assist in the return of normal economic health in the world, without which there can be no political stability and no assured peace. Our policy is directed not against any country or doctrine but against hunger, poverty, desperation, and chaos. Its purpose should be the revival of a working economy in the world so as to permit the emergence of political and social conditions in which free institutions can exist."[42]

The American government was seeking to act practically as a multilateral aid-giving agency. The Europeans were to agree among themselves what their requirements were. "It would be neither fitting nor efficacious for this Government to undertake to draw up unilaterally a program designed to place Europe on its feet economically. This is the business of the Europeans. . . . The role of this country should consist of friendly aid in the drafting of a European program and of later support of such a program so far as it may be practical for us to do so."[43]

Although the official statement was not precise about motive, the aid program had been generated in large measure out of fear of communism. The sense of danger that communism might take over countries in Western Europe came not only from the threat of Russian military aggression but also from that of internal discontents who exploited the conditions of poverty. By helping to raise European living standards, the Marshall Plan would help to create economic conditions that would sustain democracies in their stand against communism. But the American government was willing to help any government that wanted help. The Foreign Assistance Act of 1948 that embodied Marshall's proposals did not exclude communist countries; it contemplated a "plan of European recovery open to all such nations which cooperate." Still, the act strongly asserted fundamental American principles: "it is further declared to be the policy of the people of the United States to sustain and strengthen the principles of individual liberty, free institutions, and genuine independence in Europe."[44]

What was usually cited as the plan's chief economic objective was to enable the recipient countries to afford their needs when buying abroad, mainly in dollars. Aid to Europe, Howard Ellis wrote in a book published for the Council on Foreign Relations, was an instrument of fiscal policy for this purpose by the central nation in the world economy, and Charles Kindleberger saw the aid as the distribution of dollars to offset economic disequilibrium. Closing the dollar gap, however, was not considered as substantial an objective as revitalizing European productive capacity. The enabling legislation itself stated three main purposes:

1 promoting industrial and agricultural production in the participating countries;

2 facilitating the soundness of European currencies, budgets, and finances; and

3 stimulating the growth of international trade of participating countries with one another and with other countries by reducing barriers.[45]

Americans' humanitarian motives clearly entered into their support for postwar foreign aid. The early wartime polls, taken when funds were channeled primarily through UNRRA, showed that the American instinct for aid was triggered by more than anticommunism. Americans were well prepared to provide postwar aid for reconstruction, even while they still considered the Soviet Union an ally. The crisis of living and working conditions in Europe sincerely moved many Americans. When people were asked what they thought was the most important argument for the Marshall Plan, an overwhelming majority—up to 94 percent of those in favor of the plan—answered that they believed that "we should help the hungry and sick." Even after having experienced wartime shortages of butter, sugar, meat and other rationed food products, Americans had generally favored enduring shortages so that the needy people of Europe could share the supplies.[46]

In addition, Americans were not giving their goods merely to prevent a depression at home. Actually, they gave the most aid at times when domestic inflation was prevalent, and inflation was a serious concern. Economists warned of the adverse inflationary affects of spending billions abroad, and polls showed that a major reason Americans were suspicious of the plan was higher prices at home. Truman called for price control legislation, though Congress enacted only part of it. By the end of the Marshall Plan in 1952, the aid had cost the United States government—the American taxpayers—$13 billion, nearly $80 for every man, woman, and child in the United States.[47]

Americans sought to judge how well the aid had paid off. Howard K. Smith believed that Europe had needed the Marshall Plan for "survival." In 1949 he thought that this and more had been accomplished, although recovery was slow. It might not be possible for the small island nation of Britain to restore itself to its old position of power in a world of giants. But Smith was encouraged that by the end of 1948 Britain with Marshall aid had succeeded in balancing its trade. "There was much talk of British *recovery*." France had prospered: "Thanks to the workers and to capital from Marshall aid, production is fairly healthy," but he was not certain that France would not revert to its unstable position. As for Italy, its economic situation remained serious; it was one of the few countries aided by the Marshall Plan that had not yet been able to reach prewar levels of production, and it could "be an object of charity for many, many years to come." The same for Greece: "There is absolutely no chance that Greece will be able to support herself by the end of the Marshall Plan."[48]

European recovery had been expected to take a generation, but results became clear not long after Smith wrote. "Happy days," proclaimed Theodore White after his travels in the early 1950s, "seemed close at hand, and the individual triumphs of the Plan stood out crisp and brilliant." In "every country" in Europe, he could point to some outstanding project accomplished through the Marshall Plan: in Sardinia, the draining of malarial swamps that had afflicted its population with disease; in the Netherlands, the poldering off of the Zuyder Zee with new dikes, preparing to claim 128,000 acres of farmland from the sea; in France, the mechanization of French coal mines and electrification of the nation by hydropower. In Turkey, life had been modernized with ploughs, tractors, and railways, and in Africa, geologists explored areas of European colonies for raw material sources.[49]

The final report of the Marshall Plan in 1952 was full of superlatives. It was "the most daring and constructive venture in peacetime international relations the world has ever seen," having spent "the largest sum in history" on reconstruction efforts.[50]

The results could be measured in cold statistics: Industrial production was 64 percent above 1947 and 41 percent above prewar levels; steel production had nearly doubled in less than four years; coal production was slightly below the prewar level but still 27 percent higher than in 1947; aluminum, copper, and cement production were up, respectively, 69, 31, and 90 percent from 1947; food production was 24 percent above 1947 and 9 percent above prewar levels. Paul Hoffman looked at the statistics of a new Western Europe. His verdict: this comeback was "the most courageous in history." In West Germany, the American high commissioner, John J. McCloy, called the country's transformation a "miracle." West Germany had become the second-largest industrial country in Western Europe.[51]

There had also been benefit to the United States. As the Marshall Plan report stated, nearly half of the total American funds spent in Europe—about $5.5 billion— had been used to purchase industrial commodities, mostly from the United States, and another $5.2 billion had purchased food and other agricultural commodities such as cotton. More than $800 million had gone into the cost of ocean freight and goods sent to Europe.[52]

The "best illustration" of the Marshall Plan's success, according to the final report, was not in statistical, economic, or even human terms, but in an area that the plan was not specifically designed to be involved in: the Continent was "now able—even though with great sacrifice—to shoulder part of the heavy burden of rearmament." This pre-saged a great change in the character of American aid. Following the Marshall Plan, American aid to Europe became what was called "defense support," administered by the Mutual Security Agency, and it also consisted of military assistance under the Department of Defense. Because of this reallocation of resources, John Williams in *Foreign Affairs* in the summer of 1952 referred to the Marshall Plan as an "interrupted experiment." Despite its struggle to rearm, Europe still had a serious problem of foreign debt. In 1947 the United States had a huge excess of exports of $9 billion; Western Europe's gold and dollar drain was $8.5 billion. Although by 1950 America's current account surplus had virtually vanished, the problem had apparently not yet been solved, for in 1951 the American export surplus rose again, to $5 billion.[53]

Even though the costs of arms for a war-tired continent forced diversion of some resources from development, American aid did stimulate with impressive speed suc-cessful European recovery. Among the many economic indicators, one that stood out was that within five years after the war, the countries of Western Europe were producing at above prewar levels. But more than that, the people were not starving, they were not defeated or demoralized, and they had resumed a normal pace of life. They were eating regularly and working hard. They were riding the trains or driving on the open roads.

They were buying and selling goods. The Marshall Plan had helped Western European nations hold off economic collapse and rebuild a working society. In succeeding years they continued to regain vitality. Their shipping fleets were restored and they exported goods again. Finally, by encouraging the states of Western Europe to come together in a common effort, the Marshall Plan prepared the way for continuing European economic cooperation in the Common Market, which was born in the late 1950s.[54]

Point Four: World Development

The experience of giving billions of dollars in foreign aid to Europe inspired the belief that Americans could apply their aid elsewhere—in Asia, Africa, or Latin America. Criticism of the successful Marshall Plan focused not on its purpose but on its scope. In December 1949, John Kenneth Galbraith pronounced the Marshall Plan inadequate: assistance to the developing world would be needed to complement aid to Europe, and he suggested committing "the United States permanently to the role of Santa Claus." Santa Claus was what just about everyone—Henry Wallace included—was saying America should *not* be, and Galbraith hoped his audience would not be too disturbed by his suggestion. "As a matter of fact," he went on bravely, "Santa Claus is sometimes to be preferred to empty stockings." If others did not put it quite that way, they did begin to take a worldwide view of aid distribution. Marshall's goals, said the *New York Times* editors, could not be gained by dealing with "a series of particular emergencies in particular areas. There is but one emergency and it is a world emergency."[55]

To help nations develop, Americans also needed to provide more than financial resources. They had to supply the technology that would enable developing areas to increase their levels of productivity and living standards. Here was the clearest way that David Potter believed the people of plenty could benefit the world. Exports, he noticed, even technological devices like the McCormick reaper, made American abundance seem "infinitely desirable but quite unattainable." It was not productive for peoples seeking development to draw on American abundance so that it remained distinctively belonging to Americans. American aid had to teach the means to abundance.[56]

Proposed as the fourth point of President Truman's inaugural address of 1949, "Point Four," as it came to be called, was a critical undertaking in his "program for peace and freedom": "we must embark on a bold new program for making the benefits of our scientific advances and industrial progress available for the improvement and growth of underdeveloped areas. More than half the people of the world are living in conditions approaching misery. Their food is inadequate. They are victims of disease. Their economic life is primitive and stagnant. Their poverty is a handicap and a threat both to them and to more prosperous areas."[57]

In contrast, Truman continued, the United States, endowed with advanced technical know-how, was in a unique position to take the lead in furthering world development: "The United States is pre-eminent among nations in the development of industrial and scientific techniques." America's "imponderable resources in technical knowledge are constantly growing and are inexhaustible. I believe that we should make available to peace-loving peoples the benefits of our store of technical knowledge in order to help them realize their aspirations for a better life."

By helping peoples of the world increase their economic production and raise their standards of living, Truman asserted, commerce would expand for the mutual benefit of economies around the world. Greater production would help remove discontent. Improved standards of living would presumably encourage democratic governments. "Only by helping the least fortunate of its members to help themselves," Truman stated, "can the human family achieve the decent, satisfying life that is the right of all people." So Truman requested that Congress make funds available to supply developing areas with technical, scientific, and managerial knowledge, as well as financial assistance.[58]

Point Four was a favored project of Truman's. He considered it the most important policy for peace of his administration. Nothing like it had ever "before been proposed by any country in the history of the world," he later reflected. Point Four had been in his mind for two or three years, "ever since the Marshall Plan was inaugurated," he explained at a press conference. "It originated with the Greece and Turkey proposition. Been studying it ever since." He fantasized about it while looking at the large globe in his office.[59]

Point Four was not intended to be "a wholesale give-away plan," he said. Nor was it another Marshall Plan. It was a "worldwide" program of sharing the technical information "already tested and proved in the United States." Truman considered the plan a practical answer to the failure of colonialism, in that it aimed to give to other peoples rather than taking from them. Vast lands of Africa and South America presented opportunities for expansion of the world's food supply. "What we want to do under Point Four is to help develop these resources for the benefit of the people who own them." He wanted to raise people in these areas who were "still living in an age almost a thousand years behind the times."

Seeking "a foreign policy for a nation that was the free-world leader," Truman consciously modeled Point Four on Roosevelt's New Deal and on his own Fair Deal. Their administrations had proved to him that "the way to build a successful economy in which the most people enjoyed high standards of living was to keep the national resources out of the hands of special interests and in the possession of the people themselves. This was our program domestically, and I wanted to make it a permanent part of our foreign policy." But Truman admitted to other motives. Point Four was also aimed at "preventing the expansion of Communism in the free world." In addition, the development of huge sections of the world "would be as beneficial to American trade as to the areas themselves." He estimated that "an improvement of only two per cent in the living standards of Asia and Africa would keep the industrial plants of the United States, Great Britain, and France going at full tilt for a century just to keep up with the increased demand for goods and services."

The president spoke out to garner support for his plan. Talking informally to a businessmen's dinner in October 1949, he said that in the Mesopotamian Valley alone there could be a revival of the Garden of Eden in which thirty million people could live. He explained how the Zambezi River Valley in Africa could be converted into "sections comparable to the Tennessee Valley in our own country if the people of those regions only had access to the 'know-how' which we possessed."[60]

No rebellion by the American taxpayers ensued and little or no opposition in the press, only a minimum of criticism in Congress, which appropriated funds in the Act for International Development. Nor was there serious suggestion of returning to international institutions to deliver aid. Truman went through the formality of presenting the plan to the United Nations, and the Economic and Social Council endorsed it in March 1949, but the United Nations was not involved in distribution. What little consideration was granted to internationally minded thinking was blatantly critical. International economic aid giving could not be warranted, first, as *Business Week* pointedly stated in 1956, because the aid-seeking nations would be "getting something for nothing." The United States would lose control of its aid and even relatively prosperous nations would try to reach into the till. But a more important reason was that the United States would "not be rid of the 'biting the hand that feeds' feeling." It would inevitably have to put up the lion's share of an international fund, and this was the bottom line: "we must be sure that our help is for friends and not for possible enemies." Yet critics of internationally administered aid wanted unilateral aid continued, and even expanded, for one reason: "the Soviet economic challenge must be met."[61]

Point Four pleased David Potter, though he saw it as a gesture rather than a revolutionizing action, because America still controlled the large part of its export of technology through sales by private companies abroad. *Fortune,* on the contrary, saw the foreign involvement of these companies as serving the same purpose as Point Four. When Westinghouse licensed foreign manufacturers to use its techniques and processes, helping them lay out their plants and training their technicians, the corporation had been operating "its own private Point Four." As Sears, Roebuck taught industrial techniques and merchandising methods to the Brazilians, the company was "one of Point Four's most aggressive if unofficial vessels." Whether the government or industry supplied the technology, the end result was the same. But the support by the government was never enough to do the entire job contemplated. The original appropriation for Point Four was $34.5 million. Truman recognized that this amount was inadequate. In fiscal year 1952 its budget grew to $147.9 million. Yet in his State of the Union message that year, Truman declared that Point Four was not doing enough: "Our technical missionaries are out there. We need more of them. We need more funds to speed their efforts, because there is nothing of greater importance in all our foreign policy."[62]

Truman was on the whole pleased by the implementation of Point Four as only a beginning in overcoming the problems of hunger, disease, and poverty. In a flash of idealism, he had hoped it would be for all nations. "The technical assistance program was not an anti-Communist measure," he recorded. "We could have included Russia in the program if she had been willing." He never offered it that way. And he was convinced that fighting communism had been a most important result. Point Four "provided the strongest antidote to Communism that has so far been put into practice."[63]

Americans observed many concrete successes of Point Four. Technicians, who in 1953 numbered some 2,445 in thirty-five foreign lands, reported that they had helped to increase food production, improve public health, raise levels of education, and build democratic institutions. The experiences of several workers from one class of the program's four-week orientation provided examples of improving national services: A railway train dispatcher went to Ecuador to help modernize railroad procedures; a mining engineer went to Nepal to serve as a consultant to the government on mines; a meteorologist went to Liberia to assist in setting up weather stations; a housing specialist went to Colombia to consult on building shelters; a labor analyst went to Peru to help establish a public employment service.[64]

Americans noted improvement in food production. In India, agricultural techniques as instituted in the United States increased crop yields, principally of wheat. An American official distributing seeds in Liberia for cocoa, coffee, and palm oil showed the people how to produce quantities sufficient for cash crops. American aviators stopped a locust scourge in Iran in the summer of 1951 by spraying insecticide from planes. A potato blight in Ecuador was brought under control by American experts, and production increased six times. Costa Rican farmers learned the conservation technique of plowing on contours. A small canning factory constructed by a group of Burmese received technical help. In Jordan in late 1951, engineers rebuilt old Roman reservoirs to catch the rain. When an American cotton expert found that Afghan farmers had never seen long-handled hoes, he provided some and the farmers' production rose.[65]

Improvement in public health was measured. The use of DDT related to a reduction in malaria, before the latent dangers of the toxic chemical became apparent. Americans in Iran had assisted Teheran to install a water treatment plant. Iranians learned health care through film, film strips, posters, and cartoon books.[66]

Betterment in education was gauged as well. Native Indians in the Andes received basic education from American teachers. Ethiopians took advantage of equipment and technical guidance for a trade school in Addis Ababa. Around the world boys and girls learned to become carpenters, metalworkers, automobile mechanics, radio technicians, plumbers, and skilled craftsmen to benefit their societies. Americans trained the new teachers, who in turn spread their knowledge.

Americans claimed to have strengthened democratic governmental institutions. Studies to streamline public administration, similar to the Hoover Commission at home, had been organized in Brazil, Colombia, and Mexico. American experts set up a new budgetary system for the Liberian government and a new money system with a Central Bank in Saudi Arabia.[67]

Point Four was quickly—perhaps too quickly—judged a success. The resources to support it were small in comparison with the need. Even the millions of dollars appropriated for Point Four were spread thin by the many developing regions. And Point Four was limited by another drawback in its administration: one observer, Jonathan Bingham, noted that "deep down, most Americans have a tendency to believe that our way *is* the only way—or at least the best way, not only for us, but for everybody. Sometimes this arrogance is painfully obvious." After all, technical assistance was administered not through the United Nations but directly by Americans. So "it will be up to the American people to decide what is to be done—whether the Point 4 ideal is to be vigorously pursued. . . . This is an awesome responsibility."[68]

The sums of money and technical knowledge given by a wealthy power to promote the development of far-flung places were unprecedented. By the 1970s, when the quantity of American foreign aid began to shrink, the United States had spent $150 billion, two-thirds of which reached regions outside Western Europe. The Marshall Plan helped Europe recover from war, and Point Four had a measure of success in encouraging food production, public health, and education in developing countries. And in addition to government programs, large companies had privately invested capital abroad and exported know-how, establishing branch factories, and bringing managerial expertise and technical skill.[69]

Did the recipients want the aid? It was a question that the donors seldom asked, because they assumed recipients would not accept assistance if they did not want it. The receipt of aid involved a sense of pride mixed with dependence on certain necessities. David Potter was conscious of feelings of envy, but Jacques Barzun did not mind the criticism. Americans were doing right, he believed: relief, sanitation, Point Four, and similar efforts might not catch up with famine and disease, but practically and morally they were on the right path. Aid to Asia did not have to reconcile Karl Marx with Confucius or Confucius with Thomas Jefferson. What mattered was the distribution of rice. If success meant cultural intervention, Barzun said, "so be it."[70]

America backed off from distributing its aid through international organizations like UNRRA, which had given without the ties of politics or ideology. For all its good intentions, America had not contributed its aid for purely humanitarian purposes. Using its vast wealth and influence to help friends, it did not consistently give aid to those who needed it. It rejected the notion of letting the world's nations as a community advise and decide on that need. The Marshall Plan rose to a high level of humanitarianism because it offered its aid to all the nations of Europe no matter what their ideology or political alignment. But had the aid been offered through an international agency like UNRRA, which the Soviets had clearly accepted, there might have been a chance of not removing but alleviating the suspicion and fear that led to political confrontation and military rivalry.

Still, the giving of this aid was the high point of magnanimity of the American world role. The question is, would the giving of aid through international agencies have paid extra dividends of both humanitarianism and self-interest, in strengthening those institutions even as it helped the poor? A double purpose might have been accomplished. America might not have received quite so much glory and credit; it might have reaped the benefit of an ongoing and working organization that would share among the nations the distribution of aid.

The aid did not always have the intended effects. Luring or maintaining recipient nations as allies could not be guaranteed. Other peoples pursued their own interests, which sometimes coincided with American interests and sometimes did not. The United States gave billions of lend-lease dollars to the Soviet Union during World War II, but that country did not become democratic in a Western way. A couple of billion dollars in aid plus war materiel that went to the Nationalist Chinese did not prevent a communist revolution. Korea and Vietnam had been buttressed by massive amounts of aid, but with varying and uncertain success, and neither was democratic in the American tradition.

The people who received the aid ultimately determined what success it had. Europe had been badly damaged, but, as Theodore White stated poetically, "there is fire in the ashes of the old civilization." America could fan the fire to flame or allow it to fade, but the flame could not be fed from America; it had to blaze from its own sources. Without the Europeans' initiative and application of their resources, the Marshall Plan would have failed. And the sustained efforts of developing peoples made possible their early strides in the difficult process of economic advancement.[71]

Through aid, Americans were helping industrial and industrializing nations become competitors. Americans stood to gain from an increase in international trade, which was largest between industrial nations. Nevertheless, the economic revival of Europe and Japan revealed the potential impact of aid. While recovery was substantially generated from within, aid made the growth of these developed areas all the more spectacular in a relatively short time. To developing nations, the United States was providing tools of production that could be readily grasped, even if their development was temporarily less rapid than the recovery of industrial nations that had been set back by war. Helping others develop was a policy through which Americans eased a global process of modernization that was under way.

11

Cultural

Thrust

America abandoned its role as a cultural colony for that of a cultural metropolis. Instead of looking to Europe or other lands for models in medicine, mathematics, science, art, literature, and fashion, Americans developed their own creativity. Around the turn of the century, applying their economic resources and technology, Americans ceased merely to import culture and started exporting it as well. So began a cultural spread the dimensions and the intimacy of which were hitherto unknown.[1]

The development of modern communications supported the idea that the habitable surface of the planet was being drawn together. Cargo ships, passenger liners, and aircraft, as well as cables, telephones, radio transmissions, and television broadcasts vastly increased human contacts. The revolution in communication led to some startling revelations in the 1940s. It had taken Ferdinand Magellan some three years to circumnavigate the world, but propeller planes took less than four days. In 1620 the *Mayflower* had sailed for about two months to cross the Atlantic, but modern ships did it in four days and clipper planes in less than one; jet planes would reduce the transoceanic transit time to a matter of hours. In 1790 a traveler had spent eleven days going from Boston to Pittsburgh, but on modern transportation he could get to Mandalay in less time. Radio messages, traveling the distance equivalent to seven times around the globe in a single second, and the telephone or telegraph, which reached nearly any city in the world, made possible virtually simultaneous communication.[2]

Observing this smaller world by plane in 1942 on his forty-nine-day trip to four continents, Wendell Willkie announced: "There are no distant points in the world any longer. I learned by this trip that the myriad millions of human beings of the Far East are as close to us as Los Angeles is to New York by the fastest trains. I cannot escape the conviction that in the future what concerns them must concern us, almost as much as the problems of the people of California concern the people of New York. Our thinking in the future must be worldwide."[3]

After traveling for several days by rail across the North American continent in the summer of 1944, past wide plains and the Great Divide, Franklin Roosevelt reflected when he reached the West Coast: "I could not fail to think of the new relationship between the people of our farms and cities and villages and the people of the rest of the world overseas—on the islands of the Pacific, in the Far East, and in the other Americas, in Britain and Normandy and Germany and Poland and Russia itself. For Oklahoma and California, for example, are becoming a part of all these distant spots as greatly as Massachusetts and Virginia were a part of the European picture in 1778. Today, Oklahoma and California are being defended in Normandy and on Saipan; and they must be defended there—for what happens in Normandy and Saipan vitally affects the security and well-being of every human being in Oklahoma and California."[4]

When Americans formed an image of their culture newly bound together with the rest of the world, did they see their country as one among a variety of flourishing cultures, ready to exchange their skills and arts? Or did they conceive of it as a unique center of exceptional modernity? The role of Americans in their cultural contacts was a subject of discourse. Henry Luce's idea was for America to send out to every part its engineering, science, medicine, movie studios, airlines, roads, and education. As Luce looked upon America, it was ready to assert the benefits of advancement, which other peoples needed and welcomed. A report in Luce's *Fortune* in 1944 stated that whether the United States would grow "as a center of world thought and trade" depended on the efficiency of American-owned international communications, its cable, radio, and telephone facilities, as well as its movies and publications. Britain had provided "an unparalleled example of what a communications system means to a great nation standing athwart the globe."[5]

The image of America as a preeminent cultural center contrasted with Henry Wallace's dream of peoples brought together through travel and communication. In a conversation with Vyacheslav Molotov, one of Stalin's close advisers, who was visiting the United States in 1942, Wallace suggested building a great multinational highway and providing a parallel airway route from Buenos Aires in South America; northward to the United States, Canada, and Alaska, then across into Siberia and Russia and on to Europe, with branch highways and airlines into China and India, linking peoples and their cultures. Molotov's initial cautious reaction—"No one nation can do it by itself"—turned to enthusiasm about the possibility of the United Nations working in cooperation, and he thought that they would see such a route in their lifetimes. Whether they saw themselves as sharing cultures with other peoples through travel and enterprise or as bearers of an exceptional culture of their own, Americans engaged in growing international encounters.[6]

"Citizens of the World": Travelers, Businessmen, and Servicemen

The number of Americans overseas—"citizens of the world," as Franklin Roosevelt named them—burgeoned, to the extent that the 1950 federal census began to count individuals of selected groups living abroad, and the census in 1960 counted for the first time all Americans wherever they might be. By 1960 a million and a half citizens, double the estimated number in 1950, and nearly 1 percent of Americans—soldiers, seamen, diplomats, technicians, businessmen, missionaries, students, wives, and children—lived and worked outside the United States. In 1960 another million and a half Americans traveled by sea and air to foreign countries.[7]

With the upsurge in living and working in foreign places, a series in *Life* magazine entitled "Americans in the New Age of World Travel" pointed out that although Americans had gone abroad before, time and money were no longer insurmountable obstacles to the masses. While worldwide airlines made overseas visits practical, Americans had gained sufficient wealth to meet the costs. "Traveling now and paying later, a vacationing U.S. secretary or schoolteacher abroad is today no rarer than a honeymooner at Niagara Falls."[8]

The correspondent Theodore White, leaving his assignment in China in the 1940s for Europe in the early 1950s, likened the Americans he observed in these diverse foreign parts to the Roman centurions in conquered Greece and to the English, the aristocrats of travelers of the nineteenth century, welcomed for bringing their currency and their modern customs. He described the American experts coming to lecture in European universities on their latest theories of nuclear physics, and security agents scrutinizing and training other peoples in the prevention of leakage of nuclear security. He noted that labor organizers recruited by the American government exhorted European unions to organize, and that businessmen recruited by the government urged European businessmen to compete. Garment cutters of the Amalgamated Clothing Workers showed French workers how Americans cut clothes. Private emissaries showed Belgians how to dig coal, Italians to drill natural gas, Englishmen to operate modern refineries, and Indians to use ploughs.

> Where a generation ago people laughed at the British servant of empire travel-
> ing through desert or jungle carrying his tin washtub and dinner jacket, they
> now regard Americans with astonishment. Americans bring with them not the
> tin washtub and dinner jacket but a composite of all the villages and towns they
> left behind in America—to create wherever they rest their own villages-in-
> exile. Thus there is an American community life in Paris, in London, in Athens,
> in Rome, in Bonn and all the outposts of American dispersion in Europe, the
> Middle East and Asia. At their PX's, supported by the sprawling United States
> Army around the globe, they may buy in special overseas American money ev-
> erything the hometown American department store sells.[9]

Europeans told Howard K. Smith that they could tell an American at a glance anywhere in the world, regardless of physical characteristics. Among the distinct ways of this new breed of travelers were "an intense love of freedom and an unfathomable belief in the self-sufficiency of the individual and the worth of his lone enterprise." Smith looked homeward to explain the conspicuous American strain of hope and optimism—to wide-open frontiers, plentiful opportunities, and the expectation that hard work and shrewd dealing paid off, which was "not often the case in a Europe

ridden with barriers of class and tradition." Smith could not tell whether "the florid man
with a twang and a bewildered look you meet on the street" was a dirt farmer or a Texas
oilman worth ten million dollars. But Smith noted that for Americans it would make a
great difference, for success was "still the dominant national value and it is measurable
for most people in dollars and cents."[10]

Anthropologists gave scholarly study to journalistic impressions: "What is it that
makes it possible to say of a group of people glimpsed from a hotel step in Soerabaja or
strolling down the streets of Marseilles, 'There go some Americans,' whether they have
come from Arkansas or Maine or Pennsylvania, whether they bear German or Swedish
or Italian surnames?" asked Margaret Mead. She hypothesized that the answer was tied
up in notions of national character. "Not clothes alone," Mead believed, "but the way
they wear them, the way they walk along the street without awareness that anyone of
higher status may be walking there also, the way their eyes rove as if by right over the
façade of palaces and the rose windows of cathedrals, interested and unimpressed,
referring what they see back to the Empire State building, the Chrysler tower, or a good-
sized mountain in Montana."[11]

A social science study of national character by the Carnegie Corporation in the
1950s formally examined Americans abroad in Mexico, Yugoslavia, Iran, Ethiopia,
Indonesia, and Japan. Through interviews and observations, the research determined
that they carried with them "the guilt for intolerance in Arkansas or bumbling in
Washington. They likewise bask in the reflection from great achievements at Cape
Canaveral or inspiring acts of leadership in Washington. Businessmen or missionaries,
airmen or soldiers, spies, 'experts,' or diplomats, they are all, like it or not, surrogates
for the United States Secretary of State. Many play the part with a feeling of acute
embarrassment. Some learn quickly to relax in the presence of their own power. Not a
few take too seriously the notion that their image mirrors America to foreign eyes, and
feel they must settle every outstanding issue of American foreign policy every time
they talk with a stranger."[12]

The effect of all their movement abroad was to draw attention to Americans in their
fast planes and their luxurious hotels and massive bases, but not necessarily to make
Americans more cosmopolitan or more understanding of other peoples, Daniel Boorstin noted. On the contrary, Americans tended to come to their destinations in planes or
on ships operated by American companies. The illusion of these conveyances was that
their occupants never left home. As Boorstin remarked of a flight to Amsterdam from
New York's Idlewild Airport, leaving at 6:30 one evening and arriving the next morning
at 11:30, "I had flown not through space but through time." Then, when the tourist
arrived at his destination, he remained "almost as insulated as he was en route." The
"ideal tourist hotel" abroad resembled as closely as possible "the best accommodations
back home." Beds, lighting, facilities, ventilation, air conditioning, central heating, and
plumbing were all "American style," although a shrewd hotel management would make
"a special effort to retain some 'local atmosphere.'" Americans in Madrid, Istanbul,

Cairo, Santiago, and Sydney found it possible to stay in American hotels where they could eat only American food, buy American products, and stay in their rooms watching American television reruns.[13]

The government made its own practical interpretation of the characteristic presence of Americans abroad. Granting their wealth and accomplishments, President Eisenhower warned travelers to beware of acting out stereotypes of a rich and powerful people, of being "immature diplomatically—impulsive—too proud of their strength. . . . Each of us, whether bearing a commission from his Government or traveling by himself for pleasure or for business is a representative of the United States of America."[14]

Conspicuous among Americans abroad were the businessmen, who brought to their jobs more than their goods and their deals. *Life* pictured these pioneers of American business as "getting things done in a somewhat new American way." The magazine traced the trip in the 1950s of one executive, Frank White, a vice president of American Machine and Foundry. A "whirlwind example of this businessman breed," White inspected a company plant and met with the foreign minister in Italy, talked business with a Turkish banker at the Hilton Hotel in Istanbul, and made plans in London for a new AMF plant in the British Isles. He traveled abroad seven times in a year and a half, and he sold everything from tobacco machinery and skin-diving gear to atomic reactors. But he believed his job was more "than a chance to turn a profit": "I feel strongly that international business can be and sometimes is a contributing factor to the preservation of world peace. If other countries have a big enough stake in the United States and vice versa, it will become very difficult to disrupt these relations."[15]

Oil industry businessmen opened up worldwide operations, in the view of the industry analyst Leonard Fanning, because of their enterprise: "the American oilman's drive, his ability to make snap decisions as well as carefully weighed and evaluated ones, his confidence in his own ability, his ingenuity—the American flare for taking 65 pieces of nothing and making something sorely needed with them—and his frequent accomplishment of the impossible in logistics and long-range planning." The popular expression of World War II was appropriate to these apostles of big business: "The difficult we do immediately; the impossible takes a little longer." Another characteristic was "the American ability to make friends abroad when he sets his mind to it." A Middle Easterner known to Fanning had compared the landing of the Standard of California geologists on the sands of Saudi Arabia in 1933 to Christopher Columbus discovering America. The native was referring not only to the geologists' major oil discoveries but also to their part as "ambassadors of good will" among the Bedouin people. "What promise for the future this vista of amity among peoples opens up!" Fanning remarked. "The narrow view of an isolated, domestic industry is as untenable as a United States itself isolated from the Free World."[16]

As businessmen moved through foreign markets with their own cultural "baggage" of ideas and customs, they were advised by *Changing Times* to "quash your national pride in your country's accomplishments, or at least you must not permit your pride to become arrogance." *Business Week* recommended that they needed to deal with "cultural savvy," to be on guard against some national characteristics. A businessman might be motivated to act toward customers with efficiency or to speak assertively. But the businessman's call on a Bedouin customer would be rude if he did not stay at least three days, and, in dealing with a Chinese customer, he should avoid emphasizing a point or concluding a conversation by saying how good it was to talk; the Chinese might feel he had aroused anger in the American. The ways that brought praise at home might bring scorn abroad. In Liberia, the Firestone company built a modern maternity clinic for the wives of plantation workers, but the local women refused to use it, because their custom was for the husband to be present at the birth of a child and the men had not been allowed in the delivery room. At a big sugar plantation in Peru owned by W. R. Grace, the company nearly lost its entire work force by building a swimming pool; the workers ran in terror from it because they had a traditional superstitious fear of pools of water.[17]

Servicemen, too, left their mark on the countries they occupied. The soldiers were victors, but they were egalitarian victors. At the great hall of the Nazi elite in Berchtesgaden, Germany, where the leaders once met to chart plans of conquest, the American soldiers used the private liquor stock for toasts with their French allies. As the soldiers took pride in breaking down the remnants of dictatorship, they often got along well with the local peoples, giving away food, cigarettes, and candy bars. American soldiers were not mercenaries but citizens who much preferred being home to fighting away from it.[18]

As occupiers, the soldiers espoused democracy, but they often maintained a privileged position. Servicemen were feared in Tokyo: they noticed at first that the people looked on each of them as General MacArthur's "personal representative," with respect and awe. Only when the men displayed a "certain humanity" did the "extreme deference" of the locals give way to "normal politeness." American soldiers represented a law higher than that of the police, so local authorities hesitated to confront them, and one American believed that the American presence was "rapidly undermining the faith these people once had in their leaders," though not by trepidation of arms alone. "The amazing array of equipment we bring ashore, the nonchalance and easy ways of our men, and most of all the American soldier's generosity are winning the people to new ways of thinking."[19]

In Germany, the soldiers' special privileges often included living in the best houses that had been requisitioned and having maids to work in their homes. While probably more fortunate than most military personnel and families, the wife of an army captain, who lived with her husband and two children in a nine-room house with three servants, described the good life in the *Saturday Evening Post*. The family enjoyed the best food and plenty of coal, gas, and electricity—for $225 a month. She saved $300 of her husband's salary every month. The former owner of the requisitioned house had to stay on the concrete floor of a nearby garage, and the captain's wife wondered how this sort of occupation could teach the Germans the American brand of democracy. Thomas Bailey thought, "so much 'embarrassing' plenty in the midst of such misery did seem a bit like rubbing in the defeat." Mingling pride in victory and in the triumph of democracy, Bailey's black chauffeur seemed to derive "satisfaction, even a sense of power, in forcing Hitler's once proud and racially conscious *Herrenvolk* to scramble out of his path as he blared his way down the thoroughfare."[20]

As the occupation of defeated countries continued, the peoples became less servile. David Rodnick's anthropological study *Postwar Germans* found that Germans did not want the American occupiers to look down on them as inferiors. German youths were reported "bewildered" by looting American soldiers, which made America appear to them as only interested in victimizing the Germans. Sometimes the soldiers treated German girls "contemptuously" and were "rough" with them, which the girls resented. A hitchhiker Theodore White picked up expressed anger at Americans: "We see now that the conquerors who were supposed to teach Germany democracy do not mean democracy either. They show us now that in only one thing Hitler was right, that the world respects force. We find now the Russians are just as savage as Hitler, and the Americans and English are savage too, only they are savage in a gentlemanly way. They did not fight us to make democracy, but because they wanted to crush Germany forever."[21]

But the most lasting impression on the occupied peoples was not of military force but of the modern life the soldiers represented. The millions of American military personnel were seen as salesmen for American products and customs overseas, almost like businessmen. Turks, Russians, Moroccans, and "everyone everywhere" were caught looking with wonder at the simplest possessions of the Americans. Wrote one astonished citizen, Isabel Cary Lundberg, in *Harper's:* Every "soldier, sailor, flier, and marine, on beaches and atolls, in swamps and on deserts, in the port of Murmansk and the railhead at Teheran, carried his arsenal of revolutionary weapons on his person, in his knapsack, duffle bag, and foot locker. Did a single one of them regard himself as an agent of social change and revolution? Perish the thought! Yet one has only to ask what the native populations everywhere wanted of the GI, the Air Force pilot, the gob, and the Seabee. They wanted what the vast majority of the world's population, European and non-European, wants: the wrist watch, fountain pen, cigarettes, flashlight, chocolate bars, chewing gum, cameras, pocket knives, pills to kill pain, vaccines to save lives, hospital beds with clean sheets, hand soap and shaving soap, gadgets and gewgaws of every description, the jeep, the truck, and *white bread.*"[22]

In American bases in the late 1940s, Air Force fliers and ground crews, because of the machines they used, the clothes they wore, the foods they ate, and the illustrated magazines they read, appeared, "without knowing it or even wishing it, as 'the terrible instigators of social change and revolution.'" American technique became standard in auto maintenance, in airport control, and in water sanitation. The United States Armed Forces Network filled the air with jazz and news and for a while had the largest listening audience in Europe. The armies of occupation taught the Germans and the French how to make hamburgers and hot dogs.[23]

"Personal Diplomacy"

Diplomats delivered the positions of their government to foreign leaders in Paris, Léopoldville, Aden, and Calcutta, but since Wilson had traveled to Europe to participate in the conference at Versailles, United States presidents had increased their direct personal contacts with the leaders and people of different states. Roosevelt crossed the Atlantic on the U.S.S. *Quincy* on his way to Yalta, and Truman sailed to Europe on the U.S.S. *Augusta* to attend the conference at Potsdam. The presidents carried with them the accoutrements of the leader of the wealthiest nation on earth. Truman was accompanied by "at least a part of the executive branch of the government," and an escort heavy cruiser, the *Philadelphia,* moved ahead of the president's ship to make a smooth path in rough seas. "It was a wonderful crossing," he recorded. Movies were shown at night. Each morning Truman awoke early to walk around the deck. He ate a meal in every mess hall aboard the ship to talk with the men. After the ship made a record crossing on the return voyage, Truman marveled at sailing the Atlantic at a rate of 645 miles every twenty-four hours.[24]

The first president to travel abroad by air, Roosevelt, flew during the war from the Mediterranean island of Malta to Yalta on the Crimean peninsula. Truman, who turned in his plane dubbed the *Sacred Cow* for a DC-6 called the *Independence,* could not get over the rapid advance in travel. "We haven't adjusted ourselves to this speed." Eisenhower was the first to have a jet for a presidential plane. His Boeing 707, a "mammoth machine," as he described it, completely dwarfed his earlier plane named the *Columbine,* which he had once thought to be the last word in luxury, size, and speed. The jet of clean lines and sleek engines, he discovered, was a source of astonishment wherever it landed. At the airport at Mar del Plata, as the president of Argentina admired the presidential aircraft, Eisenhower thought of the Latin American custom that whenever a guest holds an object in esteem, the host must give it to him. Unhappily, Eisenhower reflected, "the plane was not mine to give away." He did the only other thing he could think of: he invited the president to ride along to the next stop, an Andean resort city. The Argentinian readily accepted.[25]

American leaders traveled abroad to lead in war, to seek peace, to make threats, to deliver aid, and to encourage good will. In World War II Roosevelt established the pattern of international meetings for coordinating Allied efforts. He conferred frequently with Churchill. Twice he met with Soviet leaders. He received a French delegation at Casablanca and the Chinese at Cairo. But Roosevelt's success in achieving cooperation against the enemy was not transferable to solving the problems of the postwar world.

Roosevelt, and Truman too, liked Stalin when they met face to face. At Stalin's visit for lunch at Potsdam, Truman was "impressed by him. . . . He looked me in the eye when he spoke." Truman confided his initial impression in his private diary: Stalin "put on a real show drinking toasts to everyone. . . . I can deal with Stalin. He is honest—but smart as hell." But after no peace agreement emerged from the meetings,

Truman felt frustrated. He wished then that he had been allowed to give his point of view to the Russian people directly, without censorship. What would he say to them if he had the chance? He would begin, "we have no desire nor are we trying to change the world to fit the pattern of our own country." American freedom "enabled our masses of people to enjoy an ever improved standard of living, free from the kind of toil that still is breaking the backs of hundreds of millions of people. I would offer American experience, American skill and American science to help lift the load from these people's backs."[26]

Eisenhower relished his "personal diplomacy." As president-elect, he made an inspection tour of Korea, carrying out his campaign pledge in October 1952 to go to that war-divided country. After Stalin's death Eisenhower attended in June 1955 a summit meeting at Geneva and, serving as chairman, met with the leaders of Britain, France, and the Soviet Union. In his second term Eisenhower made his most wide-ranging trip, from Europe to the Middle East to India. In Britain he visited the royal family in Scotland at Balmoral castle. In Germany an exuberant crowd lined the road from the airport, turning out in numbers that exceeded the populations of the towns through which he passed—and all this in a country utterly defeated by his army ten years before.[27]

Continuing on his trip, in Pakistan he had become accustomed to masses cheering and shouting. But in Afghanistan he was surprised again, experiencing "the excitement of a mob bursting out of control. Suddenly, and without warning, we found our vehicles unable to move, almost sinking in a sea of strange faces. But the faces were friendly." In India along the road from the airport, dense crowds, with carts, donkeys, and camels, began swarming around the vehicles. "It was an overwhelming experience," wrote Eisenhower. The teeming crowd "outdid in size anything I had ever seen, including those of the victory celebrations in the great cities of America and Europe." As the motorcade finally entered New Delhi, "the human sea closed in upon us and compelled a halt. For more than twenty-five minutes we could not move. Members of the Secret Service were almost helpless." Then Eisenhower saw Prime Minister Nehru forcing his way to the front of the car. Using the stick he always carried, the prime minister began laying about him, but his "lively non-violence" was to no avail. At long last, with the help of police reserves, the car began to proceed. Later a crowd of well over a half million congregated on a vast grassy field to hear Eisenhower address them. Eisenhower traveled from country to country offering tribute, not demanding it, as rulers of empires had in times past. When Pakistan's president asked for American aid, Eisenhower noted, "in one guise or other, this question was part of every business conference I held in every nation throughout the entire tour." In general his answer was always the same: He wanted "to help those nations who wanted to help themselves in raising their own living standards and combatting Communism."[28]

As a result of his global journey, Eisenhower could point to no great agreements of national security or trade. But having seen millions of people, he "never once" saw "a patently hostile face; the welcoming placards along the roadsides and the glad shouts of

'America!'—recognizable in spite of language differences—left no doubt of the friendly sentiments the teeming populations felt for our nation." The American chief executive felt rewarded by "the eagerness of whole populations to learn about America," and by a "better understanding of the peoples he, directly or indirectly, as head of the strongest nation on earth, is destined to serve." The masses he had met all shared "their favorable conception of American freedom, American purpose, and American aspirations for all men."[29]

But Americans were not always welcomed abroad. In 1958 Vice President Nixon made a trip to South America. In Peru at a university in San Marcos, he met a crowd of students demonstrating against him. He risked a confrontation because of a simple proposition: he conceived of himself as the bearer of the status of a powerful state, and he could not falter. "I recognized," he reflected, "that the United States, as a world power, should always take into consideration the sensitivities of smaller nations. While it is pleasant to be popular and liked, I have always thought that our country in its leadership should never lose sight of the goals, objectives, and aspirations of the United States itself." If the Peruvian leaders "shrank from this crisis, I thought that my actions should not be inhibited by their fears."[30]

At the university's gate Nixon got out of the car and walked directly toward the crowd of two thousand that had been yelling "Fuera Nixon" (Go home, Nixon) with an occasional "Muera Nixon" (Death to Nixon). He faced a "Communist-led gang," he called it, and those in front backed away. Nixon tried to speak, his interpreter shouting in Spanish: "If you have complaints against the United States, tell me what they are and I shall try to answer them. This is the free way, the democratic way to discuss the differences we have." For a few moments he thought he had the situation "under control," until suddenly he felt a blow to his shoulder. The crowd was throwing stones, and Nixon ordered a retreat. As he got into the car, the rocks were flying, but Nixon could not resist the temptation to stand on the rear seat while the car moved slowly away and shout, "You are cowards, you are afraid of the truth! You are the worst kind of cowards." Nixon remembered, "I felt the excitement of battle as I spoke."[31]

In 1959 Nixon made another highly publicized trip, this time to the Soviet Union, and there, within a decade after Truman had desired to address the Russian people, the vice president had this opportunity. In a speech he argued that Americans had the world's highest standard of living and so had come closest to an equitable distribution of income. It was a revolutionary conception, overturning fundamental communist theory: "The average weekly wage of a factory worker in America is $90.54," Nixon said.

> With this income he can buy and afford to own a house, a television set and car. . . . Putting it another way, there are 44,000,000 families in the United States. . . . Thirty-one million families own their own homes and the land on which they are built. America's 44,000,000 families own a total of 56,000,000 cars, 50,000,000 television sets and 143,000,000 radio sets. And they buy an

average of nine dresses and suits and fourteen pairs of shoes per family per year. . . . But what these statistics do dramatically demonstrate is this: that the United States, the world's largest capitalist country, has from the standpoint of distribution of wealth come closer to the ideal of prosperity for all in a classless society.

America was not only prosperous, but it also represented political democracy. Said Nixon, to prove his point: "President Eisenhower is one of the most popular men ever to hold that high office in our country. Yet never an hour or a day goes by in which criticism of him and his policies cannot be read in our newspapers, heard on our radio and television, or in the halls of Congress. And he would not have it any other way." There was freedom of speech: "forty hours of radio broadcasts from the Soviet Union can be heard without jamming in the United States each day." There was freedom of religion: Americans could worship at any church or no church at all. And there was freedom to travel: "We look forward to the day when millions of Soviet citizens will travel to ours and other countries in this way."[32]

Language

The power of the word, transmitted by voice and print, was immense. "English is increasingly becoming a *lingua franca,*" said *Foreign Affairs* in 1956, the modern international medium of exchange for aviation, science, technology, commerce, diplomacy, and popular culture. Great Britain had spread the language throughout the empire, but after World War II American English, boosted by American economic and political power, became prevalent. In Western Europe and Latin America the domestic use of English had become far more widespread than that of any other foreign language. In developing regions, where newly formed nations lacked a common tongue, English was especially popular. Worldwide, probably more than 270 million people could speak English, and the numbers were increasing.[33]

Americans heard their every-day expressions and idioms returned in unexpected places. Veterans who served in New Britain in the Pacific encountered local kids using American slang and cuss words, and whatever an American said to them, they always replied with "Okeydoke." Youngsters in the hills of Burma became "funny fans" when soldiers produced brightly colored comic books. Among Russians Margaret Bourke-White reported the fascination for such expressions as "tear jerker," "cracked ice," and "sob sister." A mining official in the Belgian Congo told an American his inquiry about diamonds was the "$64 question." Teachers of English in Norway changed the rules of grammar; young students were not marked incorrect, as they had been, if they wrote "honor" instead of the British "honour." But the American contribution to the English language confused some of the British, those who, it was said, were not quite certain whether Alaska was one of the forty-eight states of the union or whether the Grand Canyon was the title of a Hollywood film.[34]

Books and magazines opened a flow of information and ideas. They carried the ideas of democracy and modernization, and their impact could be shown by Thoreau's *On the Duty of Civil Disobedience* after a single copy came into the hands of Mohandas Gandhi, then a young lawyer in South Africa. But, writing in the *Department of State Bulletin* in 1955, Nelson Rockefeller, a special assistant to the president, stated that Americans had been slow to recognize the impact of their books. Rockefeller felt that books were "windows to a nation's soul" and important in making friends abroad. Books confronted communist propaganda. They also made available technical knowledge to assist in economic development. Rockefeller wanted a government program to distribute books abroad: "American world leadership" warranted "the greatest possible effort to expand the use of American books throughout the world."[35]

American books rushed into the void left by European literature after the war. The novels of Hemingway and Faulkner and the detective mysteries of Mickey Spillane became popular, and by the 1950s American exports of books had grown to three or four times what they had been before World War II. Added to the $40 million worth of American books, at wholesale prices, exported annually were millions more in British editions; in Great Britain and its dominions overseas, American books either in original or British editions circulated as freely as in the United States. Elsewhere American books were translated into other languages. The growing demand for paperback books in the United States raised expectations for a similar market for inexpensive American books abroad.[36]

Periodicals circulated among every-day readers and national leaders. An avid reader of *Life*, the Nazi Albert Speer told John Kenneth Galbraith of his dread at seeing pictures of American war plants; Speer's mastery of the American idiom included a description of his interrogation as "Grade B Warner Brothers." Writers on assignment for *National Geographic* kept encountering readers of their magazine in South Africa or the Belgian Congo. The head of the National Geographic Society discovered during a call on Zanzibar's sultan that he was already a member. By the mid-1950s, *Reader's Digest* had spread through editions in English, French, Spanish, and the Scandinavian languages, and it became either the largest or the second-largest monthly magazine of its type in England, France, Spain, and Scandinavia. All over Europe Theodore White browsed through a variety of American publications on newsstands. The *New York Herald Tribune* was published daily in Paris, and the overseas edition of the *New York Times* was available twelve hours later. *Time* and *Newsweek* appeared in overseas editions on the same day as the issues at home. The *Saturday Evening Post*, the *Ladies' Home Journal*, the *Atlantic, Harper's, True Story, True Detective*, and *Real Western* were all distributed a few days after they came out in the United States. At the French Ministry of Justice, White visited the supervisor of comic books, who took him through his files of *Sioux Boy* and *Texas Jack;* stacks of comics of cowboys or spaceships had to be scrutinized to protect the children, the minister told him.[37]

Russians were eager for American writing, when they could get hold of it. While

Margaret Bourke-White was unpacking her camera equipment, a Russian woman came in and carefully smoothed out the paper wrappings. When the Russian saw that they were pages torn from *Vogue* and *Harper's Bazaar,* she exclaimed: "We must carry these to the House of Fashion Models." American periodicals were scarce. The Soviet government did not want them handed about among the people. At a wartime American air base in Ukraine, W. L. White learned, the Soviets required that all American magazines and newspapers received by the troops be collected once a week and burned. George Kennan reported a year after the war that, aside from Tibet or Afghanistan, the Soviet Union was "more barren than any other region of news and information originating directly from American sources."[38]

Music

The mechanical means of recording and the inventions of the phonograph and record disc released far and wide a whole body of American music. Dean Acheson was moved by the influence of American music after learning of a young colleague's tour of South Asia, the Soviet Union, and the Eastern European satellites in the 1950s. However American policy might be criticized, "American jazz reigned unchallenged from Bombay through Tashkent, from Moscow to Warsaw and Belgrade." "How," the young American had asked a Pole, "can you listen to this stuff?" "Ah!" said the Pole. "You ought to hear what we have had to hear for ten years!" In remote Pacific islands Americans encountered "The Sidewalks of New York." Blacks in South Africa learned "Negro" spirituals of the United States.[39]

Jazz was a uniquely American musical form, which became "hot" around the world. In Paris, Americans heard it not merely among the circles of French intellectuals but also among the youths who assembled on the Left Bank. At a jamboree in early 1952, bands from around Western Europe played their riffs and blues, imitating American styles, in a contest. *Life* reviewed the concerts as "anything but placid." A Belgian band that dared to play reading sheet music on music stands, rather than by memory and improvisation, was "so loudly booed it could not be heard." When a French band played "sweet music," the fans "howled for blood"—"until America's Dizzy Gillespie came up and quieted them with bebop." Along with Ella Fitzgerald, Gillespie was "a hit" of the show.[40]

Recordings made musicians well known before they went abroad. Benny Goodman, the King of Swing, who headed a big band in the 1930s and 1940s, took his jazz around the world in the 1950s and 1960s. At a command performance for the king of Thailand, Goodman played his clarinet with a fifteen-man orchestra, when suddenly the king began to play the clarinet that Goodman had given him as a gift. Improvising together before the guests, the king switched to the saxophone. They played tunes, among them "Muskrat Ramble" and "Honeysuckle Rose," for about an hour. "Kings of Swing and Thailand Jive" reported the front-page headline of the *New York Times*: the two kings "all but blew the roof off Thailand's royal Amphorn Palace." "He's not bad at all—not at all," Goodman said of the twenty-nine-year-old monarch.[41]

Jazz reached the Soviet Union on contraband records and on X-ray plates, even as the 1950s issues of *Pravda* or *Izvestia* condemned the United States as the listeners' worst enemy. The people who congregated at parties in dark rooms heard Bing Crosby, Nat King Cole, Louis Armstrong, and Peggy Lee and engaged in activities that they thought rightly accompanied by American jazz: smoking Camels and using English words—"darling" and "baby." Jazz, wrote Vassily Aksyonov, a Soviet writer who came to live in the United States, was "America's secret weapon number one," broadcast every night via the Voice of America to the Soviet Union from Tangiers. He wondered, "How many dreamy Russian boys came to puberty to the strains of Ellington's 'Take the A Train.'"[42]

Goodman took his band to the Soviet Union in 1962. At the Central Army Sports Arena in Moscow, he played to about forty-six hundred listeners, including Khrushchev—the first time a Soviet leader lent respectability to jazz. Although, according to an American reviewer, the Russians did not "stomp in the aisles in any burst of enthusiasm," they "obviously enjoyed their first musical dispensation from the 'King of Swing.'" On the street by Red Square, Goodman also attracted a crowd when he took his clarinet out and began to play. About two hundred people heard "Yankee Doodle Dandy" and "Midnight in Moscow." Khrushchev and Goodman appeared at a fete held by the American embassy on July 4, and they got into an amicable debate on the merits of jazz.

"Ah, a new jazz fan," the orchestra leader said.

"No," said Khrushchev, smiling. "I don't like Goodman music. I like good music." "I am not a jazz fan, I like real music," he continued. "I don't understand jazz. I don't mean just yours. I don't even understand our own."

Goodman explained that it took time to appreciate jazz, provoking Khrushchev: "Good music should appeal at once—it shouldn't take time." Both men agreed that they liked Mozart.[43]

Khrushchev had greeted more enthusiastically the American pianist Van Cliburn, who played in the finals of the Tchaikovsky Piano Competition in Moscow in 1958 and won first prize. After his final piece, Rachmaninoff's Third Piano Concerto, the twenty-three-year-old Texan received a standing ovation. For his technical skill and romantic style, shouts of "Bravo" rang out for eight and a half minutes, until the judges permitted a violation of the contest rules and sent Cliburn out for a second bow. Wherever in Russia he went afterwards, fans and autograph seekers mobbed him. At a Kremlin reception, Khrushchev embraced Cliburn. First Deputy Premier Anastas Mikoyan remarked, "You've been a very good politician for your country. You've done better than the politicians"—and *Time* commented that Cliburn had produced a "more favorable impact on more Russians than any U.S. export of word or deed since World War II."[44]

But these were classical works, and jazz appealed especially to the young. At a cafe Goodman's band members joined in a jam session with Soviet youths. Their only criticism was that Goodman had not come fifteen years earlier, because his music was not the latest Western form.[45]

By the end of the 1950s a new creative art, rock and roll, was spread from America all over Europe by traveling bands, records, and juke boxes, as teenage boys and girls danced to the beat. In Japan, "rock 'n' roru" was popular with youths. Walking down a Tokyo street, one could hear the tune "Jailhouse Rock" emanating from a bar's jukebox. Imitators of Elvis Presley performed in coffee shops. One establishment named the "Tennessee" featured a Japanese band whose members, dressed in cowboy boots and hats, sang folk ballads.[46]

Hollywood Films

Hollywood motion pictures offered the most vivid image of modern American life to the largest number of people. American films had been in demand in virtually all overseas areas since World War I, and in the 1930s they continuously drew larger numbers of viewers than indigenous movies. Exports boomed even in the later years of World War II, to allies and liberated areas, and then worldwide in the postwar years. By the late 1950s, about half of the average receipts of films came from abroad. "We have seen the American motion picture become foremost in all the world," President Roosevelt announced in an address to the 1941 awards dinner of the Academy of Motion Picture Arts and Sciences. "We have seen it reflect our civilization throughout the rest of the world—the aims and the aspirations and the ideals of a free people and of freedom itself."[47]

Movies represented a picture of life that was flexible, energetic, egalitarian, and industrious. The very pace and clarity of American films, and the rapid-fire delivery of speech, characterized this movement and energy. The stories were of democratic life: of the plight of an American Everyman played by Gary Cooper in *Meet John Doe,* of a rural community's hope and optimism in *Our Town,* and of the whole montage of American life in *It's a Big Country.* Hollywood pictures offered foreigners impressions of American styles, slang, music, houses, cars, gadgets, kitchens, clothing, and machines. On the whole, these images represented modernity. But because American films put forth the aberrant side of behavior representing youthful toughs in gang films, convicts in gangster films, and moral degenerates in ostentatious musicals, critics questioned whether Hollywood's portrayal of American values and life should be deliberately shown in foreign lands.

The film industry supported the American war effort, during which the film producer Walter Wanger suggested that studies wanted "to make an even larger contribution to winning the war and achieving goodwill on earth" than they had. He argued that films portraying American vigor and democracy had "round-the-world value." After the war Spyros Skouras of 20th Century-Fox urged his colleagues, in *Variety,* to carry on a "missionary spirit," which would "not only be of great importance to the motion picture industry economically," but would also allow them to use the medium to help "enlighten humanity." It was "a solemn responsibility," Skouras added, "to increase motion picture outlets throughout the free world because it has been shown that no medium can play a greater part than the motion picture in indoctrinating people into the free way of life and instilling in them a compelling desire for freedom and hope for a brighter future."[48]

But Eric Johnston, the businessman who became president of the Motion Picture Association of America in 1953, found that argument hard to buy. He believed that motion pictures were effective in presenting an idea of America because they were not obvious propaganda. They reflected the freedom under which they were made. Hollywood was an entertainment business, not a propaganda factory, and "that's precisely why American movies are more popular around the world than the films of any other nation." Hollywood films showed "*all* sides of America—the good and the bad," thereby carrying "important social and ideological by-products."[49]

Hollywood films pictured what Americans represented in foreign settings and situations. In *Casablanca* (1942), Humphrey Bogart played an individualistic American nightclub owner in French Morocco who declared his unwillingness to stick his neck out for anyone, but at the end proved to be not really an isolationist at heart. He was forced to intervene in the war, and so was America. In *Blood on the Sun* (1945), James Cagney exuberantly portrayed an American reporter in prewar Tokyo, a good-hearted but independent loner who singlehandedly uncovered Japanese plans for world conquest. After the war, on-screen Americans ended up in foreign places as innocent tourists, like Katharine Hepburn as a spinster vacationing in summertime Venice in 1955. But the postwar themes of American films were largely of foreign tensions and espionage. In 1952 Tyrone Power was an earnest diplomatic agent whose Cold War espionage took him into Trieste and onto dark European trains to uncover an enemy plot for World War III.

In earlier years directors customarily shot films with foreign settings and themes in Hollywood. Using a background projection system, actors in studios were photographed in front of "transparencies" representing the streets of Paris or the foot of Mt. Fuji. After the war, moviemakers began to use foreign locales. When Cecil B. DeMille decided to remake *The Ten Commandments,* which he had originally shot in the 1920s in California as a silent black-and-white film, Paramount sent him to Egypt for two months in the fall of 1954 with a load of cameras, light reflectors, tents, furniture, costumes, and foodstuffs. The new film was shot in color, using wide-screen projection. Paramount created an ancient Egyptian city in the desert at Beni Youssef, a few miles southwest of Cairo. The city gates of Per-Ramses were 107 feet high, and from them stretched an avenue of sphinxes nearly a quarter of a mile long. Some journalists had the notion that DeMille, not satisfied with the real ancient pyramids, had built some of his own. "We did," said DeMille with the exaggerated flair of a moviemaker, "and for the very simple reason that the actual pyramids of ancient Egypt have changed in appearance in the past 3,000 years. The pyramids we built on the horizon, visible from the city gates, were white and unweathered, as the real pyramids were in Moses' time."

The moviemakers' creations did not stop with ancient wonders: Behind the set of the gates there was a city, but it was not Per-Ramses. "It was Paramount," said DeMille. There were offices, huge storage sheds for props and costumes, a medical clinic, cafeterias for the thousands of extras, tents for the Egyptian cavalry lent to the picture company by the government to act as pharaoh's army, corrals for the horses, which had to be trained for months to draw chariots without shafts, and parking space for the fleet of cars that shuttled constantly between nearby cities, studios, and lodgings for the cast.[50]

Far from deterring moviemakers, remote terrain or strange climate attracted them. The director John Huston brought Katharine Hepburn, Bogart, and a crew to the Belgian Congo to film *The African Queen* in 1950. The company built in the jungle a camp consisting of comfortable cottages, a bar with a Victrola, and a restaurant serving American-style food. The Americans brought with them sound booms and arc lights and large Technicolor cameras, made mobile in filming scenes by ingeniously constructed tracks. Each day they took their equipment and replicas of parts of the *African Queen* on a large modern raft out onto the Ruiki River. "The local blacks didn't know what in the world we were trying to do," Hepburn remembered. They had to be impressed with all this paraphernalia, but she was "sure it seemed to them utterly idiotic. Lugging stuff up the river—getting dressed up—sitting around—sitting in the *African Queen*—talking gibberish—taking little trips—and doing it over and over again—then going home. And doing the same thing again the next day. They thought we were crazy. They'd never seen a movie. Or maybe they had . . . ." She never knew for sure.[51]

Americans who traveled had a chance to observe close-up the impact of Hollywood films. Wendell Willkie believed that motion pictures had played an important role in building up the good will that foreigners held toward Americans. From films people of "every country can see with their own eyes what we look like, can hear our voices." From Natal to Chunking he was plied with questions about American motion-picture stars—questions asked "eagerly by shop-girls and those who served me coffee, and just as eagerly by the wives of prime ministers and kings."[52]

Travelers who saw Hollywood pictures abroad liked to watch the reactions of foreign audiences along with the show. Both the foreigners and their observers usually liked what they saw. In wartime China, movies with Chinese subtitles were shown to the laborers and townspeople helping to build airfields. As many as thirty thousand Chinese, few of whom had ever seen a film before, came to one showing of an American film. Before another presentation, *The Return of the Cisco Kid,* an American sergeant suggested to two other army men that they go to see it, though all three of them had seen it back home. "You wouldn't hear the thing," his comrades told him, because the audience read the Chinese subtitles aloud, making it impossible to hear the soundtrack.

Movies shown in Iran were five years old but popular in spite of an early curfew. In an Iranian theater some soldiers saw *The Big Store* with the Marx brothers. The subtitles were in French, but the film would flicker to a stop to replace the Marx brothers with Persian script explaining the action to that point. It reportedly took ten minutes to tell what happened in five minutes of screen action. By the time the Marx brothers returned to the screen, one of the soldiers had lost track of the continuity, but fortunately, he thought, "with the Marx Brothers, that doesn't matter much." After the intermission, the screen was suddenly filled with four minutes of *Gone with the Wind* in Technicolor before the operator recognized his mistake.

In Greece after the liberation of Athens, a citizen told an American of the excitement among his people at being able to see American movies again for the first time since 1940. The movie houses were advertising as coming attractions the films they had been saving ever since the Germans invaded—*The Life of Abraham Lincoln* and *The Road Back.*[53]

In Eastern Europe and the Middle East, from Warsaw to Cairo, Stanton Griffis, who served as American ambassador to four countries after World War II, attended films in local theaters and also screened them for private audiences. He made "no bones" about saying that on many occasions he had "accomplished more with good American pictures than with all the formal activities and paraphernalia of official diplomacy." He held to the conviction that American films were "an invaluable adjunct to American foreign policy."[54]

In postwar Germany films purposely showed the rudiments of democracy. Theodore White remembered going one evening to a theater in Düsseldorf to see *All Quiet on the Western Front,* a film about the hardships of soldiers in World War I. Hitler had never let his people see this when it first appeared. The audience was silent until a soldier on the screen suggested to his troops that the way to fight the war was to sell tickets to a huge stadium in which everyone could watch the generals and the statesmen who made the war fight it out themselves. All at once the people broke into a burst of laughter and applause.

In towns and cities through Western Europe White had seen Hollywood movies drawing customers and filling them with dreams similar to those of Americans—"of the penthouse, of shiny convertibles, of well-furnished homes." Hollywood films had also filled their nightmares with the "symbols of the smoking pistol, the ominous ringing of the telephone, the stab of violence puncturing the course of life."[55]

Concrete measurement of the impact of films worldwide was often sought. An estimate of the total audience for just Cecil B. DeMille's pictures from 1913 to 1959 was no less than four billion people—or about one and a half times the population of the earth at the time of his death in 1959; but no one knew for sure, because accurate counts of viewers outside movie houses were never taken. But DeMille noted the impact of his films in less tangible ways. He was surprised to find that *The Crusades,* in which Christian military expeditions sought to recover the Holy Land from the Muslims, had been popular in the Middle East. And his life of Christ, *The King of Kings,* had been widely shown in Confucian China.[56]

The Soviets were a little different in their reactions to American films. Even in World War II they seldom showed a movie that depicted middle-class American life or its standard of living. The best-known American films were Charlie Chaplin's *The Gold Rush* and *The Great Dictator,* and a Sonja Henie skating picture. The 1943 film *North Star,* Hollywood's version of life on a Soviet collective farm under German attack, was seen by Henry Wallace in the Siberian port city of Magadan; he noted it was then "the rage." When Margaret Bourke-White was in Moscow, she noticed that *The Great Waltz,* an extravagant MGM production about nineteenth-century Vienna, was bringing in capacity audiences. When W. L. White was there, the most popular foreign pictures were *Jungle* and *Thief of Bagdad.* White went to the theater hoping to see how the Russians "would react to an American picture, which gave, casually, just a fair idea of American life—an American home or well-dressed average Americans getting into cars or trains." Instead he saw *Jungle,* an adaptation of Kipling's *Jungle Book,* set in a Hindu village; the location of the other film was medieval Baghdad. He nevertheless noted that the girls and young soldiers were delighted.[57]

White thought it unlikely that even the film *The Grapes of Wrath,* which portrayed harsh depression life, would be released in Russia, because it would bewilder the Soviet audience. The Joad family in the film would not be pitied for their clothing, which was little different from Soviet clothes. "But here is a family which, not being content with its circumstances, leaves without obtaining permission and wanders a thousand miles or so without a travel permit in search of a better job. Where is the NKVD? Why aren't they stopped? Each of these offenses is worth a five-year sentence. True, the grand-mother dies on the way and obviously malnutrition contributed, but this is no rarity in the Soviet Union. . . . Above all, where did they get the car? Since it is shabby, of course, it didn't come from the Kremlin motor pool, but the fact that it will run at all proves it must have belonged to an important factory foreman for use on official business only."

A Russian woman accompanied White to a theater to see a Soviet film, and he was uncomfortable not knowing if the two men who sat nearby were NKVD agents. The woman said she was interested in American films and told him how she admired the American stars, Charlie Chaplain, Mary Pickford, and Douglas Fairbanks. Though they had appeared years previously in silent films, she asked for the names of their recent pictures. The film the American and Russian were seeing was supposed to be a comedy. "The scenes were tedious and the technique was bad." The sound and the pictures did not coordinate. "I began to think, watching this jerky business," he wrote, "what a treat it would be for this girl to see an American film—of recent vintage." So he invited her to the American embassy to see one, and of course, she wanted to go to see a new American film. But when the day came, he decided against it because it occurred to him that something he wrote later might displease the Soviets, and that the career she hoped for in Soviet movies might be jeopardized.[58]

Even well after the war, classic American films of the 1930s, confiscated from the Nazis by the Soviets, were shown to the Russian people in the absence of new Soviet films. The authorities showed the films under altered titles so as to avoid paying royalties to American studios and to present at least the facade of an ideological message: *Stagecoach* was called *The Journey Will Be Dangerous*, and *The Roaring Twenties* was *The Fate of the Soldier in America*. The films received accompanying introductions: "*The Journey Will Be Dangerous* treats the heroic struggle of the Indians against Yankee imperialism." Young viewers saw these films again and again, but to see the American stars rather than the introductions, and for a time teenagers spoke to each other in lines from American films. "Comrade Stalin made a big mistake by letting our generation see those films," one friend confided to Vassily Aksyonov; "they provided one of the few windows to the outside world from our stinking Stalinist lair."[59]

Television

The impact of films soon lessened somewhat in intensity, for by the end of the 1950s the distribution of American movies turned down worldwide. In 1961 the footage of film sent abroad fell off sharply. Films were being produced for home audiences in Italy, France, India, and elsewhere, and the downturn in American film production coincided with the dissemination of a new American means of mass entertainment and information, television. In 1948, when television was only beginning, worldwide box-office receipts of American films totaled $2.445 billion. A decade later the total was only $1.88 billion. The receipts remained well below those of earlier years. But if movies were receding in their impact, television was expanding, filling in a gap in communications.[60]

What Americans considered true about the impact of films seemed even more immediate with television. Television had the potential to reach lives at a rate unmatched by past technologies. "American TV products—for better and for worse—," appraised Wilson P. Dizard of exports of American programs in 1964, "are setting the tone for television programming throughout the world in much the same way Hollywood did for motion pictures 40 years ago." He found that the United States led "all other countries combined twice over as a program exporter." American television exports, Dizard testified before a congressional committee in 1967, made them "the main source of the 'American image' for increasing millions of people abroad." He discovered that the "daily schedule of a typical Australian television station is, particularly in prime listening hours, virtually indistinguishable from that of a station in Iowa or New Jersey."[61]

In Britain in the 1950s, viewers watched *I Love Lucy, Gunsmoke,* and *The Lone Ranger.* In Argentina in the 1960s, the favorite American imports were *The Man from U.N.C.L.E., The F.B.I.,* and *Batman.* In Belgium, American productions filled the "Top Ten," with *The Jetsons* and *The Fugitive* near the top. In Finland, American shows accounted for up to 85 percent of filmed programs. In Mexico, a survey in *Television Age* noted, "U.S. shows dominate Mexican prime time," right through the evening.[62]

As the technological breakthrough of television spread globally in the 1950s, the head of RCA and NBC radio and television, David Sarnoff, wanted no form of communication to be overlooked, especially in an offensive against communism: "the spoken word and the written word; radio and television; films; balloons and missiles to distribute leaflets; secret printing and mimeographing presses on Soviet controlled soil; scrawls on walls to give isolated friends a sense of community." His latest scheme was to mass-produce cheap, light-weight radio receivers that would be automatically tuned to receive American broadcast signals. These instruments could be made available by the million to listeners behind the Iron Curtain.[63]

Exhibitions

Industry and government presented foreign expositions and trade fairs that combined traditional cultural contacts with the technological. One mobile exhibit went on a six-thousand-mile tour of Europe, transporting its own tent, puppet theater, and motion pictures—for the express purpose of making Europeans aware of the Marshall Plan. Paul Hoffman, the Marshall Plan head, thought an effective feature of the exhibit was the "half million toy balloons" it had released into the air, each carrying a postcard with the return address of the person who sent it up. In Denmark the caravan show released about seventy thousand balloons with the message "Our hope is that one day people and goods will be able to pass the borders as freely as the balloons can move over land and sea." When some balloons landed in East Germany, Poland, Hungary, Czechoslovakia, and Lithuania, the communist government spokesmen warned that it was physically dangerous to pick up the balloons because they might explode. The local press and radio charged that the purpose of the balloons was to study air currents prior to launching a bacteriological war.[64]

To open one of the largest American expositions, the American National Exhibition in Moscow, Vice President Nixon made his trip to the Soviet Union in 1959. Nixon recalled using "the exhibition as a means of describing our way of life, our standard of living, and our aspirations to the Russian people." A huge aluminum geodesic dome, two hundred feet wide, was a highlight of the exhibition. Around the inside walls were hundreds of large photographs, and some models with explanations demonstrated features of American technology, education, labor, medicine, agriculture, space exploration, and nuclear energy. Ramac 305, an electronic brain, offered written replies in Russian to any of thirty-five hundred listed questions about the United States. A multiscreen film showed thousands of glimpses of American cities, farms, highways, shopping centers, and people at work, leisure, and worship. Surrounding the dome were hundreds of displays, many of them provided by private corporations, which had donated their products and services. Circlorama, a 360-degree motion picture, took viewers on a trip through the United States. A fashion show of everyday clothing was presented by models. There was also an entire $14,000 model home. The fair, according to *Time,* was "a wonder of U.S. planning, talent and do-it-yourself ingenuity."[65]

Touring the exhibition, Nixon took Nikita Khrushchev in front of television cameras recording the two men on video tape, and the talk heated up over the technological communications and the free spread of ideas.

Khrushchev: "Then what about this tape? If it is shown in the United States it will be shown in English and I would like a guarantee that there will be a full translation of my remarks."

Nixon, assuring him that the remarks would be translated, and adding that he would like his remarks fully translated in the Soviet Union, said: "this color television is one of the most advanced developments in communication that we have. I can only say that if this competition in which you plan to outstrip us is to do the best for both of our peoples and for peoples everywhere, there must be a free exchange of ideas. After all, you don't know everything—"

Khrushchev: "If I don't know everything, you don't know anything about communism except fear of it."

The two men walked into the kitchen of the model house, past glittering American consumer goods and appliances. They debated the merits of their respective ways of life.

Khrushchev, after Nixon pointed out a built-in panel-controlled washing machine: "We have such things."

Nixon: "This is the newest model. This is the kind which is built in thousands of units for direct installation in the houses." He explained that the house could be built for $14,000.

Khrushchev: "We have steel workers and we have peasants who also can afford to spend $14,000 for a house."

Nixon: "We do not claim to astonish the Russian people. We hope to show our diversity and our right to choose. We do not want to have decisions made at the top by government officials who say that all homes should be built in the same way. Would it not be better to compete in the relative merits of washing machines than in the strength of rockets. Is this the kind of competition you want?"

Khrushchev: "Yes, that's the kind of competition we want."

Nixon: "To me you are strong and we are strong. In some ways, you are stronger than we are. In others, we are stronger. We are both strong not only from the standpoint of weapons but from the standpoint of will and spirit."

Khrushchev: "It sounds to me like a threat. We, too, are giants. You want to threaten—we will answer threats with threats."

Nixon: "We will never engage in threats."

Khrushchev: "You wanted indirectly to threaten me. But we have the means to threaten too. . . . We want peace and friendship with all nations, especially with America."

Nixon: "We want peace too, and I believe that you do also."

Khrushchev then challenged Nixon to have the United States remove its bases from foreign lands.[66]

Because the exhibition represented a national image of democracy and modern industry, and because Nixon defended that image, he was praised at home. Said the next day's *Times*: "We believe that if the whole record of what happened and what was said yesterday can go out to the Russian people and to the captive nations, the United States need not worry about the presentation of its case." With thousands of Soviets passing through the exhibition and tickets being scalped for ten times their value, *Time* called the entire effort a resounding success: "the American fair had wowed Moscow."[67]

UNESCO

Governments had long tried to spread the influence of their national cultures to other territories, either unilaterally or bilaterally. The United States government had entered the field of overseas cultural relations in earnest only in 1938, and then not with global reach but with the intent of reaching other American states. The attempt to internationalize the multilateral exchange of culture grew out of an initiative by the United States. In March 1944 the Americans in a great conceptual leap proposed the organization of a group of nations to aid the educational and cultural reconstruction of the war-weary nations, and what finally emerged at a conference in November 1945 was ambitious and farsighted. The United Nations Educational, Scientific and Cultural Organization, or UNESCO, took form to recognize the common civilization of all peoples and the transcendence of culture beyond nationalism. In 1946 the United States joined the organization, committing itself to its objectives of promoting collaboration through education, science, and culture.[68]

Feeling ran high for American support of an international cultural organization. "I am extremely interested in this organization," Truman said in September 1946. "I think it can make the greatest contribution in the history of the world to the welfare of the world as a whole, if it really goes at it in the spirit that is intended." His rationale for the organization was that the United States would not be surrendering its own world outlook but would be sharing it: "If we can exchange educators with all the countries in the world, and send ours to those countries to show our viewpoint, it won't be long until we have the world situation as we have it in the 48 States—we don't have any difficulties, or any insoluble difficulties, between the 48 States that can't be settled on a peaceful basis."[69]

UNESCO's spread of culture was the kind of work Henry Wallace had envisioned since early in the war. Through his plan for globe-girdling airways, he made connections between the advance of scientific achievement and the exchange of culture under international auspices. The network of modern airlines linking the world's large airports, he proposed, would be under international control. He saw far-reaching economic and cultural benefits from people traveling with greater ease. They could organize new industrial projects and become acquainted with other lands, which would encourage international understanding.[70]

Americans were by and large enthusiastic about the prospects of an organization like UNESCO and the scientific and cultural programs it offered. In 1945, 84 percent of Americans favored a world agency to help schools in all countries teach children how to understand the people of other countries, and an even higher percentage was willing to have a world organization examine the books used in their own cities or counties to see if they were fair to all nations. In the spring of 1947 opinion was strong for the United States to provide money to help pay for an international broadcasting station sending radio programs around the world, to help rebuild schools and colleges destroyed in the war, to send teachers to foreign countries on exchange agreements, and to help countries exchange books, magazines, arts, and museum exhibits.[71]

American leadership helped to shape the new international organization. In 1953 the members of UNESCO elected Luther Evans, the former librarian of Congress, as its director-general, succeeding Jaime Torres Bodet of Mexico. Evans became director-general despite the fears of some nations that the United States might dominate the organization, since it already supplied about one-third of the budget.[72]

UNESCO strove to help to increase the flow and exchange of information—moral, intellectual, and technical—both to intellectuals and to entire peoples. In education, that meant arranging conferences and publications for scholars, as well as programs to eradicate illiteracy. In science, it meant research in astronomy, oceanography, geology, and geophysics, as well as medicine and public health. In culture, it meant encouragement of music, painting, architecture, theater, dance, writing, philosophy, as well as libraries, museums, art galleries, and zoos.

The program to elevate literacy became a priority for Director-General Evans. At least 44 percent of the world's adult population could not read or write, compared with 2.5 percent in the United States. Evans was heartened that the rate of illiteracy increase was slowing, apparently because of the kind of work UNESCO was doing. But the number of 700 million illiterates was growing. The "resources are often still inadequate," said Evans.[73]

All of this did not get very far, despite good intentions or right aims. UNESCO's agenda, a huge catchall of internationalist works in all areas of knowledge, was spread so thin as to have little significance in the lives of individual nations. The allocation of UNESCO's budget, of which the largest part by a considerable margin was provided by the United States in the early years, did not do much to influence even poor nations, let alone the wealthy ones, and the number of developing countries was rapidly increasing.

One of UNESCO's far-reaching projects, and one illuminating its hopes and eventually its weaknesses, was the creation of an international history of mankind. The problem of achieving an international history emerged at the opening of UNESCO's first conference in 1946 at the Sorbonne in Paris. David Hardman of the British Ministry of Education had referred to Greek and Egyptian civilizations as ancient, but the Indian lecturer, Sarvapalli Radhakrishnan, took direct issue with the inherent Western view of the history of progress moving from east to west. He took it that Hardman, through an oversight, had forgotten to mention India, whose civilization had survived; to ignore its continuing development, he charged, was to play at history. The American historian Ralph H. Gabriel was sensitive to the Indian complaint and contributed to a joint American and Indian study of their respective values. Although Gabriel wrote from the traditional consensual historical point of view about American politics, economy, and arts, this work had been inspired by a desire for comparative cultural study.[74]

The *History of Mankind,* the last volume of which was finally published in 1966, was a massive work covering prehistory and the beginnings of civilization, the ancient world, the early modern world, and the twentieth century. The twentieth-century volume, written and edited by Caroline F. Ware, an American, along with an Asian and a European, received writing and comment from committees of historians all over the globe, attempting to eliminate national prejudices and rise to a global perspective. The United States was fully represented in this volume as the powerful creator of a new world order after the decline of the European powers. The historians agreed that the United States had set standards for industrialism, capitalism, and democracy, and led the so-called free world. After World War II, the study told, the United States was in a unique position: "With her homeland undamaged and her industrial productivity enormously increased, the United States was the major source of wealth for reconstruction, as she had been for the supplying of war material." "For the first time in human history a society of abundance became a reality, not merely the myth of a golden age or utopia. The first country to experience this new phenomenon, the United States, was clearly only the vanguard in mankind's movement toward this condition." The study pictured the United States taking the lead in the United Nations and making available its money and technical aid to its allies.[75]

But American historians, though not quarreling with these findings, in the end dissented from UNESCO's efforts. William H. McNeill, who more than a decade before had assisted Toynbee in his wide-ranging history, called the book unwieldy and uneven. It was very much a political work, the very thing the authors had tried to avoid. History written by committees had straddled important issues, yet provoked an unremitting dissent from expert readers in footnotes. The Russians, who joined the project late, registered their disapproval by attaching particularly lengthy footnotes to the text.[76]

Within a decade of its founding, UNESCO seemed to be losing its appeal. As early as October 1949 Byron Dexter wrote in *Foreign Affairs* that UNESCO's work is "at an extreme pitch of confusion." The programs were vast, too thin to be absorbed, and thus unable to appeal seriously to the peoples of the world. An analysis of articles in the *New York Times* as well as the London *Times* showed that their coverage of UNESCO had dropped precipitously through the 1950s, reflecting a downturn in interest. By the mid-1950s 70 percent of Americans had never heard of UNESCO or read about it, and most of those who did were not certain of what its functions were. What attention it did receive was often critical. In 1955 *U.S. News & World Report* headlined a story "'UNESCO' under Fire—But What Is It?" Criticism grew with the fear that UNESCO was "teaching children to put 'the world' ahead of the United States."[77]

The futility of the United States to achieve its ends within UNESCO was not so much a failure to set aims as a failure to devote financial and human resources commensurate to the goals it had. There was simply a dearth of support. The lack of control over the world organization drew the federal government to take upon itself the obligation to appeal to people beyond the state borders for support of American ideas. The final rationale for turning from international auspices to unilateral activity was that the power of the United States demanded it. The concerted application of influence—in this case the dissemination of what American officials considered the attributes of their national culture—required the government to take on the activity itself. "The problem of an overseas government information service is most clearly seen as a part of the revolutionary development of the world role of the United States," Charles A. H. Thomson, an official of the War Information Office during World War II, observed in 1948. "Our international commitments and interests are now so large that it is no longer prudent to ignore any instrument whereby those commitments can be discharged and those interests safeguarded."[78]

USIA

"One can only hope—certainly an American can only hope—," wrote Archibald MacLeish in the late 1940s, "that the first nation to adapt its foreign affairs to the world of modern communication will be a nation founded upon the confidence that the people can govern themselves and of right ought to." This hope was not of an equal sharing of culture, but for direct government action: "to correct the image of that nation formed abroad by those who know it only through its soldiers or its diplomats or its men of business—through its political and military and commercial enterprise in foreign markets and in foreign places." As contemplated, the official information programs would represent the nation in all the areas of cultural relations we have already seen—through books, movies, radio, television, and exhibits.[79]

Government image making made sense to those who compared advertising to American propaganda. If an advertised image could gain support for a presidential candidate or sell an automobile, why not sell the American way of life around the earth? And as with advertising at home, the objective of the foreign information programs was not to exchange information but to project it. It was a one-way flow, a soliloquy, not a dialogue. But over the years exactly how that message was to be transmitted underwent different interpretations. In 1945 President Truman benignly formulated the American "endeavor to see to it that other peoples receive a full and fair picture of American life and of the aims and policies of the United States government." The government effort was designed to supplement American private organizations and individuals, which were already carrying the largest burden of information, in the fields of news, motion pictures, and communications; the government would not compete with them.[80]

Congress refined the objectives of the information program in 1948 by enacting the Smith-Mundt Act, which enabled the government to "promote a better understanding of the United States in other countries, and increase mutual understanding between the people of the United States and people of other countries." An information service was to disseminate abroad "information about the United States, its peoples, and its policies." An educational service was to cooperate with other nations in the exchange of persons, knowledge, technical know-how, and the arts.[81]

In contrast, in 1950 President Truman, at the recommendation of the National Security Council, called for a "Campaign of Truth," a hard-hitting program of blatant advocacy of the American point of view to counteract communist doctrines. In an address to the American Society of Newspaper Editors, Truman spoke of "a struggle, above all else, for the minds of men. Propaganda is one of the most powerful weapons the Communists have in this struggle. Deceit, distortion, and lies are systematically used by them as a matter of deliberate policy. . . . Unless we get the real story across to the people in other countries, we will lose the battle for men's minds by pure default. . . . We must make ourselves heard round the world in a great campaign of truth."[82]

Expecting to improve information operations abroad, President Eisenhower broached the issue in his first State of the Union message of February 1953. It was imperative to "make more effective all activities of the Government related to international information." Following the recommendation of a special committee, Eisenhower called for a new administrative division. In 1953 the United States Information Agency began functioning as an independent branch of government both to project the national image abroad and to advocate American policies. In 1953 the first director, Theodore Streibert, the former chairman of the board of the Mutual Broadcasting System, defined the agency's purpose: "Under this new mission, avoiding a propagandistic tone, the Agency will emphasize the community of interest that exists among freedom-loving peoples and show how American objectives and policies advance the legitimate interests of such peoples." Through both means, "objective, factual news reporting and appropriate commentaries," he aimed to present a full exposition of United States actions and policies.[83]

What led the administration to expect that the USIA would have a substantial impact on peoples around the world was the sheer size of the operation. By the late 1950s the agency, with its headquarters in Washington, was the largest national information organization in the world, having a global reach of more than two hundred branch posts, officially named a service—the United States Information Service—in the field. Under the agency's jurisdiction, the Voice of America was the largest radio system ever undertaken up to the 1950s, then transmitting regular broadcasts in native languages daily to all areas of the world by shortwave. The service operated the largest library system in the world, with branches in dozens of countries. The service operated the largest noncommercial news distribution facility in the world, with regional editions of the news sent daily by radio teletype to periodicals in Europe, Africa, the Middle East, East Asia, and Latin America. Sending abroad Hollywood films and documentaries, the service was the largest noncommercial film distributor in the world. Under its auspices, there were more educational exchanges, more scholars traveling to more places, and more people working to express an American perspective than ever before.[84]

What was the official image that Americans projected in their books, films, and shows? The photographs and models in public view were of skyscrapers, farmhouses, factories, clubs, suburbs, and churches. The displays offered examples of farm implements, automobiles, farm machinery, and home conveniences. Documentary films depicted town meetings, drugstores, schools, churches, and countless other American activities and artifacts. Even where people could not read, or read very little, they could see a picture of life in America.

Presenting this image as a composite collage of America for foreigners, the USIA's book *USA: Its Geography and Growth* appeared in the mid-1950s. The viewpoint it expressed was not unlike that of the picture book *Look at America* produced by a private publisher for citizens at home. The country was so big, the text stated, that to cross it a traveler would have to ride in a modern train speeding at a mile a minute for several days and nights. The land was so diverse that foreigners would surely find within the continental bounds someplace like home. A whole host of scenes was shown; there was "no one scene which alone represents America. The dark northern pine and the slender palm of the South, the lush green meadow and the barren wind-swept rock, the lonely isolated farmhouse and the city of a million homes—all these are America." There was a common belief, the government agency declared: the "American dream," that the inhabitants could by their efforts make life better, and that their children could do even better than the earlier generation.[85]

The intensity of the impact of the government's cultural thrust on other peoples was usually gauged by abundant testimony and figures. The USIA counted the mail response to Voice of America broadcasts, the use by newspapers of its press releases, and attendance at sponsored film showings and exhibits.[86]

Did other peoples believe the propaganda of the American government? In occupied Germany, Americans could simply poll the defeated Germans about what they thought of "the work the American occupation authorities have done in the cultural field" of radio, theater, cinema, press, and publishing. Among the former enemies, 49 percent said "very good work" or "good work," 17 percent said "fairly good work," and 33 percent said "bad work" or "very bad work." But this was merely an early and fragmentary indication of propaganda, and Americans were not likely to poll the Soviets.[87]

Impressions of the impact of propaganda on the Soviets came from personal observation. George Kennan was convinced from many sources that those who had seen *America,* the only American publication allowed in the Soviet Union, a large, profusely illustrated magazine modeled on Luce's *Life,* with color pictures printed on slick paper, were "enormously impressed by it." If circulation restrictions were lifted by the Soviet government, Kennan ventured, *America* would be the "most popular magazine" in the country. A picture spread of "an average American school, a small town, or even an average American kitchen dramatizes to Soviet readers" the fact that Americans had, "contrary to everything they are told by their propaganda, a superior standard of living and culture."[88]

Intelligence sources provided information to Ambassador Smith that led him to believe that the Russian-language broadcasts of the Voice of America, which began in February 1947, had made a favorable impact. The evidence: Following the broadcast of Truman's declaration of the need for military aid for Greece and Turkey, Soviet engineers working at the Dnieper Dam sent word to the embassy that they had heard the president's speech. From bits of conversations heard around, members of the embassy staff were convinced that Soviets listened to the Voice of America. One traveler in Byelorussia found from talking with people on the train that half of them knew of the broadcasts, and a farmer from the Caucasus discussed the programs with an American Army officer on the street. A young man visited the American Information Office in Moscow to explain that the principal audience of the Voice of America was youth. The interest of his friends in America was not the result of war contacts, but because "America represents progress—it has authority." He added that the American programs he had heard were "concrete examples of democracy in action—things which we will remember."

The reaction of the Soviet government was also a measure of the influence of propaganda. Criticism of the propaganda, not friendly support, was taken to be a positive sign. When a top Soviet commentator attacked American broadcasts, Smith cabled the State Department: "It shows that the program is on the right track. Our hearty congratulations." He believed most Russian people accepted America's version of the facts for the reason that they were familiar with the methods of their own government and secret police. When the Kremlin began to jam the American broadcasts in 1949, his belief in the impact of the Voice of America was confirmed. But if the propaganda was successfully convincing those it was intended to reach, wouldn't the level of criticism diminish rather than increase?[89]

The USIA had taken on its own part in cultural relations, but it may not have been as influential as the day-to-day attractions of the culture itself. Daniel Boorstin came to this conclusion after a trip to South Asia in 1960: in Bangalore in southern India "we had an admirable United States Information Agency library with a wide selection of books." Some 250 people a day visited the library, a considerable number of them to escape the dust, or to find a place to do their schoolwork. Some came to learn about the United States or other Western cultures. "At the same time a half-dozen motion picture houses in the city customarily showed American movies," providing images of America to "many more people and at a far greater rate than that at which the library was offering them ideas about America." Boorstin nevertheless credited the government with having had "a large part in spreading" American images. American propaganda had been "trying to create an image (we always say, of course, a 'true,' by which we mean a favorable, image) of the United States." He saw these images at the International Agricultural Fair in Delhi during the winter of 1960. "The American pavilion, a light and graceful structure, danced in the sun. Inside, it was neat and uncluttered. One of the sights most impressive to all comers was an American farm kitchen—a dazzling porcelain-and-chrome spectacle, complete with refrigerator, disposal, deep-freeze, automatic washer and dryer, and electric stove. Before it walked a procession of Indian peasant women. Long pendant earrings, bangles on arms and ankles, objects piercing their noses—these pieces of gold were their savings which they dared not put in the hands of banks. In their arms they carried barebottomed infants. They stopped and stood in bewilderment. What was this? It was the image of America."[90]

Could these people grasp the image of an American kitchen? Reinhold Niebuhr believed that "propaganda" which unduly stressed the height of the American standard of living as "proof of our social virtues" was "ineffective." The standards of living of a highly industrialized nation, he explained, were "so improbable to the imagination of impoverished peasants of the Orient, that they cannot impress their social and political attitudes."[91]

In the end it is uncertain whether the image as projected by the government was accepted by others, but not because the picture of technology, industry, or a high standard of life was accurate. For how could that image be separate from the action? The information the government distributed was supposed to be reality. But could reality be slanted in favor of the American position in world affairs? If the people of other lands liked the visitors they met, if they liked the exports, if they liked the foreign aid, if they liked the actions of the government—if they liked these manifestations, then the USIA would be irrelevant. If they did not like them, then it is doubtful whether the USIA would do much good at all. To the extent it represented the culture, it might be judged a success, or at least truthful, perhaps even more than the extent to which it influenced the thinking of others. The basis of truth seemed represented by the differences of opinion among Americans themselves. When American editorials or traveling scholars disagreed with their own government in public places, that frankness demonstrated and illustrated what freedom was. That might not be the most effective way to communicate government policy, but it was a way to communicate political democracy.

While the government spread culture abroad, George Allen, a diplomat with the USIA, admitted, "People may feel their way of life is being insidiously undermined by what they regard as irresistible encroachments by America on their way of doing things. We are not consciously pushing this Americanism as an instrument of the cold war. It's just happening." But, "to the extent that the so-called American cult does represent the real attitude and progress of the U.S., I welcome it, because I like America to be regarded as the wave of the future." The spread of American culture from the perspective of the late 1950s gathered force and speed—but not so much through the government as through the people themselves.[92]

"Is the World 'Going American'?" asked *U.S. News & World Report* in the spring of 1959. From accounts by its regional editors in bureaus around the world, the magazine reported, "America's biggest export boom is now under way. But you can't put a cash value on it—yet. The exports are intangibles: American ideas, methods and habits. They are being adopted all over the world, changing the lives of people of all ages, in all walks of life. It's a sort of 'American revolution' sweeping the globe." Foreigners eagerly sought clothes labeled "Made in U.S.A." Blue jeans were worn by people, especially teenagers, all over Europe and Japan. After Walt Disney's movie of Davy Crockett's life, "Davy Crockett" coonskin hats were seen on children at play in France.[93]

Hamburgers and hot dogs began to compete with local foods. In British pubs, patrons drank canned beer instead of draught. Consumption of canned fruit rose. In Germany and France, candy could be selected from machines. In West Germany milk bars sprang up. In France cafeterias, sandwich shops, and counters, rather than restaurants, were frequented for lunch. Factory canteens sold hundreds of thousands of meals a day, and some factories installed sandwich and soft-drink vending machines. The Japanese took to American popcorn, canned juices, and potato chips.

Europeans began to play with pinball machines. Hula hoops became a rage in Europe, but only as interest in them was fading among Americans.[94]

American automobile culture was imported along with American automobiles. A drive-in movie outside Rome had space for 750 cars and 250 motor scooters. Curb service by carhops at food stands was a familiar scene in Tokyo. Motels were opening in France and throughout Europe. Parking meters were found on Tokyo streets. There were even drive-in banking facilities. Shopping centers began to appear in France and superhighways were planned alongside ancient Roman roads. As traffic jams began to appear in London, Paris, Rome, Bonn, and Sydney, American know-how in road building was applied to plans for turnpikes and parkways.[95]

But the attraction of American culture brought with it an ironic indictment. The Asians, Reinhold Niebuhr reported in his meditations on America's cultural "hegemony in the world community," were inclined to regard American prosperity as evidence not of virtue but of "injustice." The Europeans, he added, found American culture not the essence of technical efficiency, as Americans believed, but simply "vulgar." They feigned being imperiled by the popularity of an American synthetic soft drink, as the French protested "Cocacolonialism." He believed that the "cultural aversion of France toward us expresses explicitly what most of Europe seems to feel." *Le Monde* had said that America was a "technocracy" not too sharply distinguished from the technical control of life in Russia, and Niebuhr had reason to agree. He judged "a measure of truth in the charge of similarity between our culture and that of the pure Marxists because both are offshoots of the ethos which had its rise, significantly, in the same France which is now our principal critic in Europe." America perpetuated the inventions of writing and printing, Niebuhr added, but "the further elaboration of communications in the arts of mass communication" had "led to the vulgarization of culture as well as to the dissemination of its richest prizes among the general public. Television may represent a threat to our culture analogous to the threat of atomic weapons to our civilization."[96]

Certainly other peoples were attracted to American culture as projected from Hollywood or on television, even as they criticized it as vulgar or sentimental art, as if America were responsible for the avid consumption by millions of its productions. But could the "official" USIA image of American culture as filtered through an international agency have removed some of its onesided combativeness? Would that discipline have provided an alternative, objective, campaign for "truth," one which welcomed America's perspective and allowed for a diversity of world opinion? Would American support of an international organization have counteracted the foreign belief that a nation as fortunate as America could not possibly also possess and appreciate foreign values of life?[97]

Though the extent to which American cultural institutions and ideas penetrated national cultures remains extremely difficult to ascertain, American private and government activities, whether for good or ill, whether they were enjoyed, imitated, or despised abroad, sometimes had a direct and obvious impact on the domestic cultures of other nations. The wide range of American activities that extended culture; the traders, investors, missionaries, scholars, and tourists who carried ideas and knowledge; the educational institutions and religious denominations, foundations, mass media, commercial enterprises, and individual contacts that wove a network of relationships; the businessmen who furthered the process of modernization, the missionaries who organized native churches, the government representatives who conducted foreign operations, and the soldiers who ensured the security of others—all these diffused culture. These individuals and institutions introduced new products, new technical know-how, new rapid communications, new attitudes toward society, new political thoughts, and new religious ideas. They built roads, analyzed soil, repaired equipment, ran government information programs, and healed the sick.

Americans were in a unique position of affecting foreign cultures, but a transformation of domestic cultures was not likely or desirable. A transplantation of customs from abroad could never completely replace the indigenous culture, values, and beliefs. The aversion to new and different ways, and the guilt of forswearing the ways of ancestors after the lust for the modern, made such a transformation impossible. The certain attractions of culture were offset by a repulsion. Cultural ways reaching back for centuries could not be changed inherently. Each nation was free to develop its own system, reforms, and institutions compatible with its own beliefs and culture, even if these changes were inspired by outside influences. In the final analysis, the people of various cultures could imitate unabashedly or reject forcibly what they pleased of foreign influence.

12

Political

Structure

America had provided its aid and sent goods and products abroad. The nation at first had little need to build frontier posts, to hold garrisons for patrol or defense, or to control colonial bases to protect its power. These extensions were far from the liberal and open American consensus view, which was also one of efficiency. The United States was a republic, and built on the principles of democracy, it had, long before it was a great power, opposed Europe's projection of military might to hold colonies. But armed outposts, naval ports, and missile launch sites became an integral part of the American role. The vigilance of these outposts and the forces in reserve provided the security without which the ships, airlines, trade, and communications might be rendered vulnerable. The garrisons became strategic locations in the struggle for power against competitors.

The United States had resisted European empires under the political principle of self-determination, which was given early expression by the revolt against Britain in the War for Independence. Wilson's Fourteen Points, the essential peace terms of the Allies in World War I, listed self-determination as a prime objective for the postwar world, portending the break-up of the empires of Germany, Austria-Hungary, Ottoman Turkey, and Russia. In the Atlantic Charter of World War II, self-determination was foundational. America sought "no aggrandizement, territorial or other." And although national self-determination meant independence, and democracy meant rule of a people over their own life and institutions, self-determination was bound up, in Roosevelt's mind, with democratic values; for America desired "to see no territorial changes that do not accord with the freely expressed wishes of the peoples concerned." Roosevelt believed that his Four Freedoms—the freedom of expression, the freedom of worship, the freedom from want, and the freedom from fear—were the simple essence of democracy, and all of them were to apply "everywhere" or "anywhere" in the world. He offered "no vision of a distant millennium," for America was now a committed power in the world. Truman perpetuated the belief. In October 1945 he laid out twelve fundamental points of American foreign policy, including the avoidance of territorial aggrandizement and the disapproval of territorial changes not based on popular count, and the nonrecognition of governments imposed by outside force.[1]

243

The principles of self-determination were at odds with the policies of allies that maintained imperial possessions. *Life* stirred up an international commotion in an editorial attack on the remnants of the British Empire: "Doubtless it is presumptuous for a single periodical to attempt to speak for the American people. Nevertheless, the editors of *Life* . . . make no apology for their presumption. We assure you that we do speak, in this instance, for a large portion of our 134,000,000 fellow citizens." One "thing we are sure we are *not* fighting for is to hold the British Empire together." When British news reporters and government officials criticized the article, and Edward R. Murrow on the radio from England amplified the criticism, Luce sent *Time*'s executive editor to mollify Churchill's government. Finally, Luce wrote a letter to British friends in the government and the press, stressing the common objectives of the two countries to create a postwar order. But Luce did not believe imperialism suited America. "It has been proposed that I write a redefinition of the American Century and explain that I wasn't no imperialist," Luce told an interviewer, intentionally using slang for emphasis. "I don't know who has taken worse raps than I for opposition to imperialism. . . . You can't extract imperialism from 'The American Century.'" He had assumed that the American role must be democratic, existing as "an internationalism of the people, by the people and for the people."[2]

Henry Wallace, who offered an alternative to Luce in many other uses of power, was vociferous against colonialism and for the emancipation of colonies. The subjugation of peoples went against Wallace's deep egalitarian beliefs. In the 1944 pamphlet *Our Job in the Pacific,* he wrote that America should recognize that within the British, French, and Dutch colonies of India, Burma, Malaya, Indochina, and the East Indies, people had a yearning for freedom. The United States should set the example of self-determination, Wallace believed, by extending independence to the Philippines. He supported an orderly evolutionary process of transition from colonial subjugation and "coolie economics" to self-government and an economy of opportunity.

Like Luce, Wallace proved able to shake up the British leadership. He asserted his views against the imperious attitudes of the staunch old empire builder Winston Churchill. After a lunch in May 1943, Wallace recorded in his diary that Roosevelt, Wallace, and others listened as Churchill began talking.

> He made it . . . clear . . . that he expected England and the United States to run the world and he expected the staff organizations which had been set up for winning the war to continue when the peace came, that these staff organizations would by mutual understanding really run the world even though there was a supreme council and three regional councils.
>
> I said bluntly that I thought the notion of Anglo-Saxon superiority, inherent in Churchill's approach, would be offensive to many of the nations of the world as well as to a number of people in the United States. Churchill had had quite a bit of whiskey, which, however, did not affect the clarity of his thinking process but did perhaps increase his frankness. He said why be apologetic

about Anglo-Saxon superiority, that we were superior, that we had the common heritage which had been worked out over the centuries in England and had been perfected by our constitution. . . .

I suggested it might be a good plan to bring in the Latin American nations so that the citizens of the New World and the British Empire could all travel freely without passports. Churchill did not like this.[3]

Paradoxes existed in the current thinking about the implementation of a world role: in the promotion of self-determination and the accommodation with power politics. The United States took simultaneous stands for the break-up of the British Empire and cooperation with it in wartime. The government was unwilling to alienate its allies, Britain, France, Belgium, and the Netherlands, to force the right of self-determination for the peoples of Africa and Asia. Moreover, the exercise of world power—by exporting economic prowess, granting aid, and spreading culture—threatened to undermine the principle of self-determination. Influence required the exertion of power, and self-determination required restraint. The reconciliation of these two opposing forces was a prime political and moral problem.

The American consensus was aware of the issue at the outset of the new world role. The historian Richard Hofstadter derived paradox even from Roosevelt's fervent opposition to European imperialism. Although Roosevelt believed that "imperialists"—a term he used as epithet—had been shortsighted in taking a purely exploitative view of the colonies, Hofstadter admitted that Roosevelt also recognized the possibilities for American trade in the old colonial areas—in the oil fields in Saudi Arabia, for instance. The "ruthless imperialism of the older colonial powers might be replaced by a liberal and benevolent American penetration" that would be to the advantage of American commerce and to "the natives." Thus while supporting self-determination, Roosevelt felt compelled to exert American power in other nations in support of its interests.[4]

The consensus could not quite reconcile the paradox. When Daniel Boorstin pondered the problem of the exertion of power in pursuit of self-determination for others, he argued, Americans could not force the creation of democracies. "To tell people what institutions they must have, whether we tell them with the Voice of America or with the Money of America, is the thorough denial of our American heritage. . . . An imposed democracy expresses a corroding cynicism." The tyrannies of fascism, nazism, and communism imposed themselves on others without hypocrisy, for their actions relied on force. But "if we were to become cynical in order to make Europe *seem* to stand for something better than it might on its own, we would risk losing everything, even if we should win." Americans should defend their institutions without insisting on propagating them. "We must refuse to try to export our commodity"—in order to be true to it.[5]

In examining the moral basis of self-determination, Reinhold Niebuhr questioned the practice of its preservation by the intervention of another nation. One nation could not determine the legitimacy of self-determination; each people had to do that. Americans had to use their power, to be sure, but they should not be deceived about it: "For the fact is that every nation is caught in the moral paradox of refusing to go to war unless it can be proved that the national interest is imperiled, and of continuing in the war only by proving that something much more than national interest is at stake."[6]

The organization of a political order to permit the use of power and control its abuse required effective mechanisms. The Atlantic Charter conceived of "a wider and permanent system of general security." This conception led to the proposal of any number of projects, ranging from compacts with close allies to dreams like those of H. G. Wells for a super world-state establishing law for all humankind.[7]

Anglo-American Alliance: *Union Now*

During the first two years of American involvement in World War II, plans to enhance the peace required British cooperation, because until the war, that nation's power had appeared monumental. On the surface, a combination of these two most powerful nations would preserve their common Anglo-Saxon ideals of democracy, individualism, and free enterprise. The United States and Britain were, despite divergent interests over the preservation of empire, the closest of powers, whose inhabitants spoke the same language, shared similar democratic traditions, and had common interests in the peace of the Atlantic world.

Support for a British coalition grew most recently out of the *Union Now* proposal of Clarence Streit in 1939. Streit urged the immediate consolidation of the democracies around the North Atlantic *"in a great federal republic built on and for the thing they share most, their common democratic principle of government for the sake of individual freedom."* As the founder democracies of this union, Streit named the United States, Britain and its Commonwealth, France, Belgium, the Netherlands, Switzerland, Denmark, Norway, Sweden, and Finland. These nations provided "the nucleus of world government" with overwhelming financial, monetary, economic, and political strength to assure peace. Together, with their overseas empires, these nations "own almost half the earth, rule all its oceans, govern nearly half mankind."[8]

After the loss of most of the Continental democracies to Hitler's invading armies, Streit proposed in 1941 a first step in the grandiose union: the joining of the United States with Britain and its empire, mainly Canada, Australia, New Zealand, and the Union of South Africa. The war, Streit wrote in his book *Union Now with Britain,* made this combination urgent. Although this plan was flawed by Streit's wish that the subjugated colonial peoples bolster Western democracy, Luce called the idea of "Union Now," with the United States as the senior partner, "an inspiring proposal." In 1941 James T. Shotwell, an earlier advocate of outlawing war, backed a postwar exercise of power by an "Anglo-American directorate." Dorothy Thompson was another promoter of "an Anglo-American union."[9]

After the second year of the war, the talk of Anglo-Saxon union for peace lessened.

"Two years ago," said a *Saturday Evening Post* article in 1943, "some Americans . . . pictured the Anglo-American combination as playing the postwar tune, while the Russian Bear danced to it." An Anglo-American combination was untenable, because Britain had lost power in comparison with the Soviet Union. In addition, a union founded on ethnic heritage was criticized as close to "an Anglo-Saxon counterpart of Hitler's program for a 'master race.'" The alliance with Britain was a throwback to the kind of power politics and unsettled policy of balance of power that had led to two world wars.[10]

Future plans for peace embraced other powers of the world. At minimum, peace plans encompassed a coalition of the "Big Three" or "Big Four," requiring that the United States cooperate, as far as possible, with Britain, Russia, and China not only in military matters but also in the organization of postwar programs. Allied cooperation grew from private meetings between American and British leaders like that between President Roosevelt and Prime Minister Churchill on naval ships off the shore of Newfoundland to gatherings involving Stalin at Yalta and Potsdam, and Chiang Kai-shek at Cairo.

International Organization: The United Nations

In the later war years, the favored plan for the postwar world was a new international organization. The United States took the initiative in calling for "a confederation, or an association of the United Nations," reviving the American conception of the League of Nations, created at the urging of President Wilson but rejected by Congress. Some called the new organization America's "Second Chance."[11]

The United Nations organization was in large measure the result of persistent American effort. Beginning early in the war, the United States put weight behind the creation of international organizations to deal with the economic, assistance, and social problems of the coming era. In 1943 the United States was the host country to the conference that led to the formation of the Food and Agriculture Organization. The United States sponsored the formation of the United Nations Relief and Rehabilitation Administration to deliver food and commodities to the peoples of Europe and Asia. In 1944, at Bretton Woods, the United States endorsed the United Nations Monetary and Financial Conference that planned the World Bank and the International Monetary Fund. All this was prelude to the 1945 conference at San Francisco, the United Nations Conference on International Organization.

These moves opposed the idea of spheres of influence as the impractical arrangements of days past, the remnants of the old European world order. On his return from the conference at Yalta, Roosevelt reported on March 1, 1945, that an international organization would "spell the end of the system of unilateral action, the exclusive alliances, the spheres of influence, the balances of power, and all the other expedients that have been tried for centuries—and have always failed." In their stead, Roosevelt regarded the United Nations as the foundation of postwar collective security, a cooperative organization of sovereign nations.[12]

In support of Roosevelt, Secretary of State Cordell Hull stood for a universal internationalism. In his *Memoirs,* he summarized his views against traditional aggrandizement: "I was not, and am not, a believer in the idea of balance of power or spheres of influence as a means of keeping the peace." During World War I he had studied systems of spheres of influence and balance of power, and his conclusions about their "iniquitous consequences" had stayed with him. Presuming the end of spheres of influence in World War II, Hull proposed to replace them with an international organization providing for the security of its members. He considered the principle of united action to be more important than any plans to settle specific boundary questions while war still waged. "I could sympathize fully with Stalin's desire to protect his western borders from future attack," he wrote. "But I felt that this security could best be obtained through a strong postwar peace organization."[13]

After his trip to the Moscow Conference in 1943, Hull reported to Congress in November that the powers had agreed on the establishment of the United Nations. He declared, "there will no longer be need for spheres of influence, for alliances, for balance of power, or any other of the special arrangements through which, in the unhappy past, the nations strove to safeguard their security or to promote their interests."[14]

A United Nations organization received support from policymakers in the Atlantic Charter of 1941, the Declaration of the United Nations in 1942, and the Moscow Declaration of 1943. On this matter the Republicans overwhelmingly agreed with the Democratic administration. John Foster Dulles, who headed a wartime committee of the Federal Council of Churches to help change the opinion of the country in favor of postwar international cooperation, advocated a "common concern" principle over a "sphere of influence" procedure. Each nation's leadership had to be willing to compromise, Dulles believed, to build a "political framework for a continuing collaboration of the United Nations." "If we want peace," Dulles concluded, "then we must intensify and universalize" the negotiation process.[15]

Each house of Congress passed a resolution in 1943 favoring the participation of the United States in an international organization. The House resolution, the work of J. William Fulbright, a young representative from Arkansas, was simple, reading in its entirely: "That the Congress hereby expresses itself as favoring the creation of appropriate international machinery with power adequate to establish and to maintain a just and lasting peace among the nations of the world, and as favoring participation by the United States therein through its constitutional processes."[16]

The editors of the *New York Times* were swept up in universalist optimism in February 1945, agreeing with the leaders that the proposed United Nations charter "represents a move to end the drift toward independent policies and unilateral actions, toward spheres of influence, exclusive alliances and other expedients, and to replace these methods with broader international agreements and more universal organizations in which ultimately all peace-loving nations can join. If the charter can accomplish this, it will come to be regarded as a turning point in the world's history."[17]

Public opinion strongly favored participation in an international organization. At no time since 1942 did less than two-thirds favor the step, and by the fall of 1943 only 13 percent of Americans were opposed. More than a majority of people were willing to enter the organization on an equal basis with the nation's principal allies, Britain and Russia, but not then with Germany. Americans as a whole did not favor regional security alliances, and up to over 80 percent of them during the war were prepared to give support to an international police force. After the war Americans, when asked if they thought peace would have a better chance if they relied on the atomic bomb rather than on the United Nations, agreed four to one that the United Nations was a better way.[18]

The reasons for this consensus over an international organization were based on pragmatism and hope. Roosevelt knew that the success of a comprehensive organization depended on the power that supported it. Therefore, the participation of the United States, the world's largest power, was mandatory. While a democratic principle of universality of membership lay in the parliamentary General Assembly, in which each member state would have one vote, the potential force would lie in the Security Council, in which the great powers would share the chief responsibility for peacekeeping. Roosevelt looked to the major wartime allies of Great Britain, the Soviet Union, and China, to join the United States on this council. Combining the strength of these powers, the organization would intervene whenever necessary to enforce the law to prevent aggression.

America would exert influence in favor of its interests within the United Nations, but Roosevelt knew final decisions had to be made jointly. He was willing to acknowledge that the "United States will not always have its way a hundred percent—nor will Russia nor Great Britain." This was the secret of insuring self-determination: "once there has been a free expression of the people's will in any country, our immediate responsibility ends—with the exception only of such action as may be agreed on in the International Security Organization that we hope to set up."

To this way of thinking, the United Nations would take account of the conflicting ideal of self-determination and the reality of power politics. In its innermost councils, the big states would hold the power to act, and the small states in general meeting would exert their moral force. States would retain the right of self-government but would turn over to the international body the authority to settle disputes and wars. The international body, under the guidance of the big powers but in consultation with the smallest nations, would raise an international police force. "No plan is perfect." But whatever plan was adopted, Roosevelt explained, would "doubtless have to be amended time and again over the years, just as our own Constitution has been."[19]

The resounding words that opened the UN charter, approved by the United States Senate in July 1945, seemed to disclose the international organization's debt to the United States Constitution and to the spirit of democracy in the United States: "We the peoples of the United Nations, determined to save succeeding generations from the scourge of war. . . ." The charter went on to clarify two meanings of the term *self-determination*. A state was said to have the right to choose freely its political, economic, social, and cultural system, and the people of a nation had the right to constitute themselves in a state.[20]

President Truman told the closing session of the United Nations Conference in San Franciso in June 1945 that the "Constitution of my own country came from a Convention which—like this one—was made up of delegates with many different views." He hoped for an "international bill of rights" acceptable to all nations involved in writing it, to be "as much a part of international life as our own Bill of Rights is a part of our Constitution." It would not be long, he added in 1946, "until we have the world situation as we have it in the 48 States—we don't have any difficulties, or any insoluble difficulties, between the 48 States that can't be settled on a peaceful basis." An essential tenet for the United Nations was that democracy, federalism, and the division of power would make the organization work. "If we could get the same international application of justice between nations that we have between the states in this Union," Truman asserted, "I think we could maintain the peace—that is what we are working for at any rate."[21]

Truman's thinking was direct. His sentiment that the United Nations represented "the greatest organized attempt in the history of men to solve their differences without war" had to be sincere. He carried a copy of a poem with him in his wallet—"Locksley Hall," by Alfred Tennyson. He had written out the lines in his own hand:

> Till the war-drum throbb'd no longer, and the battle-flags were furl'd
> In the Parliament of Man, the Federation of the World.
> There the common sense of most shall hold a fretful realm in awe,
> And the kindly earth shall slumber, lapt in universal law.[22]

Truman's version of history was related nearly verbatim in the works of historians. Carl Van Doren's 1948 story of the making and ratifying of the Constitution, *The Great Rehearsal*, drew out the parallel between the separate states in the 1780s and the sovereign states of the United Nations in 1940s. The task the early Americans had completed was to create out of a loose league of states a strong government overseeing federal affairs, while leaving local affairs to the states. The citizens of many nations, he observed, had likewise become convinced that "only by some similar alteration of the Charter of the United Nations" could the organization "develop from a league of states into a government capable of securing the peace and welfare of the world."[23]

Americans were open to democratic world thinking, David Riesman hypothesized, not necessarily because of the democratic traditions of their past, but because of the current tendency toward other-direction. His "other-directed man" was projecting abroad his "way of life" in a way that seemed to be left to "Realpolitik," but this individual type also concealed expediential considerations. As evidence Riesman found the testimony of a young veteran interviewed in 1947 by the University of

Michigan Survey Research Center, who was asked whether he thought the United States had given in or had its own way too much in the United Nations. He replied: "This will sound funny, but I think we are getting our own way too much." Why did he say that? "Because we don't want the other nations to feel that we are trying to take over their countries. They know that Russia wants that and I think that's why there is so much argument. But if they feel we are trying to grab, they won't trust us either." So when Americans did not get what they wanted, the young man continued, "I think that's really good because it makes the other countries feel that we're just like them and that we are having troubles too. That would make them more sympathetic to us and more friendly." Riesman had high hopes for this sensitive thought as "a real advance." His other-directed man had comprehended subtleties about the world of which "moralizer" predecessors would ordinarily have been incapable.[24]

Although Reinhold Niebuhr considered the moral imperative to be the most important impetus in bringing the world community together—more than economic interdependence or political cohesion—he struggled with a pragmatic and realistic morality. He judged that enlightened people in all nations had at least an inchoate sense of obligation to a community of humankind. A world community was a "desperate necessity." But a "common moral sense" did not have much "immediate political relevance." Significantly, he thought success in achieving world community more likely if Americans were less sure of their purity and virtue, a natural consequence of their tremendous power: "The pride and self-righteousness of powerful nations are a greater hazard to their success in statecraft than the machinations of their foes." One of the functions of the United Nations should be to restrain the preponderance of American power. The United Nations would serve as "an organ in which even the most powerful of the democratic nations must bring their policies under the scrutiny of world public opinion. Thus inevitable aberrations, arising from the pride of power, are corrected."[25]

Inherent in these analyses was a sense of anticipation about the United Nations. An international city of peace located on American soil was a symbol of American determination that the new organization be made to work. After Congress unanimously resolved in 1945 to invite the UN to establish its headquarters in this country, architectural plans were made and in 1948 the site of New York was chosen. The UN was on land donated by John D. Rockefeller and had an American architect, Wallace K. Harrison, at the head of an international team; it was built with American money, $65 million loaned by the United States government, interest-free; and it was constructed with American engineering skill, the superstructure of the Secretariat Building put up by the American Bridge Company. Finally, American support allowed the UN to function: the United States paid one-third or more of the budget in the early years.[26]

At a special session of the UN General Assembly in October 1949, held outside the still-to-be-completed UN Building on Forty-second Street, where a huge blue banner with the emblem of the United Nations hung as background, President Truman dedicated the United Nations as a "Workshop of Peace." The laying of the stone of the permanent headquarters—the three-and-a-half-ton piece of New Hampshire granite carved with the words "United Nations" in English, French, Chinese, Russian, and Spanish, and the date MCMXLIX—he said, constituted "an act of faith—our unshakable faith that the United Nations will succeed in accomplishing the great tasks for which it was created." He spoke to the sixteen thousand in the audience, including diplomats and iron workers, a group of whom looked on from the twenty-ninth floor of the Secretariat skyscraper. The Soviet foreign minister, Andrei Vishinsky, joined in the applause for Truman's speech, and with United States jets flying overhead, the president's party drove away.[27]

"The World Capitol" was in a fitting setting, in the view of popular periodicals, as part of midtown Manhattan, "associating the U.N. with the aspirations of the world of peaceful activity," and the "Tower of Peace," with its glass-and-marble facade in the new International style, represented "open diplomacy." "Six acres of glass in the U.N. building's walls let in the light of day." The beauty was egalitarian: spaciousness, economy, and efficiency were emphasized; restaurants, meeting rooms, lounges, a post office, and underground parking space were provided; statues and murals against war were on display, and in front the flags of all member states. And the building was a symbol of modernity, the shimmering Secretariat towering thirty-nine stories above the East River, the long and sweeping General Assembly Building and the clean, sharp, rectangular Conference Building, housing the UN's councils and committees, crouching low beside the river bank. Harrison was dubbed by *Time* "one of the pyramid builders of today," and *Life* displayed a spread of pictures of the vast glass side of the Secretariat Building lighted up after dark and taking "a familiar place on New York's night skyline." Students learned about the United Nations from glossy color pictures and organizational charts in textbooks, and local and foreign sightseers came to the UN in numbers that *Newsweek* characterized as an "invasion."[28]

The world organization placed no barriers to membership by communist governments. That was part of its hope: its openness to diverse opinion and readiness to accommodate earnest, frank debate. Truman and Roosevelt sought the participation of the Soviet ally. As George Kennan noted, "We didn't ask how it had come by its power—whether by fair means or foul. We didn't ask it to disavow its ideology. We didn't even object to the admission of some of its satellites." The American view was that "the U.N. was to consist of both Communist and non-Communist powers."[29]

But the Soviets were emphatic in their insistence on the right of veto in the Security Council. The Americans concurred, and because the greatest powers in the Security Council did not resolve their ideological differences, they were unable to agree on the composition of an international force, let alone other crucial issues. Truman blamed the Soviet Union as the "one nation" that had "blocked action in the United Nations by using the veto time and time again."[30]

Soviet intransigence in the United Nations did not change American principles, but it did alter American actions. The American and Soviet views of self-determination within the United Nations were in conflict. In particular, the United States refused to acknowledge the legitimacy of Soviet annexation of the Baltic states of Latvia, Lithuania, and Estonia and Soviet control of other Eastern European countries. The inability of the United Nations to ensure self-determination of these areas because of Soviet vetoes in the Security Council coaxed American leaders to act on their own. What was new was the idea that the United States had a responsibility to police international law. To counter the Soviet bloc, the United States took unilateral action to organize formally a vast free-world bloc.[31]

The Alliance System

The pressure for the United States to act on its own intensified. On March 12, 1947, when President Truman announced that the United States had to come to the aid of Greece and Turkey, he defended the action by the necessity to fight communism, not to accommodate or reform it in a universal organization. The United States had to act because of its power: "No other nation is willing and able to provide the necessary support for a democratic Greek government," he asserted. Britain had once been dominant in the region. Churchill had bargained with Stalin for recognition of British influence in Greece in exchange for Soviet dominance in Romania, Bulgaria, and Hungary. But Britain had become unable to maintain its commitments in the Balkan region.[32]

The State Department staff, reading the messages from the British government seeking relief, realized that "Britain had within the hour handed the job of world leadership, with all its burdens and all its glory, to the United States." Mindful of the strategic importance of Greece and Turkey to the security of three continents, Joseph Marion Jones remembered, "It was clear to many at the time that an enduring national conversion to the role of world leadership was taking place." And he told of consensus over the change: "American democracy working at its finest," with the administration operating "far beyond the normal boundaries of timidity," the Congress "beyond usual partisanship," and the American people "as a whole beyond selfishness and complacency." These three groups worked together "without sentimentality" to accomplish "a national acceptance of world responsibility."[33]

Truman rejected the United Nations as being too slow to act: "the situation is an urgent one requiring immediate action, and the United Nations and its related organizations are not in a position to extend help of the kind that is required." But Truman did not conceive of his doctrine as thwarting or even circumventing the United Nations. On the contrary, by helping Greece and Turkey, the United States would "be giving effect to the principles of the Charter of the United Nations," whether or not the organization actually supported the action. The goal of self-determination was intact, though now specifically defined not by a universal body but by American perception. The president's statement became known as the Truman Doctrine: "I believe that it must be the policy of the United States to support free peoples who are resisting attempted subjugation by armed minorities or by outside pressures." He believed that the "free peoples of the world look to us for support in maintaining their freedoms."[34]

Truman's vigorous call meant a reorientation of consensus thinking. Congressmen who had made the leap from isolationism to support for the international body questioned a change in policy so soon after having made a commitment to the United Nations a couple of years before. Sen. Arthur Vandenberg allowed that the independence of Greece and Turkey "must be preserved, not only for their own sakes but also in defense of peace and security for all of us." But the policy "must keep faith with the pledges to the Charter of the United Nations which we all have taken." "We must proceed as far as possible within the United Nations," said Sen. Claude Pepper of Florida, who wanted full American financial support. Sen. Harry F. Byrd of Virginia said: "If we bypass the United Nations organization, will these independent movements by America destroy the U.N.?" Anticipating this criticism, Truman had explained that while the possibility of UN aid had been considered, that body was unable to act immediately and effectively. The hopes of those who had become accustomed to a strong and resolute United Nations were nevertheless jolted. The same day Truman made his speech, Supreme Court Justice William Douglas and Sen. Carl Hatch were paying tribute to the international law represented by the United Nations before a group of the United World Federalists. Hatch deplored the retreat toward balance-of-power settlements and bilateral tactics. "For, notwithstanding our great economic and military power," he declared, "I do not believe that we, or any other nation for that matter, can maintain peace" through "the old system of balancing one nation off against another." That day, he argued, had "gone forever." The senator, nevertheless, supported Truman's policy.[35]

Defense of the Truman Doctrine drew on George Kennan's proposal that American strength be applied to prevent Soviet expansion. The United States had "it in its power," Kennan had declared, "to increase enormously the strains under which Soviet policy must operate," and so great was the pressure of that power that it might bring about "either the break-up or the gradual mellowing of Soviet power." A policy of "patient but firm and vigilant containment" had to depend primarily on American resources and traditions, Kennan argued, but he elaborated in a report of the State Department Policy Planning Staff in 1947 that with the extensive American undertakings of the occupations of Japan, Germany, and Austria, and massive aid to Western Europe, "it is clearly unwise for us to continue the attempt to carry alone, or largely singlehanded, the opposition to Soviet expansion." He believed that the United States should enhance its containing power: it was necessary that local forces assume part of the burden.[36]

Secretary of State Dean Acheson explained that although the United States, because of its productive capacity, would take the leading role in combating communism, other nations would add their support in a mutual enterprise: "The free world includes over two-thirds of the total population of the earth . . . nearly three-quarters of the world's land area. . . . The total productivity of the free world is many times that of the

Soviet Empire. And, most importantly, the free world has resources of mind and spirit incalculably greater than those under the totalitarian control of the Kremlin. . . . It would be folly for all our nations to invite war by leaving this potential of strength undeveloped and unorganized."[37]

The United States began to amass an overseas alliance system with the North Atlantic Treaty Organization in 1949. The Atlantic Ocean and the Mediterranean Sea, which for the strategists who conceived of NATO was an arm of the ocean, united the nations of Western Europe and of the Americas in a common strategic, economic, and cultural region to be protected by this alliance. It was an expansive view, taking in lands not only strung along the Atlantic coast but reaching well inland and far afield. America drew together with its "natural allies"—Belgium, Canada, Denmark, France, Greece, Iceland, Italy, Luxembourg, the Netherlands, Norway, Portugal, Spain, Turkey, and Great Britain; West Germany joined the organization in 1955.

As with the formation of the United Nations, democratic traditions became a part of the American defense of NATO. The NATO treaty, Acheson said in an address in 1949, was "the product of at least three hundred and fifty years of history, perhaps more. There developed on our Atlantic coast a community, which has spread across the continent, connected with Western Europe by common institutions and moral and ethical beliefs." Cultural similarities, he added, were the strongest of ties because of their basis in the common values of life—democracy, individual liberty, and the rule of law. Truman reapplied his rationale for the United Nations to NATO, saying that his faith in the unity among the North Atlantic nations was "borne out by our experience here in the United States in creating one nation out of the variety of our continental resources and the peoples of many lands." Consensus was not only a domestic good; it was also a good among the allies.[38]

The NATO alliance was further defended as supportive of earlier policies of foreign aid. The State Department used the pact in the official rationale as "a necessary complement to the broad economic coordination now proceeding under the European Recovery Program." Increased security would promote the economic recovery of Europe and back up Truman's doctrine of aid to resist the communist push.[39]

The State Department argued publicly that the pact would actually lead to the fulfillment of the United Nations. Collective self-defense arrangements were recognized in Article 51 of the UN Charter: the member governments had the inherent right of individual or collective self-defense against armed attack. Because, the State Department argument went on, the primary responsibility for maintaining international peace rested with the Security Council, the pact among the North Atlantic countries was "designed to help bring about world conditions which will permit the United Nations to function as contemplated at the San Francisco conference." It should "enhance the likelihood of reaching peaceful solutions to pending problems by making clear the consequences of resort to force."[40]

But the pact was at center a military instrument. Article 5 contained a pledge that each nation would bring its arms to bear in the event of an attack on others who joined the pact. An attack on one would be considered an attack on all. NATO, declared Truman, "gave proof" of the American "determination to stand by the free countries to resist armed aggression from any quarter." It was the first peacetime military alliance entered into by the United States since the Constitution, and the first formal alliance since the colonies had entered into an alliance with France in the American Revolution. Truman believed that if an organization similar to it had existed in 1914 and in 1939, the acts of aggression that had pushed the world into two wars would not have happened.[41]

Privately within the State Department, George Kennan retreated from this broad interpretation of his containment policy. He cautioned that NATO carried a serious danger that "we will deceive ourselves." A military pact could not be "the main answer to the present Soviet effort to dominate the European continent"; and, he added, the scope of that pact should be "restricted to the North Atlantic area itself." Nevertheless, he joined the harmonious chorus, saying "there *is* valid long-term justification for a formalization, by international agreement, of the natural defense relationship among the countries of the North Atlantic community."[42]

In the 1950s President Eisenhower and Secretary of State John Foster Dulles extended alliances beyond the North Atlantic. Early in the administration, Eisenhower's sentiment was that foreign policy "must be a coherent global policy." Defense in Europe and in the Americas was in principle "no different" from that in Asia. Dulles described in 1950 the appearance of a line drawn on a world map that, in effect, said: "we will fight anyone who steps across that line." Since no clear line of allies yet existed in the Pacific, Asia, and the Near and Middle East, Americans had left open "immunity to aggression" in those areas. Dulles relied on this reasoning to implement a Pacific pact, the Southeast Asia Treaty Organization, drawing the United States into alliance with Australia, New Zealand, Pakistan, the Philippines, Thailand, Britain, and France in 1954. SEATO declared that armed attack on any of the participating nations or their colonies would be regarded as a threat to the safety of others, but the agreement did not include the rigid provisions for collective defense of NATO. Similarly, the Central Treaty Organization covered the Middle East regions. CENTO developed out of the 1955 Baghdad Pact, which included Iraq, Iran, Pakistan, Turkey, and Britain, though Iraq withdrew in 1959. CENTO extended American alliances based on "agreements of co-operation."[43]

The United States took on commitments for its own defense along the borders of far-flung allied states, where containment might be accomplished through political initiatives, or by the military forces poised for confrontation. Was containment primarily political or military? And what were the risks that containment would lead to war? Kennan's proposal of containment advocated what he called "counter-force." He did not explicitly endorse military containment, but he did not define political counterforce, either. His position was ambiguous. "Soviet pressure against the free institutions of the western world is something that can be contained by the adroit and vigilant application of counter-force at a series of constantly shifting geographical and political points, corresponding to the shifts and manoeuvres of Soviet policy." In private memorandums

Kennan did not rule out the possibility of military force, but he argued that America could most effectively counter Soviet expansiveness by the force of its example, a self-confident, patient example. So although he questioned the sweeping language of the Truman Doctrine as suggesting a universal application, Kennan nevertheless supported the doctrine, hoping that it was not "a blank check to give economic and military aid to any area in the world where the communists show signs of being successful."[44]

By proposing containment, Kennan, along with officials who translated the concept into policy, ran the risk of military confrontation. Once challenged, containment—even political containment—might escalate to military force. This danger brought an early and eloquent criticism by Walter Lippmann, who dismissed the global spread of containment as a "strategic monstrosity." Lippmann agreed on the necessity of alliances in halting Soviet military threats, but he warned, the United States could not contain the expansive pressure of the Russians with ready American troops at every point. The policy could be implemented "only by recruiting, subsidizing and supporting a heterogeneous array of satellites, clients, dependents and puppets." The exertion of American power in regions other than the vital countries of Europe would squander American substance and prestige.[45]

Even critics of containment policy agreed on the necessity of taking a stand against Soviet communism at the risk of war, though they were confused about how and where containment should be applied: where to apply American pressure—in Europe, Africa, or Asia—and how to contain the Soviet Union politically without resort to military force.

The Korean War: The Military Solution

The buildup of a militant position, by which the United States became known not only for its goods, gifts, ideas, and institutions but also for its military, began modestly and reluctantly and under a measure of restraint and international control. The projection of military power was to be unpretentious, limited in size, amount, and aim. In 1947 U.S. Army and Air Force contingents went to Greece to train government forces against communist rebels. From 1948 to 1949 American planes led the Berlin airlift, bringing supplies to a city beleaguered by the Russians. In the East, American marines remained in China after World War II and helped Nationalist troops in the northern and central regions to face communist revolutionaries. The military advisers and training officers stayed until the last stages of the civil war in 1949.

When the communist forces of North Korea attacked South Korea in June 1950, that peninsular country had not been included in the unilateral American defensive perimeter as defined by Secretary of State Acheson and policymakers in the Truman administration. Nevertheless, the president interpreted the move as a threat both to world peace under the UN Charter and to American security. He quickly sent American troops to enter the conflict. To explain why American men were going to war when

America's national territory or people were not attacked directly, Truman informed the public in a radio and television address in July 1950 that the attack on the Republic of South Korea had "made it clear, beyond all doubt, that the international Communist movement is willing to use armed invasion to conquer independent nations." Communist aggression mounted "a very real danger to the security of all free nations." Later he voiced apprehension about "a monstrous conspiracy to stamp out freedom all over the world." He asserted that "the United States cannot—and will not—sit idly by and await foreign conquest."[46]

The Korean War met minimal resistance within the United States and was affirmed by consensus propositions. Directly linking Korea with containment, Kennan urged intervention. In a magazine article in 1951, he wrote that he had foreseen such communist aggressions in his "X" article of four years before. He saw the war as proof of the wisdom of both containment and rearmament.[47]

Henry Luce and his magazines firmly defended American involvement. *Life*'s position on the war was militant, furnishing editorials entitled "The Prospect Is War" and "We're in It Now." Even Henry Wallace acquiesced in the American action, quashing his once passionate hopes for peaceful cooperation with the Soviet Union and his fears of being drawn into war amid the great national awakening in Asia. After Korea, Wallace finally had had enough. He was tired of playing the part of the critic, saying that "when my county is at war and the UN sanctions that war, I am on the side of my country and the UN." From that time on Wallace muted his criticism of the fight against communism.[48]

Politicians who characterized the war as an international police action backed the collective effort. On July 5, 1950, Sen. Paul H. Douglas of Illinois said that once the United Nations had called upon its members to take military action, "any use of armed force by us was not an act of war, but instead merely the exercise of police power under international sanctions. . . . What we are really doing in Korea is to serve as a police force to carry out the decision of the United Nations that its member nations should help to repel the invasion of South Korea. We are, therefore, serving as agents of an international authority designed to protect the peace of the world and not as anarchic or self-appointed users of force."

In this perspective the war was the precedent for a permanent international police force to keep the peace thereafter. UN Ambassador Warren R. Austin said on May 28, 1951: "Thanks to the lessons of Korea, we have found the way to prevent the United Nations from ever again being caught unprepared in the face of aggression." He promised "soon to transmit to the United Nations, on behalf of the Government of the United States, a specific statement of the types and strength of the national armed forces which will be maintained by the United States of America, in accordance with our Constitutional processes, for service as United Nations units."[49]

Under the principle of UN collective security to protect the order and peace of the world community, thirty-eight member governments pledged support, and fifteen sent troops. But the operation was predominantly an American enterprise. In the Security Council the United States proposed the resolution branding North Korea the aggressor, while the Soviet Union was absent, enabling the resolution to pass. The vote for military intervention endorsed Truman's decision. Then, after the UN followed the American lead, Truman drew on reserves of wealth and resources to supply the greatest number of fighting men and the largest amount of equipment. All but one in ten of the troops were American; nine-tenths of Allied casualties were Americans.

Despite American efforts to secure greater support from its UN allies, the response was minimal. British troops in Asia were already fighting in Malaya. French troops were engaged in Indochina. The tiny units sent by Colombia, Turkey, and Thailand were marginal contributions to waging the war. The return of the Soviet representative, Jacob A. Malik, to the Security Council did not curtail the action but did increase resistance to it. The Soviet Union proposed a Korean cease-fire, withdrawal of foreign troops, and national elections to be supervised by a UN commission. The Americans and British rejected the proposal on the grounds that North Korea should be punished before it could be treated as an equal.

This was limited war, fought, in Truman's constant reminders, to avoid world conflagration, "to prevent a third world war," and waged to a draw, rather than to victory as in World War II. The reasoning that this action was to prevent general war perhaps escaped those people who viewed limited war as a threat leading to a wider conflict. But the build-up of the American military that began with Korea, although temporarily reduced after the war, did not stop then. And the new forces, despite the plans of Ambassador Austin, were not under UN auspices.[50]

Beginning with the Korean War, the government of the United States made unilateral decisions, with or without the sanction of international authority, to deploy armed forces to countries within a growing alliance and to build bases in every region of the globe. The army became entrenched abroad, the navy's fleets remained stationed in foreign ports, and air force bases became institutions on foreign soil. American military involvement ranged from all-out shooting wars to ferrying supplies and troops of allied nations in and out of battle.

From International Control to the Arms Race

Conventional force was the most visible expression of protecting the political structure of the world role. The mobilization of a great unseen destructive power, unimaginable in force, conceived in secret, and held in reserve, represented the ultimate exertion of power. One scientist who took part in the construction of nuclear weapons posed the question of rulers who held the power to alter the human environment and damage the human species, and perhaps to end its life on earth: "Should Man play God?" The temptations of Prometheus haunted the leaders in government, but, as Henry Kissinger later acknowledged, the gods of Greek mythology might punish man by fulfilling his wishes too completely. To hold these weapons and yet not fire them against enemies posed a great paradox.[51]

Right after the bombs had been exploded on Hiroshima and Nagasaki, those who looked to the United Nations turned to it to control the weapons and to redirect the energy of the atom from war to peace, and from destruction to building. These hopes for control under an international organization arose in Truman's radio address on his return from meeting with Stalin at Potsdam: "The atomic bomb is too dangerous to be loose in a lawless world. That is why Great Britain, Canada, and the United States, who have the secret of its production, do not intend to reveal that secret until means have been found to control the bomb so as to protect ourselves and the rest of the world from the danger of total destruction."[52]

In the flush of victory, Truman sought advice about the means to implement that earnest initial reaction. The scientists, statesmen, and generals who pressed for international control had to resolve which UN members would be let in on administering the secret and under what circumstances. In memos to the president, Henry Wallace proposed "the free and continuous exchange of scientific information . . . between all of the United Nations." Wallace had a penchant to see Americans as others might see them, as a nation that had demobilized but had not entirely forgone its military power after the war. "How do American actions since V-J Day appear to other nations?" he asked. With a $13 billion defense budget, the Bikini tests of the atomic bomb, production of B-29s, and the effort to secure "air bases spread over half the globe from which the other half of the globe can be bombed," Wallace could not "but feel that these actions must make it look to the rest of the world as if we were only paying lip service to peace at the conference table." How would it appear if the positions of the United States and Russia were reversed—"if Russia had 10,000-mile bombers and air bases within a thousand miles of our coastlines and we did not?" Military power, Wallace believed, was no answer to international relations. "Some of the military men and self-styled 'realists' are saying: 'What's wrong with trying to build up a predominance of force?' " Wallace countered, "In a world of atomic bombs and other revolutionary new weapons . . . a peace maintained by a predominance of forces is no longer possible." The reason, he said, was obvious. "So far as winning a war is concerned, having more bombs— even many more bombs—than the other fellow is no longer a decisive advantage. If another nation had enough bombs to eliminate all of our principal cities and our heavy industry, it wouldn't help us very much if we had 10 times as many bombs as we needed to do the same to them." Russia would soon produce the bombs. He called for international control.[53]

Before retiring from the War Department, Henry Stimson recommended to the president that the United States work out an agreement directly with the Soviet Union and Great Britain "to control and limit the use of the atomic bomb as an instrument of war." He did not like the view of Americans "having this weapon rather ostentatiously on our hip," but, on the other hand, he did not favor the full control of an international organization. On September 11, 1945, he wrote, later underscoring the points he considered the most important: *"I emphasize perhaps beyond all other considerations the importance of taking this action with Russia as a proposal of the United States—backed by Great Britain but peculiarly the proposal of the United States. Action of any international group of nations, including many small nations who have not demonstrated their potential power or responsibility in this war would not, in my opinion, be taken seriously by the Soviets."* Stimson's belief had matured beyond mistrust of Russia and on this issue he agreed with Wallace. As was scribed in his memoirs, "Granting all that could be said about the wickedness of Russia, was it not perhaps true that the atom itself, not the Russians, was the central problem?" He questioned whether it was practical to hope that the atomic "secret" could be used to win concessions from the Russian leaders and whether civilization could survive with atomic energy uncontrolled.[54]

The lines between the ways to achieve international control—whether through negotiation inside or outside an international organization—were drawn in a cabinet meeting of September 21, 1945. Stimson made his plea. Forrestal, the secretary of the navy, did not want to share the secret with anyone. Wallace argued for sharing internationally scientific knowledge, though not "factory technique or 'know how.'" Acheson supported Stimson: direct discussion was necessary with the Russians.[55]

Truman made his own determination. In a message to Congress in October, he stated that the "hope of civilization" lay "in international arrangements" to renounce the use and development of the atomic bomb. The alternative to overcoming the difficulties would be "a desperate armament race which might well end in disaster," but Truman decided not to begin discussing this problem in the United Nations, which had barely formed, until it was "functioning and in a position adequately to deal with it." He proposed to initiate discussions, first with America's "associates" in this discovery, Great Britain and Canada, and then with other nations, especially the Soviet Union, in an effort to effect an agreement on the conditions under which "international collaboration" might safely proceed.[56]

Meanwhile, calls for international control came from all over. One of the early appeals for world government was by Norman Cousins, who published "Modern Man Is Obsolete" in the *Saturday Review of Literature*. In 1946 a volume of comments appeared, entitled *One World or None*, in which Walter Lippmann called for world law applying to all nations to gain control of atomic weapons. The chancellor of the University of Chicago, Robert Hutchins, highly regarded for his educational reforms, argued forcefully in a pamphlet, *The Atomic Bomb versus Civilization*, for a "world state which the survival of mankind demands." The United States could quickly allay mistrust by agreeing to use the bomb only with the consent of the United Nations and by disclosing the "so-called secret of the atomic bomb."[57]

The major step to realize international control under a world body was the formation of a committee to draft an American atomic policy. The committee, led by Dean Acheson, in turn sought out a board of technical consultants, whose chairman, David Lilienthal, had been the head of the Tennessee Valley Authority. The final report, transmitted to the secretary of state, was formally entitled *A Report on the International Control of Atomic Energy,* often called the Acheson-Lilienthal Report. The writers carefully prepared doubting readers for their main proposition. Their proposal "may seem too idealistic . . . too radical, too advanced, too much beyond human experience." But, they asked, "What are the alternatives?" They had "no tolerable answer."[58]

The members of the committee looked to the United Nations to administer an international atomic agency. Their proposed Atomic Development Authority, internationally staffed, would be powerful. It would have "exclusive jurisdiction" to conduct all major operations in the field of energy and weapons—"all activities relating to raw materials, the construction and operation of production plants, and the conduct of research in explosives." The secretary of state endorsed the proposal, and Truman dubbed the committee's product "a great state paper."[59]

The American negotiator at the United Nations, Bernard Baruch, introduced to the member states the plan for an International Development Authority with worldwide enforcement powers: "We are here to make a choice between the quick and the dead," Baruch intoned, and he repeated with rhetorical flourish the points of the Acheson-Lilienthal plan favoring the authority. But he added a new provision, with the president's approval. Baruch demanded that the member nations not be allowed to veto proposals concerning atomic matters under its jurisdiction. The stipulation threatened discord among the big powers because they had earlier agreed to the right of veto in the innermost UN councils.[60]

Public hopes for the United Nations working out the serious problems of world peace were high. *Time* did not know if the proposal was feasible but judged the ideas to be "reasonable" and "technically sound." "International atomic control was a right and necessary objective." Even the suspicious *New York Daily News* said that the Baruch plan was best, if there had to be a plan. Walter Lippmann was pleased with everything in the plan except the call to outlaw the veto. The conclusions required "a very special kind of respectful attention, a little like that which an ancient geographer, who knew in theory, but only in theory, that the world was round, would have to pay to Columbus and Magellan."[61]

It was a dream that some refused to relinquish easily. A year later Robert Oppenheimer restated his belief in the UN's work to control nuclear weapons. Whether or not the Soviets agreed with the Americans or the Americans with the Soviets, the agreement was worth pursuing: The "basic idea of security through international coöperative development has proven its extraordinary and profound vitality."[62]

But international control failed to become a reality. The negotiations broke down when the great powers could not consent to an organization in which a single nation could control a nuclear decision with its veto. The United States had made the UN proposal, the Soviets suggested alterations, and no one was willing to negotiate the differences. Baruch left his post and the proposal died quickly.

Responsibility for the failure of serious negotiations lay with both sides, but the reasons for the U.S. refusal to seek an accord lay in the beliefs of Americans as typified by Truman—the belief in American preeminence and the need to protect it. Truman felt that the United States should maintain its front rank in nuclear weapons, and he expressed his opinion characteristically. At a county fair in Missouri he declared America's good intentions about atomic energy: "That great force, if properly used by this country of ours, and by the world at large, can become the greatest boon that humanity has ever had." By seeking the "welfare of the world" instead of the individual gains a nation could make "at the expense of another nation," Americans could "take this discovery which we have made and make this world the greatest place the sun has ever shone upon." Truman was less clear about how to work this out internationally. Meeting the press later on the porch of a lodge on Reelfoot Lake in Tennessee, Truman reviewed the policy that the United States should share its secrets because the "scientific knowledge that resulted in the atomic bomb is worldwide knowledge already."

But then he explained what he meant. He was prepared to share theory, *not* the expertise that was the American secret; "just the same as know-how in the construction of the B-29," or "the know-how to make automobiles by mass production." In these areas America should not be expected to share. Nor did he think other nations had the capability to catch up: it would not do "any good to let them in on the know-how, because I don't think they could do it, anyway." They would have to possess "the industrial plant and our engineering ability to do the job, as well as the scientific knowledge. . . . If they catch up with us on that, they will have to do it on their own hook, just as we did." Truman denied that the lack of accord between the United States and Russia was the result of the United States having the bomb and Russia not: "It isn't true—it isn't true at all. The difficulty, I think, is a matter of understanding between us and Russia. There has always been a difficulty, principally because we don't speak the same language."[63]

The United States had no intention of relinquishing its unique technical expertise, and no greater power could insist that it must. Here was another retreat from international hopes: The bomb had been an American monopoly. The United States would not freely grant its magic power to any other.

Limited war in Korea under the authority of the United Nations did not stop fears of a world war, or the preparation for such a war. The specter of war was a third world war, this time with nuclear weapons. *Collier's* magazine presented a graphic picture of what it imagined World War III would be like, devoting its full issue of October 27, 1951, to the "Preview of the War We Do Not Want." Its contributors included Pulitzer Prize–winners and national figures: Robert Sherwood, the playwright; Hanson Baldwin, the military editor of the *New York Times*; Edward R. Murrow, the CBS radio newscaster; Arthur Koestler, the political novelist who had interpreted communism in *Darkness at Noon;* Allan Nevins, the historian at Columbia University; Walter Reuther, the president of the United Auto Workers of America; Walter Winchell, the newspaper columnist; Lowell Thomas, the radio reporter; Sen. Margaret Chase Smith of Maine; and Red Smith, the sports writer of the *New York Herald Tribune*. The war plan was code named "Operation Eggnog." Its premise was blunt: "The men in the Kremlin must make the choice. They can roll up the Iron Curtain. Or they can start a war and have it shot down."[64]

Collier's imagined World War III as beginning in 1952 with an attempt to assassinate Marshal Tito of Yugoslavia. Upheaval in Yugoslavia led to the intervention of troops from Bulgaria, Romania, and Hungary, all backed by the Soviet army. Truman labeled the aggression "Kremlin inspired," while the communists called the uprising "an internal matter" of the Yugoslav people. The United States, joined by the Western powers of the United Nations, declared war. The U.S. Air Force thereupon began saturation bombing of the Soviet Union, supposedly hitting only military targets, industrial installations, and atomic bomb plants, while avoiding cities. The Soviet Union mounted attacks across the German plain, into the Baltic countries, and through the Middle East, forcing the UN troops, suffering heavy losses, to retreat. London and overseas bases were attacked with atomic bombs. Then the United States was attacked with atomic bombs for the first time when the Soviet air force hit Detroit, New York, and the atomic bomb plant at Hanford, Washington. But the Allies bravely fought back, turning the tide of war by firing atomic artillery and smashing an enemy offensive on Christmas Day, 1952, in Europe.[65]

In 1953, the Eggnog scenario continued, the United States was attacked for a second time with atomic bombs on Chicago, New York, Washington, and Philadelphia. "The American capital is missing in action," wrote the Associated Press columnist Hal Boyle. The Lincoln and Jefferson memorials were in ruins and the top of the Washington monument sheared off, as flames raged over eighteen square miles. Soviet submarines fired missiles with atomic warheads into Boston, Los Angeles, and San Francisco. In retaliation, the United States bombed Moscow at midnight, July 22, 1953, with B-36s flying from American bases. "As we looked down through the overcast," Murrow wrote in his dispatch of the Kremlin being blown up, "I saw it—something that I can only describe as the flame of a gigantic blowtorch filtering through dirty yellow gauze. . . . It was the most professional, nerveless military operation I have ever seen," exclaimed Murrow, who had witnessed the World War II German air attacks on London. The center of Moscow was destroyed and the city damaged for twenty miles around. After atomic bombs were flung back and forth between the enemies, Baldwin, in his strategic analysis, found that the extensive use of atomic bombs did not lead to atomic holocaust, because "our war was primarily against Communism and the Soviet rulers rather than the Russian people." A task force, landed behind Soviet borders in the Ural Mountains, destroyed the last remaining Soviet atomic stockpile in underground chambers and ended the Soviet capability to retaliate. "The Reds will never drop another A-bomb," Lowell Thomas recorded. After Stalin disappeared, uprisings began in the Soviet Union and its satellite nations. As a UN offensive took place on all fronts, the West gained the initiative. The Red army retreated and then disintegrated.[66]

In 1955, according to this story, hostilities ceased as the Soviet Union degenerated into chaos, and the UN set up its occupation command in Moscow, forever changing Soviet life. The survivors in the Soviet Union avidly read translations of *Collier's, Life,*

Time, Reader's Digest, the *Saturday Evening Post,* and Walter Lippmann and Walter Winchell. "Russia is no longer a vast concentration camp of 212,000,000 victims. Russia is free," wrote Winchell in his first column to "Mr. and Mrs. Russia." The Moscow ballet was replaced with *Guys and Dolls,* and among the films that opened was *The Secret Life of Walter Mitty* with Danny Kaye. Women were emancipated. They were "no longer slaves," Sen. Margaret Chase Smith reported. Labor unions were established with the assistance of Walter Reuther. Democracy was revived. The Russians were reeducated, and Alan Nevins expressed his gratification that the Ford, Rockefeller, and Carnegie foundations had pooled their resources to rehabilitate Russian science and technology. The United Nations relieved Russia through agencies named UNIHOPE, UNITOC, UNIPROD. Red Smith wrote about the camaraderie of the Moscow Olympics of 1960, by which time the Soviet Union had become a friendly state.[67]

It was a fallacy to assume that the world could quickly recover from atomic strikes destroying major cities. After millions had perished, the prospect of happy and prosperous survivors in atomic war's aftermath would be remote. But the nightmare was not so far-fetched when compared with the secret plans actually made about the same time for war with the Soviet Union. In 1949 the Joint Chiefs of Staff, with Truman's authority, made preparations for atomic war to begin in 1957. "Dropshot" was the code name of the secret document, written the year Russia exploded an atomic bomb and China fell to a communist regime. It was not a plan for preventive war to keep the Soviet Union from becoming more powerful; it was a contingency plan to prepare the country for war.[68]

The public and the secret plans for atomic war were obviously different in their narrative color and detail, but there were striking similarities—in the crises that sparked the war, the early setbacks of the United States and its allies, the successful offensive against the Soviets, the ultimate victory, and the reformation of the Soviet nation. The war in 1957 was expected to arise by miscalculation, as one side or the other failed to estimate accurately how far the other might be pushed. A sneak attack on the United States might be launched by the Soviets, with consequences far exceeding the catastrophe of Pearl Harbor.[69]

In the first phase of the war, the United States would be incapable of defending its territory. Soviet sabotage and onslaughts by air, submarine, and guided missiles would destroy industrial facilities and lives. The people had to be prepared for the resulting disruption; their unity depended on it. Mobilization of American forces would be on a scale unprecedented in any war, and the United States had to collaborate with its allies—Great Britain, the British Commonwealth, and the entire Western world—to defend vital areas and installations. But the United States would of necessity be the heart of the resistance to the Soviet aggression, and it was the ultimate Soviet objective.[70]

According to the Dropshot scenario, most of the hard fighting was supposed to take place around the perimeter of the Soviet Union. As the Soviets pushed across Europe, the United States would have to be prepared to be driven back from West Germany to Brittany, and even a beachhead there might fall. As a strategic naval and air center, Britain would be in grave danger from air and missile attacks, and atomic bombs could open it up to invasion. The oil-bearing regions of the Middle East in Saudi Arabia, Kuwait, and Iran must be held, as it was projected that in 1957 the United States at war would need more strategic materials from abroad than from domestic sources. Southeast Asia was to be kept for its resources and bases. Japan would have an industry capable of contributing little to the war effort, but the main islands and Okinana should be protected, to base American divisions.[71]

After sustaining initial losses, the United States in phase 2 of the next world war would intensify the air battle, exert unrelenting pressure on the ground "along the general line of discriminate containment," and control the seas. To counter the hordes of Soviet armed forces, the United States would be ready in 1957 with awesome new weapons—heavy bombers, guided missiles, high-speed submarines, and incendiary chemicals. It would also retaliate with atom bombs: "Our principal initial capability will lie in . . . an air offensive with atomic bombs against the USSR." "A strategic air offensive against the USSR utilizing the A-bomb supplemented with conventional bombs should be instituted immediately after the outbreak of hostilities." From a ring of bases around the Soviet citadel, the United States would launch constant attacks into the heartland.[72]

In phase 3 of the war, a major advance across the European continent would destroy occupying Soviet forces and open the way for invasion of the immense Soviet Union. The lessons of past invasions of Russia, the vastness of its territory, the magnitude of its effort in manpower and supply, all pointed to the necessity of unceasing air strikes before the initial land attack. The probable avenue for invasion was across the north German plain, through Poland and the Baltic states, and into Russia.[73]

At the end of war, the United States would enforce surrender terms. The allied troops occupying the Soviet Union would establish their rule in the cities to exercise control of the government, communications, shipping, and resources. The occupiers would reinstate new civil government.[74]

Both Dropshot and Eggnog were to conclude in a smashing victory for the country that had never lost a war, and both plans took for granted that the severe losses of atomic attack could be quickly overcome. There was little concern about whether both sides might lose in nuclear world war. Strategists concluded that to assure victory, the military had to be strengthened, and this prompted a titanic military building program over a substantial period.

While the hypothetical Eggnog and Dropshot plans took shape, the number of real weapons in the American atomic stockpile increased rapidly, after a slow start, from 2 in 1945 to 50 in 1948, 450 in 1950, and 1,350 in 1953. The new weapons deployed at home and abroad ran the gamut from atomic shells, designed for tactical use on battlefields, to the hydrogen bomb, explosive enough to level entire cities. New means to deliver warheads were devised by the Strategic Air Command, which started out in

1946 with 148 B-29 bombers, added the B-36 and B-50 in 1948, and introduced the B-52 in 1955. The force grew to over 1,500 medium-range and intercontinental bombers.[75]

Between 1953 and 1960 some 17,000 nuclear weapons were added to the stockpile, making a total of 18,500 warheads, with more on the way. The mid-1950s program of long-range ballistic missiles received high priority, and missiles eventually displaced bombers as the leading way to deliver bombs.[76]

With the failure of international control, presidents, secretaries of state, advisers, and generals thought of using these terrible, swift weapons not only in abstract war plans but also in crisis spots around the world. If Soviet communism was the ultimate threat to Allied societies, it followed that the risk of untold destruction and death was acceptable. It was an unanswered proposition: what specific threat was worth this risk?

In June 1948 the Soviets blockaded Berlin. Truman determined that the United States was "resolved to maintain its position" in the American sector of the city. In the pursuit of this policy, he asserted, the "Government is prepared to use any means that may be necessary." B-29 aircraft, officially described as atomic-capable, were deployed to bases in Britain, though they did not carry atomic weapons.[77]

On November 30, 1950, in the midst of the Korean War, the day after marines were surrounded by Chinese communist troops at the Chosin Reservoir, Truman warned in his press conference that he was contemplating using nuclear weapons:

The President. We will take whatever steps are necessary to meet the military situation, just as we always have.

Q. Will that include the atomic bomb?

The President. That includes every weapon that we have.

Q. Mr. President, you said "every weapon that we have." Does that mean that there is active consideration of the use of the atomic bomb?

The President. There has always been active consideration of its use. I don't want to see it used. It is a terrible weapon, and it should not be used on innocent men, women, and children who have nothing whatever to do with this military aggression. That happens when it is used.[78]

Two years later, President-elect Eisenhower, the former commander in World War II, who had expressed his conviction that the atomic bomb would not have to be used against Japan, threatened on his return from Korea, on December 14, 1952, to confront the enemy with "deeds executed under circumstances of our own choosing." Eisenhower recorded that he wanted "to let the Communist authorities understand that, in the absence of satisfactory progress, we intended to move decisively without inhibition in our use of weapons, and would no longer be responsible for confining hostilities to the Korean Peninsula. We would not be limited by any world-wide gentleman's agreement." So he sent Secretary of State Dulles to New Delhi in May 1953 to deliver a message to Prime Minister Jawaharlal Nehru, fully expecting the words to be relayed to China. As Dulles cabled home, he spoke of the possibility of "stronger" military activity that "might well extend the area of conflict." He did not mention nuclear weapons explicitly, and the next day Nehru pressed Dulles to be more specific about what the "end might be."[79]

Was Eisenhower actually prepared to use nuclear weapons? He brought up the issue on several occasions with his advisers and generals. In a meeting of the National Security Council on February 11, 1953, he stated that "we should consider the use of tactical atomic weapons on the Kaesong area," which he had been informed was an enemy stronghold. His advisers were divided. Gen. Omar Bradley argued that such a move would antagonize allies. Secretary of State Dulles mentioned the moral problem of these weapons, but only to contend that the distinction between nuclear and conventional weaponry should be broken down, believing an atomic bomb should be considered for use like any other weapon. Eisenhower was not convinced that nuclear weapons should be used: at the conclusion of the meeting, he "ruled against any discussion with our allies of military plans or weapons of attack."[80]

If presidents backed away from the use of nuclear weapons, others repeatedly urged their use or intimated they should be brought to bear, as the war in Korea dragged on. Maj. Gen. Emmett O'Donnell, who had overseen the Far East Air Forces Bomber Command, favored use of all weapons in the arsenal, stating publicly that "we should have cracked them and cracked them hard as soon as it was determined it was the Chinese Communist army attacking us from across the border"—a remark for which his superiors summoned him to air force headquarters in Washington. Gen. James Van Fleet believed atomic weapons could be used "unquestionably" to save Allied lives.[81]

In Congress, senators and representatives of both parties jumped on a nuclear bandwagon. Sen. Henry Cabot Lodge, Jr., who sat on the Foreign Relations Committee, proposed prompt use of atomic explosives: "if they can be used efficiently and profitably they should be used." Sen. Lyndon B. Johnson of Texas called for an ultimatum to Russia: "We are tired of fighting your stooges; we will no longer waste our substance battling your slaves; we will no longer sacrifice our young men on the altar of your conspiracies. The next aggression will be the last. . . . We will strike back with all the dreaded might that is within our control and it will be a crushing blow." Sen. Wayne Morse of Oregon favored using atomic "field weapons" as soon as they were available. Rep. Overton Brooks advocated the use of atomic shells to "bring back more of our men alive and fewer in caskets," Sen. J. Allen Frear to provide "the only alternative to an endless and inconclusive war," Sen. Zales Ecton to defend against a communist "human-tide" offensive, and Sen. Olin D. Johnston to put an end to "fighting with our right hand tied behind us."[82]

In November 1952, New York governor Thomas Dewey declared, "I personally would favor using atom artillery. . . . Oh, sure." Harold Stassen, the president of the University of Pennsylvania, determined that the use of atomic weapons even on the Kremlin itself would be "morally justified" if they could "be effectively used to assist American soldiers to escape the trap in North Korea which the outrageous lawless attack of the Communist armies closed upon them" or, most important of all, if the

Russian Politburo started World War III with world domination as its objective. Even Henry Wallace said that "Russian aggression" in Korea had caused him to change his mind. Events had "justified" the bomb, but he hoped "we never have to drop it again."[83]

Eisenhower evidently thought his threats had worked in Korea. "Soon the prospects for armistice negotiations seemed to improve," he recalled in his memoirs. Yet as the war wound down, an armistice was arrived at by negotiations, and Eisenhower never had to decide whether to use the weapons.[84]

So it is with the ultimate nuclear power and the consequent danger of war that we end our exploration of the American world role at its peak. The United States forged a global alliance system that was not an empire in the traditional sense; the principal means by which the United States established its political supremacy was by protecting other nations against rivals. America's relation with these nations was cemented by treaties and arrangements under which allies retained their sovereignty. The only territory the United States sought from them was strategic bases.

Americans continued to spread their force into every region. After the Korean War, the U.S. Seventh Fleet defended Taiwan, as Chinese communists shelled two small, rocky offshore islands, Quemoy and Matsu. In January 1955 the Seventh Fleet helped evacuate Nationalist Chinese troops and civilians from the Tachen Islands. From August to November 1958 ships convoyed supplies to Quemoy and Matsu to defend the islands again bombarded by Communist China. U.S. Marines and Army troops with naval support landed in Lebanon in 1958 to protect its government. Soon after, U.S. helicopter units arrived in South Vietnam to support its struggling combat forces.

American power, the government endeavored to convince foreign nations, would be impelled into action not for conquest but for the establishment of peace and order. The United States did not consistently insist that the issues of war and peace be confronted in international organizations to restrain the power of other nations—and of the United States. Instead, direct American involvement in foreign conflicts aimed to settle potentially disruptive international conditions. But by exemplifying self-determination and the will of the people, the United States was actually inspiring popular expressions of independence by war, if necessary. American attempts to maintain the integrity of weak developing countries and to preserve stability might paradoxically serve to strengthen the unity of rising peoples in their cause, and often against Americans.

As we have seen, consensus ideas, encompassing both the Left and the Right, supported the outward thrust of American society. Even the liberal Henry Wallace campaigned for an expansion of America's already tremendous trade. Doctrines of economic abundance were related to enterprise abroad through the growth of American exports under the ground rules of free-trade policies; the vastly increased foreign investment through private companies; and the stabilization of national currencies by a world dollar standard under the Bretton Woods Agreement. Notions of philanthropy and social welfare were related to foreign aid in the Marshall Plan, Point Four, and subsequent assistance to regions worldwide. The concepts of an egalitarian, technological society were related to the cultural expansion of travel, expositions, Hollywood films, television programs, customs, and fads. In addition, federalism and democratic beliefs were related to support for regimes in the Truman Doctrine and through a web of alliances spiraling out from the United States around the globe.

There was a falling away from genuine attempts at universal international action, to unilateral action. The rejection of the International Trade Organization was based on the image of the United States as the preeminent economic power serving as the regulator of the world's economies. Although American plans were for an ITO to promote free trade, the United States failed to accept this organization in 1950, relying instead on a general agreement for trade. In practice, the valuable investment channeled through the World Bank and the International Monetary Fund was dwarfed by enormous U.S. government transfers.

After the end of UNRRA in Europe in 1947, American aid increasingly took the form of direct programs, most notably the Marshall Plan. The United States also provided substantial aid in the technological grants of Point Four and subsequent assistance to developing regions.

Limiting involvement in UNESCO, the government instead emphasized the United States Information Agency, with the mission of projecting an official American worldview. The government enhanced private cultural relations: of individual businessmen, soldiers, and diplomats abroad; of Hollywood films and television programs; of blue jeans, jazz and rock music, and fast-food restaurants.

As the United Nations did not receive full American support, the government used the UN's weakness to justify unilateral support of regimes under the Truman Doctrine and thereafter through an alliance system that included the North Atlantic Treaty Organization, the South East Asia Treaty Organization, the Central Treaty Organization, and the Rio Pact. These plans to keep the peace led to the build-up of both nuclear weaponry and conventional arms.

If the root cause of inadequate development, starvation, and poor health was not communist activity but rather an exhaustion of physical plant and spiritual vigor, the most effective policies were the ones Henry Stimson had called for at the beginning of America's world role. These policies were directed not to the simple combating of communism but to the restoration and development of the economic health and vigor of societies. They were designed to overcome the economic and social maladjustment that made societies vulnerable to totalitarian movements. The policies of the Marshall Plan, Point Four, and exchange of culture originated because of American creativity and innovation and came about at the invitation of other peoples. The effective activities were not unilateral but by agreement among nations.

More direct means of exerting influence replaced the fledgling attempts to create international institutions. The epic global activities of the United States provided substantial benefits to other peoples. The manifestations of America's action abroad were successful when the United States exerted an irresistible force in its wealth, social life, and cultural fads that other nations wanted to emulate or follow. But as the United States moved further away from international institutions, it acted increasingly in accordance with its ethnocentric national outlook and sought to wield influence through military action, making pitfalls more likely. American internationalism was becoming ethnocentric rather than cosmopolitan.

Even direct application of American power did not always achieve the intended results. Prosperity was enhanced in widespread regions where American trade routes, investment, and currency reached. Despite instances of exploitation in pursuit of profits, the nation was actually providing the modern technology and capital that other nations needed for long-term development. American technical and financial aid stimulated Western Europe and Japan to recover economic vigor, political well-being, and national self-confidence, and new nations received considerable support in their efforts to modernize. This aid did not necessarily keep allies faithful; it often helped encourage economic competitors. American ideas and customs became known in other lands. Ultimately, the peoples of different cultures were free to accept American ways or to reassert their own cultural values. The United States took the lead in organizing a world order of general peace first through the United Nations and then through a far-flung alliance system. But the pursuit of peace diverted massive resources into the maintenance of a domestic military establishment and bases abroad. Recognition of unparalleled American strength by totalitarian enemies may have discouraged some breaches of the peace. But forceful challenges to the peace and to the authority that helped maintain it ultimately meant war.

PART IV

The

Crisis

of a

World

Role

☆ ☆ ☆ ☆

13

The

Consensus

Dilemma

Along the frontiers of influence, as they stood at the height of the world role, allies and enemies mounted challenges to America's economic growth, technical advancement, and trading prowess, to the attraction of its culture, and to its vast alliance system. Up to this point the American world role was in large part a natural progression following upon successful internal development and the failure of previous powers. Now the world role faced crises endemic to it, and the consensus approached the future with a measure of anxiety.

From the 1940s through the 1950s, the American world role emerged and developed with the consensus. How did leaders and intellectuals labor to hold together the popular consensus? How did the leaders change their thought? Was there a reemphasis of old ideas? Or was there, on the contrary, a lack of resolution for the continued application of power?

The Problem of National Purpose

In Bad Axe, a small town in eastern Michigan, not far from the shores of Lake Huron, on a spring afternoon in 1960, the citizens gathered to talk about a subject that was no longer removed from their daily lives: "America's national purpose." The people came from their farms in the flat surrounding country, and from their stores and houses in the town center. Their grassroots symposium on the nation's aims was held in the sun in front of the courthouse. The editor of the local *Huron News,* who organized the debate, in opening it told the crowd: "We must recognize, accept and support a purpose of our own."[1]

In that spring of 1960 national purpose was a subject heard across the nation at political meetings, in commencement addresses, in magazine columns, in newspaper editorials, and on radio and television. National organizations placed the topic on their agendas. The American Veterans made it the theme of their summer convention, and the Junior Chamber of Commerce called on its two hundred thousand members to further discussion throughout the country. The debate entered the presidential campaign. "Nineteen-sixty will be a campaign on national purpose," said the Republican Platform Committee chairman, Charles

Percy. "The party that can best chart the course the nation should take will win the election."[2]

The discussion of national purpose was a reaction to a loss of confidence in America's ability to solve world problems. Walter Lippmann sensed insecurity and drift: "The critical weakness of our society is that for the time being our people do not have great purposes which they are united in wanting to achieve. The public mood of the country is defensive, to hold on and to conserve, not to push forward and to create." And George Kennan in the 1950s came to concentrate his attention more on the problems of his homeland than on its Soviet adversary. His words were striking from one who had once conceived of America exerting pressure to mellow or eliminate Soviet power: "If you ask me . . . whether a country in the state this country is in today: with no highly developed sense of national purpose, with the overwhelming accent of life on personal comfort and amusement, with a dearth of public services and a surfeit of privately sold gadgetry, with a chaotic transportation system, with its great urban areas being gradually disintegrated by the headlong switch to motor transportation, with an educational system where quality has been extensively sacrificed to quantity, and with insufficient social discipline even to keep its major industries functioning without grievous interruptions—if you ask me whether such a country has, over the long run, good chances of competing with a purposeful, serious, and disciplined society such as that of the Soviet Union, I must say that the answer is 'no.'"[3]

At the request of the editors of *Life,* several leaders of consensus opinion contributed their judgment on the purpose of the nation to a symposium, whose scope of inquiry was not strictly national but international. Editor-in-chief Henry Luce introduced the discussion: the United States had become "the greatest nation in the world. But what now shall Americans *do* with the greatness of their nation? And is it great enough? And is it great in the right way?" The big question asked by Americans, he said, was, "What is the National Purpose of the U.S.A.?" That was what Americans were "worrying about"—more than the price of eggs or the merits of education. He had once devoted his publications to get Americans to accept their "greatness." Now he wanted them to know what it was for.

The participants in the Luce symposium included a poet, a professor, a corporate board chairman, an evangelist, a journalist, a politician, a foundation executive, and a strategist. Later that year, *Life* invited the two major candidates for the presidency, John F. Kennedy and Richard M. Nixon, to submit their thoughts on national purpose. The figures were a seasoned and diverse group, many of whom had been writing about the American world role since its origins after World War II, scattered on both the liberal and conservative sides of the consensus, but all fully within it: Archibald MacLeish, Clinton Rossiter, David Sarnoff, Billy Graham, Walter Lippmann, Adlai Stevenson, John Gardner, and Albert Wohlstetter. Luce summoned them all "to a national debate." It could be, said the introduction to the series in *Life,* "the most crucial debate of our generation."[4]

Luce's debate enlarged the longstanding project of the Rockefeller Brothers Fund, organized in 1956 to "clarify the national purposes and objectives." The encyclopedic study, which published its full report in 1961, grew out of the beliefs that "we had emerged as the strongest nation and the best hope of freedom in an explosive world" and that "the United States, in the middle of the twentieth century, found itself in a critical situation." The thirty consensus leaders invited by the Rockefeller Project, including Henry Luce and David Sarnoff and John Gardner of Luce's symposium, formed an Overall Panel.[5]

The search for purpose reached to the top levels of government. President Eisenhower's State of the Union message in January 1959 called for goals to guide the nation and the people. In early 1960 Eisenhower appointed a presidential Commission on National Goals. "We are now the strongest nation on earth," he said in charging the commission members. "We have found ourselves in a position in which the entire Free World looks to us for leadership and help, in the first instance against an aggressive Communist conspiracy, supported by rapidly growing economic and military strength, but more broadly in the worldwide struggle for the realization of decent conditions of life." Eisenhower viewed the commission as bipartisan, bringing together scholars and experts in various fields who would meet at the American Assembly at Columbia University. As president of Columbia a decade before, Eisenhower had lent a hand to the formation of this assembly, getting the idea for it from the deliberations he attended at the Council on Foreign Relations. Eisenhower turned to the assembly, under the direction of Henry Wriston, to better understand the American "position of world leadership."[6]

The talk about national purpose and goals was spread further by the presidential commission's report, *Goals for Americans,* and the Rockefeller Project's *Prospect for America.* The series in *Life* was reprinted as a book, *The National Purpose.* The *New York Times* published the *Life* essays in full, and columnist Arthur Krock, noting the extent of the nation's soul-searching, commented: "The news from the aquarium suggests that what this country really needs is a good 5¢ national porpoise."[7]

The search for purpose entered all disciplines. In history, Oscar Handlin edited a volume entitled *American Principles and Issues: The National Purpose.* The Republic had become great, he echoed Luce, and throughout "the land people were asking what the United States ought to do with its greatness." Seeking national purpose when America's international relationships had entered a period of "disturbance" was no different from the seventeenth-century efforts of the first colonial settlers struggling to define their distinctive character in the New World. Daniel Boorstin entered the fray, having long suspected that "our problems arise less from our weaknesses than from our strengths. From our literacy and wealth and optimism and progress." The "problem of 'national purpose'" was to Boorstin mythic, and even if it was "largely an illusion," it was "one of the most popular illusions of our time," for it alluded to great power. The power was already *there,* and Americans engaged in the luxury of wondering what to do with it. But talking about it in committees and writing collaborative works was to him not the same as taking action. Americans had not formed committees to create their success.[8]

David Riesman's essay "National Purpose" looked at the popular phenomenon as an effort to reconsider the surplus of power and affluence, or, as he expressed it in his sociological and economic jargon, "to bring the simplicity of the balance sheet into the process of deciding where the surplus of assets and choices concentrated at the top of our society should be allocated." What was new was "the widespread self-consciousness of the quest for a national purpose." Hearkening back to his other-direction thesis, Riesman added that "the effort to define America by a single idea or connected set of ideas is occurring at the same time that the country is growing greatly in population while also discovering limits to its outward reach."[9]

The labor leader Walter Reuther declared that "most important of all, we need a deeper sense of national purpose." A committee of prominent scientists, including Margaret Mead, argued in the magazine *Science* for new understanding about "what science contributes to the national purpose." And in a column in the *New York Times*, James Reston added, "if George Washington had waited for the doubters to develop a sense of purpose in the eighteenth century, he'd still be crossing the Delaware."[10]

At stake for the consensus was America's international position. The broad challenge to the United States, Lippmann wrote in 1960, encompassed "the whole field of national power," not only military power but "the power to produce wealth and the power to use wealth for education, for the advancement of science and for public as well as private ends." It was commonplace to rank the United States as "the strongest, the most influential and most productive nation in the world"—as President Eisenhower said in his Farewell Address of 1961—or as "first in the world militarily, economically, scientifically, and educationally," in Vice President Nixon's words. But a number of observers had lost confidence in the existence of an American advantage.[11]

Midway through the 1950s, a strident pioneer of realism, Hans Morgenthau, had begun calling the United States one of the two most powerful nations, approximately equal to the Soviet Union. "The United States is no longer the most powerful nation on earth," he proclaimed dramatically in 1957, "nor is it even equal in actual and prospective military power to the Soviet Union." Morgenthau expunged every reference to America's preeminence when he revised his by then classic work *Politics among Nations* in 1960. Other observers agreed. Lippmann believed that he had witnessed "the loss of American primacy among the great powers of the world" between 1953 and 1960.

Morgenthau made a direct connection between the loss of power and the absence of purpose. In 1960 he published *The Purpose of American Politics,* in which he argued that only by a strenuous reevaluation of the "national purpose" could America regain its stature. Here was a strange twist for the old realist: he was joining in the debate that considered power not as a ramification of hard material elements but as an idea—or a moral purpose. He was embracing the very collection of ideas—moralism—that his realism purported to correct. The crisis of America's world role, said the Morgenthau of 1960, was "essentially a crisis of the national purpose." Americans were unaware of their intangible, but real purpose: "It is exactly because we are no longer as sure as we used to be of what America stands for, of what distinguishes it from other nations, of what the meaning of its existence is, that we must inquire into its purpose." And the problem of loss of purpose arose from the very consensus within America: "our questioning arises from the lack of relevant controversy; . . . from a vagueness of concept which precludes controversy, for where nothing is clearly stated there is nothing to oppose." Lacking a purpose, "America would be nothing more than a complex of power and wealth without specific meaning."

Part of Morgenthau's reconsideration was a conscious effort to compensate for misinterpretations of his earlier writings. In a new preface to the 1960 edition of *Politics among Nations,* he wrote: "Against the misunderstanding of the central element of power, which, after having been underrated to the point of total neglect, now tends to be equated with material strength, especially of a military nature, I have stressed more than before its immaterial aspects, especially in the form of charismatic power, and have elaborated the discussion of political ideologies." America could regain its power—it could "indeed become again what it once was"—if it answered a question and heeded the answer: "What has brought us to this predicament, diminishing our greatness and impairing the military ramparts without which not only the greatness but the very existence of America will become a recollection of history?" Morgenthau sought the answer not in lack of money or deficiencies in scientific training, but "in the decline of the American government, of its philosophy and operations, of the very conception of what government means in a democracy."[12]

At this time of reassessment around 1960, the consensus over internationalism had solidified. Americans had become accustomed to their world position, and if there was any chance of losing power, they affirmed the need to retain it. In one poll more than half of Americans believed that the "United States should maintain its dominant position as the world's most powerful nation at all costs, even going to the very brink of war, if necessary." Republicans and Democrats, conservatives and liberals, old and young, westerners and easterners, rural folk and city dwellers, all agreed that the United States had to maintain a dominant status, short of going to war.[13]

Isolationism had ceased to be an issue. Occasional talk of a "New Isolationism," as the diplomatic historian Norman Graebner put it, meant a new "powerful tradition of unilateralism" in American foreign policy. The problem was not of remoteness but of the extent of engagement in the world. In the introductory essay of the *Life* national-purpose series, John Jessup avowed that "any lasting political purpose must take the whole great globe for its arena." Americans' "top priorities," Adlai Stevenson asserted, "must reach beyond our shores," and Archibald MacLeish conceived of the American aim as the "liberation of humanity." The presidential commission's report, *Goals for*

Americans, encouraged a global competition with the Soviet Union to "preserve and enlarge our own liberties, to meet a deadly menace, and to extend the area of freedom throughout the world."[14]

Since 1948 Gallup polls had repeatedly shown that a large proportion of Americans, ranging from nearly 40 percent to more than 50 percent, considered foreign and defense policies the most important problems confronting the United States. The polls found that more people were informed about foreign policy issues than in the past. Attitudes based on differences in class, region, and ethnicity diminished and homogeneous attitudes toward international policies took their place. The Rockefeller Panel found that "there *is* an American consensus."[15]

Almost every commentator asserted that the United States had to seize the initiative in world affairs as never before, but also that domestic troubles—among them misdirected affluence, complacency, and moral malaise—threatened to damage world functions and prestige. Foreign trials were a test of domestic strength. A lag in technology had to be closed. "If for no other reasons," stated Warren Weaver of the Sloan-Kettering Institute, "the requirements of defense make imperative a vigorous and large scientific effort." John Gardner demanded a reappraisal of the education system to raise standards and produce more physicians and engineers.[16]

The economists Herbert Stein and Edward F. Denison recommended that the American gross national product be stimulated to expand at the maximum rate possible in a free enterprise system. "We, our allies, neutral nations, and the Soviet bloc are all deeply affected by the vision of the United States as by far the world's richest and economically strongest country. It is hard to conceive a world in which this would not be true. But it seems possible that a change to a situation in which the Soviet economy is generally recognized to be growing faster than ours, not only in percentages but also absolutely, not only in spurts but steadily, and is approaching ours in total size, could have profound consequences. It could greatly strengthen the confidence of the Russians in their own system, increase the attraction of the Communist system for the independent, underdeveloped countries, worry our allies about their reliance upon us, and weaken our own morale." Accelerating "our pace in the production race" would enhance the national security.[17]

In sum, throughout the society and economy, the Rockefeller Panel's report espoused a distention of efforts: "We must accelerate our rate of growth. We must improve our educational system. We must expand our social progress in response to changing needs. We must strengthen our free institutions so that growth liberates the inner forces of individual development."[18]

In the early 1960s, polls indicated that Americans in general believed that of greater importance than dwelling on international causes—and the polls showed the people *did* think in international terms—was concentrating on building up strength and prosperity at home. The people were conscious of power. Surveys indicated that the majority wanted to improve educational standards and place greater emphasis on science and mathematics. Almost two-thirds of respondents were willing to accept higher taxes and a cut in the American standard of living to support an adequate national effort.[19]

Abroad, most consensus observers testified to the favorable results of the Truman Doctrine, the Marshall Plan, and other foundations of American policy of the late 1940s. The policies that had been mainly limited to Europe had become after the Korean War essentially unlimited in geographic range, and, in addition, intensified and augmented in all fields of international endeavor—social to military. "At whatever cost," said the president's commission, "we must maintain strategic and tactical forces of sufficient strength to deter the Communist powers" and "to cope with military aggression even on a limited scale."[20]

For the world economy, the consensus defended the postwar economic aim of a gradual reduction of tariffs and quota restrictions among industrialized states, but it had to take into account a new adversity. Since the late 1950s, the United States deficit in international payments had become chronic as expenditures mounted for military bases and economic aid. Though American exports continued to exceed imports, exports had not shown a strong upward trend in recent years, while imports had increased considerably. The United States faced growing competition from nations with low labor costs. John J. McCloy, the chairman of the board of the Chase Manhattan Bank and formerly the president of the World Bank, calculated:

> It would be a tragic result if the United States balance of payments problem became so acute as to thwart fundamental objectives of the nation's foreign policy. Indeed, to permit it to do so would be a confusion of ends and means. Today the United States stands stronger than at any time in its history, with a Gross National Product exceeding $500 billion, and possessing more than two-fifths of the free world's industrial capacity. True, United States foreign trade, while large in absolute terms, represents only a modest proportion of our total economic effort. Moreover, the nation has been called upon to accept a special responsibility as the repository for a sizable proportion to the world's currency reserves. Yet in no sense are the fundamentals governing our international economic position such as to warrant cutting back on badly needed commitments abroad of a political, military, and economic nature. On the contrary, the thing to do is to face the balance-of-payments problem squarely and take whatever action is necessary to resolve it.

Because cutbacks in foreign commitments were not foreseen at this point, economists generally offered little more than the abstract suggestion that American export trade be conducted in the world's markets with ingenuity and vigor.[21]

In maintaining cultural contacts with other lands, Americans were disturbed by a growing hostility which they had not faced when their ways had been characterized by an amiable or helpful optimism. The bestselling 1958 novel *The Ugly American*, which its authors, William J. Lederer and Eugene Burdick, called a work of fiction based on fact, told a tale of diplomatic blundering, opportunism, and incompetence. In a series of vignettes, America's economic and technological preeminence was taken for granted. As the American ambassador to the fictional southeast Asian country of Sarkhan looked out the window of his air-conditioned office in the embassy, the "only motorized vehicles he could see were trucks which had been given to the Sarkhanese government by the American military advisory group." They carried military supplies—boxes of hand grenades, bundles of barbed wire, barrels of gasoline and oil, and containers of unassembled machine guns, and "all of it made in America."

But with this sense of preeminence went a haughtiness, even if it was unconscious, in policymaking. The local populace in *The Ugly American* had grown apprehensive of the Americans who felt they had to live up to their commissaries, big cars, and cocktail parties. One American character was told just before a beating by foreign nationals, "No, you haven't got the power or the will or anything. . . . You've done nothing but lose since the end of the war. And for a simple little reason: you don't know the power of an idea. The clerks you send over here try to buy us like cattle."

The "ugly American," Homer Atkins, was actually a "good guy" who brought his practical engineering skill to the people of Sarkhan, not to their government. Physically an "ugly man" with freckled hands and black grease under his nails, he, more than the politicians obsessed with fighting communism, rose above ethnocentrism. He shared his skill with individuals, and he was outspoken with Vietnamese and American authorities who wanted to build dams and military roads. He did not believe the local people wanted "big T.V.A.'s" or military roads. He recommended they should "start small, with little things," and he followed his own advice when he went into the Sarkhan countryside to a village to help it build a pump. A local mechanic, Jeepo, who helped Atkins, told his compatriots, "This American is different from other white men. He knows how to work with his hands." But the technical adviser at the American embassy told Atkins that by working with his hands, he had "lowered the reputation of all white men."[22]

Aware of the image of the "ugly American," the President's Commission on National Goals officially recommended that "qualified" Americans in far larger numbers than ever before be encouraged to live and work in foreign lands. The presence of overseas American civilians in the next decade, the report added, had to rise if the United States was to sustain a desirable level of exports and foreign investment and carry out programs for training and technical assistance. Travelers would better represent the United States by learning languages and specialized skills. Operations of the USIA in other countries could be made more effective in picturing American life and policy to counteract distortions spread by communist propaganda. Maintaining respect for the United States abroad was a major concern of Americans, who, in mid-1960s polls, nevertheless tended to think that their image in the eyes of other peoples was high.[23]

The consensus leaders thought that aid to developing countries demanded a substantial increase in expenditures for education, technical training, and economic aid, and for the building of roads, port facilities, and utilities. In Adlai Stevenson's view, assistance should not be "on a year to year basis but for the next critical generation." Archibald MacLeish proposed a concept as bold as the Marshall Plan in Africa, Asia, and Latin America. "The tools of action—military assistance and above all economic and industrial and scientific aid" might be applied to contribute to "our liberating mission." A majority of Americans approved of foreign aid, polls showed during the 1960s, but they did not generally favor increasing it.[24]

Americans had to hold the line from Berlin to Vietnam. "We must stand firm wherever, as in Berlin, our commitments and interests are squarely opposed to those of the Soviets," the president's commission stated. Advising the commission, William Langer, a professor of history at Harvard, expressed an objective of policy: "to encourage, support and defend those forces which, in the present-day world, are working in the direction of freedom, equality and representative government." In essence reformulating the Truman Doctrine, Langer declared that the "United States should be prepared to support other nations in defending themselves against Communist or other aggression, and in protecting themselves against economic pressure or political subversion."[25]

The commentators consistently admired the lofty purposes of the United Nations, and the presidential commission listed as a "key goal" the "strengthening" of the international organization. But together they preferred major support for existing alliances ready to employ force, and the commission made it plain that the United States should not abandon "unilateral action," for "the United Nations provides a forum for Soviet propaganda and tactics of dissension, and an opportunity for Soviet vetoes to block or delay free world advances." The growing bloc of votes from the new and "uncommitted" nations, the commission noted, might turn UN decisions against American interests. In polls an overwhelming majority of Americans thought that the United States should cooperate fully with the UN, but the people backed the strengthening of alliances by taking into account the view of allies in policymaking.[26]

The emphasis of purpose was on national security. The rationale for an enlarged military was detailed by the Rockefeller Panel, which recommended that the United States devote more money, technology, and effort to building more advanced weapons, especially missiles. The "over-all United States strategic concept" lagged behind technological breakthroughs, and budget appropriations were "out of gear" with accelerating global commitments. The report maintained that "the security of the United States transcends normal budgetary considerations" and that "the national economy can afford the necessary measures." It was not enough that since the "unilateral disarmament" at the end of World War II, the United States had engaged "in a military effort unprecedented in our history in peacetime." The build-up had proved "inadequate to the challenge we confront." What made further efforts necessary was "the Communist thrust to achieve world domination." And most of the nations of the world depended on American protection: "the safety of the non-Communist world will depend on our ability, psychological and military, to engage our forces promptly and decisively in case of aggression." So it all came together: "Industrial strength" had become "a military asset only to the extent that it can provide armaments before the outbreak of war." Thus, the United States required a "growing industrial, technological, and scientific base in order to achieve a state of continual readiness for the long haul." The choice, in turn, depended on the "purpose of our leadership" and the "spirit of our people."[27]

The Confrontation with Enemies: Military

A "common denominator" among the writers on national purpose, Richard Nixon calculated, was that the nation had "mounted insufficient response to the Communist challenge to free society." Archibald MacLeish professed that the "only way freedom can be defended is not by fencing it in but by enlarging it, exercising it," and David Sarnoff called for the determination to fight the cold war "on a scale for complete victory." Next to keeping the country out of war, the polls showed, combatting world communism continued to be the greatest American concern, whether domestic or international. Most of those surveyed agreed that the United States should take a firmer stand against the Soviet Union than it had in recent years, though they did not rule out negotiation if it would contribute to peace.[28]

The challenge from the Soviet Union was founded on more than the land area the Soviets controlled, their resources, and their population. Not that these Soviet assets were not outstanding. A new map by the National Geographic Society was introduced with impressive claims: The union covered half of Europe and a third of Asia, one-seventh of the earth's land surface. The Soviet people had exploited newly discovered resources of Siberia—iron ore, tin, gold, and diamonds—and had turned virgin soil into cropland. They had built huge dams, one designed to generate twice the output of the Grand Coulee Dam, the largest producer in the United States. New industrial sites manufactured iron, steel, and chemicals. Rich petroleum fields had raised Soviet yield to approximately half that of the United States. The world's longest pipeline stretched for more than twenty-three hundred miles. Airports and intercontinental ballistic missile bases had been constructed.[29]

The rate of Soviet production was rising, and Khrushchev repeatedly asserted that communism would surpass the American system. But the number of Americans who witnessed the Soviet advances with their own eyes was small. Prospective travelers were not given visas, though some were admitted in the late 1950s. One of those was Thomas Hammond, a young professor of Russian history. He and other visitors found a nation lagging behind the United States in its economic development and standard of living but pushing on, and closing the gap. Their impression was that America was on top, though in danger of slipping. Hammond found the Russians eager to learn about the United States. Passers-by plied him with questions: "Do people live better in America?" "What are the wages of an average worker?" "How much does an American car cost?" "Do you have social security?"[30]

The Russians wanted American goods. A young man offered to buy Hammond's suit, and when he would not sell it, the teenager asked for an electric razor, jazz records, or cameras, explaining that Soviet products were poorly made. Hammond met young people who listened to smuggled records of Elvis Presley—one student's prized possession was "Jailhouse Rock"—and the American had to tell an older woman, who wanted to know about Greta Garbo's latest films, that the star had not made a film in years, to which the fan replied that the latest Hollywood films in Russian theaters were of World War II vintage.

Hammond found, along with interest in America, evidence of Soviet growth in the looming modern apartment buildings and the "Stalinist Gothic" skyscrapers like the Ministry of Foreign Affairs and Ministry of Foreign Trade building, and the Moscow University tower, where Soviet students learned the sciences. He saw technological advance in a massive forty-ton dump truck, and though a late-model automobile named the Sea Gull was on display, trucks outnumbered cars on the highways. He looked around the Moscow subway, glittering with marble, glass statuary, mosaics, and chandeliers. When one subway worker asked him if the subway in New York was as beautiful, Hammond responded that it was not but that it had four hundred stations, compared to about forty-six in Moscow. The worker's response that someday the Soviets would have five hundred stations caused Hammond to reflect: "I often heard other Soviet citizens voice pride in their accomplishments, combined with a determination to surpass the United States. They evaluate almost everything in terms of competition between the two systems."[31]

This reaction was exactly the one that Nixon brought back from his trip to Russia in 1959. Again and again he learned a lesson in what he called Soviet "determination"—"in their driving purpose to achieve for themselves a better and more abundant life." The vice president had been immediately impressed, while driving from the airport to the center of Moscow, by the astonishing amount of new building, most of it huge apartments. Nixon was taken with Khrushchev's "deep belief in the future development of the Soviet Union's vast potential," and he caught a few glimpses of this resolve: his "jet cavalcade of three new Soviet Tu-104Bs," traveling at five hundred miles an hour; and the largest Soviet machine tool plant at Novosibirsk. Yet, reminiscent of Vice President Henry Wallace's wartime trip of fifteen years before, Nixon was struck by the American equipment in the tool factory: approximately half the machines were "American-made." One of the correspondents noticed that a Cincinnati-made machine carried an instruction plate in Japanese. Nixon also noted a new scientific center, still under construction, near Novosibirsk, where scientists would work in nuclear physics, thermophysics, hydrodynamics, and electrometry.[32]

The Soviet threat emanated not from scientific and technological advances alone, but from their application to Soviet political and military power. So it was that Adm. Arleigh Burke, the chief of naval operations of the U.S. Navy, recorded in 1959: "Distinguished American visitors to the Soviet Union in recent weeks have told me that the most dangerous thing they saw in Russia is the look on the faces of the people . . . the grim look of determination, the cool and deliberate confidence of people who are going places, who know they are missing a lot of life, who know they are being forced to sacrifice both tangible and intangible human values, but who are resolute in their aim to beat the United States in everything." They expected "to gain prestige in the eyes of the rest of the world" and "to demonstrate that their way is the way of the future" by beating the United States "in athletics, in the arts, in scientific achievement, in industry, political maneuver, and everything else."[33]

The full impact of this threat came from the Soviet launch of the world's first earth satellite on October 4, 1957. Sputnik was a shock to a country accustomed to thinking its science was first. James Killian, President Eisenhower's science adviser, felt "most keenly" the "affront" to his "national pride": "I was, of course, led at once to speculate about whether this country had grievously underestimated the technological capacity of our adversaries," for "the Soviets had actually accomplished, ahead of the United States, a technological feat to which we had both directed our efforts. And this did violence to a belief so fundamental that it was almost heresy to question it: a belief I shared that the United States was so far advanced in its technological capacity that it had in fact no serious rival."[34]

The Soviets were actually cutting back their armed forces, from 5,763,000 in 1955 to 3,623,000 in 1960, with further reductions in sight. But the Soviet Union continued to compete in areas of military technology by building long-range aircraft and a missile force. The cuts in personnel, Khrushchev claimed, were offset by the increased firepower; the Soviet Union, said to have thirty-five ICBMs in 1960, was producing rockets "like sausages from a machine." The Soviet air force had some twenty thousand aircraft, and the Soviet navy was the second largest in the world, with double the tonnage of the British navy.[35]

Although Khrushchev said these forces were for defense only, high-ranking American strategists asserted that they could have no other purpose than to threaten the entire world. This perception of the Soviet Union was their overriding one. The former chief of the Strategic Air Command, Gen. Curtis LeMay, stated that the communist objective was "control of the entire world." Gen. Thomas Power of the Air Force stated in his *Design for Survival* that the "ultimate Communist objective" was " annihilation of the capitalist system and establishment of Communist dictatorship over all nations of the world." The "military aspects of the Communist threat represent just one phase of the most insidious and gigantic plot in history."[36]

Along the periphery of the Soviet Union were its European allies and China, which had become a communist regime under Mao Zedong in 1949. Unrecognized by the United States since the revolution, China had denied admittance to American reporters. But a New Zealand photographer for *National Geographic* succeeded in obtaining a visa, and his photographs, wrote an editor who had once lived in Peking, "speak for themselves: here are the big new buildings of the Communist capital and showcase city, the disciplined mass demonstrations, the refurbished facades of historic monuments. Here is something for every Westerner to ponder." Gone was the old Peking of "the great Chinese houses," the "Thieves' Market," and "ricksha boys." The new buildings—the modern pagoda-type tower of the Nationalities' Cultural Palace, the Great Hall of the People, and the giant bowl of the Peking Workers' Stadium, completed in 1959, were symbols of the future. The young Chinese girls and boys intent on learning Western languages and science might not grow up to know the old Chinese ways, but their industry and perseverance "mirror a China not to be taken lightly."[37]

China had struggled to modernize with a "great leap forward" in industrial development and had built a regimented commune system to increase agricultural production, but both efforts had fallen short. China's strength was in a people that the Chinese government described as a great human sea, formed into militia units. While China had yet to build long-range missiles, a writer for *Foreign Affairs* stated that should the Chinese obtain a modern offensive striking power, it was likely to strengthen their conviction that they, and perhaps their masses alone, could survive an atomic war.[38]

Crises ranged mainly around the borders of the Soviet Union and China on the outskirts of the American alliance system. After the Korean War, the American government did not contemplate major reductions in military aid to those allied nations gaining independent strength. Rather, the president's commission made the case to "maintain and strengthen our military alliances." The resort to an ever more awesome military position reflected a loss of patience, not of duty.[39]

Through the 1950s the policy to deter aggression whenever the Soviet Union or its allies threatened to break through was generally known as "massive retaliation." Secretary of State John Foster Dulles predicated strategic policy on a reserve of overwhelming atomic force. As Dulles put it in 1954, the United States would rely on the power "to retaliate with great force by mobile means" at places of its "own choice." The United States had to maintain its forces in a state of "instant readiness." Vice President Nixon stated that rather "than let the Communists nibble us to death all over the world in little wars" like Korea, Americans would "rely in the future primarily on our massive mobile retaliatory power."[40]

In Vietnam, Laos, and Cambodia, the enfeebled French empire was tottering. Since 1945 Vietnamese revolutionaries had renewed the struggle for the independence of their country. But the American government supported France, its ally first in NATO and later in SEATO. In 1952 a *National Geographic* reporter traveled "half around the world" to this remote "trouble spot" facing "Red China across 750 miles of frontier." He described Vietnam as a war-torn, jungle-covered land of thatched villages with bamboo gates and cramped houseboats, where the "Viet Minh," the "Communist forces," fought against the French and their local supporters. Only in the large cities like Saigon, the "Paris of the Orient," with its boulevards, outdoor cafes, parks, and palaces, did the American feel safe. The capital was romantic: "Sipping a cool drink at a sidewalk café, one watches a cosmopolitan cast of characters stroll by. . . . Like extras in a Hollywood spectacle, French officers, sailors, Foreign Legionnaires, bearded priests, black-robed nuns, Viet-Namese natives, military police, Chinese and Indian merchants, and occasional Americans make their entrances and exits." But there was "no absolute security anywhere," not in "a weird half-war of sabotage, hit-and-run guerrilla tactics, ambush, and sudden death in lonely places." And seldom did he travel even a few miles outside cities "without an armed escort." The American saw the ravages of a village at war. Arriving an hour after an attack by Viet Minh "guerrillas," he saw a dozen fires raging. "Dazed villagers wandered aimlessly about; some threw water on thatch roofs. Schoolboys carrying slates and pencils watched in speechless fright. Old people, sitting by the road, gazed with sad, unseeing eyes. Long lines of refugees trudged toward Hue, salvaged possessions on their backs." From nearby hills came the echoes of "avenging" French artillery, and from overhead the roar of French dive bombers.[41]

President Eisenhower had been adamant that American forces not be drawn into this war on the Asian mainland. "I cannot conceive of a greater tragedy for America than to get heavily involved now in an all-out war in any of those regions," he declared, "particularly with large units." Instead the United States had sent aid, and an American could see "plenty of evidence" of it. In Hanoi alone one could visit large housing projects for refugees and attend night literacy classes taught by American volunteers. One could see at Son Tây newly installed American diesel engines pump Red River water to irrigate rice fields. Throughout Indochina American experts and dollars had "aided the war-needy, erected prefabricated hospitals, provided fertilizers, and dug wells." They had "distributed medicines, provided generator-driven community radios to keep villages informed, resurfaced roads, built bridges and harbor installations."[42]

The armaments in French fortifications were also evidence of U.S. military involvement. As the French later vainly defended Dien Bien Phu in 1954, the American government deliberated on air strikes to support them, and the consideration of nuclear weapons came up again, as it had in Korea. Gen. Nathan Twining believed that they should be used. Years later he recalled: "what we thought would be—and I still think it would have been a good idea—was to take three small tactical A-bombs. . . . You could take all day to drop a bomb, make sure you put it in the right place. No opposition. And clean those Commies out of there and the band could play the 'Marseillaise' and the French would come marching out of Dien Bien Phu in fine shape." In April 1954 Adm. Arthur Radford's assistant, Capt. George Anderson, took up the matter of using tactical nuclear weapons with the counselor of the State Department, Douglas Mac-Arthur II, who reported to Secretary Dulles: "Admiral Radford wondered whether we could not go to the French and get their approval for using atomic weapons in Indochina if this became necessary." On a trip to France that same month, Dulles went so far as to broach the question of nuclear weapons with Foreign Minister Georges Bidault to relieve the besieged French troops. Bidault understood the secretary to have mentioned the possibility and told his aides so. The offer must have been vague—Dulles later pleaded that he had "no recollection whatever" of an alleged offer. The president, after all, thought it "very unlikely" that a nuclear weapon "could effectively be used in the jungles" around Dien Bien Phu. Strikes with napalm bombs would be "more effective."[43]

The crisis ended with French defeat. President Eisenhower held out against inter-

vention, pledging in a news conference that America would not become involved in war
unless Congress declared it. By international agreement at Geneva, the communist
nationals set up a state in northern Vietnam and settled on a provisional military
demarcation line dividing them from South Vietnam. But American periodicals depicted this division with scenes of refugees forced by communist infiltration to leave
their ancient thatched villages. Wearing conical hats and barefooted, they boarded U.S.
transport ships at Haiphong in the north and crossed a thousand miles of the South
China Sea to Saigon. The American sailors gave the refugees food, clothes, and candy,
and bathed the kids and played baseball with them, and made signs to wish them luck on
their "passage to freedom." The refugees received "welcome kits" of soap, towel, and
toothpaste, and tins of milk labeled "From the people of America to the people of Viet
Nam—a gift." American funds again paid for shelters for the arrivals in camps and
helped the people build new villages with U.S. technical advice and machinery. American bulldozers and other machines began clearing mountainous jungle land and draining a vast swampy area where farms might burgeon. Yet soon the American image in
Vietnam was not of bulldozers and refugee kits but of helicopters and military buildup.
By 1962 the country of sunlit patched rice fields near the South China Sea had seemed
to one American "to sink beneath us as the formation of 16 helicopters cast dragonfly
reflections on the standing water below." The trap was set for another Vietnamese crisis,
but before it closed, crises loomed elsewhere.[44]

Across the Formosa Strait, on Taiwan, the anti-Communist Chinese who had
followed Gen. Chiang Kai-shek from the mainland were building a country pictured by
an American observer as once marked by rising "domed mountains, their brushy slopes
dotted with plantings of pine, acacia, and Chinese fir" and now modernizing, boasting
increased sugar production, up-to-date factories, and plans for a cross-island highway.
And the United States provided aid as a mainspring of this industrial development.
American movies and movie stars, from Micky Mouse to Esther Williams, and Jack
Benny radio programs broadcast by the armed forces were as well-known to some
Taiwanese as to Americans, and the United States provided arms, ships, aircraft, and
advisers.[45]

In 1954 and 1955, and again in 1958, the Chinese on the mainland opened artillery
barrages on the small, rocky offshore island groups of Quemoy and Matsu, claimed by
the Taiwanese. One American reporter who flew into the fire noted shells exploding in
the terrain, ruining centuries-old temples, and he saw the islanders hide in candle-lit
holes, tunneled into the ground. Shells "burst and men died and women and children
saw their homes crumble and moved into caves to live like animals." President
Eisenhower declared that he was determined to help Chiang defend these outposts. He
agreed with Secretary Dulles in private that if "Quemoy were lost either through assault
or surrender," Taiwan would probably be conquered by "subversive and/or military
action," followed by the loss of Japan. In January 1955 Congress empowered the
president to employ the armed forces of the United States as he deemed necessary for
the protection of Taiwan and its related territories. The fleet convoyed supplies to

Quemoy and Matsu, and on the islands U.S. Army officers instructed Nationalist gun crews and offered technical assistance.[46]

In March 1955, after a trip around the "forward positions" of Southeast Asia and the West Pacific, Dulles spoke of "new and powerful weapons of precision which can utterly destroy military targets without endangering unrelated civilian centers." He warned the Chinese not to see the United States as "merely a 'paper tiger.' " The United States was ready "to stand firm and, if necessary, meet hostile force with the greater force that we possess." A few days later Eisenhower said in a news conference that he could "see no reason why" nuclear arms should not "be used just exactly as you would use a bullet or anything else." When the president told his press secretary, James Hagerty, before meeting reporters the next week that if the issue came up again, "I'll just confuse them," he was probably revealing his own state of mind about the dilemma of nuclear weapons; he had to threaten to use them in order not to have to use them. "So," Eisenhower stated publicly, "I you think you just have to wait, and that is the kind of prayerful decision that may some day face a President." He probably did not know exactly under what conditions he might use these awful weapons. One thing was sure: he was not about to use them quickly. The government sent howitzers with nuclear capability to Quemoy.[47]

An escalation of tension also occurred in Europe. A West Germany pacified by the occupation forces awakened with energy and prosperity and danger along the barbed-wire borders of the frontier between East and West. Images of change were plentiful: the old Germany of Wagnerian music festivals at Bayreuth, and the reemergent Germany of 1960 as the most productive nation in Western Europe; the old Germany of Bavarian village beer halls and churches, and the new Germany of tall steel-and-glass buildings; the old Rhine Valley castles towering above the vinelands, and the new Rhine of large freight boats passing in succession. Why had the transformation in western Germany come about? According to one American explanation, largely because of nearly "four billion dollars in U.S. aid started West Germany's wheels turning again and kept the people from starving while they picked up speed." Perhaps the biggest change came about in the German army, which under Hitler had been bent on world conquest and after World War II had been entirely disbanded, and now was rearming to become the largest standing army in Western Europe. Once again factories were under construction to turn out fighter aircraft.[48]

In divided Berlin the Americans faced the Russians in crises from 1958 to 1961. In 1958 Khrushchev delivered an ultimatum. If a new treaty was not concluded within six months by the other three Allies that had divided the city, the Soviet Union would make separate arrangements with East Germany, terminating the wartime agreements. Eisenhower told his cabinet that the United States had to "stand firm even should the situation come down to the last and ultimate decision," although neither he nor the State Department believed it would "ever be allowed to go to that terrible climax." He rejected a general mobilization. "We are certainly not going to fight a ground war in Europe," he said in a news conference. When he was asked if the United States was prepared to use nuclear weapons to defend free Berlin, the president answered: "Well, I don't know how you could free anything with nuclear weapons." But the United States might be forced to come to Berlin's defense: "I can say this," he went on: "the United States and its allies have announced their firm intention of preserving their rights and responsibilities with respect to Berlin." The threat of hostilities, he insisted, came from the Soviet side. "I didn't say that nuclear war is a complete impossibility," he explained. But he balked at nuclear weapons the same way he opposed a general mobilization: "to use that kind of a nuclear war as a general thing looks to me a self-defeating thing for all of us."[49]

The strategies that lay behind ongoing crises, the threat to go to the brink of war and the pledge never to turn back from the frontier, were embedded in consensus thought. In no case did the nation come close to using nuclear weapons in defense of territory, allies, or interests. The danger of nuclear war existed, but the leaders were caught in the paradox of nuclear weapons. They built them up in stockpiles and freely discussed their use, but they could not bring themselves to use them. The weapons had no use in warfare, not after the two that had exploded over Japan. As for political leverage, the threats wore thin. In the end these weapons were impotent for any constructive purpose other than deterrence of their use, and they had no redeeming or civilizing quality.

The Competition with Allies: Economic and Social

The challenge of awakening rivals did not yet come from within the alliance system. The system's very foundations were laid to block enemies outside, and the countries within it were placated or docile over the deployment of American force. By the late 1950s the images of American allies cast by Americans who looked out on the world and traveled through it were little different from those formed a decade earlier. The struggles and successes of peaceful allies could be seen in two countries, Britain and Japan, one once paramount and victorious in World War II, the other totally defeated.

Britain, with its decimated empire, continued to fade from its position as a great power. While the Anglo-American alliance was the cornerstone of British foreign policy, the "special" relationship with Britain alone was not the cornerstone of American global policy. An American visitor to England would barely notice that anything eventful or out of the ordinary was happening. The popular images of England endured, like the Thames, meandering through tranquil meadows and the heart of London down to the sea, and ships bringing "untold treasure: ivory from Africa, shells from the Pacific, spices from Arabia, porcelains and bronzes from the Far East."[50]

On the surface, the decline of Britain looked like a typical case of the British muddling through. But according to observers for *U.S. News & World Report,* the change was "from the position of a great world power, with a globe-girdling empire, to that of an island nation dependent almost entirely upon its own resources and ingenuity." Britain's richest colonies were already gone, and so, too, was its former military dominance. For a small country, "the cost of membership in the 'great-power club'" was becoming "prohibitive."[51]

At issue was Britain's failure to conform to the pattern that had once made Britain great, a pattern not unlike that of American success. Britain had turned to consumption rather than capitalist investment; burdensome empire as opposed to efficient trade of mass-produced goods; and an old-fashioned conventional fleet rather than a flexible modern military. *Business Week* predicted serious trouble ahead for Britain. Crowded into a small country that had to import many basic raw materials and much food, the British had failed to increase exports to maintain a comfortable balance with imports. They could no longer count on large net receipts from merchant shipping, which ran into foreign competition, and British banking had been enfeebled as London paid heavy interest on the foreign investments in its own land. Defense outlays abroad had also been rising, leading the British government to spend beyond its means. Overall Britain, which was losing rather than gaining gold and gold reserves, had no way to pay for what it needed abroad, and the adverse balance of payments damaged the domestic economy. It seemed futile to seek the past glory of empire by trying to maintain sterling as an international currency second only to the dollar—and doing this at the expense of the long-term strength of the British economy.[52]

As economic strength eroded, the empire collapsed, replaced by the British Commonwealth of Nations. The colonies that had gained independence, with the single early exception of Burma, had chosen to enter the Commonwealth. But this confederation had no constitution or rules for membership. The ties that bound it were of sentiment, and Queen Elizabeth II was the head of nearly every member state. The Commonwealth of Nations did not "amount to very much any more," reported *U.S. News & World Report.* "Britain can no longer dominate the Commonwealth, can no longer protect it, can no longer count on all its members standing by its side if Britain goes to war." At an assembly of Commonwealth prime ministers in 1960, the press took formal pictures of the queen in a long white robe surrounded by her former subjects, now, like her, the leaders of independent states, but the conference could not agree on what to do about apartheid in South Africa or much else. This meeting was to be the last, said *Time,* "at which there are as many white Prime Ministers as colored." Lacking the power to guarantee the defense of the Commonwealth members, Britain depended heavily on the United States for the defense of the home islands. The United States, from a strategic perspective, was "replacing Britain as military protector of the Commonwealth" through its ANZUS pact with Australia and New Zealand, and through SEATO. To raise Britain's rank as a great power, the government had maintained its own independent nuclear force, but development and modernization of these weapons were expensive. Britain was risking disaster by assuming obligations far beyond its capacity to sustain.[53]

While Britain was forced to consider drawing in its global ties to the Commonwealth and to the United States, it was returning to a close relationship with Continental

Europe—a radical departure for the island nation. After the outset of the Marshall Plan, the United States had encouraged Britain to join a European free-trade area or customs union. Britain had refused, insisting that British leadership of the Commonwealth ruled out membership. But Britain was impelled by the necessity of seeking trade with the rapidly advancing nations of Europe, led by France and Germany, with a vision of a united community. Although Europe had not developed "supra-nationally," *Foreign Affairs* said, Europe was adhering as a unit.[54]

Of Japan, the old image of a land of fine prints, delicate gardens, and bold calligraphy did not die easily, as a Japan of industry, enterprise, and hard work arose. Stripped of its empire, Japan was an overpopulated land of ninety-two million people on four major home islands, largely lacking raw materials. The people were poor, but their production had improved beyond prewar levels and had exceeded the expectations of the immediate postwar years. An American who had been in Tokyo at the end of the war would scarcely have recognized the place in 1958. "Today hardly a scar remains to mark the city's wartime wounds." Tokyo had become "the world's biggest metropolis"—"furiously busy by day, bright as Broadway by night, inhabited by 8,700,000 fiercely energetic citizens whose numbers are increasing by a quarter million every year." Tall buildings sprung up "like steel-and-concrete mushrooms from the compost of little wood-and-paper houses that cluster at their feet."[55]

By 1960 Japanese business was cultivating a mammoth market throughout Southeast Asia and was looking east to American markets. But American consumers, by and large, remained wary of goods made in Japan. They still thought of Japan as a maker of cheap "toy" goods, and they sought the traditional items in bulk—fish, cotton goods, bamboo products, and silk. They had also taken a liking to hibachi grills. A 1959 study of American attitudes toward Japanese imports revealed that most American buyers thought that they could find some imported Japanese mechanical and electrical products that were less expensive than American-made—cameras, radios, and shavers—and of equal quality. But Japanese sewing machines and precision equipment were considered inferior to those in America, and 78 percent of Americans thought Japanese quality poorer than American. Attempts by the Toyota Motor Company and other Japanese firms to build autos recalled earlier GI jibes: "If you strip off the floor lining, you can read the beer-can labels." While the Americans had maintained a healthy trade surplus against these products, for the first time in the postwar years, Japan narrowed its unfavorable balance of trade to nearly the break-even point with the United States, its main customer.[56]

The secret of the Japanese success, according to numerous American press accounts, lay neither in the hard-working, energetic, optimistic, and eager-to-learn character of the people, nor in their high rate of savings and capital formation and the country's low defense budget, but in imitation of the United States. Postwar Japan had been reshaped by American influence, and Americans were pleased to be emulated. *Business Week* cited the democratic reforms, economic aid, and land reform fostered by the American occupation forces. "U.S. technology was introduced through direct investment and royalty arrangements," said *U.S. News & World Report*. "Quality controls—insisted on by Americans—enabled the Japanese to live down their old reputation as producers of cheap and shoddy merchandise." *Time* reported that Japanese manufacturers, guided by American know-how, had "gone far to overcome the reputation for shoddiness formerly attached to the 'Made in Japan' label." Japan had also benefited from the war against the communists in Korea. Ever since the war, the Japanese had earned substantial amounts of dollars through American procurement of military goods, fertilizers, textiles, and machinery for other nations of Asia and for the American troops in Korea, Taiwan, and South Vietnam.[57]

Toward the end of his term in office, President Eisenhower had planned to visit Japan, but riots against a proposed new American defense treaty, confirming the American right to bases on Japanese soil, caused the trip's cancelation. In retaliation for the demonstrations, blamed on communists and leftists, some American firms boycotted or sent back Japanese televisions, electronics, radios, bicycles, carpet, and rubber slippers and planned to buy American. But across the country at big companies that sold Japanese imports, at Sears, Woolworth, and Montgomery Ward, merchants noticed little shunning of Japanese products, and the boycott was a failure. A few Americans, meanwhile, were wondering if the transistor radios shipped to America from Japan were forerunners of more, better-made, and less costly products.[58]

14

The

Internal

Crises

The tone of the Augustan period of the American world role, when the very success of the early policies after World War II widened an outlook that had never been abandoned, was set by John Kennedy's inaugural address. The president spoke shortly after noon on January 20, 1961, from a platform erected at the east front of the Capitol, immediately after taking the oath of office administered by the chief justice. It was a cold and glistening sunny day, after a snow storm the night before, and his clear words were to mark the beginning of a brilliant new era: "Let the word go forth from this time and place, to friend and foe alike, that the torch has been passed to a new generation of Americans," a generation that, having known war and a hard and bitter peace, was "unwilling to witness or permit the slow undoing of those human rights to which this nation has always been committed, and to which we are committed today at home and around the world."

It was a new generation, but the words were of reaffirmation, a continuation of the same or an expansion of it: it was a time of renewed and increased effort. "Let every nation know, whether it wishes us well or ill, that we shall pay any price, bear any burden, meet any hardship, support any friend, oppose any foe to assure the survival and success of liberty."[1]

This was how Kennedy began his administration, but Eisenhower, in ending his, had apparently anticipated these bold urgings. A few days earlier, he addressed a warning to his successor, counseling that in meeting America's prolonged "burdens" in the world, "there is a recurring temptation to feel that some spectacular and costly action could become the miraculous solution to all current difficulties. A huge increase in newer elements of our defense; development of unrealistic programs to cure every ill in agriculture; a dramatic expansion in basic and applied research—these and many other possibilities, each possibly promising in itself, may be suggested as the only way to the road we wish to travel." Eisenhower was the oldest president to leave office; Kennedy was the youngest elected to it and brought his youth and stamina to lead the national consensus he inherited. He was, Eisenhower noted, contemplating an unbounded expansion of national enterprises.[2]

The attempt at reformation of the American world role had been dramatic in the election campaign of 1960.

Richard Nixon's plea that the United States had not mounted a sufficient response to communism was coupled with his assurance that "we do have the strength, and we will develop more, to win this struggle and win it without war." John Kennedy's appeal as the Democratic candidate resulted in large measure because he took a new tack for American campaigns: he decried the steady decrease in America's relative strength. That is not to say he was not impressed by the power of the United States. "We are a great and strong country—perhaps the greatest and strongest in the history of the world," he declared. "But greatness and strength are not our natural right. They are not gifts which are automatically ours forever." Thus, "if we do not soon begin to move forward again, we will inevitably be left behind." Kennedy walked a fine line. The problem was this: "We are still the strongest power in the world today. But Communist power has been, and is now, growing faster than is our own. And by Communist power I mean military power, economic power, scientific and educational power, and political power." Sounding like Harry Truman on the hustings, he declared, "This is the greatest country in the world. But we can be still greater. This is the most prosperous country in the world. But we can be still more prosperous." Unlike Truman, he worried about declining power but did not believe it was irreversible: "Why is it that we who represent the final flowering of the human experience in self-government should be regarded as a tired country, as a country which has seen its best days?" "I think our high noon is yet to come."[3]

"What is it that Mr. Nixon and I differ on?" Kennedy asked. Nixon believed that "the United States is doing everything it should do to maintain its position in the world." Kennedy defined the contest as about those who thought American power sufficient and those who wanted to increase it, those who were satisfied with things as they were, and those who were not. Nixon was on record that the United States had to boost its efforts against communism but that Kennedy should not be "running down" the United States. The issue was who could do the most. "I am calling for greater effort . . . ," Kennedy announced. "It is not naive to call for increased strength." His message was "for a greater America, for a greater national effort for our prestige, in our defenses, in our economy, in our education, and in our efforts to peace." "I want an America that is not 'first, if,' not 'first, but,' not 'first, when,' not 'first, maybe,' but 'first,' period," the candidate declared to applause. "I want a world which looks to the United States for leadership." America should have a defense "second to none" and maintain a position as "the No. 1 productive power in the world."[4]

Kennedy criticized Nixon's efforts as inadequate. "In 1954 he tried to get us involved in a hopeless colonial war by recommending the dispatch of American troops to fight in Indochina." Nixon's goodwill trip to Latin America did not enhance but endangered the prestige of the United States by provoking demonstrations and disorder. His debate with Khrushchev was a disappointment, for "the best he could do in that Moscow kitchen was to wag his finger in Mr. Khrushchev's face and say: 'You may be ahead of us in rocket thrust, but we're ahead of you in color television.' " The United States needed more missiles.[5]

To meet the global communist challenge, Kennedy advocated a reassertion and extension of American policies. First, he wanted to stimulate the growth rate of the economy, to keep its commanding position in the world marketplace. The means "to regain our position of preeminence in the world" was "economic growth." Under President Eisenhower, "we have not been growing," Kennedy said, and "Mr. Khrushchev noted it when he promised to 'bury' us." Economic production had a dividend. With a healthy rate of growth, "we can end the gnawing doubts about our national defense." Kennedy addressed Eisenhower's restraint in defense spending, saying growth would pay many times over the cost of the vital defense programs that the Eisenhower administration had not afforded—the cost of putting the Strategic Air Command on a continuous air alert, the cost of modernizing the army and navy, and the cost of building more Polaris and Minuteman missiles.[6]

Abroad, Kennedy wanted a build-up of nuclear firepower and conventional forces to meet hostile forces on any front. Because America was the "strongest Nation on earth" and "because the Communists know it, they have succeeded in tying us up in one trouble spot after another—on their own terms, and in areas of their own choosing—and in this way preventing us from using our strength to advance freedom throughout the world." His campaign slogan was the "New Frontier," to follow Roosevelt's "New Deal." Roosevelt had denied that American frontiers lay on the Rhine, but Kennedy proclaimed, "Now in 1960, American frontiers are on the Rhine and the Mekong and Tigres and the Euphrates and the Amazon. There is no place in the world that is not of concern to all of us." He pledged: "this country has to move forward again."[7]

Expansion of Policies: Trade, Culture, and Aid

As president, Kennedy expanded the policies that had been limited in scale and locale mainly to Europe until they became essentially unlimited in geographic range and augmented in all fields of international endeavor. In trade policy, the president warned that the world role would be jeopardized without expanded exports. While American international balance of payments was "in deficit," the Common Market and Japan had become competitors, and the communist bloc had "a vast new arsenal of trading weapons." Kennedy believed that "American trade leadership must be maintained," otherwise "we cannot continue to bear the burden that we must bear of helping freedom defend itself all the way, from the American soldier guarding the Brandenburg Gate to the Americans now in Viet Nam, or the Peace Corps men in Colombia." Unless Americans had the resources to finance those great expenditures—"unless we are able to increase our surplus of balance of payments"—the United States would be faced with a hard choice.

One answer to this problem Kennedy called "negative": raising American tariffs, restricting capital, and pulling back from the world. The president would not allow adversaries this advantage. "This Administration was not elected to preside over the liquidation of American responsibility in these great years," Kennedy declared, paraphrasing Churchill on the decline of the British Empire. "There is a much better answer," he suggested: "to increase our exports, to meet our commitments and to maintain our defense of freedom. . . . In the life of every nation, as in the life of every man, there comes a time when a nation stands at the crossroads; when it can either shrink from the future and retire into its shell, or can move ahead—asserting its will and its faith in an uncertain sea. I believe that we stand at such a juncture in our foreign economic policy."[8]

Through his policies of cultural exchange and his personal travels, Kennedy sought to raise his country's image in the eyes of other peoples. Perhaps the most triumphal tour of an American statesman in this era was Kennedy's 1963 visit to Berlin, where the Soviets had recently built a wall cutting the city into East and West. On June 26 the West Berliners—three-fifths of the population—gave Kennedy what his aide Theodore Sorensen called the most overwhelming reception of his career. The great size of the crowd, their shouts and expressions of hope and gratitude, moved some in the president's party to tears—even before they surveyed the wall. On a platform outside Berlin City Hall, from which could be seen "only a sea of human faces chanting 'Kenne-dy,' 'Kenne-dy'," the young president declared:

> Two thousand years ago the proudest boast was *"civis Romanus sum."* Today, in the world of freedom, the proudest boast is *"Ich bin ein Berliner. . . ."*
>
> There are many people in the world who really don't understand, or say they don't, what is the great issue between the free world and the Communist world. Let them come to Berlin. There are some who say that communism is the wave of the future. Let them come to Berlin. And there are some who say in Europe and elsewhere we can work with the Communists. Let them come to Berlin. And there are even a few who say that it is true that communism is an evil system, but it permits us to make economic progress. *Lass' sie nach Berlin kommen.* Let them come to Berlin.
>
> Freedom has many difficulties and democracy is not perfect, but we have never had to put a wall up to keep our people in . . . .
>
> All free men, wherever they may live, are citizens of Berlin, and, therefore, as a free man, I take pride in the words *"Ich bin ein Berliner."*[9]

The crowd was clapping, waving, cheering, and roaring through the square. Kennedy himself had mixed feelings. He was, as Arthur Schlesinger described him, "first exhilarated, then disturbed," remarking on his return that if he had said, "March to the wall—tear it down," his listeners would have marched without rational reflection.[10]

The Kennedy administration's commitment of increased aid to developing regions was in the tradition of the Marshall Plan and Point Four. The Peace Corps, proposed by Kennedy to Congress in 1961, was an organization to help poor countries "meet their urgent needs for skilled manpower." To the mountains, villages, and factories of "dozens of struggling nations," Kennedy wanted American volunteers to go to work with the people who sought them. The emphasis was not only on the demonstration of their skills, the intention of Point Four, but on the personal contacts the volunteers could supply. The Peace Corps members were not career government technical advisers but by and large enthusiastic students as well as professional citizens who wanted to devote their energies and time and toil to others in the cause of development.[11]

The Peace Corps volunteers worked on projects, teaching in secondary schools or universities, running local health clinics, advising farmers about raising chickens or growing corn, or helping to plan the development of a new nation's cities. In Thailand and the Philippines, volunteers assisted in malaria eradication. In Bolivia, Malawi, Korea, and Malaysia, they initiated tuberculosis controls. In Guyana, the Ministry of Education assigned a volunteer to introduce a new math curriculum in primary schools, marking their first break with rote learning. To introduce the inductive method of teaching science in Nepal, volunteers produced science-teaching manuals. English instruction was a featured effort in Middle Eastern and East Asian countries. The program's stress on teaching was to give the peoples the know-how needed to continue on their own.[12]

Kennedy echoed the consensus calls to stand firm from Berlin to Vietnam, and to uphold the national commitments and interests squarely opposed to those of the Soviets. He took pride in the alliance system at its height, this monumental arrangement designed "to maintain the balance of power in the world." "We are trying," he stated in 1963, "to make it possible for those countries in Latin America, and in Africa, and in the Middle East, and in Southeast Asia—in fact, all around the globe, new countries, old countries, different religions, different colors—we are trying to enable them to maintain their freedom so that in this diverse world the balance of power will remain with us." His phrasing of tying together distant and scattered countries by alliance, recalling descriptions by the British of their possessions in every zone and clime, never alluded to alliances as an empire. But he did emphasize that the alliance system was centered in the United States, was an American creation, and would not exist without America; "it is the United States, and on many occasions the United States alone, which has prevented this globe from being dominated by our enemies." Without American assistance rendered to millions of people through alliances, "long ago this globe of ours would have seen the Communist advance sweep over much of what is now free."

The United States, Kennedy affirmed, was "the keystone in the arch of freedom." As he told an audience, "I think you should take pride and satisfaction in realizing that only the United States, and our power and strength and commitment, permits dozens of countries scattered all over the world to maintain their freedom. . . . It is the United States that carries this great burden, and . . . you should take pride in the fact that . . . beginning with the days of the close of World War II, it has been the United States— first in Western Europe and now in Latin America, and now in Africa, and now in the Middle East, and now in Asia, and now in SEATO, and now in CENTO, and now in NATO, and now in the OAS—that really does the heavy work that makes it possible for these institutions to survive." "Only the United States has obligations which stretch ten thousand miles across the Pacific, and three or four thousand miles across the Atlantic, and thousands of miles to the south. Only the United States—and we are only 6 percent of the world's population—bears this kind of burden."[13]

"Missile Gap": The Military Imperative

The majority of Americans had by now been shaken loose from the early international presuppositions of trade, aid, and cultural exchange that shunned the military in the years immediately following World War II. The growing Soviet capability to inflict damage with nuclear weapons on the United States intensified the determination to devise an ever more awesome military position. Through the 1950s strategists asserted nuclear supremacy to deter aggression by the Soviet Union or its allies. The policy of "massive retaliation" was predicated on a reserve of great atomic force. But for Kennedy that was not enough. He wanted to keep that retaliatory power intact and to expand it with a conventional capability to project around the globe.

The massive nuclear weapons stockpile increased by some thirty thousand warheads from 1955 to 1967, when the number reached its all-time high of thirty-two thousand. Strategic missiles were outfitted with these warheads and took the names of ancient gods holding the fate of the earth in their hands: Atlas, Titan, Thor, and Jupiter. Later came the American hero of the Revolution, the Minuteman.[14]

Fears of a "missile gap" grew out of a vague sense of lost superiority. More and more weapons had to be built in order to stay in front. The issue was not essentially deterrence of the use of these weapons by an enemy, but the maintenance of supremacy. There was little reason to fear the Russians when the United States had a monopoly of weapons, and not much reason to fear them after they had built the bomb, because they lacked the means to deliver it.[15]

The Soviet launching of Sputnik in 1957, which had aroused anxiety that the United States was deficient in diverse areas of life—technology, education, engineering, industry—led to alarm that the Soviets were ahead in missiles and that the United States had become vulnerable to Soviet attack. Nothing better represented this fear of vulnerability than the so-called Gaither Report, which warned that the Soviet Union had "probably surpassed us" in intercontinental missiles, posing a threat to the Strategic Air Command. America was still strong enough between 1959 and 1960, when Soviet bombers were few and its missiles not yet deployed, to maintain strategic superiority with the Strategic Air Command on "effective 'alert' status." That capability could be used for political advantage: *This could be the best time to negotiate from strength, since the U.S. military position vis-a-vis Russia might never be as strong again.* But the report called for quick action: "If we fail to act at once, the risk . . . will be unacceptable."[16]

In the media the missile issue became overblown, exemplifying a national mood—the mood of the assertions to regain a national purpose—that the nation was threatened, yet strong, that it had the resources and could have its influence felt if only it had the will to maintain its military forces. Chalmers Roberts gave the readers of the *Washington Post* his interpretation of the still top-secret Gaither Report as portraying "a United States in the gravest danger in its history." It pictured the nation moving, frightfully, "to the status of a second-class power." It showed "an America exposed to an almost immediate threat from the missile-bristling Soviet Union." The effects of this realization would be dire. Only through "an all-out effort" could the United States "hope to close the current missile gap and to counter the world-wide Communist offensive in many fields and in many lands."[17]

This perception of the necessity for extraordinary military efforts was present, if in the case of missiles the evidence was not. Journals picked up the issue and presented tables and charts and pictures to demonstrate the Soviet lead. Thomas R. Phillips, a retired brigadier general, asked in the *Reporter* magazine, "Is the time coming soon when the Soviet Union could launch an attack without fearing retaliation?" *Time* posed the question, "Will the missile gap mean a power gap?" The figures varied from article to article—ranging from a gap of a few hundred to several thousand missiles—but they all indicated the steady gains of the Soviets over the Americans. Stewart Alsop in the *Saturday Evening Post* was foreboding in his article, "Our Gamble with Destiny." He wondered, "Do we have the power and the courage to withstand the Kremlin's threats?"[18]

The media were alarmed because the strategic analysts were. In January 1959 Albert Wohlstetter published an article in *Foreign Affairs* entitled "The Delicate Balance of Terror." The balance of nuclear weapons, he argued, was "in fact precarious." He derided America's "deep pre-sputnik sleep." The Russians, he feared, were inclined to accept nuclear war in a crisis. Henry Kissinger also felt that a "missile gap" was perilous. He was adamant that there was no escape: "The missile gap in the period 1961–1965 is now unavoidable." His concern was with the danger of imminent "Soviet nuclear blackmail—even to the extent of threatening direct attacks on the United States."[19]

As it turned out, there was no missile gap. And soon the experts and the media caught on. In 1960, *U.S. News & World Report* imparted, "It's Russia's Turn to Worry about the 'Missile Gap'" with the coming deployment of the Polaris missile on submarines. In 1961 Lt. Gen. Bernard Schriever announced that "we are not behind the Soviet Union in the development of missiles—and I'm talking now about ballistic missiles of all types." *Newsweek* questioned, "Was There Ever a 'Missile Gap'?—Or Just an 'Intelligence Gap'?"[20]

Evidence for a missile gap was lacking in the data available from the U-2 spy plane flights over the Soviet Union. In his memoirs, Eisenhower claimed that these flights "provided proof" that the "missile gap" and the earlier "bomber gap" were nothing more than "imaginative creations of irresponsibility." If the president himself did not feel the need for crash programs, he nevertheless succumbed to the need for reinforced strategic forces: he proposed new resources for them in his next year's budget message.[21]

Whether the United States held fewer missiles than the Soviet Union was moot so long as each nation had the capability of destroying the other, and as long as each side knew it. The argument was over a growing and deep-seated misconception about power. The United States did not have an intrinsic need for more missiles than the Soviet Union if its purpose was to deter attack. The concern about the missile gap was about the paradox of nuclear weapons. America was stronger than ever before—it had more power to destroy than ever before—but it was not strong enough. It could easily obliterate the enemy, but it was not strong enough. Tremendous military power did not necessarily increase the influence of policies, so it was not strong enough.

The fallacy in the thinking that favored this build-up of nuclear weapons entered into areas of strategy. Engaging in all-out nuclear war had already become unthinkable. So, in the absence of any effective recourse to total war, a strategy of limited war was conspicuously advocated. "Limited war is thus not an alternative to massive retaliation, but its complement," Kissinger wrote in his 1957 best-seller *Nuclear Weapons and Foreign Policy*. Relying on tactical nuclear weapons to counter growing Soviet strength, Kissinger recommended: "Limited nuclear war represents our most effective strategy against nuclear powers or against a major power which is capable of substituting manpower for technology."[22]

But limited war did not necessarily lead to nuclear destruction. The use of nuclear weapons might be avoided if all-out war could be avoided. In the same year that Kissinger's book appeared, Robert Osgood's *Limited War* raised the question of how the United States could employ military power as a practical instrument of foreign policy when the destructive potentialities of war exceed any rational purpose. If Americans knew that total nuclear war would be a catastrophe but assumed that the communists were out to win military objectives, then instead of complete retaliation, Osgood reasoned, the nation needed a strategy of fighting "kept within narrow geographical bounds, and in which discrimination in the use of weapons and selection of targets would be practicable."[23]

To depreciate the possibility of a nuclear war while maintaining a strong military presence, the United States, even during the rapid accumulations in the nuclear stockpile, prepared to build up conventional forces. The government gave up trying to restrain the budget and prepared to meet the rising costs of an enlarged military. Curtis LeMay put forth the point of view: "any arms race with the Soviet Union would act to our benefit. I believe that we can out-invent, out-research, out-develop, out-engineer and out-produce the U.S.S.R. in any area from sling shots to space weapons, and in so doing become more and more prosperous while the Soviets become progressively poorer." A poll showed that after the Kennedy administration had significantly expanded American defense capability, 83 percent supported a military program at the current level of strength, if not an increase. The expansion of conventional forces continued under President Johnson.[24]

The Military-Industrial Complex: Social Costs

The expansion of nuclear and conventional forces aroused consensus concern, though only minor at first, about the damage the military inflicted on the economy and society. Eisenhower voiced this concern in his farewell address televised to the nation. On January 17, 1961, the old soldier came to question the value of a military that consumed so much of the national resources, toil, and industry:

> Until the latest of our world conflicts, the United States had no armaments industry. American makers of plowshares could, with time and as required, make swords as well. But now we can no longer risk emergency improvisation of national defense; we have been compelled to create a permanent armaments industry of vast proportions. Added to this, three and a half million men and women are directly engaged in the defense establishment. We annually spend on military security more than the net income of all United States corporations.
>
> This conjunction of an immense military establishment and a large arms industry is new in the American experience. The total influence—economic, political, even spiritual—is felt in every city, every State house, every office of the Federal government. We recognize the imperative need for this development. Yet we must not fail to comprehend its grave implications. Our toil, resources and livelihood are all involved; so is the very structure of our society.
>
> In the councils of government, we must guard against the acquisition of unwarranted influence, whether sought or unsought, by the military-industrial complex. The potential for the disastrous rise of misplaced power exists and will persist.
>
> We must never let the weight of this combination endanger our liberties or democratic processes. We should take nothing for granted.

Eisenhower was alluding not just to an insidious technological or military elite that was taking over public policy. He was talking about the nature of power itself. To his way of thinking, Americans were understandably "proud" of their national "preeminence," yet they realized that American leadership and prestige depended "not merely upon our unmatched material progress, riches and military strength, but on how we use our power in the interests of world peace and human betterment." The latter was a new conception for a president—that the exertion of influence had repercussions on the national power position. The president had come to consider the overexpansion of the military as a misuse of power and influence.[25]

Eisenhower did not want America to be known for its military might, more than the achievements of its society. The day after his farewell speech, he explained to reporters that he abhorred the image of a militaristic America. "When you see almost every one of your magazines, no matter what they are advertising, has a picture of the Titan missile or the Atlas or solid fuel or other things, there is becoming a great influence, almost an insidious penetration of our own minds that the only thing this country is engaged in is weaponry and missiles. And, I'll tell you we just can't afford to do that. The reason we have them is to protect the great values in which we believe, and they are far deeper even than our own lives and our own property, as I see it."[26]

The presidential warning against a huge military came as a surprise to many in the government who had expected a more sentimental leave taking from the retiring leader. But at his final press conference, he stressed that the "basic problem" facing the country was "what to do to keep ourselves strong and firm and yet conciliatory"—the question of power. Eisenhower had expressed these sentiments in private with uncommon passion at a time when many thought any costs could be met. In a conference with Secretary of Defense Charles Wilson and military commanders, the president stated that "true security requires a sound economy" and that "it is necessary to make a realistic appraisal of what the country will support, over an extended period of time, without loss of morale, confidence, and dynamic industrial effort upon which a sound and expanding economy depends." Later, the president discussed "the fundamental reasons why needs of our economy must always be considered. It is the nature of our Government that everyone, except for a thin layer at the top is working, knowingly or unknowingly, to damage our economy—the reason being that they see the need for more and more resources for their own Service or agency, and the valuable results that can be achieved through added effort in their own particular element. Unless there is someone who brings all of these together, the net effect is to create burdens which could sap the strength of our economic system. Similarly, there are great pressures on the military program from every particular element, and the catalytic factor provided by the Press and Congress might make it explode. In working for permanent security, we must give due consideration to the right 'take' from the economy—one which will permit the economy to remain viable and strong." In one secret conference he questioned military procurement across the board, stressing to his advisers that "our problem is keeping the economy sound for another ten years" and that "we have constantly got to ask ourselves whether we are cutting out everything that can be cut out."[27]

Eisenhower's warnings were hardly heeded by the Kennedy administration. The crises continued, and so did the buildup of conventional and nuclear forces, and the trend toward reliance on the military in crises. The confrontation that posed the greatest danger took place during the Kennedy administration, and it penetrated far within the frontiers of American influence. Cuba, the West Indian island south of Key West, invaded by American forces in the Spanish-American War, had attracted American travelers by its tropical waters and businessmen who came to own hotels, public utilities, ranches, sugar mills, and plantations. The navy maintained a base at Guantánamo Bay. But when Fidel Castro took power in 1959, he nationalized American-owned businesses, worth more than one billion dollars, and he allied his regime with the Soviet Union. After CIA-trained Cuban exiles attempted an invasion of their homeland and failed, the Soviets began to install missiles on Cuba capable of hitting deep inside the United States. An American U-2 aircraft flying over the island on October 14, 1962, caught the Soviet installations in pictures.

On October 22, President Kennedy announced: "It shall be the policy of this Nation to regard any nuclear missile launched from Cuba against any nation in the Western Hemisphere as an attack by the Soviet Union on the United States, requiring a full retaliatory response upon the Soviet Union." His pledge, he said, was consistent with "our commitments around the world." According to the president's brother Robert, who participated in the private crisis deliberations, "The possibility of the destruction of mankind was always" in the president's mind, the possibility of "World War Three," a war "fought with atomic weapons." Secretary of Defense Robert McNamara told Congress later, "we faced that night the possibility of launching nuclear weapons." Before the end of the month, the crisis culminated with the use of conventional forces— the deployment of U.S. naval forces to enforce a blockade of Cuba. Negotiations resolved the crisis when the Soviets agreed to withdraw the missiles from Cuba and the Americans in turn agreed to remove their old nuclear-armed missiles from Turkey.[28]

The Consensus Falters

Through the crises, and well into the 1960s, the consensus remained intact, and American leaders were still confident in their ability to lead, shape, and hold it together. Theodore Sorensen considered consensus to be frequently "hampered by myths and misinformation, by stereotypes and shibboleths, and by an innate resistance to innovation." But there was consensus. President Kennedy's televised explanations of his decisions—on the need for a military build-up to hold Berlin and the order to use American fleets to block ships heading to Cuba—achieved on each occasion a continuing "national consensus that discouraged any adversary's hopes for disunity." Yet Kennedy saw that the consensus could not be taken for granted. Popular opinion was potentially volatile. Kennedy's plea for fallout shelters in his 1961 discussion of Berlin ended the prevailing national apathy on civil defense, but it also "unleashed an emotional response which grew to near-hysterical proportions (before it receded once again to near-apathy)." His warnings on the presence of Soviet missiles in Cuba had to be "sufficiently somber to enlist support around the world without creating panic here at home."[29]

In the last speech of Kennedy's life, at 9:00 on the morning of November 22, 1963, he described U.S. military power to the Chamber of Commerce in Fort Worth. In the three years of his administration, he had increased the nation's defense budget by "over 20 percent; increased the program of acquisition for Polaris submarines from 24 to 41; increased our Minuteman missile purchase program by more than 75 percent; doubled the number of strategic bombers and missiles on alert; doubled the number of nuclear weapons available in the strategic alert forces; increased the tactical nuclear forces deployed in Western Europe by over 60 percent; added five combat ready divisions to the Army of the United States, and five tactical fighter wings to the Air Force of the United States; increased our strategic air-lift capability by 75 percent; and increased our special counter-insurgency forces which are engaged now in South Viet-Nam by 600 percent." These figures he presented as the tangible signs of a stronger America.

He was proud of what America under his direction had wrought. "Without the United States, South Viet-Nam would collapse overnight. Without the United States, the SEATO alliance would collapse overnight. . . . Without the United States there would be no NATO. And gradually Europe would drift into neutralism and indifference. Without the efforts of the United States in the Alliance for Progress, the Communist advance onto the mainland of South America would long ago have taken place. . . . We are still the keystone in the arch of freedom."[30]

After this breakfast talk, the president flew to Dallas, where at approximately 12:30 in the afternoon he was assassinated. In the remarks he had prepared to deliver later that day, he hearkened back to the promise he had made in Forth Worth as a candidate in 1960: to build "a national defense which was second to none." In the speech he never gave, he was adamant: "That pledge has been fulfilled."[31]

The period that had begun with great hope—for reexamination and for a new beginning with new goals, purpose, and ideals—ended in tragedy, the assassination of the young president. Kennedy was remembered for his sharp wit, energetic style, confidence, and sense of humor. He "quickened the heart and mind of the nation, inspired the young, met great crises . . . and left behind so glowing and imperishable a memory," noted Arthur Schlesinger, Jr., Kennedy's aide and biographer. James Reston observed, "He was, even to his political enemies, a wonderfully attractive human being . . . a rationalist and an intellectual." Theodore H. White told of a visit to the president's widow, Jacqueline, at the family home in Hyannis Port, Massachusetts. She mentioned the song from the musical *Camelot* that Jack liked to play before they went to sleep, telling of the "one brief shining moment" that should never "be forgot." "There'll be great Presidents again . . . ," she said, "but there'll never be another Camelot."[32]

The most extensive attempt to toughen American policy came from the radical right, whose growing strength prompted the Republicans to nominate Barry Goldwater as their presidential candidate in 1964. In 1960 Kennedy had promised to do more; Goldwater did not believe he had done nearly enough to correct the problems he had raised. Throughout the campaign, Goldwater's speeches sounded the themes of foreign failures and the decline of American prestige abroad. He despised crises and stalemates. "Until 1950," Goldwater wrote, "America had never lost a shooting war," but within ten years it had suffered repeated defeats at the hands of the communists. Goldwater's *Why Not Victory?* expressed the conservative view that mastery was possible in the cold war. By reasserting their superior strength and willpower, Goldwater argued, Americans could be victorious in any confrontation with the communist bloc, which would eventually weaken under the pressure of repeated defeats. "Our objective must be the destruction of the enemy as an ideological force possessing the means of power," he said. "Victory is the key to the whole problem; the only alternative is—obviously—defeat."[33]

Goldwater's hard-line views on foreign affairs extended the bounds of the consensus to the farthest limit in his adventurous, reckless policy proposals. Impatient with negotiation and compromise, he urged that the United States break off diplomatic relations with the Soviet Union, consider withdrawal from the United Nations, and reject any moves for arms control. By repudiating any possibility for military victory in a general war with nuclear weapons, he stayed within the prevailing view, but he did not rule out force. The fear of nuclear war, he thought, had frightened the "free world," so that it was "gradually accepting the notion that anything is better than fighting." What appeared to be a casual attitude toward war seemed to separate Goldwater from moderates, who were not so outspoken but nevertheless generally stood ready to use force if vital interests were threatened.[34]

That liberals and conservatives of such different outlooks could appeal so deeply to the public's concerns about international affairs disclosed the boundaries, not the absence, of domestic consensus. A strengthened, vigorous foreign policy could easily be identified with Eisenhower, Stevenson, Kennedy, Nixon, and Goldwater, as well as with Walter Lippmann, David Sarnoff, and Billy Graham. They did not, of course, agree on the scope of policies and the means of carrying them out. Liberals tended to advocate innovative diplomacy, backed by awesome force in reserve, while conservatives held onto hopes for absolute victory, by force if necessary. But liberals, moderates, and conservatives generally called for the United States to remain in a position of strength and to maintain an active program of international works.

In pressing for *more,* they concocted a strange mixture of what Daniel Boorstin called "braggadocio and petulance. Braggadocio—empty boasting of American power, American virtue, American know-how—has dominated our foreign relations now for some decades. It is the spirit of making the world safe for democracy, of unconditional surrender, of crusading for the American way of life—in a word, of belief in American omnicompetence." The petulance came from shame of success—men in gray flannel suits, organization men, labor racketeers, anti-intellectuals, TV watchers, comic-book readers, beatnik youth. But this irritability with success, like the success itself, supported the belief that there was nothing that Americans could not do if they only put more money into it and got it organized. American braggadocio and petulance both assumed "that a great nation like us can do whatever it wishes. They share the illusion of omnicompetence which has haunted every world power. Because we have decent political institutions, a mobile and egalitarian society, a high standard of living, and a literate populace, they say we can also be the world's greatest philosophers, the world's most amusing conversationalists, and the world's best artists. In this national arrogance perhaps our only competitors today are the Soviets, whose illusions of omnicompetence are more dogmatic than ours."[35]

Thus the consensus leaders who had been the successful architects of American internationalism after World War II attempted a reevaluation of their mission. But they lacked the initiative to correct policies on a scale commensurate with the challenge of shifting international conditions. While the limits of power were being reached, the consensus attempted to boost national power and expand the consensus and harden the country's positions. American foreign policy stressed military strength, and though the United States was gaining in that field, Americans were more insecure than before.

In the absence of victory, which had been the American way in foreign affairs and had been achieved overwhelmingly in World War II, the consensus overcompensated in a vain effort to achieve victory. It was generally agreed that the United States had to exert greater effort and resources on foreign policies. Millions of dollars more had to be appropriated and effort expended to ensure that the United States kept up with and moved ahead of the Soviet Union or any other country in the race of scientific knowledge, economic production, and arms.

An initial modesty of action had led to a drive for grandiose actions. The eminently successful policies of the past continued to influence those of the present in a worldwide expansion of American power. Consensus policy lacked a recognition of the overextension of power when intervention spread to become global, marked by the great watershed of Korea and followed by the crises of the 1950s and 1960s.

It was not just the where but also the how of power that had become overextended and misapplied. The efficiency and ease with which the world role had taken shape yielded to crisis. The world role would no longer be perpetuated mainly by the intercourse of trade and culture, but had to be enforced by armament. The end result: the nagging fears that the world role was in crisis led to the conclusion that the nation needed more weaponry of all sorts, conventional and nuclear. There had to be more of everything, to be sure: more education, more technological research, more production, more trade, more aid, more cultural exchange, more military—more across the board, without considering the relative merits of each demand. There was no clear-sighted analysis of the value and detriment of each case.

Finally, American policy as developed by the consensus fell into stagnation, if not complacency, in the 1950s, while national endeavors encountered setbacks. It lacked the creativity and generosity of purpose of the immediate postwar period. Toward the end of the decade, the consensus advocated essentially a reaffirmation or extension of earlier ways. The consensus, which had distinguished itself in dealing with the previous challenges to American internationalism, could not adapt to the conditions that confronted internationalism as it was developing. Policy had become committed to maintaining the status quo and had failed to take into account revolutionary change in large parts of the world. No basic change in the domestic and foreign policies that had been formulated in the 1940s took place. No significant innovations, no fundamentally different ideas, no rethinking of old ideas, not to mention redefinition of the whole national purpose, occurred. Consensus ideas, to a considerable extent, had become irrelevant to the position of America in the world.

15

The

Dissenters

Forming in the late 1950s and expanding in the 1960s, a host of groups within the polity confronted the majority consensus opinions. Civil rights advocates sought equal rights for minorities, university students attacked the consensus complacency, youths rejected conventional morality, and leftist intellectuals denounced the underlying assumptions of consensus economics, sociology, and historical ideology. The result was a social schism and an intellectual discord that were symptomatic of national crisis. Where did this dissent come from, after a period of placid consensus and general harmony and after concerted thinking toward the formation, expansion, and maintenance of a world role? What was the radical criticism that branded orthodox ideas as the source of the nation's foreign crises? And how did the old consensus respond to this criticism?[1]

The New Left

There had been radicals and reformers before: some in the consensus had named Henry Wallace and his followers "radicals," though they had served to expand the consensus that accepted internationalism rather than break it; and before them, the Progressives had sought reform in the early part of the century. One historian of the New Left, Staughton Lynd, traced modern American radicalism back to the Founding Fathers, who, though they had tolerated slavery and based political rights on private property, had, after all, mounted a revolution that articulated demands in the radical language of inalienable rights. But this historical continuity, he admitted, had an ahistorical intention: use of the past to give direction to the recent radicalism. None of this radical version of "Whig" history explained why radicalism had subsided in the postwar years as the consensus for an American world role arose.[2]

C. Wright Mills coined the term "New Left" to connote the early movement in the United States. In 1960 Mills wrote a letter to the British *New Left Review*, complaining of the dearth of fervent progressive ideas. He looked for the agent of change in the postwar world in "the young intelligentsia," not in the working class, which he thought was satiated with its record earnings and would not alter the way things were. From Mills's manifesto, the young leftists took a name and, perhaps, a sense that they were doing the unprecedented and unique. The new radicalism, as the historian Howard Zinn argued, came from "nowhere in the world but cotton fields, prison cells, and the minds of young people reflecting on what they see and feel."[3]

The new movement, then, followed in the footsteps of the old radical Progressivism and Marxist communism, exemplified by the writers Upton Sinclair, Jack London, and John Reed, and by those who as youths had flirted with socialism and later joined the consensus—John Dos Passos, Reinhold Niebuhr, and Walter Lippmann. But the new discontents were different. Whereas the Old Left had resisted America's rising industrialism and the economic monopolies that came with it, the New Left opposed a persistent and global American presence. The Old Left had followed Marx's theory that material relations of life and class struggle were at the center of human history and had looked with favor on the planned economy of the Soviet Union during the Depression of the 1930s. The New Left, on the other hand, was neither pro-Soviet nor communist, yet it did not accept the American world role and the military establishment that defended it. The Old Left had criticized munitions manufacturers in World War I, but a weak military did not warrant its full attention. The New Left attempted to reapply the senescent economic interpretation of events to attacks on the excess of world power.

The New Left started out less rigid and intolerant than the Old Left had been. For the most part, it was undogmatic. Marx was rewritten. It would not do to conceive of the United States as being in the throes of class struggle. The New Left had become accustomed to prosperity, rising real wages, and middle-class status. New Leftists accepted that the abundance that increased with production offered the means to overcome poverty. The focus of the new thought was not on the means of production but rather on the uses of that production and on consumption. It refused to accept the expansion of trade and investment and the exercise of power through alliances, bases, and nuclear weapons.

The new radicals did not join in the consensus celebration, as many of their forebears had done. The old never approached the magnitude and zeal of the new. The influence of the Old Left and latter-day Progressives had been eclipsed in the 1940s by the emerging consensus in World War II. The outward postwar successes, along with the widespread fear of associating with revolutionary communists, caused the number of radical intellectuals to dwindle. The young radicals had been born after Henry Wallace had re-formed the Progressive party in the late 1940s to challenge Harry Truman for the presidency, or they were too young to remember that campaign. Some remembered Adlai Stevenson and idolized him for his wit and intellect in the 1952 and 1956 presidential campaigns. But they carried their protest far beyond any bounds that had constrained Wallace and Stevenson.

The New Left had another vision. As the socialist leader Michael Harrington wrote:

> There is a familiar America. It is celebrated in speeches and advertised on
> television and in the magazines. It has the highest mass standard of living the
> world has ever known.
>
>   In the 1950's this America worried about itself, yet even its anxieties were
> products of abundance. The . . . familiar America began to call itself "the afflu-
> ent society." There was introspection about Madison Avenue and tail fins; there
> was discussion of the emotional suffering taking place in the suburbs. In all
> this, there was an implicit assumption that the basic grinding economic prob-
> lems had been solved in the United States. In this theory the nation's problems
> were no longer a matter of basic human needs, of food, shelter, and clothing.
> Now they were seen as qualitative, a question of learning to live decently amid
> luxury.
>
>   While this discussion was carried on, there existed another America. In it
> dwelt somewhere between 40,000,000 and 50,000,000 citizens of this land.
> They were poor. They still are.

Harrington did not challenge the existence of power and wealth. What he focused on
were "the strangest poor in the history of mankind," existing within "the most powerful
and rich society the world has ever known." No one before had effectively called for
action commensurate with the long-ignored problem of poverty. Harrington's purpose,
and, in a larger sense, that of the New Left, was to create radical change.[4]

The intellectuals who inspired the radical vision attacked domestic and foreign
self-satisfaction. The economist Ben Seligman satirized the old-fashioned consensus
worship of big business, expressed as a litany: "the American Way of Life yields a high
standard of living; there are 135 million radios; we can always outproduce the Russians; economic success is founded in efficiency; business is conducted in a spirit of
service; and, above all, these attainments come about because of the System." Seligman
found these boasts wanting; so did Robert Theobald, an economist who argued that the
United States had paid heavy social costs for its affluence. Although 1960 was memora-
ble for the beginning of a debate on "The National Purpose," Theobald was dissatisfied
with the consensus contentions. The discussion had failed to generate even a clear
statement of the issues. While he admitted the "general agreement on the need to
reconsider our way of life, . . . few radically new policies were suggested." He called
for entirely new constructs. Priority had to be given not to generating new wealth and
power, the need for which Theobald recognized as "mythology," but to distributing to
everyone sufficient food, clothing, and shelter, and to providing a reasonable standard
of living to the unemployed as well as to students, writers, artists, visionaries, and
dissenters.[5]

The social critic Paul Goodman addressed the increasing numbers of students at
colleges and universities who were grappling with the problems of alienation, absurdity, and meaninglessness in their lives and institutions. Degrading education for the

"positive damage" that schools did to the young, Goodman placed the failure squarely on the attitudes of a wealthy and powerful modern society. "Within the United States, we have reached a point of productivity when it becomes absurd to use the rate of growth and the Gross National Product as measures of economic health," he declared. Unqualified growth did "more harm than good." Goodman threw out the school curricula manipulated by "social goals and National Goals." He rejected the consensus acceptance of atomic bombs and the cold war as "normal politics." He had little use for the push toward the development of ever more sophisticated technology since the Korean War and "hysterically since Sputnik." Science and technology education, he argued, had little value for the population at large, and as he saw it technology had been misapplied in America's imperial expansion abroad in the late 1960s.[6]

The radical philosopher Herbert Marcuse attacked the "advanced industrial society" that had become "richer, bigger, and better" but was "irrational." Born in Berlin and educated in Germany, he came to the United States to lecture and write on his philosophy of rebellion. Technological productivity, he believed, was "destructive of the free development of human needs and faculties, its peace maintained by the constant threat of war, its growth dependent on the repression of the real possibilities for pacifying the struggle for existence—individual, national, and international." Social domination over the individual was much greater than ever before. Society had forced stifling consensus on individuals: "the general acceptance of the National Purpose, bipartisan policy, the decline of pluralism, the collusion of Business and Labor within the strong State" were all repressing social change. The "affluent society" was accompanied by "moronization, the perpetuation of toil, and the promotion of frustration." Marcuse tore apart the "irrationality of the whole"—the "waste and restriction of productivity; the need for aggressive expansion; the constant threat of war; intensified exploitation; dehumanization." He left the reader with images of American society in which contrived attractiveness hid the terror: "highly classified nuclear plants and laboratories become 'Industrial Parks' in pleasing surroundings; Civil Defense Headquarters display a 'deluxe fallout-shelter' with wall-to-wall carpeting ('soft'), lounge chairs, television, and Scrabble, 'designed as a combination family room during peacetime (sic!) and family fallout shelter should war break out.'" Marcuse argued that abolishing poverty and misery mattered more than guns, butter, and television.[7]

The shift of American power from economic and social to military determinants was central to the chronicles of C. Wright Mills. Mills was a father of dissent who began within the consensus and later moved outside. In the late 1950s, he rejected the nearly uncritical acceptance of America's military among the consensus thinkers. In *White Collar*, he had already in 1951 criticized the conformist mores of the new class of affluent workers, whereas consensus thinkers had lauded them. Yet Mills respected America's new success. His work is the door through which we may pass from solid consensus to troubled dissent.

Mills's concern with the growth of military power surfaced in his early book on labor unions. In *The New Men of Power*, he predicted in 1948 that if the "sophisticated conservatives" had their way, "the next New Deal will be a war economy rather than a welfare economy. . . . The establishment of a permanent war economy is a long-time trend." He soon felt vindicated. By the time he wrote *The Power Elite* in 1956, Mills believed that the war economy had become a fact. He placed the military establishment at the center of a corrupt hierarchy together with the political machinery and big corporations, a critique given credence by President Eisenhower's warning of an inordinate military-industrial complex.[8]

But it was in his 1958 book, *The Causes of World War Three,* that Mills gave vent to his preoccupation with the extent of the military in American life. Whereas *The Power Elite* was a book of sociological description and scholarship, *The Causes of World War Three* was the book of passion and prescription: he agonized that the United States was heading toward war. The "thrust toward World War III" was "a defining characteristic of our epoch." War was "no longer an interruption of peace; in our time, peace itself has become an uneasy interlude between wars; peace has become a perilous balance of mutual terror and mutual fright." It had not always been so, even as late as World War II.[9]

War's outbreak, he feared, was imminent: "Tomorrow morning . . . the equipment of a U.S. radar man somewhere in Canada mechanically fails, or under extreme pressure of time he mistakes a dead satellite or a stray meteor for an incoming ballistic missile. He tracks it toward the industrial heart of the U.S.A. In a few minutes his alarm is out, and in a few more—about fifteen minutes in all, we are told—the planes of the Strategic Air Command, from several dozen bases tucked in as close as they can get to the U.S.S.R., zero in on Soviet industries and cities. . . . SAC drops its stuff. Or the missile is launched. The Americans have massively retaliated. The Russians retaliate massively. A few hours later the world is a radioactive shambles, a chaos of disaster." Would anyone, he questioned, be around even to wonder, "what were the causes of World War III?"

Mills's book answered his own question: The causes of this war were inherent in the internal institutions of the United States. "The ethos of war is now pervasive." Preparation for war shaped scientific endeavor, swelled the national budget, limited intellectual effort, dominated spiritual life, and replaced traditional diplomacy. The drive toward war was official. The small ruling circle of the power elite geared the whole society for war. Though the ruling circles of executives, politicians, and lawyers had once been distrustful of the warlords of Washington, the military had become "the largest and most expensive feature of government." Virtually "all political and economic actions" were now "judged in terms of military definitions of reality."[10]

Mills vigorously criticized the consensus that blandly accepted this military view. Consensual foreign policy, he believed, had failed. "Acheson and Dulles are in continuity; bipartisan foreign policy has become bipartisan default of policy." Intellectuals, many perhaps fearful of being thought "Unpatriotic," had fallen in with the elite leaders and became nationalist propagandists. Their "realism" Mills called "crackpot realism." But he heard no debate of alternatives.

The military was what America had become known for abroad. The causes of

World War III, Mills contended, were not inherent in abstract international relations. The causes were seated "mainly in the U.S.A." American foreign policy had become part of the condition in which the military was tied to American economic interests. Instead of imaginative political and economic programs, it relied on what Mills called a "doctrine of violence." "The doctrine of Massive Retaliation has become massive nonsense."[11]

Mills tried to understand. In considerable part, he believed, the power elite had been molded by the events that transpired during and after World War II as problems centered on economic depression shifted to international problems centered on war. The elite was unified because of a similar "psychology" of its members in which security had merged with economics and institutions formed to give vent to these beliefs. An example Mills cited was the Quemoy crisis, in which Congress abdicated its part in the decisions that bordered on war. The same was true of the 1958 turmoil in Lebanon and of the recurring Far Eastern troubles. In this book, Mills was angry: "the strategic outlook is the idiot's outlook."

Toward the end of *The Causes of World War Three*, Mills lost some of the clarity in his argument concerning the relationship between the military and capitalist business. Was the problem, as he indicated at the outset, in the military itself, in its mindset and its growing force, or in the traditional elite, especially businessmen? His early studies of the Old Left and of Marx himself were reasserted in his ideas about ways to restrain the military through changes in the United States economy. He proposed a centralized Soviet-style economy to control American science—"the socialization of the scientific and technical apparatus of society"—without questioning why the Soviet Union was a massively armed power with such an economy. Mills had no final answers.[12]

But as Mills saw it, revolt was essential. The stakes were war or peace. To get change started, Mills attacked consensus intellectuals, and this was new. This was blatant dissension by one of the circle of intellectuals who had once been sympathetic, if not supportive. He turned on the political indifference of Galbraith's "affluent society" and criticized religionists like Niebuhr who merely followed the mainstream view of a "realistic" world role.

Mills could foresee no effective dissent in the society, aware though he was of his transitional situation in this, his last book. "The epoch in which we stand is pivotal." "We are at the very end of the military road," he wrote. "It leads nowhere but to death." Mills died suddenly of a heart attack in 1962, at the age of forty-five. War had become absurd, but the military build-up was continuing, and the protest was only beginning.[13]

All of this counterpoint was alien and hostile to the consensus, which, as we have seen, expected and wanted *more,* more of the same—more technology, more production, more military, and more trade, aid, cultural exchange, and alliances. The radicals, on the other hand, opposed more of a world role and wanted *less*: they opposed the intervention in the Korean War, atomic tests, and increasing military exploitation in place of meeting social needs. What was wrong with America, they believed, was traceable to consensus international politics and to the failure to break out of old patterns. To the New Left way of thinking, theories of power based on the global dominance of corporate capitalism and a nuclear arms race threatened to bring on World War III.

New Left Historical Interpretation

The most sustained, analytical attack on consensus foreign relations came from a group of diplomatic historians who followed William Appleman Williams, a young assistant professor of history at the University of Wisconsin. In the late fall of 1957, Williams wrote a critique of American world affairs in the *Nation*. Williams looked back sixteen years to the eve of American involvement in World War II. He feared that, supported by a consensus "chorus of enthusiastic liberal and conservative intellectuals" and shared by big corporate executives, labor leaders, and politicians of every ideological bent, Henry Luce's American Century idea had indeed come to characterize America's power role in world affairs. By 1957, however, Williams observed "considerably less rhetoric in the style of doing things 'as we see fit,'" chiding Luce by paraphrasing the words of his original editorial. During the 1950s, it was apparent, something had gone awry. The reason was plain: a crisis of confidence. In 1957 the State Department had forbidden forty-seven American students to visit Communist China by decreeing that the trip would be "subversive of United States foreign policy." Williams believed that Americans were actually subverting themselves and their own democratic traditions. The "American Century," he proclaimed, was in "crisis."[14]

From this point the New Left attempted a total reevaluation of the American world role. In 1959 some graduate students influenced by Williams began work on the journal *Studies on the Left*, which presented historical studies and accounts of current economic and social problems. The historians publishing in *Studies on the Left*, including Williams's former Wisconsin student Lloyd C. Gardner, interpreted past economic conflict that had racked American history in the tradition of Marx and Progressives like Charles Beard. And the New Left was forced to admit that a cold war consensus existed over fundamentals that had enabled the country to succeed until then. But the New Left also opened up new areas for discussion.[15]

The Left doubted no less than the consensus, at least at first, the gigantic dimensions of American power or the capacity of the United States to assume the leadership of the Western nations. To the New Left a slackness in American production or weapons programs had not produced the crisis beginning in the late 1950s and continuing into the 1960s. Rather, the crisis had developed and matured during a period when the United States had enjoyed a significant economic and military advantage over the Soviet Union, which had been devastated by World War II. The United States was a free-world colossus, uninjured at home, possessing an economy enriched by its wartime exports, and armed with a poised military. The crucial factor, Williams explained, was the way Americans interpreted their relative power advantage as an *"absolute* superiority," and the manner in which they sought to use their "supposed supremacy." Assuming that it enjoyed absolute strength, the United States took an aggressive stance toward the Soviet Union, which alone among nations threatened the American position. The United States refused to negotiate with, cooperate with, or aid the Soviet Union in the years when it did hold a relative advantage. The New Left took direct aim at the frontiers of influence, and at the policy of containment, as stated by Kennan and interpreted by his followers. *"The assumption that the United States has the power to force the Soviet Union to capitulate to American terms is the fundamental weakness in America's conception of itself and the world,"* emphasized Williams. Thus crash programs to build increased inventories of weapons, as newly advocated by the consensus, would serve only to compound the basic weakness. The problem, then, was not so much the nature of power as the use of power.[16]

Williams led the New Left in professing that the nation had to revise its central assumptions fundamentally. Any effort to explain the "crisis in The American Century" by either political party within the consensus would be doomed to failure. Williams advocated an entirely new consensus formed along New Leftist lines. The result would be a break with the imperial American foreign policy of the past. Talk about either idealism or realism, heard so often after World War II, was now apparently irrelevant. According to Williams, "It is essential, in short, to abandon the bipartisan imperialism of Thomas Jefferson and Theodore Roosevelt. America is neither the last best hope of the world nor the agent of civilization destined to destroy the barbarians. We have much to offer, but also much to learn. And the basic lesson is that we have misconceived leadership among equals as the exercise of predominance over others. Such an outlook is neither idealism nor realism; it is either self-righteousness or sophistry. Either is an indulgence which democracy cannot afford."[17]

The New Leftists offered an opportunity to rise above the old Marxist materialist interpretation of history. They examined a broad base of social and economic forces in their analysis of imperialism. In the age when the colonial empires of Europe were dying, the radical left frequently characterized American policy as the "Open Door Policy," which took its name from the Open Door Notes drafted by Secretary of State John Hay in 1899 and 1900. To the powers of Britain, Germany, France, Italy, Japan, and Russia, Hay had stated American principles: support of Chinese self-determination and equal access of American trade to China. Distilling the conglomeration of idealistic and practical motives, pressures, and theories of imperial expansion, the Open Door Policy became for Williams the substantive principle of American foreign relations in the twentieth century.

But, despite attempts to make it otherwise, the central distinguishing assumption of radical criticism was that the roots of American expansionism were embedded in the economic structure. Even if the radicals tried to avoid the caricature that limited the "economic factor" to the pursuit of money, they traced policy interests to a capitalist economy. From the internal demands of a system operated for profit, the rest of the radical critique followed dialectically. As Gabriel Kolko wrote about the formative goals of World War II, the "American economic war aim was to save capitalism at home and abroad." "At every level of the administration of the American state, domestically and internationally, business serves as the fount of critical assumptions or goals and strategically placed personnel." To Williams, ideals expressed by businessmen and national leaders that American economic policies would uplift other peoples along with bettering Americans was a central rationale of capitalist expansion, but the exploitive effect of capitalist policy was the same. Foreign policy was an extension of the needs of American capitalism or the beliefs of the leaders about the measures that were necessary to satisfy those needs.[18]

In this analysis, the essence of American policy manifesting capitalism abroad was, therefore, aggressive imperialism. The search for raw materials and constantly expanding markets engendered imperialism to ensure the economic, political, and social health of the nation. On close examination, the Open Door policy was economic. "Open Door expansion," David Horowitz agreed, "represented the natural policy of a newly great economic power" seeking competition in foreign markets. The reasoning of the "Open Door," according to Kolko, "assumed the general interest of the world was synonymous with that of the United States," but actually formed the basis of a United States–dominated world economic order.[19]

So pervasive were these policies that, to the New Left, Henry Wallace, the archcritic of the Truman Doctrine and the Marshall Plan in the 1940s, was well within the consensus. Wallace had supported the orthodox line of American economic policy, pushing for the growth of American trade abroad. In the New Left accounts, Wallace, concerned about another depression, consistently urged overseas economic expansion as a new frontier. In pursuit of the Open Door, Wallace was little different from Herbert Hoover. The only leader whom Williams cited as disagreeing with Wallace was the conservative Republican Robert Taft, who worried that Wallace's economic policies might provoke the Soviets into war. Williams did recognize that Wallace had protested the cold war policies toward Russia and that the attacks on Wallace had been vicious. Wallace had sought a less strident approach to persuade the Russians to modify their assumptions about postwar cooperation. But Williams kept returning to Wallace's beliefs concerning the assertion of American economic strength.[20]

It followed that American post–World War II policies, as scrutinized by the New Left, were misdirected. Foreign trade and investment were exploitive because of innate American needs. The New Left balked at the benefits to other peoples who wanted or accepted American capital investment and who learned from technology and organization. Foreign investment on an unprecedented scale was, according to Horowitz, intended to keep other lands "open to penetration and domination by United States capital." Kolko wrote, "By any criterion, what we call United States investment abroad is much more foreign resources mobilized in American hands, generating its own capital in a manner that pyramids the American penetration of the world economy." While Williams acknowledged that foreign investment might have increased the gross national product of a foreign area, he judged that much of the added wealth immediately ended up in the United States. There was no way that other peoples could win. The expansion of international corporations based in the United States had the same exploitive effects, the argument went on, as the influx of investment.[21]

The New Left assumption about foreign aid programs was that they offered a solution to America's economic difficulties by preventing the loss of markets. While not ruling out a measure of generosity toward the peoples of Western Europe, Williams found the primary meaning of the Marshall Plan in America's need for economic expansion to maintain domestic prosperity. Aid was to Kolko "a tool for penetrating and making lucrative the Third World in particular and the entire nonsocialist world in general." Through adroit use of aid and loans, Kolko theorized, the United States increased its agricultural exports, thwarted retaliation, gained raw materials, and kept a sizable share of manufacturing exports.[22]

The New Leftists devoted little attention to cultural exchange. They emphasized economic policy, along with the political policy and recently ascendant military dimension of America's world role, which were traced to economic imperatives. The assertion of American power along the frontiers of interests where they came up against the Soviet borders therefore threatened the Soviet Union's defenses in Eastern Europe. Containment was a proposal to extend the functioning domestic economic system abroad, and, Williams stated, the "policy of containment was supplemented in 1947 by the Truman Administration's stress on the necessity of economic expansion." The Truman Doctrine and the Marshall Plan "were the two sides of the same coin of America's traditional program of open-door expansion." By offering loans and grants to other nations, including the Soviet Union after World War II, the United States was largely attempting to receive political concessions and support for American policies. The United Nations was no answer, for even it had been corrupted by American power: American plans for an international organization to keep the peace, in Kolko's account, had been based implicitly on the belief "that the rest of the world would gladly welcome the world organization as part of an American-led century that would redound to the universal weal." The problem was that if Americans were "about to declare the American century, the Russians and British would resist."[23]

Although the New Left recognized that American policies had been intended to win victories without waging wars and had not been conceived or designed to carry out a policy of military intervention, the radical movement criticized the nation's increasing dependence on military force. During the period of demobilization after World War II, a military mentality had been scheming about the atomic bomb. The possession of the bomb had not "prompted American leaders to get tough with Russia," Williams said, "but rather their open-door outlook which interpreted the bomb as the final guarantee that they could go further faster down that path to world predominance." After the loss of the atomic monopoly, plans for intervention on a less than total scale were nonetheless abhorrent to the New Left. The development of war industries produced profits for capitalist investors at home and hardware to protect international capitalism abroad. The result of the exertion of influence on the world, Sidney Lens supposed, was the developing of the military as "the central feature of American life," another foible of "the American Century." Military interventions in Korea, Guatemala, Lebanon, Cuba, and the Dominican Republic aimed at protecting American business ventures and investment in politically unstable regions. Williams warned in the early 1960s that the United States had become impaled on the dilemma of empire: "It could resort to war or it could disengage." He offered no alternative option.[24]

The root of American problems and the tragedy that followed in the wake of American policies, in the radicals' complaint, was the open-door outlook based on an economic definition of the American world role, so that the New Left was already denying its promise; its worldview was not very different from that of earlier complainers. The critique was of an imperialist strategy that maintained an integrated world order, by force if necessary, and that ultimately brought the United States into conflict with the Soviet Union and its satellites. Lloyd Gardner assumed that "the United States was more responsible for the *way* in which the Cold War developed" than the Soviet Union.[25]

The United States was caught in a dilemma in which it could do nothing right or constructive. American goals could only be implemented, according to Kolko, by setting the United States "against the Soviet Union, against the tide of the Left, and against Britain as a coequal guardian of world capitalism—in fact, against history as it had been and had yet to become." With the aim of maintaining a monopoly of power and a world at peace, America gradually "stood revealed more and more unambiguously as the conservative guardian of the international status quo," Horowitz said. It followed that an imperial United States ended up opposing revolutions by the peoples of developing nations, even if they were plagued by starvation, political oppression, or social needs, because these revolutions might upset the order of American influence.[26]

The consequence of unending foreign crises was sure to be frustration, discouragement, or panic. But the most troubling threat of all was the loss of the status of preeminence, and that was why Horowitz singled out as foremost among the setbacks of the 1950s the launching of Sputnik, which had struck a blow not only at the analyses of containment but also at the belief in the "American Century," at the "very heart of that peculiarly American conception of history, the hegemony of the American Way in the modern world." The United States was in a trap in which the persistence of an "American Century," wrote Herbert Aptheker, would "continue to produce setback after setback for the U.S. government." The New Left, in contrast to the consensus, did not question whether American preeminence existed but whether it had any value at all.[27]

Whatever the scholarly merits of their work, criticized by some reviewers for shoddy methods and stacked evidence, the New Left philosophers, sociologists, and historians provided the conceptual formulation of dissent. They did not create the movement, but they did influence a generation of young radicals, who not only had ideas of their own but also brought about concrete change.

16

The

Activists

Groups of young men and women still reaching their maturity dreamed of putting some of the New Left ideas into action. They were not cloistered scholars, and though many of these activists attended colleges and in the main they were well educated, they turned to activism in student organizations and in the civil rights protests in the South and in northern cities. The young radicals came into their own as rebels against the old consensus. They wished to build a new society.

Student Protesters

When Tom Hayden, who was born in Detroit and grew up in its middle-class suburb of Royal Oak, went off to school at the University of Michigan in 1957, he came to Ann Arbor with the goal of becoming a journalist, and he imagined himself as a future foreign correspondent. He was, he recalled, "following the American dream." He chose a different course. While covering the 1960 Democratic convention as an editor of his college newspaper, he wondered why he was only chronicling events instead of participating in them. He became intrigued by a network of students concerned with issues of civil rights and nuclear disarmament. He joined in their early protests and became a theoretician of their rising movement. Hayden acknowledged a debt to Mills and Marcuse "as prophets of a new social order"; he did not embrace traditional Marxism. He was attracted to John Kennedy for the idealism he aroused, and for his efforts to create a Peace Corps, which represented to Hayden an alternative to the suicidal arms race and an anticommunist obsession that had led to militarism. It was "a way out of the Cold War." But his enthusiasm faded quickly once Kennedy was in office, as this peaceful effort "became wedded to American foreign policy as a whole."[1]

In 1962, at Port Huron in eastern Michigan, a few hundred miles to the south of Bad Axe, where the local debate of national purpose had taken place not two years before, Hayden joined a Students for a Democratic Society meeting. There, at a camp on the windy shores at the extreme end of Lake Huron, where Hayden had gone perch fishing with his father as a boy, he wrote of the new generation's restless discontent with the world it had inherited.

320

Along the shoreline of trails that led through trees to the sandy beach, he drafted the Port Huron statement that gave voice to the intellectual mind of the New Left student activists and became their classic declaration. He had a view of America in the world.

> When we were kids the United States was the wealthiest and strongest country in the world; the only one with the atom bomb, the least scarred by modern war, an initiator of the United Nations that we thought would distribute Western influence throughout the world. Freedom and equality for each individual, government of, by, and for the people—these American values we found good, principles by which we could live as men. Many of us began maturing in complacency.
>
> As we grew, however, our comfort was penetrated by events too troubling to dismiss. First, the permeating and victimizing fact of human degradation, symbolized by the Southern struggle against racial bigotry, compelled most of us from silence to activism. Second, the enclosing fact of the Cold War, symbolized by the presence of the Bomb, brought awareness that we ourselves, and our friends, and millions of abstract "others" we knew more directly because of our common peril, might die at any time.[2]

Hayden contested the validity of a consensus debate on national purpose. The United States rested in "national stalemate, its goals ambiguous and tradition-bound."As Hayden watched the Kennedy administration unfold, he considered the "call to 'service'" not an allusion to idealism but a crass expression of "defending the free world from Communism." Kennedy was part of the politics of "status quo," in which government activity was rationalized by the cold war and anticommunism. Hayden did not find it surprising that the far right, typified by Barry Goldwater, espoused "Victory over Communism." But Hayden contended that anticommunism had become an umbrella under which to protest "liberalism" and "internationalism." He fully recognized that the "vast majority" of the people regarded the "temporary equilibriums of our society and the world as eternally functional parts." But the reassurances of consensus politicians and their stagnation of thought did not discourage Hayden from seeking experimentation or hoping for an enlarged activist following. He had gone to Newark, New Jersey, in 1967 to help blacks obtain better housing, welfare, and political power, and in the summer riots in that city he learned something about the potential of organized violence and the disorder that ghetto residents could create by attacking stores, neighborhood institutions, and business districts. Attacks with "paint or bullets" could change the status quo, though he affirmed that "only politics and organization can transform it."[3]

Following William Appleman Williams, Hayden professed that the economic and military investments of the United States in the cold war contradicted its peaceful intentions. The activists did not believe that America could be both an empire and a

democracy. They opposed American imperialism for corrupting democracy. They believed Americans had been as imperialistic toward the blacks within their society as
toward developing nations. When Hayden looked at the national war economy and its
international trade, the connection in his mind was that America was racist at home and
abroad and was protecting an empire of poverty and privilege. He saw a direct relationship between domestic and world affairs, but it was very different from the relationship
the consensus found. The "American empire" was set to "become more of a military
state, taxing and drafting its own people and consequently stifling any real aspirations at
home." At stake was the nation's preeminence. "From the early forties to the early
sixties, the period in which the present younger generation was shaped, there was no
doubt that the American Empire was the most powerful in the world." But, as Hayden
stated, *"The world we see is one in which a decadent and super-rich American empire,
with its principles of racial superiority, private property, and armed might, is falling
apart. We want to join the new humanity, not support a dying empire."* [4] Their own view
of "internationalism" led them to identify with peoples whom the government defined
as enemies.

Hippies

Another group of radicals, the hippies, followed in the bohemian tradition of the
beatniks, the drifters of the "beat" generation of the 1950s. The hippies lived on the
fringe of society and sociologists called their activity the counterculture. But the hippies grew into a movement that spread through society and brought new attitudes to it.
Preaching love and peace and the beauty of flowers, they turned their restlessness to
nonviolent rebellion against the way things were. They rebelled against the conformity
of the silent and lonely crowd of the 1950s. They were interested in music and poetry,
rather than split-level homes in the suburbs and white-collar office jobs.[5]

The bohemians of the New Left set themselves apart from their parents. These
refugees from consensus established their own life, centering their revolt in San Francisco and New York. The poet of the beatniks was Allen Ginsberg, who represented
their art—shunned at first by the established writers and poets. As a shy youth in
Paterson, New Jersey, he at first wrote romantic and introspective poems about death
and sunsets. Suddenly, as he neared thirty, in 1955 and 1956, in San Francisco, Ginsberg wrote the rough and angry poem "Howl," bemoaning "the best minds of my
generation destroyed by madness." In the poem "America" he wrote "America I've
given you all and now I'm nothing." He defined his relation to his country and deplored
what he thought it was becoming: "America when will we end the human war?"

America when will you be angelic?
When will you take off your clothes?
When will you look at yourself through the grave?
When will you be worthy of your million Trotskyites?

America why are your libraries full of tears?
America when will you send your eggs to India?
I'm sick of your insane demands.

Here was an obscure and failed America that was in opposition to the promises of Archibald MacLeish.[6]

The hippies looked to the New Left for whatever serious, organized body of ideas they could use. They called America racist and imperialistic, and they were entirely impatient with the ineffective liberalism of the consensus that represented the middle class. At one meeting between the New Left and what Abbie Hoffman called the "Old Left," he felt conspicuous as a hippie dressed in beads, boots, bellbottoms, and a cowboy hat, and sensed the "vibrations as very mixed." Hoffman was bored with the talk, until one of his hippie cohorts kicked the conference table over, shouting, "Take off your ties, they are chains around your necks. . . . You're gonna make a revolution?" The Old Left still was tied in many ways to the consensus, and the hippies wanted to be separate: "They do socialism," Hoffman reflected, "we blow pot in the grass, they do imperialism, we go swimming, they do racism, we do flowers for everybody." But the new radicals avowed not to be Marxists—and thought little of Russia. "Same as here," Hoffman said. "Dull, bureaucratic-sterile-puritanical."[7]

Among these hippies, Hoffman sought to organize a group called Yippies, for the Youth International Party, but they lacked institutional organization. He discussed their radical intellectual origins, citing Herbert Marcuse, who said the hippie flower children had found "the answer" and who reportedly smoked hashish. Hoffman referred to Paul Goodman and quoted the economist Robert Theobald: American society would have to entitle its people to more than a guaranteed income, and then soon enable anyone simply to go into a store and take "what you wanted." He knew Ginsberg and had read his poetry. Hoffman's cohort Jerry Rubin saw hippies as an expression of "the break-down of the affluent society"—the phrase of John Kenneth Galbraith.[8]

The hippie movement could not be traced to intellectuals alone. Indeed, the hippies thrived on avoiding philosophic thought. They followed their feelings and instincts and sought the gratification of pleasure. A hippie who had grown up in affluence, Rubin traced the making of his civil disobedience to his fifth year, when he was walking down the street with his grandmother. "I want an ice cream cone," he said. When she said, "no, supper will be soon," Rubin started screaming and ran into the middle of the street, clutching the trolley car tracks until he got his ice cream. He admitted to being "spoiled" as a child. Hoffman, alias "Free," recollected stealing cars at the age of fifteen. At seventeen he was thrown out of school for hitting a teacher and was stabbed in the leg in a gang fight.[9]

Popular culture was a strong influence on the radicals. Hoffman liked *Planet of the Apes*, "a trip and a half," he described it, which ended with the image of the Statue of Liberty in ruins and the realization that America had been destroyed by the nuclear weapons it had been the first to create. He found "fantastically compelling" *Viking*

Queen, Rosemary's Baby, 2001, and *Wild in the Streets.* The people Hoffman respected as influences on him included W. C. Fields, the Marx Brothers, Alfred Hitchcock, Che Guevara, and the Beatles.[10]

The movement did not just seek access to consensus media; it depended on it. As the movement spread by buttons, posters, stickers, and sweatshirts, it received attention in the large-circulation magazines *Time* and *Life,* whose founder, Henry Luce, actually became intrigued with the drug culture and tried LSD. Radicals also appeared on the widely watched television shows and spread their views through bestselling books, poetry, art, and rock and folk music. They sponsored workshops on drugs and communes. The hippie leaders got their message out against consensus world political goals through the consensus media.[11]

The New Left, activists, and hippies were representatives of a fragmenting consensus society that had held together over the world role a diversity of groups regardless of age, gender, ethnic group, race, geographic region, and economic class. Groups that had long been firmly within the consensus were seeking their own existence distinct from it.

Youths

As Hayden recognized, a minority of youth joined the New Left, and so too did only a small proportion of youth enter communes or become deeply immersed in the counterculture. But youths differentiated themselves from the earlier generation of consensus by their own conventions. They wore long hair and patched jeans. They began to take drugs, and the mores and sexual relations became more casual. Without becoming part of the New Left and the hippies, the youths appropriated much of their culture and worldview. And because of the postwar baby boom that was reaching teenage years, the median age of the population, according to the census, had reversed for the first time in American history. As the number of teenagers in the population increased to a record number, so did the power of youth, or the power that youth perceived it had.

A new art form of the young, whether radical or hippie, even moderate or conservative, gave them a means of expression: rock and roll. This music that burst on the scene in the early 1950s was different than that of the earlier consensus generation in World War II, which had rallied the nation to the cause as popular singers like Bing Crosby and big bands like Benny Goodman's performed for the troops. The composer Irving Berlin produced "God Bless America," and Frank Loesser, "Praise the Lord and Pass the Ammunition." Although early rock songs were of young love, school, and life on the beach—songs like Bill Haley's "Rock around the Clock" and Elvis Presley's "Love Me Tender"—a few singers of folk music, like Pete Seeger, carried on the 1930s tradition of topical protest songs, and in the 1960s rock songs turned political. Groups like the Beatles, the Rolling Stones, Jefferson Airplane, and the Grateful Dead sang of street fights, rebellion, hippie life, and foreign crises.[12]

Jerry Rubin hypothesized that the New Left movement sprang from rock music: "Music to free the spirit. Music to bring us *together*. . . . *Rock 'n' roll marked the beginning of the revolution.*" He singled out the songs of Bob Dylan and the Beatles. Abbie Hoffman credited rock music, specifically Bob Dylan, the Beatles, and the Doors, with his nonconformist hippie ideas. In rock, America was the first nation: Hoffman wondered why Cuban radio stations, which he listened to, did not play it. But this music carried its message throughout the society at large. Observed *Time* magazine: "Where once teen-agers were too busy frugging to pay much heed to lyrics, most of which were unintelligible banshee wails anyway, they now listen with ears cocked and brows furrowed. The rallying cry is no longer 'I wanna hold your hand,' but 'I wanna change the world.'" And the *New York Times Magazine* told its readers that the time had come to start listening to this music, because of what its message revealed about "how young people are thinking about love, peace, freedom, sex, drugs, Vietnam."[13]

The cold war had no "Yankee Doodle," "Battle Hymn of the Republic," or "Over There." Rather, the crises abroad brought an ever-present foreboding, as in "Eve of Destruction," written by a teenager named P. F. Sloan in 1965:

> The Eastern world, it is explodin'
> Violence flarin', bullets loadin'
> You're old enough to kill but not for votin'
> You don't believe in war, but what's that gun you're totin'
> And even the Jordan River has bodies floatin'
> But you tell me, over and over again, my friend,
> Ah, you don't believe we're on the eve of destruction.[14]

Some mainstream radio stations attempted to censor "Eve of Destruction" because of its message against foreign military intervention and the values of an armed society. A Los Angeles disk jockey, Bob Eubanks, said, "How do you think the enemy will feel with a tune like that No. 1 in America?" Some stations allotted equal time to the song, "The Dawn of Correction" in response:

> The Western world has a common dedication,
> To keep free people from Red domination.
> Maybe you can't vote, boy, but man your battle stations,
> Or there'll be no need for votin' in future generations.[15]

Bob Dylan, in his twenties, was one of the earliest and most vocal troubadours of the young New Left, echoing the movement's sentiments when he wrote about the evils of war and the social ills within America that had led the country into crises. He had expressed his fears of the escalation of war to nuclear catastrophe in "A Hard Rain's A-Gonna Fall," written during the 1962 Cuban missile crisis, which the nation's policymakers hailed as well managed, but which was to Dylan the height of folly.[16]

Dylan sang bitterly against the establishment that manufactured weapons of war

for profit and recalled President Eisenhower's 1961 warning against the increasing
influence of a military-industrial complex. To Dylan the masters of war included those
who "build all the guns," "build the death planes," and "build the big bombs" while
hiding "behind desks" and in mansions. Dylan's words to them were: "I hope that you
die," and "your death'll come soon." Dylan depicted the cold imagery of "young
people's blood" flowing "out of their bodies" and "buried in the mud." He sang of total
futility and of the "worst fear," the "Fear to bring children into the world," because of
the senseless and brutal killing.[17]

Dylan's songs spurned the government decision makers' line that the Communists
were in a worldwide conspiracy. His view of anticommunism was that it was not much
more than paranoia. In "With God on Our Side," Dylan observed that politicians had led
the nation into Indian wars, the Spanish-American War, World War I, and World War II
for reasons he could not fathom. Following all the fighting of World War II that had
been justified as God's will, he noted, "We forgave the Germans / And we were
friends / Though they murdered six million." Now the Germans were on God's side,
but the Russians were not, and all the confused, wearisome hatred had been diverted
against the Russians. He mocked the propaganda against the Soviets, along with the
proposition that Americans fought under divine direction. Dylan had been told to hate
the Russians, to be ready for war, "And accept it all bravely / With God on my side."[18]

Songs also urged change to reverse the sad conditions of crisis and war. The people
who supported the leaders and fought in war were, in the song "The Universal Soldier"
by Buffy Sainte-Marie, an American Indian, ultimately the ones to end it. The American soldier, along with his counterparts in Canada, France, Russia, and Japan, could
refuse to serve. Dylan's "Subterranean Homesick Blues" followed Paul Goodman's
Growing up Absurd in urging revolt against the way things were in schools and in the
government: "Don't follow leaders," Dylan said. "You don't need a weather man / To
know which way the wind blows." And Dylan had wondered, "how many times must
the cannon balls fly / Before they're forever banned? / The answer, my friend, is
blowin' in the wind."[19]

These words and music expressed the youthful restless moods in a time of crowded
summer streets and music-filled cafes of New York's Greenwich Village or the Haight-
Ashbury section of San Francisco. A dream of the young remained that of Pete Seeger,
who for many years had been singing of "the strangest dream": "the world had all
agreed, to put an end to war." That dream meant questioning the consensus politics that
threatened it.[20]

Women

In the 1950s, when Betty Friedan started writing for women's magazines, she found
that editors had the idea that women were interested in neither politics nor life outside
the United States. Politics, for women, she observed, concerned Mamie Eisenhower's

clothes or the Nixons' home life. It had not always been so. During World War II the *Ladies' Home Journal* carried substantive articles on international affairs like "Can the U.S. Have Peace after This War?" by Walter Lippmann. But during the postwar years articles on politics pandered to women as housewives. One editor worked on a piece that tried to bring the atomic bomb "down to the feminine level by showing the emotions of a wife whose husband sailed into a contaminated area." A proposed article for another leading women's magazine was "How to Have a Baby in an Atom Bomb Shelter."[21]

In her 1963 critique of women in society, *The Feminine Mystique,* Friedan was adamant that women could not be sheltered from the world. They were caught up in the same anxieties and tensions that David Riesman described as prevalent in the society that had become intrinsically connected to the world. But she objected to Riesman's suggestion, derived from Freudian psychology, that women need not seek their own autonomy through productive contribution to society—they might better help their husbands hold on to theirs. Friedan directed stern criticism at Margaret Mead, who had once supported the war effort of World War II by writing *And Keep Your Powder Dry* and had disseminated Freudian theory that demeaned women.[22]

The consensus had been numbing and somnambulistic.

There was, just before the feminine mystique took hold in America, a war, which followed a depression and ended with the explosion of an atom bomb. After the loneliness of war and the unspeakableness of the bomb, against the frightening uncertainty, the cold immensity of the changing world, women as well as men sought the comforting reality of home and children. . . .

We were all vulnerable, homesick, lonely, frightened. A pent-up hunger for marriage, home, and children was felt simultaneously by several different generations; a hunger which, in the prosperity of postwar America, everyone could suddenly satisfy.

At home, women, forced by consensus society, "shrugged off the bomb, forgot the concentration camps, condoned corruption, and fell into helpless conformity. . . . It was easier, safer, to think about love and sex than about communism, McCarthy, and the uncontrolled bomb." She compared the American home to a "comfortable concentration camp," and the women its captives.[23]

Friedan inspired women's groups in their dissent from the consensus. With the founding in 1966 of the National Organization of Women (NOW), a new generation of radical feminist intellectuals produced their own literature. Kate Millett saw the problem of America in the world as rooted in American society's patriarchy. The military, along with industry, technology, universities, science, political office, and finance—in short, "every avenue of power within the society"—was "entirely in male hands." The repercussions of half the populace, the female half, controlled by the half that was male, and elder males dominating younger females, involved violence and war. The rationale that accompanied the "imposition of male authority euphemistically referred to as 'the battle of the sexes' " resembled the "formulas of nations at war, where any heinousness is justified on the grounds that the enemy is either an inferior species or really not human at all."[24]

The feminists argued that women offered a less warlike worldview than men. Male-oriented consensus society did not, Friedan was convinced, have the answers to postwar problems of crisis and nuclear weapons. "Girls who grew up playing baseball, baby-sitting, mastering geometry—almost independent enough, almost resourceful enough, to meet the problems of the fission-fusion era—were told by the most advanced thinkers of our time to go back and live their lives as if they were Noras, restricted to the doll's house by Victorian prejudice." Friedan wanted women to commit themselves to world issues that had previously involved mostly men. What was needed was a "national educational program, similar to the GI bill," for women who wanted to continue their education and pursue careers. But would there be less conflict if women gained positions of power?[25]

One feminist engaged Margaret Mead in debate on the issue that women were more pacific than men. Mead had maintained that, though women were not inherently submissive types, neither were they inherently nonviolent. Women could kill too, but they should not at the risk of becoming like what they abhorred. The feminists, in turn, were advocating revolution against the militaristic male society. Mead argued that a women's revolution must not take place. The feminist wrote: The "revolution-talk in general upsets her: we might be bringing fascism down upon us—blacks, Latins, Asians, but especially women, are provoking fascism." Mead nevertheless believed that women, after being "underground" for thousands of years, were "beginning to surface."[26]

Civil Rights Leaders

The dissenters against the complacent consensus joined with the civil rights movement that struggled to overcome the oppressive remnants of slavery—restricting blacks from voting and segregating them from the mainstream of American life. The foremost leader of this movement, Martin Luther King, Jr., a Christian minister, came to prominence by leading the protest against the Montgomery, Alabama, Bus Company in 1955. The arrest of a black woman for refusing to give up her seat on a bus to a white man made an activist of King, who had only that year been a scholar finishing his Ph.D. at Boston University. A year later the black boycott of Montgomery city buses succeeded in ending segregation of the riders. But King's nonviolent struggle for equal rights went on.[27]

King viewed his struggle as part of a world development. In Africa, Asia, South America, and the Caribbean, he saw the masses rising up. The "determination of Negro Americans to win freedom from all forms of oppression springs from the same deep longing that motivates oppressed peoples all over the world," King wrote. The connection between the racial crisis in America and the larger world crisis was evident in King's nonviolent resistance, inspired by the teachings of Gandhi, who had successfully led the protest that overturned British colonial rule in India.[28]

National power added to the significance of the American black movement. "America, the richest and most powerful nation in the world, can well lead the way in this revolution of values," King wrote. But King found American foreign policy lacking because of the racism at home. Slavery had spread to America with the same European imperialism that had plundered Africa. In the United States the misbegotten nineteenth-century Teutonic and Anglo-Saxon race theories, he feared, were prevalent even in the 1960s. A white woman told King that while she wanted blacks to have the right to vote and to have good jobs and decent homes, she would not want her daughter "to marry a Negro"; to which King retorted, "It is the Teutonic Origins theory warmed over."[29]

First King used the principles of American foreign policy to expose the evils of racism. The American government's advocacy of free elections in Europe was "hypocrisy" when free elections were not held "in great sections of America," he wrote in 1958. He noted that Americans found "nothing strange about Marshall Plan and technical assistance to handicapped peoples around the world" while blacks at home were wanting. He suggested that Americans should "do no less for our own handicapped multitudes." But not content with using foreign policy as a model for domestic betterment, King looked to reform foreign policy too.[30]

For King, racism and its "perennial ally," economic exploitation, explained the most crucial international issue of his generation: the rise of developing nations in the midst of cold war. His prime example was the government of South Africa's policy of apartheid. The tragedy of South Africa could not have happened without complicity: "it is the fact that the racist government of South Africa is virtually made possible by the economic policies of the United States and Great Britain." King liked President Kennedy but criticized him for making "little or no attempt to deal with the economic aspects of racist exploitation." Billions of dollars in trade and military alliances were maintained under "the pretext" of fighting communism in Africa.[31]

Like the prophets of ancient times, King called out a warning: If Americans were not determined to root out "the last vestiges of racism in our dealings with the rest of the world, we may soon see the sins of our fathers visited upon ours and succeeding generations. For the conditions which are so classically represented in Africa are present also in Asia and in our own back yard in Latin America." Throughout Latin America he found a "tremendous resentment of the United States," and that resentment was "strongest among the poorer and darker peoples of the continent." The life and destiny of Latin America were "in the hands of United States corporations. . . . Here we see racism in its more sophisticated form: neocolonialism."[32]

King adhered to the hope that America would redirect its power for good. "Somehow we must transform the dynamics of the world power struggle from the nuclear arms race, which no one can win, to a creative contest to harness man's genius for the purpose of making peace and prosperity a reality for all the nations of the world." In short, Americans had to turn the arms race into a "peace race." Only the United States had this opportunity. No "colored nation," including China, showed "even the potential of leading a violent revolution of color in any international proportions." Ghana, Zambia, Tanganyika, and Nigeria were "so busy fighting their own battles against poverty, illiteracy and the subversive influence of neo-colonialism" that they offered "little hope" to Angola, Southern Rhodesia, and South Africa, "much less to the American Negro." "The hard cold facts today indicate that the hope of the people of color in the world may well rest on the American Negro and his ability to reform the structure of racial imperialism from within and thereby turn the technology and wealth of the West to the task of liberating the world from want."[33]

King wanted to achieve the goals of the civil rights movement around the world nonviolently. He favored the United Nations, and through it disarmament of nuclear and all weapons. "The United Nations is a gesture in the direction of nonviolence on a world scale." And he was for foreign aid. He believed that America and other developed nations had "a moral obligation" to provide technical assistance as well as capital to the "underdeveloped" areas, initiating "a massive, sustained Marshall Plan" for Asia, Africa, and South America. If the rich nations would allocate for development just two percent of their gross national products annually for a period of ten or twenty years, "mankind would go a long way toward conquering the ancient enemy, poverty."[34]

> This is a great hour for the Negro. The challenge is here. To become the instruments of a great idea is a privilege that history gives only occasionally. Arnold Toynbee says in *A Study of History* that it may be the Negro who will give the new spiritual dynamic to Western civilization that it so desperately needs to survive. I hope this is possible. The spiritual power that the Negro can radiate to the world comes from love, understanding, good will, and nonviolence. It may even be possible for the Negro, through adherence to nonviolence, so to challenge the nations of the world that they will seriously seek an alternative to war and destruction. In a day when Sputniks and Explorers dash through outer space and guided ballistic missiles are carving highways of death through the stratosphere, nobody can win a war. Today the choice is no longer between violence and nonviolence. It is either nonviolence or nonexistence. The Negro may be God's appeal to this age—an age drifting rapidly to its doom. The eternal appeal takes the form of a warning: "All who take the sword will perish by the sword."

King called for "a world-wide fellowship" and he spoke of love: "Love is the key that unlocks the door which leads to ultimate reality."[35]

For his nonviolent stands and marches, King's home was dynamited and his family threatened. He won the Nobel Peace Prize in 1964. After the mid-1960s, militant civil rights leaders became impatient with King's nonviolence and called for "black power," a concept King abhorred. In breaking with King over black power, Stokely Carmichael urged a "new consciousness" among black people—"pride, rather than shame, in blackness"—and presented a political "ideology" to end racism and to avoid "prolonged destructive guerrilla warfare." "We blacks must respond in our own way, on our own terms, in a manner which fits our temperaments."[36]

In his book *Black Power,* which he wrote with Charles V. Hamilton, Carmichael saw the struggle for civil rights and American "black liberation" as part of a world struggle. "Black Power means that black people see themselves as part of a new force, sometimes called the 'Third World.'" He wanted American blacks to "hook up" with liberation struggles. The cause of the blacks of Johannesburg was the responsibility of American blacks, who had to oppose the effort of the United States to protect white prestige.[37]

The ghettos in American cities were economic colonies of a racist society, Carmichael contended, and although black people were legal citizens of the United States, they ranked as "colonial subjects in relation to the white society." Thus "institutional racism" had another name: "colonialism." The analogy, Carmichael admitted, was not perfect. The internal colonies were not physically separated from the "Mother Country." But as in the English, French, Italian, Portugese, and Spanish colonies, blacks were subordinated to whites, and while the United States did not exploit raw materials of blacks for export, the whites exploited the black communities of the United States for their human labor. "Black people in the United States have a colonial relationship to the larger society, a relationship characterized by institutional racism."[38]

The rule of American city ghettos, Carmichael said, was not unlike that of Sierra Leone in British West Africa. "The man in the ghetto sees his white landlord come only to collect exorbitant rents and fail to make necessary repairs, while both know that the white-dominated city building inspection department will wink at violations or impose only slight fines. The man in the ghetto sees the white policeman on the corner brutally manhandle a black drunkard in a doorway, and at the same time accept a pay-off from one of the agents of the white-controlled rackets. He sees the streets in the ghetto lined with uncollected garbage, and he knows that the powers which could send trucks in to collect that garbage are white. When they don't, he knows the reason: the low political esteem in which the black community is held. He looks at the absence of a meaningful curriculum in the ghetto schools—for example, the history books that woefully overlook the historical achievements of black people—and he knows that the school board is controlled by whites. . . . He is faced with a 'white power structure' as monolithic as Europe's colonial offices have been to African and Asian colonies."[39]

So Carmichael, unlike King, saw little redeeming about American power, and little of value to transform. "Perhaps the most vicious result of colonialism—in Africa and this country—was that it purposefully, maliciously and with reckless abandon relegated the black man to a subordinated, inferior status in the society. The individual was considered and treated as a lowly animal." Even when the black man had participated in wars to defend the country, repeatedly demonstrating loyalty, "the embedded colonial mentality" continued to deny him equal status in the social order.[40]

Therefore, America had little to offer the world. The adoption of "middle-class" American ways was not the answer for blacks in America any more than it was for blacks in Africa, because to Carmichael that meant assimilation or acceptance of the white man's civilization. "As with the black African who had to become a 'Frenchman' in order to be accepted, so to be an American, the black man must strive to become 'white.'" To Carmichael, that was a reinforcement of racism in the United States. The answer was not integration with whites. The answer was black community at home and abroad, organized around the precepts of black power.[41]

The dissenters and activists provided substantial insights into the expansion of American power and interests in the period after World War II. The conceptual reach of the New Left, radical scholars, activists, hippies, feminists, and black leaders revealed serious flaws in the American international role. Their dissent made it apparent that the political elite of the consensus had no monopoly of the argument. The government had complacently followed the direction of the great innovations at the outset of the cold war—the Truman Doctrine, containment, and the Marshall Plan—on an uncertain course that was already encountering serious problems.[42]

The power of a nation derived in large part from its productive enterprise, and economic considerations were clearly paramount in the New Left analysis of trade and investment policies. But this analysis did not show that the motivation of policy was on the whole economic or that American policy could be reduced entirely to imperialism in the Marxist sense of projecting a problem-ridden capitalist economy abroad. Overseas cultural activities and even the foreign aid programs of the Marshall Plan, Point Four, and Peace Corps were not totally economic in motivation, especially as fear of Communist Russia gripped the nation. And altruism could not be disregarded, either. Political, cultural, and ideological considerations had to be taken into account in the study of the uses of power. How power was used had a great deal to do with how it would be received.

The discussion by the New Left of American imperialism reflected the pervasiveness of American influence, especially in less developed countries. American business sought profits, government technicians dislocated ancient cultures, and Americans sometimes expressed condescending attitudes toward people who had not achieved their success. Then, too, the American military held bases and maintained fleets in many countries. The impact of American intrusions threatened to disrupt indigenous institutions and life.

At the same time, the New Left failed to explain the precise nature of economic imperialism or its relation to the military. Americans might seek raw materials abroad, but the losses that the Near East or Latin America suffered in oil and other natural resources were over time in large part offset by their gains in modernization and living standards. American enterprises exported goods and built factories, but the technology was learned by employees in oil refineries, sugar mills, electronics industries, and other businesses. Americans sought investment income by lending capital abroad, but the investment was frequently welcomed as a means of economic development, especially in the beginning of the world role, when the United States was the principal source of investment worldwide. Later, other nations increasingly had the financial resources to oblige with foreign investments, whether or not the United States did, and the demand for capital did not let up. Many countries benefited from foreign technology and capital, as opposed to American institutions and models of social structure.

The dissenters forced Americans to question the validity of prevailing foreign policies, but the New Leftists were less clear about what they accepted than about what they were against, and they did not succeed in creating a fundamental, let alone radical, revision of American relations with the world through the early 1960s. Dissensions within the New Left itself, while it was a growing force throughout the decade, kept it from forming a leftist consensus. The radical Left's writings were expressed in passionate but often negative or combative tones, resembling axe grinding.[43]

New Left provocations finally rehabilitated a form of isolationism, urging that the United States rid itself of world involvement. Only through forced retardation could the nation escape the dangers of reaching for a universal state—expending high military costs, building international corporate systems, and sacrificing liberty at home and the self-determination of small nations abroad. William Appleman Williams felt that Americans should responsibly give other "peoples of the world a chance to make their own history. . . . If that be isolationism, then the time has come to make the most of it." The New Left relied heavily on such spontaneous feelings. Radicals should recognize, Williams said, that they "may not be able to provide wholly satisfactory resolutions of all the problems. . . . We do not have all the answers now, and it is profoundly unradical to assume that we will devise them in our own time."[44]

The continued hardening of consensus policy forced the New Left to argue that nothing less than a total restructuring of American institutions could result in an acceptable foreign policy. Above all, the capitalist way of life, with its investment in private or corporate enterprises, had to be abandoned. Finally, Williams came to recommend that Americans return to a government modeled on the Articles of Confederation, a step that he determined was the only way to jettison empire. In place of the United States a loose federation of regional socialist communities might be constructed. The Left's promise of new creativity was unfulfilled.[45]

As for the hippies' thinking on world affairs, Abbie Hoffman began his *Revolution for the Hell of It* with a letter from his mother, dated November 1967, after she had read in *Time* and the *New York Times* about her son and his fellow bare-chested hippies calling for mass fornication. "I used to be so proud of all that you kids did, but now I just don't know. If you didn't have *such potential,* it would be different, but how can you waste what you have on such trash?????? I can't understand it at all!" It was a plea across the generations. The young people had no direction. *"You* are acting like children!" she exclaimed. They were tearing apart the system, not trying to build it anew: "If you *have* to make *Time* why can't it be for *something decent???*" Hippies had little to offer beyond "dropping out." The absurdity of his position was evident in his own self-mockery.

It was like a confused game. It was a revolution without rational purpose, of absurdity—like Dada, an international movement that after the turn of the century rejected customary beliefs among European artists and writers, and that had a radical doctrine without form. Hoffman once came to a New York City police station to demand that the police arrest him along with some blacks brought in for smoking pot. The police tried to ignore him until he kicked in the captain's trophy-case window and was arrested. Hoffman was advocating anarchy—a word as good as any, Hoffman silently agreed, when the judge used it in court. But Hoffman's explanation of why he committed the provocative act was even more revealing than this confession: he told his friends he did it because "it was fun," not out of principle. "To my brothers I tell the real truth, which is that I don't know why I did it. They smile because they know any explanation I give is made up."[46]

The escape of the hippies and the retreat of the New Left were no answers to the maintenance of world involvement. Both were troubled reactions to ways they did not like. These children of the affluent society wanted to do anything to be free. But theirs was freedom lacking in rationale, and they had no clear vision of the alternative society that they wanted to build.

It was the civil rights movement as represented by Martin Luther King that offered hope, but a hope that had little chance of transforming the consensus foreign policy at that time. King's talk of love and brotherhood sounded naive and idealistic to the realists, not the words of a man who was serious about meeting the challenges of war and communism. Nonviolence could not succeed against a ruthless communist enemy, was the common retort to King's gospel. Tactics that might integrate lunch counters in the American South, it followed, could never defend European cities against Soviet armies and hold strategic outposts in Asia against insurgents. King's vision transcended the ethnocentric tendencies of black power, but his prophetic hopes and the inspiration he gave, which had changed domestic life, had little immediate effect on American foreign policy.

Both the consensus and the New Leftists were deficient in new thought at this time of crisis. The consensus stressed a hardening of the American position. Having successfully met the challenge of the immediate postwar world to recognize and use American power in a mission of internationalism, the consensus intractably maintained the attitudes and institutions of dominant power despite changing world conditions. Unless new conceptions could be developed while flexibility was still feasible, the consensus was apt to fail conspicuously in determining the future course. In the early days of the opposition, the consensus did not seriously rebut the New Left, which seemed an aberration, a deviation from what was right and normal, an apparition that might vanish or a mental derangement that deserved no more respect than the New Left showed the consensus.

Perhaps it was quixotic for the hippies and activists to take on an established and powerful consensus, but they stood to gain. The dissenters, however, had not shown the necessary creativity to develop a new national outlook or to create a new unanimity in the country.

American power began to decline as soon as it reached its peak. At the point of greatest power and productive capacity, as the nation exerted its might and diverted its resources toward a tremendous military, a division of purpose disrupted the social harmony. Ultimately, the rise of the opposition to the consensus epitomized the beginnings of a loss of the harmony that had sustained the nation's world role after World War II. A serious schism was developing as consensus ideas faltered and proved unable to master the problems of declining power.

PART V

The

Decline

of a

World

Role

☆ ☆ ☆ ☆

17

Discord

at

Home

and

Abroad

At mid-century President Truman dismissed doomsayers who complained that the American world role would not be lasting and that the Republic was "on the way out": "They don't know what they are talking about." He believed that the United States was "only at the beginning of very great things" and compared America's present world position to the rise of the British Empire. In the late 1840s the duke of Wellington had allowed that he was content to die because the British Empire was declining. Yet, continued Truman, Disraeli and Gladstone built an expanded realm after Wellington's death. Truman did not choose to consider the eventual decline of that empire. Although he did conjecture, "Another country will eventually come along that may be greater than ours," the idea was abstract and remote. The outlook then was of a flourishing nation. Decline might become a possibility, but it was not inevitable.[1]

By the 1970s the scope and perceptions of the American world role had altered radically from its earlier stages. The United States relinquished its status as trading house of the world, and the American dollar, symbolic of power, was devalued under pressure from other nations. The country cut back on developmental and technological aid to other lands. Alliances expired and the military, despite its lingering exertions, began to withdraw from foreign bases.

The consensus expression of the leaders and people that was instrumental in explaining the world role from its beginning through its development and crisis may also tell us something about its end. The orthodox leaders, who maintained the world role by affirming the foundational economic, cultural, and foreign aid policies and by extending the military, and the dissenters, who fought these exertions at every turn, had opposing ideas about America's preeminent place in the world, about the nature of its power, what it consisted of and how strong it was, and how the nation's influence should be expressed. The consensus precepts that had been conceived and manifested in earlier years faced change and dispute. We should examine the dialogue between the consensus and those who opposed it, for if the consensus reformulated some of its ideas, we also need to consider whether the New Leftists ever rose above the part they played as protesters. Why did the world role end?

"Is America in Decline?"

Echoes of paramount power were clear in the 1960s. President Lyndon Johnson's account of American strength in 1964 excelled any of his predecessors: "America today is stronger than it has ever been before. It is stronger than any adversary or combination of adversaries. It is stronger than the combined might of all the nations in the history of the world. And I confidently predict that strength will continue to grow more rapidly than the might of all others." He attributed this awesome power not to the nation's factories, fields, workers, and character, but unabashedly to its military. And his documentation was statistical and quantitative.

The first area of strength the president emphasized was that the United States had "nuclear superiority." In three years, it had increased its nuclear power on alert "2½ times." The United States had more than a thousand fully armed ICBMs and Polaris missiles "ready for retaliation." It had eleven hundred strategic bombers, many of them equipped with air-to-surface missiles. "Against such force the combined destructive power of every battle ever fought by man is like a firecracker thrown against the sun," and the nuclear arsenal continued "to grow." But that was not all. The second area of strength Johnson emphasized was the capability to fight conventional wars. The United States had raised the number of divisions ready for combat by 45 percent. They could be moved swiftly around the world by an airlift capacity that had increased by 75 percent. The number of tactical aircraft had risen by more than 30 percent. The third area of strength was the ability to defeat terrorists and guerrillas. The United States had special forces trained for this duty around the world, and behind them five brigade-size support divisions stood ready. The fourth and final area was the development of new weapons. Science and technology had been applied to a Minuteman II missile with twice the accuracy of the first Minuteman. The United States was also developing the Lance missile, the EX-10 torpedo, the F-111 long-range aircraft, the A7A attack plane, a new battle tank, and a new antitank missile system. "And that effort is without parallel in all the world."[2]

In 1970 President Nixon's declaration that the United States was "the richest and strongest nation in the history of the world" resembled the claims of Harry Truman in the 1940s. The president's assistant and later secretary of state, Henry Kissinger, likewise stated as inescapable the "fact that the United States disposes of the greatest single aggregate of material power in the world." To explain the sources of this power, Kissinger drew on his work as a professor of government at Harvard. For two decades after 1945, he determined, American power had been based on "the assumption that technology plus managerial skills gave us the ability to reshape the international system." Those attributes of power, Kissinger explained, were no longer of exceptional magnitude. The overwhelming factor was military force, he calculated, particularly the gargantuan arsenal of nuclear warheads and ballistic missiles. At the same time, Nixon and Kissinger began to inform Americans that the era of their predominance, which had been dependent on American resources as well as prescriptions, had passed.[3]

On a sultry late-summer Sunday evening in Washington in August 1971, President Nixon addressed the nation from the White House to explain that the United States had to accept a new relation to the rest of the world. He listed a series of problems confounding the strength of the nation: unemployment, industries that lagged in production, inflation that had driven up the cost of living, an enfeebled dollar overseas, and a serious deficit in the nation's balance of payments. At the end of World War II, Nixon asserted, America had been unchallenged in the world. The "economies of the major industrial nations of Europe and Asia were shattered" and the United States had drawn on its wealth and power to aid the recovery of their strength. "Today, largely with our help, they have regained their vitality. They have become our strong competitors." America did not possess overwhelming economic strength; "now that other nations are economically strong, the time has come for them to bear their fair share of the burden of defending freedom around the world. The time has come for exchange rates to be set straight and for the major nations to compete as equals. There is no longer any need for the United States to compete with one hand tied behind her back." What followed was startling to those who had been accustomed to the way things were. The president speculated, "Whether this Nation stays number one in the world's economy or resigns itself to second, third, or fourth place . . . whether we hold fast to the strength that makes peace and freedom possible in this world, or lose our grip. . . ."[4]

Nixon was articulating a sensitivity to a changing national stature. Before the end of December 1971, the *New York Times* ran a page-one story by Max Frankel declaring that "the United States does not labor alone in the reconstruction of power relationships and may not be dominant in the process any more. The era initiated by World War II has ended." The "politics of the world" was "in flux"; American power was "declining." *Time* and *Life*, whose pages Henry Luce had once dedicated to the glory of power, had a difficult time coping with America's diminished influence, but *Life* made an attempt in 1971: "The pattern of world power has changed its shape. We must begin to think about our world in a new way." The emerging world did not have one great center of power, which Luce had promoted, or two centers of power, which the editors admitted having grown used to. A world "dominated and divided" by two nuclear superpowers had been "losing definition for some time," but the realization came after the fact. Foreign policy had previously "consisted in marshaling the will, ideas and money" to help friends and resist enemies, but the "end of that era finds us with our resources strained, our prestige reduced and our dollar dangerously weak."[5]

The problems of rebuilding strength proved infinitely more difficult than using power that already existed. Polls showed that the public, which had supported the costs of maintaining the world role, believed that their country had lost rather than gained ground during the late 1960s and early 1970s. The awareness of national regression was evident among groups regardless of political party, income, education, or age.[6]

The decline of material power was a problem in the main for the leaders of the orthodox consensus and their followers, rather than for the radical dissenters who were either silent on this complex problem or especially slow to express it. Tom Hayden finally wrote in 1980: "Our former power in the world is collapsing, and with it our economic security and sense of purpose." The dissenters were not terribly concerned with the creation of material power. Though, like the consensus, they had taken for granted the existence of that power, they were incessantly critical of it and condemned the misuse of its elements: the waste of resources, the exploitation of labor, and the alienation brought about by automated technology. The dissenters sought to redistribute power, not to diminish it. Their small movement, though growing in the 1960s until the early 1970s, had few assets beyond their intellectual and moral energy, in opposition to the government, the military, finance capital, and heavy industry. They had prepared to fight a monster, and it seemed inconceivable to them that the monster's power might be weakening.[7]

In the coming years American decline would be denied by some members of the orthodox leadership. In 1979 Cyrus Vance, President Jimmy Carter's secretary of state, decried the "distorted proposition" that "America is in a period of decline in the world." It was "wrong as a matter of fact but dangerous as a basis for policy." Yet in making this declaration Vance acknowledged that American sway was not what it had been. He sought balance in placing American power at a lower level than it had been. "There can be no going back to a time when we thought there could be American solutions to every problem," the secretary argued. But there was no balance. Through the 1970s Ronald Reagan insisted that the United States was no longer "number one"; "we're becoming number two in military strength." As president in the 1980s he looked curiously at the early postwar period, when "we had a monopoly on nuclear weapons and could have tried to dominate the world, but we didn't." In Reagan's telling of history, his administration had by the end of its first term restored the nation to a new equilibrium: "we halted America's decline," he said.[8]

The adjustment of 1971 did not halt world change, nor did subsequent attempts to reckon with it. For the orthodox consensus, declining power was not a passing phenomenon. It kept recurring. In 1979 *Business Week* prepared a special issue entitled "The Decline of U.S. Power," which stated that the "U.S. has been buffeted by an unnerving series of shocks that signal an accelerating erosion of power and influence." The editors wondered about the "causes of decline" and were awed by the complexity of the problem. They concluded that "by most criteria"—political, economic, monetary, and military—"the U.S.—the colossus that emerged after World War II—is now clearly facing a crisis of the decay of power." *U.S. News & World Report* presented the same jumble of factors: "U.S. military supremacy is dwindling. The once-almighty dollar is a shrunken image of its former worth, and American know-how seems to offer no escape from chronic inflation and trade deficits—or from bondage to Middle East oil, either."[9]

An intellectual movement arose around the notion of decline. In 1976, the year of America's bicentennial celebrations, Richard Rosecrance edited a collection of essays, *America as an Ordinary Country*. "The *Pax Americana* is over," he wrote. The "United States is now only first among equals, *primus inter pares* among nations." The United States had been reduced to the position of "'ordinary' or 'average' nation," he reasoned, because it could not be expected to take on its accustomed responsibility for world peacekeeping, or to support the world economy and sustain an international financial structure founded on the dollar. America's role "as maintainer of the system is at an end." The intellectuals pressed on in the 1980s. In August 1987, Paul Kennedy at Yale wrote a piece entitled "The (Relative) Decline of America" for the *Atlantic Monthly,* and that year published a sweeping book, *The Rise and Fall of the Great Powers.* His thesis was that as many nations had risen and fallen since the 1500s, the United States was the latest of them to enter a stage of relative decline, while other nations were on the rise. The idea of an "American Century," he wrote, was over. *Newsweek* queried in a title story, "Is America in Decline?" and the *New York Times Magazine* repeated the question as the title of its own cover story. The editors of *Foreign Affairs* noted that "the issue of American decline is striking a sensitive nerve."[10]

The people too had views about what was altering their national stature. In 1975 the Harris poll asked a cross section of the American people to reflect on the past sources of the nation's "greatness" and the changes they had undergone. According to this poll, the major contributions of the past included the elements of rich natural resources (91 percent agreed this was so); industrial know-how and scientific progress (90 percent); a hard-working people (87 percent); and military strength (80 percent), along with success in fighting wars (71 percent). There were also the intangible elements: people of different ideas respecting the rights of others (77 percent) and free education for all qualified students (75 percent). But when the question was asked about the future, the people felt that nearly every element was on the decline. Americans believed that they no longer possessed abundant resources and were not as hard-working or as technologically competent as they had been. The biggest drop in the people's estimation concerned rich natural resources, down 12 percent; hard-working people, down 9 percent; and industrial know-how, down 4 percent. Military strength was down 7 percent, and success in fighting wars, down 10 percent. In the 1980s the anxiety among the people grew. In discussing their views about their national standing, respondents tried to understand what was diminishing it and why: 45 percent worried, "We are slipping dangerously"; 27 percent said, "We are still No. 1, but other nations are catching up with us very quickly"; 16 percent said, "We are in a period of long-term economic decline." After years of being accustomed to preeminence, a remarkably small share, 8 percent, affirmed, "We are No. 1 and will remain the strongest, most dynamic economy in the world."[11]

No one could agree on why all this was happening or what to do about it. At the forefront of those who had once named themselves realists and who had promoted the consensus issues of a growing world role and now faced its retreat, Hans Morgenthau pressed for a reappraisal not only of the dispersal of world power but, significantly, of what constituted it. Morgenthau knew that his pursuit, begun in the 1940s, to create a science of power had attracted many followers, but now he chose to disassociate himself from those who had turned his study into what he called a pseudoscience. They had proposed their theoretical models of "systems analysis," "feedback," "input," and "output" and had attempted to reduce power to rudimentary quantifiable factors. But by quantifying power, they neglected the critical psychological forces that interfered with their models and statistics. He called for recognition of the complexity of power. He redefined power as "a quality of interpersonal relations that can be experienced, evaluated, guessed at" but was "not susceptible to quantification."[12]

The study of power was not a science, after all, Morgenthau came to realize, at least not according to the method of the natural sciences. He had once found theorists mired in history; since then they had gone to the opposite extreme and been "repelled by history." They were instead fascinated by the rational models of natural science, with which they sought to rationalize politics. Morgenthau retorted that their wayward models hearkened back to a Newtonian universe that contemporary science had left far behind. Politics, domestic and international, was "susceptible to a radically different kind of understanding from that which is appropriate to the world of nature."

Power was not the only end of mankind's affairs, Morgenthau had learned, because, he believed, people were also moral and spiritual. Once he had tried to subordinate the spirit to power, but now he had a rather different emphasis. "When we try to understand politics, we are dealing, it is true, with men in the aggregate, but with men per se—that is, as spiritual and moral beings—whose actions and reactions can be rationalized and quantitatively understood only on the lowest level of their existence. Thus what the contemporary theories of politics endeavor to exorcise as deficiencies in view of an ideal, pervasively rational theory are in truth only the ineradicable qualities of the subject matter itself. A theory that does not take them into account transforms itself into a dogma, a kind of metaphysics, regardless in what empirical or mathematical garb it is clothed."[13]

The overemphasis on material power was a predicament that Morgenthau, whatever his intention, had been a prime mover in creating. It had led him to emphasize America's dominant power and later its weakening power. Having already in the 1950s reduced the United States from the world's most powerful nation to one of the two most powerful, he had no patience with those who in the late 1960s maintained trust in American paramountcy. He took issue with Zbigniew Brzezinski, a member of the Policy Planning Council of the State Department, who declared in the summer of 1967: "This is truly the American decade." Impressed by the power of American military force, economic investments, global trade, technology, and respect abroad, Brzezinski argued that the United States should use its power to promote order in this decade while it still could. This conception, in Morgenthau's wry observation, had "whittled down Henry Luce's 'American Century' of twenty years ago to 'the American Decade.'"[14]

But when the diminution of influence did not cease a decade later, Morgenthau's concern grew. "When one reflects upon the place of the United States among the nations, one cannot escape the conclusion that, regardless of the objective facts of military power, the American position has declined," he wrote in an article entitled "The Pathology of American Power." Morgenthau's reexamination of national strength had to be faced by policymakers. Observing that shifts in strength had set the international system in tumult, Kissinger meditated: "Clearly, there is an urgent need to analyze just what is understood by power—as well as by balance of power." A full assessment of international affairs, he believed, required treatment of diverse historical traditions, social values, and economics, but these factors transcended the scope of his study and the usual thinking of political scientists or historians. What were the changing criteria of power?[15]

Consensus Support for War

The assessment of decline begins on the farthest frontier of the American alliance system, where the North Vietnamese and Vietcong inhabitants warred for control of the southern region of their country, set apart after the French left the colony. The effort at national unification by a Soviet ally living under a communist system was an intolerable blow against the American alliance, and the United States entered the conflict; and from the military exertions in that region, American power began an inexorable, reluctant, and groping retreat. The military retreat that began in Southeast Asia continued from other places and was accompanied by a withdrawal of trade, investment, and aid.

The Vietnam War, limited in scope, fought in the jungles of a divided Southeast Asian nation, and reaching into the adjacent countries of Indochina, signaled the end of the predominant American global role. Although less cataclysmic than the world war that had spawned American internationalism, the Vietnam conflict was profoundly revolutionary in nature. In the longest and the second-most-costly conflict in American history, the tremendous might of the American military machine with its technologically sophisticated armaments could not force a successful conclusion to the war. Was this military exertion the cause of decline?

Presidents Kennedy and Johnson had led the nation into the Vietnam War on the assumption that the American people would remain unified against the communist foe. A year after ascending to the presidency, Johnson found, as he noted in his memoirs, that there "*was* a consensus—a broad, deep, and genuine consensus among most groups within our diverse society—which would hold together, I hoped and prayed, long enough for the important tasks to be accomplished." Johnson labored to preserve that consensus in the 1964 presidential campaign, stating his expectation that "all Americans are going to support their country in defending our interests in the world. I have seen no evidence that our action in Viet-Nam should be made a partisan matter. I am exceedingly pleased with the unanimity with which the Congress and the people— and, if you will pardon me, the press—supported this movement."[16]

The United States went to war in Vietnam as a consequence of a protracted series of events. When the Vietnamese fought against the French in 1945, Ho Chi Minh appealed to the United States for help, but President Truman failed to respond. President Eisenhower decided not to intervene with military force to prevent the defeat of the

French forces at Dien Bien Phu in May 1954, and though he acquiesced in the Geneva agreement of July 1954 dividing Vietnam at the seventeenth parallel, he rejected the all-Vietnamese election in 1956 that had been called for under the agreement. The Kennedy administration backed the coup that ended with the assassination of the allied southern leader Ngo Dinh Diem in November 1963. The American military support for South Vietnam, which until 1960 had consisted of a few hundred advisers for training the army, increased to 17,000 personnel involved in covert war at the end of 1963. Then, early in 1965, the United States began to bomb North Vietnam. Thirty-five hundred marines landed at Da Nang in March; in July the number of combat troops was 75,000. The number continued to climb from month to month until it reached more than 510,000 early in 1968.

Essentially, American involvement in the war reflected an agreed-upon outlook—a consensus view—on the world, a view perpetuated by the president's decision making. The view accepted by Congress and the public was of the free world leader forced to resist the imminent takeover of parts of the planet by communist forces, and the focal point was the weak borderland in the frontier that ran through Vietnam. Johnson had told the people in his campaign in 1964 that his policies were unyielding, though peaceful; he was not going to send American boys to fight an Asian war. But war was the risk that the consensus faced. The official story of the war in the 1960s was that it was the product of every president's policy, regardless of party or world vision. Johnson hearkened back, "For ten years Presidents Eisenhower and Kennedy, and I have been actively concerned with threats to the peace and security of the peoples of Southeast Asia from the communist government of North Vietnam. President Eisenhower sought, and President Kennedy sought, the same objectives that I still seek."[17]

The leaders expected the consensus to be molded by the same assumptions and beliefs that had successfully united broad segments of the population over international affairs since the world role took shape. Kennedy, who never made a definitive public pronouncement about American policy in Southeast Asia, represented the United States as being, "as it has since 1945, the keystone of the arch of freedom all around the world." Americans "defending the freedom of Viet-Nam" were among those maintaining "the freedom of countries stretching all the way around from South Korea in a great half-circle to Berlin." Johnson extended that global perspective in 1964, saying that "the challenge that we face in southeast Asia today is the same challenge that we have faced with courage and that we have met with strength in Greece and Turkey, in Berlin and Korea, in Lebanon and in Cuba."[18]

The official rationale of the American effort in the war differed little from the norms that had been fundamental to American strategy. Johnson upheld the high principle of the right of self-determination for small states: "We want nothing for ourselves—only that the people of South Viet-Nam be allowed to guide their own country in their own way." Expressing outrage when several North Vietnamese torpedo boats attacked the USS *Maddox* in the Gulf of Tonkin in August 1964, the president also invoked the right of self-defense: "Aggression by terror against the peaceful villagers of

South Viet-Nam has now been joined by open aggression on the high seas against the United States of America." The justification was uncertain because American destroyers had been mounting clandestine attacks against North Vietnam, but he coupled American and South Vietnamese interests and ordered strikes against North Vietnamese naval bases. The Gulf of Tonkin Resolution, passed at Johnson's request by Congress in 1964 to authorize him to take all necessary measures in Vietnam, avowedly supported the controlling beliefs: "naval units of the Communist regime in Vietnam" had "deliberately and repeatedly attacked United States naval vessels," and the United States was attempting to assist "the peoples of southeast Asia to protect their freedom" against communist aggression.[19]

Based on these intellectual, even mythic assumptions, ingrained in the psyches of the leaders and their consensus followers, the war was an eminently rational step, the final recourse after the pacific exertions of American influence had been rebuffed and thwarted. Dean Rusk, secretary of state under both Kennedy and Johnson, contributed to the formulation of the war, but only after, he argued, the ways of peace—the support of investment capital, foreign aid, cultural importation, and diplomatic leverage—had failed. Americans, having demonstrated their willingness to aid others who were threatened, as in Greece and Korea, Rusk believed, had a "sense of responsibility" that knew "no geographical barriers." His countrymen were determined to support their commitments under SEATO, which did not include South Vietnam as a member but did cover the country by protocol in "the treaty area," according it military protection. Rusk regretted that the huge sums spent on arms had not been spent "on the development of the human and material resources of the area—the harnessing of the great Mekong River for the enrichment of the lives of all the people of this area, the building of great highways to bind the peoples of this area together in friendly intercourse, the improvement of the lot of the people themselves, those living in the country, cities, towns and villages—their health, their welfare and their education."[20]

But to Rusk, North Vietnam was an exception to the group of newly independent nations that had "come into being under the impulse of Western ideas" and aspired to democratic principles. On the contrary, North Vietnam was a renegade nation under the control of communist agitators. Because the small state of South Vietnam had no capability to make an adequate defense against aggression, Rusk asserted, the United States had the self-appointed responsibility, well known since the Truman Doctrine, which he echoed in his own formal statement: "to assist free nations of this area who are struggling for their survival against armed minorities directed, supplied and supported from without." Toward this end, Rusk put forth, the United States had been preparing its conventional military forces to deal with guerrilla warfare in South Vietnam.[21]

Johnson formed the image of Vietnam as a nation under communist siege during his 1961 mission there as vice president; he delivered a letter to the government from President Kennedy pledging American support. He returned to Vietnam as president, making two trips in strict secrecy. On his last trip, two days before Christmas 1967, during a stay in Manila, he slipped into Cam Ranh Bay, one of the great American military bases. The commander-in-chief's heavily screened, protected views of the country were not of the alluvial plains of the Mekong Delta, or of the forests of ebony and bamboo, or of the people living in the villages or working in the rice paddies, but were limited to the confines of the American enclave: the unfurled flags, the regimented barracks, and the lines of soldiers at attention. The Vietnamese, who were excluded from the base, had little idea what the commotion was about.[22]

Johnson rode around the base on the back of a jeep and walked through hospital corridors meeting the wounded. He awarded medals to Gen. William Westmoreland and the American ambassador, Ellsworth Bunker. Squinting into the sun, he addressed the assembled military men at Christmastime: "I can bring you the assurance of what you have fought to achieve: The enemy cannot win, now, in Vietnam. He can harass, he can terrorize, he can inflict casualties—while taking far greater losses himself—but he just cannot win. . . . The enemy is not beaten but he knows that he has met his master in the field. He is holding desperately—he is trying to buy time—hoping that our Nation's will does not match his will."[23]

The Dissenters Increase

For Johnson, the will of the nation was crucial to victory in the war, but even as the government anticipated that the consensus would remain firm over world affairs, the solidarity of the group in thought weakened. While the militant force of the United States failed to gain the victory Johnson desired in Vietnam, the dissenters protested the hardening consensus policies. The warnings and fears of the New Leftists seemed to them to have come true. They were at once surprised at how quickly and overwhelmingly the reversal of national fortunes had occurred; self-congratulatory that they had been right all along; and troubled by what had come to pass.

The Vietnam War brought prominence and influence to the New Left. For the thinkers who gave intellectual energy to the movement, the war vindicated the warnings they had been making since the late 1950s that American foreign policies had taken on what William Appleman Williams called a terrifying momentum toward disaster. Although countless Americans might have sincerely believed with President Johnson that their policy was peace, Williams argued, they were caught in the contradiction that no true peace could be achieved until other peoples honored historic American principles. "And so, quite naturally, once again to war to uphold the principle of self-determination, to secure the necessary access to the world marketplace, and to help the poor and the weak." The result of misguided purpose and tragic misuse of great power was, to Williams, "the horrible reality of the ever increasing death and devastation in Vietnam," which galvanized growing numbers of Americans to demand an end to the terror. Williams leveled this criticism of the war having known war. A graduate of the U.S. Naval Academy, he was a veteran of the Navy in World War II, but to him the "pulverizing destruction of a tiny nation in the name of self-determination, and the related barbarization of the once proud American Army, were gruesome and shameful ways to learn the nature of disaster."[24]

The New Left critics claimed that the Vietnam intervention confirmed their analyses of a global imperial system based in the United States. The United States had extended its power into the vacuum left by French withdrawal. But America's ruthlessness in waging a war with the most modern weaponry ever developed was a specter of imperial arrogance that exceeded the abuse of power of any former empire. Britain had once held the entire subcontinent of India with a few thousand troops. America had mobilized hundreds of thousands of soldiers to quell the rebellion of a population that was a fraction of India's. David Horowitz thought the "savage aggression" of the United States revealed more vividly than any previous military intervention the lengths to which it would go to maintain its imperial "international system," and Gabriel Kolko argued that the United States had fought in Vietnam with "increasing intensity to extend its hegemony over the world community."[25]

The war provoked questions for the New Left not only about the nature of foreign policy but also about the domestic society relating to corporate production fueling the war effort. The New Left account of the American presence in Vietnam as essentially a result of domestic economic needs of employment and profits that had to be satisfied in foreign markets explained what it saw as the ruthlessness of American imperialism. Although Vietnam was not in itself a large market, the sophisticated version of the argument was that the United States had to fight there to protect a global imperial trading system—even though that position ignored the other strategic, historical, and social formulations of the world role.

Imperialism, the thinkers of the Left expected, would force fundamental change in the American capitalist economy and domestic life. The visionaries among them thought that they glimpsed the signs of the beginning of a radical social movement. Teach-ins by professors began at universities in 1965. Draft resistance grew, and young men burned their draft cards in defiance of the law. Protests and riots shattered the complacency of the earlier decade. They looked toward "an open door for such a revolution in America."[26]

Tom Hayden's anger grew as he tried to make sense of the escalating war. Drawing on New Left intellectuals and his own experience, he looked for the roots of the American empire's "invasion" of Indochina in the national war economy and its international trade. He related the "defining conflict of our times" to the racism and poverty he had seen with his own eyes within the cities of America.[27]

Hayden's opposition to the war was reinforced by the illegal trip he made with Staughton Lynd, a Yale professor, to North Vietnam in 1965. From the moment their plane flying low over the China border brought them into Vietnam, the young men gained an image of the country distinctly different from that of Lyndon Johnson—"of delicately manicured fields, interrupted by areas of dense vegetation, a countryside developed with obvious care by generations of people." As they drove into Hanoi from the city's small airport, the people were tending fields on both sides of the road and working in the huge paddies. "If they were the quaking targets of the U.S. Air Force," the Americans did not see it. "In fact, if anyone was feeling an emotional shock it was ourselves as we entered this little world forbidden to Americans, so unknown to our people and so exposed to our military power."[28]

Lynd and Hayden saw a Vietnam that was not merely an armed camp of soldiers and cement-and-dirt bomb shelters, but also a working and determined society at war—a society that was to their eyes gentle yet hardened, sentimental yet ironic. At sunset one day, they drove south out of Hanoi for about an hour to see the war damage, fearing an air attack by their own country. They reached a bridge that had been bombed out and a town where a nursery school had been devastated by rockets. They saw the wreckage of a pagoda and talked to a monk. As they moved through broken bricks under the dark skies, "viewing the reality of war for the first time, it was difficult to believe that anything was real: the bombing, the school, the night, our own presence on such forbidden ground." Their reports echoed the American World War II dispatches from Britain, but this time the Americans had dropped the bombs.

Good will toward Americans had been disillusioned. "We like Americans," one man told Hayden, "because of their practical minds. We like Americans because of . . . Lincoln. . . . We like the American people because of their industry and science. If there was no bombing and strafing, our factory might have developed quicker." With these words, the man broke down: "The word American means something beautiful to us, but it has been difficult to say since the intervention."

Hayden sensed the Vietnamese will never to be beaten and defiance against the economic and military strength of the United States. The American troops, safe inside their guarded compounds and barracks, were vulnerable in the countryside. "We are confident," he was told, "that whatever the number of troops brought to Vietnam, the United States will not win." The Vietnamese people would "limit" the effectiveness of "most modern American weapons," including the B-52. The tactic of the "spiked trench," the Vietnamese informed him, hindered the mobility of U.S. troops, who encountered "incalculable numbers of holes—trenches filled with spikes made of bamboo" and, groping for traps with poles and prods, could not be quick on the ground. "It is impossible for a helicopter to land in a jungle; the same with a tank in a quag-mire."[29]

Hayden returned to the United States to find cities occupied by troops putting down rioters. There was war both at home and abroad, in Hayden's eyes. American bombers in Vietnam, he believed, carried on a tradition of Western imperialism that had begun with Columbus, who after all had been searching for Asia, and extended to the Indochinese the wars of genocide against the Indians on the American frontier. Hayden vented his resentment at the scale of imperial arrogance: American bombing was unprecedented in human history, the most concentrated bombing of civilian targets ever executed. The air attack on Guernica in Spain by the fascists thirty-five years before, when the world had been outraged by the deaths of eighty civilians, paled in comparison to the United States exploding more tons of air, ground, and sea munitions in Southeast Asia than it had in all of World War II. The only way to end a people's war, Hayden concluded, was to obliterate the people.[30]

In frustration, Hayden supported the communist nationals, who were trying to build a new society, and their revolutionary zeal inspired him. Following Williams, he believed that Americans thought they were fighting for self-determination but were actually fighting against it. "What America has been fighting in Vietnam is not 'aggression from the North' nor a 'civil war,' as the doves like to insist, but a *successful revolutionary nation, as valid in its claim to self-determination as any in history.*"[31]

The Radical Discontent

Far from the charred fields of Vietnam, the clouds of war cast a shadow over American society. The radicals' darkened image of this society exacerbated the unrest and defiance of authority that was breaking it apart. In the mid-1960s Allen Ginsberg began work on a long and ambitious work, *The Fall of America,* in which he wrote of his zigzagging travels across the United States by car, train, and bus. He packed his poems with the scenery of an America he saw enhanced or distorted by marijuana smoking and accompanied by rock music on the radio—he cited the songs of Bob Dylan, the Beatles, and the Kinks, and the tune Eve of Destruction. He mocked the nation's leaders for their sad folly as he watched them dig deeply into a hole: Robert McNamara for his wrong guesses, Dean Rusk and Maxwell Taylor for advocating war, and Lyndon Johnson for the bad advice he accepted. He lashed out at the violence condoned by Hanson Baldwin, *"The distinguished military Editor of the New York Times,"* for printing that the allies were winning and that the enemy was being hurt. But, he thought, "Arguing with a schizophrenic is hopeless."

One of his poems opened on a train crossing the American midsection in the summer of 1966, a train passage not unlike that made by Jacques Barzun over a decade before. And the intent to capture America was not different from Archibald MacLeish's—though the war had disillusioned MacLeish too, for he now questioned whether the Great Republic had betrayed its promise as a Great Power. But Ginsberg's image was radically changed. This landscape was not celebratory, expansive, and grandiose; it was introverted, twisted, and confused. The scene of "Iron Horse" opened, as had Barzun's *God's Country and Mine,* behind a closed window shade on a railway car. Barzun opened his shade to look out right away; Ginsberg hesitated, focusing on himself inside.

> This is the creature I am!
>> Sittin in little roomette Sante Fe train
>> naked abed, bright afternoon sun light
>>> leaking below closed window-blind . . . .

When he eventually turned to "watch the landscape" outside, he saw nothing notable—
a truck driver, "a tree," spinach fields. Instead, with an inner strife and the pursuit of
self-gratification he describes came outward preoccupation in war, but the country was
wrong, uninformed, and misdirected, he thought. Everyone he encountered on the train
liked the war but him.

> A consensus around card table beer—
>> "It's my country,
>>> better fight 'em over there than here,"
>> afraid to say "No it's crazy
>>> everyone's insane—
>>>> This country's Wrong,
>>> the Universe, Illusion."

>> Soldiers gathered round
>>> saying—"my country
> and they say I gotta fight,
>> I have no choice,
>>> we're in it too deep to pull out,
>>>> if we lose,
>> there's no stopping the Chinese communists,
>>> We're fightin the communists, aren't we?
>>> Isn't that what it's about?"

On this journey, he realized the stakes were finally the fall of America:

> Lightning's blue glare fills Oklahoma plains,
> the train rolls east
>> casting yellow shadow on grass
>>>> Twenty years ago
> approaching Texas
>> I saw
>>> sheet lightning
>>>> cover Heaven's corners
>> Feed Storage Elevators in gray rain mist,
>>> checkerboard light over sky-roof
> same electric lightning South
>> follows this train
>>> Apocalypse prophesied—
> the Fall of America
>> signaled from Heaven—

Here in 1966 was this troubled poet on a train, the major poet of the Beat Generation,
prophesying what the proper leaders would never believe:

Too late, too late
> the Iron Horse hurrying to war,
>> too late for laments
>>> too late for warning—[32]

Young Americans thought differently about their American landscape than their elders once had. In his mid-twenties in 1968, Jacob Brackman, chosen by *Esquire* as a spokesman for his generation, caught the film on television that he had first seen in 1952, when he started going to the movies alone: MGM's *It's a Big Country*. He felt "short-circuited back to a past" he "scarcely recalled." This movie full of the optimistic, confident images of a big country set Brackman thinking about how America had changed—or perhaps how he or his generation had changed—in the sixteen years during which he had entered young manhood and angry youths had burned city blocks, students had occupied great universities, and draft resisters had gone into exile in Canada. He wrote in almost stream of consciousness: "At night, sometimes, I used to think about how lucky I was to have been born here. My own relation to America was strong and clear. Of course I knew that there were imperfections, vast ones, but I thought almost everybody good . . . wanted to change what was bad. I was ready to work, too, and I thought of our problems: 'We'll lick 'em.'"

In the film, "'Indians' were mentioned once," in a recitation of all the different kinds of Americans. Although it was a "'sweeping panorama' no Negro was seen. . . . Squalor was a homey testing ground for pluck, a purgatory short enough to make heaven seem the cozier. The Korean War did not exist. . . . I went to lots of movies as a kid; I could never have guessed that this one, for all its garish mediocrity, influenced me as much, or confirmed as much for me, as any book I ever read." It was not so much that Brackman disbelieved the film as that its image of America had become increasingly remote from reality. "I wish I could have seen it annually, throughout my adolescence, to graph my departure from its lovely vision." He parted company with those who saw poverty as a toughening up on the road to success, racism as a dying aberration in the South, and war as forced on Americans by ruthless foreigners. The new generation, Brackman thought, saw these problems not as accidental but as institutional, imbedded in American society, requiring enormous change and new definitions of living and maturity.[33]

Abbie Hoffman too found a tarnished image of America, and he contrasted it to the one Lyndon Johnson projected in a picture book compiled in 1966 called *This America*. It was a book full of Great Society views—of farms, cities, and faces—accompanied by a text of Johnson's impressions. The first double-page photograph was a black-and-white scene of the stark, open plains, captioned: "For this is what America is all about." To Hoffman, Johnson had made a mess even of this picture book, let alone the society. How could a desolate landscape that looked "like the other side of the moon, cold, sterile, not a living, breathing thing" be what America was all about? It was clear that Johnson had in mind a symbol for the frontier's uncrossed desert or the unclimbed ridge of tomorrow, but Johnson's platitudes left Hoffman unmoved.[34]

Hoffman's own image of America, devoid of any grandeur, emerged in a description of the ins and outs of traveling across "Amerika" on "$0 a day." Even the spelling was meant to liken America to a fascist state to be resisted, and in turn exploited. Hoffman encouraged hippies hitchhiking cross-country to steal from restaurants or to hoodwink supermarkets by eating in the aisles. Or they could go on welfare, which Hoffman thought was so easy to get in many states that "anyone who is broke and doesn't have a regular relief check coming in is nothing but a goddam lazy bum."[35]

Despite this absurd vision of their "Amerika," the hippies became a social force against the war. They tended to be nonviolent and escapist, seeking revolution in drugs rather than overt subversion of the government. The hippies shared the leftist radicals' opposition to the Vietnam War, but they lacked further unity. "I was once in the New Left," Hoffman said, "but I outgrew it. Or perhaps it outgrew me. We differ on many things." He did not like "the concept of a movement built on sacrifice, dedication, responsibility, anger, frustration and guilt." Instead, he advocated more sex, drug taking, and quitting school and jobs. The hippie life appealed to the thousands of youths who, like Hoffman, attended mass concerts, where they listened to rock music, smoked marijuana, and sought love.[36]

Beneath the hippies' levity seethed anger at the senselessness of the killing and destruction of war. The romantic pursuit of peace and love—"Do your own thing" and "Make love, not war"—was a mockery of the "realism" of military policy. Hoffman compared John Foster Dulles to the Nazi Adolf Eichmann, who was convicted of war crimes by an Israeli court and hanged in 1962. As the hippies, like the Left, turned against the leaders of their own nation, they empathized with the enemies. They idolized Mao Zedong of China and Che Guevara and Fidel Castro of Cuba. Hoffman rooted for the Vietcong as underdogs in their attack on the U.S. Embassy, a feat that "crew-cut generals in shiny limousines and million-dollar planes that zoom by" had thought impossible. "America will lose more than its face in Vietnam rice paddies hunting jackknife warriors with napalm machines. Where will be our Alamos? Where even our brave men planting flag on Iwo Jima hilltop?"[37]

Martin Luther King came to oppose the war slowly, first speaking out against it in the spring of 1967, reluctant to hurt his cause of civil rights at home by criticizing the nation abroad. But when he did oppose the war, he was vociferous exactly because of civil rights. The poverty programs for the poor, both black and white, were diminished because of the war priorities. He regretted that young black men were fighting eight thousand miles away "to guarantee liberties in Southeast Asia which they had not found in southwest Georgia and East Harlem." In addition, King opposed the war because, as he walked among the agitated young men who rioted in city ghettos and told them of his nonviolent principles, they asked—rightly, King thought—"what about Vietnam?" They asked whether "our own nation wasn't using massive doses of violence to solve its problems." King believed that he could never again raise his voice "against the violence of the oppressed in the ghettos without having first spoken clearly to the greatest purveyor of violence in the world today: my own government."[38]

King applied his belief in nonviolence directly to Vietnam. His thoughts went to the enemy people living through the war, and he sought to understand their concerns and to give them voice. "They must see the Americans as strange liberators." The Vietnamese had quoted the American Declaration of Independence to proclaim their independence, but the American government "felt then that the Vietnamese people weren't ready for independence." The Americans were not only fighting against their own ideals but had fallen victim to "deadly Western arrogance." The people of Vietnam knew America by the bombs it dropped, the concentration camps it put Vietnamese into, the water it poisoned, the crops it killed, and the casualties from its firepower.

King's judgment was that the United States had "no honorable intentions in Vietnam." Its "minimal expectation" was to occupy Vietnam "as an American colony. . . . Somehow this madness must cease. We must stop now. I speak as a child of God and brother to the suffering poor of Vietnam. . . . I speak for the poor of America who are paying the double price of smashed hopes at home and death and corruption in Vietnam."[39]

King called on everyone "of humane convictions" to "protest": "We are at the moment when our lives must be placed on the line if our nation is to survive its own folly." The war was a symptom of disease within "the American spirit." The war was corrupting American society, but not as in Paul Goodman's description in *Growing up Absurd* of "spiritual emptiness": the malady was explicit "spiritual evil." King knew that some radicals glorified violence, and he felt that the "extreme conduct" of the hippies illuminated "the negative effect of society's evils on sensitive young people." Yet he hoped for some redeeming qualities from these dissenters. The hippies might contribute their "vision of peaceful means to a goal of peace." From the radicals might come commitment, "the burning sense of urgency, the recognition of the need for direct and collective action."[40]

The war united these radicals—the intellectuals, students, and hippies, civil rights advocates, feminists, and pacifists, young and old, affluent and poor—and they came together in thought and on the streets in huge demonstrations. The Pentagon, the center of military command, was a prime target. On a brisk fall day in bright sunshine on October 21, 1967, more than fifty thousand demonstrators marched through the nation's capital to the Pentagon. They came up against lines of Federal marshals backed by soldiers armed with rifles fixed with bayonets. The surging crowd shouted obscenities and threw eggs and bottles. At the rally at the Lincoln Memorial before the trek to the Pentagon, the pediatrician Bejamin Spock had said that the enemy "is Lyndon Johnson, whom we elected as a peace candidate in 1964, and who betrayed us within three months, who has stubbornly led us deeper and deeper into a bloody quagmire in which uncounted hundreds of thousands of Vietnamese men, women and children have died, and 13,000 young Americans, too." A student activist led the crowd in a chant of "Hell, no, we won't go." Reporters noted that only a sprinkling of the participants were past the age of thirty, and the youths carried signs: "LBJ—how many kids did you kill today?" "Where Is Oswald When We Need Him?" Jerry Rubin was an organizer of the protest, and the hippies requested a permit to levitate the Pentagon three hundred feet off the ground by chanting ancient Aramaic exorcism rites. Seeking to delegitimize the Pentagon by mocking it, they fantasized that they could raise the building into the air, where it would turn orange and vibrate until its evil emissions had fled. The accommodating administrator who heard their request gave permission for them to raise the building a maximum of ten feet. Hoffman described the situation absurdly: "The Pentagon vibrates and begins to rise . . . . Sergeant Pepper asks the band to play *The Star Spangled Banner*."

As the crowd built up around the Pentagon, flying wedges of the demonstrators rushed toward an entrance. A final desperate charge breached the security lines and met the rifle butts of the guards inside. At least ten invaders managed to penetrate the building before they were repulsed.

Some 250 people, including the novelist Norman Mailer and the feminist Dagmar Wilson, were arrested. As darkness fell, the protesters built bonfires and burned draft cards.[41]

The Consensus Breaks

When old assumptions and aspirations had lost their ability to keep diverse groups together, many members of the old consensus rejected their once virtually uncritical support of policies abroad. The aging consensus thinkers of the late 1940s and 1950s watched the bitter experience of Vietnam and its devastating repercussions at home. For a group that had guided the country at a pinnacle of power, the specter of tragic discord provoked grave doubts. This was not the way consensus policies had been meant to develop. In their disenchantment, some turned to the precepts of the New Left to comprehend the loss of the American position abroad. If their increasing numbers did not march in the streets or participate in protest rallies that drew tens of thousands in the cities of New York and Washington, they sided with the radicals to pursue the common end of altering the American world role as it had developed.[42]

Consensus historians began to divide among themselves, but they commonly approached America at a crossroads. By the time Daniel Boorstin was finishing the third and final volume of his *The Americans* in 1973, he all but ignored the Vietnam War, which did not fit in with the keynote of destiny that had begun his first book in 1957, on the colonies. The final volume concluded with a section on America as a great power, and Boorstin still wrote about destiny and mission, to which he added a "sense of momentum," meaning that the size and speed of the nation had continued to increase in the world. The American boast, he said, was how big everything was here and how fast everything moved. "The United States was a large and speedy nation; Americans knew it, and for the most part, they loved it." Growth was still "ever more and faster," and that seemed to have become "the nation's whole purpose." In his occasional essays, Boorstin disparaged the dissenters as the "New Barbarians," but there was no sense of decline here, only perpetual expansion, as if the momentum were not in America's world role but in his own thesis.[43]

Although Boorstin held firm, his fellow consensus historians had doubts. In the late 1960s Richard Hofstadter, a pioneer of the consensus school who had seen American power as a clear reflection of democratic harmony, tackled an analysis of domestic turmoil that he considered overdue. He concluded his *American Violence* with the present predicament. "In fact almost everything depends upon external forces which no one dares to predict: the tempo at which we disengage from Vietnam, the national and international response to our undisguisable failure there, and our ability to avoid another such costly venture." Hofstadter never resolved his disturbed feelings before his early death in 1970. Like him, Arthur Schlesinger, Jr., who had felt that the hope of the world lay in the American experience, now observed that it did not offer the outside world all that much. The "American failure in Vietnam" was "an expensive and horrible education," teaching him that even a superpower could not "run two crusades at once— that we cannot wage even a small war against an underdeveloped country and at the same time move creatively to meet the problems of our own land."[44]

Historical concern about decline received attention in Andrew Hacker's *The End of the American Era*. In 1970 Hacker—whose father, Louis M. Hacker, had written *The Triumph of American Capitalism* in 1940—took a bleak view: not just America's power was at stake, but also its very nationhood and survival. "A nation's decline may be under way even as its power and prosperity seem at their greatest." Hacker saw decline in the corporations that were breeding "superfluous" unemployed Americans; in racial violence that threatened civil war; in self-indulgent individualism that made the people unfit for consensus; in families that were torn by divorce and a weakening of parental authority; in diminished standards among scholars that produced trivia rather than knowledge. The beguiling thesis of postwar consensus historians like Hartz—that America's lack of a feudal past exempted it from constraints—had led to an individualism of self-indulgence lacking in patriotism. Americans had been instructed that "America was different, that what has happened to other nations could never happen to us." Expectations of exceptionalism only resulted in bewilderment when war brought it all home: "The growing unpopularity of the Vietnam involvement resulted chiefly because many Americans began to sense that their nation no longer had a lesson to impart." He concluded, "America's history as a nation has reached its end."[45]

Under the impact of foreign policy debacles, historical parallels between American internationalism and the exploits of past world empires recalled that Greece, Rome, and the British Empire had not been eternal. President Nixon traveled around the country in the early 1970s to warn Americans that he sensed the United States had reached a point not unlike that faced by past great empires at their peaks. Nixon's study of history had taught him that after empires had achieved affluence and risen to world greatness, they declined; he permitted himself to think about what Truman never had the patience to consider: "I think of what happened to Greece and Rome. . . . What has happened, of course, is that great civilizations of the past, as they have become wealthy, as they have lost their will to live, to improve, they then have become subject to the decadence which eventually destroys a civilization. The United States is now reaching that period." His warning of decline was entwined with a fear that the United States would lose the first war in its history in Vietnam.[46]

Kissinger, knowing that Nixon had read Toynbee, gave him an edition of Spengler's *Decline of the West*, explaining that he wanted to introduce the president to another approach to civilization. While not agreeing entirely with Spengler's conclusion, Kissinger was stimulated by the perception that civilizations rise and fall, following "a certain rhythm and a certain sequence of events." Trained as a historian, Kissinger was "conscious of the fact that every civilization that has ever existed has ultimately collapsed," and he admitted to having "a sense of the inevitability of tragedy." As a statesman he was compelled to act on the assumption that problems had to be solved, but Americans were challenged by "huge problems." The reason he discussed Spengler with President Nixon was "to emphasize that the manifestations of events which come up in the form of tactical decisions are very often quite misleading and that a statesman has to understand what the trend of events is" in the context of the "total culture."[47]

The United States "now stands for what Rome stood for," Toynbee had stated during a 1960s North American lecture trip on the eve of the buildup of military forces in Vietnam. "Rome consistently supported the rich against the poor in all foreign communities that fell under her sway; and, since the poor, so far, have always and everywhere been far more numerous than the rich, Rome's policy made for inequality, for injustice, and for the least happiness of the greatest number. America's decision to adopt Rome's role has been deliberate. . . . I miss the enthusiasm and the confidence that made the old revolutionary America irresistible." America, he said, had risen to a high position in its turn after Britain. "The British have, I should say, already made all those mistakes that the Americans are now making, or may now be in danger of making. Britain's position in the World in the nineteenth century had, after all, a good deal in common with America's position in the World today. The load on British shoulders then was not, I suppose, as heavy as the present load on American shoulders. Your present position is a bit more lonely and a good deal more responsible than ours has ever been. Still, we have had a foretaste of your present experience; and it has been a close enough foretaste to throw a present-day Englishmen into a fit of fear and trembling."[48]

Toynbee had once envisioned the United States dividing the world with the communist bloc, but he was left in awe at the frustration of United States power in Vietnam. The United States had brought to bear against this little country "the mightiest military machine that there has ever been so far," and all the resources of American science and technology had been applied to arming of that military with "ingeniously inhuman weapons." No country in history had ever been devastated more ruthlessly than Vietnam, Toynbee said, evidently including states like Carthage, wiped out of existence by Rome. Yet, he puzzled, North Vietnam and the Vietcong had successfully withstood the huge deployment of American military might, a whole inventory of conventional weapons that included napalm bombs. More than that, they had "thrown the American forces in Vietnam on the defensive; their latest feat has been to shake the stability of the dollar." How, he wondered, had the Vietnamese achieved this?[49]

The reason, Toynbee observed, was that America's image of itself in the world was a mirage. The Vietnamese were not the advance guard of monolithic world communism on the march, because that monolith did not exist. The force with which Americans had joined in battle was not world communism but Vietnamese patriotism. The Vietnamese were fighting a foreign intruder the way Americans had once fought their own Revolutionary War. The Americans were not fighting a crusade but "a modern colonial war of the kind that was waged by European powers for more than four centuries," beginning with the Spanish conquest of Mexico and Peru and continuing until France's failure to hold Algeria by force of arms. Once full of clear-sighted idealism, Americans had denounced European colonialism, "and this on the whole with justice," Toynbee added. Now the United States had "started to try to build up a colonial empire" of its own in eastern Asia. Americans might reject that charge, but, Toynbee found, they had already accomplished the first step toward their empire by setting up their own puppet "native" governments. No matter how Americans viewed their presence in Vietnam, to the Vietnamese "European" meant "Western," and "Western" included "American." Toynbee agreed with the Vietnamese: "America has embarked on colonialism at the moment when colonialism has been proved to be no longer practicable." The implications of American colonialism were astounding, he wrote, for even if the Americans prevailed, they had lost. The "Vietnamese resistance movement has made history; and this piece of history could not be undone even if Vietnam were to be wiped out." In Vietnam the Americans had challenged a "spiritual force," and their only salvation was to admit a terrible mistake, for "the sands are running out."[50]

By the time he died in 1975, Toynbee's disillusion with America as a world power was nearly complete. Toward the end of 1972 James Reston looked him up in St. James' Square in London for a judgment about where things then stood in world history, and though he found the old gentleman in his eighties rather frail and his hair turned white, his eyes were bright and energetic. He talked to Reston like a schoolmaster, caring but skeptical, and the subject of America made the teacher not only disappointed but sad: "It was, he says, the new Jerusalem, the great center of both power and idealism. But now, particularly since the war in Vietnam, it seems very much like the other imperial powers, more interested in its power than in its ideals." America had offered so much, and still did with its invention and modern technology and the trade it had fostered, even as other nations had matched its technology and surpassed it in trade surpluses. Toynbee even found some hope in the elusive dreams of the hippies for a peaceful ideal world. A consolation to him was that some of the young were "rejecting the materialistic goal of life and turning to simpler ways." But on the whole he seemed "pessimistic about the West" and hoped "not for a revival of orthodox faith, but for an ethical reformation" that would come out of the spiritual needs of the contemporary Western world. He would not be present to see this reformation, the aged man said, but he believed in the regeneration of nations.[51]

The radical Left and other discontents found much to ponder in Toynbee's interpretations of world history. David Horowitz, agreeing wholeheartedly with the Englishman's comparison between the United States and Rome, rephrased his words in 1965 so that they applied directly to America. American policy, he stated bluntly, "made for inequality, for injustice, and for the least happiness of the greatest number." What might be misleading Americans, Sen. J. William Fulbright stated in 1966, was the idea of "being responsible for the whole world . . . just as the sense of universal responsibility turned the heads of ancient Romans and nineteenth-century British." The uses and abuses of power ultimately became a question of decline. Sen. Eugene McCarthy turned around the classic formula of the 1940s from the perspective of the late 1960s: "throughout history, mighty nations have learned the limits of power. There are lessons to be learned from Athens, from Rome, from sixteenth-century Spain, and from England and France in this century."[52]

A prosperous American society had been characterized by David Riesman as outward-looking. By 1969 he had come to believe that Americans should not simply "shift away from spending on war and preparation for war" but should further divert wealth to meet pressing domestic needs, including health care, housing, welfare, and control of environmental pollution. The costs of meeting these needs, "even if the war in Vietnam were to be ended," Riesman feared, "would greatly exceed even our massive production in the foreseeable future." And David Potter reflected on the corresponding social dissatisfaction that troubled his people of plenty. What had happened to the postwar America that had progressed "on many fronts—industrial, and technological, and scientific"—and "had passed from triumph to triumph," assuring Americans of the "invulnerability" of their political system? He worried that the domestic protest and divisiveness endangered "our public policy as never before."[53]

In one of the last essays he wrote before his death in 1971, Reinhold Niebuhr considered his disillusion with the realist view of power he had advocated in the early postwar era. Rebellious ideas that he had begun to develop in the late 1950s had been verified by the war in the 1960s. "Perhaps there is not so much to choose between communist and anticommunist fanaticism," he remarked, "particularly when the latter, combined with our wealth, has caused us to stumble into the most pointless, costly and bloody war in our history." Niebuhr remembered that his support of realism had inadvertently helped bring about the current tragic consequences, for that realism was, "like all realism, excessively consistent. It is one of the mysteries of human nature that while most of us are unconscious of an inevitable mixture in our motives, we try to atone for this error by a too consistent emphasis on 'the law in our members which wars against the law that is in our minds.' "[54]

In Congress, a number of Republican and Democratic senators, led by Senator Fulbright, were repulsed by the war. As chairman of the Senate Foreign Relations Committee, he used its investigative authority to develop an alternative source of interpretation to the administration. The evolution in his thought began in 1964, when he believed that the regime of South Vietnam might be bolstered to prosecute the war, that withdrawal of American troops was unrealistic, and that an expansion of the conflict should not be ruled out. "It should be clear to all concerned that the United States will continue to defend its vital interests with respect to Vietnam," he stated with an assurance that sounded like Lyndon Johnson's. By 1966 Fulbright had boldly asserted that the United States had overextended itself in Vietnam and had come to suffer from the corrosive effects he described in *The Arrogance of Power*. The United States was following a grotesque policy in Vietnam to prove that it would not have its power intimidated. While as yet he thought that no responsible critic of the war or any member of the Senate advocated a disorderly American withdrawal and abandonment of South Vietnam, he favored a "peace short of victory." "It is precisely because of America's enormous strength and prestige that we can afford to be magnanimous in Vietnam."[55]

As the war dragged on without success, by the early 1970s Fulbright recognized in Vietnam a futile crusade that had drained Americans of confidence and strength. America was a "crippled giant." "How did the United States, the greatest and strongest nation on the face of the earth, allow itself to be reduced" to such circumstances? He objected to the explanation of policymakers that the United States had global responsibilities which compelled it to bear burdens that no one else would. "Power is a narcotic, a potent intoxicant, and America has been on a 'trip,'" he said, using a word popular among hippie and radical drug users. About ending the war, he stated categorically: "It does not matter a great deal *how* it is ended."[56]

George Kennan came to believe that his entire containment principle had been misunderstood by policymakers. Long out of government, he lamented the overemphasis on military power by those who had come to make the decisions of war and peace, and the overextension of power in regions that overstretched the globe, as far as Vietnam. He felt "like one who has inadvertently loosened a large boulder from the top of a cliff and now helplessly witnesses its path of destruction in the valley below, shuddering and wincing at each successive glimpse of disaster." In his own mind, Kennan wrestled over how clearly he had foreseen the danger of war in 1947. But he took refuge in the belief that he could not have clarified what he meant at the time, because of his official position in government.

Later Kennan admitted that the errors of omission in his article were so egregious that he bore "responsibility for the greatest and most unfortunate of the misunderstandings to which they led." In the late 1960s, as he read over Walter Lippmann's 1940s attacks on the Mr. "X" article, he came so far as to believe that Lippmann had actually said what Kennan himself had wanted to say. The misunderstanding between them, he reflected, was "almost tragic in its dimensions." Lippmann's criticism of the universalism of the Truman Doctrine, and of the militaristic risks of containment, were points that Kennan appropriated, admitting that they "would figure prominently in my own later writings. He saw them, for the most part, long before I did. I accept blame for misleading him." Containment had been twisted and distorted into a militaristic overextension of power, and its use by policymakers was all wrong: "I emphatically deny the paternity of any efforts to invoke that doctrine today," he wrote in 1967, "in situations to which it has, and can have, no proper relevance."[57]

Among the public, during the Kennedy presidency and the early years of the Johnson administration, many Americans barely noticed the intervention in Vietnam. Opinion predominantly supported the war; then it shifted dramatically. In 1968, 62 percent of those surveyed supported fighting on, while 31 percent wanted to end the war. In 1971 a clear majority of 55 percent wanted the United States to disengage from Vietnam even at the risk of an eventual communist takeover, while 36 percent favored continuing the war. An emergent but undeveloped counterconsensus, supported by the young and inspired by the New Left, threatened to oppose the old consensus over the issue of the war. In 1971 those in their twenties were more opposed to continuing the American effort than any other age group, even though as recently as 1968 nearly three-fourths of them had favored fighting to ensure the survival of a noncommunist regime in South Vietnam. Partisan differences between Democrats and Republicans were consistently nonexistent. The war was singled out by two out of three Americans as the issue that had sparked the radical protest in the streets.[58]

After 1968, a year marked by assassinations, massive rioting, and demonstrations at home and by the communist Tet offensive in Vietnam, the rising group of dissenters resulted in a schism that divided and troubled the country and impeded action by the leaders as in no other war since the United States had become a world power. The New Left spoke of revolution, while the inflexible consensus leaders took a stand for "law and order." The divisions widened. The dissenters posed a threat to the effectiveness of the government policies. As president, Nixon found that the "American domestic consensus" had been "strained by 25 years of global responsibilities." The difference was "very fundamental" between his decision to invade Cambodia and prolong the Vietnam War, Nixon stated, and the decisions leaders had once made for victory in World War II, for a conclusion to the action in Korea, and for the removal of Soviet nuclear missiles from Cuba. In previous decisions "the American people were not assailed by counsels of doubt and defeat from some of the most widely known opinion leaders of the Nation."[59]

In the eyes of the government and its supporters, the dissenters had to be discredited or silenced, and the loyal members of the old consensus stood together. Having established the correctness of its policies, the government had incapacitated itself from questioning them. At first the consensus did not take the New Left seriously, treating it like a bothersome mosquito rather than a hive of bees on the swarm. The consensus respected the right of small groups to protest under protection of the Constitution and the courts. When the escalation of the war continued in 1965, the government did not respond significantly. Even after the demonstration at the Pentagon, President Johnson at a press conference in November 1967 was mild, if agitated, in his rebuke of domestic adversaries: "There has always been confusion, frustration, and difference of opinion when there is a war going on." He talked about the American Revolution, which about a third of the people had opposed. He recited the opposition of New England states to the War of 1812, the bitter speeches in Congress against the Mexican War, the pressure on Lincoln to work out a compromise with the seceding southern states in the Civil War, and the problems endured by Wilson in World War I. But, in retrospect, Johnson contended, these wars had been right, and now, he was adamant, he too was right, regardless of public opinion. He did not then realize that the building opposition would be stronger than at any time since the Civil War itself. "We believe very strongly," he stated, "in preserving the right to differ in this country, and the right to dissent. . . . We welcome responsible dissent. . . . I have never said anyone was unpatriotic. I don't question these people's motives. I do question their judgment. I can't say that this dissent has contributed much to any victories we have had."[60]

Within the Johnson administration it largely fell to McGeorge Bundy, the president's brilliant assistant for national security, to defend the government's policies against critics on several occasions. Johnson dubbed him "my debater," and he became what *Time* called "a chief public articulator of U.S. aims and purposes." Early on, when the administration was almost complacent about the criticism as part of the dialogue in a free society, Bundy participated in debates at universities and against serious consensus critics.[61]

One of Bundy's most riveting exchanges was in 1965 with Hans Morgenthau, the intellectual giant of power politics, who already thought the Vietnam War misguided. The debate, which included other participants, was moderated by Eric Sevareid and broadcast on CBS television. Why did Bundy want to risk public debate of official policy in wartime? Certainly no such debate would have been necessary after Pearl Harbor. Bundy was there, he said, "Most of all because I believe with all my heart that the policy which the United States is now following is the best policy in a difficult and dangerous situation and the one which best serves our interests and the interests of the world, the interest of peace."

"I am opposed to our present policy in Vietnam," Morgenthau countered, "on moral, military, political and general intellectual grounds." This was for him more than a question of one of the greatest powers in the world fighting a minor power; his old theories of power might have been expected to predetermine the outcome of such a conflict. Now he was talking about morality again, and he was convinced that the policy could not achieve the results desired by the administration. Quite to the contrary, he went on, "it will create problems much more serious than those which we have faced in the recent past."

Bundy, quoting the president, cited the need to keep a commitment to help defend the Vietnamese, and also to strengthen world order around the globe, "from Berlin to Thailand." The argument of a commitment did not count, Morgenthau replied, because the United States had in effect installed the government in Saigon, the Diem regime. It was as if "we have contracted with ourselves," not the Vietnamese. Furthermore, the Vietnamese demonstrated no abundant public support for the American intervention.

Bundy and Morgenthau disputed the fundamental nature of the war. Morgenthau insisted that the conflict was a civil war that did not warrant American intervention. A revolt in the South was being aided by the North. Bundy said that Morgenthau was simply wrong. It was an international war, and Ho Chi Minh had announced it to be so.

Morgenthau was concerned about the consequences of American policy. Americans, he said, were in Vietnam to contain communism, according to the notion that "if we don't stop it there we will have to stop it elsewhere"—"in Hawaii or perhaps in California." Americans were in Vietnam as part and parcel of Kennan's containment policy, which was bound to fail in Asia. In Europe "you could draw a line across a map and tell the Soviet Union, 'Until here and not farther.'" The struggle in South Vietnam had no bearing on "whether or not Indonesia will go Communist, or Tanzania in Africa will go Communist, or Colombia will go Communist." The problem was the overextension of the United States: "the success of our policy of military containment in Europe" had "led us into the fallacy to apply the same instruments to a situation which is entirely different and where such instruments cannot succeed."

As for a future course, Bundy insisted that Americans should stay in Vietnam until the task was done. Morgenthau's stand: "I think our aim must be to get out of Vietnam, but to get out of it with honor."[62]

Less than a year later, in early 1966, Bundy resigned from the White House staff and left government. Only in 1968, during the closing days of the administration, did he declare his doubts. Even while defending his 1965 decisions in 1968, he proposed reducing the number of troops and halting the bombing, not because of the damage to Vietnam but because of the damage to America. Americans "must begin to lift this burden from our lives," said Bundy, now the president of the Ford Foundation, in a symposium on law, liberty, and progress at DePauw University in Indiana. Further escalation of the war was no option; its "penalties upon us all are much too great." Americans would not support the cost and sacrifice for another period of years. "It is now plainly unacceptable that we should continue with annual costs of $30 billion and an annual rate of sacrifice of more than 10,000 American lives. It is equally wrong to accept the increasing bitterness and polarization of our people." He felt "a special pain in the growing alienation of a generation which is the best we have had. So we must not go on as we are going." American power was overwhelming, Bundy said, but the "primitive but tightly controlled" North Vietnamese society and its military had not been broken by the force already applied by the United States. Only nuclear weapons might achieve a military solution, he suggested, but that course had been rejected as the "worst kind of folly." No foreign force could win this battle.[63]

Domestic Schism

But the strict consensus discipline of the New Left and hippies had begun, and they felt it. After the Chicago riots in 1968, the disorder in the streets across the nation worried those in power, even some who supported the dissenters' ends. Committees of notables investigated the revolt and demanded to know the reasons for the end of consensual tranquility. One was the National Commission on the Causes and Prevention of Violence; another was the House of Representatives Committee on Un-American Activities. In 1968 both forums asked the radicals to defend their radicalism, to those whose power they challenged. As Bundy had defended the orthodox view, Tom Hayden defended the dissenting view.[64]

This time, to their faces, Hayden questioned the very legitimacy of his elders in government, and of their hearings and their authority. "Frankly, I think that it is very difficult for a person in my position to believe that you are actually prepared to study the real causes of violence as I see them in the country. There are no young people on the commission, no student activists, no draft resisters, no outspoken critics of the draft." Why had he come? To state for the record that "the sources of violence in this country are to be found in the war on Vietnam" and to instruct his interrogators that they should be studying the war rather than student protest movements, draft resistance, or the antiwar movement. "And in a deeper sense," he went on, "violence in this country stems from a system which is sick, which is racist, which apparently has a boundless ambition to police the world, which is therefore losing authority and legitimacy in the eyes of millions of young people in this country and many millions more of people around the world, a system which relies more and more on the use of force, on the use of police to maintain itself rather than relying on consent or persuasion or traditional techniques of democracy."[65]

Hayden pleaded for defiance of the government because the war had been decided upon without the consent of the people, and he implicated more than merely a "small presidential circle that meets on Tuesdays for lunch at the White House." He assumed, as did C. Wright Mills, that foreign policy was the product of a power elite, combining "the Pentagon, the armed services, the intelligence operations, defense contractors, and private investors," agencies that were "essentially private and independent bureaucracies shielded from, and secret from, the public." Hayden further believed that they interfered in "the internal politics of other nations without the knowledge of the American public" and obtained "billions of dollars for their own purposes without public accountability."

In consequence, politicians had relinquished their authority. Dean Rusk, Lyndon Johnson, Richard Nixon, and Hubert Humphrey were "already finished," because they had "no respect from wide sections of the American people." Hayden compared this leadership to the Nazis who had controlled the people of Germany, the majority of whom had been uninformed about what was going on. In both cases, Hayden argued, the government was illegitimate. Therefore, Americans had a right to resist the manufacturers of armaments, just as the Germans should have resisted the Nazis who controlled gas chambers.

These assertions ruffled the leaders, many of whom had fought against the very totalitarian governments Hayden compared them to. Didn't Hayden deep down think these comparisons between a democratic republic like America and a dictatorship as brutal as Nazi Germany were far-fetched? Hayden admitted no doubts. He pressed his belief that his radical movement was a way for the people to voice their will after being thwarted in elections by politicians who made the decisions for war in secret. Hayden did not think that he was taking his freedom for granted.[66]

Resistance, Hayden stressed, was not illegal. The war was illegal. The authorities were "immoral, illegal, unconstitutionally constituted." That was justification enough for protest: "To say that we were acting illegally is to say that the manufacturer of napalm is legal, that the war in Vietnam is legal, that the system is operating according to law." That is why the New Left considered violence against the authority of the consensus. When asked if he approved of violence, Hayden responded that he "would not morally condemn a person who engages in such sabotage because I understand the way he feels." Hayden was not a disciple of King's nonviolence, but he did not insist on force, either. Yet he did believe that the right to be violent against the United States derived from American violence in Vietnam. The American government had "no right to lecture people to be nonviolent." Hayden declared that he believed less in violence than did the government.[67]

By 1968 the New Left had finally been taken seriously, and the orthodox leaders feared it for the consequences of its dissent. It was no longer dismissed as being on the fringe, and the consensus tried to repress it. Hayden had testified voluntarily before Congress; in 1968 he and fellow radicals—leaders of students, activists, and hippies— were put on trial before a judge and jury, for conspiracy to incite a riot across state lines at the Democratic National Convention in Chicago. Hayden maintained that he was not on trial merely for his actions but for his "disrespectful identity," for all that he stood for against a corrupt and repressive consensus society. He did not see himself alone on trial but also his generation and his country after he had to endure "a nightmare and an awakening . . . something out of Kafka's imagination—six months of living in Judge Hoffman's neon oven; a trial that symbolized the beginning of full-scale political repression in the United States."[68]

The protesters had not come to Chicago to riot, they pleaded; they had not pro- voked violence—the police had, by deliberately creating the major confrontations. The police had cleared Lincoln Park each night to enforce a curfew, driving people into the streets and covering the park with gas. They had marched with swinging clubs into a seated group in the Grant Park bandshell after someone had pulled down the American flag; and they had smashed into a peaceful, chanting crowd that was clogging the intersection in front of the Hilton Hotel. The rebels, Hayden said, were "the new-style niggers" who bore the brunt of the violence.

The defendants openly disrespected the court. They mocked it in press confer- ences, demonstrations, and speeches, although the court could not punish the defen- dants for exercising freedom of speech outside. They complained that the jury was not of their peers; no young people or blacks sat on the jury, no hippies or even what Hayden called "a young 'mod.'" "From now on, even middle-class white children would no longer be safe from the paranoid wrath of the older, entrenched generation."[69]

The dissenters expected further repression by the government—but only as their own movement increased in influence. Abbie Hoffmann goaded the authorities to become increasingly repressive. "People run off to Hanoi to collaborate with the enemy. Everybody's smoking pot on the streets. People go on TV and radio shows and spell out in detail plans of sabotage. And simultaneously there is repression." He relished the prospect that the increase of both revolt and repression would produce highly volatile conditions on which he and his movement would thrive. The failure of the war gave his movement strength: "You see, there is no solution to the Vietnam war. To leave or to stay is a defeat."[70]

The pressures of the New Left and the activities in the street were felt at the center of authority in the White House. There was a climate of suspicion among the aides, reaching all the way to the president. Secretary of State Kissinger grew deeply troubled by the breakup of consensus, so much so that he believed "the fundamental problem in our foreign policy" was "to restore the national consensus on our broader purposes in the world." He feared that a "loss of confidence in our own country would inevitably be mirrored in our international relations." Nixon strove through television speeches to gain support from a "Silent Majority," which he supposed existed mainly in the Midwest and longed for a successful conclusion to the war. He called on Americans to be "united against defeat. Because . . . North Vietnam cannot defeat or humiliate the United States. Only Americans can do that."[71]

One of the president's aides, Jeb Stuart Magruder, reacted with animosity toward the critics: the leaders felt "shaken by antiwar demonstrations" and a "wave of bombings." The fear of society unraveling, not by foreign forces but by protesters within, had led those in privileged positions to listen to a plan proposed by Gordon Liddy at a meeting with Attorney General John Mitchell. What Liddy called "mugging squads" could "rough up hostile demonstrators" and "kidnapping squads" could "seize radical leaders"—Liddy mentioned Jerry Rubin and Abbie Hoffman—and "hold them in a 'safe house' in Mexico during the Republican Convention." Mitchell rejected this part of the proposal, but other hostile tactics were used against the dissenters: a list of Nixon administration enemies, phone taps, violence by police against protesters, CIA surveillance, Internal Revenue Service harassment, and, finally, the burglary of the Watergate headquarters of the Democratic party.[72]

Startlingly, Americans expressed in polls a new and urgent concern. One in four listed national disunity or political instability as a fear for the country in 1971. Almost half of Americans believed that the unrest over the military force was serious enough to lead to a "real breakdown." The schism in American society, the polls further showed, was not of party, economic class, ethnic group, or race. Americans had divided fundamentally over the nation's international mission. Fear of breakdown was expressed by all segments of the population—young and old, learned and poorly educated, rich and poor, whites and nonwhites. The unrest was not dismissed as merely the agitation of radical firebrands. Americans as a whole, not unlike the New Left, saw ingrained causes in the failure of national institutions. The suspicion of Americans' traditional ways mandated changes.[73]

The Vietnam War was not the only reason for the end of America's world role. The divisions and discord at home shattered the consensus that had forged American international preeminence, and those divisions were no less important in ending the world role than the nation's first defeat in war. The bitter experience of property ruined, wounds inflicted, lives lost, and human misery destroyed some of the Americans' most cherished consensus beliefs about power, victory, and transforming the societies of distant countries. The consensus had held to an image of the United States that had represented the qualities of attraction afforded by its modern continental nation, its productive capacity, its wealth, and its social harmony. But the war had repercussions at home.

18

The

Military

Costs

The Pentagon, the command center of arsenals and forces from Vietnam to the Mediterranean, was a striking symbol of American military might, to which both the consensus and the radical opposition looked, one with awe and pride, the other with regret and revulsion. Constructed during World War II, it was the world's largest office building. The concrete-and-limestone edifice was three times the size of the Empire State Building, and the U.S. Capitol could fit into any one of its five sides. Worldwide radio communications and the world's largest private branch telephone exchange, linking some 40,000 telephones, along with 15,000 miles of pneumatic tubes and 2,100 intercoms kept Pentagon personnel informed day and night in the event of crisis or attack. The Pentagon was a practically self-sufficient city of 31,300 inhabitants, fed in six cafeterias, ten snack bars, and a pavilion in the central courtyard, and served by two hospitals, an officers' club, a gymnasium, Turkish baths, and four bowling alleys. The military headquarters had four workers assigned the task of replacing the 600 lightbulbs that burned out each day, while another four were professional clock-watchers, caring for the master control that synchronized the building's 4,000 clocks. The Pentagon's television-radio studio produced three national programs each week. Marveling at the simplicity of the structure and the complexity of its organization, *Time,* in a cover story on the Pentagon, called it "unique on the face of the known world" and the "materialization of the military mind. . . . It is the brain of the U.S.'s armed might." The positive view of the Pentagon was countered by the dissenting one of C. Wright Mills, who related this symbol of "the scale and shape of the new military" to "the American means of violence" that had been enlarged, centralized, and complicated by a worldwide bureaucratic structure, controlled by "the men of violence: the United States warlords." The Pentagon was a chief target of radical protest.[1]

"The Greatest Aggregation of Power": The Military

The criteria of declining power lay not simply in crude material elements. Substantial military power had been evident in the latter period of the world role, even as the nation

369

had been defeated at arms. The United States had amassed a greater power to destroy than ever before. It was a gross increase in military force, not necessarily relative to the nations that were concurrently gaining in the modern armament of guns, bombs, and missiles. Yet the increase in power was global, reaching into all areas, and it was total: the arsenals of the United States, if ever fully deployed, had the capability to destroy its enemies and civilization everywhere.

The Vietnam War first exposed to the realists serious economic and social problems, though not in the early years. With conscious determination as the world role progressed, military leaders had been preparing the United States for war, until by the time of Vietnam they supervised what Secretary of Defense Robert McNamara claimed was "the greatest aggregation of raw power ever assembled by man." Awesome, overwhelming military power had become the norm. The military had increased in a great thrust with few breaks since the onset of the Korean conflict in 1950. The number of warships rose from 812 in 1960 to 976 in 1968. The number of aircraft reached 15,327. The United States was then ahead of the Soviet Union in the number of major naval combat vessels and of aircraft in the Air Force, and despite the longstanding realist fear of the size of the Soviet military, the United States had also mustered the advantage in personnel over Soviet forces.[2]

The nuclear superiority of the United States over the Soviet Union, as McNamara admitted in 1967, was actually greater than the government had planned or deemed necessary. The much-belabored missile gap, which Kennedy had pressed as an issue in the 1960 campaign, McNamara was now forced to admit, was bogus. In the nuclear arsenal ready for retaliation, American power had more than doubled since 1960. In 1967 the number of nuclear warheads reached a peak of 32,000; the following year a diminution in the number of warheads began as old weapons were retired. Nonetheless, the quantity of intercontinental ballistic missiles increased, from 934 in 1965 to nearly 1,054 in 1970, and so did the number of Polaris submarine-launched missiles.[3]

The scale of the country's preparations for war was underscored by the costs of military expenditure, amounting to nearly 10 percent of the gross national product. This disbursement was larger than the GNP of entire nations: in 1970 the United States defense budget of $83 billion exceeded the gross national products of Belgium, $18.1 billion; Sweden, $21.3 billion; and Italy, $61.4 billion. Moreover, according to the economist Robert Heilbroner's calculations, American military expenditure in the 1960s regularly exceeded the total of all personal income taxes; accounted for one-quarter of all federal public works; provided more than 20 percent of all manufacturing jobs in seven states; and subsidized about one-third of all research in the United States.[4]

The trend toward reliance on military power was noticeable abroad in the increasing expenditure in allied states on military grants and aid, rather than on worldwide economic, humanitarian, and cultural pursuits. Payments for the military dwarfed the government's expenditure on these other areas of the world role and accounted for up to half of the federal budget, so that from the end of World War II to the end of the Vietnam

War in the 1970s, the United States government spent over $1,000 billion on the military.[5]

The Economic Costs

The commonplace consensus defense of this military spending had been propounded by the realists since the formulation of NSC 68 and the Korean War: No cost should be spared for defense. The debate of national purpose in 1960 reinforced that axiom. In the 1960 presidential campaign, Kennedy renewed the call for a buildup of arms to perpetuate the world role, and Johnson took the same stance when he became president. "No one should doubt for a moment," Johnson vowed, "that we have the resources and the will" to defend the global interests that the United States had assumed since World War II, "as long as it may take." The United States, McNamara determined, was "well able to spend whatever it needs to spend on national security." The costs, whatever their level, would have the effect of expanding the production of the economy, not placing undue demands on it.[6]

An early critique of these propositions was by Seymour Melman at Columbia University. In 1965 he scrutinized the impact of military expenditure on American society: "A process of technical, industrial, and human deterioration has been set in motion. . . . The price of building colossal military power, and endlessly adding to it, has been the depletion of American society, a process now well advanced in industry, civilian technology, management, education, medical care, and the quality of life."[7]

Melman's formulation was decidedly out of step for 1965: The communists had to be met with military force, the orthodox intoned as doctrine. Besides, American industry and trade were booming. Yet Melman persisted in his views, and he marshalled evidence in a follow-up study in the late 1960s:

1 In 1968, 6 million dwellings were grossly substandard, mainly in the cities.

2 10 million Americans suffered from hunger in 1968–1969.

3 The United States ranked 18th among nations in 1966 in infant mortality rate.

4 In 1967, 40.7 percent of the young men examined were disqualified for military service, many for medical reasons.

5 In 1950, 109 physicians practiced in the United States per 100,000 of the population; in 1966 only 98 did.

6 About 30 million Americans were trapped in an economically under-developed sector of the society.[8]

This was the kind of criticism that the dissenters on the left had cited to argue that the federal government had consistently put defense above the standard of life, taking military resources from efforts to alleviate poverty, to improve health, and to advance public services. Appalled at the "economic waste of war," C. Wright Mills had hoped to replace the "permanent war economy" by a "permanent peace economy." The choices of the New Left usually divided between "guns" and "butter."[9]

But a dimension of the problem usually escaped the orthodox and dissenters alike. The capacity of the United States to carry the burden of the military or to divert its costs to the social welfare depended on the ability to afford the expenditures. The dynamic state of the American economy lulled the orthodox into complacency that it would provide whatever was necessary for defense. Nor did the New Left consider the conservation of power a prime concern. Melman, whose analysis was followed by the Left, warned of adverse consequences along with poverty: America's metal-working machinery was aging; the railroads had nothing to compare with the Japanese and French fast trains; and the United States merchant fleet ranked twenty-third in the age of its vessels. But to the Left, as to the orthodox, the effects of military spending on the world role itself were not by any means clear in the 1960s.[10]

Since World War II, the cost of military preparations had only intermittently concerned the maverick economist John Kenneth Galbraith, who as an inspector of the Strategic Bombing Survey examining bombed-out German factories had challenged the usual Air Force thinking, telling officers that the war had cost America far more in output than it had cost Germany. In his 1967 book *The New Industrial State,* he backed off his contrary provocations and essentially expressed the orthodox reasoning. He agreed that spending on weaponry had served to improve the technology that might be useful for civilian production. Yet he was firm that arms expenditures had no unique value for increasing demand. If the conflict with the Soviet Union could be shifted from weapons competition to scientific and engineering competition, he suggested, the effect would be equally "satisfactory."[11]

In his 1969 book *How to Control the Military,* Galbraith finally let loose against the ascendant military beliefs that the conflict with communism was "man's ultimate battle," and that the national interest was "total," that of humanity "inconsequential." The military had become "an unlimited partner in the arms industry" and "a controlling voice in foreign policy." It had "reversed constitutional process in the United States—removed power from the public and Congress to the Pentagon." Recalling Eisenhower's warning about the military-industrial complex, Galbraith maintained that any "general or admiral who rose to fame before World War II would be surprised and horrified to find that his successors in the profession of arms are now commercial accessories of General Dynamics." He urged restraining the bloated military by getting it under the firm political control of the president and Congress.[12]

Galbraith's change in thought foreshadowed the orthodox consensus concern about the continuing defense costs and the effects on society of the military consumption of natural resources, social energy, and capital funds. Toward the end of the Vietnam War, the United States Steel Corporation applied to the government for financial relief, contending that World War II had caused domestic deposits of high-grade iron ore and coal to be exhausted earlier than it had anticipated. As a result, the company had incurred extra expenses in using low-quality raw materials. The company sought a refund from the government for amounts paid as income taxes and Korean War excess-profits taxes and interest for the year 1950. The government made its case to the Supreme Court that a tax break would set a bad precedent, but the Court let stand the decision of lower courts that U.S. Steel could gain relief for this rapid depletion of resources. Post–World War II military technology and hardware regularly consumed mounting quantities of mineral and petroleum resources.[13]

The military required—and usually got—skilled experts and specialists. "That anyone, on the grounds of principle, should refuse his services to the Pentagon or Dow Chemical was nearly unthinkable," Galbraith wrote from personal experience. Social scientists responded "eagerly to invitations to spend the summer at RAND. They devoted their winters to seminars on the strategy of defense and deterrence." A military fixation controlled an enormous amount of the thought, energy, and talent of a generation of scientists and educators. Many were attracted by the allure of weapons development and strategy. Even their opponents, those whose passion was peace and who saw the dangers of nuclear weapons and were drawn into a crusade for arms control, were preoccupied by what they abhorred. While America was educating fewer scientists than other technologically advanced nations, the work of many of its scientists concentrated on the military and its suppliers rather than on bringing efficiency to industry.[14]

The American people paid for the military expenditure by diverting enormous quantities of financial capital into it—enough capital in four years alone during the Vietnam buildup in the late 1960s to purchase all the equipment, machinery, and facilities owned by all American manufacturers combined. Meanwhile, Japan and West Germany invested in civilian research and development at far higher rates than the United States. The greatest performer in industrial growth since World War II was Japan, which had nearly no military establishment and spent only 1 percent of its GNP on the military. West Germany had grown far more rapidly than the United States, applying a much smaller proportion of its GNP to defense. At the other extreme, the Soviet Union, which spent the largest proportion of its GNP on the military, was entering a state of economic stagnation.[15]

The proponents of high military spending continued to argue that large outlays might spur economic growth, creating employment and ensuring stability. But the trend toward the military as the foundation of power at the expense of other elements was not a subject that the old realists preferred to dwell on. Early in the Vietnam War the leaders were unshaken in their conviction that the war could be paid for with ease. Their rationale was defended by the editors of *Fortune,* who, working their way through the tangled issue, reconsidered the World War II lesson of Galbraith: "The costs to the enemy of repairing the damage are picayune compared to the costs to the U.S. of doing the damage." There was the bizarre image of machine guns mounted on helicopters firing up to 18,000 rounds per minute into treetops, and B-52s operating at a cost of more than $1,300 per hour per plane, flying ten hours round-trip from Guam to South

Vietnam to strike at an enemy that had no large encampments visible from the air. *Fortune* recognized the limits of the kind of force hailed by McNamara when he said, "The bomb tonnage that is resulting is literally unbelievable." Still, the magazine did not see any severe damage of military spending to the United States: "Only a rich nation can afford to wage war at ratios so very adverse. But the U.S. *is* a rich nation. If there is a great disparity between the bomb power dropped and the economic value of the targets, there is also a great disparity between the wealth and power of the U.S. and of the enemy. The cost of the bombs is small in relation to the G.N.P. of the U.S., and the damage they do is sometimes substantial in relation to the G.N.P. of North Vietnam, or to the resources available to the Vietcong." Yet the high costs of winning the war could create "economic strains."[16]

The Vietnam War accelerated the erosion of natural resources and the drain of capital, and military spending did not promote widespread technological innovation with the social benefit of a machine tool or printing press. During the war, in 1971, the trade of the United States fell into deficit, weakening confidence in the dollar. The war, the economist Leonard Silk stated categorically, "sealed the doom of the postwar world monetary system that had been built on a strong dollar and fixed exchange rates between the dollar, gold and other currencies." Spending on the war, along with re-newed domestic social programs, caused the prices of American goods to become less competitive. "Tragically," Paul Samuelson wrote, "the post-1965 Vietnam escalation" had created "Vietnam inflation," which hindered America's trade position long after the war.[17]

The economic strains of war did not yet appear to the old realists to be anything other than temporary. As the war ended, the overseas military expenditures that had risen significantly, C. Fred Bergsten forecast in *Foreign Affairs* in 1972, were "coming down," and the trade and currency misfortunes were sure to turn around.[18]

Still the specter of defeat in Vietnam did not curb military power. The realist calls for military growth continued in the 1970s, bound up with the fears of declining power or loss of superiority. In 1971, a defense panel appointed by President Nixon stated, "In a dramatic shift in the balance of power, largely unnoticed by the public, the quarter century of clear U.S. strategic superiority has ended." The United States was in danger of becoming "a second-rate power."[19]

Even President Jimmy Carter, who believed that the United States should make a clear commitment to the principle of human rights to correct the corrupted image of Vietnam, nevertheless increased the defense budget. "We must pay whatever price is required to remain the strongest nation in the world. That price has increased as the military power of our major adversary has grown."[20]

In 1976 Ronald Reagan contended that the United States was no longer "number one" in military power, and in extemporaneous comments, he charged that the United States was already in second place. The exact date that he believed the United States began its military decline was not clear, but Reagan looked to the period of the Vietnam

War as a turning point. "Since the mid-1960s," he said, "we have, as a nation, frittered away a clear military superiority over the Soviet Union."

Once Reagan became president in the 1980s, he carried out an expansion of every service and claimed that he had rebuilt American strength with each passing year of his presidency: The "state of our Union is stronger than a year ago and growing stronger each day," he proclaimed in 1986. His State of the Union Message of 1988 declared "a complete turnabout, a revolution. Seven years ago, America was weak . . . . Today America is strong." But again his view of America was primarily military: "We've rebuilt our defenses" and made America "strong." Toward the end of his administration, Reagan stated, "I had a plan . . . to deal from strength. That was why I was so much a believer in refurbishing our military and our strength."[21]

But offsetting the boast of increasing military strength was a sense of general economic decline. The United States eventually went into debt to pay for the military buildup. The national debt doubled between 1980 and 1985, as military expenditures outstripped the growth of any other major sector, including health and agriculture. The United States required foreign capital to cover the accumulating debt. Foreign investment from nations within the alliance system—Japan and the NATO nations—thus subsidized the federal defense budget.

By the 1980s Seymour Melman felt his theories had been vindicated. His *Profits without Production* continued the chronicle he had begun twenty years before of the danger of the mililtary-industrial complex. By now the consequences of defense spending, he argued, had become obvious. With the Pentagon commanding vast resources and unconcerned about the cost of armament, American business had lost its worldwide reputation for "Yankee know-how" in automobiles and machine tools. Not only was military expenditure depriving children of food, but it was also severely damaging the whole economy. It threatened to turn America into a "second-rate industrial country."[22]

Galbraith too now further appreciated the detrimental impact of military costs. He recalled that John Maynard Keynes had once proposed that pound notes be buried in abandoned coal mines, because digging them up would be beneficial to employment and consumer spending. Galbraith drew the lesson: "Weaponry of vast cost that was unusable because of its nearly infinite destructive power was now, and increasingly, serving the same economic purpose as the buried money."[23]

New critics produced additional evidence. In the late 1970s a study by Ruth Sivard found that military expenditures were "more damaging to the economy than has been assumed in the past." They retarded economic growth because they did not add to the economy's productive capital stock. Diminished growth, in turn, meant a loss of job opportunities. Furthermore, military requirements, she calculated, damaged the environment.[24]

In 1983 the Nobel Prize–winning economist Wassily Leontief completed his quantitative study *Military Spending,* which applied his out-put, in-put theory of economic activity to the military sector. His computer data, covering developing regions and developed countries like the United States, convinced him that the American economy was not exempt from the debilitating economic effects of military spending. The "potential for the civilian economy" would be increased by applying military resources "directly to selected civilian objectives." He concluded that with "decreases in military spending, outputs of most goods and services increase."[25]

Gradually these warnings on the dangers of military spending entered mainstream opinion. The *New York Times* declared its position: The "dream" of military force had "put the economy at risk."[26]

President Reagan had urged the public to back arms increases, saying that any cuts would pose a threat to the United States. But in at least one poll, in 1987, Americans came to see economic strength as more important than military strength in assuring American influence in the world. Asked to pick the most important foreign policy goal, 62 percent of the people chose "Strengthening our economy to be more competitive with other countries." Naming the greatest threat to the future, more people said it would come from domestic economic problems than from terrorism or military attack.[27]

But the United States could not easily relinquish its military paramountcy, even as its economic dominance slipped away. The government was not content with foreign capital resources expended on the military through the budget deficit, and in the early 1980s it sought Japanese technology to improve its weaponry. The Japanese had steadfastly refused to provide this technology under a ban on arms exports. Finally, on the eve of an otherwise uneventful three-day visit by President Reagan to Japan in November 1983, the Japanese gave in to the longstanding American requests and agreed to export technology for military purposes, including heat-resistant ceramics, lasers, and fiber optics. The initial Japanese interest in defense collaboration with the United States was not military but commercial: to apply new technologies to civilian products. And military contractors expressed concern that the United States was "opening the door to the same sort of Japanese competition that crippled the American auto and steel industries."[28]

So it was easier for the government to build up the military than for the society to repair its declining economic advantage in the world markets. C. Fred Bergsten raised unprecedented geopolitical questions in *Foreign Affairs* in 1987. "Can the world's largest debtor nation remain the world's leading power? Can a small island nation that is now militarily insignificant and far-removed from the traditional power centers provide at least some of the needed global leadership? Can the United States continue to lead its alliance systems as it goes increasingly into debt to the countries that are supposed to be its followers?" Military spending gave the appearance of great power, even as the United States ceased to have a favorable balance of trade and then lost its status as world creditor, cut its foreign aid, and allowed the global system of alliances to crumble. Military power was designed to compensate.[29]

The Social Determinant

No innate characteristic in the American economy or society explained why America should rely so heavily on the military. America had become a great power without undue dependence on the military, but after a glorious victory in World War II and a short-lived return to peace, a warrior mentality asserted itself. How did this remarkable reversal in the nature of power come about? How, in particular, did it come about in a country that had traditionally been suspicious of military power and was known instead for its modern industrial goods, the latest technology, and altruistic aid?

The answers lie in the consensus acceptance of the society's military, economic, and bureaucratic institutions. Leaders of the state and the military informed the consensus of the necessity for extraordinary action to exert control in a series of crises. Henry Steele Commager, the historian of national character, was sobered to think during the Korean conflict that war had become normal and peace abnormal. During the first 175 years after the Revolution, Commager figured, the United States had been engaged in major wars for 25 years—one year out of every seven. Yet from the start of America's active participation in World War II in 1941 through the end of its involvement in Vietnam in 1973, the country had been engaged in some form of military conflict abroad for 29 years, with only three years of respite. The all-out wars, police actions, and interventions were not restricted to any continent or region, as American forces became caught up in World War II, Korea, and Vietnam; in civil wars in China and Greece, where American soldiers trained troops and provided combat advice; and in rebellions, landing forces in Lebanon in 1958 and in the Dominican Republic in 1965. Only in 1956, 1957, and 1959 was the United States without foreign military involvement.[30]

Commager looked for changing qualities of the people of the United States when confronted by war and cold war. Americans, he believed in 1951, had been a peaceful, democratic, nonmilitary people—amateur fighters, not professional or mercenary or members of a military caste attaching special significance to the uniform. Although he ignored the Mexican, Spanish, and Indian conflicts, he argued that because the army largely demobilized after wars, Americans had placed their civil life above the military and implemented that quality constitutionally. But Commager noted a possible threat: never before in the nation's history had the military "exerted so much influence or exercised so much power." Americans had been unprepared for war—their major wars had more often than not taken them by surprise—but in a world troubled by war they had entered a period of a peacetime draft, general military service, continuous officer training, immense military appropriations, and "the concentration of a substantial part of production and of scientific research on military needs." The persistence of this preparedness over time, Commager predicted, would profoundly affect the national life. Americans had usually been convinced that the wars they were fighting were just, that they were upholders of the right, not aggressors, and they had never lost a war. And in their moral certitude, Commager judged, they fought wars as they operated their industry, farms, and government. "They like large-scale organization; they prefer to fight with machinery, with the best and the most arms and equipment; they reveal in war as in peace an immeasurable inventiveness and ingenuity."

The historian left open the question what would eventuate if the people did not believe in their cause. But he provided a clue. In each of the earlier major conflicts of American history, including World War II, the neophyte military nation, the United States had beaten its well-prepared rivals. In Vietnam, where the Americans were the military experts, well prepared, well equipped, and well trained in the latest weaponry, they lost.[31]

In the 1970s, Commager wondered: "we who heretofore have not been able to face even the possibility of defeat are now required to take the possibility of annihilation into our calculations." When fateful decisions were made under the shadow of the atomic weapon, Commager returned to the idea of a military mentality that had once been absent from his assessment of the American character but that was by necessity becoming a preoccupation—though to what end? "Can we who have been living off our political—and, to some extent, our moral—capital build up new political, scientific, technological and moral resources in time to stave off disaster? The prospects are not encouraging."[32]

The rationalization of the new attitude of the military as a primary instrument of power was recognized by Alistair Cooke, the long-time observer of national character and mores, who imagined in 1973 that most people under forty assumed that the United States had "always been a military mammoth." Like Commager, Cooke located a turning point in American attitudes in World War II, when they began looking on war not as an emergency disruption of life but as a profession. Yet the transformation to a military mode of thinking was not complete then.

After the "soldiers got out of uniform and all but the smallest stock of weapons was scrapped," Cooke noted, the atomic bomb caused Americans to become infatuated by their military power. In the nineteenth century, he reflected, the British navy had dictated the Pax Britannica. But because the first use of a nuclear bomb on Japan had caused a worldwide moral revulsion against its further use, the United States became "the first supreme power that could not use its ultimate weapon." Throughout the 1950s and well into the 1960s, "the triumphant feeling persisted that America could dictate a Pax Americana" even without resorting to the bomb, by deploying marines, technicians, "paramilitary" groups, and arms. In Vietnam "the American elephant could make the earth tremble, but it couldn't conquer the ants who lived on it."

Cooke presented a novel image of the modern-day American character: Two young men arrive at a ground-level shack, show their identification cards, descend in an elevator, and prove they know the combination to launch missiles. Part of a worldwide network, "from the White House through the National War Command, through Omaha and the bombers to the farthest nuclear sub," they had been trained "to keep what is surely the loneliest, and could be the last, vigil of human warfare. Yet these doomsday warriors look no more like soldiers than the soldiers of the Second World War looked like conquistadors. . . . You see the type in small variations everywhere. . . . They may have capacious bow-window bellies or be as reedy as beans. They can wear glasses. They stand around, at sea, at a ground base, or deep in a missile silo, and they 'program' their incomprehensible jargon into consoles, dictating out of large manuals, throwing switches, watching a run of lights, announcing with all the dramatic flair of an inventory clerk that the first missile is 'away' and presumably about to destroy Moscow or Peking."

The men were ordinary Americans, Cooke noted, but they held the unbelievable power of a suicidal nuclear war. "They have families, they play pool or go bowling on their off nights, they do carpentry and gardening, they follow the football scores. . . . They have had thorough psychiatric tests, which are periodically repeated." And these individuals ranked as part of a power elite. "For the greatest danger is that the technology of the unthinkable war will enchant its practitioners, growing so subtle and mighty as to acquire a momentum all its own, which mere men will be powerless to subdue."[33]

The gradual consensus acceptance of this change in the character of American power came about with the development of what Ralph E. Lapp called the weapons culture, in which economic and technological power became directed toward military production. "It is no exaggeration to say that the United States has spawned a weapons culture which has fastened an insidious grip upon the entire nation," Lapp wrote in 1968. "Gradually the U.S. involvement with defense industry has proceeded to the point where weapons-making begins to dominate our society. . . . A central problem for democracy is the control of this military-industrial complex that has grown in influence as its political connections have ramified." The modern military establishment did not exist without the disciplined acquiescence of the citizenry.[34]

No evidence existed of generals secretly manipulating the civilian government, or of manufacturers running the military. C. Wright Mills's theory of the hierarchy of the power elite may have inferred conspiracy in a small circle of highly placed people occupying positions in American society from which they "look down upon" and "mightily affect" the "everyday worlds of ordinary men and women." The elite warlords, corporation chieftains, and political directorate were in "command" of the major "organizations of modern society." But Mills denied a conspiracy of "an easily located set of villains." His conception of a power elite did "*not* rest upon the assumption that American history since the origins of World War II must be understood as a secret plot, or as a great and co-ordinated conspiracy of the members of this elite. . . . There is nothing conspiratorial about it."[35]

Civilian leaders, the presidents and secretaries of defense, listening to the military services, wielded the authority that expanded the military. The government elected by the people initiated and maintained the enlarged military, through a complex of bureaucratic connections that reached from government into industry and into states and communities. The people's obedience to military priorities came from the hardening images of the earlier stages of the world role: of a communist world threatening every region of the globe with armies, and of the United States as the principal power with the economic wealth, ships, air force, and missiles to stop this menace. The delegation of resources to the military and its industrial suppliers relied on the continuing determination of elected representatives and of the mass of people, whether laborers, scientists, or scholars.

The devotion of resources, social energy, and economic production to America's world role told something about the priorities of the nation. Americans could invest in schools, hospitals, highways, factories, cities, suburbs, personal comforts and pleasures, jewelry, and yachts. They could invest in the operation and defense of a world role. To some extent the amounts spent for aid or war or farming or music were disparate and not strictly comparable or interchangeable. Still, because the available funds were not infinite, spending money on some things might impoverish others.

Martin Luther King saw the military costs of the Vietnam War destroy his hope for society. "There were experiments, hopes, new beginnings," he said of the government's poverty program. Then came the war, and he "watched the program broken and eviscerated as if it were some idle political plaything of a society gone mad on war," and he "knew that America would never invest the necessary funds or energies in rehabilitation of its poor so long as adventures like Vietnam continued to draw men and skills and money like some demoniacal destructive suction tube." Learning that the "mis-estimate of the war budget" amounted to $10 billion for a single year, he calculated that the error alone was more than five times the entire commitment for the antipoverty programs. The cost of $332,000 for each enemy killed was incomprehensible to King: what lives could be transformed, what tragedy averted, if Americans would simply cease the killing in Vietnam, he declared. "The security we profess to seek in foreign adventures we will lose in our decaying cities. The bombs in Vietnam explode at home; they destroy the hopes and possibilities for a decent America." He dwelled on the "wasteland" until he died of an assassin's bullet in 1968. American abundance was being "squandered."[36]

Over time, the proportion of GNP that went into defense and the military amounted to about one-tenth. But looked at as lost social and economic investment—resources which might have been directed into profitable enterprises that would grow and multiply, as the United States had been doing during its rise to power, as England had done during its ascendancy, and as Japan was currently doing—the cost of obsolescent weaponry or destruction was enormous. If the percentage of GNP for the military was equal to the GNP of entire nations, the lost proportion of productive enterprise was equal to the GNP of many more nations. The lost productive value, both at home and abroad, had a dragging effect on the progress of advancing technology, overcoming poverty, husbanding resources, and encouraging art. Those benefits would have multiplied in value, and they would have had the effect of sustaining the world role, but the expenditure on armaments had undermined the world role that they were supposed to protect.

The mental inertia of the old adherents to consensus prevented them from comprehending the changing world about them. They still looked on foreign competition or the resistance in Vietnam as an accident, regarded their industry as the best, were pleased by the results attained in science, and were satisfied with the status quo. They failed to perceive that beyond the national boundaries the methods of organization and administration had altered throughout the world.

The New Left strengthened its attack on big business and the inflated military. William Appleman Williams had talked about the regionalization of American power, about an Articles of Confederation–type constitution that would make it more difficult for the central government to create and exercise military power. But that was a utopian notion. It is also uncertain to what extent hippies like Abbie Hoffman cared whether the United States was a world power or not. But children of that world power—the acceptance of internationalism having transpired before many of their births—knew no other condition, and they were less concerned with the elements producing that power than with its uses. The new generation desired the consumption of power in ways other than the military adventures that the orthodox leaders were committed to.

The criteria for the process of demise were found fundamentally in the division and discord over American internationalism that had arisen both outside and inside American society and that had been exposed in the Vietnam War. When Galbraith considered "why America's influence and that of the Soviets" were "in retreat," he rejected economic reasons as paramount. True, the "economic system of the United States and that of the Soviet Union have not in the last years been turning in the kind of performance that would make them the lodestar for the rest of the world. Both are highly organized, and both are struggling with the sclerotic tendencies that are inherent in all organizations, public or private, socialist or nonsocialist. But the main reason for the shared decline in influence is, without question, the unbounded and universal determination of people to govern themselves." The will or spirit of the people was instrumental. These urgings for self-determination had turned against the United States in places like Vietnam. Even as the American holdings of military power were increasing, other nations had gained a larger scope for autonomous action.[37]

In the mid-1980s, near Jay Mountain on a remote, wooded plot in the Adirondacks was a long-abandoned silo, a launching pad for Atlas intercontinental missiles. Once at the forefront of weapons technology, the silo had been one of seventy-two Atlas sites, nestled in the northeast forests or buried beneath the desert in the Southwest, built at a cost of $1.6 billion. Inside the control room, a 1966 telephone directory rested on a shelf. Dust clung to the console in the subterranean vault where a five-member Air Force crew had once stood twenty-four-hour watch at the launch controls. Beneath the sediment of twenty years, the words "Commit Start" remained legible on a metal lid covering the lock that activated the firing mechanism. Nearby, the ninety-ton doors of a silo were stuck open and the 170-foot-deep hole was filled with water. These were the ruins of the image of modern America as an arsenal, fortified by missile bases loaded with consoles, switches, and lights and staffed by young soldiers, which Alistair Cooke had seen only a decade earlier. But already the missiles had fallen into disuse and their silos into wreckage. Meanwhile, factories had deteriorated into rusted rubble as well. So, with a schism over what the nation valued and to what degree, we turn to a consideration of what the nation dedicated its resources and energies and life to, and to what that tells us about the kind of nation it is.[38]

19

Criteria

of

Declining

Power

For the first time since the United States had surpassed Britain as the world's leading economic producer in 1880, it embarked on a long-term decline relative to other nations. After the close of World War II, the United States had produced nearly 50 percent of the world economy, measured by estimates of national product; by 1971 the figure had fallen to less than 30 percent. "Twenty-five years ago, at the end of World War II," President Nixon asserted in the early 1970s, "we were unchallenged in the world, militarily and economically. As far as competition was concerned, there was no one who could possibly challenge us. But now that has changed." The position of leadership was "jeopardized."[1]

While the growth of the United States was at a rate lower than that of all other major industrial nations, except Britain, American officials praised the absolute levels of gross national product. The GNP, which had doubled during World War II, doubled again by 1957 and yet again by 1969. In 1970 President Nixon celebrated the achievement of the world's first trillion-dollar economy by giving a talk with clenched fist about economic strength and national greatness. Nixon was supposed to have watched the new Commerce Department "G.N.P. clock"—a large board of blinking lights and numbers—flash the trillion-dollar statistic, conveniently at noon, on December 15, but he was late. "When it became clear that Mr. Nixon would not arrive on time," reported the *New York Times,* "departmental technicians worked madly to turn the machine back. But it seemed to develop a life of its own, flashing the trillion-dollar figure at 12:02, and when the President arrived at 12:07, $2.3 million more had been added to the total." "Paul Mc-Cracken," the chairman of the Council of Economic Advisors, "told me that it is moving at the rate of $2,000 a second," Nixon said on his arrival. "By this reasoning," the *Times* figured, "the clock should have jumped only $600,000 during the five minutes between 12:02 and 12:07, suggesting that it may have been working overtime in the excitement of the moment." By the conclusion of his talk, the clock had jumped $5 million more.[2]

Nixon's glorification of the GNP came at a time when the concept of its continual growth was under attack by the New Left and counterculture who found little value in production and innovations of science and technology. Paul

Goodman warned against engaging in "a rat race of highly competitive, unnecessary busy-work with a meaninglessly expanding Gross National Product." Eventually, Paul Samuelson too recognized an unsolved problem of modern economies, "the quality of life versus mere GNP growth." Some economists challenged not only the virtue of growth but its very possibility, as a Massachusetts Institute of Technology team reported in *The Limits of Growth* in 1972.[3]

The American percentage of world production did not reach a plateau and settle there. During the 1970s the share slid from over 26 percent to 24 percent, and neared 20 percent in the 1980s. The proportion of the old foundation industries of steel, automobiles, and commercial aircraft also shrank. In the decade following 1972, the American share of total world production of motor vehicles fell from 32 to 19 percent, and of steel from 20 to 12 percent.[4]

The standard of living, measured by total output per person, lagged in in 1973 behind Switzerland, Sweden, Denmark, and West Germany. Switzerland produced nearly $7,000 a person, the United States just above $6,000. By the measurement of time at work required to buy a select assortment of food and consumer goods, the United States still ranked highest. In subsequent years, however, the United States fell further down the list arranged by per capita output, behind the small oil-producing state of Kuwait in the 1970s and behind Japan in the 1980s.[5]

The decline of the American proportion of the world economy did not depend fundamentally on the inflationary and recessionary consequences of business cycles and government monetary policy. The business cycles continued revolving whether the nation was increasing or decreasing its percentage of world production. The nation's territorial extent, bounteous resources, large skillful population, and technological ability all had contributed to America's material power. We again turn our attention to them, to examine issues of their changes, absolute and relative.

The Factors of Production: Land, Labor, Technology

The toll of time and abuse on the continent were symptomatic of the ravages of decay. In her 1960s bestseller *Silent Spring,* Rachel Carson pictured the landscape of "the heart of America" as she had known it, a checkerboard of farms with grain fields and hillside orchards and green tillage. In autumn, the blaze of oak, maple, and birch stood out from the reaches of the pines. In winter, dried weeds rising above the snow attracted birds who fed on the berries. "So it had been from the days many years ago when the first settlers raised their houses, sank their wells, and built their barns." So it had remained until World War II. But that was not the vision any longer. Carson described the indiscriminate use of pesticides since the 1940s as a blight that had crept over the land: "There was a strange stillness. The birds, for example—where had they gone? . . . It was a spring without voices. . . . The roadsides, once so attractive, were now lined with browned and withered vegetation as though swept by fire. . . . Even the streams were now lifeless." The environment of earth, rivers, and air had been assaulted, but by "no enemy action," Carson wrote. "The people had done it themselves."[6]

In the late 1960s and 1970s an ecological movement railed against the killing of wildlife, the felling of timber, the eroding of topsoil and pasture, the stripping of the earth for mines, and the spraying of dangerous pesticides on croplands, forests, and gardens. The economist Robert Theobald noted that the postwar period, which had begun with national pride in the capability to force the habitat into patterns the people desired, was ending with Americans having to grasp the finiteness of their natural endowments and their interdependence on the rest of the world. He lauded the New Left and the hippies as showing an alternative path in their concerns with the abuse of technology and increasing consumption and their new awareness of their environment. Still, for Americans as a whole, "the destruction of a forest by pollution will not appear in calculations of the Gross National Product at all unless money is spent to save the trees."[7]

The evidence ecologists provided was just the same as that the geopoliticians had once presented as success: the growing population, rising energy consumption, industrial production, and highway construction. Americans were consuming one-third of all raw materials consumed each year in the world. In the 1970s Americans burned more energy than Japan, Britain, Germany, and Russia combined. The American consumption of earth and energy had been widely equated with the status of the United States as the richest, strongest country in the world. But that very consumption—57 percent of the world output of natural gas, 42 percent of its silver, 35 percent of its aluminum—undermined American self-sufficiency. The United States had come to demand more than it produced.[8]

The early limits of natural plenty were difficult for a people who had known abundance to comprehend. In 1972 *U.S. News & World Report* branded the United States as an emerging "have-not" nation. "Hard facts show the U.S. is leaning more and more on other countries for the raw materials that are so vital to its status as the world's most prosperous land." The United States had become dependent on foreign supplies for most of its tin, bauxite, cobalt, platinum, and diamonds, which were needed for tools, engines, chemicals, and telecommunication equipment—the products of a highly technological nation. But the most serious depletion was in fuel supply. "Concern is growing that the United States—the most industrialized country in the world—will be hard pressed to get the oil and gas it needs in the years immediately ahead." In the 1970s the United States required foreign supplies for nearly half of its oil.[9]

The end to self-sufficiency raised the question of how a great power denied resources could exercise a world role. In 1973 the Organization of Petroleum Exporting Countries (OPEC) boosted the price of petroleum and declared an embargo against the United States as one of the nations that had supported Israel in its war with Egypt and Syria. Unlike crises of the past, this one found the United States unable to meet its demand for oil by rapidly expanding its own production. In the winter of 1973–1974, when homes were cold and cars waited in long lines at gas stations, President Nixon urged Americans "to regain the strength that we had earlier in this century, the strength of self-sufficiency." He wanted to increase the production of energy within the nation's borders, because America's part in the world was at stake: "Our ability to meet our own energy needs is directly limited to our continued ability to act decisively and independently at home and abroad in the service of peace, not only for America but for all nations in the world." He called for a commitment of national resources and technology to an endeavor that he named "Project Independence," to be comparable to the Manhattan Project, so that by the end of the decade the United States would have the potential to meet its needs "without depending on any foreign energy sources." But the call went unheeded, and the dependence on foreign supplies continued.[10]

The depletion of resources marked a watershed in America's material situation. By the stark geopolitical thought prevalent earlier in the era, the raw materials taken from the land reduced an American advantage. Sinews of power had become subject to foreign control. But how then did one explain the advances of Japan, an island nation with little coal and no oil? It had moved very far industrially. Obviously, the need to import fuel and minerals was not decisive in the erosion of material power.

Lagging productivity triggered inquiries into the competitiveness of American workers. In President Nixon's Labor Day address of September 1971, he hearkened back to the "work ethic" of the past, to which he attributed the rise of "a poor nation of 3 million people, over a course of two centuries" to "the position of the most powerful and respected leader of the free world. . . . We are told that it doesn't matter whether America continues to be number one in the world economically and that we should resign ourselves to being number two or number three or even number four." He found Americans wondering: "What's happening to the work ethic in America today? What's happening to the willingness for self-sacrifice that enabled us to build a great nation, to the moral code that made self-reliance a part of the American character, to the competitive spirit that made it possible for us to lead the world?" His admonition was for a return to the values of hard work: "Nations, like people, never really stand still," the president preached. "As change accelerates, they compete successfully and move ahead, or they relax and they fall behind."[11]

The culture of abundance challenged the previously dominant idea of a Puritan, work-directed ethic. "Is hard work going out of style?" asked educators and social scientists in the 1970s. For the New Left, who followed social thinkers like C. Wright Mills, Paul Goodman, and Herbert Marcuse, the question was whether the people *wanted* to compete to achieve the dubious end of increased production. Hippies shunned production as tiresome and oppressive, inimical to finding satisfaction in their lives. Business managers faulted workers who abandoned the belief that the one who worked hard would be justly rewarded. At General Motors, where absenteeism at plants had more than doubled during the 1960s, Chairman James Roche complained that "higher absenteeism is a by-product of the affluence of the 'sixties." David Riesman's opinion was that "the relative lack of challenge that abundance produces makes it harder for many to find . . . meaning" in their work.[12]

In 1972 confrontation over the work ethic came to a head in a strike against a General Motors plant in Lordstown, Ohio. Management intended this plant as "a classic American response to the challenge of imported autos turned out by low-wage labor in modern West German and Japanese factories." Completed in 1970, the plant was one of the most modern, automated, and efficient in America, crammed with sophisticated machines and time-saving procedures to turn out more than one hundred Chevrolet Vegas every hour. In the interest of efficiency and profits, management set the goal to lay off 350 workers. Angry laborers argued that management was already forcing them "to work too hard and too fast." They could not keep up with the work coming down the assembly line. They fell behind in the installation of parts and cars were actually sabotaged, with ignition keys snapped off. Said *Newsweek* of the striking plant workers, whose average age was twenty-three and who appeared along the line with shoulder-length hair, "Afros," and "mod" clothing, they bore a "hallmark of much of today's youth: a rather cavalier attitude toward the work ethic, and no tolerance at all for the nit-picking discipline of the assembly line."[13]

As competition from abroad increased, comparisons of characteristic American work habits with those of other industrial peoples became frequent in the 1980s. A feature story entitled "U.S. vs. Japan: Can American Workers Win the Battle?" in *U.S. News & World Report* pitted the workers of the two rivals "in a battle for supremacy. How well they do their jobs is likely to be a major factor in whether Japan can overtake the U.S. as the world's No. 1 economic power. The evidence so far is that the Japanese are gaining fast." One survey rated Japanese workers above American workers in a variety of characteristics that observers of "national character" had once ascribed to Americans: quality-consciousness, hard work, honesty, loyalty, basic skill, reliability, and cooperativeness; the Americans had the advantage only in initiative, ambition, and advanced skill. A number of indices pointed out that the Japanese work week was longer than that in America, payroll costs per hour were lower, and productivity growth was higher. The sociologist Ezra Vogel stated bluntly: Americans used to think that the Japanese "could make junk but not good products, then they could make radios and transistors but not big things like televisions, then they could make televisions but not automobiles, then automobiles but not high technology. The latest phase has us saying they aren't creative enough to be good at software, and they can't handle the service sector. I wouldn't bet on that."[14]

In 1983 a government commission on education reported that the nation's "once unchallenged preeminence in commerce, industry, science, and technological innova-tion" was being lost. "What was unimaginable a generation ago has begun to occur— others are matching and surpassing our educational attainments. If an unfriendly for-eign power had attempted to impose on America the mediocre educational performance that exists today, we might well have viewed it as an act of war. As it stands, we have allowed this to happen to ourselves." The United States could no longer rely on "an abundance of natural resources and inexhaustible human enthusiasm." "Our nation is at risk," the report declared. The risk was not only that the "Japanese make automobiles more efficiently than Americans" or that American machine tools were "displaced by German products." It was of a "redistribution of trained capability throughout the globe."[15]

Illiteracy was increasing. Some twenty-three million American adults were functionally illiterate according to simple tests of everyday reading and writing skills. Student performance on the College Board's standardized Scholastic Aptitude tests declined steadily for a generation, from 1963 to the 1980s. And international comparisons of student achievement revealed that American students were never first or second in comparison with other industrialized nations, and were often last. If given a map without legends, not two out of three of seventeen-year-old high school students could find France. Fewer than a third of high school seniors knew in which half of the nineteenth century the Civil War occurred, nor did students know the international affairs of recent history: a third did not know that the United States supplied economic aid to Europe after World War II, and barely half knew of the American part in the Korean conflict.[16]

The Japanese, in contrast, received credit for making educational strides unheard of in the United States. Most Japanese three- and four-year-olds attended private pre-elementary schools. The Japanese school year was longer than the American—by one count up to sixty days—and so was the school day. After school, Japanese students attended extra classes for exam preparation. They were more disciplined than their American counterparts. After a visit to Japanese schoolrooms in 1985, Terrel Bell, the former American secretary of education, remarked, "The Japanese educational system is superior to ours, if you measure quality by academic achievement in such areas as literacy and command of mathematics and science."[17]

What a remarkable question it was for the *New York Times* science correspondent, Malcolm Browne, to ask: "Do Asians have genetic advantages, or does their apparent edge in scientific skills stem from their special cultural tradition?" He did not hearken back to social Darwinist notions but asserted that environment, rather than biology, conditioned the Asian advantage. Asians studied with discipline and family support. Imbued with their traditional values, they flourished in an environment of creative freedom.[18]

Alistair Cooke had vehemently denied any hint of American decadence in his work on national character in 1952. But Cooke, whose point of comparison was his native Britain in decline, had grown pessimistic: "In America, the race is on between its vitality and its decadence. This happens to all great empires." Technology had cut the demands on labor's time and toil and enabled laborers to increase their productivity, even with a shortened work week. But this growth of productivity suggested the efficiency of organization and capital equipment, rather than the degree of physical effort.[19]

By the 1970s the United States no longer served as the supplier of the world's high-technology manufactured goods. The warnings were strong that the lead in technology, that distinct capability exemplified by the record of automobiles, airlines, and electronics, was slipping from the nation's grasp. In 1975 Robert Sarnoff, the chairman of RCA and the son of the founder, forecast before his company was eventually broken up "a serious technology gap" for the United States. James Roche, the General Motors chairman, feared that America no longer enjoyed "the technological edge over other advanced countries." By the beginning of the 1980s, Simon Ramo, the chairman of TRW-Fujitsu, had detected that America's technology was in "disturbing decline."[20]

The dissenters associated a retardant technology with protection of the environment and escape from alienation and exploitation. But the slide in technology required a general change in attitude. "For half a century the U.S. has led the world in 'technology'—translating know-how into goods that have served the country and brought in hundreds of billions of dollars from sales abroad," stated an article titled "Now It's a 'Technology Gap' That Threatens America," in *U.S. News & World Report* in 1971. The "U.S. technological position in the world not only is stagnant, but probably is deteriorating." A prime measure of a nation's inventiveness, patent applications, were more numerous per capita during the 1970s in West Germany, the Netherlands, and Sweden than in the United States. Patents awarded to Americans peaked in 1971, after which the number issued annually dropped throughout the decade.[21]

American steel makers, after World War II a symbol of national enterprise and power, were an ailing industry. In 1986 Walter Williams, the chief executive of the Bethlehem Steel Corporation, who had begun at the company as an engineer in the midst of a post–World War II building boom that made it one of the giants of American industry, watched wreckers tear down one of the blast furnaces he had designed and constructed thirty years before. The company eventually stopped making steel in its giant mills in Bethlehem, Pennsylvania, altogether. Companies went bankrupt as Americans bought bulky and heavy steel products that cost less even when shipped from plants overseas thousands of miles away. The idea that the seeds of the steel industry's woes were "in the outcome of World War II" at first seemed fantastic, because the war had stimulated steel production. But while Japan and Europe had totally rebuilt their steel mills after the war, employing modern technique, American companies for the most part continued to operate old facilities until they became uncompetitive and obsolete. Mills closed, throwing laborers out of work. One reporter, who walked through the ghostlike remains of a deserted plant in the late 1980s, questioned "whether the nation's steelmakers will survive."[22]

After World War II, the people of New Delhi had marveled at five-year-old Chevrolets, and Europeans had paid a high price for a car simply because it was American, while Americans had no serious interest in foreign models. In 1949 only two Volkswagens were imported into the United States; the records do not show any Japanese imports that year. But by the 1970s, as Americans bought small, fuel-efficient, clean, and cheap foreign models, Henry Ford II said, "I frankly don't see how we're going to meet the competition," adding: "Wait until those Japanese get a hold in the central part of the U.S."—an admission that might have stunned his grandfather, the innovator of mass-produced cars and an epitome of competitive energy. The Ford annual report of 1971 was a warning to stockholders. "American industry cannot possibly stay competitive if the American people and their representatives decide that the time has come to stop trying." No "nation can compete in world markets for industrial products unless it is able to invest heavily in research and development and in efficient, modern plants and equipment." America was losing "its place of leadership."[23]

A decade later, Henry Ford II gave up his chairmanship of the company. "We let our quality go bad," he said. "We got careless, we got sloppy, we built lousy quality cars." Shortly afterward, Toyota, America's leading automobile importer, proclaimed the Japanese triumph in a full-page advertisement. "Back in 1957 we brought our first two cars to America. And took them home again," ran the bold line beneath a picture of two awkward, strange-looking 1950s Japanese imports. Since Americans had belittled the cars as overpriced, underpowered, and built like tanks, Toyota admitted starting over. "We stretched our technology farther than we had ever stretched it before. . . . And one day we did it: we made a better car. And the rest, as they say, is history."[24]

In the production of airplanes, from the four-engined piston-powered planes to the jets numbered 707 to 747, and in the expansion of airlines, the United States had long taken the lead. Airlines had prodded technology from aircraft manufacturers and established routes worldwide, in the way Juan Trippe pioneered Pan American airways. The decision in the early 1970s not to build a supersonic passenger aircraft, the SST, marked a previously unknown broad antitechnological feeling in the United States and a lack of faith that technology could succeed in meeting the serious problems of the jet's pollutants and high operating costs. Instead, the British and French development of supersonic jets supplied the most advanced civil air transportation of the world. When President Nixon visited the Azores for meetings with the French president Georges Pompidou late in 1971, he arrived on *Air Force One,* a conventional Boeing jet, and the French president arrived on a supersonic Concorde. Nixon greeted Pompidou with a handshake and "I saw your Concorde, congratulations." "I only wish we had made the plane ourselves," Nixon later told the French leader.[25]

In 1985, Pan Am sold to United Airlines the Pacific routes that Juan Trippe had audaciously charted with his flying boats. The company had made the sale, according to the report to stockholders, because of its difficulty competing in a volatile international industry. Pan Am was not a "'shrinking' airline," the report protested. But Pan Am had relinquished its role as a worldwide carrier and in 1991 it sold its last European routes. Before the end of that year, its cash depleted, the enterprise that had been synonymous with American aeronautical influence shut down. "Sayonara Pan Am" was the headline of an advertisement by Japan Air Lines. "For over thirty years, Pan Am has been Japan Air Lines' biggest competitor across the Pacific. Now the time has come to bid farewell to a most worthy opponent."[26]

Although American electronics started commercial television networks and developments in tape recording and stereo, by the 1970s the United States had become dependent on imports of electronic equipment, mostly from Japan. The electronics industry was in a declining position when in 1985 the chairman of Sony advised Americans that the United States lacked an inventive, can-do attitude, like that of Japan. "The very day we finish one invention, we begin improving it. We are never satisfied." For example, he claimed that "Sony made the compact disc," the "most significant innovation since Thomas Edison invented the phonograph." The Japanese industrialist had not been intimidated by the larger American companies, believing his outstanding achievement was his personal decision to sell products with the Sony name in America. "We had developed a transistor radio. In seeking distribution in the U.S., I met the purchasing officer of a big, big company. He said, 'If you agree to take off Sony's name and put on our name, we will make a big order.' It was an attractive number, too— enough to keep us busy for a year. Our people in Tokyo even agreed to it. But I insisted on Sony's name. I lost that order, and he said, 'You are stupid, because our name has been around for 50 years.' I said to him, 'Fifty years ago, how many people knew your company's name?' Because I was insistent, we established Sony's name." One piece of advice he would not give. When a reporter asked him, "What comes next?" he refused to answer. "You are asking me for my trade secrets."[27]

Yet technology fostered new ways of growth. It could redress the exhaustion of resources by generating energy from the sun and tides. Technology further increased the efficiency that would raise the standard of living while reducing the hard toil of labor. The United States maintained a lead in computer technology. Other nations learned and adapted know-how that Americans had been first to develop, just as the United States had received its early technological instruction from Britain.

What was draining resources and creativity from the enhancement of productive endeavors? It is possible that the United States might have improved its situation through certain choices; for as we know from the conditions in existence during America's development, ameliorating any one of these factors might have increased material production and wealth. The nation might have ventured investment in new sources of energy; or the people might have worked harder and longer hours, and consumed less and saved more; or the government and people might have invested in new and productive technology, from high-speed computers to industrial robots. As late as World War II the people had worked longer hours than in peacetime, restricted consumption, and increased savings, which they invested in technology and the building of new factories. The price of this development was the delay of gratification of leisure and material comforts, but it also offered the promise of future reward. Affluence and comfort and the pursuit of things not merely productive—art, music, and philosophy—did not conflict with productivity. Neither did the world role, which was to enhance the nation's position and growth, providing outlets for national energy and expertise. But its collapse followed the failure within. The nature of the exertion of this world role deserves analysis for the costs of its maintenance and the weariness of the public to maintain it.

Global Losses: Trade Deficit, Currency Devaluation, and Debtor Status

After World War II the United States had a huge surplus in its balance of trade, a gold stock totaling more than that of the rest of the world, and the basic currency of international exchange, the dollar, which transcended its fiscal importance as a symbol of power and stability. No more.

In 1971 the United States encountered the first deficit in its balance of merchandise trade since 1893. The problem was more severe and complex than the balance-of-payments issue, which had been pressing since the late 1950s. The payments deficit had been acceptable while the world had a dollar shortage and American trade burgeoned. It was the direct result of the conscious governmental decision-making to ship gold and hand out short-term IOUs in support of military forces abroad and of the economies of poor allies. The trade deficit was a failure of the national society to compete in the world.[28]

The warnings of those who saw the trade deficit coming were weak and late, and they went unheeded. Secretary of Commerce Maurice Stans went before a congressional committee in July 1971 to explain his forecast of the first negative trade balance of the century: the demand for raw materials and "low-technology" products was growing, while America's trade in agricultural products and high-technology goods remained stagnant. Showing a chart that plotted the nation's trade surplus to zero, he spoke prophetic words: "In 1971 the trade surplus may disappear altogether." At these hearings, Stans was echoed by John R. Pierce, an executive of Bell Telephone Laboratories, who pointed to the nation's technological deterioration. "For more than a quarter of a century we have taken technological preeminence and our industrial strength for granted, as if no action, domestic or foreign, could threaten them," he declared. "Now they are threatened, and so is our power to do the things that would make our world better." Representative John W. Davis, the subcommittee chairman, feared that "winter is coming" for American trade. No one knew what to do. Nothing was done.[29]

By the end of 1971, exports brought in $42,770 million; but imports cost Americans $45,459 million, forcing the deficit. Added to the debit side were the amounts that American travelers spent in other countries, a transfer that had been going on for years. On the credit side, the funds that Americans lent abroad yielded investment income in excess of their expenditures. When all the payments were tallied that year, the debit balance included government expenditures abroad, the largest of which were military transactions, totaling $6,468 million. The costs of stationing foreign troops and maintaining bases were not offset by the credits of private enterprise, and the trade in goods and services was no longer a source of income to wipe out the foreign outlays.[30]

The story of the sea change in the total value of goods that entered and left the country—of America's first trade deficit in the century—appeared on January 26, 1972, on page 45 of the *New York Times*. Although there was "no doubt" of the "underlying deterioration" of the nation's trade position, there was some denial. The story suggested that the deficit might be the result of dock strikes that had temporarily distorted export statistics. For technical monetary reasons, C. Fred Bergsten thought it inconceivable that the "bulk of the deterioration in the U.S. trade surplus" was the consequence of more than "purely temporary factors." He thought that the exchange rates of European and Japanese currencies would correct the imbalance. *Fortune* rationalized that the trend of prices rising less rapidly in the United States than in its major trading partners would show "favorable effects" in the trade figures. Besides, the Japanese were eliminating many of their quotas on imports of American-made goods and had promised to restrict voluntarily their exports of textiles to the United States.

All at once, some experts who had formerly seen trade underpinning America's world role—as a means of exercising a progressive influence and of funding overseas aid—argued that a trade surplus was simply unnecessary to sustain it. Writing in *Foreign Affairs,* Bergsten noted that if the Nixon administration wanted a large trade surplus to maintain its international power, it was ignoring the evidence that Britain's trade had frequently been in deficit during the century of the Pax Britannica, and the world role of the United States had survived the sharp decline in its trade balance as early as the late 1950s. Bergsten did not then confront the problem of Britain's decline or question the long-term consequences of current adverse trends. *Fortune* reported that the United States was earning so much on its foreign investments that other countries had to export more than they imported from the United States to obtain enough dollars to pay Americans their dividends. On balance, *Fortune* assured its readers, "There's no need to panic."[31]

Through the decade, the trade winds blew ill. The nation's imports did not subside but swelled. Whereas the trade books had once shown credits in nearly every category of export and with nearly every part of the world, just the opposite became the usual. The United States bought more than it sold of oil and gas, machinery, automobiles, telecommunications, clothes, iron and steel goods. It was buying more than it sold from Canada and Mexico, and all of South America; Britain, West Germany, and all of Western Europe; Japan, South Korea, Taiwan, and the rest of Asia; and all of Africa— so the deficit stretched to nearly every part of the world. The largest deficit was with Japan, the next largest with Canada. A sizable part of the trade deficit was with developing nations. Moreover, as trade fell into a deficit, it had become increasingly important to the economy—11 percent of GNP by 1985 as opposed to 5 percent after World War II.[32]

The faltering of trade set off speculation as to its causes. Even with rising real wages abroad, foreigners, according to Paul Samuelson, could "produce for themselves more cheaply than we have been producing for them. Hence they can outsell us increasingly in third markets, and can even begin to outsell us in our home markets."[33]

One might look afar for the changes in trade, but John Kenneth Galbraith held up a mirror to the United States. With the perspective of time, the father of the "affluent society" saw economic ideas as a reflection of the world in which they developed, whether those ideas belonged to Adam Smith or Karl Marx, and he realized that his own ideas of unbridled affluence that had characterized an era were prematurely dated. With a touch of weariness, he meditated on the aged industrial countries with "old and putatively senile" industries. The business organization of the United States was threatened by the young, flexible, and aggressive enterprises of Japan, Korea, Singapore, and Brazil, and potentially India. American expense for foreign products was "a marked subtraction from effective demand at home."[34]

The effects were obvious. Pictures in *National Geographic* and the daily press showed that automobiles and radios in the jungles and villages of developing countries were no longer likely to be of American make, but German or Japanese. In the early 1970s, Volkswagens appeared on the streets of Bangladesh and, closer to home, in Baja California. Until then the buses on the streets of Santiago, Chile, were mainly American-built; the new diesel buses were European. Chinese farmers were seen standing next to new Japanese trucks, and natives of other lands were holding Japanese portable radios. Toyota trucks took foreign laborers to work at the Al Ahmadi oil fields in Kuwait. A Datsun pickup was the preferred mode of transportation over camels or Plymouths for Bedouins in Saudi Arabia. Black workers at the South African border were in a Mitsubishi truck. The Red Cross jeeps fording the Torola River in a remote Salvadoran province were Nissan. There were still American things to be observed in developing countries—indeed, these lands emerged as America's largest market—but sometimes the products were the remains of the old days, such as a decayed 1940 Chevrolet spotted in Surabaja, Java, about thirty years after it was the latest design.[35]

Americans in large numbers turned in the 1970s and 1980s from General Motors and Ford cars to those of foreign make. Instead of Kodak cameras, people bought West German ones. Instead of RCA televisions, they bought Japanese Sony models. The most unlikely things came from the most unlikely places—baseball gloves from Taiwan and steel from Brazil. Sen. Robert Kasten was especially disturbed when he saw in the Senate gift shop postcards showing the Iwo Jima monument. The cards were printed in Japan. "We thought we knew which side won that battle. But now we know who's really winning."[36]

The Japanese lit up Times Square. Since the late 1960s the large, bright signs of American companies in the advertising mecca had come down, including those of *Time* and *Life*, Camel, Pepsi-Cola, Kleenex, Scripto pens, Knickerbocker beer, Chevrolet, Canadian Club, Admiral TV, and Lucky Strike. The signboards of Japanese manufacturers selling in America arose in their place. After Sony had created a display in 1972, up went signs for Fuji films, TDK Electronics, Toshiba high-technology devices, Canon U.S.A. cameras, AIWA America stereo components, Casio computers, Panasonic audio and video equipment, and VCX video cassettes. Where Fuji Film mounted a spectacular electric exhibit on the Forty-third Street corner, a "Buy More Bonds" sign had hung on V-J Day in 1945.[37]

The classical pattern in trade had been broken, that of an advanced industrial nation importing raw materials for conversion to useful goods in its factories. In the 1970s machinery and manufactured goods replaced oil as the top American import, and the automobile industry was benefiting from the voluntary import restraints of Japanese corporations. Now Lee Iacocca of the Chrysler Corporation had to wonder whether America had been reduced to a colony again, this time of Japan: "We send Japan low-value soybeans, wheat, corn, coal and cotton. They send us high-value autos, motorcycles, TV sets and oil-well casings. It's 1776 and we're a colony again."[38]

In a 1980s cover story, "The Yankee Trader: Death of a Salesman?" *U.S. News & World Report* suggested a metaphor of America's severe decline in trade: the disenchanted salesman, Willie Loman, in Arthur Miller's 1949 *Death of a Salesman*. Americans once thought they could outsell the world, but America's declining trade meant "a historic turn in its fortunes. The nation that has long taken pride in its Yankee-trader image now finds itself falling behind in the global marketplace." Unless it became more competitive, America as a salesman would die.[39]

Finally, Japan offered to help Americans in a way the United States had helped the Japanese after World War II: to increase purchases of foreign goods. The Japanese prime minister, Yasuhiro Nakasone, just as President Truman had done in the 1940s, asked his people to buy foreign goods. It was a rare appeal to the Japanese, but the results, according to an American in Tokyo a day later, were not entirely satisfactory. The opinion was widespread that "Americans just do not make products as well as the Japanese do." It was a strange reversal from the earlier times. A sushi chef from Yokohama said that although he was happy to buy foreign golf clubs and whisky, he bought Japanese cars. American telephones looked "old-fashioned" to the Japanese, and failed to sell. The image of the United States was of a country from which "any product that requires attention to detail, anything to do with mechanical quality control, anything to do with meticulousness and workmanship," was "suspect."[40]

Devaluation of the Dollar

As trade plunged into deficit, the dollar came under attack as the leading world currency. President Nixon's dramatic late-summer 1971 address declaring America's new relation to the world announced that the dollar would not be redeemable in gold. "We must protect the position of the American dollar as a pillar of monetary stability around the world," he vowed. But by ending the dollar's guaranteed support in gold, the president was closing a quarter-century period since the Bretton Woods agreement of 1944 that had witnessed the dollar as the main currency of world trade and commerce. The more dollars the United States spent abroad for goods or sent as foreign or military aid, the less welcome they became, so the dollar shortage became a dollar glut. In addition, the United States had shipped abroad its gold stocks. In 1971 the United States held less than half the gold it had after World War II. The government had initially tried to use its political influence to stave off the nations that demanded devaluation, but it could not protect economic power through artificial means.[41]

This was big news, dramatically reported. Trade had slowly and quietly slid into deficit with more of a whimper than a bang. But the devaluation of the dollar brought banner headlines in the *New York Times*. "A World Effect," said the paper of Nixon's unilateral change in the twenty-five-year-old monetary system. "Nixon's Economic Gamble" was the cover story in *Time,* which wistfully reminisced about an era that had ended: there was one "seemingly immutable fact of life. The U.S. dollar has remained the one major currency with an unquestioned and stable international value. Last week all that changed perhaps forever." The dollar had been "dethroned as the world's dominant currency." Only three months before, Treasury Secretary John Connally had stoutly told a Munich bankers' conference that "the dollar would not be devalued." Now there was no turning back.[42]

It was hard at first for leaders to realize the reduced status of their currency. The president blamed international money speculators for "waging an all-out war on the American dollar." Gold payments would be suspended "temporarily." He claimed not to be devaluing the dollar, though he acknowledged that the effect would be the same: it would raise the price of foreign cars and other imports. As Connally explained, the president's action did not "mean a devaluation." That depended on what other nations did. In his judgment, the dollar would rise vis-à-vis some currencies and decline vis-à-vis others. "It can't do anything but breed confidence."[43]

But others were struck by a cold reality. Leonard Silk wrote of Nixon's speech on August 15, 1971, that post–World War II American economic policy could be said to have ended on that date. Regardless of the quick economic benefits that might accrue from the president's move, the end of an "American-led" world monetary system defied disbelief. "We just ended the Bretton Woods system forever," said Arthur M. Okun, who as chairman of the Council of Economic Advisers under President Johnson had labored strenuously to maintain the system as a symbol of national stature. The fixed-exchange system of the dollar set in 1944, Paul Samuelson said, "became part of history."[44]

Before the end of December 1971, the heads of the leading industrial nations met in Washington, where, at the Smithsonian Institution, the national museum, Nixon accepted a formal devaluation of the dollar. The mission of the gathering was to arrange a new Bretton Woods Agreement, this time without the United States at the center of the world economy. Nixon sententiously told the representatives that whereas at the time of the Bretton Woods conference the United States was "predominant in economic affairs in the world," now "instead of just one strong economic nation, the nations of Europe, Japan and Asia, Canada and North America, all . . . are strong economically, strong competitors." Because negotiations took place among "equally strong nations insofar as their currencies were concerned," the dollar was formally depreciated mainly against the mark and the yen and floated against these and other currencies. Henceforth the dollar would be valued and devalued like any other currency. But confidence in the currency at a low level was not guaranteed. Its fluctuation was inherent in the Smithsonian agreement, and the dollar, according to Prof. Lorie Tarshis of Stanford University, had "lost its magic."[45]

The decline in the value of the dollar, which had the effect of reducing the cost of American-made goods abroad, was supposed, according to economic theory, to attract foreign buyers of American goods. Money held in foreign currencies was likely to come pouring back into America. The devaluation and deficits would be temporary setbacks after a brief adjustment. In one broad leap, Treasury Secretary Connally projected that the American trade deficit might be reversed, returning "our balance of trade and balance of payments to a favorable position." Paul Samuelson believed devaluation would work like a trick for American trade. "No longer can Japanese industries count upon flooding the American market with an increasing volume of their exports." The opposing view, neither as popular nor as hopeful, expressed by a businessman, Frazer B. Wilde, was that despite the devaluation "we are going to have a continuing problem on the trade balance. . . . Some of our major specialties, such as airplanes and electronics, will be a reduced factor in the future in producing exports."[46]

Within a year of the devaluation, the press was asking, "Is the dollar headed for more trouble?" It was. The American currency fell in value through the 1970s, the continuing crises blamed on the onslaughts in foreign-exchange markets. The dollar would rise again, and then fall to record postwar lows in the 1980s: Against the yen and the mark, the dollar fell in value to less than half of what it had been, from 3.65 marks in 1970, when the Bretton Woods Agreement was still strong, to 1.7 marks in the 1980s, and from 357.65 yen to near 100—a decline over an extended period not unlike that of the pound after World War II. The plight of the depreciated dollar was depicted in a cartoon in the *New York Daily News*: A man carried a box to his attic full of American dollars and put them next to a box of Confederate dollars. "Someday they'll rise again!" he said, shuffling away.[47]

The fundamental problems of producing competitive goods had not been solved, and the foreign-policy columnist C. L. Sulzberger understood the political ramifications: "The present crisis of the dollar has a symbolic significance transcending its purely financial aspects, for the dollar has come to be accepted as the quintessential token of United States power." Into the 1970s and 1980s, as the trade deficit worsened, no monetary maneuvers provided relief, for whether the dollar increased or decreased in value, the deficit continued unabated.[48]

Debtor Nation

That was not the end of troubles. American overseas investment was deteriorating, though this predicament was far from the minds of the financial experts of the early 1970s who thought the consolation in the trade deficit was that the United States had spread capital and bought into the industry of nearly every country of the world. Their perception of American investment in multinational corporations was that the return would provide the United States with the surplus wealth it needed for its world activity. Some economists at the Harvard Business School reasoned that the United States should become a service economy and live off its foreign investment income. An economist at the Brookings Institution wrote similarly: It did not matter that the United States had a deficit in its trade. Like Britain in the twentieth century, the United States could and should live off the income from its foreign assets. By this argument, which conveniently overlooked British decline, the United States could forget the notion of exporting goods, and instead import manufactured goods from less advanced lands.[49]

The tables had turned on the United States as the flow of capital abroad ebbed and foreign investment money increased at home. The investment took many forms: sums for plants, real estate, banks, financial institutions, government securities, and corporate stocks. Mammoth European and Japanese multinational companies established facilities in the United States. In a 1978 speech before the National Press Club, Chairman G. William Miller of the Federal Reserve Board warned that the United States was headed for economic decline if it continued to consume overindulgently rather than invest. "Will we neglect investment . . . for future generations?" he asked. "Will the legacy of our time be an economic desert?"[50]

In 1985 the United States became a net debtor to the rest of the world for the first time since 1914; a year later it became the largest debtor in the world, and all at once the greatest debtor in history. The commentator David Gergen asked in astonishment: "Us? The wealthiest, most dynamic economy in the world?" The Federal Reserve chairman, Paul Volker, warned that the predicament was "ominous." Only now did C. Fred Bergsten see a precedent for America's diminishing world position in the perceptible decline of Britain in the 1920s. But most coverage of this turning point was not dramatic. The *Wall Street Journal* buried the story on page 3 under the staid headline "Current Account Gap Grew in Quarter, Confirming U.S. Is Net Debtor Nation," and the *New York Times* placed its report in the business section. That week President Reagan was asked in a news conference whether he was disturbed that for the first time in seventy years the United States had become a debtor nation. "Are we?" the president responded. "Should we care?" asked the *Times* editorial. "In theory, no," but "in practice, yes."[51]

Consumers were generally aware that Mercedes-Benz, Toyota, Volkswagen, Sony, and Shell Oil had foreign origins. But many did not know, as Earl Fry pointed out in 1980 in *Financial Invasion of the U.S.A.,* that some of the everyday products they used were "controlled by foreign interests." Common foods, such as Libby fruits and vegetables, Keebler cookies, Stouffer cakes, Nestlé's chocolates, and Good Humor and Baskin-Robbins ice cream, were owned by overseas concerns. The supermarket chains A & P and Grand Union were connected to foreign firms, as were the clothing stores Gimbels and Saks Fifth Avenue. Medical companies supplying Alka-Seltzer and Pepsodent toothpaste were purchased by foreigners. The *New York Post, Village Voice, Parents' Magazine, Esquire, New West, New York,* and Bantam paperback publishers were all foreign-owned. In addition, Clorox, Borax, SOS soap pads, Kiwi polish, Bic pens and lighters, Kool cigarettes, Magnavox, and Capitol records were among the popular goods that had strong foreign linkages.[52]

The names on the lists of foreign-owned companies changed, as firms were bought and sold, merged and divested, but the foreign-buying trend continued in the 1980s. Foreign investment came from all over the globe, primarily from Britain, Japan, Canada, West Germany, the Netherlands, and Saudi Arabia. *Newsweek* reported that foreigners were "buying America" because they had an abundance of capital, which America lacked. "It's the savings of a Bavarian innkeeper who can earn only 3.5 per cent a year at his bank at home; it's the British Airways pension fund, which owns a shopping center in Houston. It's the oil money of Iranians, among them a sister of the Shah, who have bought so many of the million-dollar homes in the Trousdale Estates section of Beverly Hills that the natives call it 'the Persian Gulf.' And it's the Eurodollars in the coffers of polyglot multinationals in Stockholm and Stuttgart, using the profits from their exports to the U.S. to build and buy factories here. The Germans make Volkswagen Rabbits in a Pennsylvania factory that Chrysler had to abandon. The Japanese bottle Coca-Cola in New Hampshire, raise cattle in Utah and make soy sauce in rural Wisconsin." It was not the rich American bringing capital to other lands. Now *Newsweek* told the story of one American's Italian cousin landing at Kennedy Airport in New York City with $700,000 in his suitcase. Over the phone he struck a deal with a realty company for a Fifth Avenue office building.[53]

"America on the Auction Block," trumpeted *U.S. News & World Report.* The "'For Sale' sign" was up across the United States, and foreign investors were "on a shopping spree" from coast to coast. *Time,* in its cover story "The Selling of America," offered three words of advice for foreigners: "Buy! Buy! Buy!" The article pictured the United States as "a huge shopping mart in which foreigners are energetically filling up their carts. . . . Never before have U.S. citizens witnessed so many familiar landmarks and trademarks passing into foreign hands."[54]

That foreign buyers bailed out or purchased firms that had "America" in their name or had a prestigious national image was a sign of how important their funds were as a source of capital. BankAmerica negotiated a sale of $350 million of new securities to Japanese financial companies to replenish its supply of capital. After a German publisher bought Doubleday, the Penguin Publishing Company of London bought the New American Library. General Electric sold its stake in RCA's record company to a West German concern, which already owned 25 percent of it. American Motors had been owned by France's Renault before it ceased to have an independent existence when sold to Chrysler in the 1980s. Bruce Springsteen, who recorded the popular rock song "Born in the USA," released by CBS records, found that his company had been sold to Sony.[55]

The money the Japanese had piled up from their foreign trade surplus also flowed into financial institutions until it hardly surprised a Citicorp official that the "U.S. banks' preeminence is being dissolved by the aggressiveness of the Japanese." In 1968 the largest bank in the world was Bank of America, and six of the world's top ten banks were American. In 1987 the largest bank in the world was Dai-Ichi Kangyo Bank, seven of the top ten banks were Japanese, and the largest American lender, Citibank, ranked seventeenth. The Japanese bought billions of dollars' worth of U.S. Treasury bonds. They bought private bonds. They bought stocks. The Nippon Life Insurance Company acquired a sizable stake in Shearson Lehman Brothers. A bank like Sumitomo could easily buy the American houses of Salomon, Merrill Lynch, and Goldman.[56]

So too with real estate. The Dai-Ichi Mutual Life company—whose building General MacArthur had commandeered for his headquarters after World War II—purchased a large part of Citicorp's headquarters in New York, setting a record for a single financial commitment made for an American property by an investor from Japan. The Japanese bought Chase Plaza in Los Angeles, the Paine Webber building in Boston, and the Exxon Building, ABC's headquarters, the Tiffany building, and Rockefeller Center in New York.[57]

American companies were not toughening up lethargic nineteenth-century European companies anymore, since in a progression after Chrysler left Europe, Firestone pulled out of Switzerland, and ITT left France. Foreign companies, more likely than not from Japan, were streamlining American firms. A *Wall Street Journal* case study of foreign takeovers investigated the television manufacturer Motorola, after it became part of Matsushita Electric Industrial Co. in 1974. The reporter found the Japanese incredulous at the backwardness of American industrial technique. "The Japanese had been aware that Quasar"—the name the Japanese gave the firm—"had manufacturing and quality-control problems, but hadn't been aware of their magnitude": Expenses for warranty repairs were at least double and sometimes quadruple those for Japanese sets. So the Japanese removed the incompetent American management and sent over Japanese executives. They began heavy capital spending, totaling $15 million, to modernize the plant, as Motorola had not invested in it since the late 1960s. They increased efficiency on the assembly lines, replacing the old conveyor belts with stoppable ones, so that a worker could finish a task correctly before sending his completed work down the line. The Japanese also brought their technological advancement to the American product. They redesigned Quasar television sets so that they could be made on automated equipment that matched equipment in other Matsushita plants. New labor relations were begun with the nonunion workers. Efforts were made to make the surroundings more comfortable by adding lights and fans to improve ventilation. Employees were also given brooms and were expected to clean up after themselves. The company held ten-minute meetings twice a day between foremen and line workers to discuss production. Productivity rose 25 percent; the rejection rate was down from 20 percent under American management to 2 percent.[58]

Foreign companies employed increasing numbers of Americans. On *Newsweek*'s cover those facing unemployment could read: "Your Next Boss May Be Japanese." Perhaps 250,000 Americans worked "for Japan Inc., making it one of the largest and fastest-growing employers in the United States. . . . The Japanese will no longer be the inscrutable, seemingly invulnerable economic rival across the ocean. They will be across the street." As they moved in, they were met with resistance to their growing influence: "Some don't like what the Japanese did to Pearl Harbor; others, what they did to Detroit." Yet the magazine offered advice to employees who wanted to win over a Japanese boss: "Eat sushi, work long hours, be patient."[59]

The United States eventually imported technology and management skills in an effort to compete. The decision of General Motors to seek assistance from Toyota to produce a new subcompact emphasized the shortcomings of American manufacturing technique. Assembled at a GM plant in Fremont, California, the car would not only be of Toyota design but would also have a Toyota engine and transmission, and the entire operation would be supervised by a Toyota executive. GM's need for help from a company that its executives had hardly deigned to notice not many years before raised the question of why this corporation, once studied as the model of scientific manage-ment, could not produce a high-quality small car on its own. "The reason for turning to the Japanese is simple," said the manager of Chevrolet. "With their lower production costs, Japanese manufacturers can sell small cars at prices that American manufacturers can only match by selling at a loss." By recognizing the "pre-eminence of Japanese companies as the world's masters at making small cars," the Americans might learn from them.[60]

Shorn of their income from foreign trade and investment, Americans sought relief from the costs and burdens of providing aid. In 1971, for the first time since the beginning of the Marshall Plan in 1948, the Senate refused to pass in some form a foreign-aid measure requested by an administration. Sen. Mike Mansfield lamented an "end of the foreign aid program as initiated after World War II in the Marshall Plan." "The era of General Marshall's brave new world is over," C. L. Sulzberger noted. In the 1980s Vice President George Bush met with Egyptian president Hosni Mubarak to tell him that domestic budget imbalances made it impossible for the United States to provide the aid he requested. And when Secretary of State George Shultz visited Africa, a Nigerian reporter, citing the cuts in American aid to Africa, asked whether they were motivated "by racism or economics." Shultz simply explained America's budget prob-lems, saying, "If you think you have troubles here, you should see our troubles with our budget." Japan took over as the world's principal donor.[61]

Nations growing in economic strength, it followed as if axiomatically, gained cultural influence. Half a world away from Japan, the *New York Times* reported, "Japa-nese power soars in New York." It was the new cultural power that accompanied Japanese wealth. The 10:30 p.m. train to North White Plains out of Grand Central Station had a new name: the "Orient Express," the reporter called it, because many of its passengers were Japanese who had lingered in Japanese restaurants to send telexes to home offices in Tokyo. The sixty thousand Japanese who lived in the New York area had formed their own restaurants, bars, newspapers, television programs, country clubs, and private schools. The "Asian influence" had grown in American arts, theater, dance, music, fashion, and film. At New York nightclubs, "Asians . . . , particularly the Japanese, are preferred customers, bringing cash and cachet." The newspaper noted "a shift in the way the Japanese relate to Americans. No longer deferential to American skill, the Japanese appear to have acquired a new confidence and seem less eager to adopt American ways than to bring Japanese convention to New York." "Japanese don't feel so intimidated by Americans anymore," said one Japanese. "They know

America has a problem. It is a matter of economic power. It affects their attitude." Said another, "We have learned so much from the United States. Now we have the reverse situation. Americans can learn from us."[62]

In the balance sheet of America's world role, the United States from World War II until the 1970s received income from its trade. But these funds hardly compared to the outlays for aid, grants, and military ventures. As other nations had grown in competitiveness, the United States had expanded its world programs—the Korean War, the Vietnam War, NATO and alliance expenses, and military aid. Eventually the United States spent assets accumulated during its rise to support its role, and it went into debt.

The reasons for the deterioration in America's international position were not that America's civilian foreign aid programs had worked wonders abroad, and that the outflow of direct foreign investment and technology had provided other nations with knowledge and expertise. These activities did not determine that the recipients would outproduce the United States in automobiles, steel, and televisions. On the contrary, the activities enlarged total world trade, and the United States stood to gain along with many nations. When America was rising in England's latter days of great power, England came to be surpassed in productivity by a number of nations. It did not channel its financial and social energies into productive enterprise as it had done before, as the United States was then doing—or as Japan would do.

The failure of the society to compete effectively was evidence that American decline was not the result of the revival of other nations alone. The Japanese had not grasped some secret that had been unknown to the Americans. They were doing essentially what Americans themselves had done. They worked hard for future reward, applied technology to production, put capital into production of high-quality goods at low cost, and provided most of their population a sense of well-being with the fair and even distribution of wealth. They traded hard abroad and kept their defense forces small and lean.

The fall from economic dominance left the United States without sufficient wealth to take care of unlimited foreign commitments and at the same time to handle its domestic needs. The relative decline in production, then, related to the changes in the factors of production—the raw materials, technology, and capital resources—that had made possible the rise to power. The United States was beset by misguided use of resources, low savings, wanton consumption, and a loss of quality and efficiency in production. The yielding of power was very much at the choosing of the Americans, who preferred the indulgence of consumption, whether on luxuries or on foreign undertakings, to the imagination and discipline of production. That opened the way for another power to surpass them.

The bottom line was this: The American surplus on current private account was no longer large enough to cover world programs. If America needed to finance its world role out of current income, how long could it afford to do so if it lost the source of its foreign income? The maintenance of a world role within its income meant that the United States, having lost its surplus in trade, would have to lower its standard of living or import capital and go into debt to foreign nations—the same nations it was supposed to be protecting within its area of influence.

Dollars expended on private domestic requirements were not necessarily withheld from world purposes. Some things were productive and some were not, whether at home or abroad. Investment in industry would yield returns for future growth, and the development of other nations would reap general benefits. The difference between the effect of improving the domestic and world societies was immaterial: the result was improving factory productivity, cleaning the air and environment, and adding teachers to the staffs of schools, whether in New York or Bolivia. The issue was what enhanced the human condition, progress, and power—for these are the essence of a world role that made for legitimacy in the eyes of other peoples. The nation did not damage its world role because of its total overseas commitments, but only some. Americans had financed foreign involvements and had at the same time lived well at home, but overconsumption and war had forced choices between preparation for war and factories, hospitals, houses, fashions, and food—at home and elsewhere.

20

The

New

World

At dusk on June 30, 1977, two years after American helicopters had taken flight from the roof of the U.S. embassy in Saigon, abandoning Vietnam, the flags of the remaining member nations of the Southeast Asia Treaty Organization were lowered for the last time at the Bangkok headquarters. The central command terminated all functions, the building was sold to the Thai government for its Foreign Ministry, and the secretary-general left his office. SEATO, which Dwight Eisenhower and John Foster Dulles had conceived in 1954 as remaining in force indefinitely, had dissolved itself.[1]

The alliance that John Kennedy had told Americans to take pride in and that Lyndon Johnson and his advisors had cited as justification for the defense of South Vietnam was ultimately more of a legal symbol of global influence than a mutual security pact. In 1975 the Thai and Filipino governments recommended that SEATO be phased out, and the leaders of Malaysia, Singapore, and Indonesia viewed the organization as obsolete. Pakistan had withdrawn years earlier, France had suspended its support, and Britain had kept no significant military presence east of Suez. After the defeat of the United States in Vietnam, the Asian members thought it extremely unlikely that the Americans would send another expeditionary force to Asia. So the American frontiers of interest crumbled. CENTO was disbanded in 1979, over the objections of the American secretary of state. And when New Zealanders voted to ban from their territory all nuclear weapons, including those on American warships, the United States suspended military ties and ANZUS faded away in the 1980s.[2]

The United States had assumed the role of successor to the European world system that had passed with World War II. The American world role in turn ended. The balance of power had altered as other lands became stronger. In a survey of the newly emerging world, the question we should bear in mind is this: To what extent was the decline of the American world role the result of the growth of other nations, and to what extent was it the result of actions of its own choosing? In his 1970 report to the Congress and the nation on American foreign policy, President Nixon declared: "The postwar period in international relations has ended. Then, we were the only great power whose society and economy had escaped World War II's massive destruction." With the close of that era, the vision ended of the United States as "the richest and most stable country, without whose initiative and resources little security or progress was possible."[3]

The Common Market

In Western Europe, out of the war rubble Europeans had built modern industry, housing, and transportation. By the 1960s, declared *Time,* the "'economy of abundance,' once a U.S. phrase and fact, was visible in other lands. . . . A wartime G.I.—or even 1954's tourist—would hardly recognize the place." Throughout West Germany, closed military installations became industrial plants; along the Rhine oil refineries and petrochemical facilities were monuments to Europe's new business firms. France's damaged port of Rouen had new docks, new bridges, new housing developments for the employees who worked in refineries, yielding three times their prewar capacity, and in new plastics and textile plants. To the south, the land opposite Venice's lagoon had emerged as a top industrial center, producing vast quantities of aluminum. Germany, France, and Italy had grown at much faster rates than the United States; Germany's annual growth rate of 8.6 percent from 1950 to 1960 was more than double that of the United States. With the integration of nations in the European Common Market—West Germany, France, Italy, the Netherlands, Belgium, Luxembourg, and eventually Britain—a great economic power arose in the 1960s, challenging C. L. Sulzberger to describe Europe, including Britain, as a new superpower that might eventually wield concerted political power. It was already "the greatest commercial superpower of them all."[4]

Individually, the European nations did not mount great power, but together they did. Britain had collapsed from the world's mightiest empire to a little nation, which press reports in America characterized as the "Sicily of the North Sea" or the "Pakistan of Europe." After World War II Britain had been Europe's richest major nation. But with the lowest growth rate in the Western industrial world, Britain was overtaken by France and Germany and fell down the list of producers until it lagged with Italy. Having ceased to be a formidable force of its own in the world, and certainly no longer a superpower, as William T. R. Fox had thought a mere three decades before, Britain joined the Common Market in 1971, ending a centuries-old aloofness from the Continent and severing special political ties with the United States, which no longer sufficed to promote British interests.[5]

American interest in old England dwelled on its recent history, for if such a precipitous decline could happen to that power, might it not happen to the United States? This question would have been unthinkable a mere few years before. Then there had been no comparison between the nations: One was a continental giant with the shining assets of modernity, and the other was a crowded island with industry that had failed to modernize. But now Max Lerner, reporting from London, observed: "The symptoms of the British malady are economic, but its roots are political, psychological, intellectual and moral. This could, of course, be said of the United States as well, and there are signs that America may be following the same road to sickness as Britain and that in 20 years it could arrive at the same outcome." The " 'Little Englanders' have had their way and have their twilight day now. When the horizons shrink, the men grow smaller."[6]

Why had Britain failed to keep growing? This was a postwar puzzle. American commentators hardly knew where to begin to sort it out. They listed a number of reasons, including the ineptitude of British businessmen, the self-indulgence of British workers organized into unions, the failure to control welfare services, the high taxes that had prevented the accumulation of capital, and the vain defense of the pound as a major currency and a trapping of empire. Even the cheerful temperament of the British was blamed for perhaps lulling them into a false sense of security.[7]

The deficit in British trade was running at millions of pounds a month, leaving the docks of British ports desolate and segments of the working population impoverished. Britain's losses overseas were financed by foreign money deposits in London, mainly from the developing countries it had once dominated and from Japan. In 1974 the former banker of the world obtained a $1.2 billion dollar credit—not from the United States but from Iran—to help finance its trade deficit. The largest center of Japanese engineering in Europe was in Britain, around Newcastle, a city once known for coal mining and shipbuilding. After Nissan built a state-of-the-art automotive plant near the city in 1986, twenty other Japanese firms followed suit. In the 1980s the Victoria and Albert Museum, a repository for the artifacts of British greatness, tried to get the backing of Japanese companies to keep open its nostalgic galleries to the past.[8]

With its economic outlook diminished, Britain belatedly cut defense spending. The American government unhappily recognized that Britain's international policing days were over. In the 1970s the British government decided, despite NATO protests, to remove the bulk of its naval and air forces from the Mediterranean, completing a move begun in 1947 with its withdrawal from Greece and Turkey. Lacking the wealth to patrol the world's sea lanes, Britain closed bases and cut forces from Malta to Singapore and Hong Kong. The naval base near Cape Town in South Africa was given up, and frigates were withdrawn from the West Indies. On a late June afternoon under showery skies in 1977, the foreign correspondent R. W. Apple, Jr., observed the royal fleet, assembled to pay tribute to Queen Elizabeth II in a jubilee celebration, "much reduced in scope but still the heir to the rich tradition of Drake and Nelson." The queen on the afterdeck of the royal yacht *Britannia* watched through binoculars as submarines, minesweepers, frigates, destroyers, cruisers, and small craft passed in review. Despite the impressive display, Apple noted the "inescapable signs of the change that has swept over Britain." In 1953, when the queen was crowned, the Royal Navy had been the second largest in the world. In the 1970s, with less than one-third as many ships, it had been surpassed by both the Soviet and the Chinese fleets. "The British think little about their navy nowadays," the reporter mused.[9]

Still, Britain's entry into the Common Market added considerably to the total power of the European union. With a third of the world's trade, the Common Market had double the trade volume of the United States. It held gold and foreign exchange reserves at least three times larger than those of the United States. Although the United States had for years enjoyed a trade surplus with Europe, in the 1970s it began buying more goods from the Common Market countries than it sold to them.

The European superpower had emerged because of its economic strength, but it soon played an increasingly independent role outside NATO, even though it did not have complete political cohesion or a mighty military, despite the nuclear forces Britain and France clung to. To stem the growth of that independence, in 1973 Secretary of State Henry Kissinger envisioned a plan to strengthen European ties to the American alliance during the "Year of Europe," so called because "the era that was shaped by decisions of a generation ago is ending." He grasped one point that was part of the government's policy thereafter: "The revival of western Europe is an established fact, as is the historic success of its movement toward economic unification." In the next decade, steps toward European union strove toward free and open trade and common currency.[10]

Russia

The Soviet Union was the second-greatest industrial nation during the 1970s, and until then it had been growing much faster than the United States. Even as the Soviet growth rate slowed, the Soviet Union had surpassed the United States in the staple commodities of steel, oil, pig iron, coal, cement, tractors, cotton, and wool. *Newsweek* gave credit to the "new champion": In 1971 "Khrushchev's boast had finally come true." For the first time since 1895, the United States was not the world's largest steel producer. The Soviet Union produced 133 million tons of steel, compared to the 120.2 million tons produced in the United States. In 1974 the Soviet Union became the world's top oil producer with 3.4 billion barrels, pushing the United States into second place with 3.2 billion. Even Soviet commercial seapower outranked that of the United States in total tonnage of vessels. When the *New York Times* announced that the Soviet Union had seized world leadership in steel production, fulfilling a fifty-year-old ambition, the paper asked, "Will the over-all American industrial lead continue for long?"[11]

In the 1970s the Soviet standard of living had risen, but unevenly and at a slow pace. A *National Geographic* journalist on a trip to Leningrad discovered that even if food prices were exorbitant by American standards, an industrial worker's family might well own a television, a phonograph, and a record collection, including songs of Western singers, one favorite being Tom Jones. The American further admitted that the vast Union of Soviet Socialist Republics had risen "to the status of a superpower," but he pointed out that the country's burdensome bureaucracy had failed to meet shortages of consumer goods and housing. He witnessed no major changes in the abuses of censorship and abridgement of personal liberty.[12]

The Soviet Union had unceasingly confronted the United States with a large army, and it proceeded to construct a modern navy to challenge American ships on the high seas and in the Mediterranean. In the early 1970s it possessed 1,618 ICBMs compared to 1,054 for the United States. But Nixon decided that the United States was ready to accept approximate parity in nuclear weapons. Because each of the two nuclear nations had "the power to destroy humanity," the president urged that it was in the interests of each to recognize that building additional weapons did not provide advantage. This reasoning produced the Strategic Arms Limitation Treaty in May 1972, an agreement without precedent, by which, as Kissinger noted, the world's two most powerful nations, divided by ideology, history, and conflicting interests, mutually restrained armaments.[13]

The detente of the 1970s did not proceed smoothly, not after the Soviet Union invaded Afghanistan and a second SALT treaty went unratified. But in the mid-1980s a new leader, Mikhail Gorbachev, embarked on a domestic revolution that reached into every area of life. Observing that Soviet economic growth had fallen behind that of the West, he hoped to turn the national resources from waging cold war to domestic production. Gorbachev intended this change to overcome Soviet backwardness, which bothered one American on his arrival in Moscow. His hotel "did not have an automated registration-and-reservation service—the kind we take for granted in the United States." The impression he gained during his stay was that the Soviet economy was "low-tech." The Soviet Union was "a Third World country with rockets." Gorbachev's restructuring of the economy, which he called *perestroika*, partially dismantled the government's central planning bureaucracy and instituted free-market reforms.[14]

In Soviet society, the openness of *glasnost* allowed students to question strict doctrinal interpretations of history. They engaged in discourse with teachers and found fault with communism. Historians revealed long-classified secrets of Stalin-era labor camps, and they exchanged views of the past with American scholars. George Orwell's novel of totalitarian dictatorship, *1984*, which had been banned for forty years, was published in 1988. Rock music received new legitimacy. One band popular among Soviet youths by the name of Avtograf, according to an American review, recalled "American rock 15 years ago." Yet at a concert at Olympic Stadium in Moscow, Soviet young people heard the touring American musician Billy Joel, and they danced in the aisles and pressed toward the stage. The evangelist Billy Graham preached to believers in an Orthodox church in Moscow. Broadcasts of the Voice of America were no longer jammed. Soviet television presented a show of satire called *Montazh,* described by one observer as the "Soviet equivalent" of *Saturday Night Live.* The NBC *Today* show and *Nightly News* were allowed to make live broadcasts with few travel restrictions. A Soviet dissident who had fled his country twelve years before returned to Moscow in 1987 for an eight-day visit; he came away with a clear impression that the intelligentsia, scientists, doctors, and engineers of his acquaintance had a new attitude and a sense of commitment to stand against the bureaucracy.[15]

The Soviet Union never buried the American economy as Khrushchev had threatened, and in high technology it had failed. Soviet legions and nuclear weaponry had no advantage in a condition of deterrence where both sides had sufficient weapons to destroy each other. Soviet tyrannical rule was mellowing less because of direct pressure from the United States than because of the internal pressures if its own society to modernize. So George Kennan had lived to see come to pass his prediction that time would run out on the Soviet regime built by Stalin and Lenin. A fundamental threat to the American world role came not from the enemy but from allies within the old hegemonic frontiers of influence.[16]

Japan

In a part of the globe that after World War II was ravaged and developing and unlikely to mount a challenge to the United States, a new power arose. By the late 1960s Japan had become the world's third-largest economic power. In the early 1970s the stated goal of Japanese government and business leaders was not merely to close the diminishing gap with the Soviet Union but to rival the United States in wealth. *U.S. News & World Report* noted in 1970: Japan was "convinced that it can and will replace the U.S. as the richest nation in the world. . . . Japanese ambitions are unconcealed. The energetic islanders are clearly determined to be *Ichiban*—Number One." Estimates of how long it would take to reach this goal ranged from thirty to fifty years, somewhere around the end of the century, but the magazine found agreement among both Japanese and Westerners that "Japanese competition confronts the U.S. with the toughest challenge it has ever had." After all, the annual growth rate of Japan's gross national product through the postwar period approached 10 percent, nearly three times that of the United States, and it climbed to 11.1 percent between 1960 and 1969.[17]

The National Geographic Society, which had routinely dispatched observers to investigate hinterland cultures, in the mid-1970s sent one to ask the Japanese "about the secrets of their success." "Who will own the 21st Century?" the society's journal asked. The reporter had the impression that, despite Japan's rising productivity, the Japanese standard of living was not high in Western terms. The Japanese worked hard at jobs six days a week. They lived simply, not lavishly. Their homes were small and compact. Clothes dryers were rare and electric dishwashers almost nonexistent.[18]

Yet their very frugality enabled the Japanese to save for the future and promoted Japanese success. Before the 1970s were over, the sociologist Ezra Vogel had written a book called *Japan as Number One,* and in 1986 he suggested in *Foreign Affairs* that the world was on the verge of a "Pax Nipponica." After his first trip to Japan in the 1960s, Vogel had "not even questioned the general superiority of American society and American institutions," but now he wrote, "Future historians may well mark the mid-1980s as the time when Japan surpassed the United States to become the world's dominant economic power."[19]

In the 1980s, Japan surpassed the Soviet Union in economic production. It was the world's largest producer of ships, automobiles, and televisions. It had the largest corporation in the world. It had the largest banks. It had the largest stock market. It was the most successful trader on earth. It was the world's greatest creditor. It was calculated to be the world's richest nation in total assets, domestic and foreign. It became the greatest financial power in the world. Thus before the end of the 1980s Clyde Prestowitz wrote *Trading Places*, presenting the proposition that Japan had gained much of the prestige that America had lost.[20]

With Britain declining, and Americans wondering why, they also wondered why Japan had the strength to challenge the United States. The United States had possessed all the advantages in resources, population, science and technology, and industrial plant; Japan was one of the poorest countries in the world in oil, coal, iron ore, and the minerals of modern industry, and its population was less than half that of the United States. But Japanese success was ascribed to several factors. Cheap labor was one. Japanese employees and salesmen worked tirelessly and aggressively for wages Americans would not accept. That work ethic gave the Japanese an advantage, but it was not the only reason for the competition presented to the United States, because Japanese labor costs were higher than elsewhere in Asia and were on a par with European costs. Eventually they rose to the American level.[21]

Some detractors blamed the Japanese for borrowing American science. But the Japanese adapted American innovations and turned them into salable products, as the Americans had once raided British and European technology, and eventually the Japanese made their own technological advances. As the world's thriftiest savers, the Japanese invested heavily in their businesses and in research for new products. They were not profligate consumers who spent on luxury or for the moment, as Americans were increasingly wont to do. American businessmen faulted Japanese tariffs for the failure of their exports to Japan. Only eighteen Chevrolet Corvette cars were sold in Japan in 1972 because, they said, the price in the United States was $5,500 and in Japan $17,000. Import duties played a part in the restraint of trade, but so did legal agreements and price-fixing. Finally, the Japanese were criticized for their freedom from heavy expenditures for defense because Japan's constitution—written under American supervision after the war—forbade the country from establishing a military, and the United States was protecting it under defense agreements. That allowed the Japanese to raise capital.[22]

But the Japanese found virtue in their own success. A strong cultural consensus existed among them to develop technology and to increase production. The Japanese orientation toward voluntary group agreement and behavior was important to the culture, and the people joined in a concerted effort that valued innovation and profit. At 8 o'clock one morning an American, standing in a Matsushita TV factory, observed the workers line up and begin to sing the company song:

For the building of a new Japan,
Let's put our strength and mind together,
Doing our best to promote production,
Sending our goods to the people of the world,
Endlessly and continuously,
Like water gushing from a fountain.
Grow, industry, grow, grow, grow!

Even the executives and scientists were supposed to sing this song. The corporate group loyalty contributed to efficiency and teamwork in pursuit of trade.[23]

Japanese success prompted *U.S. News & World Report* to raise the question thirty years after Pearl Harbor: "Who Really Won World War II in Asia?" The article proposed that the history books might have had it wrong in stating that the United States had won a clear victory: "In a strict military sense, the United States and its allies won. . . . But if winning means which nations ended up 30 years later holding positions of strength in Asia, then I think you have to say that Japan and the Communists in China were the big winners." In 1985 Theodore H. White, who had witnessed General Mac-Arthur oversee the Japanese surrender on board the U.S.S. *Missouri,* reminisced about that day in one of his last published pieces before he died: The Americans were "bedazzled by the splendor of the day—for here was American power at its zenith." The "power was all ours and stretched, visibly, as far as the eye could see." But had it been an illusion? So much had changed: "Today, 40 years after the end of World War II, the Japanese are on the move again in one of history's most brilliant commercial offensives, as they go about dismantling American industry. Whether they are still only smart, or have finally learned to be wiser than we, will be tested in the next 10 years. Only then will we know who finally won the war 50 years before."[24]

Japan had achieved the capability of new world influence not because of its limited military but by virtue of its position in the world economy. Sony, which had been a repairer of radio sets after World War II, had been built into a giant industrial conglomerate, as had Honda, Panasonic, and Canon. Japanese companies became world traders, leaving evidence of their products on every continent. West Germans bought Japanese cameras. From Afghanistan to Bolivia, Japanese trucks outsold the competition. In America, their production had gained easy access to markets in steel, electronics, and automobiles. Sony and Panasonic televisions and radios, Honda motorcycles, and Toyota and Datsun automobiles became commonplace. As the world's largest banker, Japan's overseas investments were greater than any other nation's. The yen became a leading international currency.

The presence of Japanese businessmen abroad had first increased in Southeast Asia and Thailand and became visible in Africa, along with technical experts. In Zaire, Japanese mining engineers dug for copper ore. The Japan Overseas Cooperation Volunteers, similar to the American Peace Corps, sent young people to developing nations. In Ethiopia, Japanese technicians vaccinated villagers against smallpox, and near its border in Kenya they helped build a Nairobi–Addis Ababa highway. In Kenya, Japanese taught girls sewing. With an eye on the developed world, the Japanese who owned the Alaska Lumber and Pulp Company employed American lumberers to provide the raw material for Japanese photographic film and for houses. The Japanese owned hotels in Honolulu in a district known locally as "Little Tokyo." They bought businesses and skyscrapers on the American coasts and in the heartland.[25]

China

But Japan's story, as big as it was, might not have been the biggest story. Japan showed what other nations, even poor ones, were capable of, and the Japanese quickly faced competition from new nations manifesting dynamism in the Pacific region. Since the early 1960s, Taiwan, South Korea, Singapore, and Hong Kong had grown in production and trade. Their populations, once poor, came to rank with the most affluent in the world. In Taiwan's capital, Taipei, high-rise office buildings went up. "American-style department stores, with everything from videocassette recorders to expensive clothing imported from Europe, are crammed with shoppers," read one American report. But though the stores were in the American fashion, the products were mainly Japanese. In the streets of Seoul, clogged with oxen twenty years before, cars were so numerous they could barely move. Hong Kong boomed "as an emporium of trade and light industry." Its harbor was filled not, as in the old days, with junks but with great ships. Huge textile mills produced twenty-four hours a day. An American visited executive suites atop new skyscrapers to meet "successful capitalists" who had once been "poverty-stricken farmers." Back on the street, he looked for a ricksha and realized that this "old trademark of the Orient" was "doomed to disappear." Ricksha pulling was considered a degrading occupation, and the government issued no more licenses.[26]

These Asian nations precipitated an extraordinary shift in the world's centers of power. Beginning in 1980 the United States traded more with Asia than with Western Europe, marking a major historical reorientation centuries after the Europeans had encountered the New World seeking trade. And that trade was in deficit with Asia. Korea rose rapidly in world trade by shipping to foreign markets inexpensive autos, electronics, and clothing, becoming a strong competitor with Japan. Hong Kong, the world's top exporter of clothing, was also exporting its own industrial products, and it came to bank 10 percent of the world's sterling reserve. Singapore had become a major financial center. Starting with few raw materials, unskilled populations, and little knowledge of advanced science, these countries prospered by buying materials abroad and placing high value on education, a work ethic, and frugality and savings. Their GNPs grew at up to 10 percent a year. Their standards of living rose and Americans reported from the East of the coming "Pacific Century." How would it be otherwise once China emerged as Japan, Singapore, and Hong Kong had emerged?[27]

After the Cultural Revolution of the 1960s, China had lagged in economic development, but in the 1970s China was no longer a latent dragon that might on some future day stir from its sleep. *National Geographic* still showed farmers plowing fields behind water buffaloes and lotus-filled ponds, but it also pictured Shanghai as an industrial center of billowing smokestacks that produced the goods of the nation's busiest port, crowded with modern freighters. A country historically plagued by famine and subsistence levels of consumption now produced enough to feed its population of one billion people, with amounts left over to export abroad. China had increased its productivity at an annual rate matched by only a handful of other modern nations. As technological efficiency grew, the nation raised capital in China's first "stock market."[28]

Observers characterized the Chinese people in pursuit of a better life. They saw mud huts of the peasants had been replaced by brick homes. In the streets of Canton, banned human-powered rickshas had been superseded by bicycles, trucks, taxis, and buses. The exotic enchantment of distant pagodas remained, but vanished were the mandarins and most of the beggars, robbers, and opium dens. The old trains in which people had been herded like cattle were gone; the trains were efficient and immaculate. In the first five years of the 1980s, living standards doubled.[29]

In the 1980s other travelers to China brought back photographs that showed the people had forgone dressing in Mao suits. Instead, children appeared in embroidered dresses and overalls, women in colorful prints and jewelry, and businessmen sported monogrammed shirts under three-piece worsteds. "Hotels throb with disco music or deliver Muzak. In the street, there is the incessant ringing of bicycle bells, the blare of car horns and the grinding of construction equipment." Boom boxes played rock music. "In the midst of this new cacophony, however, is one sound that was eerily absent in the early 1970's. Laughter can now be heard in the lanes and alleyways, as can the sounds of TV's, VCR's, neighborhood anger and family joy." The most important change was the increasing outlets for individual expression.[30]

In 1982 a young traveler, Mark Salzman, who had graduated that spring from Yale, went to Changsha in Hunan Province, where he taught English at the Medical College. He still witnessed traditional scenes, once familiar to Theodore White: On the train, he looked out the window and saw "a group of peasants walking alongside the railroad tracks with a huge pig tied to a wheelbarrow that had a wooden wheel." One moment he saw "rice paddies, vegetable patches and fishponds," and several hundred yards later the train came to a halt in his destination, the provincial capital. In the city he caught glimpses of carpenters, wool spinners, key makers, and bicycle repairmen at work. He also noted that the electricity failed, the buses and trains were overcrowded, and the government and postal services were entangled in bureaucracy. But Salzman had another interest in China, an abiding tradition for the Chinese but one forcing a new Western perception of a self-assertive and inwardly strong China: martial arts. He became a pupil of one of the nation's kung fu experts. Here was the image of the new China: young men in sweatsuits engaging in furious armed combat.[31]

Another traveler, Harrison Salisbury, discovered that the bestselling author in China was not Mao Zedong, Deng Xiaoping, or any other Communist leader. It was Lee

Iacocca, the Chrysler chairman, whose autobiography had sold hundreds of thousands of copies. "Not every young Chinese wants to grow up to be Lee Iacocca," Salisbury conceded, "but a startling number would like to go that way." One college student asked him, "What's wrong with being a millionaire?" Salisbury did not believe that China could reach economic parity with the West in less than a hundred years, but it was "slowly modernizing major industry," and the Chinese accepted profit making at home and expanding trade with the West as their road to progress.[32]

In foreign affairs various press reported that China was "breaking out of isolation." In the 1960s China had fired its first atomic bomb, and ten years later it had built up a limited nuclear stockpile, maintaining perhaps fewer than two hundred bombs. Yet China was in "no rush to join the arms race, preferring to invest in more economic development rather than in weapons." Since launching its first space satellite in 1970, a 380-pound device that circled the globe playing "The East Is Red," Chinese scientists had developed a program that in 1986 offered to launch American satellites. "Most Americans think of China as the land of the bicycle"; but China had "suddenly become a player in the high-stakes game of commercial space launchings."[33]

China reentered the international community at the United Nations. In 1971 China was seated in the body despite the objections of the American delegate, George Bush. He failed to rally support to forbid the entrance of China if Taiwan was expelled. China's inclusion in the world body with a permanent seat on the Security Council meant, the *Wall Street Journal* editorialized, the "decline in the political power of the United States relative to the rest of the world, a decline that has been under way for some years."[34]

In 1972, to reopen contacts with China that had been broken for a generation, President Nixon undertook an extraordinary trip to meet Chairman Mao Zedong and Premier Zhou Enlai, and he toasted them in the Great Hall of the People in Beijing, offering "friendship." He visited the Great Wall and declared that the vast construction was a symbol of "what China in the future can become." Nixon became concerned with China as an industrial power of unparalleled potential. He left the country with one "awesome" impression: "the disciplined but wildly—almost fanatically—enthusiastic audience at the gymnastic exhibition" in Beijing, which confirmed his belief that "we must cultivate China during the next few decades while it is still learning to develop its national strength and potential." Otherwise, the president worried, China might one day be the "most formidable enemy that has ever existed in the history of the world."[35]

When historians of the next century wrote about the present, Nicholas Kristof posited in *Foreign Affairs,* they might conclude that the great world-changing event of the time was the rise of China. Though the United States had possessed the world's largest economy since the nineteenth century, at present trajectories China, the fastest-growing economy in the world, would displace it in the first half of the twenty-first century and become "the number one economy in the world." An ominous historical comparison was made between the United States and China. "There was once a nation founded upon the principles of reason and moral responsibility. Blessed with an industrious people and abounding in natural resources, it became one of the most prosperous and self-sufficient nations on earth. Eventually, however, having grown accustomed to ease and plenty, too many of its people grew self-indulgent. Foreigners were quick to exploit this weakness by selling them illicit drugs." In time, the once great and noble nation withered in strength. Paul Harvey's capsule account of what happened to China in the nineteenth century served as a metaphor of modern America. If "you think this story is about 20th century America—you're wrong," he wrote ironically. Yet China had reversed its centuries-long decline.[36]

China was "awakening." Or, as a senior vice president of the World Bank said: "The sleeping giant is not sleeping any more. It is taking giant strides."[37]

The Developing World

New nations, more than forty of them, stretching across the southern regions of the globe, with a total of more than one billion people, arose out of the crumbled colonial empires of Europe. The independent Africa of the 1970s contrasted sharply with perceptions of the Africa of only a decade before, when the continent, said a roving correspondent for *U.S. News & World Report*, still "seemed a dark, mysterious, even frightening part of the world . . . no more than a vast jungle, dominated by hordes of black men unable to govern themselves." "Witch doctors are giving way to the economists these days," and poisoned arrows had been set aside for modern weapons of war. In Zaire, the Belgian Congo until 1960, the vestiges of colonialism were torn down, even a statue of the explorer Henry Morton Stanley. An American visitor commented that Zaire was looking away from colonialism toward independence and the development of mineral wealth buried in the world's largest reserves of cobalt and industrial diamonds. It was also seeking to expand its industry through foreign investment. In the 1970s Goodyear began to build a factory and Gulf Oil was drilling wells offshore, but the Europeans reasserted their presence with British Leyland, Renault, and Unilever.[38]

South African mines remained a major source of rare minerals, and American dependence on them had grown. But the white government discriminated against the majority of the citizens, forcing blacks to live in townships or homelands. In the 1970s *National Geographic*, changing its editorial policy of accentuating the positive in every land, eventually characterized South Africa as the "Land of Apartheid." American businesses, including General Motors and International Business Machines, had sought to use their capital as a progressive force for development and employment. But the United States began to withdraw its business from South Africa for the very reason it had once used to defend investment: to exert leverage for better working conditions, and to offer an example of what a society of equality should be. Helping to end the rigid and ruthless practice of segregation, Congress forbade new investment, and GM and IBM cut off funds or sold factories.[39]

To achieve common ends not possible individually, developing nations combined into regional and resource organizations. In 1960 the several Arab nations had collectively formed the Organization of Petroleum Exporting Countries. With the huge revenue from oil sales, the OPEC nations underwent a renaissance. By 1973 Abu Dhabi had one of the highest per capita incomes in the world. In Oman, major public medical services, which had been given by the American Reformed Church Mission, were provided free by the government to all Omanis.

In the 1980s the last American to preside over the world's largest oil company, the Arabian-American Oil Company, or Aramco, once the property of Exxon, Texaco, Mobil, and Chevron, handed over power to its first Saudi boss. The towns where the American Aramco workers lived had been replicas of American suburbs, with supermarkets, movie theaters, an American television network, a hospital, a golf course, and neat streets with names like Canyon Road and Rolling Hills. One observer described them in the 1970s as shining "like little jewels compared with nearby Saudi towns of Dammam and Al Khobar and much of the rest of what was then underdeveloped Saudi Arabia." By the 1980s, the main American town, compared with Al Khobar's sleek highways, modern supermarkets, and video stores, looked "shabby." Saudi workers who once strove to live in the Aramco towns came to spurn them for better, bigger Saudi homes, many with swimming pools and marble stairs.[40]

The Relativity of Rise and Decline:
"What the World Thinks of America"

For much of the world, images of modernity had become real. Tractors, tall buildings, airplanes, automobiles, and streamlined railroads were not unique to the United States. In 1947 the London *Economist* had pictured America as the world's colossus, the only prosperous superpower. In a periodic update in 1991, entitled "A Better Yesterday," the British journal provided perspective from a formerly preeminent nation that had declined. "America now is not self-confident, not sure of its greatness. It feels the pressure of the outside world on its violate shores, and it fears a debilitating fragmentation within them." The article contrasted the 1940s image of the Industrial Expressway, connecting Detroit with the new Willow Run bomber factory—the artery of probably the "world's greatest centre of high-technology manufacturing"—to the road's potholed, dilapidated condition. "Among young Europeans—and young Japanese—visitors to America today, it is common to hear the view that America is a bit old-fashioned." Young Italians were saying, "*America e qui*"—America is here—"as if the modernity for which they once crossed an ocean is now available in Turin and Milan."[41]

Rising nations no longer saw America as a principal teacher. From the point of view of the Japanese, Americans had not girded themselves for the long-term future. American products were just not very good, said the Japanese who felt that their own attention to detail and service assured that "Made in Japan" stood for quality; "Made in America" was a fine imprint for sporting goods and trinkets but not for heavy industry or electronic goods—a total reverse of the situation in the 1940s. The Japanese were giving Americans lessons in elementary economics instead of the other way around. "As I listen to American complaint," a Japanese professor said to an audience in the United States, "it seems to me that the Americans are too eager to try to find a scapegoat in Japan, without becoming very serious. So I would like to suggest that the Americans should become serious now, because the U.S. situation is serious, and also, to have a long-term view." A Japanese businessman added that he was hearing Americans say that "the Japanese are saving 18%, we save only 5%; the Japanese should start . . . consuming more. We spend so much money on military, the Japanese spend only 1% of GNP; therefore the Japanese should spend more on the military." He did not assume that America was right.[42]

To the ascending nations, their advancement meant providing a world service. America seemed to be suffering from the old European disease of stagnation and old age, to be turning into a place for sightseeing and viewing cultural antiquities and for establishing markets to sell manufactured products. The Japanese might have had a nostalgia for American culture, but they were exasperated by what they regarded as American decline, a tendency to seek comfort rather than science, consumption rather than production and trade. The attitude that the days of "learning" and "catch-up" for Japan were over was captured by George Packard in *Foreign Affairs*: "For Japanese leaders, America has become a clumsy ally—almost an embarrassment. . . . Meanwhile, Japan serves as a scapegoat. 'What is wrong with making good products?' an official protested privately. . . . Nobody is forcing the American people to buy our goods.' "[43]

American cultural services still held attractions. The leading theme of the report by *Newsweek* on "What the World Thinks of America" was that the great engines of American culture drove on unimpaired, "pouring out to the world 265 million servings a day of Coca-Cola and an infinitude of hamburgers embedded in a double infinitude of sesame-seeded buns." But even here the reporters expressed the fear that, as "the world's leading nation," the United States "so often finds itself in the position of peering over its shoulder to make sure it is still being followed."[44]

In habits, clothing, and fads, American things remained popular. "No cigarette in Europe has quite the cachet of a Marlboro, for which Europeans are willing to pay twice or more what local brands cost; and a good place to smoke it, of course, is McDonald's. Those quintessential American garments, T shirts and NFL jerseys, are standard street dress from Mexico City to Manila." Television was the largest cultural export, but the medium's technology and its message came from different sources: The set itself might be made in Taiwan or Korea, but "chances are most of the entertainment programs it shows will be as American as the Super Bowl, which . . . was broadcast to 23 nations, from Thailand to Costa Rica." Americans were not exporting machinery as much as plots: "Africans tune in 'The Jeffersons' to view white American producers' fantasies of black American life; European connoisseurs of duplicity can choose between 'Dallas' and 'Dynasty.' " One Chinese comrade from Szechuan Province thought that his people might learn from that great "scientific and educational program from America, the 'Man from Atlantis.'" By majorities ranging from 55 percent in Japan to 83 percent in Mexico, polls found a "great deal" of American influence on television, movies, and pop music in their countries, exceeding the perceived American impact of science and business.

The government did not match this private spread of culture: "We get 'Ironside,' but no plays by Arthur Miller or Tennessee Williams," complained an Egyptian journalist. "Where is the Cleveland Orchestra?" The problem was that the USIA's budget for cultural activities was insufficient. Similarly, an American ambassador to Italy thought the United States had not taken advantage of what he called "public diplomacy." He found the *Federalist Papers* long out of print in Italy, yet 90 percent of the country's television entertainment was American.

But in the end American culture folded into the host country's own. So thoroughly had goods like hamburgers, colas, and blue jeans entered into other nations that they were often regarded as part of the common cultural heritage of humankind, in the way that few bothered to recall the British origins of what had become the standard Western business suit. *Newsweek* considered the Japanese child who, on his way from the airport to a hotel in Los Angeles, was heard to exclaim: "Look, Mommy, they have McDonald's in America, too."[45]

The findings of one of the secret surveys that the USIA had been conducting in Europe for twenty-two years, as disclosed by the *New York Times*, told a story that contrasted with Wendell Willkie's impressions on his travels some thirty years before: "while there is still a large reservoir of good will toward the United States in West Europe," it was "at its lowest level." Among the British, only 34 percent were favorably inclined—a record low since the 1950s; among the Italians, 41 percent—a record low; among the French, 38 percent, and among the West Germans, 57 percent—near-record lows. Distraught USIA officials prepared a second analysis of the survey, but it did not significantly change the results. The explanation for these findings was enlightening: "The prevailing view is that America has already reached its peak or is in fact on the way down in the things that make a country outstanding." But if America had lost its productive dynamism, it continued to warrant regard as a democracy and to garner respect for its people.[46]

Unlike Europeans or Japanese, developing peoples—as glimpsed in a poll taken in Mexico—still held American technical progress in high esteem. The view from Mexicans was that the best attributes of the American economy included its lack of inflation, its high employment, and its technology. More than this material development, Mexicans admired American democracy and its system of government. But finally, they considered their own way of life and social values far superior.[47]

When President Nixon looked out on the world in 1971, he formulated the proposition: "instead of just America being number one in the world from an economic standpoint, the preeminent world power, and instead of there being just two super powers, when we think in economic terms and economic potentialities, there are five great power centers in the world today." He cited the United States, Western Europe, Japan, Russia, and China. The "United States, as compared with that position we found ourselves in immediately after World War II, has a challenge such as we did not even dream of. Then we were talking about the dollar gap; then we were talking about the necessity of—putting it in terms of a poker game—that the United States had all the chips and we had to spread a few of the chips around so that others could play. We did it. . . . But now when we see the world in which we are about to move, the United States no longer is in the position of complete preeminence . . . now we face a situation where four other potential economic powers have the capacity, have the kind of people—if not the kind of government, but at least the kind of people—who can challenge us on every front."[48]

The growth in Western Europe and Japan, which pointed the way for the development of other nations, was a fundamental cause of the change in America's international position. It is the nature of power to be relative. But in exploring the relative status of the nations, we have entered into a conundrum about the criteria of declining power. Looking at Britain we have seen that the leading nation of the nineteenth century had declined into one that was inconsequential relative to the most powerful, though it had grown in its own right. In national product Britain had come to produce far more wealth than when it was the workshop of the world; its nuclear arsenal made the firepower of its once-dominant navy seem ineffective or superfluous. But this absolute increase in power did not necessarily increase its relative power. Similar comparisons can be made between nations at their relative peaks and their modern counterparts, which became more powerful absolutely, but less powerful relatively, because of the advancement elsewhere of science and technology, economic production, and military weaponry: the Roman Empire under Augustus compared with modern Italy, or the Chinese empire before 1500 with modern China, and so on. The United States had grown absolutely, but it was less powerful relative to other nations as they grew in strength.

Yet these relative shifts in power do not explain why nations rise and decline. We have looked within nations to understand their development. Internal dynamism accounted for the changing relative power of Britain and Japan after World War II. Both nations were islands off the coast of a continental mass. Neither nation had a superabundance of natural resources. They had roughly comparable populations. Britain had begun the postwar period as a victorious great power, though hit hard by war; Japan as an impoverished and defeated country. But within a generation Japan had advanced far beyond Britain in technological expertise, economic production, standard of living, and influence on the life of other countries through the sale of its goods and export of its capital. Britain held onto some vestiges of world power with its nuclear weapons and a navy, and in a symbolic way with a seat in the Security Council of the United Nations, but it was a nation in retreat. Japan had the capability for an expanded military beyond the defense forces assembled under a constitution that outlawed militarism; certainly Japan could afford a far stronger military than Britain could muster. Japan had gained extraordinary advantages; Britain had lost them.

At the end of World War II certain factors enabled the United States to be a principal power, rather than Brazil, Australia, or India. Now certain factors had enabled Japan to surpass the United States in key aspects of a world role, as the world's banker and most successful trader, producer of some major industrial and high-technology goods, and donor of aid. Brazil and South Korea became competitive trading nations. The internal dynamism of rising states was clearly the result of more than proximity to the Atlantic world, massive land area, large population, or even the amount of capital with which the states began, and it was certainly not due to the size of their military, at least not in Japan.

The rise of the rest of the world had been an interest of the United States. The new world held out the promise of bettering the human condition. The 1945 world of destruction built anew was in part a tribute to the success of America's policies of trade and capital investment, aid through the Marshall Plan and Point Four, and democratic and egalitarian institutions. America was creating competition, but it was failing to compete and to continue the primary contribution it had made for so many years as a generating force of social and economic dynamism. As the weaknesses and problems that had hindered nations in many regions had not made America strong—though these conditions had magnified this situation—the recovery of other lands did not make America weak.

The growing strength of other nations would not relatively weaken the United States if it were to continue to develop and to invest its social energy and economic wealth in innovative enterprise and magnanimous activity. Prospering nations might not restrict the material growth of another but contribute to it. The expectation of American trade, aid, and culture was that they would not only improve the condition of countries around the world but also reap benefits at home. The United States might have continued its creative scientific, cultural, and economic activity to the extent that it had in its formative days as a world power, or, for that matter, as Britain had done in the nineteenth century, or as Japan came to do.

The Ending World Role

After the Vietnam War a matrix of problems that came close to the substance of power haunted the American world role—the political repercussions of military defeat and dislocated economic conditions of low growth and unemployment—and the pivotal problem of the state of the consensus. The revolt against the orthodox thinking that had evolved after World War II was a rejection of the world role as it had taken form in policies. Some consensus hardliners were sensitive to a mood that tended toward isolationism, stemming from the belief that Americans had paid a high price for its world role and had recovered few rewards. A commentator in *Foreign Affairs* found that the 1960s had "produced a new school of isolationism. . . . The old kind of American idealism is gone—and with it the sense of world mission." President Nixon expressed consternation over what he saw as the conversion of former "international-ists" into "neo-isolationists." The analyst Robert Tucker believed that the likely conse-quences of "a new isolationism" would be the end of the "preponderant role" America had played since World War II. For Tucker, isolationism turned principally "on the willingness to enter into—or, in the present context, to retain—military commit-ments." Isolationism was "anti-interventionism."[49]

But the issue was ill defined. The issue was no longer whether the nation was isolationist or internationalist. It was—as it had been since the end of World War II and even as the decline in power diminished policy choices—over what kind of interna-tionalism the nation was to represent. So thought some weary internationalists who had earlier supported the United Nations Charter and the agencies of world organization, UNRRA and UNESCO, and then transferred their primary support to the Truman Doctrine, the Marshall Plan, and NATO. One of them, William Fulbright, before he retired from the Senate, came to favor a conception of internationalism that he believed had been held by Franklin Roosevelt and the leaders of the generation who had brought the United States out of nineteenth-century isolation. He did not think that there was "the slightest chance of the United States returning to the isolationism of the prewar years." Americans were "inextricably involved with the world politically, eco-nomically, militarily and—in case anyone cares—legally. . . . The charge of 'neo-isolationism' is an invention of people who confuse internationalism with an intrusive American interventionism, with a quasi-imperialism."[50]

The central manifestations of American internationalism—the economic enter-prise, technological grants, foreign aid, or political objectives—had not embittered the mass of people against internationalism. In national election campaigns, candidates consistently accepted an active role for the United States in the world. Without taking an inconsistent stance, Americans elected candidates who strongly avowed peace. In 1940 the people reelected Franklin Roosevelt, who ran on his record for peace and declared his hate of war. In 1952 Truman did not run for reelection and Eisenhower pledged to go to Korea. Even in 1964 on the eve of the Vietnam buildup, the Democratic incumbent Lyndon Johnson countered the Republican Barry Goldwater's insistent calls for bombing North Vietnam with the statement: "we are not going north and drop bombs at this stage of the game." He would not have "American boys to do the fighting for Asian boys." Johnson did not carry out his pledge for peace, nor did he run for reelection in 1968, and Nixon won that year with the claim that he had a secret plan to end the war.[51]

The consensus had not expected that the world role would lead to war. It was to create practical development, improved living standards, and democratic societies through trade and goods, technological aid, managerial skills. But to block the spread of communism, the national government added the apparently realistic effort of waging war to stave off threats to the general peace. So impatiently, and perhaps with a loss of some of the confidence that their progressive ways would prevail, Americans turned to military solutions. Yet arms did not solve the deep-rooted problems of development, the lack of food, education, production, and medicine. And America no longer radiated the economic, cultural, and political qualities of attraction that had once characterized the society.

Force had negligible effect in vindicating a general acquiescence in America's power. The United States gained little support from its allies in Vietnam, and even Britain, which had initially supported the war, became disenchanted. The United Nations had no part in waging the war. The lack of international cooperation was a major difference from the Korean War, which had been fought under the auspices of the international organization. After the war, the Asian alliances fell apart.

Dissent and disillusion at home combined with defeats and the blunting of power abroad. The acceptance by the majority of Americans of the precepts against the extended military intervention ultimately limited the prospects of the world role as it had taken form. The consensus that had earlier solidified around a role supported by economic production divided over seeking military solutions to foreign problems, and economic prowess shifted to countries that were grasping new manufacturing mastery. War and constant preparation for war were weakening the nation's power from within.

Although misled by their leaders at the outset, the American people possessed the will to turn against their designs when the expenditure of power under their authority resulted in disaster. Toward the end of his life, one of the founders of the world role, Dean Acheson, wondered what had gone wrong. Distressed by the country's mood, especially among the young people, of "depression, disillusion, and withdrawal from the effort to affect the world around us," he wrote the memoirs he once vowed never to write, to tell his tale of the past heroic age of "large conceptions" and "great achievements," the "product of enormous will and effort." "Its hero is the American people," he wrote, led by Truman and Marshall. But since that period of creation, the rulers had failed. Lyndon Johnson, whose dreams of a Great Society were destroyed by the vain pursuit of the Vietnam War, wandered through the corridors of the empty White House offices on the last night of his term. He returned to his ranch in the Texas hill country, wrote his memoirs, and let his hair grow long in the fashion of the hippies. Robert McNamara refused to talk about Vietnam in public until forced to do so more than a decade later in a court of law. Dean Rusk left government, his career ended. Richard Nixon lost control of the government in the Watergate scandal and became the first president to resign in disgrace. Their successors, Gerald Ford and Jimmy Carter, inherited a weakened presidency.[52]

The revolutionary disruption by the dissenters died. The youthful activists had thought their movement would last, but how could a movement based on youth continue as they aged? The maturing New Left critics had no way to cope with declining American power. The monster was gone and they had nothing to fight. As America became a debtor nation, the Left still clung to its old platitudes of arrogance and imperialism. But if other nations were outstripping the United States in trade and were turning the country into a market, were they doing so by superior virtue or by aggressive economic tactics? Some of the dissenters lost their old idealism. Jerry Rubin became an entrepreneur running his own networking business for investment bankers and lawyers. David Horowitz became a conservative commentator who scorned the New Left for its inchoate attack against authority leading to the social problems of crime and drugs. Abbie Hoffman committed suicide. The dissenters, who had built no new consensus, saw no center to American life. As the loss in Vietnam showed Tom Hayden that America was not the policeman of the world, the devaluation of the dollar meant to him that America was no longer the banker to the world. For him, the long path of the frontier had ended.[53]

The consensus that had formed in World War II, once broken in Vietnam, never reformed in the next generation. Discussions of consensus usually lamented the loss of the former harmony and cohesion. "Where has the consensus on American foreign policy gone?" asked the diplomat and policy analyst Herbert Spiro in 1979. A *Time* essay in 1983 said of the postwar creed of internationalism that had been "dominant, almost consensual": "Viet Nam destroyed that consensus. It did something more. It destroyed the sense of equilibrium that underlay that consensus, and introduced a period of volatility that is with us to this day."[54]

Political divisions of Left and Right and of party combined with divisions among minorities who had constituted the consensus and had in common their opposition to the Vietnam War. Women, African-Americans, Hispanic-Americans, Asian-Americans, and Native Americans continued to emphasize their diversity. Their minority efforts had begun as a means to adjust past grievances of discrimination. But these multiple divisions by gender, race, ethnicity, and other categories became indicative of the waning American optimism about the nation's prospects. Americans, who had generally believed that all groups would have a better life in the future than their forebears, emphasized their group differences as a means of competing for public resources and political representation. They sought separate interests above consensual interests, as if to carve out a larger piece of a shrinking pie. Arthur Schlesinger, who had at the outset lauded the virtues of the vital center in forming the American destiny, noted, "The rising cult of ethnicity was a symptom of decreasing confidence in the American future."[55]

Not only had the center fractured, but the political system oscillated between extremes. The Left rose and crested, and then the Right, in response. The reaction against Vietnam drove the Democratic party to the left in 1972, when George McGovern campaigned to bring America home from foreign entanglements, and in 1976 Jimmy Carter devoted his administration to exercising restraint abroad. A countervailing uneasiness about weakening power turned the Republican party to the right with the election of Ronald Reagan in 1980.

The leadership made continuous calls for the restoration of consensus. Reagan, knowing that support for his foreign policy was not as cohesive as that accorded his predecessors thirty years earlier, hearkened back to the old "bipartisan consensus" that included the Democratic party of Roosevelt, Truman, and Kennedy. "No legacy would make me more proud than leaving in place a bipartisan consensus" toward foreign policy, Reagan said, "a consensus that prevents a paralysis of American power from ever occurring again."[56]

But a majority of Americans eventually disapproved of Reagan's foreign policy, after marines he had sent to Lebanon were killed, and later the Reagan administration became entangled in the Iran-Contra scandal. In 1988 Henry Kissinger and Cyrus Vance, former secretaries of state of each party, collaborated in writing an article for *Foreign Affairs* that decried the loss of the bipartisan consensus that had accepted "global responsibilities" since 1941, and the appearance of the "growing number of Americans" who wanted the United States to be less active internationally. At jeopardy were American international interests and "the cause of freedom." The people lamented their own loss of consensus, which they saw, according to one poll, as the main reason for their nation's "apparent decline" in world affairs. Within the society the loss of dominance was at first almost imperceptible, during a wave of the rhetoric of "standing tall" accompanied by military buildup. Yet officials and journalists who studied public opinion found no consensus of the kind Gabriel Almond had discovered after World War II. As George Quester wrote in his *American Foreign Policy: The Lost Consensus*, "debate has now replaced consensus." The psychological adjustment to that disagreement among the people was slow but inexorable.[57]

No return to isolation was possible. But there was no consensus on foreign affairs, or on the kind of internationalism that was cosmopolitan. In the 1980s the United States shunned the international organizations whose formation it had championed in World War II and took a unilateral approach. The United States fell deeply in arrears in the payment of its financial obligation to the United Nations. The United States quit UNESCO. The United States voided the ruling of the World Court that it had violated Nicaraguan sovereignty by mining harbors, and the government threatened to end formally American recognition of the court's authority in political cases. President Reagan suggested that the United Nations consider itself free to move from New York City, whereas once Americans had pledged this location to demonstrate their support of the organization. Despite the hostility, the people still liked the UN as a principle. While a majority agreed that the UN was doing a "very good" or a "good" job, vast majorities believed that the United States should remain in the UN and that the world body itself should keep its headquarters in the country. In 1991 the UN mandated that the United States and its allies wage war in the Persian Gulf, liberating Kuwait, which Iraq had overrun the year before. The American-led attack demonstrated the potential of collective action, but the war was not fought under the UN flag nor under its command. For the first time since the American Revolution, the United States accepted financial aid from other countries to fight a war.[58]

Americans left behind a dual legacy: first, of an example of modern technology and democratic institutions. The once-conquered nations of Germany and Japan advanced in democracy and modernized industry until they outperformed the United States in productivity growth and in the surplus of trade. The former enemies Russia and China turned toward the democratic ways for which the United States had stood. The Iron Curtain fell. The Berlin Wall was torn down, and vacant watch towers along it remained as artifacts of the abandoned frontier. So too did walls and barriers of barbed wire come down in Hungary and Czechoslovakia and throughout Eastern Europe. Soviet tanks were loaded onto railroad cars headed back to Russia. In China's Tiananmen Square the people raised a Goddess of Liberty like that in New York harbor, only to be harshly put down; but their yearning for democracy remained.

The Soviet Union entered a new revolution while the people of Moscow demonstrated for reform within sight of the Kremlin. The last president of the old union, Mikhail Gorbachev, resigned from his position, and the first elected president of Russia, Boris Yeltsin, moved into Gorbachev's office without giving him a chance to clean it out first. The communist hammer-and-sickle flag was torn down all over the country. The statues of Marx and Lenin and Felix Dzerzhinsky, the godfather of the Soviet secret police, were toppled, and Leningrad changed its name back to Saint Petersburg. The Moscow McDonald's introduced Russians to the "chizburger" served by young "management trainees." Teens wanted Western styles and music; and Russians sought foreign-made VCRs, Walkman cassette players, and automobiles. The Soviet empire fell apart and republics broke off from central control. The Soviet Union ceased to exist.

World alignments were in flux again, like after World War II, now with Russian leaders pleading for American foreign aid. American fliers were in Moscow unloading cargo planes of food and medical supplies for Russians, just as they had once airlifted goods to Berlin in 1948 to make a stand against the Russians. And Russia agreed to accept help from the United States in dismantling the nuclear weapons it had stockpiled in an arms race with the Americans. Only now the United States was not the main center of capital and foreign aid for Russia, nor was it the main supplier of VCRs, television sets, or automobiles.

Modern technology and democratic institutions were not the entire legacy. The legacy of America in Vietnam was not democracy or education or prosperity, but bomb craters and a defoliated landscape. Even a generation after the war had ended, Vietnam remained a nation in which the lingering scars were human and physical. The bridge over the Red River that linked the interior with Haiphong harbor still showed the haphazard repairs completed after the damage by American bombers. In Laos, gaping craters in the Plain of Jars had become fishponds. Unexploded bombs lay in wait, and one of the thousands of belated casualties of the war, a nine-year-old girl, was wounded and partially blinded in 1983 when a small bomb exploded, killing her brother and two other children. Vietnamese development belatedly followed that of other Pacific rim countries. The people wanted the amenities of Western life—blue jeans, shoes, and cassette recorders—and talked about *Gone with the Wind*, which was shown on television. But billboards over a Hanoi square featured Sony of Japan and Samsung of South Korea, and the streets were filled with Honda motorcycles. The U.S. embassy in Saigon, its bronze plaque a trophy of war in a museum, had been commandeered by the Vietnam State Oil Company, and the United States was one of the last nations to have relations with the new Vietnam. Americans came to search crash sites for remains. And one American visiting a smoke-filled pagoda saw a middle-aged woman who pointed to a photo of a young man, holding a little boy, next to a young woman holding a baby. "Then she made a gesture—bombs."[59]

The decline of the world role, as with its rise, was reflected in the state of the consensus over what was important and to what degree, whether the pursuit of territory, economic production, or military at home or abroad. Power did not lie in any one of these. Rather, entwined with them all was belief about what might be accomplished. The era of American preeminence concluded not with the end of history and the fulfillment of national manifestations of abundance, aid, cultural exchange, and self-determination, nor with the end of military power. It concluded with the breakup of consensus and with the nation expending its resources, skilled labor, and wealth in unproductive ways and alienating parts of the world by the use of military force. A nation that refused to accept these domestic and international relationships stood to doom itself.

EPILOGUE

We have come a long way in our exploration of the American world role, from its origins, through its flourishing, with the institution of order that it established, and finally to its decline. It has taken us from a pinnacle of wealth, power, and idealism to a depth of tragedy and defeat bearing the seeds of a new beginning. We have encountered a tangle of motives and thoughts, hope and disillusionment, of a crowd of individuals caught up in world events, all connected with the myths of the age—the myths of power and of realism, of consensus and dissent, and of destiny and mission. What have we learned? What have we derived from this history that illuminates our present condition? Do we learn from myth after all, or do we close our minds to it as merely abstract, without sense, and without ties to reality? And do we really know what the past was, or is history itself a fable not quite agreed upon? We proceed with care, knowing that we try to establish a meaningful order out of the mythic material of the past.

We began with two particular myths, and we return to them. It was not simply reality itself—even in an age of realism—that shaped the national behavior in the world. These myths existed as ways of perceiving reality, and they offered perspectives on the meaning of the world role regarding the dynamics of rise and decline and the consequences of worldwide activities, what succeeded and what failed. The first myth offered was that of the "American Century," an idea of American leadership as a preeminent power in the postwar era. The second myth was the "Century of the Common Man," a vision of an egalitarian society of common men and women seeking common interests.

Of these myths, which one most closely characterized the international relations of the era? As for the Century of the Common Man, there were substantial American efforts to cooperate with a multitude of peoples in an organization, centered in the United Nations, that would resolve international disputes and crises. But the United States came to rely most heavily on an alliance system under its own leadership. The United States unilaterally provided foreign aid and cultural services surpassing those of any other nation. These programs did not take form in international organizations but originated in the United States—the Marshall Plan to assist war-torn Europe in the late 1940s, the Point Four program and the Peace Corps to help developing countries to modernize. The century of the common people was an outward-looking, often courageous consciousness, but this approach to international relations pressed by Henry Wallace fell out of favor; he was rejected in the 1948 presidential election and recanted his views during the Korean War. If his temperament was right, he lacked tact and restraint, and he did not mold an American consensus to win political leadership. Fear of communism and pride in power were major causes for the defeat of the Century of the Common Man.

The history of the postwar years is in a sense the history of the victory of one kind of thinking over the other. Implementation of policies associated with the Century of the Common Man did not consume the greatest human efforts in an era of cold war and realpolitik. Wallace had set high standards for the United States, and he did not consider carefully the possibility of Soviet deception or recalcitrance. In the early 1960s Wallace implied that Truman had been right to fire him as secretary of commerce, but before he died in 1965, he came to believe that the Vietnam War had proven him right after all in his stand for the common people. After twenty years, he felt vindicated.

It was the program of an American Century that was triumphant. The American Century vision saw the postwar world chiefly in power relationships, with the United States as dominant. From that all else followed. After the war the confrontation between the American and Soviet superpowers in the cold war did not necessarily weaken the applicability of the myth. On the contrary, it vindicated the stand that the United States had to take extraordinary steps to protect Western democracy. The purveyor of this vision, Henry Luce, correctly foresaw America's economic expansion and free-trade policies, cultural spread, foreign-aid distribution, and political support for friendly countries. Luce forecasted and later supported the Marshall Plan and Point Four. Through these policies he saw a dominant United States acting unilaterally in pursuit of its interests, without an international organization serving as an intermediary. When Luce espoused political support for friendly countries, although he did not at first realize it, he was inferring military support later evident in the Truman Doctrine and containment theory. The postwar alliance system and the wars in Korea and Vietnam followed. Luce refined some of his ideas before his death in 1967, but he never questioned his main propositions. As the United States entered the Vietnam War, its paramountcy seemed no less assured than victory. But that war signaled the end of paramountcy, and by the end of the cold war, the world role founded on it could not be sustained.

Each of these reproductions of the external world, set forth as guides to action by society, corresponded in some degree to the reality of the external world. Neither totally represented reality. A world in which America was omnipotent never existed. But overestimations of preeminent power led to the crisis of overextension. If the American Century was a central myth of this era of preeminence among nations, and the American preeminence it characterized was in decline, then the myth could not be sustained and the image of preeminence would not provide a guide to action in accordance with the way the world was. Its propositions would be untrue.

We have sought in this inquiry to apprehend ideas and events that were obscure to us, to link previously unconnected pieces of the origins and development of the world role. The central issues of our study are, as Charles Beard once said, elusive and perhaps unknowable. But again and again, in periods of rise and decline, we have seen that the world role depended on something more fundamental than military force and economic might. What, then, was the impetus to the world role?

We recall the myths of origin—the explanations for the world role at its outset according to the elemental forces of the continental domain, the abundant natural resources, the large population, the efficient technology, the production and wealth, and the armaments. The myths reflected the initial stress placed by the consensus of leaders and people on investing their capital and enterprise in developing the land, skills, and technology and creating a dynamic economy and native arts, all of which enabled the nation to lead in innovation. After World War II the consensus determined to direct national creativity and energy to enlarged possibilities abroad in trade, aid, and culture. The military had shown its valor and potential destructive force in World War II. But Americans had not relied on armed might as a foundation of power before that war, and after the war they reduced their military services as they had after earlier wars. Not until the Korean War did the military begin growing rapidly, unfettered by the resistance Americans had once put up to it.

The emergence of a consensus around international policy was significant. Consensus belief set the nation on a new course. The United States began its world role because of a consensus in the society over internationalism, supported fundamentally by modern industry and manifested in commerce and aid, not a destructive military.

Consensus beliefs were caught up in anticommunism, fueled by the dread of totalitarianism, collectivism, and Soviet expansion. But another premise was fundamental: that American self-awareness was no less responsible for the national development in the world. The idea of Henry Stimson was that what really mattered in the American world role would matter even if the Soviet Union did not exist. The domestic society explained the potential of America's world activity as much as external threats.

The consensus perception of world affairs received strong intellectual support from many fields. Historical traditions and impressions of modernity alike, which exuded confidence for large world undertakings, were represented by some of the prevailing economic, social, and religious interpretations of internationalism. Economic doctrines of a "people of plenty" and the "affluent society," sociological theories of "other-direction" and a "power elite," and religious tenets of brotherhood and "Christian realism" explicitly extended domestic thought into an international worldview. They were reflected abroad in the spread of technology and capital through multinational corporations, the offer of science, movies, customs, and fads, and the generosity of the Marshall Plan.

But why did the world role decline? Why did a nation of great power, with vast domestic resources and foreign institutions, face decline? Our quest led us to the crisis of consensus belief and confusion over recurring turmoil. The period of foreign crises, one following another, from Berlin, to Dien Bien Phu, to Quemoy and Matsu, to Lebanon, to Cuba, to Vietnam, followed the gradual overextension of hardline attitudes of a preeminence through military security. Consensus foreign policies had served their purpose or had met resistance in warfare, further forcing the consensus to increase the firmness of its position. The government was conserving a world role and resisted change. An aroused minority of dissenters—New Left intellectuals, students, and activists—challenged the mainstream with their own sort of idealism. They criticized the disintegrating consensus as a symbol of selfish capitalistic policies and military intervention, demanding change and threatening rebellion. For the United States to recognize limits abroad, it had to dismiss deeply rooted domestic customs. But the views of neither group were completely defensible, and both the consensus and its critics failed to provide satisfactory answers to continuing international problems.

The demise of the world role coincided with a weakening of America's economic strength relative to other nations. The United States had been the biggest creditor in the world and the most successful exporter as well, but it began to suffer a deficit in its trade and later became a debtor nation in world investment. Yet material considerations alone did not signal the end of America's world role as it had developed after World War II. Military strength had vastly increased, but it was not necessarily effective in carrying out policies. The military lingered as the outstanding element of power, as the nation maintained an enormous defense establishment to support troops on foreign soil, a global navy and air force, and a huge nuclear arsenal.

Lost in the pursuit of military power in competition with the Soviet Union was the old emphasis on the investment of social energy and capital in innovative enterprise, which had been fundamental to American power and had made possible a mighty military, as well as productive choices. Massive military expenditures drained, perhaps debased, the deeper sources of American social and economic power. Former enemies and docile states within the area of American hegemony, principally Japan and Germany, took hold of the initiative for dynamic social and economic development. They beat the United States in the trade of mass-production goods once uniquely American not only in the markets of developing countries but even in its own domestic market, and surpassed it in providing developmental capital and aid to the world.

The failure was of belief within. With the torturous debacle of military intervention in Vietnam, the domestic division between the orthodox consensus and the dissenters widened. Groups of diverse ideologies, ethnicities, and parties focused on what separated them as opposed to what brought them together. The increasing overemphasis on military might was not only ineffective but also damaging to domestic industrial capability, and it further disturbed the cohesion of the domestic society, thereby thwarting the prospects that the United States would remain a dominant power. The nation lost its economic footing and moral stability.

The national power was declining for many reasons: foreign markets were lost to enterprising competitors and the excess of imports over exports drained wealth from home; the nation was reduced to a debtor in the world financial markets; the popular culture of art, music, and film became a degree more materialistic and violent; the sense of magnanimity in aid was replaced by a fear of loss; the society faced problems of drugs, crime, decay of the inner cities, declining educational levels, and a deteriorating environment; and the nation turned to defense, rather than to its own example as a dynamic society, to make its influence felt.

But in all these cases there was a failure of national spirit. The society was divided over what is important and lasting and what is not: over the importance of work and investment of money and resources into future innovation and production, over the value of giving and sharing one's resources with the less fortunate, over the need for creating art and music, over the fears that spawned increased quantities of weapons. The society turned to the consumption of resources at home and abroad to maintain a self-indulgent economy and to wage war or prepare for war. Defeat in war then added a terrible blow to the world role.

So the clash between the mainstream orthodox, who resisted change, and the radicals, who impelled it, effectively ended the world role. No reconstituted consensus of domestic alliances took form. But in the expression of divergent ideas over what should be done in the world, and in this tension of resistance and inciting, came the possibility of creativity and forward movement. The answer did not lie in the course pursued by the orthodox thinkers who looked back in reverence to the days of glory and wanted to conserve them even by the blatant use of military force. Nor did the answer lie in the course propounded by the dissenters, who condemned the past of great power regardless of the benefits it had offered. The danger in these approaches was that the past would be regarded as either venerable or worthless. One way wanted to perpetuate by destructive means what had been; the other wanted to obliterate it.

Having developed the sources of the world role within the homeland, how, then, did the nation behave? In building power, earlier generations had done better than their successors. They created a center of unsurpassed productivity. But even as the United States had been unchallenged in world trade and capital reserves, the nation had preferred to be aloof from world political affairs. A consequence of the isolationist tradition became the trial of participation in World War II. The Americans could no longer ignore the larger political world in which they were dwellers. The achievement of inner strength was not sufficient to go it alone in the world.

So internationalism ensued. But what kind of internationalism? The United States had never joined the League of Nations, and mere membership of the League would not have been sufficient to prevent a second world war; the United States would have had to lend its full support with its allies to stopping aggressors when they violated international law. Nor did the United States put its full influence behind the United Nations organization or, conversely, allow other nations to restrain American power. Instead of that restraint, the United States created a world structure of its own.

Americans offered benefits to other societies. Their generosity with their wealth and expertise was not devoid of altruism or service, though the results might not always have been as expected. Trade, investment, and currency, despite degrees of exploitation, provided advanced technology and capital that other countries could use for long-term development, which helped some of them become competitors. The involvement of American culture in other lands left their peoples ultimately free to accept American ways, music, art, literature, and ethics; to accept the ways of French, Japanese, African, or other cultures; or to reassert their own cultural values. The stimulation provided by American financial and technological aid did not necessarily gain and hold faithful allies, but it did help reduce the dependence of recipient nations on foreign indus-trialized goods. Ironically, the successful pursuit of general peace forced the diversion of massive resources into the maintenance of a military establishment, operation of foreign bases, and, ultimately, prosecution of war. An internationalism of preeminence was eventually manifested mostly in the military and intervention. The United States did not fully try the cosmopolitan internationalism envisioned in World War II—of nations cooperating in arranging restraints and checks and balances. That internationalism did not become a habit of life.

The misrepresentations of a preeminent state in the world reflected the uncon-scious bias of an American-centered worldview. Even if unintentional, the bias was an error of balance and proportion, through omissions and exaggerations, reproduced from traditional misconceptions of Manifest Destiny and ethnocentrism. An uncon-scious pattern of consensus thinking imposed a distorted perspective on history, chart-ing out a future fashioned according to an American framework. Implicit in this perspective was the Americanization of other regions of the world over a span of time in an American Century, without necessarily having the consent of the other people who shared the time and space. Americans generally took for granted that their nation was in possession of a superior way, and they did not fully comprehend the life of peoples outside their borders. The viewpoint of international relations as stemming from do-mestic conditions in response to foreign threats did not permit Americans to enlarge the objectives of their society to make them commensurate with the stature of a world nation. The unilateral moves and bilateral and multilateral agreements originated by Americans did not eventually lead to the establishment of a lasting, effective world system at the time of America's decline from preeminence.

Both the benefits and the misrepresentations of the world role and their conse-quences were manifested in the spread of American influence. The trade and capital investment of a great producer and creditor were tools both for profits and for the development and growth of nations, but huge corporations dominating the politics and lives of other peoples, or failing to reinvest profits in productive facilities or toward the welfare of the host country, had no long-term value in enhancing the common stock of resources, labor, or wealth. On the other hand, by its concentration of wealth and reinvestment of it, the United States had set a standard in products available nowhere else and had supplied technologically advanced goods to large numbers of people. By redistributing sums of its wealth in aid, loans, and investment, and by spreading goods and technology, the United States was providing a service to the world.

The United States did not fall behind simply because of this redistribution. All stood to benefit from it. But the United States ceased to be the leading innovator in technological know-how and product development, as it moved from efficient production to consumption. Part of this trend was the siphoning of resources into the military. Over time this diversion weakened the United States: Abroad, the military bases that were operated under alliances, sometimes with dictatorships lacking popular support, provided perceived enemies with the very ammunition they needed to condemn the United States and expand their revolutionary movements. The irony is that the forsaking of economic power for military power did not strengthen America as intended but weakened it: Domestically, the United States might indeed have been stronger than it was at its fall from preeminence if it had been more pacific and cosmopolitan than military and ethnocentric. The country would eventually buy outside basic commodities it once produced.

In the provision of aid by sharing wealth and assisting with technology, again, the greatest benefits were not from exploitation or from expectation of political returns but from satisfying humane obligations. The Marshall Plan, motivated by political and humanitarian sentiments, served to rebuild a civilization and to overcome conditions of poverty that threatened unrest and another war. The plan was humane and cost-effective: it promoted general prosperity for all, including the United States, and general peace. After this extraordinary beginning, the United States made only a superficial effort in its aid commitments to developing nations. Despite the Point Four program and others that followed, the government devoted far more resources to defense than to support that would build economies and alleviate poverty. Meanwhile, many of the poor nations felt the need to spend their spare resources on armament—India and Pakistan had even desired or achieved nuclear weapons—in supposed emulation of the big powers.

Aid was counterproductive when used as a stealthy means to control poor nations. Its application mainly to entice nations to follow America's leadership reinforced alliances. However feasible control might be, it would lead to resistance against the giver. Benefits were lost by withholding or withdrawing aid for lack of patience. A genuine program applied principally in an effort to overcome poverty, ignorance, and disease had the advantage of reducing discontent that led to turmoil and war. Because trade was greatest among the most prosperous nations, it enlarged the prosperity of all. By working for the technological development and capital growth of others, the rich were achieving their own enrichment. But perhaps the most important purpose of aid was supplied by a poll of the American people during the Marshall Plan: the largest group supported that aid simply because it was right to help those who were hungry and sick. The want of the poor impoverished the rich; the gain of the poor benefited the rich. National self-interest coalesced with a sense of morality.

In addition, science and technology contributed to the exchange of ideas, culture, and interests that had the potential to draw together the inhabitants of the globe. A communications revolution created worldwide services of telephones, motion pictures, radio, and television. Medical research discovered drugs to prevent diseases and plagues. Transportation advances contributed to forcing peoples to live in close proximity—black and white, Easterner and Westerner, Catholic and Protestant, Muslim and Hindu. Science had sent people into space, from where they observed a small blue-and-white globe uniting peoples regardless of their differences, the way someone might have once seen a village in a valley from the crest of a hill.

Science had also developed terrible weapons of warfare. Whereas the world's peoples had marveled at American cultural interchange and at an American walking on the moon, many of them were outraged at the use of advanced weaponry against those who lacked it and at the stockpiling of weapons sufficient to destroy not only enemies but the innocent as well. The application of science had the ability both to repel peoples and to attract them.

Finally, an international political community offered the means of settling disputes and furthering relations. But conflicts among the great powers arose in the Security Council and in the economic and social agencies of the United Nations, sometimes stifling international cooperation rather than encouraging it, and some nations refused to join in common activities, including the raising of peace-keeping forces. Shunning the United Nations, Americans organized an alliance network and global economic system centered in the United States. The nation then offered its economic, technical, and cultural assistance directly to friendly states. Americans acted virtually alone in Vietnam and took international self-assertion to its limits. Still, nationalism even among small countries succeeded in curbing the predominance of a superpower.

The alliance system had been organized not to expedite disputes but to support unilateral action. The nation's armies stationed around the world might be sanctioned by foreign governments, but if not by the will of the local people, they met resistance. Finally, even though the military was armed with the latest weaponry, no domestic vitality, productivity, and inner strength derived from overarmament. This was not the spirit of a nation that had spread its influence at the outset of its world role through the trade and activity of the people who went about their lives building and producing. In cases where the United States promoted self-determination and development of peoples, it generally succeeded. The Americans had been welcomed as liberators in occupied Western European and East Asian countries in World War I and World War II, and for their postwar contributions to rebuilding. At the end of the cold war the peoples of Eastern Europe and Russia embraced the democratic ways represented by the United States and the Western democracies. Where self-determination was abridged or development retarded, as in Vietnam, Americans failed.

The world entered a period in which the old statuses of power and ways of thinking were shaken. The international system founded on first one dominant power, then two powers, and finally several, was in turmoil. Great powers were not unchallenged and lesser powers grew in stature. The many exerting nationalisms, each projecting separate policies into the world, had created a potentially unmanageable situation, not unlike the one that Americans had encountered on the eve of World War II. By the time

America had become a debtor and had met reverses as the world's police force, the American order was unsustainable.

Out of the time of chaos emerged the need for creativity. The ethnocentricity of a world state was not able to last. An echoed call for an American, Russian, Chinese, German, or Japanese Century did not present a promising basis on which to make future policy. Many nations grasped modern technology, and the weapons had become far too formidable. The common challenge was to evoke a pluralistic world while at the same time supplying an integrating concept other than that of dominant power of one nation.

What prospects, then, are opened up? Here we might take a clue from Walter Lippmann, who once wrote that when Britain was in decline, it had the United States to fall back on for protection and support. The United States, he pointed out, had no other big nation to depend on. Therefore, Americans, with some anxiety and impatience, had to act the part of an independent, dominant power, which their nation did for the good part of a century. The weakness of this argument becomes apparent with the decline of American preeminence, something that was initially difficult for the realists to foresee, so struck were they by the material assets of a continental nation.

The United States might have avoided its turn from the road not taken, toward cosmopolitan internationalism, which had laid the groundwork for an international order in the event of the erosion of American power. The United States eventually reached the point, as stated by Richard Nixon, where the vision of it as the richest and most stable country, without whose initiative and resources little security or progress was possible, had ended. The example of a preeminent nation putting its full support behind cosmopolitan internationalism might have had enormous, though not immediately apparent, benefits for the United States and other countries. The irony is that the cosmopolitan internationalism which realists said would display weakness would actually have left the United States at the end of its preeminence in a stronger power position—in terms of its material strength, internal cohesion, and international legitimacy.

For one thing, cosmopolitan internationalism would have benefited the American economy, though it did not seem so when the economy had been exceptionally successful. The United States had proposed formation of the International Trade Organization to regulate world trade, but withdrew its support because it did not want to listen to debtor and deficit nations. The United States, so its leaders thought, obviously knew better. The organization had been conceived to adjudicate any unfair advantage. But when the United States itself became a debtor and deficit nation, it formally complained that it was unfairly being exploited by more advanced trading nations. Where was the United States to turn to settle its complaints? Where was the ITO when the United States needed it? It eventually would have offered the United States a way to improve its trade deficit and its debtor status in cooperation with other nations, just as the organization was supposed to have helped nations in a similar situation before the United States rejected it.

In the area of aid, the Marshall Plan, perhaps the high point of American relations, could have had extraordinary additional effects beyond assisting Europeans, by contributing to international cooperation. The Soviets had opposed American unilateral aid but not its aid through UNRRA. Soviet acceptance and participation in the Marshall Plan would have pulled the rug out from under the spreading cold war. The Marshall Plan distributed through the United Nations was not about to become government policy, because of the fear, no doubt correct, that short-term setbacks would be frustrating and irritating. The United States might have had its own way less than it did during its heyday, but the distribution of resources would have been devoted to development and long-term benefits might have been monumental.

As for political relations, instead of listening to world opinion about what constituted proper international behavior, the United States went its own way and fought in Vietnam and lost. It would not have gone to war in Vietnam had it listened to its allies and to world opinion, to Vietnamese opinion in the elections called for in the Geneva settlement, or to an American citizenry that voted for a peace candidate in 1964. The war was based on a misguided and ethnocentric view of the world held by a preeminent nation acting as it pleased. A respect for international opinion would have spared the United States the trauma of defeat in war and the disruption of its economy and the unity of society.

Nothing was inviolable about the United Nations. If one nation did not cooperate with the world's nations, other nations could have proceeded without it in a reformed international organization or formed another. Correcting problems between nations that they had been unable to resolve themselves was the primary function of an international organization, which might have acted as a regulator of the exchange of trade, aid, culture, and goodwill. For peace could not be sought in the abstract. American presidents said they waged war to achieve peace, but peace was also the determined application of power through trade, economic aid, and culture. Nations were interrelated in a network of giving and taking, buying and selling, and by a humanness that transcended communism and capitalism. And that essential conception of interdependence takes us back to our starting point, the study of myth, a people's beliefs.

Views of interdependence went against the grain of the established strategic thinking, and the United States had left-over extensive interests from its period of preeminence that blocked the acceptance of interdependence. The orthodox dismissed conceptions of interdependence with incredulity, if not contempt. But a curious feature of its world involvement is that the United States, which had been effective and prospered through trade, investment, and cultural exchange, came to rely on war and military activity to advance American interests and values. The pursuit of preeminence or superiority of a powerful nation by force or the ability to wage violence did not create a similar prosperity.

The way to power was the same at home and abroad, and it was through attributes altogether different from the pride and force that are normally associated with power: it was through intellect, creative imagination, compassion, and empathy toward other cultures; in a word, magnanimity. Great power was based not on quick advantage or cleverness of strategic advantage. Great power was expressed with a capacious spirit that did not exclude the fate of other peoples. That required a new consensus—not for the nation to go its own way, for such a course would lean toward the ethnocentric, but toward a more successful relationship with other societies.

Looking back on the two particular myths, we might hypothesize that if Americans had wanted this era to be the American Century, they would have had to work toward making it the Century of the Common People, not just within the frontiers of the United States but in other lands as well. Without the internal power of natural resources and social dynamism, the problem would have been moot. By virtue of its power the United States could take actions other nations could not; it could project its might in arms even to the other side of the globe, and it could offer the benefits of its technology, economy, and culture to other societies. But the choices created by this power were not America's alone. The development of other peoples had to be their own, albeit aided by American technology and capital and its example of self-determination.

The American Century overestimated the nature of unilateral power, forgetting its relative qualities and the interests and desires of allies and rivals alike. The Century of the Common Man was an idealistic sentiment which overlooked the hostilities and ideas that divided the world's people into sovereign nations. The harmonious use of power with the interests of peoples in their own self-determination and economic development stood the strongest chance for a common peace. But, again, that did not mean the United States would decline in power if it continued to reinvest in its own economic and social dynamism.

Neither the American Century nor the Century of the Common Man, then, fully comprehended the world as it was. Neither view applied to the needs of world problems at the end of the era of U.S. preeminence. These old myths were limited to the frame of a century that was passing and to the conception of the United States as a preeminent power, which was ending. To seek new myths one might try to return to the years of World War II, when old ideas gave way and creative thought was applied to world problems. Another myth at the time, by Wendell Willkie, was One World, a vision of an international community of nations, based on the precepts that there were no distant points in the world any longer, that all peoples were tied together by modern technology, and that future thinking had to be worldwide.

But returning to this old myth is not satisfactory either. It was an abortive attempt at world order. The world had indeed become one technologically, in communication among peoples, and in the ability to send military force across national borders; but it had not become one on a psychic plane. Such consciousness was lagging behind the realities of technological development. No concept had yet recognized the common humanity of peoples and the plurality of the earth's societies. In the tension between the new realities and the failure of old myths lay the need for new, enduring myths.

The United States was preeminent for only a moment of history, one powerful state among nations and empires over time, holding land, propagating population, making science, producing wealth, raising armies, waging war, espousing beliefs and faith. Because states, nations, and empires of the past have declined, we might expect that in the future, as in the past, old states will retreat and new states rise, manifesting their world roles. Rising states take hold of new myths, inventions, discoveries, exercising power where the earlier powers have left only a void. But there is no certainty that with the passage of time a society must lose its sense of innovation or seek to impose its will on other nations by force.

In international activity, certain areas of the American vision pointed toward a supranational outlook, though an emergent global era could not be realized alone in American life and thought. The generation of technologically advanced goods and services and their free flow among nations created potential for human progress. The technical and artistic skills of engineers, scientists, doctors, movie makers, entertainers, airline pilots, road builders, and teachers provided human needs to people who wanted them. Food production and living standards were capable of being raised to help the poor and hungry. A respect for world opinion expressed through procedures and institutions to help realize common interests might enable the great powers to restrain military power and the weak countries to receive protection in a pluralistic world.

What mattered was what was remembered and emulated, not what was resisted, by nations that progressed, not by ones in decline. What mattered was creation in philosophy, science, agriculture, industry, medicine, art, song, architecture, writing, morality, and charity, in which lay something of the immortal that lives on after the civilization itself is gone. For even if America should finally fail, it might pass on as legacy its techniques of commerce, communication, and democracy to others who valued them, the way it once profited from earlier civilizations. In those connections lies the continuation of human history and the emergence of global civilization.

NOTES

Prologue

1 Major works on Manifest Destiny include Weinberg, *Manifest Destiny,* and Merk, *Manifest Destiny and Mission.* Early references to Manifest Destiny include the first appearance of the phrase in O'Sullivan's editorial, "Annexation," in *United States Magazine, and Democratic Review,* July–August 1845, 5–10. Pratt, "Origin of 'Manifest Destiny,'" 795–98, traced the first use of the term, and his "John L. O'Sullivan and Manifest Destiny," 213–34, recounted its passage into the national vocabulary. An article that contributed to the wide usage of the term was "'Manifest Destiny' Doctrines," *Niles' National Register,* Jan. 22, 1848, 334–36. Later sources on Manifest Destiny and imperialism include Fiske's "Manifest Destiny," 578–90, reprinted in *American Political Ideas,* 101–52; Schurz, "Manifest Destiny," 737–46; and Powers, "War as a Suggestion of Manifest Destiny," 173–92. Shortly after the turn of the century, references to the term included Chittenden, "Manifest Destiny in America," 48–59; and Bardin, "'Manifest Destiny' in the Caribbean."

2 F. Turner, "The Significance of the Frontier in American History," in *Frontier in American History,* 1–38, 213, 306. On Turner's frontier thesis and the influence of the frontier experience on foreign policy, see W. Williams, "Frontier Thesis and American Foreign Policy," 379–95; and Kaplan, "Frederick Jackson Turner and Imperialism," 12–16. On Turner's lack of precision in defining the frontier, see Billington, *American Frontier Thesis,* 18.

3 F. Turner, *Frontier in American History,* 219, 246. See also 242, 267, 315.

4 F. Turner, *Frontier in American History,* 37–38; Sharp, "Three Frontiers," 369–77; Seymour Martin Lipset, "The Turner Thesis in Comparative Perspective: An Introduction" and Marvin W. Mikesell, "Comparative Studies in Frontier History," in Hofstadter and Lipset, *Turner and the Sociology of the Frontier,* 9–14, 152–71.

5 Darwin, *On the Origin of the Species* and *Descent of Man,* 1:172–73. Part of Darwin's passage is quoted from Zincke, *Last Winter in the United States,* 29. In *Descent of Man,* Darwin had other observations about the United States. If the country continued to double in population every 25 years, its 30 million people would increase in 657 years to cover the whole land area of the globe so thickly that four men would have to stand on each square yard (1:126). Darwin also thought that European settlers in the United States underwent a slight but rapid change in appearance (1:237). His subsequent research seemed to confirm his view that the bodies and limbs of immigrants became elongated. During the Civil War, he reported in a later edition (New York, 1896), regiments of German immigrants were too small for the ready-made clothes manufactured for the American market (196).

6 Hofstadter, *Social Darwinism,* 146–73; Pratt, "'Large Policy' of 1898," 219–42, and "The Ideology of American Expansion," in

Craven, *Essays in Honor of William E. Dodd*, 335–53. "The New Manifest Destiny" was the title of chap. 1 of Pratt's *Expansionists of 1898.*

7 Fiske, *American Political Ideas*, 143–44; Burgess, *Political Science*, 4, 39, 45; Strong, *Our Country*, 159–80.

8 U.S. Congress, Senate, Sen. Beveridge speaking on policy regarding the Philippines, 56th Cong., 1st sess., Jan. 9, 1900, *Congressional Record*, 33:711; T. Roosevelt, *Winning of the West*, 3, and *Rough Riders*, 48–50; Demolins, *Anglo-Saxon Superiority*, published in Paris as *A quoi tient la supérioirité des Anglo-Saxons.* On Roosevelt as a student of Burgess at Columbia, see Beale, *Theodore Roosevelt and the Rise of America*, 27, 312.

9 Stoddard, "Racial Realities in Europe," 14; Grant, *Passing of the Great Race;* Stoddard, *Rising Tide of Color.*

10 T. Roosevelt, *Theodore Roosevelt's Speeches in Europe*, 102; Stoddard, *Rising Tide of Color*, 263; Grant, *Passing of the Great Race*, 227–28.

11 A. Smith, *Wealth of Nations*, 2:69–73.

12 Marx, *Capital*, 1:765; Lenin, *Imperialism*, 15, 67, 114.

13 C. Beard, *Economic Basis of Politics*, 103–7, and his great work, *Economic Interpretation of the Constitution*, now found wanting.

14 C. Beard, *Idea of National Interest*, 89–120.

15 C. Beard, *Economic Basis of Politics*, 106–14.

16 On beliefs of the people regarding foreign policy, see Bailey, *Man in the Street;* Almond, *American People and Foreign Policy;* Osgood, *Ideals and Self-Interest in America's Foreign Relations;* Halle, *Civilization and Foreign Policy;* Divine, *Second Chance.* The part the public can play in foreign policy can be seen in Lippmann's *Public Opinion and Foreign Policy, U.S. Foreign Policy,* and a later pessimistic work, *Essays in the Public Philosophy.*

17 On intellectual traditions of myth and symbol in American history, see Hollinger, "Historians and the Discourse of Intellectuals," in Higham and Conkin, *New Directions in American Intellectual History*, 42–63. Informative contributions include H. N. Smith, *Virgin Land: The American West as Symbol and Myth*, and J. Ward, *Andrew Jackson: Symbol for an Age.* A critique of these studies is by Kuklick, "Myth and Symbol," 435–50. On the theory of myth, see McNeill, "Mythistory, or Truth, Myth, History, and Historians," 1–10; Roelofs, *Ideology and Myth;* and Cassirer, *Symbol, Myth, and Culture.*

18 Some work has been done on the relation between a culture and the ideas of foreign affairs. A study looking closely at State Department cultural programs is Ninkovich, *Diplomacy of Ideas.* A comparative study is by Iriye, *Power and Culture.* Interpretive studies include Dallek, *American Style of Foreign Policy,* and Rosenberg, *Spreading the American Dream.*

19 Standard histories of the cold war include an early study by McNeill, *America, Britain, & Russia.* A valuable series is Feis, *Churchill-Roosevelt-Stalin; Between War and Peace;* and *Japan Subdued,* revised as *Atomic Bomb and the End of World War II;* along with his *From Trust to Terror.* Other useful studies include Donnelly, *Struggle for the World, The Cold War;* M. Herz, *Beginnings of the Cold War;* Lukacs, *New History of the Cold War;* Neumann, *After Victory;* Seabury, *Rise and Decline of the Cold War;* and Halle, *Cold War as History.* Leading revisionist works include W. Williams, *Tragedy of American Diplomacy;* Fleming, *Cold War and Its Origins;* Aptheker, *American Foreign Policy;* D. Horowitz, *Free World Colossus;* G. Kolko, *Politics of War;* L. Gardner, *Architects of Illusion;* and Alperowitz, *Atomic Diplomacy.* Notable attempts to move beyond revisionist

accounts written during the cold war include Gaddis, *United States and the Origins of the Cold War,* and Yergin, *Shattered Peace.*

On the need for further study of the social and cultural aspects of international affairs, see Donald W. White, "The Nature of World Power in 'American History: An Evaluation at the End of World War II," *Diplomatic History* 11 (Summer 1987): 181.

20 Toynbee, *Study of History,* 9:581–83. See also Donald W. White, "The 'American Century' in World History," *Journal of World History* 3 (Spring 1992): 105–27.

21 Luce, "American Century," 61–65, repr. in *American Century.*

22 Wallace, "Price of Free World Victory," 9–13; "Price of Free World Victory: The Century of the Common Man," 482–85; and in *Century of the Common Man,* 14–23.

23 On the life and thought of Luce, see Swanberg, *Luce and His Empire;* Kobler, *Luce;* and Neils, *China Images in the Life and Times.* On Wallace, see Lord, *Wallaces of Iowa;* Markowitz, *Rise and Fall of the People's Century;* Walker, *Henry A. Wallace and American Foreign Policy;* and Walton, *Henry Wallace, Harry Truman, and the Cold War.* On discussion of the American Century, see Thompson, "The American Century," *New York Herald Tribune,* Feb. 21, 1941, 17; Sherwood, comments published in Luce, *American Century,* 79–89; Kirchwey, "Luce Thinking," *Nation,* March 1, 1941, 229–30; N. Thomas, "How to Fight for Democracy," 58–59; C. Beard and M. Beard, *American Spirit,* vol. 4: The Rise of American Civilization, 573–77; Mead, *And Keep Your Powder Dry,* 205, 252; Niebuhr, *Discerning the Signs,* 11, 78; U.S. Congress, House, Rep. Martin J. Kennedy speaking to create a committee to preserve and propagate democracy, 77th Cong., 1st sess., Feb. 27, 1941, *Congressional Record,* 87:1496–97, 1502; and Kennedy speaking on "The American Century," 77th Cong., 1st sess., March 5, 1941, *Congressional Record,* 87: 1828–31.

24 Padover, "American Century?" 85–90; H. J. Morgenthau, *Politics among Nations,* 115; Baldwin, *Price of Power,* 130–41, 327–28; Flanders, *American Century,* 96; Taft, *Foreign Policy for Americans,* 17; Truman, *Public Papers,* 1952–53, 424.

25 F. D. Roosevelt to Henry Wallace, Aug. 30, 1943, and Eleanor Roosevelt to Henry Wallace, July 31, 1942, Franklin D. Roosevelt Library; Wallace, *Price of Vision,* 76–81; "Comments," in Wallace, *Price of Free World Victory,* 32, 34; Blum's introductory essay, *Price of Vision,* 28–29, 54; H. Cantril, *Public Opinion,* 711–12, 1057, 1062. See *Prelude to War,* the first film of Frank Capra's *Why We Fight* series for the government, and *The Price of Victory,* a documentary about Wallace's Century of the Common Man speech (both films released by the Office of War Information, 1942). The Academy Award–winning feature film *Gentleman's Agreement* (1947) contrasted the "American Century" with "everybody's century" of "people all over the world."

26 Luce, "American Century," 61–62; Wallace, *Century of the Common Man,* 14, 16–17.

27 Luce, "American Century," 62–64.

28 Wallace, *Century of the Common Man,* 15, 17–18.

29 Luce, "American Century," 64; Wallace, *Century of the Common Man,* 14, 17–18.

30 Wallace, *Century of the Common Man,* 19–20. To some critics the differences between the American Century and the Century of the Common Man were obscure. Macdonald, "(American) People's Century," 294–310, comparing these concepts in 1942, found no significant differences between them. What Macdonald did find was noticeable agreement between the Left and the Right on these aims for the postwar world. Comparing the two concepts again in 1948, Macdonald, *Henry Wallace: The Man and the Myth,* 31–35, 70–72, explained that the difference between Wallace and Luce was one of tact. Luce put "bluntly" what Wallace was essentially saying vaguely. "Mr. Wallace, meet Mr. Luce,"

Macdonald summarized. One historian, Markowitz, has taken strong exception with this assertion in the *Rise and Fall of the People's Century,* 53–54. Luce wrote Wallace that he thought their differences were minimal, and Wallace was conciliatory. See Henry R. Luce to Henry A. Wallace, May 14, 1942, and H. A. Wallace to Henry R. Luce, May 16, 1942, Time, Inc., Archives. The differences did impress some observers. The foreign correspondent Edward R. Murrow, from his post in London, wrote that the fate of European diplomacy and postwar peace would depend on whether Luce or Wallace "is the forerunner of the American policy of tomorrow" (Edward R. Murrow to Eric Sevareid, Aug. 26, 1942, Papers of Eric Sevareid, Library of Congress).

31 Luce, "American Century," 65; Wallace, *Century of the Common Man,* 20.

32 Luce, "American Century," 65; Wallace, *Century of the Common Man,* 20–21.

33 Luce, "American Century" 65; Wallace, *Century of the Common Man,* 19–20.

34 Luce, "American Century," 65; Wallace, *Century of the Common Man,* 15, 20.

35 Luce, "American Century," 65; Wallace, *Century of the Common Man,* 20.

Chapter 1

1 The early strategic boundaries of the U.S. are traced in Lippmann, *U.S. Foreign Policy,* 11–26, 109. The Joint Chiefs of Staff later used language remarkably similar to Lippmann's when describing America's defensive area in *Foreign Relations of the United States,* 1947, 1:739. On Feb. 3, 1939, Roosevelt denied he believed that "the American frontier is the Rhine" *(Public Papers,* 1939, 114–15); but in private he said that "our first line of defense is really the small countries of Europe that have not yet been overwhelmed by the Nazis" (Ickes, *Secret Diary,* 2:571); he was soon making similar statements in public *(Public Papers,* 1940, 635–36; 1941, 388). Churchill's famous "iron curtain" speech is in *Sinews of Peace: Post-War Speeches,* 100–101. Acheson explained the "defensive perimeter" in an address to the National Press Club, Washington, D.C., on Jan. 12, 1950, printed as "Crisis in Asia—An Examination of U.S. Policy," *Department of State Bulletin,* Jan. 23, 1950, 115–16.

2 See Council on Foreign Relations, *Documents on American Foreign Relations* for the texts of the North Atlantic Treaty, 1949, 612–15; the Philippines Treaty of Mutual Defense, 1951, 262–65; Security Treaty with Japan, 1951, 266–67; the Southeast Asia Collective Defense Treaty, 1954, 319–23; and the Baghdad Pact, 1955, 342–44, and 1959, 396–99. Eisenhower's comment is in Memorandum of Discussion at the 179th Meeting of the National Security Council, Friday, January 8, 1954, *Foreign Relations of the United States,* 1952–1954, 13:952; Eisenhower, *Public Papers,* 1954, 421.

3 F. D. Roosevelt, *Public Papers,* 1944–45, 405. Some of the argument of Part I of this book was made in Donald W. White, "The Nature of World Power in American History; An Evaluation of the End of World War II," *Diplomatic History* 11 (Summer 1987); 181–202.

4 Hopkins, "What Victory Will Bring Us," 21. See also Welles, *Time for Decision,* 413.

5 Truman, *Public Papers,* 1945, 213.

6 Ibid., 1948, 327, 502, 730–31. See also 287, 304, 312, 336, 359, 362, 378, and 491 for similar statements.

7 Luce, "American Century," 63–64; Johnson, "Whose War Aims?" 102; MacNeil, *American Peace,* 155–56; Scherman, "Last Best Hope," 111, condensed from *Atlantic Monthly.* See also Brunauer, "Power Politics and Democracy," 109–10.

8 Memorandum by the Secretary of Defense (Forrestal) to the National Security Council, July 10, 1948, *Foreign Relations of the United States,* 1948, 1:589–92; Report to the President by the National Security Council, NSC 20/4, ibid., 1948, 1:668; A Report to the President Pursuant to the President's Directive of January 31, 1950, ibid., 1950, 1:252–62. NSC 68 was the work of a joint study group of the State and Defense departments headed by Paul Nitze; the completed study was forwarded to Truman on April 7, 1950, and was approved by him on Sept. 30. A Report to the National Security Council, Basic National Security Policy, NSC 162/2, Oct. 30, 1953, Dwight D. Eisenhower Library. These lists recurred in the documents and memorandums prepared by the Joint Chiefs of Staff, National Security Council, and early postwar government officials. The Joint Chiefs in 1946 listed the need for "outlying bases," maintenance of "industries essential to the national war effort," and stockpiling of "critical strategic materials," in Memorandum Prepared by the Joint Chiefs of Staff, March 27, 1946, *Foreign Relations of the United States,* 1946, 1:1164. See also Report to the National Security Council by the Executive Secretary (Souers), NSC 7, March 30, 1948, ibid., 1948, 1:548–49. Forrestal's interest in the nature of power preceded his becoming secretary of defense, and during World War II he had begun a course on this subject for navy officers. See Forrestal, *Forrestal Diaries,* 6. Out of the experience of this navy course, H. Sprout and M. Sprout edited *Foundations of National Power.*

9 The argument that the U.S. became a world power at the Declaration of Independence is set forth in Bailey, "America's Emergence," 1–16; J. Adams, *Works,* 7:226–27, letter to Count de Vergennes, July 13, 1780. Studies chronicling the development of the U.S. as a great power usually concentrate on the late nineteenth century: e.g., May's *Imperial Democracy* and F. R. Dulles's *Prelude to World Power.* Dulles traced subsequent developments in *America's Rise to World Power.*

10 McKinley, *Speeches and Addresses,* 588. Gladstone's comparison is in "Kin beyond Sea," 181.

11 Wilson, *Public Papers: The New Democracy,* 1:371, and *Public Papers: War and Peace,* 1:640, 2:18, 89; Hoover, *State Papers,* 1:270–71, and *New Day,* 91–92.

12 Studies on realism in American foreign policy include J. Herz, *Political Realism;* Carleton, "Wanted: Wiser Power Politics," 194–206; Niebuhr, *Christian Realism;* and Kenneth Thompson, *Political Realism.* These are closely related to studies of national interest: Beard's pioneering *Idea of National Interest;* H. J. Morgenthau's *In Defense of the National Interest;* and Schuman's "International Ideals," 27–36.

13 Spykman, *America's Strategy,* 11.

14 Ibid., 11–19, 446–72.

15 W. Fox, *Super-Powers,* 2–11, 20–21.

16 H. J. Morgenthau, *Politics among Nations,* vii. Other editions of this famous philosophical textbook appeared in 1954, 1960, 1967, and 1973. On Morgenthau, see the memorial essay by Arthur M. Schlesinger, Jr., in Schwab, *United States Foreign Policy,* ix–xvi. Works on the nature of political power contemporary with Morgenthau's but with different perspectives include B. Russell, *Power;* Carr, *Twenty Years' Crisis;* Ferrero, *Principles of Power;* de Jouvenel, *On Power;* Lasswell and Kaplan, *Power and Society.*

17 H. J. Morgenthau, *Politics among Nations,* 8, 13–19.

18 H. J. Morgenthau, *Scientific Man,* 203.

19 Gallatin, *Peace with Mexico,* 25–27; Sumner, *Essays,* 2:295; H. J. Morgenthau, *Politics among Nations,* 18–20.

20 Olcott, *Life of William McKinley,* 2:109–11. Olcott recollected the president's words from an interview with him on Nov. 21, 1899, printed in *The Christian Advocate,* Jan. 22, 1903.

21 Wilson, *Public Papers: The New Democracy,* 1:67, 69. See also *Public Papers: War and Peace,* 1:259.

22 Wilson, *Public Papers: War and Peace,* 2:309.

23 Kennan, *American Diplomacy,* 95–96, 100–103; and *Realities of American Foreign Policy.* His cable to the Secretary of State calling for realism, Feb. 22, 1946, is in *Foreign Relations of the United States,* 1946, 6:708. See also Cook and Moos, "Foreign Policy: The Realism of Idealism," 343–56, and *Power through Purpose: The Realism of Idealism.* Moos, an educator at Johns Hopkins University, was a consultant in the White House in 1957 and 1958, and assistant to the president from 1958 to 1960.

Chapter 2

1 Jones, *Fifteen Weeks,* 46.

2 An important survey of readings treating the countries and regions of the world is H. Sprout and M. Sprout, *Foundations of National Power* (1945), later brought up to date with readings of the quickly shifting international situation as of 1951. A post–World War II analysis of international power relationships is Baldwin, *Price of Power,* 23–55.

3 Kissinger reviewed the origins of this system in *World Destroyed.*

4 Acheson, *Present at the Creation,* xvii, 3–8, 726; and *Power and Diplomacy,* 3–8.

5 E. Fischer, *Passing,* 176–77; Holborn, *Political Collapse of Europe,* ix–xi, 87–110.

6 W. Fox, *Super-Powers,* 12–13, 17; Baerwald, "Future of Europe," 416; Holborn, *Political Collapse of Europe,* x. See also Memorandum by the Under Secretary of State for Economic Affairs (Clayton), The European Crisis, May 27, 1947, *Foreign Relations of the United States,* 1947, 3:230. See also Dallin, *Big Three.*

7 Brinton, *United States and Britain,* 3–23.

8 Brodie, "How Strong Is Britain?" 432–49. A study of the decline of Britain and the corresponding rise of the United States is by Lionel Gelber, *America in Britain's Place.* One might compare the thesis of this book to the later study by Clyde Prestowitz, *Trading Places,* on the United States and Japan.

9 Murrow, *This Is London,* 161, 181, 203–4, 227.

10 Winant, *Letter from Grosvenor Square,* 4, 52–58; Byrnes, *Speaking Frankly,* 93. See also Childs, "London Wins the Battle," 129–52.

11 H. Roberts and Wilson, *Britain and the United States,* 1–2, 72–75, 81, 96; W. Fox and A. Fox, *Britain and America;* J. Williams, "British Crisis," 1–17; UN, General Assembly, *Preliminary Report of the Temporary Sub-Commission on Economic Reconstruction,* 132–37; Memorandum by the Joint Chiefs of Staff to the State-War-Navy Coordinating Committe, April 29, 1947, *Foreign Relations of the United States,* 1947, 1:737–38. See also Ward, "Britain in the Shadow."

12 H. Sprout and M. Sprout, "Command" and *Toward a New Order.*

13 India's special place in the empire is related in L. Fischer, *Empire;* Fischer's talk with the British general is on p. 29. Churchill is quoted in the *New York Times,* Nov. 11, 1942, 4, and also in Fischer, *Empire,* 45, 66.

14 The Chargé in the United Kingdom (Holmes) to the Secretary of State, Jan. 7, 1950, *Foreign Relations of the United States,* 1950, 3:1601.

15 Henry, "War's Wake," 1–32; UN, General Assembly, *Preliminary Report of the Temporary Sub-Commission on Economic Reconstruction*, 9–10, 15, 17, 24, 28, 96–97, 107–9.

16 Henry, "War's Wake," 1; W. Jacobs, "Where Do the People Live," 354–55.

17 "Britain: Blitz by General Winter," *Newsweek*, Feb. 17, 1947, 36–37, and "Visitor from Siberia," 37; "Europe: The Cold Hands, the Empty Plates," *Newsweek*, Jan. 20, 1947, 36.

18 Clay, *Decision in Germany*, 21, 32; Murphy, *Diplomat among Warriors*, 257, 264; " Berlin," *Life*, July 23, 1945, 19–27; Truman, *Memoirs*, 1:341; Truman, *Off the Record*, 52.

19 F. D. Roosevelt, *Public Papers*, 1941, 389; Galbraith, "Germany Was Badly Run," 173.

20 The text of the Morgenthau plan, Suggested Post-Surrender Program for Germany, Sept. 1, 1944, is in *Foreign Relations of the United States*, The Conference at Quebec, 1944, 86–90, and the memorandum on the treatment of Germany initialed at Quebec by Roosevelt and Churchill, Sept. 15, 1944, is on pp. 466–67. For State and War department opposition to the plan, see Hull, *Memoirs*, 1602–22; and Stimson and Bundy, *On Active Service*, 568–83.

21 JCS/1067, Directive to SCAEF Regarding the Military Government of Germany in the Period Immediately Following the Cessation of Organized Resistance (Post-Defeat), Sept. 22, 1944, is in *Foreign Relations of the United States*, The Conferences at Malta and Yalta, 1945, 143–54. This paper was the basis for the final directive issued in April 1945. For a redraft, see *Foreign Relations of the United States*, 1945, 3:378–88. For the text of the directive, as released in October 1945, see "Military Government of Germany," *Department of State Bulletin*, Oct. 21, 1945, 596–607. For Clay on implementing JCS/1067, see *Decision in Germany*, 10–19.

22 Truman, *Memoirs*, 1:341, 361–62; Clay, *Decision in Germany*, 44–45; Truman, *Public Papers*, 1945, 174–75.

23 Jackson, *Nürnberg Case*, 7–8, 30–31; Jackson, *Case Against the Nazi War Criminals;* Radin, "Justice at Nuremberg," 369–84.

24 Byrnes, *All in One Lifetime*, 368–69, and his address delivered in Stuttgart on Sept. 6, 1946, "Restatement of U.S. Policy on Germany," *Department of State Bulletin*, Sept. 15, 1946, 501; Rodnick, *Postwar Germans*, 219.

25 Acheson, " Current Situation in Germany," *Department of State Bulletin*, May 8, 1949, 585–88. For perspective on the "tug-of-war" over Germany between the Eastern and Western powers, see Craig, "Germany between the East and the West" and Schorske, "Dilemma in Germany."

26 Hersey, "Home to Warsaw," 16–20; UN, General Assembly, *Preliminary Report of the Temporary Sub-Commission on Economic Reconstruction*, 153–54. See also Lane, *I Saw Poland Betrayed*, 20–27.

27 "Allies Enter Vienna," *Life*, Sept. 3, 1945, 34–35; Henry, "Tale of Three Cities," 641–69.

28 Burnett, "Yank Meets Native," 105–28. The organization of the *Foreign Relations of the United States* series for 1947 reflects this conception of the developing world; the colonial areas are grouped not geographically in their own regions but as subheadings under the ruling European powers.

29 Boggs, "Africa: Maps and Man," *Department of State Bulletin*, Sept. 18, 1943, 188; Smyser, "São Tomé," 657–80.

30 Moore, "Britain Tackles," 311; "The National Geographic's New Map of Africa," *National Geographic* 97 (March 1950): 396–99; Moore, "White Magic," 321; UN, General Assembly, *Preliminary Report of the Temporary Sub-Commission on Economic Reconstruction*, 179.

31 Moore, "White Magic," 321–62, and "Britain Tackles," 311–51; Grosvenor, "Safari through Changing Africa," 145–98, and "Safari from Congo to Cairo," 721–71.

32 Moore, "Busy Corner," 197–223, and "Cities," 725–66; Groves, *Now It Can Be Told*, 33–37, 170–73.

33 "Job Before Us," *Fortune*, April 1944, 121; "Submarine Shells California Oil Plant" and "Coast Blacked Out," *New York Times*, Feb. 24, 1942, 1; "Attack on the U.S.," *Time*, March 2, 1942, 9. The *Times*, Feb. 26, 1942, 1, reported that on Feb. 25 Los Angeles feared Japanese planes were attacking and anti-aircraft batteries fired barrage after barrage into the predawn darkness.

34 "Little Industry, Big War," *Fortune*, April 1944, 165–68, 295–309; J. Cohen, "Japanese War Economy," 361–70.

35 McKelway, "Reporter with the B-29s," 26–39; Cary, *War-Wasted Asia*, 61, 249; U.S. Strategic Bombing Survey, *Effects of Atomic Bombs on Hiroshima and Nagasaki*, 3–9. For an extended discussion, see Committee for the Compilation of Materials on Damage Caused by the Atomic Bombs in Hiroshima and Nagasaki, *Hiroshima and Nagasaki*.

36 T. White and Jacoby, *Thunder out of China*, xi–xiii.

37 MacArthur, *Reminiscences*, 278.

38 Proclamation Calling for the Surrender of Japan, Approved by the Heads of Government of the United States, China, and the United Kingdom, July 26, 1945, *Foreign Relations of the United States*, The Conference of Berlin (The Potsdam Conference), 1945, 1474–76; Instructions to General of the Army Douglas MacArthur, (Message No. 1), *Foreign Relations of the United States*, 1945, 6:712; Bisson, *Prospects for Democracy*, 1–2.

39 "The Japs Get MacArthur's Orders" and "The Japanese Mind in Defeat," *Life*, Sept. 3, 1945, 23–27; Brines, *MacArthur's Japan*; Bisson, *Prospects for Democracy*, 17.

40 Haring, *Japan's Prospect*, 25; Cary, *War-Wasted Asia*, 78; U.S. Department of Commerce, *Historical Statistics*, 903, 905.

41 MacArthur, *Soldier Speaks*, 188; T. White and Jacoby, *Thunder out of China*, xiii.

42 Rowe, *China among the Powers*, 1–7, 167.

43 Ibid., 23–33; Cressey, *Asia's Lands and Peoples*, 44; Fairbank, *Trade and Diplomacy*, 1:4. See also Hoover, *Memoirs: Years of Adventure*, 66–72.

44 T. White and Jacoby, *Thunder out of China*, 26, 169.

45 Winfield, "This Is China," 8–9, 12–13; Hsü, *Rise of Modern China*, 686, 708–10; Hogan, "Shanghai," 91–92.

46 Buck, *American Unity and Asia*, 77–78; and "China Faces the Future" in *What America Means to Me*, 67–86.

47 "U.S. Bases in China Held to Be Vital," *New York Times*, Sept. 1, 1947, 6; T. White and Jacoby, *Thunder out of China*, xiii, 199.

48 Barnett, "Profile of Red China," 230–43; Winfield, "China's Basic Problems," 2–5; Wallace, *Toward World Peace*, 93–95; "Seven Years of Valley Forge," review of *Thunder out of China*, by T. White and Jacoby, *Time*, Oct. 28, 1946, 110–13; T. White, *In Search of History*, 206–12, 240–41; Elson, *World of Time, Inc.*, 140–52; Memorandum by the Policy Planning Staff, Sept. 7, 1948, *Foreign Relations of the United States*, 1948, 8:149–50.

49 "Japan Surrenders to Allies, Signs Rigid Terms on Warship; Truman Sets Today As V-J Day," *New York Times*, Sept. 2, 1945, 1; "Annamites Curb French," Sept. 11, 1945, 6; "Indo-China Fights Return of French," Sept. 22, 1945, 2.

50 This famous reexamination of American objectives, A Report to the President Pursuant to the President's Directive of January 31, 1950, April 7, 1950, known as NSC 68, is in *Foreign Relations of the United States, 1950*, vol. 1; the "Background to the Present Crisis" is on pp. 237–38.

51 Stimson and Bundy, *On Active Service*, 383; "The Time to Act Is Now," *New York Times*, June 24, 1941, 18; "Turnabout in Russia" and "Russia's 'Economic Wound,'" *Fortune*, December 1942, 102–8; "As Russia Marches West," *New York Times*, Jan. 28, 1945, 4, p. 8.

52 "Our Own Baedeker," *New Yorker*, Feb. 10, 1945, 17–18; Schwarz, "How Much Oil Has Russia?" 736, 739.

53 Eisenhower, *Crusade in Europe*, 469; Harriman and Abel, *Special Envoy*, 257; Bourke-White, *Shooting the Russian War*, 265, 269; UN, General Assembly, *Preliminary Report of the Temporary Sub-Commission of Economic Reconstruction*, 174–75.

54 Scholz, "Need We Fear Russia's Economic Strength?" 3–7; "Turnabout in Russia" and "Russia's 'Economic Wound,'" *Fortune*, Dec. 1942, 102–8; Wohl, "Transport," 470–74; Willkie, *One World*, 63–64; East, "How Strong Is the Heartland?" 78.

55 Johnston, *We're All in It*, 108–9; W. White, *Report on the Russians*, 43, 47, 49–50.

56 W. White, *Report on the Russians*, 22, 25, 149, 155, 204.

57 Scholz, "Need We Fear Russia's Economic Strength?" 3–7.

58 W. Smith, *My Three Years*, 39, 131, 139.

59 Baldwin, *Price of Power*, 35; Willkie, *One World*, 59; W. White, *Report on the Russians*, 165.

60 Bergson, "Russian Defense Expenditures," 373–76; "Russia's Edge in Men and Arms," *U.S. News & World Report*, April 2, 1948, 23; "The Power behind Red Diplomacy," *Newsweek*, March 29, 1948, 28–32; Baldwin, "19 Million in World Armies, Forty-Nation Survey Shows," *New York Times*, May 12, 1947, 1, 14; Eisenhower, *Papers*, 7:1106; Evangelista, "Stalin's Postwar Army Reappraised," 110–38.

61 "The Chargé in the Soviet Union (Kennan) to the Secretary of State," Feb. 22, 1946, *Foreign Relations of the United States*, 1946, 6:696–709.

62 H. K. Smith, *State of Europe*, 69–70.

Chapter 3

1 Spykman, *America's Strategy*, 7–8; "Geography Is Fate?" *Time*, April 20, 1942, 90–96; Strausz-Hupé, *Geopolitics*, viii.

2 Mackinder, "Geographical Pivot of History," 421–37; Mackinder, *Democratic Ideals and Reality* (1942), originally published in 1919 to apply his geographic theories to help organize the peace after World War I, was republished during World War II to help with the problems of peacemaking. Later Anthony J. Pearce, an assistant professor at New York University, edited Mackinder's *Democratic Ideals and Reality* (1962) to guide strategic thinking on the Soviet Union. Mackinder carried his theories further in "Round World," in *Foreign Affairs* in 1943. On American perspectives of German geopolitics, see Weigert, "Haushofer and the Pacific," 732–42; and S. Neumann, "Fashions in Space," 276–88. An investigation into the origins and development of the so-called science is Weigert's *Generals and Geographers*.

3 Eliot wrote the Foreword to the 1942 ed. of Mackinder's *Democratic Ideals and Reality*, vii–xi. Renner redesigned the postwar world in "Maps for a New World," *Collier's*,

June 6, 1942, 14–16, 28. Reaction to Renner was, "Renner's Balloon," *Time*, June 15, 1942, 25–26; and "How to Make a Map," *Time*, July 13, 1942, 42–44. Weigert and Stefansson collected a series of articles on American political-geographical postwar planning in *Compass of the World* (1944). Weigert, Stefansson, and Harrison edited an updated work, *New Compass of the World* (1949). A text of geopolitics was Whittlesey's *Earth and the State*. A critical view of geopolitics, blasting its development from a science into a study of German totalitarian plans for world domination, was Gyorgy's *Geopolitics*.

4 Spykman, *Geography of the Peace*, 8–18; MacNeil, *American Peace*, 170.

5 Strausz-Hupé, *Geopolitics*, x–xi.

6 U.S. Department of Commerce, *Statistical Abstract*, 1946, 4.

7 F. D. Roosevelt, *Public Papers*, 1940, 391; Truman, *Public Papers*, 1945, 203. The State Department's concern with foreign bases is seen in *Foreign Relations of the United States*, 1947, 1:708–12, 766–70, and 3:657–87; 1948, 3:169–351, 682–715.

8 U.S. Department of Commerce, *Statistical Abstract*, 1946, 4; 1947, 3.

9 Lapp, *Must We Hide?* 9; "Boomerang Seen in Hydrogen Bomb," *New York Times*, Feb. 12, 1950, sec. 1, p. 6. See also Coale, *Problem of Reducing Vulnerability;* Kindall, *Total Atomic Defense.*

10 H. Sprout and M. Sprout, *Foundations of National Power* (1951), 426. See also U.S. Army, *Geographical Foundations of National Power, Army Service Forces Manual*, 26–29; Dewhurst and Associates, *America's Needs and Resources*, 573. On America's natural resource position in the postwar world, see Mather, *Enough and to Spare.*

11 Leith, Furness, and Lewis, *World Minerals and World Peace*, 1–4, 32–38; Stein, *World the Dollar Built*, 11.

12 Leith, Furness, and Lewis, *World Minerals and World Peace*, 39–41.

13 Ickes, "What the U.S.A. Is Worth," 87–88; Dewhurst and Associates, *America's Needs and Resources*, 578–93; Leith, Furness, and Lewis, *World Minerals and World Peace*, 46.

14 Leith, Furness, and Lewis, *World Minerals and World Peace*, 45.

15 Ibid., 38, 45–46; Dewhurst and Associates, *America's Needs and Resources*, 597–98; Formula for the Determination of a National Stockpile, JCS 626/3, Jan. 22, 1948, Records of the United States Joint Chiefs of Staff, National Archives.

16 Mather, "Petroleum—Today and Tomorrow," 603–9; Ickes, "We're Running out of Oil," 26–27, 84–85; "Mr. Ickes' Arabian Nights," *Fortune*, June 1944, 123–29, 273–80; "Oil: The First Agreement," *Fortune*, October 1944, 113–14; Fanning, *Foreign Oil*, 3–12, 319.

17 Groves, *Now It Can Be Told*, 170–76.

18 Ickes, "What the U.S.A. Is Worth," 31, 88.

19 J. Davis, "Fifty Million More Americans," 420; Hauser and Taeuber, "Changing Population," 12; U.S. Department of Commerce, *Historical Statistics*, 8, 105–6; U.S. Department of Commerce, *Statistical Abstract*, 1951, 94. Because of discrepancies in data in the annual *Statistical Abstract* series and *Historical Statistics*, a supplement to it, this study cites the data in *Historical Statistics*, which have undergone correction and supersede earlier figures. Where statistics are unavailable in *Historical Statistics*, they are cited in the *Statistical Abstract.*

20 U.S. Department of Commerce, *Historical Statistics*, 8; Hauser and Taeuber, "Changing Population," 21; J. Davis, "Fifty Million More Americans," 416–17, 420.

21 U.S. Department of Commerce, *Historical Statistics*, 11, 19; J. Davis, "Fifty Million More Americans," 421.

22 U.S. Department of Commerce, *Historical Statistics*, 382; Commager, *American Mind*, 407.

23 R. Turner, "Technology and Geopolitics," 9; A. Compton, "Science and Our Nation's Future," 207–8.

24 Colton, "Winning the War," 705–36; Dewhurst and Associates, *America's Needs and Resources*, 685.

25 Einstein, in Benjamin, *I Am an American*, 43–44.

26 A. Compton, "Science and Our Nation's Future," 208.

27 Ogburn, *Technology and International Relations*, v–vi; U.S. Department of Commerce, *Historical Statistics*, 957–59.

28 Kendrick, *Productivity Trends*, 1; Acheson, *Power and Diplomacy*, 29; Thomas C. Blaisdell, Jr., and Eugene M. Braderman, "Economic Organization of the United States for International Economic Policy," in Harris, *Foreign Economic Policy*, 37; Truman, *Public Papers*, 1949, 356. Consideration of the economic determinants of national power was by W. Rostow, *Process of Economic Growth*, and by Deutsch, *Nationalism and Social Communication*.

29 The American percentage of the world's manufacturing production is in League of Nations, Economic, Financial and Transit Department, *Industrialization and Foreign Trade*, 13.

30 Lippmann, "Need for Enlightened Business Leadership," 5; Report by the Policy Planning Staff, Review of Current Trends, U.S. Foreign Policy, Feb. 24, 1948, *Foreign Relations of the United States*, 1948, 1:524; Harris, "Issues of Policy," in Harris, *Foreign Economic Policy*, 5; MacNeil, *American Peace*, 155. See also James, *One World Divided*, 179, 181. Revised GNP statistics are in U.S. Department of State, Bureau of Public Affairs, *Planetary Product*, 1977–78, i.

31 Clough, *American Way*, 185–90. For a similar list of factors of production, see also Conference on Economic Progress, "Consumption—Key to Full Prosperity," *ADA World* 12 (May 1957): 3M.

32 Among the early economists who turned to the ever-improving statistical methods to explain American growth was Simon Kuznets, with his study, *National Income*. A path-building study comparing national product to related data for labor, capital, and other factors of production from 1869–78 to 1944–53 was Abramovitz, *Resource and Output Trends*. A major contribution to analysis of the factors affecting the growth of the economy from 1909 to 1958 was Denison, *Sources of Economic Growth*. Denison applied a similar methodology to compare the factors of production in the United States and eight Western European countries from 1950 to 1962 in *Why Growth Rates Differ*. The statistics cited are from U.S. Department of Commerce, *Historical Statistics*, 8, 127, 681. For capital data see Kuznets, *Capital in the American Economy*, 64–65. For the extraction of natural resources, see Leong, "Index of the Physical Volume Production of Minerals," 15–29.

33 Kuznets in a later study, *Economic Growth of Nations*, 303–7, concluded after decades of study: The growth of industrial countries had entered "a *new* economic epoch that reflects the emergence of a new group of factors large enough to dominate growth over a long period." For productivity he looked largely to increase in knowledge that related to new science and technology.

34 U.S. War Production Board, *War Production in 1944*, 22–24; F. D. Roosevelt, *Public Papers*, 1944–45, 40; only seven years before Roosevelt had seen "one-third of a nation ill-housed, ill-clad, ill-nourished," in *Public Papers*, 1937, 5.

35 "It's Wonderful," *Fortune*, October 1945, 125; UN, Statistical Office, *National and Per Capita Incomes of Seventy Countries*, 14–16; Potter, *People of Plenty*, 81–83; Deutsch, *Nationalism and Social Communication*, 36, 40.

36 Chester Bowles, "Blueprints for a Second New Deal," in Harris, *Saving American Capitalism*, 13; Stein, *World the Dollar Built*, 18.

37 MacNeil, *American Peace*, 155.

38 U.S. Department of Commerce, "The Economy in the Third Year of War," *Survey of Current Business*, February 1945, 3; Atwood, "Miracle of War Production," 694. For GNP statistics see U.S. Department of Commerce, *Historical Statistics*, 224. Compare with the calculations of Kuznets, *National Product*, revised as *National Product in Wartime*.

39 "Steel," *Fortune*, May 1945, 121.

40 F. D. Roosevelt, *Public Papers*, 1940, 202, 234; 1944–45, 165–66, 287. Some criticism of the initial proposal is found in "Machine Tools Needed for Defense Program Will Take Year to Produce, Stillwell Warns," *New York Times*, May 17, 1940, 37; and Arthur Krock, "Production for Defense Is President's Problem," ibid., May 19, 1940, sec. 4, p. 3; U.S. Department of Commerce, *Historical Statistics*, 768.

41 Memorandum Prepared by the Joint Chiefs of Staff, March 27, 1946, *Foreign Relations of the United States*, 1946, 1:1162; NSC 68, in *Foreign Relations of the United States*, 1950, 1:256, 258; A Report to the National Security Council, Basic National Security Policy, Oct. 30, 1953, NSC 162/2, Dwight D. Eisenhower Library; U.S. Department of Commerce, *Historical Statistics*, 1116.

42 H. Roberts and Wilson, *Britain and the United States*, 102.

43 NSC 68, in *Foreign Relations of the United States*, 1950, 1:261; Baldwin, *Price of Power*, 105, 323.

44 Eisenhower, *Crusade in Europe*, 2.

45 U.S. Department of Commerce, *Historical Statistics*, 1141; Marshall, *Selected Speeches and Statements*, 124–25, 202. For Soviet manpower figures, see Evangelista, "Stalin's Postwar Army Reappraised," 115.

46 U.S. Department of Commerce, *Statistical Abstract*, 1940, 150, and 1946, 224; Forrestal, "Will We Choose Naval Suicide Again?" 9–11, 90; "Forrestal Says Navy Will Get 28,000 Combat Planes in 1944," *New York Times*, April 4, 1944, 27; "Navy to Ask Rise in Fleet Tonnage," Feb. 1, 1945, 13.

47 Truman, *Public Papers*, 1945, 431; "Navy Day, 1945," *Time*, Oct. 29, 1945, 26–28; "Power & Peace," *Time*, Nov. 5, 1945, 19; *New York Times*, Oct. 28, 1945, 1, which had a banner headline; "City Turns Out by the Millions for Navy Day; Truman Reviews Fleet, Charts Foreign Policy" was the headline in the *New York Herald Tribune*, Oct. 28, 1945, 1, and the headline over a spread of pictures was "The Most Triumphant Navy Day in the Navy's—and in New York's—History," 3.

48 U.S. Department of Commerce, *Statistical Abstract*, 1950, 213; U.S. Strategic Bombing Survey, *Over-all Report (European War)*, 107; Galbraith, *Life in Our Times*, 201, 204–6, 226.

49 Eisenhower, *White House Years*, 1:8, 78–79; U.S. Department of Commerce, *Historical Statistics*, 1141; Hanson W. Baldwin, "19 Million in World Armies, Forty-Nation Survey

Shows," *New York Times*, May 12, 1947, 1, 14; U.S. President's Advisory Commission on Universal Training, *Program for National Security.*

50 Truman, *Public Papers*, 1945, 432; "Sea Power of U.S. Has No Close Rival," *New York Times*, May 12, 1947, 14; U.S. Department of Commerce, *Statistical Abstract*, 1954, 244; Von Karman, *Where We Stand*, iv. See also Arnold, *Global Mission*, 615.

51 Truman, *Public Papers*, 1945, 197, 199; John Hersey, "Hiroshima," *New Yorker*, Aug. 31, 1946, 32. The magazine devoted its entire issue to that one article, which was republished as a book, *Hiroshima* (1946).

52 Stimson, "Decision to Use the Atomic Bomb," *Harper's*, February 1947, 102, and for further argument that the dread of many more bombs ended the war, see K. Compton, "If the Atomic Bomb Had Not Been Used," 54–56; Bernstein, "Postwar Myth," 38–40; U.S. Strategic Bombing Survey, *Japan's Struggle to End the War*, 10–13.

53 Truman, *Memoirs*, 1:421; Arnold Wolfers, "The Atomic Bomb in Soviet-American Relations," in Brodie, *Absolute Weapon*, 113.

54 For a German explanation of American success in building a bomb, see Heisenberg, "Research in Germany," 214. See also Goudsmit, *Alsos*. On Japan's atomic program, see Nishina, "Japanese Scientist Describes the Destruction of His Cyclotrons," 145, 167, who also found that Japan did not have the industrial power, even before the war, to produce atomic bombs; and the letter from Karl T. Compton to Secretary of War Robert P. Patterson, in the *New York Times*, Dec. 6, 1945, 3. On the development of Soviet atomic energy, see Kramish, *Atomic Energy in the Soviet Union.* For the Acheson-Lilienthal report, see U.S. Department of State, Committee on Atomic Energy, *Report on the International Control of Atomic Energy*, ix, 2.

55 U.S. Atomic Energy Commission, *In the Matter of J. Robert Oppenheimer: Transcript of Hearing*, 467; Record of the Meeting of the Joint Congressional Committee on Atomic Energy, Washington, July 20, 1949, *Foreign Relations of the United States*, 1949, 1:491; Baldwin, *Price of Power*, 67–68; Truman Scored for Doubting Russians Have Atomic Bomb," *New York Times*, Jan. 28, 1953, 1.

56 Truman, *Public Papers*, 1945, 212; Eisenhower, *Crusade in Europe*, 443; Eisenhower, *White House Years*, 1:312–13.

57 Early recognition of the dilemma of the power of nuclear weapons was by Brodie, *Absolute Weapon*, 21–107. The paucity of nuclear weapons after World War II, long a secret, is recorded in Lilienthal, *Atomic Energy*, 1–3; he had written of this earlier in obscure terms in his *Journals*, 2:165–66; see also Hewlett and Duncan, *Atomic Shield, 1947/1952*, vol. 2: *History of the United States Atomic Energy Commission*, 47. American nuclear weapons stockpile figures are compiled in Cochran, Arkin, and Hoenig, *Nuclear Weapons Databook*, vol. 1: *U.S. Nuclear Forces and Capabilities*, 6, 15.

58 Secret discussion in government includes, United States Policy on Atomic Warfare, NSC 30, Sept. 10, 1948, *Foreign Relations of the United States*, 1948, 1:624–28; A Report to the National Security Council, Basic National Security Policy, NSC 162/2, Oct. 30, 1953, Dwight D. Eisenhower Library. For war plans, see Evaluation of Current Strategic Air Offensive Plans, JCS 1952/1, Dec. 21, 1948, and Long Range Plans for War with the USSR—Development of a Joint Outline Plan for Use in the Event of a War in 1957 (Short Title—"Dropshot"), JCS 1920/5, Dec. 19, 1949, Records of the United States Joint Chiefs of Staff, National Archives.

On Truman's consideration of use of the bomb, see his *Public Papers*, 1950, 727, and Truman, *Memoirs*, 2:395–96; Truman, *Off the Record*, 304; Truman, *Strictly Personal and Confidential*, 31. Eisenhower discusses the issue in his *White House Years*, 1:178–81.

Chapter 4

1 Acheson, *Grapes from Thorns*, 74.

2 Tocqueville's *Democracy in America* was originally published in 1835. A text revised by Francis Bowen and edited by Phillips Bradley was published in the United States at the end of World War II. Anthologies containing the works of foreign travelers in America included Commager, *America in Perspective*, and Handlin, *This Was America*.

3 Brogan, *American Character*, ix, xi–xxi, 163.

4 Cooke, *One Man's America*, 4–5, 37, 39, 41. Other British accounts are by Pope-Hennessy, *America Is an Atmosphere*, 11, 21, 31, 102; Hutton, *Midwest at Noon*, ix–xiii; and C. Roberts, *And So to America*.

5 Bruckberger, *One Sky to Share*, 106, 126, 130, 149, 178; and his *Image of America*. See also Maurois, *From My Journal*, for another French view.

6 Hector St. John de Crèvecoeur, *Letters from an American Farmer* (repr. 1951), 43; Commager, *America in Perspective*, xi–xii, and Commager, *American Mind*, 3–5, 409–11, 443. Other historical studies of national character include Parkes, *American Experience*; Schlesinger, *Paths to the Present*; H. N. Smith, *Virgin Land: The American West as Symbol and Myth*; Potter, "The Quest for the National Character" in Higham, *Reconstruction of American History*, 197–220; and Perry, *Characterically American*.

7 Mead, *And Keep Your Powder Dry*, 24, 26, 27; and her "National Character," in Kroeber, *Anthropology Today*, 642, 662.

8 Gorer, *American People*, 18–19, 227, 246.

9 Buchanan and Cantril, *How Nations See Each Other*, 45–59, based on an international survey prepared under the auspices of UNESCO. Coleman, "What Is American?" 492–99, collected from books and periodicals statements that certain characteristics or principles were distinctly American. Potter, *People of Plenty*, attempted to combine the resources of foreign observers, historians, anthropologists, and social psychologists. Riesman, with Denney and Glazer, *Lonely Crowd*, investigated salient strata in the population. Riesman reviewed trends in the field in "The Study of National Character: Some Observations on the American Case," in his *Abundance for What?* 584–603.

10 Commager, *American Mind*, 430–32.

11 Ibid., 432–33.

12 Lippmann, *Public Opinion and Foreign Policy*, 9; Almond, *American People*, 3, 28; Bailey, *Man in the Street*, 2. Bailey similarly emphasizes the role of public opinion in *Diplomatic History of the American People* (1946, with earlier editions in 1940 and 1942). See also Markel, *Public Opinion and Foreign Policy*; Lazarsfeld, Berelson, and Gaudet, *People's Choice*; Dahl, *Congress and Foreign Policy*; Cohen, *Press and Foreign Policy*.

13 F. D. Roosevelt, *Public Papers*, 1940, 547; 1944–45, 35–36.

14 Reston, *Prelude to Victory*, ix–x, 129.

15 Lippmann, *U.S. Foreign Policy*, 3–5.

16 An early chronicle on isolationism was by W. Johnson, *Battle against Isolation*. Later studies include Langer and Gleason, *Challenge to Isolation*; Adler, *Isolationist Impulse*; DeConde, *Isolation and Security*; and Jonas, *Isolationism in America*.

17 F. D. Roosevelt, *Public Papers*, 1944–45, 32, 524; Wallace, *Democracy Reborn*, 176; Wendell L. Willkie, Text of Address at the United China Relief dinner, New York,

March 26, 1941, in *New York Times,* March 27, 1941, 12; Taft, "Senator Taft's Peace Program," 8; Luce, "American Century," 63; Lippmann, *U.S. Foreign Policy,* 45–46, 69–70.

18 F. D. Roosevelt, *Public Papers,* 1941, 514–16; U.S. Congress, Senate, Declaration of War with Japan, 77th Cong., 1st sess., Dec. 8, 1941, *Congressional Record,* 87:9505–6; House, War Resolution, 77th Cong., 1st sess., Dec. 8, 1941, *Congressional Record,* 87:9520–37; "Unity in Congress," *New York Times,* Dec. 9, 1941, 1; and James B. Reston, "Capital Swings into War Stride," ibid., Dec. 9, 1941, 5.

19 Lodge, *Storm Has Many Eyes,* 26–27, 56–57.

20 Vandenberg, *Private Papers,* 1; U.S. Congress, Senate, Senator Vandenberg speaking on "American Foreign Policy," 79th Cong., 1st sess., Jan. 10, 1945, *Congressional Record,* 91:164–68.

21 Hoover and Gibson, *Problems of Lasting Peace,* 159, 162, 181, 183, 268, 277; Hoover, *40 Key Questions,* 31.

22 Lindbergh, *Wartime Journals,* 560–61, 566–67; "United We Stand," *New York Times,* Dec. 9, 1941, 30; Nov. 14, 1945, 2, and Nov. 19, 1945, 5.

23 "War with Japan," *New York Times,* Dec. 8, 1941, 22; "United We Stand," Dec. 9, 1941, 30; "No Comfort for Our Enemies," Nov. 8, 1942, sec. 4, p. 10; "Our Second Chance," April 9, 1941, 24.

24 F. D. Roosevelt, *Public Papers,* 1942, 32, and 1944–45, 34; "National Ordeal," *Time,* Dec. 15, 1941, 18.

25 H. Cantril, *Public Opinion,* 367, 1055–59; Bruner, *Mandate from the People,* 31–38.

26 Truman, *Memoirs,* 1:436–37; "President Joins Capital's Gaiety," *New York Times,* Aug. 15, 1945, 3.

27 "Japan Surrenders, End of War!"; "All City 'Lets Go,'" *New York Times,* Aug. 15, 1945, 1, 5; "V-J Revelry Erupts Again with Times Sq. Its Focus," Aug. 16, 1945, 1, 6; "Japanese War Ends" and "Seething City Hails Victory, Millions Out," *New York Herald Tribune,* Aug. 15, 1945, 1.

28 "America Leads," *New York Times,* Aug. 14, 1945, 20; "Problems of Peace," Aug. 16, 1945, 18.

29 "Victory Celebrations," *Life,* Aug. 27, 1945, 21–27, and "The Meaning of Victory," *Life,* Aug. 27, 1945, 34; "Days to Come," *Time,* Aug. 27, 1945, 19.

30 "The Peril of Victory," *New Republic,* Aug. 20, 1945, 203–4.

31 Truman, *Public Papers,* 1946, 431. On internationalism see the valuable study by Divine, *Second Chance,* which focuses on international organizations.

32 Truman, *Public Papers,* 1948, 260; Vandenberg, *Private Papers,* 552; "Lodge Says Parties See Abroad As One," *New York Times,* Feb. 13, 1947, 3; NSC 68, *Foreign Relations of the United States,* 1950, 1:252–54.

33 "Lodge Urges U.S. Aid UNO," *New York Times,* March 21, 1946, 2; "Lodge Says Parties See Abroad As One," Feb. 13, 1947, 3; "Nonpartisan Policy Advocated by Lodge," Sept. 3, 1948, 15; "The Strongest Force," *Time,* April 26, 1948, 20; Vandenberg, *Private Papers,* 552–53, 577–78.

34 A. Schlesinger, Jr., *Vital Center,* ix–x, 219, 255.

35 Truman, *Memoirs,* 2:505–7; Eisenhower, *White House Years,* 1:84. See also Eisenhower, *Public Papers,* 1953, 2; Kennan, *Realities of American Foreign Policy,* 104–5.

36 Bruner, *Mandate from the People,* 52–55; Gallup, *Gallup Poll,* 1:431, 521–22, 653–54, 719, 723–24, 751; 2:791–92, 794, 839, 888.

37 Lippmann, *Essays in the Public Philosophy,* 16–20.

38 Wriston, *Diplomacy in a Democracy,* 61, 72, 80.

39 The concept of legitimacy is represented in Ferrero, *Principles of Power;* de Jouvenel, *On Power,* considers legitmacy, 23–25; B. Russell, *Power,* distinguishes between leaders and followers, 16–34.

40 Willkie, "Our Reservoir of World Respect and Hope," 34–39. Willkie delivered this speech over the radio on Oct. 26, 1942. He adapted his address in his *One World.*

41 Willkie, *One World,* 157–58, 161.

42 Buck, *American Argument,* 119–20.

43 H. Miller, *Air-Conditioned Nightmare,* 2:xxvii.

44 "Imperialism or Indifference?" *Economist,* May 24, 1947, 785.

45 MacArthur, *Reminiscences,* 272–77.

46 Eisenhower, *Crusade in Europe,* 461–62; Harriman and Abel, *Special Envoy,* 277.

47 Molotov, *Problems of Foreign Policy,* 212–13.

48 Lane, *I Saw Poland Betrayed,* 176–77.

49 Yank Staff, eds., *Yank* (1947), 103, 125, 145–47.

50 R. Smith, *OSS,* 353–54. See also Herring, *America's Longest War,* 1.

51 Roper, *Where Stands Freedom?* introduction, 15–16, and table to question 3.

52 Ibid., 16–17, and table to questions 4–6.

53 Buchanan and Cantril, *How Nations See Each Other,* v–viii, 38–44, and Appendix D, 125–216.

Chapter 5

1 Goldman, *Crucial Decade—and After,* v–vi, 28, 34.

2 U.S. Congress, House, Committee on Foreign Affairs, *Strategy and Tactics of World Communism,* iii. See also I. Lederer, *Russian Foreign Policy;* Hunt, *Theory and Practice of Communism.*

3 Marshall, "Problems of European Revival and German and Austrian Peace Settlements," *Department of State Bulletin,* Nov. 30, 1947, 1027.

4 "If War Comes," *New York Times,* Aug. 24, 1939, 18; F. D. Roosevelt, *Public Papers,* 1940, 93.

5 Truman is quoted in *New York Times,* June 24, 1941, 7; "Russia after 25 Years," ibid., Nov. 7, 1942, 14; "Two-Thirds of the Ukraine," *Time,* Sept. 29, 1941, 19.

6 F. D. Roosevelt, *Public Papers,* 1941, 401–2; 1942, 103; 1943, 558; 1944–45, 99.

7 Davies, *Mission to Moscow,* xv–xviii, 67, 357; and his "The Soviets and the Post-War," *Life,* March 29, 1943, 49–55.

8 Willkie, *One World,* 84, 102; his "We Must Work with Russia—Willkie," 5, 25; Walsh, "What the American People Think," 518.

9   Wallace, *Soviet Asia Mission,* 20, 192–93. See also his "Beyond the Atlantic Charter," *New Republic,* Nov. 23, 1942, 667–69.

10 F. R. Dulles, *Road to Teheran,* v, 1, 129–30, 151–52, 260–61.

11 Perry took part in a discussion, "Russia's Foreign Policy," Sept. 12, 1943, on the NBC Radio's *University of Chicago Round Table,* no. 286, printed as a pamphlet, 2–4, 16–17. Another program in this series was "Death of the Comintern," *University of Chicago Round Table,* no. 272, June 6, 1943.

12 "The U.S.S.R.," *Life,* Mar. 29, 1943, 20; "The Peoples of the U.S.S.R.," 23; "The Father of Modern Russia," 29; "Red Leaders," 40. Davies, "Soviets and the Post-War," 49–55, was in this issue.

13 "D.A.R. Makes History at Chicago Meeting," *Life,* May 18, 1942, 34–45.

14 "The Fortune Survey," *Fortune,* Feb. 1942, 98; H. Cantril, *Public Opinion,* 961–62.

15 Chamberlin, "Russia: An American Problem," 155–56; see also his "Russian Enigma," 225–34; W. White, *Report on the Russians,* "Introduction," 236.

16 President Roosevelt to the British Prime Minister (Churchill), April 11, 1945, *Foreign Relations of the United States,* 1945, 5:210.

17 Wallace, *Soviet Asia Mission,* 246–47; Wallace, "Where I Was Wrong," 46. Italics in original.

18 Eleanor Roosevelt, quoted in U.S. Congress, House, Committee on Foreign Affairs, *Strategy and Tactics of World Communism,* 55.

19 Truman, *Memoirs,* 1:82.

20 Truman, *Mr. President,* 51–52; Harriman and Abel, *Special Envoy,* 453–54.

21 Atkinson, "Russia 1946," 85–94. The original articles, edited by the author for *Life,* July 22, 1946, appeared in the *New York Times* as "Russia Bars Amity with U.S., Returned Times Writer Says," July 7, 1946, 1, 6; "Socialist World Soviet Aim, Times Moscow Writer Says," July 8, 1946, 1, 8; "Soviet Seen Wanting Peace Despite Its Air of Challenge," July 9, 1946, 1, 6.

22 J. F. Dulles, "Thoughts on Soviet Foreign Policy," *Life,* June 3, 1946, 113. Part 2 of the article was in the June 10, 1946 issue, 118–30.

23 Truman, *Public Papers,* 1947, 178; 1948, 290. See also 1949, 112–13.

24 The Chargé in the Soviet Union (Kennan) to the Secretary of State, Feb. 22, 1946, *Foreign Relations of the United States,* 1946, 6:696, 699, 700, 706; Kennan, "Sources of Soviet Conduct," 566–82.

25 H. Cantril, *Public Opinion,* 523, 963–64; Walsh, "What the American People Think," 514; Kennan, *Memoirs,* 1:357–59.

26 Walsh, "What the American People Think," 513–15 , 520–22; Walsh, "American Attitudes Toward Russia," 189.

27 Walsh, "American Attitudes toward Russia," 189–90.

28 The Chargé in the Soviet Union (Kennan) to the Secretary of State, Feb. 22, 1946, *Foreign Relations of the United States,* 1946, 6:708.

29 H. Cantril, *Public Opinion,* 962, 964.

30 Katz and Cantril, "Analysis of Attitudes toward Fascism and Communism," 356–66; W. White, *Report on the Russians,* 205–6.

31 C. L. Sulzberger, "Red Army Officers Symbolize New Era," *New York Times,* June 6, 1943, sec. 1, p. 13, and Brooks Atkinson, "Red Army Raises Officers' Rations," ibid., Sept. 16, 1945, sec. 1, p. 35. L. Fischer provides further evidence in *Great Challenge,* 198–202.

32 Walsh, "What the American People Think," 520.

33 H. Cantril, *Public Opinion,* 962; Willkie, *One World,* 64–68.

34 Kennan, *Memoirs,* 1:557; W. Smith, *My Three Years,* 126–28; Fischer, *Great Challenge,* 222.

35 Johnston, "My Talk with Joseph Stalin," 8–9; and his *We're All in It,* 89–90.

36 W. Smith, *My Three Years,* 98.

37 Kennan, *Memoirs,* 1:190–95.

38 H. K. Smith, *State of Europe,* 54; A. Schlesinger, Jr., *Vital Center,* 146–47.

39 W. White, *Report on the Russians,* 108–9, 220–21.

40 Johnston, "My Talk with Joseph Stalin," 8.

41 Bourke-White, *Shooting the Russian War,* 105–11.

42 Eisenhower, *Crusade in Europe,* 473.

43 Willkie, *One World,* 83.

44 Atkinson, "Russia 1946," 86–87, 91–92.

45 H. Cantril, *Public Opinion,* 744; Kennan, *Memoirs,* 1:542.

46 The Chargé in the Soviet Union (Kennan) to the Secretary of State, Feb. 22, 1946, *Foreign Relations of the United States,* 1946, 6:701.

47 H. K. Smith, *State of Europe,* 38; Holborn, *Political Collapse of Europe,* 190; Byrnes, *Speaking Frankly,* 204; Report by the National Security Council on the Position of the United States with Respect to Soviet-Directed World Communism, NSC 7, March 30, 1948, *Foreign Relations of the United States,* 1948, 1:546–47.

48 Welles, *Time for Decision,* 332–34. For a retrospective view, see George F. Kennan, "The View from Russia," in Hammond, *Witnesses to the Origins of the Cold War,* 29.

49 H. Cantril, *Public Opinion,* 132, 1169.

50 W. Smith, *My Three Years,* 50–54, 129; H. Cantril, *Public Opinion,* 311.

51 H. K. Smith, *State of Europe,* 318–19, 340, 344–47.

52 Report by the National Security Council on the Position of the United States with Respect to Soviet-Directed World Communism, NSC 7, March 30, 1948, *Foreign Relations of the United States,* 1948, 1:546; Report by the National Security Council on U.S. Objectives With Respect to the USSR To Counter Soviet Threats to U.S. Security, NSC 20/4, Nov. 23, 1948, *Foreign Relations of the United States,* 1948, 1:663; Acheson, *Pattern of Responsibility,* 20; Truman, *Public Papers,* 1950, 734; Truman, *Memoirs,* 1:412; J. F. Dulles, *War Or Peace,* 2; Eisenhower, *White House Years,* 1:8.

53 Acheson, *Pattern of Responsibility,* 23; Report by the National Security Council on U.S. Objectives With Respect to the USSR To Counter Soviet Threats to U.S. Security, NSC 20/4, Nov. 23, 1948, *Foreign Relations of the United States,* 1948, 1:666–67.

54 Report by the National Security Council on the Position of the United States with Respect to Soviet-Directed World Communism, NSC 7, March 30, 1948, *Foreign Relations of the United States,* 1948, 1:546–47.

55 Wallace, *Soviet Asia Mission,* 21, 188–89.

56 Ibid., 84–85, 117–20, 129–30.

57 U.S. Congress, House, Committee on Foreign Affairs, *United States Foreign Policy for a Post-War Recovery Program: Hearings before the Committee on Foreign Affairs,* 80th Cong., 2d sess., 1948, pt. 2, pp. 1610, 1619; U.S. Congress, House, Committee on Foreign Affairs, *Extension of European Recovery Program: Hearings before the Committee on Foreign Affairs,* 81st Cong., 1st sess., 1949, pt. 2, p. 597. Rep. John Davis Lodge, a Connecticut Republican, was a grandson of Henry Cabot Lodge and brother of Sen. Henry Cabot Lodge, Jr.

58 U.S. Congress, Senate, Senator Joseph McCarthy speaking about Communists in Government Service and reading his speech at Wheeling, West Virginia, 81st Cong., 2d sess., Feb. 20, 1950, *Congressional Record,* 96:1954.

59 J. McCarthy, *America's Retreat from Victory,* 109, 132, 168.

60 Truman, *Public Papers,* 1950, 163, 234–35, 268. See also 572. On the extremes of "consensus," see Freeland, *Truman Doctrine and the Origins of McCarthyism.* "The practices of McCarthyism were Truman's practices in cruder hands, just as the language of McCarthyism was Truman's language, in less well-meaning voices" (360).

61 Truman, *Public Papers,* 1952–53, 634.

62 A Report to the President Pursuant to the President's Directive of January 31, 1950, NSC 68, April 7, 1950, *Foreign Relations of the United States,* 1950, 1:237–44, 249.

63 Stimson, "Challenge to Americans," 6, 10; and Stimson and Bundy, *On Active Service,* 651–55. George Kennan made a similar point when he cabled from the Soviet Union, "Much depends on health and vigor of our own society. World communism is like malignant parasite which feeds only on diseased tissue. This is point at which domestic and foreign policies meet. Every courageous and incisive measure to solve internal problems of our own society, to improve self-confidence, discipline, morale and community spirit of our own people, is a diplomatic victory over Moscow worth a thousand diplomatic notes and joint communiqués." The Chargé in the Soviet Union (Kennan) to the Secretary of State, Feb. 22, 1946, *Foreign Relations of the United States,* 1946, 6:708.

Chapter 6

1 *PM,* April 10, 1945, 2. The passage is also in *Actions and Passions,* 4–6.

2 Kennan, "Sources of Soviet Conduct," 581–82. Part of this chapter appeared originally in Donald W. White, "History and American Internationalism: The Formulation from the Past after World War II," *Pacific Historical Review* 58 (May 1989): 145–72.

3 Standard histories and texts by leading historians of the period carry on these general themes: Morison and Commager, *Growth,* 2:795–96; Casner and Gabriel, *Story of American Democracy,* v, 463, 543, 551, 566–67; Parkes, *American Experience,* 331, 335; Hofstadter, Miller, and Aaron, *United States,* 730, 756–57; and Faulkner and Kepner, *America,* 854, 878–79.

4 Early notions about the westward sweep of empire are recorded by H. N. Smith, *Virgin Land,* 8–10, and by LaFeber, *New Empire,* 84; H. B. Adams, "Germanic Origin of New England Towns," *Johns Hopkins University Studies in Historical and Political Science,* no. 2, esp. pp. 23–24. Even Frederick Jackson Turner, a student of Adams, began his doctoral dissertation on trading posts in Wisconsin with the economic institutions of Phoenician civilization, carried forward by the empires of the Greeks, Etruscans, Romans, and British: "Character and Influence of the Indian Trade," *Johns Hopkins University Studies*

in Historical and Political Science, 9th ser. On Turner's significant debt to the study of classical historical theory, see Fulmer Mood's introduction to Turner, *Early Writings,* 20–29; and Hofstadter, *Progressive Historians,* 51–52, 64–71. The theory is evident in Wilson, *Public Papers: College and State,* 1:43; T. Roosevelt, *Works* (1914), 1:391–92; Coolidge, *Autobiography,* 46–47.

5 F. D. Roosevelt, *Whither Bound?* 6–12; his education is described in Burns, *Roosevelt,* 10–16, and in A. Schlesinger, Jr., *Crisis of the Old Order,* 320–25; Truman, *Memoirs,* 1:119; Eisenhower, *At Ease,* 39–43.

6 J. Burns, *Roosevelt,* 13; Hull, *Memoirs,* 33–36; Eisenhower, *At Ease,* 64.

7 Truman, *Memoirs,* 1:127–32; Eisenhower, *Public Papers,* 1954, 373–74; Lippmann, *U.S. Foreign Policy,* x–xii.

8 Marquis W. Childs, "Evaluation," 1, in B. Adams, *America's Economic Supremacy.*

9 Billington, *Westward Expansion,* 15–34, and also his work with Lowenberg and Brockunier, *United States;* T. Roosevelt, *Works* (1926), vol. 8, *The Winning of the West,* 5–7.

10 Becker, *How New Will the Better World Be?* 87–88.

11 Flanders, *American Century,* 1.

12 Truman, *Memoirs,* 1:120; *Mr. President,* 10, 47, 86; and *Public Papers,* 1949, 389–90.

13 Lippmann, "American Destiny," 73.

14 Luce, "American Century," 64.

15 Padover, "American Century?" 85–90; Schuman, *Commonwealth of Man,* 202–3. C. Beard and M. Beard, *American Spirit,* 4:573–77, also discussed the American Century.

16 H. B. Adams, "Germanic Origin," 23–24; Gabriel, *Course of American Democratic Thought* (1956), v; Rossiter, *Seedtime of the Republic,* 440.

17 F. D. Roosevelt, *Public Papers,* 1940, 568–69; Wallace, *Century of the Common Man,* 14–15; Truman, *Mr. President,* 85, 106.

18 Sherwood, "Front Line," 21, 103.

19 Hull, *Memoirs,* 175.

20 Pargellis, *Quest for Political Unity,* v–vi, vii–xi; Robert R. Palmer, "Humanity and Nationality, 1780–1830," 139; Quincy Wright, "The Historic Circumstances of Enduring Peace," 361–73; Brinton, *From Many One,* preface and 3, 13, 16, 101–2.

21 The major historical work of UNESCO in which one can trace the role of the United States in world history is Ware, Panikkar, and Romein, *Twentieth Century,* vol. 6: *History of Mankind: Cultural and Scientific Development.* Criticism of the Western view of the history of progress moving from east to west is by the Indian lecturer Sarvapalli Radhakrishnan in UNESCO, *Reflections on Our Age,* 115–16. For discussion and criticism of the history of mankind in progress, see Laves and Thomson, *UNESCO: Purpose Progress Prospects,* 241–43, and Shuster, *UNESCO: Assessment and Promise,* 29–31. The unfavorable reaction to this massive work can be seen in the review by William H. McNeill in *American Historical Review* 73 (June 1968): 1479–80. In another UNESCO project, a joint American and Indian comparative study of their values in national life, the American historian Ralph Henry Gabriel wrote *Traditional Values in American Life* (Prepared for the United States National Commission for UNESCO), a study of American politics, law, religion, education, society, science, economy, and arts, and their ties mainly to Britain and before that to ancient Rome and Greece.

22 Toynbee, *Study of History* (1934–59); Somervell's abridged edition appeared in 2 vols. (1947, 1957); "A Study of History: A Brilliant English Thinker Named Toynbee Sees the Past in Terms of the Challenges and Responses That Make and Break Civilizations," *Life,* Feb. 23, 1948, 118–33; Lerner, *Actions and Passions,* 140. Lerner wrote this in his essay "Toynbee: History as Poetry and Religion as Bulwark," originally published in *PM,* May 2, 1948. *Time* ran several pieces on Toynbee, including a cover story, "The Challenge," March 17, 1947, 71–81; "The Chariot to Heaven," April 5, 1948, 58–60; and "Invaluable 10%," Oct. 30, 1950, 71. He was treated as a celebrity in its "People" column, March 1, 1948, 32. *Harpers, Newsweek, Scientific American, Saturday Review, New Republic, Atlantic Monthly, American Scholar,* and other magazines carried articles about Toynbee as well.

23 Toynbee, "Present Point in History," 191; and "The Dwarfing of Europe," based on a lecture in London on Oct. 26, 1926, in *Civilization on Trial,* 110–13.

24 Toynbee, "The International Outlook," based on a lecture in London at Chatham House on May 22, 1947, in *Civilization on Trial,* 131.

25 Ibid., 144; Toynbee, quoted by H. J. Morgenthau, *In Defense of the National Interest,* 155–56.

26 Toynbee, "Encounters between Civilizations," 293–94. This essay was based on the first lecture in a series at Bryn Mawr College in 1947.

27 Lerner, *America as a Civilization,* 882, 934–37. Two "debates" between Toynbee and Lerner were "Is America a Civilization?" *Shenandoah* 10 (Autumn 1958): 3–45, and "Is There an American Civilization, Distinct from Europe's?" *Western World,* December 1958, 29–39. David Potter tried to comprehend the differences between them in "Is America a Civilization?" in *History and American Society,* 222–27. It is interesting to trace the criticism of Toynbee by American historians: Charles A. Beard, review of *A Study of History,* vols. 1–3, *American Historical Review* 40 (January 1935): 307–9; Willson H. Coates, review of the abridged version of *A Study of History,* vols. 1–6, ibid. 53 (October 1947): 75–76; Hans Kohn, review of *Civilization on Trial,* ibid. 54 (October 1948): 90–91; Carlton J. H. Hayes, review of *The World and the West,* ibid. 59 (October 1953): 173; Franklin L. Baumer, review of *Toynbee and History: Critical Essays and Reviews,* ed. by M. F. Ashley Montagu, ibid. 62 (April 1957): 595–96; Gerhard Masur, review of *Toynbee's Approach to World Politics,* by Henry L. Mason, ibid. 65 (April 1960): 650–51; Crane Brinton, review of *America and the World Revolution and Other Lectures,* ibid. 68 (April 1963): 758–59. See also Luce, *Ideas,* 70.

28 Handlin, *Chance or Destiny,* 3; Truman, *Public Papers,* 1949, 299.

29 Higham, "Cult," 93–100, and "Beyond Consensus," 609–25; Turner, *Frontier in American History,* 1–38; Hofstadter, *American Political Tradition,* vii–x; Commager, *American Mind,* 437. An edited collection of essays that investigates the consensus school is Higham, *Reconstruction of American History.* Gabriel's *Course of American Democratic Thought* (1940, rev. 1956) forecast an attitude that became familiar after World War II. Among the leading works of the consensus school are Hofstadter, *American Political Tradition;* Hartz, *Liberal Tradition in America;* Boorstin's trilogy *Americans* and *America and the Image of Europe;* and Handlin, *Americans: A New History.*

30 Hofstadter, *American Political Tradition,* viii; Boorstin, *Genius of American Politics,* 1; and Boorstin, *Americans: The Colonial Experience,* 4.

31 Schlesinger, *Age of Jackson,* ix–x.

32 Hartz, *Liberal Tradition,* 3, 5, 50, 284, 308–9.

33 Boorstin, *Genius of American Politics,* 180–81; and *Americans: The Colonial Experience,* vii, 1–4.

34 A. Schlesinger, Jr., review of *American Political Tradition,* by Hofstadter, *American Historical Review* 54 (April 1949): 612–13; H. N. Smith, review of *Course of American Democratic Thought,* by Gabriel, *Mississippi Valley Historical Review* 43 (December 1956): 468–69.

35 Lippmann, *U.S. War Aims,* 209; F. D. Roosevelt, *Public Papers,* 1942, 351, 416, 425; 1943, 111–14; 1944–45, 331; Truman, *Mr. President,* 93; and *Public Papers,* 1945, 139, 142, and 1950, 329–30; Parkes, *American Experience,* 331. Truman justified the National Historical Publications Commission's work publishing vital records and papers of American history by the relevance of the American past to the current danger abroad, in *Public Papers,* 1951, 340–41. Other examples of applying the American past to internationalism include: Sherwood, "Front Line," 103–4, on the Declaration of Independence and U.S. power; Shotwell, "After the War," 34, on the Bill of Rights as the basis for an International Bill of Rights; Wallace, *Century of the Common Man,* 14, on the Civil War and Allied victory in World War II ("This is a fight between a slave world and a free world. Just as the United States in 1862 could not remain half slave and half free, so in 1942 the world must make its decision for a complete victory one way or the other.").

36 H. N. Smith, *Virgin Land,* 188; Sanford, *Quest for Paradise,* 229.

37 See Truman, *Mr. President,* 81–84; and, on Marxist distortions of history, *Public Papers,* 1952–53, 1120.

38 Eisenhower, *At Ease,* 40–43; and *Public Papers,* 1960–61, 775. Louis XV's reign contributed to the decline of the crown's authority, and Louis XVI was the last Bourbon king.

Chapter 7

1   Vosburgh, "This Is My Own," 113, 115–16, 122, 125–26, 128. Part of this chapter appeared originally in Donald W. White, "'It's a Big Country:' A Portrait of the American Landscape after World War II," *Journal of the West* 26 (January 1987): 80–86.

2   Acheson, "Quality of American Patriotism," *Department of State Bulletin,* May 1, 1950, 696, 698.

3   Barzun, *God's Country and Mine,* 3–5, 10, 25, 240, 344. Passages critical of America are found on pp. 48–49, 53–54, 272–93.

4   Gunther, *Inside U.S.A.,* ix–xi. See also the earlier works in his "Inside" series, *Inside Europe* (1936), substantially revised several times; *Inside Asia* (1939); and *Inside Latin America* (1941). An essay that discussed Gunther's book in the context of the times was by Allan Nevins, "America in 1947—and After," 140–48.

5   Burman, *It's a Big Country,* 3–4, 245–46.

6   Dos Passos, *State of the Nation,* 1–5, 62. On his writing, see the literary analysis by Wagner, *Dos Passos,* and the biography by Ludington, *John Dos Passos.*

7   Dos Passos, *Prospect before Us,* 276, 372–74.

8   MacLeish, *Collected Poems,* 335, 343–47. The original post-World War II edition included his poems up to 1952. "Colloquy for the States" is dated 1943, but he also published a version earlier in the war in *Atlantic Monthly,* October 1939, 484–87. On MacLeish's life and work, see Falk, *Archibald MacLeish.*

9   MacLeish, *Freedom,* 24–25, 29.

10 Look Editors, *Look at America,* 8–14.

11 *National Geographic* articles include Borah, "Nebraska, the Cornhusker State," 513–42; Atwood, "Potomac, River of Destiny," 33–70; F. Simpich, "Grass Makes Wyoming Fat,"

153–88; Atwood, "Northeast of Boston," 257–92; Burnett, "Cape Cod People and Places," 737–74; F. Simpich, "More Water for California's Great Central Valley," 645–64; Walker, "Aroostook County, Maine, Source of Potatoes," 459–78; F. Simpich, "Louisiana Trades with the World," 705–38; Shreve, "Saguaro, Cactus Camel of Arizona," 695–704; F. Simpich, "South Dakota Keeps Its West Wild," 555–88.

12 Caldwell and Bourke-White, *Say, Is This the U.S.A.,* 4–5, 158–63; Bourke-White, *Photographs,* 138–53, 180–85.

13 Bourke-White, "New Way," 128–40.

14 On the landscape in film, see T. Thomas, *Hollywood and the American Image.*

15 Martin A. Jackson, "The Uncertain Peace: *The Best Years of Our Lives* (1946)," in O'Connor and Jackson, *American History/American Film,* 147–65.

16 See Wood, *America in the Movies.*

17 Bosley Crowther, review of *It's a Big Country, New York Times,* Jan. 9, 1952, 25. See also Brackman, "My Generation," 129.

18 H. Miller, *Air–Conditioned Nightmare,* 1:10–17, 20, 23; 2:xv, xviii–xx. Italics in original.

19 Kennan, *Memoirs,* 2:61–89.

Chapter 8

1 Wirth, "Consensus and Mass Communication," 2. Good overviews of the growth and popularity of consensus theory include I. Horowitz, "Consensus, Conflict and Cooperation," 177–88; McClosky, "Consensus and Ideology," 361–82.

2 Dahl, *Preface to Democratic Theory,* 132–33; Lipset, *Political Man,* 22; Theodore M. Newcomb, "The Study of Consensus," in Merton, Broom, and Cottrell, *Sociology Today,* 277. A symposium on consensus is Griffith, Plamenatz, and Pennock, "Cultural Prerequisites," 132. Tocqueville, *Democracy in America,* 1:392, observed that a society can "exist only when a great number of men consider a great number of things under the same aspect, when they hold the same opinions upon many subjects, and when the same occurrences suggest the same thoughts and impressions to their minds"; see also 1:322–23; and 2:8–12. Tocqueville was quoted by McClosky, "Consensus and Ideology," 361, and by I. Horowitz, "Consensus, Conflict and Cooperation," 179. Lipset, *Political Man,* 24–28, contrasted Tocqueville with Karl Marx as an important thinker of consensus.

3 Dahl, *Preface to Democratic Theory,* 132; Key, "Public Opinion and the Decay of Democracy," 481–94.

4 Dahl, *Who Governs?* 314; Parsons, *Sociological Theory,* 251.

5 On the extent and solidarity of consensus, see McClosky, "Consensus and Ideology," 363; Newcomb, "Study of Consensus," 279. Critiques of consensus theory include Prothro and Grigg, "Fundamental Principles of Democracy," 276–94; Jackman, "Political Elites, Mass Publics," 753–73. See also Higham, "Cult," 93–100.

6 For American life and thought in the late 1940s and 1950s, see Hart, *When the Going Was Good!* and P. Carter, *Another Part of the Fifties.* For intellectual trends of the 1950s, see D. Bell, *New American Right,* expanded and updated as *Radical Right,* including essays by Daniel Bell, Richard Hofstadter, David Riesman, Talcott Parsons, and Seymour Martin Lipset. Compare this collection with the retrospective view by Pells, *Liberal Mind in a Conservative Age,* which declares a preference for certain works including those of David Riesman, William Whyte, John Kenneth Galbraith, Paul Goodman, Daniel Bell, Dwight Macdonald, Louis Hartz, Daniel Boorstin, and C. Wright Mills (x). For poll data, see H.

Cantril, *Public Opinion*, 367, 1055–59; Bruner, *Mandate from the People*, 31–38; Almond, *American People*, xxii–xxv.

7 U.S. Department of Commerce, *Historical Statistics*, 135, 210, 224, 225, 263, 796.

8 Potter, *People of Plenty*, 78–90.

9 "Abundance and the Mission of America," in ibid., 128–41.

10 Ibid., 134, 136, 141.

11 Galbraith, *Affluent Society*, 9.

12 Galbraith, *American Capitalism*, 1–2; "J.K. Galbraith Says: It's No Sin to Be Rich," *Business Week*, Feb. 23, 1952, 120–27.

13 Galbraith, *Life in Our Times*, 174–75, 264.

14 Galbraith, "The American Economy: Its Substance and Myth," in Chase, *Years of the Modern*, 151–74; Galbraith, *American Capitalism*, 1–9.

15 Galbraith, *American Capitalism*, 118, 123–29, 141–43.

16 Galbraith, *Affluent Society*, 252–53. See also chap. 8 of Galbraith, *American Capitalism*, entitled "The Unseemly Economics of Opulence," 101–13.

17 Galbraith, "American Economy," 151; Galbraith, "Germany Was Badly Run," 173–78, 196–200; Galbraith, "Challenges of a Changing World," 49–51.

18 Galbraith, "Rival Economic Theories in India," 587–89. See his *Ambassador's Journal* for his experiences in India in the 1960s.

19 Galbraith, "Rival Economic Theories in India," 590–93, 595–96.

20 Potter, "Between Two Worlds," review of *The Affluent Society*, by Galbraith, *Saturday Review*, June 7, 1958, 32.

21 Riesman, with Denney and Glazer, *Lonely Crowd*. His reworked and abridged edition considered in greater detail American national life in relation to the world situation. See Mills, *White Collar;* Whyte, *Organization Man*.

22 Riesman, *Lonely Crowd*, 3–35.

23 Ibid., 10–31.

24 Ibid., 18, 23, 373.

25 Ibid., 199–208.

26 Ibid., 204.

27 Ibid., 204–5.

28 Ibid., 17, 34–35.

29 Mills, *New Men of Power*, 3.

30 Mills, *White Collar*, 357. For an overview of Mills's writings and life, see the "Introduction" by Irving Louis Horowitz to Mills, *Power, Politics and People*, 1–20.

31 Mills, *White Collar*, 63–76, 279–80, 340.

32 Ibid., 328.

33 Mills, *Power Elite*, 3–9.

34 Ibid., 13, 22–25.

35 Mill, *Causes of World War Three*, 15–17, 21, 172.

36　Mills, "Bounteous New Man," review of *People of Plenty,* by Potter, *Saturday Review,* July 16, 1955, 19; "The Big Bad Americans," review of *The Power Elite,* by Mills, *Time,* April 30, 1956, 116. See also "A 'Moralist's' View," review of *The Power Elite, Newsweek,* April 23, 1956, 101–2.

37　Peale, *Power of Positive Thinking,* 12–13; Eisenhower, *Public Papers,* 1953, 1. See also Hutchinson, "President's Religious Faith," 362–69. For a sociological view of religious activity in the 1950s, see Herberg, *Protestant-Catholic-Jew.*

38　On Niebuhr's hope for religious revival in a time of cold war, see his "Is There a Revival of Religion?" 13, 60–63.

39　Niebuhr, *Christianity and Power Politics,* 33–34.

40　Niebuhr, *Does Civilization Need Religion?* 1–18. On Niebuhr's life and thought, see June Bingham, *Courage to Change,* written by an associate of Niebuhr's, and R. Fox, *Reinhold Niebhur,* a full biography making use of unpublished sources.

41　Niebuhr, *Christianity and Power Politics,* 40–41, 46.

42　Niebuhr, "American Pride and Power," 393–94; *Faith and History,* 161; *Christian Realism,* 128.

43　Niebuhr, "Why Is Communism So Evil," in his *Christian Realism,* 33–42; and *Irony of American History,* 1.

44　Ibid., 1–16, 22–23.

45　Tillich, *Protestant Era,* ix–x.

46　Ibid., 189–90.

47　Eisenhower, *Public Papers,* 1954, 372–75, 381.

48　A Report to the President Pursuant to the President's Directive of January 31, 1950, NSC 68, April 7, 1950, *Foreign Relations of the United States,* 1950, 1:262–63.

Chapter 9

1　W. White, *Report on the Russians,* 18–19.

2　Bailey, *Marshall Plan Summer,* 17–18, 53, 71, 129; T. White, *Fire in the Ashes,* 363.

3　Grosvenor, "Safari from Congo to Cairo," 747; Moore, "White Magic," 321, 322; Grosvenor, "Safari through Changing Africa," 184, 186; Douglas, "West from the Khyber Pass," 1–44; Klemmer, "Lend-Lease and the Russian Victory," 505; Moore, "Cities," 746.

4　W. White, *Report on the Russians,* 44, 124; Bourke-White, *Shooting the Russian War,* 77; Wallace, *Soviet Asia Mission,* 32, 34, 35, 43, 56, 86.

5　Bidwell, "Imports," 93; Lundberg, "World Revolution, American Plan," 40.

6　Harris, *Foreign Economic Policy,* vii, 5; Hansen, *America's Role,* 178; "Serve U.S. First, Thus Aid World, Harriman Urges," *New York Times,* May 1, 1947, 1. See also Lary, *United States in the World Economy,* 27–31.

7　Potter, *People of Plenty,* 135, 139.

8　Letiche, *Reciprocal Trade Agreements,* 26. See also Hirschman, *National Power and the Structure of Foreign Trade.* For trends in the value of exports and imports, see U.S. Department of Commerce, *Historical Statistics,* 884–86.

9　Heilbroner, "Our Foreign Trade Crisis," 387.

10 Ibid.

11 John B. Condliffe, "America's Foreign-Trade Policy," in Zurcher and Page, *America's Place*, 23.

12 Hansen, *America's Role*, 135; H. Morgenthau, in U.S. Congress, Senate, Committee on Banking and Currency, *Bretton Woods Agreements Act: Hearings before the Committee on Banking and Currency*, 79th Cong., 1st sess, 1945, 6.

13 Luce, "American Century," 65; Luce, *Ideas*, 241; Wallace, *Sixty Million Jobs*, 135.

14 Bruner, *Mandate from the People*, 70–71, 76–77.

15 Slichter, "Foreign Trade," 684; Manson, *Controlling World Trade*, 137; Wilcox, *Charter for World Trade*, 13.

16 Bruner, *Mandate from the People*, 73, 76, 77.

17 Hansen, *America's Role*, 88.

18 Hull, "War and Human Freedom," *Department of State Bulletin*, July 25, 1942, 644–46; Hull, *Memoirs*, 1177–78.

19 F. D. Roosevelt, *Public Papers*, 1941, 315; Hull, *Memoirs*, 975–76, 1153, 1211–12, 1721.

20 Wallace, *Democracy Reborn*, 205, 218; Wallace, *Price of Vision*, 169, 173–74, 409–10, 542.

21 Luce, "American Century," 65; Luce, *Ideas*, 241–42.

22 Slichter, "Foreign Trade," 688–89; Galbraith, "European Recovery," 168, 172.

23 Bruner, *Mandate from the People*, 67–81; Gallup, *Gallup Poll*, 1:505; 2:1151–52, 1155, 1180–81, 1267, 1301.

24 Harriman, *America and Russia*, 47. For requests to extend the trade agreements, see Truman, *Public Papers*, 1947, 151–52; and Eisenhower, *Public Papers*, 1954, 354–55.

25 Diebold, "Merchant Marine Second to None?" 711–20; "1,900 Ships, 100,000 Planes in '43 Will Double U.S. Output for War," *New York Times*, April 29, 1943, 1, 12. See also Gorter, *United States Merchant Marine Policies*.

26 "Post-War Shipping on Big Scale Urged," *New York Times*, Jan. 12, 1943, 15.

27 "Back in the Major League," *Time*, July 2, 1951, 83; "Trans-Atlantic Record," *New York Times*, July 8, 1952, 26; Truman, *Public Papers*, 1952–53, 436.

28 Palmer, "Building of S.S. United States," 28; "S.S. United States: First Lady of the Seas," *Newsweek*, June 30, 1952, 82–84.

29 Palmer, "Building of S.S. United States," 14.

30 "Superliner Begins Her First Crossing," *New York Times*, July 4, 1952, 1, 6; "The United States Sets Speed Mark Crossing Atlantic," July 7, 1952, 1, 3; "New Queen of Seas Stirs Admiration," July 8, 1952, 29, 51; "Port Hails the United States as New Speed Queen," July 16, 1952, 1, 5; "New Speed Dashes for Liner Barred," July 16, 1952, 5; "Queen of the Seas," *Time*, July 14, 1952, 26.

31 U.S. Department of Commerce, *Historical Statistics*, 119–20; "Airlines Leading Atlantic Travel," *New York Times*, Nov. 23, 1958, sec. 5, p. 14. See also U.S. Congress, House, Congresswoman Luce speaking on "America in the Post-War Air World," 78th Cong., 1st sess., Feb. 9, 1943, *Congressional Record*, 89:759–63.

32 "Clipper Skipper," *Time*, March 28, 1949, 84–92.

33 Trippe, *Foreign Trade*, Address delivered in New York City, Oct. 26, 1943, 1–10; Trippe, *Ocean Air Transport*, 3.

34 Trippe, *A Plan for the Consolidation of All American-Flag Overseas and Foreign Air Transport Operations* (n.p., 1943), Pan American World Airways Archives, New York; U.S. Congress, Senate, Committee on Interstate and Foreign Commerce, *Consolidation of International Air Carriers (Chosen Instrument): Hearings before a Subcommittee of the Committee on Interstate and Foreign Commerce*, 80th Cong., 1st sess., May–June 1947. See also Trippe's testimony before the Senate Committee on Commerce, in *To Create the All-American Flag Line, Inc.: Hearings before the Subcommittee on Aviation, Committee on Commerce*, 79th Cong., 1st sess., March–May 1945.

35 "'Round World Trip Begun by Clipper," *New York Times*, June 18, 1947, 13; "Airliner Ends Round-the-World Trip, in 13 Days, 3 Hours, 10 Minutes," July 1, 1947, 51.

36 "Daily Jet Flights to Europe Start," *New York Times*, Oct. 27, 1958, 23; "707 Jet Outruns the Comet at Sea," Nov. 19, 1958, 3.

37 Paul A. Samuelson, "Disparity in Postwar Exchange Rates," in Harris, *Foreign Economic Policy*, 408.

38 "Go Abroad, Young Man!" *Changing Times*, February 1953, 17–19.

39 Herbert Feis, "The Investment of American Capital Abroad," in Zurcher and Page, *America's Place*, 83.

40 Galbraith, "European Recovery," 172–73.

41 Luce, *Ideas*, 242–43. For a similar view of Westinghouse, see Johnston, *We're All in It*, 185.

42 Luce, *Ideas*, 200; Wallace, *Soviet Asia Mission*, 162–86; Galbraith, *Life in Our Times*, 366. See also Wallace, "What We Will Get out of the War," 22–23, 98–104; Wallace, *Democracy Reborn*, 200.

43 Johnston, "My Talk with Joseph Stalin," 3–4, 6–7.

44 Johnston, *We're All in It*, 185–87.

45 U.S. Department of Commerce, *Historical Statistics*, 869; Barber, *American Corporation*, 19–21, 233–85; "Go Abroad, Young Man!" 17.

46 For growing foreign concern over U.S. investment, see Servan-Schreiber, *American Challenge*, with a foreword by Arthur Schlesinger, Jr., vii–xii; McGhee, Summary of an address delivered at Düsseldorf on June 30, 1966, published as "Role of American Business in Germany," 408–10.

47 "Compass of Enterprise," *Fortune*, February 1950, 69.

48 "The Esso Handicap," ibid., 73–75, 136–41.

49 "Westinghouse Abroad," ibid., 76–78, 142–48.

50 "Sears, Roebuck in Rio," ibid., 78–80, 151–56; Potter, *People of Plenty*, 80.

51 Hansen, *America's Role*, 145.

52 Samuelson, *Economics*, 376; Hansen, *America's Role*, 169.

53 C. P. Kindleberger, "International Monetary Stabilitzation," in Harris, *Postwar Economic Problems*, 379–80.

54 Mikesell, *Foreign Exchange*, 404; "Dollar Shortage Forever," *Newsweek*, Aug. 16, 1948, 67; "Perils of Boom in Exports," *United States News*, May 16, 1947, 44.

55 Heilbroner, "Our Foreign Trade Crisis," 389, 390; Galbraith, "European Recovery," 169.

56 Condliffe, "America's Foreign-Trade Policy," in Zurcher and Page, *America's Place*, 32; Heilbroner, "Our Foreign Trade Crisis," 388.

57 Truman, *Mr. President*, 11, 13.

58 Eisenhower, *Public Papers*, 1953, 684–85.

59 U.S. Department of State, *Together We Are Strong*, Commercial Policy Ser. 144, p. 4; "No Imports Would Make Life Drab, State Department Booklet Shows," *New York Times*, Dec. 15, 1952, 1.

60 Bruner, *Mandate from the People*, 75–77.

61 "Westinghouse Abroad," *Fortune*, February 1950, 142.

62 Hansen, *America's Role*, 8.

63 J. Williams, "Currency Stabilization: American and British Attitudes," 235, 243–44; J. Williams, "Currency Stabilization: The Keynes and White Plans," 658.

64 U.S. Congress, Senate, Committee on Banking and Currency, *Bretton Woods Agreements Act: Hearings before the Committee on Banking and Commerce*, 79th Cong., 1st sess., 6, 7; Lary, *United States in the World Economy*, 19–20; Allan G. B. Fisher, "The International Monetary Fund and the International Bank for Reconstruction and Development," in Harris, *Foreign Economic Policy*, 241.

65 Hansen, *America's Role*, 90.

66 H. Morgenthau, "Bretton Woods and International Coöperation," 184; Roosevelt, *Public Papers*, 1944–45, 548. Roosevelt used the phrase "rendezvous with destiny" when accepting the nomination of the Democratic party for his second term, June 27, 1936 (*Public Papers*, 1936, 235).

67 U.S. Department of State, *Proposals for Expansion of World Trade and Employment*, 1.

68 Dam, *GATT: Law and International Economic Organization;* Gallup, *Gallup Poll*, 1:695.

69 See Wilcox, *Charter for World Trade*.

70 Hansen, *America's Role*, 94; Truman, *Public Papers*, 1946, 475; "Questions and Answers on the Proposed International Trade Organization," *Department of State Bulletin*, Jan. 9, 1949, 40.

71 U.S. Department of State, *Proposals for Expansion of World Trade and Employment*, 23–28.

72 Hansen, *America's Role*, 99; Wilcox, *Charter for World Trade*, 153–60; Acheson, "Economic Policy and the ITO Charter," *Department of State Bulletin*, May 15, 1949, 624.

73 N. Burns, "American Farmer and the ITO Charter," *Department of State Bulletin*, Feb. 20, 1949, 215; "Questions and Answers on the Proposed International Trade Organization," 38–39.

74 "Questions and Answers on the Proposed International Trade Organization," 35.

75 Acheson, "Economic Policy and the ITO Charter," 624, 626.

76 N. Burns, "American Farmer and the ITO Charter," Feb. 20, 1949, 215, 220; "Questions and Answers on the Proposed International Trade Organization," 63.

77 Acheson, "Economic Policy and the ITO Charter," 623–24; "Future Administration of GATT," *Department of State Bulletin*, Dec. 18, 1950, 977.

78 Wallace, "We Must Save Free Enterprise," 12–13, 51–54; Wallace, *Democracy Reborn*, 268–73; H. A. Wallace to F. D. Roosevelt, Feb. 5, 1943, Franklin D. Roosevelt Library. See also Wallace, "Wallace Defines 'American Fascism,'" 7, 34–35.

79 Luce, "American Century," 65, and *Ideas*, 145–46, 241–42; "ITO Charter," *Fortune*, July 1949, 61–62.

80 "ITO Charter," 61–62.

81 Eisenhower, *Public Papers*, 1954, 355; "World Trade: Peril Points and Politics," *Time*, May 24, 1954, 26–27.

Chapter 10

1 Curti, *American Philanthropy Abroad*, vii–viii; Boorstin, *Americans: The Democratic Experience*, 559–79; H. K. Smith, *State of Europe*, 290–91.

2 Hofstadter, *American Political Tradition*, 327, 345.

3 Luce, "American Century," 65; Luce, "Food: We Could Eat Less," 34.

4 Wallace, *Century of the Common Man*, 19; *Democracy Reborn*, 204, 217; H. A. Wallace to Arthur Krock, n.d., Cordell Hull Papers, Library of Congress. See also Arthur Krock, "Election Trend Arouses New Spirit in Congress," *New York Times*, Nov. 29, 1942, sec. 4, p. 3; and "Mr. Wallace's Vision of the Post-War World," Dec. 24, 1942, 14. For an example of Hull's lack of enthusiasm for Wallace's proposals, see Cordell Hull to Henry A. Wallace, June 2, 1943, Hull Papers.

5 Wallace, "What We Will Get out of the War," 100–103; Wallace, *Democracy Reborn*, 183–84, 241; Wallace, "Way to Abundance," review of *The Tennessee Valley Authority*, by David E. Lilienthal, *New Republic*, March 27, 1944, 414–16. For Luce's view of TVA, see Luce, *Ideas*, 244.

6 Galbraith, "European Recovery," 165–66.

7 Potter, *People of Plenty*, 139–41.

8 Niebuhr, *Irony of American History*, 41–42.

9 F. D. Roosevelt, *Public Papers*, 1940, 607–8.

10 Winant, *Letter from Grosvenor Square*, 143.

11 Klemmer, "Lend-Lease and the Russian Victory," 499–512.

12 Stettinius, *Lend-Lease*, 328–29.

13 Bruner, *Mandate from the People*, 84–86, 91.

14 F. D. Roosevelt, *Public Papers*, 1943, 500–509. Italics in original.

15 Wallace, *Democracy Reborn*, 204.

16 Bruner, *Mandate from the People*, 88–90. Italics in original.

17 Ibid., 90–92.

18 Welles, *Time for Decision*, 385; "U.S. Provided 71% of UNRRA Supplies," *New York Times*, Sept. 26, 1946, 13.

19 "Text of La Guardia UNRRA Acceptance Speech," *New York Times*, March 30, 1946, 5; "La Guardia As Head of UNRRA to Seek Wheat from Peron," 1, 5.

20 Truman, *Public Papers*, 1945, 464, 467; 1946, 215; "La Guardia Bids Truman Farewell," *New York Times*, July 12, 1946, 20; "La Guardia on Way to Overseas Tour," July 15,

1946, 7; "Food-Drive Dramatizer," *United States News,* April 5, 1946, 64; "La Guardia's Hungry World," *New Republic,* April 1, 1946, 428–29.

21 *New York Times,* July 27, 1946, 1; "Famine after UNRRA," *New Republic,* Aug. 12, 1946, 139; "Russia," *United States News,* April 5, 1946, 65.

22 E. Rostow, "Great Transition," 144.

23 H. K. Smith, *State of Europe,* 227–28; "Wherry Leaves Austria: Insists Army Could Supply Relief Better Than UNRRA," *New York Times,* Dec. 4, 1946, 16.

24 Memorandum by the Under Secretary of State for Economic Affairs (Clayton), The European Crisis, May 27, 1947, *Foreign Relations of the United States,* 1947, 3:232. Italics in original.

25 "Self-Finance Seen for Relief Nations," *New York Times,* July 31, 1946, 2; "U.S. Opposes Role in Joint Relief Aid," Nov. 29, 1946, 8.

26 Truman, *Public Papers,* 1947, 149–50. See also 159–61, 447.

27 "World Food Survey Shows Where Aid Still Is Needed; War's Hunger Aftermath Hitting Hardest at China, Greece, Hungary, Italy, Poland, Yugoslavia—End of UNRRA a Blow," *New York Times,* Feb. 3, 1947, 1, 10–11.

28 Truman, *Public Papers,* 1946, 106–8, 135–36, 215; 1947, 149–50. See also "The World's Food Problem," *New York Times,* Feb. 4, 1947, 24.

29 Truman, *Public Papers,* 1947, 179. A novel history of the domestic politics associated with foreign aid policy formulation of the late 1940s is Freeland, *Truman Doctrine and the Origins of McCarthyism.*

30 Wallace on the subject of aid to Greece and Turkey, recorded in U.S. Congress, *Congressional Record,* 80th Cong., 93:A1329.

31 La Guardia, Radio broadcasts over WINS, March 1–Sept. 20, 1947, typescript, New York University Library, March 15, p. 2; March 29, pp. 3–4; April 12, p. 6; May 10, pp. 2–3. His last statement on this issue was on his June 7 broadcast.

32 Bailey, *Marshall Plan Summer,* 116, 120.

33 H. K. Smith, *State of Europe,* 13–14, 94, 98.

34 Lippmann, "Today and Tomorrow" column, March 15, 1947, Walter Lippmann Papers, Yale University Library; "Warning to Russia," *New York Times,* March 13, 1947, 26; "Text of Hoover Report to Truman Urging the Restoration of German Industry," ibid., March 24, 1947, 4. For newsmagazine coverage of Europe in crisis, see "The Great Frost," *Time,* Feb. 10, 1947, 30; "Blackout," *Time,* Feb. 17, 1947, 30–31; "Much That Is Inevitable," *Time,* Feb. 24, 1947, 30; "Europe: In the Path of the Third Horseman," *Newsweek,* March 3, 1947, 30–35; "Europe: Misery on V-E Plus Two Years," *Newsweek,* May 19, 1947, 38–40; "World Unrest as U.S. Problem," *United States News,* Feb. 28, 1947, 19–21; "The Food Outlook for 1947," *United States News,* March 14, 1947, 21–22.

35 Lippmann, "Today and Tomorrow" column, April 5, 1947, Walter Lippmann Papers, Yale University Library.

36 "Pangs," *New Republic,* April 21, 1947, 6–7; "Putting World on Its Feet: America's New Responsibility," *United States News,* March 21, 1947, 11–12; James Reston, "U.S. Studies Shift of Help to Europe As a Unit in Crisis," *New York Times,* May 25, 1947, 1; "Full Funds for the Hungry," May 18, 1947, sec. 4, p. 8; "A 'Continental Plan,'" May 26, 1947, 20.

37 Bailey, *Marshall Plan Summer,* 21, 60, 86, 88–89, 101, 109.

38 Memorandum by the Joint Chiefs of Staff to the State-War-Navy Coordinating Committee, with Appendix, "United States Assistance to Other Countries from the Standpoint of National Security," May 12, 1947, *Foreign Relations of the United States, 1947,* 1:734–50. Italics in original.

39 The Director of the Policy Planning Staff (Kennan) to the Under Secretary of State (Acheson), May 23, 1947, *Foreign Relations of the United States,* 1947, 3:223–30.

40 Memorandum by the Under Secretary of State for Economic Affairs (Clayton), The European Crisis, May 27, 1947, *Foreign Relations of the United States,* 1947, 3:230–32.

41 Marshall, *European Initiative Essential to Economic Recovery,* 1–3.

42 Ibid., 4.

43 Ibid., 5.

44 Foreign Assistance Act of 1948.

45 Ellis, *Economics of Freedom* 534–37; Kindleberger, *Dollar Shortage,* 252; Foreign Assistance Act of 1948.

46 Roper, *Where Stands Freedom?* 25–26; H. Cantril, *Public Opinion,* 218–20; Truman, *Public Papers,* 1947, 437–38, 452–53, 456–58, 464.

47 Harris, *European Recovery Program,* 185–206; Roper, *Where Stands Freedom?* 26; Truman, *Public Papers,* 1947, 86, 333–34, 492–98, 532–34.

48 H. K. Smith, *State of Europe,* 35, 91, 149, 222, 226. Italics in original.

49 T. White, *Fire in the Ashes,* 67.

50 "Achievements of the Marshall Plan," *Department of State Bulletin,* Jan. 14, 1952, 43.

51 Ibid.; P. Hoffman, *Peace Can Be Won,* 89–90; McCloy, "Western Germany's Progress under Marshall Plan," *Department of State Bulletin,* Jan. 14, 1952, 45–46.

52 "Achievements of the Marshall Plan," 44.

53 Ibid., 43; J. Williams, "End of the Marshall Plan," 593–94, 597–98.

54 Ellis, *Economics of Freedom,* 467–76; H. Price, *Marshall Plan and Its Meaning,* 398–401.

55 Galbraith, "European Recovery," 170–74; Wallace, *Soviet Asia Mission,* 238–39; "Our Duty in Europe's Crisis," *New York Times,* June 8, 1947, sec. 4, p. 12.

56 Potter, *People of Plenty,* 139–41.

57 Truman, *Public Papers,* 1949, 114.

58 Ibid., 114–15.

59 Truman, *Memoirs,* 2:230–31.

60 Truman, *Mr. President,* 225–26, 249–50; Truman, *Memoirs,* 2:231–34, 238; Truman, *Public Papers,* 1949, 118–19; 1950, 467–68; 1952–53, 13. The remarks to the Businessman's Dinner Forum were off the record and not included in his *Public Papers.* See *Public Papers,* 1949, 533.

61 "To Meet the Soviet Challenge," *Business Week,* May 26, 1956, 204.

62 Potter, *People of Plenty,* 139; "Westinghouse Abroad" and "Sears, Roebuck in Rio," *Fortune,* February 1950, 76, 80; Truman, *Memoirs,* 2:234–39; Truman, *Public Papers,* 1952–53, 13.

63   Truman, *Memoirs*, 2:239.

64   J. B. Bingham, *Shirt-Sleeve Diplomacy*, 131–32.

65   Ibid., 41–81.

66   Ibid., 82–103.

67   Ibid., 104–18, 129–44.

68   Ibid., 202, 240–41.

69   See U.S. Department of Commerce, *Historical Statistics*, 872–75; and *Statistical Abstract*, 1979, 853–57.

70   Barzun, *God's Country and Mine*, 101–2.

71   T. White, *Fire in the Ashes*, 390.

Chapter 11

1   McMurry and Lee, *Cultural Approach;* Thomson and Laves, *Cultural Relations*. For background to this period, see Rosenberg, *Spreading the American Dream*.

2   Staley, *World Economy in Transition*, 3–20; Buell, *Isolated America*, 246–48.

3   Willkie, *One World*, 2.

4   F. D. Roosevelt, *Public Papers*, 1944–45, 202–3.

5   Luce, "American Century," 65; "U.S. and World Communications," *Fortune*, May 1944, 130, 278.

6   Wallace recorded the talk with Molotov in his diary, June 3, 1942, in *Price of Vision*, 85–86, and related it in an address at the Congress of American-Soviet Friendship, Madison Square Garden, New York, Nov. 8, 1942, in Wallace, *Democracy Reborn*, 199, after President Roosevelt gave him approval to make it public (*Price of Vision*, 122). See also Wallace, "What We Will Get out of the War," 22–23, 98–100; and his *Soviet Asia Mission*, 237–38.

7   F. D. Roosevelt, *Public Papers*, 1944–45, 524; U.S. Department of Commerce, Bureau of the Census, *U.S. Census of Population: 1960*.

8   "Americans in the New Age of World Travel," *Life*, June 15, 1962, 63.

9   T. White, *Fire in the Ashes*, 359–61.

10   H. K. Smith, *State of Europe*, 72–73.

11   Mead, *And Keep Your Powder Dry*, 27.

12   Cleveland, Mangone, and Adams, *Overseas Americans*, vi.

13   Boorstin, *Image or What Happened to the American Dream*, 94–99.

14   Eisenhower, *Public Papers*, 1953, 686.

15   "Emissary of American Business on the Go," *Life*, Dec. 23, 1957, 22–24.

16   Fanning, *Foreign Oil*, 318–19.

17   "Go Abroad, Young Man!" *Changing Times*, February 1953, 18; "Getting along with Foreigners," *Business Week*, June 9, 1956, 75–86.

18   Yank Stuff, eds., *Yank* (1947), 236–37.

19 Cary, *War-Wasted Asia*, 50, 73.

20 Berry, "Army Wife," 24–25, 119–22; Bailey, *Marshall Plan Summer*, 64–65, 70.

21 Rodnick, *Postwar Germans*, 99, 106; T. White, *Fire in the Ashes*, 130–33. See also Bailey, *Marshall Plan Summer*, 131.

22 Lundberg, "World Revolution, American Plan," 39–40. Italics in original.

23 Ibid., 40.

24 T. White, *Fire in the Ashes*, 373; Truman, *Memoirs*, 1:332–35; Truman, *Off the Record*, 59.

25 Truman, *Off the Record*, 146; Eisenhower, *White House Years*, 2:415, 489, 527–28.

26 Truman, *Memoirs*, 1:342; Truman, *Off the Record*, 53; Truman, *Mr. President*, 241–42.

27 Eisenhower, *White House Years*, 1:510–15; 2:416, 420.

28 Ibid., 2:494–95, 498–504.

29 Ibid., 2:512–13, 567.

30 Nixon, *Six Crises*, 200.

31 Ibid., 201–3. See also "Stones—and a Warning," *Time*, May 19, 1958, 29.

32 Nixon, *Six Crises*, 259–60; "Eisenhower Message and Nixon Speech to Soviet People," *New York Times*, July 25, 1959, 2. For Nixon's speech broadcast on Russian television and radio, see "Nixon Tells Russians End of Fear Depends on Krushchev Tactics," *New York Times*, Aug. 2, 1959, 1, 24.

33 Lacy, "Rôle of American Books Abroad," 405–17; *World Almanac 1950*, 574.

34 "Is the World 'Going American'?" *U.S. News & World Report*, March 23, 1959, 81; Burnett, "Yank Meets Native," 105–6, 109; Bourke-White, *Shooting the Russian War*, 49; Moore, "White Magic," 360–61; Yank Editors, *Best from Yank* (1945), 36.

35 Rockefeller, "Need for Expanding Use of U.S. Books Overseas," *Department of State Bulletin*, Oct. 17, 1955, 616; Lacy, "Rôle of American Books Abroad," 405–7, 414.

36 T. White, *Fire in the Ashes*, 364; Lacy, "Rôle of American Books Abroad," 409, 413.

37 Galbraith, *Life in Our Times*, 209, 211–12; Moore, "White Magic," 324; Grosvenor, "Safari through Changing Africa," 198; Grosvenor, "Safari from Congo to Cairo," 721, 724; Yank Editors, *Best from Yank* (1945), 221; T. White, *Fire in the Ashes*, 361, 362–64.

38 Bourke-White, *Shooting the Russian War*, 35, 37; W. White, *Report on the Russians*, 170–71; *Foreign Relations of the United States*, 1946, 6:686.

39 Acheson, "Culture after Breakfast," 34; Burnett, "Yank Meets Native," 105; Moore, "Busy Corner," 201.

40 "Le Jazz, Still Hot in Paris," *Life*, April 28, 1952, 125–29.

41 "Kings of Swing and Thailand Jive," *New York Times*, Dec. 7, 1956, 1, 19.

42 Aksyonov, *In Search of Melancholy Baby*, 12–13, 18.

43 "Benny Goodman's Moscow Concert Pleases but Puzzles Krushchev," *New York Times*, May 31, 1962, 1, 21; "One-Man Session by Goodman Attracts a Crowd in Red Square," June 2, 1962, 8; "Krushchev Visits U.S. Embassy Fete," July 5, 1962, 1, 4.

44 "Russians Cheer U.S. Pianist, 23," *New York Times*, April 12, 1958, 1, 12; "U.S. Pianist, 23, Wins Soviet Contest," April 14, 1958, 1, 18; "U.S. Pianist Plays for Soviet Chiefs,"

April 15, 1958, 42; "Cliburn Continues As Toast of Soviet," April 16, 1958, 39; "The Fruits of Victory," *Newsweek,* April 28, 1958, 56; and the *Time* cover story, "The All-American Virtuoso," May 19, 1958, 59.

45 "Benny Goodman's Moscow Concert Pleases but Puzzles Khrushchev," 21; Krushchev Visits U.S. Embassy Fete," 4.

46 "Is the World 'Going American'?" 81; Martin, "Biggest City in the World," 94, 95.

47 Guback, *International Film Industry,* 3–15; Thomas, *Hollywood and the American Image.* For background to American film abroad, see Kristin Thompson, *Exporting Entertainment;* F. D. Roosevelt, *Public Papers,* 1941, 40.

48 Wanger, "OWI and Motion Pictures," 100–110; *Variety,* Jan. 7, 1953, 15.

49 Johnston, "H'wood Still Best U.S. Ambassador Despite Some Contrary Opinions," *Variety,* Jan. 7, 1953, 5, 65; U.S. Congress, Senate, Committee on Foreign Relations, *Overseas Information Programs of the United States,* 83d Cong., 1st sess., pt. 2, 236.

50 DeMille, *Autobiography,* 350, 424–27.

51 Hepburn, *Making of "The African Queen,"* 38–39, 53–54.

52 Willkie, *One World,* 159.

53 Yank Editors, *Best from Yank* (1945), 29, 73, 221.

54 *Variety,* Jan. 7, 1953, 65.

55 T. White, *Fire in the Ashes,* 12, 363.

56 DeMille, *Autobiography,* 281–82, 344, 414, 422.

57 Wallace, *Soviet Asia Mission,* 34; Bourke-White, *Shooting the Russian War,* 58; W. White, *Report on the Russians,* 33–34.

58 W. White, *Report on the Russians,* 59–61, 63–64.

59 Aksyonov, *In Search of Melancholy Baby,* 17–18.

60 "Scented Movies Use Hundreds of Chemicals in an Effort to Lure Fans Back by Nose," *Wall Street Journal,* Jan. 6, 1960, 6.

61 Dizard, "American Television's Foreign Markets," 58, 63; U.S. Congress, Howe, Committee on Foreign Affairs, Subcommittee on International Organizations and Movements, *Modern Communications and Foreign Policy,* 90th Cong., 1st sess., 1967, 59; Schiller, *Mass Communications.*

62 Dizard, "American Television's Foreign Markets," 60–63; "Is the World 'Going American'?" 76; "Global Report," *Television Age,* July 3, 1967, 32–36, 60–69; "World Laps up U.S. TV Fare," *Business Week,* April 23, 1960, 129, 131.

63 Sarnoff, *Program,* 28, 31.

64 P. Hoffman, *Peace Can Be Won,* 144–46.

65 Nixon, *Six Crises,* 259; "The U.S. in Moscow," *Time,* Aug. 3, 1959, 14; "U.S. Gives Soviet Glittering Show," *New York Times,* July 25, 1959, 2.

66 "Nixon and Khrushchev Argue in Public As U.S. Exhibit Opens; Accuse Each Other of Threats," ibid., July 25, 1959, 1, 2; "The Two Worlds: A Day-Long Debate," 1, 3.

67 "The U.S. in Moscow," 14; "Opening Day at Sokolniki," *New York Times,* July 25, 1959, 16.

68 Tripp, "UNESCO in Perspective," 323–83; Laves and Thomson, *UNESCO: Purpose Pro-*

gress Prospects; Shuster, *UNESCO: Assessment and Promise;* Sewell, *UNESCO and World Politics.*

69 Truman, *Public Papers,* 1946, 433.

70 Wallace, "What We Will Get out of the War," 98–100; H. A. Wallace to F. D. Roosevelt, Feb. 5, 1943, Franklin D. Roosevelt Library. See also Wallace, *Price of Vision,* 105–6.

71 H. Cantril, *Public Opinion,* 187; Sewell, *UNESCO and World Politics,* 321–25.

72 "New Director for UNESCO," *Scientific American,* September 1953, 73–74.

73 Evans, "Almost Half the World's Adults Can't Read," 43–46.

74 UNESCO, *Reflections on Our Age,* 115–16; Ralph Henry Gabriel, *Traditional Values in American Life* (Prepared for the United States National Commission for UNESCO).

75 Ware, Panikkar, and Romein, *Twentieth Century,* vol. 6: *History of Mankind: Cultural and Scientific Development,* 3, 27, 104. See also 224, 245, 389, 951.

76 McNeill, review of *The Twentieth Century,* by Caroline F. Ware et al., *American Historical Review* 73 (June 1968): 1479–80; Laves and Thomson, *UNESCO: Purpose Progress Prospects,* 241–43, and Shuster, *UNESCO: Assessment and Promise,* 29–31, discuss the controversy of the work in progress.

77 Dexter, "Yardstick for UNESCO," 56; Sewell, *UNESCO and World Politics,* 318–21, 325; "'UNESCO' under Fire—But What Is It?" *U.S. News & World Report,* Nov. 4, 1955, 67–68.

78 Thomson, *Overseas Information Service,* 363.

79 MacLeish, "Introduction" to McMurry and Lee, *Cultural Approach,* viii–ix; Dizard, *Strategy of Truth;* Henderson, *United States Information Agency;* Stephens, *Facts to a Candid World.*

80 Truman, *Public Papers,* 1945, 253.

81 Smith-Mundt Act of 1948.

82 Truman, *Public Papers,* 1950, 260–64.

83 Eisenhower, *Public Papers,* 1953, 18; Streibert is quoted in Henderson, *United States Information Agency,* 65–66.

84 On the dimensions of USIA, see Dizard, *Strategy of Truth,* 48, 71–74, 123–24, 137.

85 U.S. Information Agency, *U.S.A.: Its Geography and Growth,* Foreword and 5, 7, 35, 126.

86 Dizard, *Strategy of Truth,* 186–200; R. Rubin, *Objectives of the U.S. Information Agency,* 24–31; Henderson, *United States Information Agency,* 284–91.

87 H. Cantril, *Public Opinion,* 153.

88 The Chargé in the Soviet Union (Kennan) to the Secretary of State, Jan. 30, 1946, *Foreign Relations of the United States,* 1946, 6:686–87.

89 W. Smith, *My Three Years,* 178–82. For similar reports by Smith, see *Foreign Relations of the United States,* 1947, 4:533–34, 545–46, 647–48.

90 Boorstin, *Image or What Happened to the American Dream,* 241–43.

91 Niebuhr, *Irony of American History,* 116.

92 "Is the World 'Going American'?" 83.

93 Ibid., 74, 77.

94 Ibid., 74, 76, 77, 78, 81, 82.

95 Ibid., 76, 77, 78, 81, 83.

96 Niebuhr, *Irony of American History*, 57–59.

97 Ibid., 59.

Chapter 12

1 F. D. Roosevelt, *Public Papers*, 1940, 672; 1941, 314–15; Truman, *Public Papers*, 1945, 433–34.

2 "An Open Letter from the Editors of *Life* to the People of England," *Life*, Oct. 12, 1942, 34; italics in original; Vernon Bartlett, "A Communication: A Journalist Member of Parliament Replies to *Life*'s Open Letter to the English People," *Life*, Oct. 26, 1942, 24; Elson, *Time Inc.*, 463, and *World of Time Inc.*, 22–27; Publisher's Note in Luce, *American Century*, 45; Luce had used these words in "American Century," 64.

3 Wallace, *Our Job*, 35–39; *Price of Vision*, 208.

4 Hofstadter, *American Political Tradition*, 344–45.

5 Boorstin, *Genius of American Politics*, 187–89. Italics in original.

6 Niebuhr, *Irony of American History*, 5, 36.

7 F. D. Roosevelt, *Public Papers*, 1941, 315.

8 Streit, *Union Now*, 2, 6–7. Italics in original.

9 Streit, *Union Now with Britain;* Thompson, "War for What?" 159; Luce, "American Century," 63; Shotwell, "After the War," 34.

10 Bess, "Let's Quit Pretending," 37; Morley, "For What Are We Fighting?" 42.

11 Hopkins, "What Victory Will Bring Us," 88; Range, *Franklin D. Roosevelt's World Order;* F. Davis, "Roosevelt's World Blueprint," 20–21, 109–10; F. D. Roosevelt, *F.D.R.: His Personal Letters*, 2:1366–67; Whitton, *Second Chance;* Divine, *Second Chance*, 4. See also Stromberg, *Collective Security.*

12 F. D. Roosevelt, *Public Papers*, 1944–45, 586.

13 Hull, *Memoirs*, 1166, 1170, 1452–53.

14 Hull, "Address by the Secretary of State before Congress Regarding the Moscow Conference," *Department of State Bulletin*, Nov. 20, 1943, 343.

15 J. F. Dulles, "America's Role in the Peace," 2–6; and his "Political Cost of Peace," 8–9.

16 U.S. Congress, House, "Participation in World Peace," 78th Cong., 1st sess., Sept. 21, 1943, *Congressional Record*, 89:7703–29.

17 "A New Turn for America," *New York Times*, Feb. 18, 1945, sec. 4, p. 8.

18 Bruner, *Mandate from the People*, 38–52; H. Cantril, *Public Opinion*, 373–75, 905–17; Roper, *Where Stands Freedom?* 32; Roper, *You and Your Leaders*, 55.

19 F. D. Roosevelt, *Public Papers*, 1944–45, 580–81, 585.

20 U.S. Congress, Senate, 79th Cong., 1st sess., 1945, *Congressional Record*, 91:7941.

21 Truman, *Public Papers*, 1945, 139, 142; 1946, 433; Truman, *Mr. President*, 56.

22 Truman, *Mr. President*, 204, 206, 245.

23 Van Doren, *Great Rehearsal*, viii.

24 Riesman, *Lonely Crowd*, 204–5. The interview is found in the pamphlet by the University of Michigan, Survey Research Center, *Four Americans Discuss Aid to Europe*, 13.

25 Niebuhr, "Illusion of World Government," 379–88; *Irony of American History*, 136.

26 "The World Capital," *New York Times*, Dec. 26, 1945, 18; "World Capitol: Five Stages," *New York Times Magazine*, Dec. 30, 1951, 6–7; "Cheops' Architect," *Time*, Sept. 22, 1952, 78, 81.

27 "Truman Urges U.N.'s Atom Plan Unless Better One Is Offered; Lie Lays Stone of Headquarters," *New York Times*, Oct. 25, 1949, 1, 6; "The Dream Made Visible," Oct. 25, 1949, 26; "U.N. Dedicates a World Capital," *Life*, Nov. 7, 1949, 33.

28 "World Capitol: Five Stages," *New York Times Magazine*, Dec. 30, 1951, 6; "Tower of Peace," *New York Times Magazine*, March 5, 1950, 24–25; "Simple Geometry," *Time*, June 13, 1949, 51; "U.N. Assembly Gets New Home," *Life*, Oct. 27, 1952, 34–35; "Cheops' Architect," *Time*, Sept. 22, 1952, 78; "New Lights in New York," *Life*, March 26, 1951, 62–67; "U.N. Invasion . . . Sight-Seers Take over the Global Capitol," *Newsweek*, March 9, 1953, 32–33.

29 Kennan, "Let Peace Not Die of Neglect," 38.

30 R. Russell, *United Nations Experience;* Truman, *Public Papers*, 1948, 187.

31 Osgood, *Alliances and American Foreign Policy.*

32 Truman, *Public Papers*, 1947, 177.

33 Jones, *Fifteen Weeks*, 7–9.

34 Truman, *Public Papers*, 1947, 177–80.

35 "Truman Acts to Save Nations from Red Rule; Asks 400 Million to Aid Greece and Turkey; Congress Fight Likely but Approval Is Seen," *New York Times*, March 13, 1947, 1, 2; "Congress Is Solemn; Some Hold Truman Plan Is Blow to U.N.—All but Marcantonio Applaud," 1, 4; James Reston, "Truman's Speech Likened to 1823 and 1941 Warnings," ibid., 3; "Warning to Russia," 26; "The President's Policy," March 14, 1947, 22, "Stronger U.N. Held Only Key to Peace," March 13, 1947, 9.

36 Kennan, "Sources of Soviet Conduct," 575, 581–82; Report by the Policy Planning Staff, Résumé of World Situation, Nov. 6, 1947, *Foreign Relations of the United States*, 1947, 1:772–73.

37 Acheson, *Pattern of Responsibility*, 291–92.

38 Acheson, "Meaning of the North Atlantic Pact," *Department of State Bulletin*, March 27, 1949, 385; Truman, *Public Papers*, 1949, 197–98.

39 "The North Atlantic Pact," *Department of State Bulletin*, March 20, 1949, 342–50. It was excerpted as Statement on the North Atlantic Pact by the Department of State, March 20, 1949, *Foreign Relations of the United States*, 1949, 4:240–41.

40 Ibid.

41 Truman, *Memoirs*, 2:240, 250; Truman, *Public Papers*, 1949, 196–98, 433.

42 Memorandum by the Director of the Policy Planning Staff (Kennan), Nov. 24, 1948, *Foreign Relations of the United States*, 1948, 3:283–89. Italics in original.

43 Eisenhower, *Public Papers*, 1953, 13; John Foster Dulles, *War or Peace*, 205–6.

44 Kennan, "Sources of Soviet Conduct," 576; The Director of the Policy Planning Staff

(Kennan) to the Under Secretary of State (Acheson), May 23, 1947, *Foreign Relations of the United States,* 1947, 3:229. On the meaning of Kennan's containment, John Lewis Gaddis argued in "Containment: A Reassessment," 873–87, that it was essentially correct, even if nebulous and misunderstood. Kennan himself has explained in his *Memoirs* that containment was not meant to be military, as he said in a letter, "George Kennan on Containment Reconsidered," published in *Foreign Affairs* 56 (April 1978): 643–47.

45 Lippmann, *Cold War,* 18, 21–23.

46 Truman, *Public Papers,* 1950, 537; 1951, 223.

47 Kennan, "Let Peace Not Die of Neglect," 10, 38–41.

48 For *Life*'s militant stand on the Korean War, see "The Prospect Is War," *Life,* Dec. 11, 1950, 46; "We're in It Now!" *Life,* Dec. 18, 1950, 34; "Let's Get Down to Cases!" *Life,* Jan. 8, 1951, 14. On Luce, see Elson, *World of Time Inc.,* 291–92. Wallace's comments were given over the BBC, April 13, 1947, during a visit in England for a series of lectures, cited in *New York Times,* April 14, 1947, 1. On Wallace, see Walton, *Henry Wallace, Harry Truman, and the Cold War,* 349–51.

49 See Schuman, *Commonwealth of Man,* 411–12.

50 Truman, *Public Papers,* 1951, 223. See also 229, 316.

51 Moss, *Men Who Play God,* 14; Kissinger, *Nuclear Weapons and Foreign Policy,* 3.

52 Truman, *Public Papers,* 1945, 212–13.

53 Wallace to Truman, Sept. 24, 1945, and Wallace to Truman, July 23, 1946, in Wallace, *Price of Vision,* 485–87, 591–95.

54 The Secretary of War (Stimson) to President Truman, Sept. 11, 1945, *Foreign Relations of the United States,* 1945, 2:40–44; Stimson and Bundy, *On Active Service,* 641, 642–46. Italics in original.

55 For accounts of the cabinet meeting, see Acheson, *Present at the Creation,* 123–24; Stimson and Bundy, *On Active Service,* 668; Forrestal, *Forrestal Diaries,* 94–96; Wallace, *Price of Vision,* 483–84.

56 Truman, *Public Papers,* 1945, 362–66.

57 Cousins, "Modern Man Is Obsolete," 5–9, reprinted as *Modern Man Is Obsolete*; Masters and Way, *One World or None*; 66–75; Hutchins, *Atomic Bomb versus Civilization,* 10–11.

58 U.S. Department of State, Committee on Atomic Energy, *Report on the International Control of Atomic Energy,* vii–x, 31.

59 Ibid., iii, 32–33; Truman, *Memoirs,* 2:6.

60 Baruch's speech to the United Nations Atomic Energy Commission was published as "Proposals for an International Atomic Development Authority," *Department of State Bulletin,* June 23, 1946, 1057–62.

61 "Beyond the Bomb," *Time,* June 24, 1946, 25; Lippmann, "Today and Tomorrow" column, June 18, 1946, Walter Lippmann Papers, Yale University Library. See also Elson, *World of Time Inc.,* 137–39; Henry Luce Memos, Sept. 13, 1945, Nov. 12, 1945, Nov. 16, 1945, Time, Inc., Archives.

62 Oppenheimer, "International Control of Atomic Energy," 250.

63 Truman, *Public Papers,* 1945, 378–88.

64 *Collier's,* Oct. 27, 1951, 17. *Life* also presented "The War We May Fight," May 28, 1951, 76–107.

65 *Collier's,* Oct. 27, 1951, 14.

66 Ibid., 19, 20, 22, 29.

67 Ibid., 37, 38, 39, 40, 41, 62, 83.

68 The original JCS document of Dropshot is in Record Group 218, Records of the United States Joint Chiefs of Staff, National Archives, and the text is published in A. Brown, *Dropshot.*

69 A. Brown, *Dropshot,* 41, 139.

70 Ibid., 49, 60–61, 124, 131–33.

71 Ibid., 137–59.

72 Ibid., 56, 108–15, 138, 159–61.

73 Ibid., 165–68.

74 Ibid., 168–69, 242–46.

75 Cochran, Arkin, and Hoenig, *Nuclear Weapons Databook,* vol. 1: *U.S. Nuclear Forces and Capabilities,* 6–11, 15.

76 Ibid., 11–12, 15.

77 The Secretary of State to the Embassy in the United Kingdom, July 20, 1948, *Foreign Relations of the United States,* 1948, 2:971.

78 Truman, *Public Papers,* 1950, 727. On Truman's consideration of use of the bomb, see Truman, *Memoirs,* 2:395–96; Truman, *Off the Record,* 304; Truman, *Strictly Personal and Confidential,* 31. That Truman recollected threatening to use nuclear weapons against the Soviet Union in the 1946 Iran crisis is reported in "Good Old Days," *Time,* Jan. 28, 1980, 13, but the evidence for his ultimatum is not in the record.

79 "Texts of Eisenhower's Statements on Trip to Korea," *New York Times,* Dec. 15, 1952, 6; Eisenhower, *White House Years,* 1:181; Secretary Dulles, Memorandum of Conversation, May 21, 1953, U.S. Department of State (Declassified); For the President from the Secretary, Incoming Telegram, May 22, 1953, Whitman file, Dulles-Herter series, Dwight D. Eisenhower Library.

80 *Foreign Relations of the United States,* 1952–54, 15:769–70. See also 825–27, 1653–55.

81 "O'Donnell Favors Using All Weapons," *New York Times,* Jan. 19, 1951, 7; "Air Force Calls O'Donnell on His Bombing Remarks," Jan. 20, 1951, 3; "Atomic Arms Use Explained," Feb. 14, 1953, 2.

82 Ibid., Oct. 12, 1951, 17; "U.S. Reported Weighing Korea Use of Atom Bomb," Oct. 14, 1951, 38; "Atom Weapons Use Urged," Oct. 16, 1951, 32; "New Battle Bombs Hailed by Senator," Nov. 10, 1951, 5; "Atom Bomb Use in Korea Asked," Nov. 13, 1951, 3; "Air War Risk Weighed," Nov. 25, 1951, sec. 1, p. 5.

83 Ibid., Dec. 2, 1950, 14; "Wallace Says Korea Justifies Atom Bomb," Aug. 11, 1950, 8; Nov. 3, 1952, 13.

84 Eisenhower, *White House Years,* 1:181.

Chapter 13

1 "Nationwide Response to National Purpose," *Life,* July 11, 1960, 90–100; *Huron Daily Tribune,* June 27, 1960, 1, and "Pictures of Local Meeting Shown in Life Magazine," *Huron Daily Tribune,* July 7, 1960, 1.

2 "Nationwide Response to National Purpose," 90. See Jeffries, "Quest for National Purpose," 451–70.

3 Walter Lippmann, "The Confrontation," *New York Herald Tribune,* Sept. 17, 1959, p. 20, repr. in *Foreign Policy Bulletin* 39 (Oct. 15, 1959): 21; Lippmann is quoted by John K. Jessup in "A Noble Framework for a Great Debate" in Life Editors, *National Purpose,* 1; George Kennan, quoted in Goldman, *Crucial Decade–and After,* 342–43.

4 The *Life* series "The National Purpose" began with a spread of colorful patriotic photographs and the introductory article by John K. Jessup, the magazine's chief editorial writer, "A Noble Framework for a Great Debate," *Life,* May 23, 1960, 22–41. The other contributors and their articles included Archibald MacLeish, "We Have Purpose . . . We All Know It" and Adlai Stevenson, "Extend Our Vison . . . to All Mankind," *Life,* May 30, 1960, 86ff.; David Sarnoff, "Turn the Cold War Tide in America's Favor" and Billy Graham, "Men Must Be Changed before a Nation Can," *Life,* June 6, 1960, 108ff.; John W. Gardner, "Can We Count on More Dedicated People?" and Clinton Rossiter, "We Must Show the Way to Enduring Peace," *Life,* June 13, 1960, 98ff.; Walter Lippmann, "The Country Is Waiting for Another Innovator" and Albert Wohlstetter, "A Purpose Hammered out of Reflection and Choice," *Life,* June 20, 1960, 114ff. A *Life* editorial stated the magazine's position a week after the last contribution and shortly after President Eisenhower canceled a visit to Japan because of riots against American policy: "Japan and American Purpose," *Life,* June 27, 1960, 32. The editors requested the Democratic and Republican presidential candidates to relate their impressions: John F. Kennedy, "We Must Climb to the Hilltop," *Life,* Aug. 22, 1960, 70B–77; Richard M. Nixon, "Our Resolve Is Running Strong," *Life,* Aug. 29, 1960, 86–94. The series of articles ran in the *New York Times.* James Reston wrote on national purpose for the paper, June 20, 1960, 28. With the exception of the articles of the presidential candidates, the selections quickly appeared in the book by Life Editors, *National Purpose,* with a forword by Luce, v–vi. All of the essays, along with selected historical documents, appeared in Handlin, *American Principles and Issues.* Goldman ended *Crucial Decade—and After* with an epilogue emphasizing the discussions of "national purpose" in 1960 (341–46). See also Elson, *World of Time Inc.,* 463–64.

5 Rockefeller Brothers Fund, *Prospect for America,* xv–xvii.

6 Eisenhower, *Public Papers,* 1959, 10–11. The commission took form along the lines of the "Memorandum Concerning the Commission on National Goals," Feb. 7, 1960, ibid., 1960–61, 159–61. Eisenhower also considered the purpose of the commission in his "Letter to Dr. Henry Wriston on His Acceptance of the Chairmanship of the Commission on National Goals," Feb. 7, 1960, 158–59. Eisenhower talked about the commission's organization at the American Assembly, a study affiliate of Columbia University, and his part in the American Assembly's creation while he was the university's president, in "Remarks at Dorado, Puerto Rico, at a Meeting of the American Assembly," March 4, 1960, 277–82. He also wrote a "Letter to Dr. Henry M. Wriston on the Progress Made by the Commission on National Goals," July 22, 1960, 585–86. The report of the U.S. President's Commission on National Goals, *Goals for Americans.*

7 "Nationwide Response to National Purpose," 90; U.S. President's Commission on National Goals, *Goals for Americans;* Rockefeller Brothers Fund, *Prospect for America;* Life Editors, *National Purpose.*

8 Handlin, *American Principles and Issues,* v–vi; Boorstin, *Image or What Happened to the American Dream,* vii–viii. See also H. J. Morgenthau, *Purpose of American Politics.*

9 Riesman, "National Purpose," in *Abundance for What?* 19–27.

10 Reuther, "Sense of National Purpose," 15–20; American Association for the Advancement of Science, Committee on Science in the Promotion of Human Welfare, "Science

and Human Welfare," 68–73; "National Purpose: Reston's Analysis," *New York Times,* June 20, 1960, 28.

11 Lippmann, in Life Editors, *National Purpose,* 132; Eisenhower, *Public Papers,* 1960–61, 1036; Nixon, *Speeches, Remarks, Press Conferences, and Study Papers,* 26.

12 Morgenthau, *Purpose of American Politics,* 3-7, 33; Morgenthau, "Decline of American Power," 14, also repr. in Morgenthau's *Impasse,* 46–55; Lippmann, "Today and Tomorrow" column, Jan. 19, 1960, Walter Lippmann Papers, Yale University Library. Compare Morgenthau's first edition of *Politics among Nations* (1948), 8, with his third edition (1960), Preface to the Third Edition, and p. 22.

13 Free and Cantril, *Political Beliefs of Americans,* 91–93.

14 Graebner, *New Isolationism,* v–vii; Life Editors, *National Purpose,* 15, 32, 48; U.S. President's Commission on National Goals, *Goals for Americans,* 2.

15 Almond, *American People,* xxii–xxv; Rockefeller Brothers Fund, *Prospect for America,* xx. Italics in original.

16 U.S. President's Commission on National Goals, *Goals for Americans,* 15; Warren Weaver, "A Great Age for Science," in ibid., 113; John W. Gardner, "National Goals in Education," in ibid., 81–100.

17 Herbert Stein and Edward F. Denison, "High Employment and Growth in the American Economy," in ibid., 175, 176.

18 Rockefeller Brothers Fund, *Prospect for America,* 251.

19 Free and Cantril, *Political Beliefs of Americans,* 52, 62–66; Almond, *American People,* xxiii.

20 U.S. President's Commission on National Goals, *Goals for Americans,* 18.

21 John J. McCloy, "Foreign Economic Policy and Objectives," in U.S. President's Commission on National Goals, *Goals for Americans,* 352–53.

22 W. Lederer and Burdick, *Ugly American,* 11–12, 24, 205, 208, 226–27, 228. See chap. 22, "A Factual Epilogue."

23 U.S. President's Commission on National Goals, *Goals for Americans,* 15, 17–18; Free and Cantril, *Political Beliefs of Americans,* 77–78.

24 Life Editors, *National Purpose,* 32, 47; U.S. President's Commission on National Goals, *Goals for Americans,* 16–17; Free and Cantril, *Political Beliefs,* 72–75.

25 U.S. President's Commission on National Goals, *Goals for Americans,* 18; William L. Langer, "The United States Role in the World," in ibid., 301.

26 U.S. President's Commission on National Goals, *Goals for Americans,* 20; Free and Cantril, *Political Beliefs of Americans,* 63–64.

27 Rockefeller Brothers Fund, *Prospect for America,* 93, 96, 99, 100, 102.

28 Nixon, in Handlin, *American Principles and Issues,* 9; Life Editors, *National Purpose,* 45, 50; Free and Cantril, *Political Beliefs of Americans,* 83–86.

29 "Russia Today," *National Geographic* 118 (December 1960): 887–88.

30 Hammond, "Firsthand Look at the Soviet Union," 353–57.

31 Ibid., 357–407.

32 Nixon, "Russia as I Saw It," 715–17, 725, 731–35.

33 Burke, "Threat Confronting Us," 334.

34   Killian, *Sputnik, Scientists, and Eisenhower,* 2–3.

35   International Institute for Strategic Studies, *Military Balance,* 1960, 2–6. The title varies. The organization was originally known as the Institute for Strategic Studies.

36   LeMay, *America Is in Danger,* 242; Power, *Design for Survival,* 43, 52. See also Twining, *Neither Liberty Nor Safety,* 4, 267.

37   Shor, "City They Call Red China's Showcase," 192–223.

38   Powell, "Everyone a Soldier," 100–111.

39   U.S. President's Commission on National Goals, *Goals for Americans,* 19.

40   J. F. Dulles, "Policy for Security and Peace," 353–64; "Text of Nixon Reply to Stevenson Attack on the Administration," *New York Times,* March 14, 1954, 44.

41   G. Long, "Indochina Faces the Dragon," 287–316.

42   Eisenhower, *Public Papers,* 1954, 253; G. Long, "Indochina Faces the Dragon," 317–18.

43   Nathan Twining, John Foster Dulles Oral History Collection, 29–30, Princeton University Library; *Foreign Relations of the United States,* 1952–54, 13:953, 1150, 1270–72, 1447–48, 1928.

44   Eisenhower, *Public Papers,* 1954, 306; Samuels, "Passage to Freedom in Viet Nam," 858–74; Chapelle, "Helicopter War in South Viet Nam," 722–54.

45   F. Simpich, Jr., "Changing Formosa," 327–64.

46   Shor, "Life under Shellfire on Quemoy," 414–38; Eisenhower, *White House Years,* 2:691–93. Eisenhower and Dulles earlier worked out their position in papers to each other: Memorandum for the Secretary of State, April 5, 1955, John Foster Dulles Papers, White House Memoranda series, and John Foster Dulles to the President, April 8, 1955, Dwight D. Eisenhower Library.

47   J. F. Dulles, "Report from Asia," *Department of State Bulletin,* March 21, 1955, 459–60, 463; Eisenhower, *Public Papers,* 1955, 332, 358; Eisenhower, *White House Years,* 1:477–78.

48   Conly, "Modern Miracle," 735–91.

49   Minutes of Cabinet Meeting, March 13, 1959, Whitman file, Eisenhower Diary series, box 25, Dwight D. Eisenhower Library; Eisenhower press conference of March 11, 1959, in Eisenhower, *Public Papers,* 1959, 243–45, 252.

50   W. Price, "Thames Mirrors England's Varied Life," 45–93.

51   "Looking for New Role in World—Britain Faces Major Shift," *U.S. News & World Report,* Feb. 8, 1960, 52–53.

52   Webb, "Britain Faces Prosperity," 189–91; "Trouble Ahead for the British Economy," *Business Week,* Jan. 14, 1961, 76–77.

53   "Will the British Commonwealth Hold Together?" *U.S. News & World Report,* May 9, 1960, 80–81; "The Lengthening Shadow," *Time,* May 16, 1960, 24–25; "The Commonwealth Holds a Meeting," *New York Times Magazine,* May 15, 1960, 22.

54   Camps, "Britain, the Six and American Policy," 112–22.

55   Martin, "Biggest City in the World," 24, 25; Shor, "Japan: The Exquisite Enigma," 733–77.

56   "Japan Looks East," *Fortune,* June 1959, 79; "Buying Japanese," *Business Week,* Sept. 19,

1959, 150; "Japan Wins New Global Status," *Business Week,* Jan. 16, 1960, 24; "Japan's Miracle," *U.S. News & World Report,* April 20, 1959, 80–83.

57 "Japan Wins New Global Status," *Business Week,* 24; "Japan After 15 Years: The American Way—But Anti-American Violence," *U.S. News & World Report,* June 20, 1960, 79; "Fast Drive from Japan," *Time,* Aug. 17, 1959, 83; "Yen for Japan's Goods," *Time,* July 4, 1960, 76; "Japan's Miracle," 82.

58 Reischauer, "Broken Dialogue with Japan," 11–26; "Yen for Japan's Goods," *Time,* July 4, 1960, 76; "Japan Looks East," *Fortune,* June 1959, 80.

Chapter 14

1 J. F. Kennedy, *Public Papers,* 1961, 1. The term *Augustan period* relates to the era of Augustus Caesar during the Pax Romana and to the neoclassical period in England, and may well apply to this period of American history.

2 Eisenhower, *Public Papers,* 1960–61, 1037.

3 Nixon, *Speeches, Remarks, Press Conferences, and Study Papers,* 7; J. F. Kennedy, *Speeches, Remarks, Press Conferences, and Statements,* 51–52, 401–2, 510, 986, 1030; and his *Strategy of Peace.*

4 J. F. Kennedy, *Speeches,* 341, 398, 402, 534. For Nixon's critique, see his *Speeches,* 860–61, 982.

5 Ibid., 874, 881.

6 Ibid., 986–87.

7 Ibid., 522, 789, 1068. See also "Kennedy Calls for Sacrifices in U.S. to Help the World Meet Challenges of 'New Frontier,'" *New York Times,* July 16, 1960, 1, 6–7. On Kennedy's foreign policy exertions, see Paterson, *Kennedy's Quest for Victory,* and Fairlie, *Kennedy Promise.*

8 J. F. Kennedy, *Public Papers,* 1962, 357–61.

9 Ibid., 1963, 524–25; Sorensen, *Kennedy,* 600–601. Italics in original.

10 A. Schlesinger, Jr., *Thousand Days,* 884–85.

11 J. F. Kennedy, *Public Papers,* 1961, 143–46.

12 Carey, *Peace Corps,* 115–22; V. Adams, *Peace Corps in Action;* Textor, *Cultural Frontiers.*

13 J. F. Kennedy, *Public Papers,* 1961, 732; 1963, 861.

14 Cochran, Arkin, and Hoenig, *Nuclear Weapons Databook,* vol. 1: *U.S. Nuclear Forces and Capabilities,* 12, 15.

15 Bottome, *Missile Gap;* Licklider, "Missile Gap Controversy," 600–615.

16 Gaither report, Deterrence and Survival in the Nuclear Age: Report to the President by the Security Resources Panel of the Science Advisory Committee, Nov. 7, 1957, White House Office, Office of the Special Assistant for National Security Affairs, NSC series, Dwight D. Eisenhower Library. Italics in original. See Halperin, "Gaither Committee and the Policy Process," 360–84.

17 "Enormous Arms Outlay Is Held Vital to Survival," *Washington Post,* Dec. 20, 1957, A1, A19; Roberts, *First Rough Draft,* 149–50.

18 Phillips, "Growing Missile Gap," 10–16; "The Coming Missile Gap," *Time*, Feb. 8, 1960, 18; Alsop, "Our Gamble with Destiny," 23, 114–18. For varying estimates of the gap, see Bottome, *Missile Gap*, esp. Appendix A.

19 Wohlstetter, "Delicate Balance of Terror," 211–34; Kissinger, *Necessity for Choice*, 26, 39.

20 York, "In Space, It's Russia; In Weapons, 'U.S. Is Catching up Fast,'" 64–66; "It's Russia's Turn to Worry about the 'Missile Gap,'" *U.S. News & World Report*, Feb. 22, 1960, 45–47; Schriever, "1960—Best Year We've Had in the Missile Business," 69–71; "Is World Balance in Missiles Shifting to U.S.?" *U.S. News & World Report*, Jan. 23, 1961, 62–68; "Was There Ever a 'Missile Gap'?—Or Just an 'Intelligence Gap'?" *Newsweek*, Nov. 13, 1961, 23.

21 Eisenhower, *White House Years*, 2:547.

22 Kissinger, *Nuclear Weapons and Foreign Policy*, 145, 199–202.

23 Osgood, *Limited War*, 5.

24 LeMay, *America Is in Danger*, 94; Free and Cantril, *Political Beliefs of Americans*, 90.

25 Eisenhower, *Public Papers*, 1960–61, 1035–40.

26 Ibid., 1045–46.

27 Ibid., 1047; Memorandum of Conference with the President, Dec. 22, 1954, Whitman file, Eisenhower Diary series; Memorandum of Conference with the President, April 2, 1956, Whitman file, Eisenhower Diary series; Memorandum of Conference with the President, Dec. 8, 1960, Whitman file, Eisenhower Diary series, Dwight D. Eisenhower Library.

28 Billard, "Guantánamo: Keystone in the Caribbean," 420–36; J. F. Kennedy, *Public Papers*, 1962, 806–9; R. Kennedy, *Thirteen Days*, 127; U.S. Congress, House, Committee on Appropriations, *Department of Defense Appropriations for 1964: Hearings before a Subcommittee of the Committee on Appropriations*, 88th Cong., 1st sess., 1963 30–31.

29 Sorensen, *Decision-Making in the White House*, 45–47.

30 J. F. Kennedy, *Public Papers*, 1963, 889–90.

31 Ibid., 1963, 897–98. Kennedy repeated the words, "not 'first, but,' not 'first, if,' not 'first, when,' but first—period."

32 A. Schlesinger, Jr., *Thousand Days*, xi; James Reston, "Why America Weeps" and "John Fitzgerald Kennedy," *New York Times*, Nov. 23, 1963, 1, 7, 28; T. White, "For President Kennedy: An Epilogue," *Life*, Dec. 6, 1963, 158–59.

33 Goldwater, *Why Not Victory?* 23, 33–34, 169–70.

34 Ibid., 31; Hofstadter analyzed the Goldwater campaign using unpublished press releases in *Paranoid Style in American Politics*, 93–141.

35 Boorstin, *America and the Image of Europe*, 13–15.

Chapter 15

1 A critique of post–World War II consensus thought is found in Lowi, *End of Liberalism* and *Politics of Disorder*. A pioneering work that studies the New Left is Unger, *Movement*. Bacciocco, *New Left in America*, emphasizes the ideas of the movement. Its development is traced in Jacobs and Landau, *New Radicals*. A debate including Daniel Aaron, Tom Hayden, Richard Rovere, and Dwight Macdonald is "Confrontation: The

Old Left and the New," *American Scholar*, 567–88. A history of the currents of 1960s politics and thought is Matusow, *Unraveling of America*.

2 Lynd, *Intellectual Origins of American Radicalism*, v–vii.

3 Mills, "Letter to the New Left," 18–23; Zinn, *SNCC*, 273.

4 Harrington, *Other America*, 1, 174.

5 Theobald, *Challenge of Abundance*, ix, 3–4, 11, 108; also his *Rich and the Poor, Free Men and Free Markets*, and *Economics of Abundance;* Seligman, *Economics of Dissent*, 190.

6 Goodman, *Compulsory Mis-education*, 9, 14, 105, 141, 180; *Growing up Absurd;* and *Community of Scholars*. See also Goodman, *Like a Conquered Province*, viii.

7 Marcuse, *One-Dimensional Man*, ix–x, xii, 242, 248, 252; also *Essay on Liberation* and *Counterrevolution and Revolt*.

8 Analyses of American society by C. Wright Mills include his early work, *New Men of Power*, 248–49; *White Collar;* and *Power Elite*.

9 Mills, *Causes of World War Three*, 1–2, 62. See also a book of essays published after his death, *Power, Politics and People*.

10 Mills, *Causes of World War Three*, 2, 21–23, 44–45.

11 Ibid., 4–6, 7, 47, 89.

12 Ibid., 23–24, 27, 49, 96, 98, 101–5, 111.

13 Ibid., 4, 7, 136, 142, 148.

14 W. Williams, "American Century," 297–98. Irwin Unger wrote a historiographical critique of the New Left school in American history, " 'New Left' and American History." A collection of essays by New Left historians is in his *Beyond Liberalism*.

15 See, for example, L. Gardner, "From New Deal to New Frontiers," in the first issue of *Studies on the Left* (Fall 1959), 29–43. See also his *Economic Aspects*.

16 W. Williams, "American Century," 299–300. Italics in original.

17 Ibid., 298, 301. Williams discussed the American Century in his provocative study *Tragedy of American Diplomacy* (1959), 147, 152, 166, 179, 182. Williams also cited it in his *America Confronts a Revolutionary World*, 169–70.

18 W. Williams, *Tragedy of American Diplomacy* (1959), 207; G. Kolko, *Politics of War*, 252; *Roots*, 26. See also J. Kolko and G. Kolko, *Limits of Power*.

19 D. Horowitz, *Empire and Revolution*, 58; G. Kolko, *Politics of War*, 265.

20 W. Williams, *Tragedy of American Diplomacy* (1962), 237–38, 261, 266.

21 D. Horowitz, *Empire and Revolution*, 234; G. Kolko, *Roots*, 73–74; W. Williams, *Tragedy of American Diplomacy* (1962), 293.

22 W. Williams, *Tragedy of American Diplomacy* (1962), 271; G. Kolko, *Roots*, 77–78.

23 W. Williams, *Tragedy of American Diplomacy* (1962), 269–70; G. Kolko, *Politics of War*, 279.

24 W. Williams, *Tragedy of American Diplomacy* (1962), 230, 295; Lens, *Forging of the American Empire*, 380.

25 L. Gardner, *Architects of Illusion*, ix–x. Italics in original.

26 G. Kolko, *Politics of War,* 624–25; D. Horowitz, *Empire and Revolution,* 227.

27 D. Horowitz, *Free World Colossus,* 301; Aptheker, *American Foreign Policy,* 120, 184.

Chapter 16

1 In chaps. 1–3 of his memoirs, *Reunion,* Hayden traces his growing up in the 1950s and the beginnings of the movement; his comment on pursuing the American Dream is on p. 16; Hayden, *Trial,* 9–10; Hayden, *Rebellion and Repression,* 22–23.

2 "The Port Huron Statement" is published in Jacobs and Landau, *New Radicals,* 150–62; Hayden, *Reunion,* 83–84.

3 Jacobs and Landau, *New Radicals,* 151, 162; Hayden, *Rebellion in Newark,* 70–71.

4 Hayden, *Trial,* 10, 33, 97, 124. Italics in original.

5 Roszak, *Making of a Counter Culture.*

6 Ginsberg, *Collected Poems,* 126, 146.

7 A. Hoffman, *Revolution for the Hell of It,* 34–36, 58. He wrote under the pseudonym Free.

8 Ibid., 30, 37, 175, 183; J. Rubin, *Growing (up) at Thirty-Seven,* 79.

9 J. Rubin, *Growing (up) at Thirty-Seven,* 58–59; A. Hoffman, *Revolution for the Hell of It,* 199.

10 A. Hoffman, *Revolution for the Hell of It,* 53, 66, 201.

11 Ibid., 105–6.

12 Belz, *Story of Rock;* London, *Closing the Circle.*

13 J. Rubin, *Do It,* 17–19; A. Hoffman, *Revolution for the Hell of It,* 9, 30, 201; Italics in original; "Message Time," *Time,* Sept. 17, 1965, 102; Kramer, "It's Time to Start Listening," 80.

14 "Eve of Destruction," written by P. F. Sloan, sung by Barry McGuire, *Eve of Destruction,* Dunhill Records.

15 "Message Time," 102.

16 "A Hard Rain's A-Gonna Fall," written and sung by Bob Dylan, *The Freewheelin' Bob Dylan,* Columbia Records. On Dylan and his work see Dylan, *Lyrics,* and Herdman, *Voice without Restraint.*

17 "Masters of War," written and sung by Bob Dylan, *The Freewheelin' Bob Dylan,* Columbia Records.

18 "With God on Our Side," written and sung by Bob Dylan, *The Times They Are A-Changin'.*

19 "The Universal Soldier," written by Buffy Sainte-Marie, sung by Donovan, *Fairy Tale,* Hickory Records; "Subterranean Homesick Blues," written and sung by Bob Dylan, *Bringing It All Back Home;* Goodman, *Growing up Absurd;* "Blowin' in the Wind," written and sung by Bob Dylan, *The Freewheelin' Bob Dylan.*

20 "Last Night I Had the Strangest Dream," written by Ed McCurdy, sung by Pete Seeger, *Pete Seeger Sings and Answers Questions at the Ford Hall Forum Boston Massachusetts,* Broadside Records.

21 Friedan, *Feminine Mystique,* 50–52. Friedan refers to Lippmann, "Can We Win the

Peace?" *Ladies' Home Journal*, January 1944, 22–23. She also mentioned Harold Stassen, "Stalin at Midnight," July 1947, 36–37, 116–21. She might also have noted articles in the same magazine by women writers like Dorothy Thompson, "War for What?" 6, 158–59. On the women's movement of the 1960s and its relation to cold war policies, see Swerdlow, *Strike for Peace*.

22 Friedan, *Feminine Mystique*, 123–27, 145–47, 180. Some of Mead's ideas on women that Friedan critiqued are in *And Keep Your Powder Dry*, 99–114.

23 Friedan, *Feminine Mystique*, 182–88, 282–87, 305–9.

24 Millett, *Sexual Politics*, 25, 46.

25 Friedan, *Feminine Mystique*, 125, 370.

26 Morgan, *Sisterhood Is Powerful*, xxxviii.

27 King, *Stride toward Freedom; Testament of Hope*.

28 King, *Stride toward Freedom*, 84–85, 191.

29 King, *Where Do We Go from Here*, 71, 73–74, 89, 188.

30 King, *Stride toward Freedom*, 222; *Why We Can't Wait*, 149.

31 King, *Where Do We Go from Here*, 173, 174.

32 Ibid., 174–75.

33 Ibid., 57, 185.

34 Ibid., 178–79, 184.

35 King, *Stride toward Freedom*, 224; *Where Do We Go From Here*, 190.

36 Carmichael and Hamilton, *Black Power*, vi–ix.

37 Ibid., x–xi.

38 Ibid., 5–6.

39 Ibid., 9–10.

40 Ibid., 23, 25.

41 Ibid., 30–32.

42 Critical analyses of the New Left are Maddox, *New Left and the Origins of the Cold War*, and Tucker, *Radical Left and American Foreign Policy*.

43 Considering the negativism of the New Left is Waltzer, "Young Radicals: A Symposium," 129–63.

44 W. Williams, *Roots of the Modern American Empire*, xxiv, 451.

45 W. Williams, *America Confronts a Revolutionary World*, 181–200; Alperovitz, "Notes toward a Pluralist Commonwealth," 28–48.

46 A. Hoffman, *Revolution for the Hell of It*, 3–5, 18–20. Italics in original. See also 55–56. Hoffman's mother refers to "The Banners of Dissent," *Time*, Oct. 27, 1967, 23–29.

Chapter 17

1 Truman, *Mr. President*, 81–84.

2 L. B. Johnson, *Public Papers*, 1963–64, 742–43; his statement on power also appeared in

his *My Hope for America*, 74. The *New York Times* gave front-page coverage to this speech, "President Says U.S. Power Tops Any Enemy Group," June 4, 1964, 1, 27.

3 Nixon, *Public Papers*, 1970, 409; Kissinger, *American Foreign Policy*, 57–58.

4 Nixon, *Public Papers*, 1971, 886–91. See also 844–45, 925–26.

5 Max Frankel, "The U.S. at an Era's End: Signs in Many Nations Show Change in the World's Power Relationships," *New York Times*, Dec. 22, 1971, 1, 16; "Our New Five-Cornered World," *Life*, Aug. 6, 1971, 4. See also C. L. Sulzberger, "New Balance of Peace," *New York Times*, Nov. 15, 1972, 47; "Out of Sorts with the World," *Life*, Nov. 12, 1971, 4.

6 A. Cantril and Roll, *Hopes and Fears*, 25–29.

7 Hayden, *American Future*, 1.

8 Vance, "Meeting the Challenges of a Changing World," *Department of State Bulletin*, June 1979, 16–19. On Reagan, see *New York Times*, May 11, 1976, 23; and Reagan, *Public Papers*, 1984, 40–44. For a similar assessment, see his *Public Papers*, 1981, 1063.

9 "The Decline of U.S. Power," *Business Week*, March 12, 1979, 36–37; "America—Declining Power?" *U.S. News & World Report*, Nov. 27, 1978, 56.

10 Rosecrance, *America as an Ordinary Country*, 11; P. Kennedy, "(Relative) Decline of America," 29–38, and his *Rise and Fall of the Great Powers;* "Is America in Decline?" *Newsweek*, Feb. 22, 1988, 62–63; Schmeisser, "Is America in Decline?" 24–27, 66–96; Moynihan and Schlesinger, "Debunking the Myth of Decline," 34–36, 52–53; "Introduction," *Foreign Affairs* 66 (Spring 1988): 678; Brzezinski, "America's New Geostrategy," 680–99; and W. Rostow, "Book Review Essay," 863–68. For the continuing debate over the perceptibility of decline, see the contrary opinions of Luttwak, who had earlier written on the strategic statecraft of the Roman Empire during its rise and decline, and Bartley, "Is America on the Way Down?" 15–27.

11 "America's Sources of Greatness," *New York Post*, Nov. 28, 1975, 21; "Anxiety in America's Heartland," *U.S. News & World Report*, April 25, 1988, 24.

12 H. J. Morgenthau, *New Foreign Policy*, 140–41; *Truth and Power*, 241–48.

13 H. J. Morgenthau, *New Foreign Policy*, 141–42.

14 H. J. Morgenthau, "A Talk with Senator McCarthy," *New York Review of Books*, Aug. 22, 1968, 14; repr. in his *Truth and Power*, 193. Brzezinski's edited remarks appeared in "Implications of Change," *Department of State Bulletin*, July 3, 1967, 19–23, and are quoted here from Morgenthau's *New Foreign Policy*, 19; H. J. Morgenthau, "Pathology of American Power," 3.

15 Kissinger, *American Foreign Policy*, 16, 61.

16 L. B. Johnson, *Vantage Point*, 41; and *Public Papers*, 1963–64, 940.

17 L. B. Johnson, *My Hope for America*, 67. See also his *Public Papers*, 1963–64, 929.

18 J. F. Kennedy, *Public Papers*, 1963, 412; L. B. Johnson, *Public Papers*, 1963–64, 930.

19 L. B. Johnson, *Public Papers*, 1963–64, 927; 1965, 395; U.S. Congress, Senate, 88th Cong., 2d sess., 1964, *Congressional Record*, 110:18471.

20 Rusk, *Winds of Freedom*, 179–80.

21 Ibid., 4, 181, 343.

22 L. B. Johnson, *Vantage Point*, 53–54, 363; "Johnson Backs Military Leaders More Firmly Than Ever in Vietnam Visit," *New York Times*, Dec. 24, 1967, 4.

23 L. B. Johnson, *Public Papers,* 1967, 1184–87.

24 W. Williams, *Tragedy of American Diplomacy* (1972), 303–4.

25 D. Horowitz, *Empire and Revolution,* 230; G. Kolko, *Roots,* 131–32.

26 W. Williams, *Tragedy of American Diplomacy* (1972), 312. Several works pictured American society in the throes of a revolution: Lewis, *Comes the Revolution;* Berger and Neuhaus, *Movement and Revolution;* Reich, *Greening of America;* Slomich, *American Nightmare.*

27 Hayden, *Love of Possession,* 4–6.

28 Lynd and Hayden, *Other Side,* 57.

29 Ibid., 69, 74–76, 185.

30 Hayden, *Love of Possession,* 5, 32–34, 98–100.

31 Ibid., 90. Italics in original.

32 Ginsberg, *Collected Poems,* 369, 382, 398–99, 432–33, 441–42, 444–45, 490–91. Italics in original. On MacLeish, see his "A Great Power—Or a Great People?" *New York Times,* Nov. 19, 1972, sec. 4, p. 11.

33 Brackman, "My Generation," 127–29. As for the reference to "no Negro," the film included an extended newsreel-like tribute to blacks, who were nevertheless segregated into this part. Another episode did include a Korean War veteran. Perhaps scenes were cut in a film version edited for television.

34 A. Hoffman, *Revolution for the Hell of It,* 178; L. B. Johnson, *This America,* 12–13. The photographs in the book were taken by Ken Heyman and the text was from the president's speeches.

35 A. Hoffman, "America on $0 a Day," 49–55.

36 A. Hoffman, *Revolution for the Hell of It,* 3–4, 61.

37 Ibid., 13–14, 82–84.

38 King, *Trumpet of Conscience,* 22–24.

39 Ibid., 25–27, 30–31.

40 Ibid., 31–32, 37, 41, 49.

41 "Guards Repulse War Protestors at the Pentagon," *New York Times,* Oct. 22, 1967, sec. 1, pp. 1, 58; "The Banners of Dissent," *Time,* Oct. 27, 1967, 23–29; A. Hoffman, *Revolution for the Hell of It,* 42–47.

42 Disenchantment with American policy among mainstream policymakers and scholars is evident in Pfeffer, *No More Vietnams?*

43 Boorstin, *Americans: The Democratic Experience,* 557–98; his *Decline of Radicalism,* 121–34; and *Democracy and Its Discontents.* See also Boorstin, "'American Century'—Myth vs. Reality," 64–67.

44 Hofstadter and Wallace, *American Violence,* 40; A. Schlesinger, Jr., *Crisis of Confidence,* 185, 192–93. See also Schlesinger's *Bitter Heritage,* and Handlin, *Distortion of America,* ix–xi.

45 A. Hacker, *End of the America Era,* 3, 7, 76, 208, 230; L. Hacker, *Triumph of American Capitalism.*

46 Nixon, *Public Papers,* 1971, 812. See also 768, 845.

47 Kissinger was interviewed by William F. Buckley, Jr., on *Firing Line*, PBS, Sept. 13, 1975; "Partial Transcript of an Interview with Kissinger on the State of the Western World," *New York Times*, Oct. 13, 1974, 34–35; the interview also appeared in *Department of State Bulletin*, Nov. 11, 1974, 629–42.

48 Toynbee, *America and the World Revolution*, 78, 92–93.

49 Arnold J. Toynbee, "Colonialism and the United States," in Houghton, *Struggle against History*, xxxii.

50 Ibid., xxxiii–xxxviii.

51 James Reston, "Professor Toynbee Looks to the Future," *New York Times*, Dec. 6, 1972, 47. Toynbee had written with favor of the hippie movement in his three-part series for the *San Francisco Chronicle*, concluding with "Hippie Revolt on War," May 18, 1967, 1, 18.

52 D. Horowitz, *Free World Colossus*, 434; Fulbright, *Arrogance of Power*, 19; E. McCarthy, *Limits of Power*, 238. "The Score: Rome 1,500, U.S. 200," *Time*, Aug. 23, 1976, 58–59, draws similar historical parallels.

53 Riesman, *Lonely Crowd*, "Twenty Years After—A Second Preface" (1970), xviii; Potter, "Social Cohesion and the Crisis of Law," in *History and American Society*, 389–418.

54 Niebuhr, "Toward New Intra-Christian Endeavors," 1662–63.

55 Fulbright, *Old Myths and New Realities*, 41–44; *Arrogance of Power*, 182, 199.

56 Fulbright, *Crippled Giant*, 100, 102.

57 Kennan, *Memoirs*, 1:356–61, 367.

58 A. Cantril and Roll, *Hopes and Fears*, 31–50.

59 Nixon, *Public Papers*, 1970, 409; 1971, 220.

60 Johnson, *Public Papers*, 1967, 1051–53.

61 "The Use of Power with a Passion for Peace," *Time*, cover story on McGeorge Bundy, June 25, 1965, 26.

62 "Vietnam Dialogue: Mr. Bundy and the Professors," *CBS News Special Report*, CBS TV, June 21, 1965. Participants: McGeorge Bundy, Hans Morgenthau, Zbygniew Brzezinski, Edmund O. Clubb, Guy J. Pauker, John. D. Donoghue; moderator: Eric Sevareid.

63 Bundy, Remarks at DePauw University, Oct. 12, 1968, in *Law, Liberty and Progress* (n.p.: DePauw University, n.d.), 2, 4, 5–7, 11, 16.

64 Hayden, *Rebellion and Repression* includes the testimony by Tom Hayden before the National Commission on the Causes and Prevention of Violence, and the House Un-American Activities Committee.

65 Hayden, *Rebellion and Repression*, 21–22.

66 Ibid., 26–27, 31, 36–37, 178–79.

67 Ibid., 31, 44–45, 72, 75.

68 Hayden, *Trial*, 4. See also Hayden's "The Trial," *Ramparts*, July 1970, the entire issue.

69 Ibid., 9, 15–17, 64–65, 77.

70 A. Hoffman, *Revolution for the Hell of It*, 60–61.

71 Kissinger, *American Foreign Policy*, 7, 194–95; Nixon, *Public Papers*, 1969, 909.

72 J. Magruder, *American Life,* 178–79, 196–97; J. Rubin's wish that he had been kidnapped to increase his credibility is in *Growing (up) at Thirty-Seven,* 8.

73 A. Cantril and Roll, *Hopes and Fears,* 31–36.

Chapter 18

1 "The House of Brass," *Time,* July 2, 1951, 16–19; Mills, *Power Elite,* 186–87.

2 McNamara, *Essence of Security,* 87, 144; U.S. Department of Commerce, *Statistical Abstract,* 1972, 257; International Institute for Strategic Studies, *Military Balance,* 1969–70, 1–10. See also L. B. Johnson, *Public Papers,* 1963–64, 742–43.

3 McNamara, *Essence of Security,* 57–58; Cochran, Arkin, and Hoenig, *Nuclear Weapons Databook,* vol. 1: *U.S. Nuclear Forces and Capabilities,* 12, 15; Nixon, *Public Papers,* 1970, 173.

4 Heilbroner, *Limits of American Capitalism,* 105.

5 U.S. Department of Commerce, *Historical Statistics,* 1116.

6 McNamara, *Essence of Security,* 88; L. B. Johnson, *My Hope for America,* 68.

7 Melman, *Our Depleted Society,* 3–4.

8 Melman, *Pentagon Capitalism,* 1–3.

9 Mills, *Causes of World War Three,* 121.

10 Melman, *Pentagon Capitalism,* 3.

11 Galbraith, *New Industrial State,* 338–40.

12 Galbraith, *How to Control the Military,* 18, 54–55, 61.

13 "U.S. Steel Tax Case," *New York Times,* Feb. 23, 1972, 64.

14 Galbraith, *How to Control the Military,* 34.

15 U.S. Department of Commerce, *Statistical Abstract,* 1975, 316, 734; Kruzel, *American Defense Annual,* 209–20.

16 Bowen, "Vietnam War," *Fortune,* 119–22.

17 Leonard Silk, "America in the World Economy," in Rosecrance, *America as an Ordinary Country,* 160; Samuelson, *Economics* (1973), 715, 719.

18 Bergsten, "New Economics and U.S. Foreign Policy," 202.

19 "U.S. Superiority Has Ended," *U.S. News & World Report,* April 5, 1971, 49–50.

20 Iklé, "What It Means to Be Number Two," 72–84; J. Carter, *Public Papers,* 1980–81, 2977.

21 On Reagan, see *New York Times,* May 11, 1976, 23; Reagan, *Public Papers,* 1986, 125; 1988, 84–85; and Reagan, "I Had a Plan . . . to Deal from Strength," 31.

22 Melman, *Profits without Production,* xviii, 3–4, 238. See also his "The Butter That's Traded off for Guns," *New York Times,* April 22, 1985, A19.

23 Galbraith, *Economics in Perspective,* 257.

24 Sivard, *World Military and Social Expenditures,* 1978, 11–13.

25 Leontief and Duchin, *Military Spending,* 3, 64, 66.

26 "Ike's Lesson, Unlearned," *New York Times,* Jan. 21, 1986, A30. See also Flora Lewis, "'You Will!' I Won't!" ibid., Aug. 10, 1984, A25.

27 "U.S. Poll Puts the Economy over Military in Importance," ibid., Nov. 11, 1987, A26.

28 "U.S. to Get Japanese Arms Technology," ibid., Nov. 9, 1983, A3; "Japan to Sell U.S. Arms Technology," July 3, 1985, A7.

29 Bergsten, "Economic Imbalance," 771.

30 Commager, *Living Ideas in America,* 605; "3 Peaceful Years in 3 Decades," *U.S. News & World Report,* Feb. 12, 1973, 24–25.

31 Commager, *Living Ideas in America,* 605–8.

32 Commager, "200 Plus 1," 6.

33 Cooke, *Alistair Cooke's America,* 335, 353, 356, 359–63.

34 Lapp, *Weapons Culture,* 12, 171.

35 Mills, *Power Elite,* 3–4, 27, 292, 294. Italics in original.

36 King, *Trumpet of Conscience,* 22–23; King, *Where Do We Go from Here,* 86.

37 Galbraith, "Second Imperial Requiem," 92.

38 "Old Missile Silos: A Burden for Buyers," *New York Times,* June 3, 1987, B1; Cooke, *Alistair Cooke's America,* 359–63.

Chapter 19

1 Nixon, *Public Papers,* 1971, 669, 895. See also Peterson, "America: Still the Top Producer, But . . . ," 34–37. Herman Kahn predicted future American GNP in a piece in *U.S. News & World Report,* May 9, 1983, A42.

2 U.S. Department of Commerce, *Historical Statistics,* 224–25; Nixon, *Public Papers,* 1970, 1134–36; "Nixon Is 5 Minutes (or $2.3-Million) Late at Rite for $1-Trillion G.N.P.," *New York Times,* Dec. 16, 1970, 1, 31.

3 Goodman, *Compulsory Mis-education,* 75; Samuelson, *Economics* (1973), ix; Donella Meadows, *Limits to Growth.*

4 "U.S. in the World Economy: The Changing Role," *U.S. News & World Report,* Sept. 10, 1984, 60–61.

5 "After Many Years As Richest Nation . . . ," *U.S. News & World Report,* Sept. 24, 1973, 66–67.

6 Carson, *Silent Spring,* 1–3, 5–9. Works criticizing the exploitation of the environment include Udall, *Quiet Crisis;* Ekirch, *Man and Nature in America;* R. Rienow and L. Rienow, *Moment in the Sun;* A. Adams, *Eleventh Hour;* and Mines, *Last Days of Mankind.*

7 Theobald, *Habit and Habitat,* 1–11, 31.

8 "U.S. Becoming a 'Have Not' in Raw Materials—What To Do?" *U.S. News & World Report,* Dec. 4, 1972, 81–84. On the growing dependence of the United States on natural resources from abroad, see L. Brown, *World without Borders.*

9 "U.S. Becoming a 'Have Not' in Raw Materials," 81; "As the U.S. Runs Low on Oil and Gas," *U.S. News & World Report,* March 27, 1972, 35.

10 Nixon, *Public Papers,* 1973, 916–22; "U.S. Oil Shortages Seem Unavoidable to Many Analysts," *New York Times,* Feb. 17, 1987, A1 D5.

11 Nixon, *Public Papers, 1971*, 934–37.

12 Ginzberg, "Is Hard Work Going out of Style?" 52–53; "Spotlight on 'Productivity'—Why It's a Key to U.S. Problems," *U.S. News & World Report*, Oct. 4, 1971, 26–27; Riesman, 1969 preface to *Lonely Crowd* (1970), xix.

13 "G.M.'s Vega Plant Closed by Strike," *New York Times*, March 7, 1972, 42; "The Bullet Biters," *Newsweek*, Feb. 7, 1972, 65–66.

14 "America vs. Japan: Can U.S. Workers Compete?" *U.S. News & World Report*, Sept. 2, 1985, 40–42; Vogel, "'Copy the Japanese,'" 45.

15 U.S. National Commission on Excellence in Education, *Nation at Risk* 5–7.

16 Ibid., 8–9; Ravitch and Finn, *What Do Our 17-Year-Olds Know?* 49, 51, 71.

17 T. Bell, "Japanese Schools: 'There Is Much We Can Learn,'" 43; "Memorizing vs. Thinking," *Newsweek*, Jan. 12, 1987, 60–61.

18 Malcolm W. Browne, "A Look at Success of Young Asians," *New York Times*, March 25, 1986, C3.

19 Cooke, quoted in *U.S. News & World Report*, July 6, 1987, 13.

20 "Sarnoff Sees Gap in Technology," *New York Post*, June 5, 1975, 16; Roche, "American Business Is Plainly in Trouble," 92; Ramo, *America's Technology Slip*, 63.

21 "Now It's a 'Technology Gap' That Threatens America," *U.S. News & World Report*, June 7, 1971, 22; Ramo, *America's Technology Slip*, 51.

22 "Steel Woes—How Acute?" *New York Times*, Oct. 17, 1977, 51; "The Fight to Save Bethlehem," May 21, 1986, D1, D6; "LTV Problems Stir Concerns On Survival of Steel Industry," July 28, 1986, A1, D11.

23 Henry Ford II, quoted in "Despite Detroit's Minicars, The Imports Keep Booming," *U.S. News & World Report*, June 7, 1971, 18; Henry Ford II and Lee A. Iacocca, "To the Stockholders, Ford Motor Company, *Ford Annual Report, 1971*, 2.

24 Henry Ford II, quoted in "Why G.M. Needs Toyota," *New York Times*, Feb. 16, 1983, D3; Toyota ad, ibid., May 6, 1986, D9.

25 W. Magruder, "For the SST," 68; "Nixon and Pompidou Meet in Azores, but Hope for Early Accord Fades," *New York Times* Dec. 14, 1971, 10; Nixon, *Public Papers, 1971*, 1185.

26 "Pan Am Plans Sale of Pacific Routes to United Airlines", *New York Times*, April 23, 1985, A1, D19; Pan Am Corporation, *Annual Report, 1985*, 3; "Its Cash Depleted, Pan Am Shuts," *New York Times*, Dec. 5, 1991, D1, D6; Japan Air Lines ad, Feb. 11, 1986, B20.

27 Morita, "Sometimes a Problem Is Overexaggerated," 51–52.

28 U.S. Department of Commerce, *Historical Statistics*, 884–85.

29 "First U.S. Deficit in Trade Since '93 Called Possible," *New York Times*, July 28, 1971, 1, 55.

30 For a discussion of the American trade balance in 1971, see Paul A. Samuelson, *Economics* (1973), 655–59.

31 *New York Times*, Jan. 26, 1972, 45; Bergsten, "New Economics and U.S. Foreign Policy," 202–4; "The Trade Surplus That Vanished," *Fortune*, August 1971, 22; Rose, "U.S. Foreign Trade," 109.

32 U.S. Department of Commerce, *Statistical Abstract*, 1987, 791–95.

33 Samuelson, *Economics* (1973), 716.

34 Galbraith, *Economics in Perspective*, 1–2, 256–57, 294–95.

35 M. Long, "Baja California's Rugged Outback," 548–49; "What's Cooking? Don't Sniff, It's a Diesel Stew," *New York Times*, July 13, 1987, A4; Terrill, "Sichuan," 288–89; "Reporter's Notebook: Costly, Uneasy Kuwait," *New York Times*, July 28, 1987, A1; Alireza, "Women of Saudi Arabia," 436; "Pretoria Hoists a Human Shield," *U.S. News & World Report*, Aug. 18, 1986, 8; P. White, "A Little Humanity," 677.

36 Robert Kasten, quoted in *U.S. News & World Report*, June 29, 1987, 9.

37 "Japanese Light up Times Sq." *New York Times*, March 2, 1982, D21.

38 Iacocca, "We're a Colony Again," 63.

39 "The Yankee Trader: Death of a Salesman?" *U.S. News & World Report*, April 8, 1985, 64.

40 "Nakasone Urges Japanese People to 'Buy Foreign,'" *New York Times*, April 10, 1985, A1; "The Wary Shoppers of Japan," April 12, 1985, D1, D18.

41 Nixon, *Public Papers*, 1971, 888.

42 *New York Times*, Aug. 16, 1971, 1; "Nixon's Grand Design for Recovery," *Time*, Aug. 30, 1971, 4–18.

43 Nixon, *Public Papers*, 1971, 888–89; "Excerpts from Connally News Conference on Nixon Administration Economic Steps," *New York Times*, Aug. 17, 1971, 16.

44 Leonard Silk, "America in the World Economy," in Rosecrance, *America as an Ordinary Country*, 159–61; *New York Times*, Aug. 16, 1971, 15; Samuelson, "At Last, Devaluation," 37.

45 Nixon, *Public Papers*, 1971, 1196; Lorie Tarshis, quoted in *New York Times*, Dec. 22, 1971, 54.

46 "Excerpts from Connally News Conference," 16; Samuelson, "At Last, Devaluation," 37; Frazer B. Wilde, quoted in *New York Times*, Dec. 15, 1971, 95.

47 "Is the Dollar Headed for More Trouble?" *U.S. News & World Report*, July 10, 1972, 20; *New York Daily News*, Jan. 7, 1988, 38.

48 C. L. Sulzberger, "An End and a Beginning," *New York Times*, Oct. 10, 1971, sec. 4, p. 15.

49 Krause, "Why Exports Are Becoming Irrelevant," 62–70; Robert Gilpin, "The Multinational Corporation and American Foreign Policy," in Rosecrance, *America as an Ordinary Country*, 185; Rose, "U.S. Foreign Trade," 186.

50 Miller, "Federal Reserve Chief's Blueprint," 72.

51 "A Nation in Debt," *U.S. News & World Report*, Feb. 18, 1985, 80; "Suddenly, the International Debt Crisis Is Close to Home," *New York Times*, March 3, 1985, sec. 4, p. 3; Bergsten, "Economic Imbalances," 794; "Current Account Gap Grew in Quarter, Confirming U.S. Is Net Debtor Nation," *Wall Street Journal*, Sept. 17, 1985, 3; "U.S. Turns into Debtor Nation," *New York Times*, Sept. 17, 1985, D1, D29; Reagan, *Public Papers*, 1985, 1107–8; "America in Hock to the World," *New York Times*, Feb. 21, 1984, A22.

52 Fry, *Financial Invasion of the U.S.A.*, 3. See also M. Tolchin and S. Tolchin, *Buying into America*.

53 U.S. Department of Commerce, *Statistical Abstract*, 1987, 780; "The Buying of America," *Newsweek*, Nov. 27, 1978, 78–88. See also Prestowitz, *Trading Places*.

54 "America on the Auction Block," *U.S. News & World Report*, March 30, 1987, 56–57;

"For Sale: America," *Time*, Sept. 14, 1987, 52. See also "For Sale America," *Readers Digest*, July 1988, 69–72.

55 "BankAmerica Confirms Investment by Japanese," *New York Times*, Oct. 8, 1987, D1, D19; "Penguin Agrees to Buy New American Library," Oct. 1, 1986, C23; "G.E. to Sell Its Holding in RCA/Ariola Records," Sept. 10, 1986, D1, D5; "A.M.C.'s Long, Hard Struggle," March 10, 1987, D1, D9; "Sony to Buy CBS Records for $2 Billion in Cash," Nov. 19, 1987, D1, D5.

56 "Is Bigger Better in Banking?" *U.S. News & World Report*, Oct. 12, 1987, 52–53; "Japanese Thrust in Wall Street," *New York Times*, March 25, 1987, D1, D4.

57 "Japanese Pushing up Prices of U.S. Commercial Property," *New York Times*, Dec. 15, 1986, A1, D5.

58 "Buying of America," *Newsweek*, 79–81; "Takeover by Japanese Hasn't Hurt after All, Quasar Workers Find," *Wall Street Journal*, Oct. 10, 1978, 1, 41.

59 "Where the Jobs Are," *Newsweek*, Feb. 2, 1987, 42–48.

60 "Why G.M. Needs Toyota," *New York Times*, Feb. 16, 1983, D1, D3; "Chevy Turns to the Japanese," Oct. 6, 1983, D1, D3.

61 "Foreign Aid Bill Beaten," *New York Times*, Oct. 30, 1971, 1, 10; C. L. Sulzberger, "Nothing Fails Like Success," ibid., April 28, 1973, 33; "Bush Tells Cairo Aid Can't Increase," Aug. 5, 1986, A3; "African Press Greets Schultz with Doubts, Jan. 12, 1987, A3.

62 "Japanese Power Soars in New York," *New York Times*, June 9, 1987, B1, B8; "At New York Nightclubs, It's In to Be Asian," Jan. 2, 1989, 15, 20.

Chapter 20

1 "SEATO, 23 Years Old, Pulls down Its Flags," *New York Times*, July 1, 1977, A3; C. L. Sulzberger, "An Alliance That Never Was," June 29, 1977, A23.

2 "CENTO and SEATO; Some Old Alliances Fade Away," ibid., May 22, 1977, sec. 4, p. 4.

3 Nixon, *Public Papers*, 1970, 116, 118. Nixon's report was reprinted by Bantam books as *United States Foreign Policy for the 1970's: A Strategy for Peace* in 1970.

4 "World Business: Hard Work and Vast U.S. Investment Begin to Pay Off," *Time*, Dec. 28, 1959, 52–53; U.S. Department of Commerce; *Historical Statistics*, 225; Sulzberger, "The Shape of Europe to Come: I," *New York Times*, Aug. 9, 1972, 37.

5 "British Economy Facing Uphill Fight," *New York Times*, Sept. 6, 1974, 45.

6 Max Lerner, "Can Britain Survive?" *New York Post*, Sept. 29, 1975, 31; his "How Britain Could Wake," ibid., Oct. 1, 1975, 59; and his "British Twilight," ibid., March 4, 1974, 29.

7 "The British Failure," *New York Times*, March 10, 1974, sec. 3, p. 13; "Britain Adrift: Are the Old Values a Handicap, or the Saving Grace?" Oct. 9, 1985, A1, A16; "Will There Always Be an England?" *Frontline*, PBS, June 10, 1986.

8 "Britain Obtains Loan from Iran; Revamps Taxes to Aid Economy," *New York Times*, July 23, 1974, 1, 51; "Thatcher's Self-Help Revolution," *U.S. News & World Report*, May 9, 1988, 38; "After Dusting Cobwebs of Victoriana, Goodbye," *New York Times*, Sept. 30, 1987, A4.

9 "Britain Confirms Cuts in Defense Spending and Provokes a Protest by NATO," *New York Times*, March 20, 1975, 5; R. W. Apple, Jr., "British Fleet Pays Tribute to Queen," ibid., June 29, 1977, A3.

10 Henry A. Kissinger, "The Year of Europe," *Department of State Bulletin,* May 14, 1973, 593–98.

11 Samuelson, *Economics* (1967), 707; "The New Champion," *Newsweek,* Feb. 7, 1972, 35; "Putting America on Its Metal," *New York Times,* Jan. 30, 1972, sec. 4, p. 4; "Soviet Is World's Top Oil Producer," Sept. 4, 1975, 57; "Soviet Merchant Fleet 5th in World, Ahead of U.S.," Dec. 27, 1972, 78; "Can Russia Surpass America?" *U.S. News & World Report,* May 15, 1972, 29–32.

12 La Fay, "Russia's Window on the West: Leningrad," 636, 652.

13 Laird, "Why Soviet Arms Worry U.S.," 41–46; Nixon, *Public Papers,* 1972, 664; Kissinger, "Remarks," *Department of State Bulletin,* July 10, 1972, 40–49.

14 "Revolution 1987, Soviet Style," *New York Times,* July 1, 1987, A26; "Gorbachev's Revolution," *U.S. News & World Report,* Nov. 9, 1987, 68–79, and "Lenin's Dream Gone Berserk," March 7, 1988, 78.

15 "Students in a Moscow School Debate the Once-Undebatable," *New York Times,* Oct. 20, 1988, A1, A10; "Gorbachev Sets the Beat for Soviet Rock," *U.S. News & World Report,* Feb. 8, 1988, 8; "In Moscow, A New Era?" *New York Times,* July 29, 1987, A2, and "Moscow Saturday Night," Sept. 26, 1988, A22; "Gorby's Gamble: Experts Hopeful," *New York Post,* Oct. 31, 1987, 13.

16 Kennan, "Communism in Russian History," 176.

17 "Japan's Drive to Outstrip U.S.," *U.S. News & World Report,* April 6, 1970, 26–28; "Japan's Drive to Pass U.S. as Top Industrial Power," ibid., April 26, 1971, 60–63.

18 McDowell, "Those Successful Japanese," 326, 327, 341.

19 Vogel, *Japan as Number One,* viii; "Pax Nipponica?" 752; Prestowitz, *Trading Places,* 3–25.

20 Prestowitz, *Trading Places,* 3–25; "When Japan Speaks, the World Listens," *U.S. News & World Report,* May 19, 1986, 65–66; "Japan Is Said to Be Richest," *New York Times,* Aug. 22, 1989, D3.

21 McDowell, "Those Successful Japanese," 332.

22 Ibid., 342; Fallows, "Behind Japan's 'Free Ride' to Prosperity," 12. *Science* devoted its issue of July 18, 1986, to an examination of the rapid advances in Japanese science. On trade, see Bergsten and Cline, *United States–Japan Economic Problem.*

23 McDowell, "Those Successful Japanese," 333.

24 "Who Really Won World War II in Asia?" *U.S. News & World Report,* Dec. 13, 1971, 67; T. White, "Danger from Japan," 19, 22; Fallows, "Is Japan the Enemy?" 31–37.

25 McDowell, "Those Successful Japanese," 338–39, 347, 358. See also Fallows, "Is Japan the Enemy?" 31–37.

26 Reed, "Asia's Four Little Dragons," 131–35; Judge, "Saturday's Child, Hong Kong," 541–44, 550–51.

27 "Southeast Asia Talks Face Major Shift," *New York Times,* Dec. 14, 1987, A14; "Asia's Newest Success Story," *U.S. News & World Report,* Nov. 3, 1986, 55–56; Linder, *Pacific Century.* See also the cover topic, "The Pacific Century?" of *Foreign Affairs* 72 (November/December 1993).

28 Topping, "Return to Changing China," 808, 816–17, 822–23; "China: New Long March, New Revolution" and "One Leads, a Billion Follow," *U.S. News & World Report,* Sept. 8, 1986, 28–29, 70.

29 Topping, "Return to Changing China," 801–33.

30 Arne J. de Keijzer, "The Old China, and the New," *New York Times,* June 1, 1988, A31.

31 Salzman, *Iron and Silk,* 7–12, 17, 26, 40–43, 61–62, 83–84.

32 Salisbury, "Stand by for a Billion Iacoccas," 30.

33 "China: New Long March, New Revolution," *U.S. News & World Report,* Sept. 8, 1986, 26, 31; "China's Proud Space Program," *New York Times,* May 19, 1986, D10.

34 "Changing Alignments," *Wall Street Journal,* Oct. 27, 1971, 22.

35 Nixon, *Public Papers,* 1972, 369, 370; Nixon, *RN: The Memoirs,* 577.

36 Kristof, "Rise of China," 59; Harvey, "There Was a Nation . . . ," 51.

37 "One Leads, a Billion Follow," *U.S. News & World Report,* 70; ibid., Sept. 14, 1987, 9.

38 "Up from Chaos: Black Africa after 10 Years of Freedom," *U.S. News & World Report,* July 6, 1970, 52–55; "Black Africa a Decade Later," *Time,* Feb. 1, 1971, 37–39; Putman, "Yesterday's Congo, Today's Zaire," 398, 407, 423. Recognition of the looming growth of vast regions of the world was by Heilbroner, *Great Ascent.*

39 Judge, "Zulus: Black Nation in a Land of Apartheid," 738–75.

40 Azzi, "Oman," 205, 222; "Successors Ready, U.S. Oilmen Bow out of Their Saudi Empire," *New York Times,* April 1, 1989, 4.

41 "A Better Yesterday," *Economist,* Oct. 26, 1991, 3–4.

42 "Thunder from the East: The U.S.-Japanese Trade War," *Adam Smith's Money World,* WNET-TV, April 16, 1986.

43 Packard, "Coming U.S.-Japan Crisis," 358; Linder, *Pacific Century,* 68.

44 "What the World Thinks of America," *Newsweek,* July 11, 1983, 44–52.

45 Ibid., 44–52.

46 "Poll in West Europe Finds U.S. Prestige Lowest in 22 Years," *New York Times,* Oct. 21, 1976, 1, 44.

47 "Mexicans, in a Poll, Say They Consider U.S. to Be a Friend," *New York Times,* Nov. 17, 1986, A1, A8.

48 Nixon, *Public Papers,* 1971, 804–7.

49 A. Cantril and Roll, *Hopes and Fears,* 29, 41–42; J. Johnson, "New Generation of Isolationists," 136, 139; "Excerpts from the Interview Granted by President Nixon on Foreign Affairs," *New York Times,* March 10, 1971, 14; Tucker, *New Isolationism,* 12–13, 36–37, 95. See also Steel, "Spheres of Influence Policy," 107–18; Roskin, "What 'New Isolationism'?" 118–27; Laqueur, *Neo-Isolationism and the World of the Seventies;* "Is America Going Isolationist?" *U.S. News & World Report,* June 28, 1971, 24–31; L. B. Johnson, *America Tomorrow.*

50 Fulbright, *Crippled Giant,* 160–61.

51 L. B. Johnson, *Public Papers,* 1963–64, 1164. See also 1390–91.

52 Acheson, *Present at the Creation,* xvii; L. B. Johnson, *Vantage Point,* 560; Nixon, *RN: The Memoirs,* 1088–90.

53 J. Rubin, *Growing (up) at Thirty-Seven,* 1–2, 7; Collier and D. Horowitz, *Destructive Generation,* 11–17; Hayden, *American Future,* 1–3, 12.

Notes to Pages 423–26

54 Spiro, *New Foreign Policy Consensus?* 7; "What Ever Became of the American Center?" *Time,* Dec. 19, 1983, 89; Chace, "Is a Foreign Policy Consensus Possible?" 1–16.

55 A. Schlesinger, Jr., *Disuniting of America,* 41. See also "The Fraying of America," *Time,* Feb. 3, 1992, 44–49.

56 Reagan, *Public Papers,* 1987, 454; 1988, 90.

57 Kissinger and Vance, "Bipartisan Objectives," 899–900; "Is America Better off These Days?" *U.S. News & World Report,* April 2, 1984, 26–27; "Foreign Policy Costing Reagan Public Support," *New York Times,* Sept. 30, 1983, A1, A8; Quester, *American Foreign Policy,* 1–4, 255; Rosenau and Holsti, "U.S. Leadership in a Shrinking World," 368–92; and Holsti and Rosenau, *American Leadership in World Affairs.* See also "America's Upbeat Mood," *Time,* Sept. 24, 1984, 10–17. No consensus existed on the past either. See "The Lessons of Vietnam," *Newsweek,* May 16, 1988, 40; "History and Hindsight: Lessons from Vietnam," *New York Times,* April 30, 1985, A1, A6; Stanley Karnow, "Why Interest in the Vietnam War Is Rekindled," *New York Times,* April 15, 1985, A19; Ben Wattenberg, "Vietnam: The Myths They Tell," *New York Post,* April 13, 1985, 19. Both sides of the argument over Vietnam are in Lomperis, *War Everyone Lost—and Won.*

58 "U.N. Tells Reagan It Must Have U.S. Money," *New York Times,* Oct. 28, 1987, A5; "U.S. to Pay $90 Million Owed to U.N. to Ease Budget Crisis," Nov. 24, 1987, A1; "U.S. to Withdraw from UNESCO Role at End of Month," Dec. 20, 1984, A1, A10; "U.S. Voids Role of World Court on Latin Policy," April 9, 1984, A1, A8; "U.S. Plans to Quit World Court Case on Nicaragua Suit," Jan. 19, 1985, 1, 4; "U.S. Plans to Quit the World Court in Political Cases," Oct. 7, 1985, A1, A6; "5-Nation Poll on U.N. Finds Hope and Frustration," June 26, 1985, A8; "Foreign Policy Costing Reagan Public Support," Sept. 30, 1983, A1, A8; "U.S. Has Received $50 Billion in Pledges for War," Feb. 11, 1991, A13.

59 "The End of the U.S.S.R.," *Time,* Dec. 23, 1991, 18–22; Edwards, "Mother Russia," 2–37; P. White, "Hanoi," 558–93; "Saigon," 604–21; and "Laos," 776–77, 787, 789.

Manuscript Sources

Dulles, John Foster. Papers. Princeton University Library, Princeton, N.J.

Eisenhower, Dwight D. Papers. Dwight D. Eisenhower Library, Abilene, Kan.

Hull, Cordell. Papers. Library of Congress, Washington, D.C.

Joint Chiefs of Staff. Records. Modern Military Branch, National Archives, Washington, D.C.

Kennedy, John F. Papers. John Fitzgerald Kennedy Library, Boston, Mass.

LaGuardia, F. H. Radio Broadcasts. New York University Library, New York, N.Y.

Lippmann, Walter. Papers. Yale University Library, New Haven, Conn.

Luce, Henry. Papers. Time, Inc., Archives. New York, N.Y.

Pan American World Airways. Archives. New York, N.Y.

Roosevelt, Franklin D. Papers. Franklin D. Roosevelt Library, Hyde Park, N.Y.

Time, Inc. Archives. New York, N.Y.

Truman, Harry S. Papers. Harry S. Truman Library, Independence, Mo.

U.S. Department of State. Archives. Washington, D.C.

Wallace, Henry A. Papers. University of Iowa Library, Iowa City.

Periodicals

Magazines

American Magazine.
Architectural Forum.
Atlantic Monthly.
Business Topics.
Business Week.
Changing Times.
Christian Century.
Collier's.
Commentary.
Commonweal.
Decision.
Economist.
Esquire.
Fortune.
Free World.
Harper's.
Ladies' Home Journal.
Life.
Look.
Nation.
New Republic.
Newsweek.
New Yorker.
Ramparts.
Reader's Digest.
Saturday Evening Post.
Saturday Review.

Science.
Scientific American.
Television Age.
This Week Magazine.
Time.
U.S. News & World Report (United States News).
Variety.
Vital Speeches of the Day.
Western World.

Journals

American Historical Review.
American Political Science Review.
American Quarterly.
American Scholar.
American Sociological Review.
Annals of the Academy of Political and Social Science.
Antioch Review.
Bulletin of the Atomic Scientists.
Christianity and Crisis.
Department of State Bulletin.
Dissent.
Far Eastern Surrey.
Foreign Affairs.

Foreign Policy.
Foreign Policy Bulletin.
Foreign Policy Reports.
Harvard Business Review.
International Conciliation.
International Security.
Journal of Abnormal and Social
     Psychology.
Journal of American History (Mississippi Valley
     Historical Review).
Journal of Politics.
Military Affairs.
National Geographic.
Nature.
New York Review of Books.
Pacific Historical Review.
Political Science Quarterly.
Proceedings of the Academy of Political
     Science.
Public Interest.
Public Opinion Quarterly.
Review of Politics.

Review of Radical Political Economics.
Shenandoah.
Social Forces.
Social Science.
Studies on the Left.
Television Quarterly.
Thought.
Virginia Quarterly Review.
Yale Review.

Newspapers

Huron Daily Tribune.
New York Daily News.
New York Herald Tribune.
New York Post.
New York Times.
PM.
San Francisco Chronicle.
Wall Street Journal.
Washington Post.

Public Opinion Polls

Bruner, Jerome S. *Mandate from the People.* New York: Duell, Sloan and Pearce, 1944.
Buchanan, William, and Hadley Cantril. *How Nations See Each Other: A Study in Public Opinion.* Urbana: University of Illinois Press, 1953.
Cantril, Albert H., and Charles W. Roll, Jr. *Hopes and Fears of the American People.* New York: Universe Books, 1971.
Cantril, Hadley, ed. *Public Opinion, 1935–1946.* Princeton, N.J.: Princeton University Press, 1951.
Free, Lloyd A., and Hadley Cantril. *The Political Beliefs of Americans: A Study of Public Opinion.* New Brunswick, N.J.: Rutgers University Press, 1967.
Gallup, George H. *The Gallup Poll: Public Opinion, 1935–1971.* 3 vols. New York: Random House, 1972.
Katz, Daniel, and Hadley Cantril. "An Analysis of Attitudes toward Fascism and Communism." *Journal of Abnormal and Social Psychology* 35 (July 1940): 356–66.
Roper, Elmo. *Where Stands Freedom? A Report on the Findings of an International Survey of Public Opinion.* New York: Time, 1948.
———. *You and Your Leaders: Their Actions and Your Reactions, 1936–1956.* New York: William Morrow, 1957.
University of Michigan, Survey Research Center. *Four Americans Discuss Aid to Europe: Illustrative Interviews from a National Survey.* Study no. 18. Ann Arbor: University of Michigan, 1947.
Walsh, Warren B. "American Attitudes toward Russia." *Antioch Review* 7 (Summer 1947): 183–90.
———. "What the American People Think of Russia." *Public Opinion Quarterly* 8 (Winter, 1944): 513–22.

Government Documents

League of Nations. Economic, Financial and Transit Department. *Industrialization and Foreign Trade.* Geneva: League of Nations, 1945.
UNESCO. *Reflections on Our Age: Lectures Delivered at the Opening Session of UNESCO at the Sorbonne University Paris.* New York: Columbia University Press, 1949.

United Nations. General Assembly. *Preliminary Report of the Temporary Sub-Commission on Economic Reconstruction of Devastated Areas.* Lake Success, N.Y., 1947.

United Nations. Statistical Office. *National and Per Capita Incomes of Seventy Countries in 1949 Expressed in United States Dollars.* New York: Statistical Office of the United Nations, 1950.

U.S. Army. *Geographical Foundations of National Power. Army Service Forces Manual,* M103. Washington, D.C.: U.S. Government Printing Office, 1944.

U.S. Atomic Energy Commission. *In the Matter of J. Robert Oppenheimer: Transcript of Hearing before Personnel Security Board, Washington, D.C., April 12, 1954, through May 6, 1954.* Washington, D.C.: U.S. Government Printing Office, 1954.

U.S. Congress. *Congressional Record,* 1940–. Washington, D.C.

U.S. Congress. House. Committee on Foreign Affairs. Subcommittee on International Organizations and Movements. *Modern Communications and Foreign Policy.* 90th Cong., 1st sess. Washington, D.C.: U.S. Government Printing Office, 1967.

U.S. Congress. House. Committee on Appropriations. *Department of Defense Appropriations for 1964: Hearings before a Subcommittee of the Committee on Appropriations.* 88th Cong., 1st sess. Washington, D.C.: U.S. Government Printing Office, 1963.

U.S. Congress. House. Committee on Foreign Affairs. *Extension of European Recovery Program: Hearings before the Committee on Foreign Affairs.* 81st Cong., 1st sess. Washington, D.C.: U.S. Government Printing Office, 1949.

U.S. Congress. House. Committee on Foreign Affairs. *The Strategy and Tactics of World Communism.* 80th Cong., 2d sess. House Document no. 619. Washington, D.C.: U.S. Government Printing Office, 1948.

U.S. Congress. House. Committee on Foreign Affairs. *United States Foreign Policy for a Post-War Recovery Program: Hearings before the Committee on Foreign Affairs.* 80th Cong., 2d sess. Washington, D.C.: U.S. Government Printing Office, 1948.

U.S. Congress. Senate. Committee on Banking and Currency. *Bretton Woods Agreements Act: Hearings before the Committee on Banking and Currency.* 79th Cong., 1st sess. Washington, D.C.: U.S. Government Printing Office, 1945.

U.S. Congress. Senate. Committee on Commerce. *To Create the All-American Flag Line, Inc.: Hearings before the Subcommittee on Aviation.* 79th Cong., 1st sess. Washington, D.C.: U.S. Government Printing Office, 1945.

U.S. Congress. Senate. Committee on Foreign Relations. *Overseas Information Programs of the United States.* 83d Cong., 1st sess. Washington, D.C.: U.S. Government Printing Office, 1953.

U.S. Congress. Senate. Committee on Interstate and Foreign Commerce. *Consolidation of International Air Carriers (Chosen Instrument): Hearings before a Subcommittee of the Committee on Interstate and Foreign Commerce.* 80th Cong., 1st sess. Washington, D.C.: U.S. Government Printing Office, 1947.

U.S. Department of Commerce. Bureau of the Census. *Historical Statistics of the United States: Colonial Times to 1970.* Washington, D.C.: U.S. Government Printing Office, 1975.

U.S. Department of Commerce. Bureau of the Census. *Statistical Abstract of the United States,* 1940–. Washington, D.C.: U.S. Government Printing Office, 1941–.

U.S. Department of Commerce. Bureau of the Census. *U.S. Census of Population: 1960.* Washington, D.C.

U.S. Department of Commerce. *Survey of Current Business,* 1945.

U.S. Department of State. Bureau of Public Affairs. *The Planetary Product,* 1977–78. Department of State Publication 8994. Washington, D.C., 1979.

U.S. Department of State. Committee on Atomic Energy. *A Report on the International Control of Atomic Energy.* Prepared for the Secretary of State's Committee on Atomic Energy, David E. Lilienthal, Chairman. Department of State Publication 2498. Washington, D.C.: U.S. Government Printing Office, 1946.

U.S. Department of State. *Foreign Relations of the United States,* 1940–. Washington, D.C.: U.S. Government Printing Office, 1959–.

U.S. Department of State. *Proposals for Expansion of World Trade and Employment.* Washington, D.C.: U.S. Government Printing Office, 1945.

U.S. Department of State. *Together We Are Strong*. Commercial Policy Series 144. Washington, D.C.: U.S. Government Printing Office, 1952.

U.S. Information Agency. *USA: Its Geography and Growth*. London: John Murray, 1960.

U.S. National Commission on Excellence in Education. *A Nation at Risk: The Imperative for Educational Reform*. Washington, D.C.: U.S. Government Printing Office, 1983.

U.S. President's Advisory Commission on Universal Training. *A Program for National Security*. Washington, D.C.: U.S. Government Printing Office, 1947.

U.S. President's Commission on National Goals. *Goals for Americans*. Washington, D.C.: Prentice-Hall, 1960.

U.S. Strategic Bombing Survey. *The Effects of Atomic Bombs on Hiroshima and Nagasaki*. Washington, D.C.: U.S. Government Printing Office, 1946.

U.S. Strategic Bombing Survey. *Japan's Struggle to End the War*. Washington, D.C.: U.S. Government Printing Office, 1946.

U.S. Strategic Bombing Survey. *Over-all Report (European War)*. Washington, D.C.: U.S. Government Printing Office, 1945.

U.S. War Production Board. *War Production in 1944*. Washington, D.C.: U.S. Government Printing Office, 1945.

Works by the Presidents

Adams, John. *The Works of John Adams*. Ed. Charles Francis Adams. 10 vols. Boston: Little, Brown, 1850–56.

Carter, Jimmy. *Public Papers of the Presidents of the United States, Jimmy Carter, 1977–81*. Washington, D.C.: U.S. Government Printing Office, 1977–82.

Coolidge, Calvin. *The Autobiography of Calvin Coolidge*. New York: Cosmopolitan Book Company, 1931.

Eisenhower, Dwight D. *At Ease: Stories I Tell to Friends*. Garden City, N.Y.: Doubleday, 1967.

———. *Crusade in Europe*. Garden City, N.Y.: Doubleday, 1948.

———. *The Papers of Dwight David Eisenhower*. Ed. Alfred D. Chandler, Jr., and Louis Galambos. Baltimore: Johns Hopkins University Press, 1970–.

———. *Public Papers of the Presidents of the United States, Dwight D. Eisenhower: Containing the Public Messages, Speeches, and Statements of the President, 1953–61*. Washington, D.C.: National Archives and Records Service, General Services Administration, n.d.

———. *The White House Years*. 2 vols. Garden City, N.Y.: Doubleday, 1963–65. Vol. 1: *Mandate for Change, 1953–1956* (1963). Vol. 2: *Waging Peace, 1956–1961* (1965).

Ford, Gerald R. *Public Papers of the Presidents of the United States, Gerald R. Ford. Containing the Public Messages, Speeches, and Statements of the President, 1974–77*. Washington, D.C.: U.S. Government Printing Office, 1975–79.

Hoover, Herbert. *The Memoirs of Herbert Hoover: Years of Adventure, 1874–1920*. New York: Macmillan, 1951.

———. *40 Key Questions about Our Foreign Policy*. Scarsdale, N.Y.: Updegraff Press, 1952.

———. *The New Day: Campaign Speeches of Herbert Hoover 1928*. Stanford University, Calif.: Stanford University Press, 1928.

———. *The State Papers and Other Public Writings of Herbert Hoover*. 2 vols. Ed. William Starr Myers. Garden City, N.Y.: Doubleday, Doran, 1934.

Hoover, Herbert, and Hugh Gibson. *The Problems of Lasting Peace*. Garden City, N.Y.: Doubleday, Doran, 1942.

Johnson, Lyndon B. *American Tomorrow: "Will We Hang Together or Hang Separately?"* New York: New York University, Graduate School of Business Administration, 1971.

———. *My Hope for America*. New York: Random House, 1964.

———. *Public Papers of the Presidents of the United States, Lyndon B. Johnson: Containing the Public Messages, Speeches, and Statements of the President, 1963–69*. Washington, D.C.: U.S. Government Printing Office, 1965–70.

———. *This America*. Photographed by Ken Heyman. New York: Random House, 1966.

———. *The Vantage Point: Perspectives of the Presidency, 1963–1969*. New York: Holt, Rinehart and Winston, 1971.

Kennedy, John F. *Public Papers of the Presidents of the United States, John F. Kennedy: Containing the Public Messages, Speeches, and Statements of the President*, 1961–63. Washington, D.C.: U.S. Government Printing Office, 1962–64.

———. *The Speeches, Remarks, Press Conferences, and Statements of Senator John F. Kennedy*, 1960. Freedom of Communications, Final Report of the Committee on Commerce, United States Senate, Prepared by Its Subcommittee of the Subcommittee on Communications. Washington, D.C.: U.S. Government Printing Office, 1961.

———. *The Strategy of Peace*. Ed. Allan Nevins. New York: Harper & Brothers, 1960.

———. "We Must Climb to the Hilltop." *Life*, Aug. 22, 1960, 70B–77.

McKinley, William. *Speeches and Addresses of William McKinley: From His Election to Congress to the Present Time*. New York: D. Appleton, 1893.

Nixon, Richard M. "Our Resolve Is Running Strong." *Life*, Aug. 29, 1960, 86–94.

———. *Public Papers of the Presidents of the United States, Richard Nixon: Containing the Public Messages, Speeches, and Statements of the President*, 1969–74. Washington, D.C.: U.S. Government Printing Office, 1971–75.

———. *RN: The Memoirs of Richard Nixon*. New York: Grosset & Dunlap, 1978.

———. "Russia as I Saw It." *National Geographic* 116 (December 1959): 715–50.

———. *Six Crises*. Garden City, N.Y.: Doubleday, 1962.

———. *The Speeches, Remarks, Press Conferences, and Study Papers of Vice President Richard M. Nixon*, 1960. Freedom of Communications, Final Report of the Committee on Commerce, United States Senate, Prepared by Its Subcommittee of the Subcommittee on Communications. Washington, D.C.: U.S. Government Printing Office, 1961.

———. *United States Foreign Policy for the 1970's: A New Strategy for Peace*. New York, N.Y.: Bantam Books, 1970.

Reagan, Ronald. "I Had a Plan . . . to Deal from Strength." *U.S. News & World Report*, Dec. 7, 1987, 31–32.

———. *Public Papers of the Presidents of the United States, Ronald Reagan*, 1981–89. Washington, D.C.: U.S. Government Printing Office, 1982–91.

Roosevelt, Franklin, D. *F.D.R.: His Personal Letters*. Ed. Elliott Roosevelt. 4 vols. New York: Duell, Sloan and Pearce, 1947–50.

———. *The Public Papers and Addresses of Franklin D. Roosevelt*, 1928–45. 13 vols. New York: Random House, Macmillan, and Harper & Brothers, 1938–50.

———. *Whither Bound?* Boston: Houghton Mifflin, 1926.

Roosevelt, Theodore. *The Rough Riders*. New York: P. F. Collier & Son, 1899.

———. *Theodore Roosevelt's Speeches in Europe*. New York: C. S. Hammond, n.d.

———. *The Winning of the West: An Account of the Exploitation and Settlement of Our Country from the Alleghenies to the Pacific*. 2 vols. New York: Scribner's, 1926 (orig. 1889–1896).

———. *The Works of Theodore Roosevelt*. National Edition. 20 vols. New York: Scribner's, 1926.

———. *The Works of Theodore Roosevelt: Presidential Addresses and State Papers*. New York: P. F. Collier & Son, 1914.

Truman, Harry S. *Memoirs*. 2 vols. Garden City, N.Y.: Doubleday, 1955–56. Vol. 1: *Year of Decisions* (1955). Vol. 2: *Years of Trial and Hope* (1956).

———. *Mr. President: The First Publication from the Personal Diaries, Private Letters, Papers and Revealing Interviews of Harry S. Truman*. New York: Farrar, Straus and Young, 1952.

———. *Off the Record: The Private Papers of Harry S. Truman*. Ed. Robert H. Ferrell. New York: Harper & Row, 1980.

———. *Public Papers of the Presidents of the United States, Harry S. Truman: Containing the Public Messages, Speeches, and Statements of the President*, 1945–53. Washington, D.C.: U.S. Government Printing Office, 1961–66.

Truman, Harry. *Strictly Personal and Confidential: The Letters Harry Truman Never Mailed*. Ed. Monte M. Poen. Boston: Little, Brown, 1982.

Wilson, Woodrow. *The Public Papers of Woodrow Wilson.* Ed. Ray Stannard Baker and William E. Dodd. 6 vols. New York: Harper & Brothers, 1925–27. Vols. 1–2: *College and State: Educational, Literary and Political Papers (1875–1913)* (1925). Vols. 3–4: *The New Democracy: Presidential Messages, Addresses, and Other Papers (1913–1917)* (1926). Vols. 5–6: *War and Peace: Presidential Messages, Addresses, and Public Papers (1917–1924)* (1927).

Works by the Secretaries of State

Acheson, Dean. "Crisis in Asia—An Examination of U.S. Policy." *Department of State Bulletin,* Jan. 23, 1950, 111–18.
———. "Culture after Breakfast." *Reporter,* Sept. 19, 1957, 34–35.
———. "The Current Situation in Germany." *Department of State Bulletin,* May 8, 1949, 585–88.
———. "Economic Policy and the ITO Charter." *Department of State Bulletin,* May 15, 1949, 623–27.
———. *Grapes from Thorns.* New York: Norton, 1972.
———. "The Meaning of the North Atlantic Pact." *Department of State Bulletin,* March 27, 1949, 384–88.
———. *The Pattern of Responsibility.* Ed. McGeorge Bundy. Boston: Houghton Mifflin, 1952.
———. *Power and Diplomacy.* Cambridge: Harvard University Press, 1958.
———. *Present at the Creation: My Years in the State Department.* New York: Norton, 1969.
———. "The Quality of American Patriotism." *Department of State Bulletin,* May 1, 1950, 696–98.
———. "United States Policy toward Asia." *Department of State Bulletin,* March 27, 1950, 467–72.
Byrnes, James F. *All in One Lifetime.* New York: Harper & Brothers, 1958.
———. "Restatement of U.S. Policy on Germany." *Department of State Bulletin,* Sept. 15, 1946, 496–501.
———. *Speaking Frankly.* New York: Harper & Brothers, 1947.
Dulles, John Foster. "America's Role in the Peace." *Christianity and Crisis* 4 (Jan. 22, 1945): 2–6.
———. "The Political Cost of Peace." *International Journal of Religious Education* 20 (October 1943): 8–9.
———. "Policy for Security and Peace." *Foreign Affairs* 32 (April 1954): 353–64.
———. "Report from Asia." *Department of State Bulletin,* March 21, 1955, 459–64.
———. "Thoughts on Soviet Foreign Policy and What to Do about It." *Life,* June 3, 1946, 112–26; June 10, 1946, 118–30.
———. *War or Peace.* New York: Macmillan, 1950.
Hull, Cordell. "Address by the Secretary of State before Congress Regarding the Moscow Conference." *Department of State Bulletin,* Nov. 20, 1943, 341–45.
———. *The Memoirs of Cordell Hull.* 2 vols. New York: Macmillan, 1948.
———. "The War and Human Freedom." *Department of State Bulletin,* July 25, 1942, 639–47.
Kissinger, Henry A. *American Foreign Policy.* New York: Norton, 1974 (orig. 1969).
———. *The Necessity for Choice: Prospects of American Foreign Policy.* New York: Harper & Brothers, 1961.
———. *Nuclear Weapons and Foreign Policy.* New York: Published for the Council on Foreign Relations by Harper & Brothers, 1957.
———. "Remarks by Dr. Kissinger." *Department of State Bulletin,* July 10, 1972, 40–49.
———. "The Year of Europe." *Department of State Bulletin,* May 14, 1973, 593–98.
———. *A World Restored: Metternich, Castlereagh and the Problems of Peace, 1812–22.* Boston: Houghton Mifflin, 1957.
Kissinger, Henry, and Cyrus Vance. "Bipartisan Objectives for American Foreign Policy." *Foreign Affairs* 66 (Summer 1988): 899–921.

Marshall, George C. *European Initiative Essential to Economic Recovery*. Department of State Publication 2882. Washington, D.C.: U.S. Government Printing Office, 1947.

———. "The Problems of European Revival and German and Austrian Peace Settlements." *Department of State Bulletin*, Nov. 30, 1947, 1024–28.

———. *Selected Speeches and Statements of General of the Army George C. Marshall*. Ed. H. A. DeWeerd. Washington: Infantry Journal, 1945.

Rusk, Dean. *The Winds of Freedom: Selections from the Speeches and Statements of Secretary of State Dean Rusk, January 1961–August 1962*. Ed. Ernest K. Lindley. Boston: Beacon Press, 1963.

Stettinius, Edward R., Jr. *Lend-Lease: Weapon for Victory*. New York: Macmillan, 1944.

Stimson, Henry L. "The Challenge to Americans." *Foreign Affairs* 26 (October 1947): 5–14.

———. "The Decision to Use the Atomic Bomb." *Harper's*, February 1947, 97–107.

Stimson, Henry L., and McGeorge Bundy. *On Active Service in Peace and War*. New York: Harper & Brothers, 1948.

Vance, Cyrus R. "Meeting the Challenges of a Changing World." *Department of State Bulletin*, June 1979, 16–19.

Works by Intellectuals and Commentators

Aaron, Daniel, Tom Hayden, Ivanhoe Donaldson, Richard Rovere, Dwight Macdonald. "Confrontation: The Old Left and the New." *American Scholar* 36 (Autumn 1967): 567–88.

Abramovitz, Moses. *Resource and Output Trends in the United States since 1870*. National Bureau of Economic Research, Occasional Paper 52, 1956.

Adams, Alexander B. *Eleventh Hour: A Hard Look at Conservation and the Future*. New York: G. P. Putnam's Sons, 1970.

Adams, Brooks. *America's Economic Supremacy*. With a New Evaluation by Marquis W. Childs. New York: Harper & Brothers, 1947.

Adams, Herbert B. "The Germanic Origin of New England Towns." *Johns Hopkins University Studies in Historical and Political Science*, no. 2. Baltimore: Johns Hopkins University, 1882.

Adams, Velma. *The Peace Corps in Action*. Chicago: Follett, 1964.

Adler, Selig. *The Isolationist Impulse: Its Twentieth-Century Reaction*. New York: Abelard-Schuman, 1957.

Aksyonov, Vassily. *In Search of Melancholy Baby*. New York: Random House, 1987.

Alireza, Marjanne. "Women of Saudi Arabia." *National Geographic* 172 (October 1987): 422–53.

Almond, Gabriel A. *The American People and Foreign Policy*. New York: Harcourt, Brace, 1950 and 1960.

Alpervotiz, Gar. *Atomic Diplomacy: Hiroshima and Potsdam, The Use of the Atomic Bomb and the Confrontation with Soviet Power*. New York: Simon and Schuster, 1965.

———. "Notes toward a Pluralist Commonwealth." *Review of Radical Political Economics* 4 (Summer 1972): 28–48.

Alsop, Stewart. "Our Gamble with Destiny." *Saturday Evening Post*, May 16, 1959, 23, 114–18.

American Association for the Advancement of Science, Committee on Science in the Promotion of Human Welfare. "Science and Human Welfare." *Science*, July 8, 1960, 68–73.

Aptheker, Herbert. *American Foreign Policy and the Cold War*. New York: New Century, 1962.

Arnold, H. H. *Global Mission*. New York: Harper & Brothers, 1949.

Atkinson, Brooks. "Russia 1946." *Life*, July 22, 1946, 85–94.

Atwood, Albert W. "The Miracle of War Production." *National Geographic* 82 (December 1942): 693–715.

———. "Northeast of Boston." *National Geographic* 88 (September 1945): 257–92.

———. "Potomac, River of Destiny." *National Geographic* 88 (July 1945): 33–70.

Azzi, Robert. "Oman, Land of Frankincense and Oil." *National Geographic* 143 (February 1973): 204–29.

Bacciocco, Edward J., Jr. *The New Left in America: Reform to Revolution, 1956 to 1970*. Stanford, Calif.: Hoover Institution Press, 1974.

Baerwald, Friedrich. "The Future of Europe." *Thought* 19 (September 1944): 402–20.

Bailey, Thomas A. "America's Emergence as a World Power: The Myth and the Verity." *Pacific Historical Review* 30 (February 1961): 1–16.

———. *A Diplomatic History of the American People.* New York: Appleton-Century-Crofts, 1946 (orig. 1940).

———. *The Man in the Street: The Impact of American Public Opinion on Foreign Policy.* New York: Macmillan, 1948.

———. *The Marshall Plan Summer: An Eyewitness Report on Europe and the Russians in 1947.* Stanford, Calif.: Hoover Institution Press, 1977.

Baldwin, Hanson W. *The Price of Power.* New York: Published for the Council on Foreign Relations by Harper & Brothers, 1947.

Barber, Richard J. *The American Corporation: Its Power, Its Money, Its Politics.* New York: Dutton, 1970.

Bardin, James C. "'Manifest Destiny' in the Caribbean." *Sea Power* 9–10 (December 1920–January 1921).

Barnett, A. Doak. "Profile of Red China." *Foreign Policy Reports* 25 (Feb. 15, 1950): 230–43.

Baruch, Bernard M. "Proposals for an International Atomic Development Authority." *Department of State Bulletin,* June 23, 1946, 1057–62.

Barzun, Jacques. *God's Country and Mine: A Declaration of Love Spiced with a Few Harsh Words.* Boston: Little, Brown, 1954.

Baumer, Franklin L. Review of *Toynbee and History: Critical Essays and Reviews,* ed. by M. F. Ashley Montagu. *American Historical Review* 62 (April 1957): 595–96.

Beale, Howard K. *Theodore Roosevelt and the Rise of America to World Power.* Baltimore: Johns Hopkins University Press, 1956.

Beard, Charles A. *The Economic Basis of Politics.* New York: Knopf, 1945.

———. *An Economic Interpretation of the Constitution of the United States.* New York: Macmillan, 1935.

———. *The Idea of National Interest: An Analytical Study in American Foreign Policy.* New York: Macmillan, 1934.

———. Review of *A Study of History,* vols. 1–3, by Arnold J. Toynbee. *American Historical Review* 40 (January 1935): 307–9.

Beard, Charles A., and Mary R. Beard. *The American Spirit: A Study of the Idea of Civilization in the United States.* Vol. 4: *The Rise of American Civilization.* New York: Macmillan, 1942.

Becker, Carl L. *How New Will the Better World Be? A Discussion of Post-War Reconstruction.* New York: Knopf, 1944.

Bell, Daniel, ed. *The New American Right.* New York: Criterion, 1955.

———. *The Radical Right.* Garden City, N.Y.: Doubleday, 1963.

Bell, Terrel. "Japanese Schools: 'There Is Much We Can Learn.'" *U.S. News & World Report,* Sept. 2, 1985, 43.

Belz, Carl. *The Story of Rock.* New York: Oxford University Press, 1972.

Benjamin, Robert Spiers, ed. *I Am an American: By Famous Naturalized Americans.* Freeport, N.Y.: Books for Libraries Press, 1970 (orig. 1941).

Berger, Peter L., and Richard John Neuhaus. *Movement and Revolution.* Garden City, N.Y.: Doubleday, 1970.

Bergson, Abram. "Russian Defense Expenditures." *Foreign Affairs* 26 (January 1948): 373–76.

Bergsten, C. Fred. "Economic Imbalances and World Politics." *Foreign Affairs* 65 (Spring 1987): 770–94.

———. "The New Economics and U.S. Foreign Policy." *Foreign Affairs* 50 (January 1972): 199–222.

Bergsten, C. Fred, and William R. Cline. *The United States-Japan Economic Problem.* Washington, D.C.: Institute for International Economics, 1985.

Bernstein, Barton J. "A Postwar Myth: 500,000 U.S. Lives Saved." *Bulletin of the Atomic Scientists,* June/July 1986, 38–40.

Berry, Lelah. "An Army Wife Lives Very Soft—in Germany." *Saturday Evening Post,* Feb. 15, 1947, 24–25, 119–22.

Bess, Demaree. "Let's Quit Pretending." *Saturday Evening Post,* Dec. 18, 1943, 9–10, 37–39.

Bidwell, Percy W. "Imports in the American Economy." *Foreign Affairs* 24 (October 1945): 85–98.

Billard, Jules B. "Guantánamo: Keystone in the Caribbean." *National Geographic* 119 (March 1961): 420–36.

Billington, Ray Allen. *The American Frontier Thesis: Attack and Defense.* Washington, D.C.: American Historical Association, 1971.

———. *Westward Expansion: A History of the American Frontier.* New York: Macmillan, 1949.

Billington, Ray Allen, Bert James Lowenberg, and Samuel Hugh Brockunier. *The United States: American Democracy in World Perspective.* New York: Rinehart, 1947.

Bingham, Johnathan B. *Shirt-Sleeve Diplomacy: Point 4 in Action.* New York: John Day, 1954.

Bingham, June. *Courage to Change: An Introduction to the Life and Thought of Reinhold Niebuhr.* New York: Scribner's, 1961.

Bisson, T. A. *Prospects for Democracy in Japan.* New York: Macmillan, 1949.

Boggs, S. W. "Africa: Maps and Man." *Department of State Bulletin,* Sept. 18, 1943, 188–96.

Boorstin, Daniel J. *America and the Image of Europe: Reflections on American Thought.* Cleveland: World, 1960.

———. "'The American Century'—Myth vs. Reality: Interview." *U.S. News & World Report,* Oct. 19, 1970, 64–67.

———. *The Americans: The Colonial Experience.* New York: Random House, 1958.

———. *The Americans: The Democratic Experience.* New York: Random House, 1973.

———. *The Americans: The National Experience.* New York: Random House, 1965.

———. *The Decline of Radicalism: Reflections on America Today.* New York: Random House, 1969.

———. *Democracy and Its Discontents: Reflections on Everyday America.* New York: Random House, 1974.

———. *The Genius of American Politics.* Chicago: University of Chicago Press, 1953.

———. *The Image or What Happened to the American Dream.* New York: Atheneum, 1962.

Borah, Leo A. "Nebraska, the Cornhusker State." *National Geographic* 87 (May 1945): 513–42.

Bottome, Edgar M. *The Missile Gap: A Study of the Formulation of Military and Political Policy.* Rutherford, N.J.: Fairleigh Dickinson University Press, 1971.

Bourke-White, Margaret. "A New Way to Look at the U.S." *Life,* April 14, 1952, 128–40.

———. *The Photographs of Margaret Bourke-White.* Ed. Sean Callahan. Boston: New York Graphic Society, 1972.

———. *Shooting the Russian War.* New York: Simon and Schuster, 1942.

Bowen, William. "The Vietnam War: A Cost Accounting." *Fortune,* April 1966, 119–23, 254–59.

Brackman, Jacob. "My Generation." *Esquire,* October 1968, 127–29.

Brines, Russell. *MacArthur's Japan.* Philadelphia: Lippincott, 1948.

Brinton, Crane. *From Many One: The Process of Political Integration, The Problem of World Government.* Cambridge: Harvard University Press, 1948.

———. Review of *America and the World Revolution and Other Lectures,* by Arnold J. Toynbee. *American Historical Review* 68 (April 1963): 758–59.

———. *The United States and Britain.* Cambridge: Harvard University Press, 1945.

Brodie, Bernard. "How Strong Is Britain?" *Foreign Affairs* 26 (April 1948): 432–49.

Brodie, Bernard, ed. *The Absolute Weapon: Atomic Power and World Order.* New York: Harcourt, Brace, 1946.

Brogan, D. W. *The American Character.* New York: Knopf, 1944.

Brown, Anthony Cave, ed. *Dropshot: The United States Plan for War with the Soviet Union in 1957.* New York: Dial Press/James Wade, 1978.

Brown, Lester R. *World without Borders.* New York: Random House, 1972.

Bruckberger, R. L. *Image of America.* Trans. C. G. Paulding and Virginia Peterson. New York: Viking, 1959.

————. *One Sky to Share: The French and American Journals of Raymond Leopold Bruckberger.* Trans. Dorothy Carr Howell. New York: P. J. Kenedy & Sons, 1952.

Brunauer, Esther Caukin. "Power Politics and Democracy." *Annals of the American Academy of Political and Social Science* 216 (July 1941): 109–16.

Brzezinski, Zbigniew. "America's New Geostrategy." *Foreign Affairs* 66 (Spring 1988): 680–99.

————. "The Implications of Change for United States Foreign Policy." *Department of State Bulletin,* July 3, 1967, 19–23.

Buck, Pearl S. *American Argument.* New York: John Day, 1949.

————. *American Unity and Asia.* New York: John Day, 1942.

————. *What America Means to Me.* New York: John Day, 1943.

Buell, Raymond Leslie. *Isolated America.* New York: Knopf, 1940.

Bundy, McGeorge. *Danger and Survival: Choices About the Bomb in the First Fifty Years.* New York: Random House, 1988.

————. *The McGeorge Bundy Statement on Vietnam at the DePauw University Symposium on Law, Liberty and Progress,* Oct 12, 1968. N.p., n.d.

Burgess, John W. *Political Science and Comparative Constitutional Law.* 2 vols. Boston: Ginn, 1890–91.

Burke, Arleigh A. "The Threat Confronting Us." *Vital Speeches of the Day,* March 15, 1959, 332–35.

Burman, Ben Lucian. *It's a Big Country: America off the Highways.* New York: Reynal, 1956.

Burnett, Wanda. "Cape Cod People and Places." *National Geographic* 89 (June 1946): 737–74.

————. "Yank Meets Native." *National Geographic* 88 (July 1945): 105–28.

Burns, Edward McNall. *The American Idea of Mission: Concepts of National Purpose and Destiny.* New Brunswick, N.J.: Rutgers University Press, 1957.

Burns, James MacGregor. *Roosevelt: The Lion and the Fox.* New York: Harcourt, Brace, 1956.

Burns, Norman. "The American Farmer and the ITO Charter." *Department of State Bulletin,* Feb. 20, 1949, 215–20.

Caldwell, Erskine, and Margaret Bourke-White. *Say, Is This the U.S.A.* New York: Duell, Sloan and Pearce, 1941.

Camps, Miriam. "Britain, the Six and American Policy." *Foreign Affairs* 39 (October 1960): 112–22.

Carey, Robert G. *The Peace Corps.* New York: Praeger, 1970.

Carleton, William G. "Wanted: Wiser Power Politics." *Yale Review* 41 (December 1951): 194–206.

Carmichael, Stokely, and Charles V. Hamilton. *Black Power: The Politics of Liberation in America.* New York: Random House, 1967.

Carr, Edward Hallett. *The Twenty Years' Crisis, 1919–1939: An Introduction to the Study of International Relations.* London: Macmillan, 1946.

Carson, Rachel. *Silent Spring.* Boston: Houghton Mifflin, 1962.

Carter, Paul A. *Another Part of the Fifties.* New York: Columbia University Press, 1983.

Cary, Otis, ed. *War-Wasted Asia: Letters, 1945–46.* Tokyo: Kodansha, 1975.

Casner, Mabel B., and Ralph H. Gabriel. *The Story of American Democracy.* New York: Harcourt, Brace, 1950.

Cassirer, Ernst. *Symbol, Myth, and Culture: Essays and Lectures of Ernst Cassirer, 1935–1945.* Ed. Donald Phillip Verene. New Haven: Yale University Press, 1979.

Chace, James. "Is a Foreign Policy Consensus Possible?" *Foreign Affairs* 57 (Fall 1978): 1–16.

Chamberlin, William Henry. "Russia: An American Problem." *Atlantic Monthly,* February 1942, 148–56.

————. "The Russian Enigma." *Harper's,* August 1942, 225–34.

Chapelle, Dickey. "Helicopter War in South Viet Nam." *National Geographic* 122 (November 1962): 722–54.

Chase, John W., ed. *Years of the Modern: An American Appraisal.* New York: Longmans, Green, 1949.

Childs, Marquis W. "London Wins the Battle." *National Geographic* 88 (August 1945): 129–52.

Chittenden, H. M. "Manifest Destiny in America." *Atlantic Monthly,* January 1916, 48–59.

Churchill, Winston S. *The Sinews of Peace: Post-War Speeches.* Ed. Randolph S. Churchill. Boston: Houghton Mifflin, 1949.

Clay, Lucius D. *Decision in Germany.* Garden City, N.Y.: Doubleday, 1950.

Clee, Gilbert H., and Alfred di Scipio. "Creating a *World* Enterprise." *Harvard Business Review* 37 (November–December 1959): 77–89.

Cleveland, Harlan, Gerard J. Mangone, and John Clarke Adams. *The Overseas Americans.* New York: McGraw-Hill, 1960.

Clough, Shepard B. *The American Way: The Economic Basis of Our Civilization.* New York: Crowell, 1953.

Coale, Ansley J. *The Problem of Reducing Vulnerability to Atomic Bombs.* Princeton, N.J.: Princeton University Press, 1947.

Coates, Willson H. Review of *A Study of History,* by Arnold J. Toynbee. Abridgment of vols. 1–6. *American Historical Review* 53 (October 1947): 75–76.

Cochran, Thomas B., William M. Arkin, and Milton M. Hoenig. *Nuclear Weapons Databook.* Vol. 1: *U.S. Nuclear Forces and Capabilities.* Cambridge, Mass.: Ballinger, 1984.

Cohen, Benjamin C. *The Press and Foreign Policy.* Princeton, N.J.: Princeton University Press, 1963.

Cohen, Jerome B. "The Japanese War Economy: 1940–1945." *Far Eastern Survey* 15 (Dec. 4, 1946): 361–70.

Coleman, Lee. "What is American? A Study of Alleged American Traits." *Social Forces* 19 (May 1941): 492–99.

Collier, Peter, and David Horowitz. *Destructive Generation: Second Thoughts about the Sixties.* New York: Summit Books, 1989.

Colton, F. Barrows. "Winning the War of Supply." *National Geographic* 88 (December 1945): 705–36.

Commager, Henry Steele. *The American Mind: An Interpretation of American Thought and Character since the 1880's.* New Haven: Yale University Press, 1950.

———. "200 Plus 1." *Parade,* July 3, 1977.

Commager, Henry Steele, ed. *America in Perspective: The United States through Foreign Eyes.* New York: Random House, 1947.

———. *Living Ideas in America.* New York: Harper & Brothers, 1951.

The Committee for the Compilation of Materials on Damage Caused by the Atomic Bombs in Hiroshima and Nagasaki. *Hiroshima and Nagasaki: The Physical, Medical, and Social Effects of the Atomic Bombings.* Trans. Eisei Ishikawa and David L. Swain. New York: Basic Books, 1981.

Compton, Arthur H. "Science and Our Nation's Future." *Science,* March 2, 1945, 207–9.

Compton, Karl T. "If the Atomic Bomb Had Not Been Used." *Atlantic Monthly,* December 1946, 54–56.

Conference on Economic Progress. "Consumption—Key to Full Prosperity." *ADA World* 12 (May 1957): 3M.

Conly, Robert Leslie. "Modern Miracle: Made in Germany." *National Geographic* 115 (June 1959): 735–91.

Cook, Thomas I., and Malcolm Moos. "Foreign Policy: The Realism of Idealism." *American Political Science Review* 46 (June 1952): 343–56.

———. *Power through Purpose: The Realism of Idealism as a Basis for Foreign Policy.* Baltimore: Johns Hopkins University Press, 1954.

Cooke, Alistair. *Alistair Cooke's America.* New York: Knopf, 1973.

———. *One Man's America.* New York: Knopf, 1952.

Council on Foreign Relations. *Documents on American Foreign Relations, 1949–1962.* New York: Published for the Council on Foreign Relations by Harper & Brothers, 1950–63.

Cousins, Norman. *Modern Man Is Obsolete.* New York: Viking, 1945.

———. "Modern Man Is Obsolete: An Editorial." *Saturday Review of Literature,* Aug. 18, 1945, 5–9.

Craig, Gordon A. "Germany between the East and the West." *Proceedings of the Academy of Political Science* 23 (May 1949): 221–31.

Craven, Avery, ed. *Essays in Honor of William E. Dodd by His Former Students at the University of Chicago*. Chicago: University of Chicago Press, 1935.

Cressey, George B. *Asia's Lands and Peoples: A Geography of One-Third the Earth and Two-Thirds Its People*. New York: McGraw-Hill, 1944.

Crèvecoeur, Hector St. John de. *Letters from an American Farmer*. New York: Dutton, 1912; repr. 1951.

Curti, Merle. *American Philanthropy Abroad: A History*. New Brunswick, N.J.: Rutgers University Press, 1963.

———. *The Growth of American Thought*. New York: Harper & Row, 1964.

Dahl, Robert A. *A Preface to Democratic Theory*. Chicago: University of Chicago Press, 1956.

———. *Congress and Foreign Policy*. New York: Harcourt, Brace, 1950.

———. *Who Governs? Democracy and Power in an American City*. New Haven: Yale University Press, 1961.

Dallek, Robert. *The American Style of Foreign Policy: Cultural Politics and Foreign Affairs*. New York: Knopf, 1983.

Dallin, David J. *The Big Three: The United States, Britain, Russia*. New Haven: Yale University Press, 1945.

Dam, Kenneth W. *The GATT: Law and International Economic Organization*. Chicago: University of Chicago Press, 1970.

Darwin, Charles. *The Descent of Man, and Selection in Relation to Sex*. 2 vols. New York: D. Appleton, 1871; rev. ed., 1896.

———. *On the Origin of the Species by Means of Natural Selection, or The Preservation of Favoured Races in the Struggle for Life*. London: John Murray, 1859.

Davies, Joseph E. *Mission to Moscow*. New York: Simon and Schuster, 1941.

———. "The Soviets and the Post-War." *Life,* March 29, 1943, 49–55.

Davis, Forrest. "Roosevelt's World Blueprint." *Saturday Evening Post,* April 10, 1943, 20–21, 109–10.

Davis, Joseph S. "Fifty Million More Americans." *Foreign Affairs* 28 (April 1950): 412–26.

DeConde, Alexander, ed. *Isolation and Security*. Durham, N.C.: Duke University Press, 1957.

DeMille, Cecil B. *The Autobiography of Cecil B. DeMille*. Englewood Cliffs, N.J.: Prentice-Hall, 1959.

Demolins, Edmond. *Anglo-Saxon Superiority: To What It Is Due*. New York: R. F. Fenno, 1898.

Denison, Edward F. *The Sources of Economic Growth in the United States and the Alternatives before Us*. New York: Committee for Economic Development, 1962.

———. *Why Growth Rates Differ: Postwar Experience in Nine Western Countries*. Washington, D.C.: Brookings Institution, 1967.

Deutsch, Karl W. *Nationalism and Social Communication: An Inquiry into the Foundations of Nationality*. New York: Technology Press of the Massachusetts Institute of Technology and John Wiley & Sons, 1953.

Dewhurst, J. Frederic, and Associates. *America's Needs and Resources*. New York: Twentieth Century Fund, 1947.

Dexter, Byron. "Yardstick for UNESCO." *Foreign Affairs* 28 (October 1949): 56–67.

Diebold, William, Jr. "A Merchant Marine Second to None?" *Foreign Affairs* 21 (July 1943): 711–20.

Divine, Robert A. *Second Chance: The Triumph of Internationalism in America during World War II*. New York: Atheneum, 1967.

Dizard, Wilson P. "American Television's Foreign Markets." *Television Quarterly* 3 (Summer 1964): 57–73.

———. *The Strategy of Truth: The Story of the U.S. Information Service*. Washington, D.C.: Public Affairs Press, 1961.

Donnelly, Desmond. *Struggle for the World, The Cold War: 1917–1965*. New York: St. Martin's, 1965.

Dos Passos, John. *The Prospect before Us*. Boston: Houghton Mifflin, 1950.

———. *State of the Nation*. Boston: Houghton Mifflin, 1944.

Douglas, William O. "West from the Khyber Pass." *National Geographic* 114 (July 1958): 1–44.

Dulles, Foster Rhea. *America's Rise to World Power: 1898–1954*. New York: Harper & Row, 1954.

———. *Prelude to World Power: American Diplomatic History, 1860–1900*. New York: Macmillan, 1965.

———. *The Road to Teheran: The Story of Russia and America, 1781–1943*. Princeton, N.J.: Princeton University Press, 1944.

Dylan, Bob. *Lyrics, 1962–1985*. New York: Knopf, 1985.

East, W. Gordon. "How Strong Is the Heartland?" *Foreign Affairs* 29 (October 1950): 78–93.

Edwards, Mike. "Mother Russia on a New Course." *National Geographic* 179 (February 1991): 2–37.

Ekirch, Arthur A., Jr. *Man and Nature in America*. New York: Columbia University Press, 1963.

Ellis, Howard S. *The Economics of Freedom: The Progress and Future of Aid to Europe*. New York: Published for the Council on Foreign Relations by Harper & Brothers, 1950.

Elson, Robert T. *Time Inc.: The Intimate History of a Publishing Enterprise*. Vol. 1, 1923–1941. New York: Atheneum, 1968.

———. *The World of Time Inc.: The Intimate History of a Publishing Enterprise*. Vol. 2, 1941–1960. New York: Atheneum, 1973.

Evangelista, Matthew A. "Stalin's Postwar Army Reappraised." *International Security* 7 (Winter 1982/1983): 110–38.

Evans, Luther. "Almost Half the World's Adults Can't Read." *New York Times Magazine,* March 16, 1958, 43–46.

Fairbank, John King. *Trade and Diplomacy on the China Coast: The Opening of the Treaty Ports, 1842–1854*. 2 vols. Cambridge: Harvard University Press, 1953.

Fairlie, Henry. *The Kennedy Promise: The Politics of Expectation*. Garden City, N.Y.: Doubleday, 1973.

Falk, Signi Lenea. *Archibald MacLeish*. New York: Twayne, 1965.

Fallows, James. "Behind Japan's 'Free Ride' to Prosperity." *U.S. News & World Report,* July 28, 1986, 12.

———. "Is Japan the Enemy?" *New York Review of Books,* May 30, 1991, 31–37.

Fanning, Leonard M. *Foreign Oil and the Free World*. New York: McGraw-Hill, 1954.

Faulkner, Harold Underwood, and Tyler Kepner. *America: Its History and People*. New York: McGraw-Hill, 1950.

Feis, Herbert. *The Atomic Bomb and the End of World War II*. Princeton, N.J.: Princeton University Press, 1966.

———. *Between War and Peace: The Potsdam Conference*. Princeton, N.J.: Princeton University Press, 1960.

———. *Churchill-Roosevelt-Stalin: The War They Waged and the Peace They Sought*. Princeton, N.J.: Princeton University Press, 1957.

———. *From Trust to Terror: The Onset of the Cold War, 1945–1950*. New York: Norton, 1970.

———. *Japan Subdued: The Atomic Bomb and the End of the War in the Pacific*. Princeton, N.J.: Princeton University Press, 1961.

Ferrero, Guglielmo. *The Principles of Power: The Great Political Crises of History*. New York: G. P. Putnam's Sons, 1942.

Finletter, Thomas K. *Power and Policy: U.S. Foreign Policy and Military Power in the Hydrogen Age*. New York: Harcourt, Brace, 1954.

Fischer, Eric. *The Passing of the European Age: A Study of the Transfer of Western Civilization and Its Renewal in Other Continents*. Cambridge: Harvard University Press, 1943.

Fischer, Louis. *Empire*. New York: Duell, Sloan and Pearce, 1943.

———. *The Great Challenge*. New York: Duell, Sloan and Pearce, 1946.

Fiske, John. *American Political Ideas: Viewed from the Standpoint of Universal History*. New York: Harper & Brothers, 1885.

———. "Manifest Destiny." *Harper's New Monthly Magazine,* March 1885, 578–90.

Flanders, Ralph E. *The American Century.* Cambridge: Harvard University Press, 1950.

Fleming, D. F. *The Cold War and Its Origins: 1917–1960.* 2 vols. Garden City, N.Y.: Doubleday, 1961.

Ford Motor Company. *Ford Annual Report, 1971.* Dearborn, Mich.: Ford Motor Company, n.d.

Forrestal, James. *The Forrestal Diaries.* Ed. Walter Millis. New York: Viking, 1951.

———. "Will We Choose Naval Suicide Again?" *Saturday Evening Post,* June 24, 1944, 9–11, 90.

Fox, Richard Wightman. *Reinhold Niebuhr: A Biography.* New York: Pantheon, 1985.

Fox, William T. R. *The Super-Powers: The United States, Britain, and the Soviet Union—Their Responsibility for Peace.* New York: Harcourt, Brace, 1944.

Fox, William T. R., and Annette Baker Fox. *Britain and America in the Era of Total Diplomacy.* Center of International Studies, Memorandum no. 1. Princeton University: Center of International Studies, 1952.

Freeland, Richard M. *The Truman Doctrine and the Origins of McCarthyism: Foreign Policy, Domestic Politics, and Internal Security, 1946–1948.* New York: Knopf, 1972.

Friedan, Betty. *The Feminine Mystique.* New York: Norton, 1963.

Fry, Earl H. *Financial Invasion of the U.S.A.: A Threat to American Society?* New York: McGraw-Hill, 1980.

Fulbright, J. William. *The Arrogance of Power.* New York: Random House, 1966.

———. *The Crippled Giant: American Foreign Policy and Its Domestic Consequences.* New York: Random House, 1972.

———. *Old Myths and New Realities and Other Commentaries.* New York: Random House, 1964.

Gabriel, Ralph Henry. *The Course of American Democratic Thought: An Intellectual History since 1815.* New York: Ronald Press, 1940; rev. ed., 1956.

———. *Traditional Values in American Life.* Prepared for the United States National Commission for UNESCO, N.p., n.d.

Gaddis, John Lewis. "Containment: A Reassessment." *Foreign Affairs* 55 (July 1977): 873–87.

———. *The United States and the Origins of the Cold War, 1941–1947.* New York: Columbia University Press, 1972.

Galbraith, John Kenneth. *The Affluent Society.* Boston: Houghton Mifflin, 1958.

———. *Ambassador's Journal: A Personal Account of the Kennedy Years.* Boston: Houghton Mifflin, 1969.

———. *American Capitalism: The Concept of Countervailing Power.* Boston: Houghton Mifflin, 1952.

———. "Challenges of a Changing World." *Foreign Policy Bulletin* 38 (Dec. 15, 1958): 49–51.

———. "The Decline of American Power." *Esquire,* March 1972, 79–84, 160–63.

———. *Economic Development.* Cambridge: Harvard University Press, 1964.

———. *Economics in Perspective: A Critical History.* Boston: Houghton Mifflin, 1987.

———. "European Recovery: The Longer View." *Review of Politics* 12 (April 1950): 165–74.

———. "Germany Was Badly Run." *Fortune,* December 1945, 173–79, 196–98.

———. *How to Control the Military.* Garden City, N.Y.: Doubleday, 1969.

———. *A Life in Our Times: Memoirs.* Boston: Houghton Mifflin, 1981.

———. *The New Industrial State.* Boston: Houghton Mifflin, 1967.

———. "Rival Economic Theories in India." *Foreign Affairs* 36 (July 1958): 587–96.

———. "The Second Imperial Requiem." *International Security* 7 (Winter 1982/1983): 84–93.

Gallatin, Albert. *Peace with Mexico.* New York: Bartlett & Welford, n.d.

Gardner, John W. "Can We Count on More Dedicated People?" *Life,* June 13, 1960, 98, 100, 109, 111.

Gardner, Lloyd C. *Architects of Illusion: Men and Ideas in American Foreign Policy, 1941–1949.* Chicago: Quadrangle, 1970.

———. *Economic Aspects of New Deal Diplomacy.* Madison: University of Wisconsin Press, 1964.

———. "From New Deal to New Frontiers: 1937–1941." *Studies on the Left* 1 (Fall 1959): 29–43.

Gelber, Lionel. *America in Britain's Place: The Leadership of the West and Anglo-American Unity.* New York: Frederick A. Praeger, 1961.

Ginsberg, Allen. *Collected Poems, 1947–1980.* New York: Harper & Row, 1984.

Ginzberg, Eli. "Is Hard Work Going out of Style?" *U.S. News & World Report,* Aug. 23, 1971, 52–56.

Gladstone, W. E. "Kin beyond Sea." *North American Review* 127 (September–October 1878): 179–212.

Goldman, Eric F. *The Crucial Decade—and After: America, 1945–1960.* New York: Vintage, 1960.

Goldwater, Barry M. *Why Not Victory? A Fresh Look at American Foreign Policy.* New York: McGraw-Hill, 1962.

Goodman, Paul. *The Community of Scholars.* New York: Random House, 1962.

———. *Compulsory Mis-education.* New York: Horizon Press, 1964.

———. *Growing up Absurd: Problems of Youth in the Organized System.* New York: Random House, 1960.

———. *Like a Conquered Province: The Moral Ambiguity of America.* New York: Random House, 1967.

Gorer, Geoffrey. *The American People; A Study in National Character.* New York: Norton, 1948.

Gorter, Wytze. *United States Merchant Marine Policies: Some International Implications. Essays in International Finance,* no. 23. Princeton, N.J.: International Finance Section, Department of Economics and Sociology, Princeton University, 1955.

Goudsmit, Samuel A. *Alsos.* New York: Henry Schuman, 1947.

Graebner, Norman A. *The New Isolationism: A Study in Politics and Foreign Policy since 1950.* New York: Ronald Press, 1956.

Graham, Billy. "Men Must Be Changed before a Nation Can." *Life,* June 6, 1960, 109, 121, 122, 124, 126.

Grant, Madison. *The Passing of the Great Race: Or the Racial Basis of European History.* New York: Scribner's, 1916.

Griffith, Ernest S., John Plamenatz, and J. Roland Pennock. "Cultural Prerequisites to a Successfully Functioning Democracy: A Symposium." *American Political Science Review* 50 (March 1956): 101–37.

Grosvenor, Elsie May Bell. "Safari from Congo to Cairo." *National Geographic* 106 (December 1954): 721–71.

———. "Safari through Changing Africa." *National Geographic* 104 (August 1953): 145–98.

Groves, Leslie R. *Now It Can Be Told: The Story of the Manhattan Project.* New York: Harper & Row, 1962.

Guback, Thomas H. *The International Film Industry: Western Europe and America since 1945.* Bloomington: Indiana University Press, 1969.

Gunther, John. *Inside Asia.* New York: Harper & Brothers, 1939.

———. *Inside Europe.* New York: Harper & Brothers, 1936.

———. *Inside Latin America.* New York: Harper & Brothers, 1941.

———. *Inside U.S.A.* New York: Harper & Brothers, 1947.

Gyorgy, Andrew. *Geopolitics: The New German Science.* Berkeley: University of California Press, 1944.

Hacker, Andrew. *The End of the American Era.* New York: Atheneum, 1970.

Hacker, Louis M. *The Triumph of American Capitalism: The Development of Forces in American History to the End of the Nineteenth Century.* New York: Simon and Schuster, 1940.

Halle, Louis J. *Civilization and Foreign Policy: An Inquiry for Americans.* New York: Harper & Brothers, 1955.

———. *The Cold War as History.* New York: Harper & Row, 1967.

Halperin, Morton H. "The Gaither Committee and the Policy Process." *World Politics* 13 (April 1961): 360–84.

Hammond, Thomas T. "Firsthand Look at the Soviet Union." *National Geographic* 116 (September 1959): 352–407.

Hammond, Thomas T., ed. *Witnesses to the Origins of the Cold War.* Seattle: University of Washington Press, 1982.

Handlin, Oscar. *The Americans: A New History of the People of the United States.* Boston: Little, Brown, 1963.

————. *Chance or Destiny: Turning Points in American History.* Boston: Little, Brown, 1955.

————. *The Distortion of America.* Boston: Little, Brown, 1981.

————. *This Was America: True Accounts of People and Places, Manners and Customs, as Recorded by European Travelers to the Western Shore in the Eighteenth, Nineteenth, and Twentieth Centuries.* Cambridge: Harvard University Press, 1949.

Handlin, Oscar, ed. *American Principles and Issues: The National Purpose.* New York: Holt, Rinehart and Winston, 1961.

Handlin, Oscar, Hans J. Morgenthau, Daniel Callahan, Saul K. Padover, and R. Paul Ramsey. *Dissent, Democracy and Foreign Policy—a Symposium.* Headline Series, no. 190 (August 1968): 3–47.

Hansen, Alvin H. *America's Role in the World Economy.* New York: Norton, 1945.

Haring, Douglas G., ed. *Japan's Prospect.* Cambridge: Harvard University Press, 1946.

Harriman, W. Averell. *America and Russia in a Changing World: A Half Century of Personal Observation.* Garden City, N.Y.: Doubleday, 1971.

Harriman, W. Averell, and Elie Abel. *Special Envoy to Churchill and Stalin, 1941–1946.* New York: Random House, 1975.

Harrington, Michael. *The Other America: Poverty in the United States.* New York: Macmillan, 1962.

Harris, Seymour E. *The European Recovery Program.* Cambridge: Harvard University Press, 1948.

Harris, Seymour E., ed. *Foreign Economic Policy for the United States.* Cambridge: Harvard University Press, 1948.

————. *Postwar Economic Problems.* New York: McGraw-Hill, 1943.

————. *Saving American Capitalism: A Liberal Economic Program.* New York: Knopf, 1948.

Hart, Jeffrey. *When the Going Was Good! American Life in the Fifties.* New York: Crown, 1982.

Hartz, Louis. *The Liberal Tradition in America: An Interpretation of American Political Thought since the Revolution.* New York: Harcourt, Brace & World, 1955.

Harvey, Paul. "There Was a Nation . . . ." *Reader's Digest,* January 1989, 51–53.

Hauser, Philip M., and Conrad Taeuber. "The Changing Population of the United States." *Annals of the American Academy of Political and Social Science* 237 (January 1945): 12–21.

Hayden, Tom. *The American Future: New Visions beyond Old Frontiers.* Boston: South End Press, 1980.

————. *The Love of Possession Is a Disease with Them.* New York: Holt, Rinehart and Winston, 1972.

————. *Rebellion and Repression: Testimony by Tom Hayden before the National Commission on the Causes and Prevention of Violence, and the House Un-American Activities Committee.* New York: World, 1969.

————. *Rebellion in Newark: Official Violence and Ghetto Response.* New York: Random House, 1967.

————. *Reunion: A Memoir.* New York: Random House, 1988.

————. *Trial.* New York: Holt, Rinehart and Winston, 1970.

————. "The Trial." *Ramparts,* July 1970.

Hayes, Carlton J. H. Review of *The World and the West,* by Arnold Toynbee. *American Historical Review* 59 (October 1953): 173.

Heilbroner, Robert L. *The Great Ascent: The Struggle for Economic Development in Our Time.* New York: Harper & Row, 1963.

————. *The Limits of American Capitalism.* New York: Harper & Row, 1966.

————. "Our Foreign Trade Crisis." *Harper's,* November 1947, 385–92.

Heisenberg, W. "Research in Germany on the Technical Application of Atomic Energy." *Nature* 160 (Aug. 16, 1947): 211–15.

Henderson, John W. *The United States Information Agency.* New York: Praeger, 1969.

Henry, Thomas R. "A Tale of Three Cities." *National Geographic* 88 (December 1945): 641–69.

————. "War's Wake in the Rhineland." *National Geographic* 88 (July 1945): 1–32.

Hepburn, Katharine. *The Making of "The African Queen": Or How I Went to Africa with Bogart, Bacall and Huston and Almost Lost My Mind.* New York: Knopf, 1987.

Herberg, Will. *Protestant-Catholic-Jew: An Essay in American Religious Sociology.* Garden City, N.Y.: Doubleday, 1955.

Herdman, John. *Voice without Restraint: A Study of Bob Dylan's Lyrics and Their Background.* New York: Delilah Books, 1981.

Herring, George C. *America's Longest War: The United States and Vietnam, 1950–1975.* New York: John Wiley & Sons, 1979.

Hersey, John. *Hiroshima.* New York: Knopf, 1946.

———. "Hiroshima." *New Yorker,* Aug. 31, 1946, 15–68.

———. "Home to Warsaw." *Life,* April 9, 1945, 16–20.

Herz, John H. *Political Realism and Political Idealism: A Study in Theories and Realities.* Chicago: University of Chicago Press, 1951.

Herz, Martin F. *Beginnings of the Cold War.* Bloomington: Indiana University Press, 1966.

Hewlett, Richard G., and Francis Duncan. *Atomic Shield, 1947/1952.* Vol. 2: *A History of the United States Atomic Energy Commission.* N.p.: U.S. Atomic Energy Commission, 1972.

Hewlett, Richard G., and Oscar E. Anderson, Jr. *The New World, 1939/1946.* Vol. 1: *A History of the United States Atomic Energy Commission.* University Park: Pennsylvania State University Press, 1962.

Higham, John. "Beyond Consensus: The Historian as Moral Critic." *American Historical Review* 67 (April 1962): 609–25.

———. "The Cult of the 'American Consensus.'" *Commentary* 27 (February 1959): 93–100.

Higham, John, ed. *The Reconstruction of American History.* London: Hutchinson, 1962.

Higham, John, and Paul K. Conkin, eds. *New Directions in American Intellectual History.* Baltimore: Johns Hopkins University Press, 1979.

Hirschman, Albert O. *National Power and the Structure of Foreign Trade.* Berkeley: University of California Press, 1945.

Hoffman, Abbie. "America on $0 a Day." *Ramparts,* February 1971, 48–55.

——— [Free]. *Revolution for the Hell of It.* New York: Dial, 1968.

Hoffman, Paul G. *Peace Can Be Won.* Garden City, N.Y.: Doubleday, 1951.

Hofstadter, Richard. *The American Political Tradition: And the Men Who Made It.* New York: Knopf, 1948.

———. *The Paranoid Style in American Politics and Other Essays.* New York: Knopf, 1965.

———. *The Progressive Historians: Turner, Beard, Parrington.* New York: Knopf, 1969.

———. *Social Darwinism in American Thought, 1860–1915.* Philadelphia: University of Pennsylvania Press, 1944.

Hofstadter, Richard, William Miller, and Daniel Aaron. *The United States: The History of a Republic.* Englewood Cliffs, N.J.: Prentice-Hall, 1957.

Hofstadter, Richard, and Seymour Martin Lipset, eds. *Turner and the Sociology of the Frontier.* New York: Basic Books, 1968.

Hofstadter, Richard, and Michael Wallace, eds. *American Violence: A Documentary History.* New York: Knopf, 1970.

Hogan, Pendelton. "Shanghai after the Japs." *Virginia Quarterly Review* 22 (Winter 1946): 91–108.

Holborn, Hajo. *The Political Collapse of Europe.* New York: Knopf, 1951.

Holsti, Ole R., and James N. Rosenau. *American Leadership in World Affairs: Vietnam and the Breakdown of Consensus.* Boston: Allen & Unwin, 1984.

Hopkins, Harry L. "What Victory Will Bring Us." *American Magazine,* January 1944, 20–21, 87–88.

Horowitz, David. *The Free World Colossus: A Critique of American Foreign Policy in the Cold War.* New York: Hill and Wang, 1965.

———. *Empire and Revolution: A Radical Interpretation of Contemporary History.* New York: Random House, 1969.

Horowitz, Irving Louis. "Consensus, Conflict and Cooperation: A Sociological Inventory." *Social Forces* 41 (December 1962): 177–88.

Houghton, Neal D., ed. *Struggle against History: U.S. Foreign Policy in an Age of Revolution.* Introduction by Arnold J. Toynbee. New York: Washington Square Press, 1968.

Hsü, Immanuel C. Y. *The Rise of Modern China.* New York: Oxford University Press, 1970.

Hunt, R. N. Carew. *The Theory and Practice of Communism: An Introduction.* New York: Macmillan, 1951.

Hutchins, Robert M. *The Atomic Bomb Versus Civilization.* The Human Events Pamphlets, no. 1. Washington: Human Events, 1945.

Hutchinson, Paul. "The President's Religious Faith." *Christian Century,* March 24, 1954, 362–69.

Hutton, Graham. *Midwest at Noon.* Chicago: University of Chicago Press, 1946.

Iacocca, Lee. "We're a Colony Again, This Time of Japan." *U.S. News & World Report,* April 16, 1984, 63–64.

Ickes, Harold L. *The Secret Diary of Harold L. Ickes.* 3 vols. New York: Simon and Schuster, 1953–54.

———. "We're Running out of Oil." *American Magazine,* January 1944, 26–27, 84–85.

———. "What the U.S.A. Is Worth." *American Magazine,* August 1943, 30–31, 87–90.

Iklé, Fred Charles. "What It Means to Be Number Two." *Fortune,* November 20, 1978, 72–84.

International Institute for Strategic Studies. *The Military Balance,* 1960–. London: International Institute for Strategic Studies, 1960–.

Iriye, Akira. *Power and Culture: The Japanese-American War, 1941–1945.* Cambridge, Mass.: Harvard University Press, 1981.

Jackman, Robert W. "Political Elites, Mass Publics, and Support for Democratic Principles." *Journal of Politics* 34 (August 1972): 753–73.

Jackson, Robert H. *The Case against the Nazi War Criminals.* New York: Knopf, 1946.

———. *The Nürnberg Case.* New York: Knopf, 1947.

Jacobs, Paul, and Saul Landau. *The New Radicals: A Report with Documents.* New York: Random House, 1966.

Jacobs, W. D. "Where Do the People Live." *Commonweal,* Jan. 18, 1946, 354–55.

James, Preston E. *One World Divided: A Geographer Looks at the Modern World.* Waltham, Mass.: Blaisdell, 1964.

Jeffries, John W. "The 'Quest for National Purpose' of 1960." *American Quarterly* 30 (Fall 1978): 451–70.

Jessup, John K. "A Noble Framework for a Great Debate." *Life,* May 23, 1960, 22–41.

Johnson, Gerald W. "Whose War Aims? The President May State Lofty Ideals But Only the American People Can Make a Lasting Peace." *Life,* Nov. 2, 1942, 96–98, 100–106.

Johnson, James A. "The New Generation of Isolationists." *Foreign Affairs* 49 (October 1970): 136–46.

Johnson, Walter. *The Battle against Isolation.* Chicago: University of Chicago Press, 1944.

Johnston, Eric. "H'wood Still Best U.S. Ambassador Despite Some Contrary Opinions." *Variety,* Jan. 7, 1953, 5, 65.

———. "My Talk with Joseph Stalin." *Reader's Digest,* October 1944, 1–10.

———. *We're All in It.* New York: E. P. Dutton, 1948.

Jonas, Manfred. *Isolationism in America, 1935–1941.* Ithaca, N.Y.: Cornell University Press, 1966.

Jones, Joseph M. *The Fifteen Weeks.* New York: Viking, 1955.

Jouvenel, Bertrand de. *On Power: Its Nature and the History of Its Growth.* New York: Viking, 1949.

Judge, Joseph. "Saturday's Child, Hong Kong." *National Geographic* 140 (October 1971): 540–73.

———. "The Zulus: Black Nation in a Land of Apartheid." *National Geographic* 140 (December 1971): 738–75.

Kaplan, Lawrence S. "Frederick Jackson Turner and Imperialism." *Social Science* 27 (January 1952): 12–16.

Kendrick, John W. *Productivity Trends: Capital and Labor.* National Bureau of Economic Research, Occasional Paper 53, 1956.

Kennan, George F. "America and the Russian Future." *Foreign Affairs* 29 (April 1951): 351–70.

———. *American Diplomacy, 1900–1950.* Chicago: University of Chicago Press, 1951.

———. "Communism in Russian History." *Foreign Affairs* 69 (Winter 1990/1991): 168–86.

———. "George Kennan on Containment Reconsidered." *Foreign Affairs* 56 (April 1978): 643–47.

————. "Let Peace Not Die of Neglect." *New York Times Magazine,* Feb. 25, 1951, 10, 38–41.

————. *Memoirs.* 2 vols. Boston: Little, Brown, 1967–1972.

————. *Realities of American Foreign Policy.* Princeton: N.J.: Princeton University Press, 1954.

————. "The Sources of Soviet Conduct." *Foreign Affairs* 25 (July 1947): 566–82.

Kennedy, Paul. "The (Relative) Decline of America." *Atlantic Monthly,* August 1987, 29–41.

————. *The Rise and Fall of the Great Powers: Economic Change and Military Conflict from 1500 to 2000.* New York: Random House, 1987.

Kennedy, Robert F. *Thirteen Days: A Memoir of the Cuban Missile Crisis.* New York: Norton, 1969.

Key, V. O., Jr. "Public Opinion and the Decay of Democracy." *Virginia Quarterly Review* 37 (Autumn 1961): 481–94.

Killian, James R., Jr. *Sputnik, Scientists, and Eisenhower: A Memoir of the First Special Assistant to the President for Science and Technology.* Cambridge: MIT Press, 1977.

Kindall, Sylvian G. *Total Atomic Defense.* New York: Richard R. Smith, 1952.

Kindleberger, Charles P. *The Dollar Shortage.* New York: Technology Press of MIT and John Wiley & Sons, 1950.

King, Martin Luther, Jr. *Stride toward Freedom: The Montgomery Story.* New York: Harper & Row, 1958.

————. *A Testament of Hope: The Essential Writings of Martin Luther King, Jr.* Ed. James Melvin Washington. San Francisco: Harper & Row, 1986.

————. *The Trumpet of Conscience.* New York: Harper & Row, 1968.

————. *Where Do We Go from Here: Chaos or Community?* New York: Harper & Row, 1967.

————. *Why We Can't Wait.* New York: Harper & Row, 1964.

Kirchwey, Freda. "Luce Thinking." *Nation,* March 1, 1941, 229–30.

Klemmer, Harvey. "Lend-Lease and the Russian Victory." *National Geographic* 88 (October 1945): 499–512.

Kobler, John. *Luce: His Time, Life, and Fortune.* Garden City, N.Y.: Doubleday, 1968.

Kohn, Hans. *American Nationalism: An Interpretative Essay.* New York: Collier, 1961 (orig. 1957).

————. Review of *Civilization on Trial,* by Arnold J. Toynbee. *American Historical Review* 54 (October 1948): 90–91.

Kolko, Gabriel. *The Politics of War: The World and United States Foreign Policy, 1943–1945.* New York: Random House, 1968.

————. *The Roots of American Foreign Policy: An Analysis of Power and Purpose.* Boston: Beacon Press, 1969.

Kolko, Joyce, and Gabriel Kolko. *The Limits of Power: The World and United States Foreign Policy, 1945–1954.* New York: Harper & Row, 1972.

Kramer, Rita. "It's Time to Start Listening." *New York Times Magazine,* Sept. 17, 1967, 80–82, 87, 92.

Kramish, Arnold. *Atomic Energy in the Soviet Union.* Stanford, Calif.: Stanford University Press, 1959.

Krause, Laurence B. "Why Exports Are Becoming Irrelevant." *Foreign Policy,* no. 3 (Summer 1971): 62–70.

Kristof, Nicholas D. "The Rise of China." *Foreign Affairs* 72 (November/December 1993): 59–74.

Kroeber, A. L., ed. *Anthropology Today: An Encyclopedic Inventory.* Chicago: University of Chicago Press, 1953.

Kruzel, Joseph, ed. *American Defense Annual, 1986–1987.* Lexington, Mass.: D. C. Heath, 1986.

Kuklick, Bruce. "Myth and Symbol in American Studies." *American Quarterly* 24 (October 1972): 435–50.

Kuznets, Simon. *Capital in the American Economy: Its Formation and Financing.* Princeton, N.J.: A Study by the National Bureau of Economic Research, Published by Princeton University Press, 1961.

————. *Economic Growth of Nations: Total Output and Production Structure.* Cambridge: Harvard University Press, 1971.

———. *National Income and Its Composition, 1919–1938.* 2 vols. New York: National Bureau of Economic Research, 1941.

———. *National Product in Wartime.* New York: National Bureau of Economic Research, 1945.

———. *National Product: War and Prewar.* Our Economy in War, Occasional Paper 17. New York: National Bureau of Economic Research, 1944.

Lacy, Dan. "The Rôle of American Books Abroad." *Foreign Affairs* 34 (April 1956): 405–17.

La Fay, Howard. "Russia's Window on the West: Leningrad." *National Geographic* 139 (May 1971): 636–73.

LaFeber, Walter. *America, Russia, and the Cold War, 1945–1971.* New York: John Wiley & Sons, 1972 (orig. 1967).

———. *The New Empire: An Interpretation of American Expansion, 1860–1898.* Ithaca, N.Y.: Cornell University Press, 1963.

Laird, Melvin R. "Why Soviet Arms Worry U.S." *U.S. News & World Report,* March 27, 1972, 41–46.

Lane, Arthur Bliss. *I Saw Poland Betrayed: An American Ambassador Reports to the American People.* New York: Bobbs-Merrill, 1948.

Langer, William L., and S. Everett Gleason. *The Challenge to Isolationism, 1937–1940.* New York: Published for the Council on Foreign Relations by Harper & Brothers, 1952.

Lapp, R. E. *Must We Hide?* Cambridge, Mass.: Addison-Wesley, 1949.

———. *The Weapons Culture.* New York: Norton, 1968.

Laqueur, Walter. *Neo-Isolationism and the World of the Seventies.* New York: Library Press, 1972.

Lary, Hal B. *The United States in the World Economy: The International Transactions of the United States during the Interwar Period.* Washington, D.C.: U.S. Government Printing Office, 1943.

Lasswell, Harold D., and Abraham Kaplan. *Power and Society: A Framework for Political Inquiry.* New Haven: Yale University Press, 1950.

Laves, Walter H. C., and Charles A. Thomson. *UNESCO: Purpose Progress Prospects.* Bloomington: Indiana University Press, 1957.

Lazarsfeld, Paul F., Bernard Berelson, and Hazel Gaudet. *The People's Choice: How the Voter Makes up His Mind in a Presidential Campaign.* New York: Columbia University Press, 1948.

Lederer, Ivo J., ed. *Russian Foreign Policy: Essays in Historical Perspective.* New Haven: Yale University Press, 1962.

Lederer, William J., and Eugene Burdick. *The Ugly American.* New York: Norton, 1958.

Leith, C. K., J. W. Furness, and Cleona Lewis. *World Minerals and World Peace.* Washington, D.C.: Brookings Institution, 1943.

LeMay, Curtis E., with Dale O. Smith. *America Is in Danger.* New York: Funk & Wagnalls, 1968.

Lenin, V. I. *Imperialism: The Highest Stage of Capitalism.* New York: International Publishers, 1939.

Lens, Sidney. *The Forging of the American Empire.* New York: Thomas Y. Crowell, 1971.

Leong, Y. S. "Index of the Physical Volume Production of Minerals, 1880–1948." *Journal of the American Statistical Association* 45 (March 1950): 15–29.

Leontief, Wassily, and Faye Duchin. *Military Spending: Facts and Figures, Worldwide Implications and Future Outlook.* New York: Oxford University Press, 1983.

Lerner, Max. *Actions and Passions: Notes on the Multiple Revolution of Our Time.* New York: Simon and Schuster, 1949.

———. *America as a Civilization: Life and Thought in the United States Today.* New York: Simon and Schuster, 1957.

Letiche, J. M. *Reciprocal Trade Agreements in the World Economy.* New York: King's Crown Press, 1948.

Lewis, Edward W. (Ted). *Comes the Revolution.* New York: Arbor House, 1971.

Licklider, Roy E. "The Missile Gap Controversy." *Political Science Quarterly* 85 (December 1970): 600–615.

Life Editors. *The National Purpose.* New York: Holt, Rinehart and Winston, 1960.

Lilienthal, David E. *Atomic Energy: A New Start.* New York: Harper & Row, 1980.

————. *The Journals of David E. Lilienthal,* 1939–81. 7 vols. New York: Harper & Row, 1964–83.

Lindbergh, Charles A. *The Wartime Journals of Charles A. Lindbergh.* New York: Harcourt Brace Jovanovich, 1970.

Linder, Staffan Burenstam. *The Pacific Century: Economic and Political Consequences of Asian-Pacific Dynamism.* Stanford, Calif.: Stanford University Press, 1986.

Lippmann, Walter. "The American Destiny." *Life,* June 5, 1939, 47, 72–73.

————. "Can We Win the Peace?" *Ladies' Home Journal,* January 1944, 22–23.

————. *The Cold War: A Study in U.S. Foreign Policy.* New York: Harper & Brothers, 1947.

————. "The Confrontation." *Foreign Policy Bulletin* 39 (Oct. 15, 1959): 21.

————. "The Confrontation." *New York Herald Tribune,* Sept. 17, 1959, p. 20.

————. "The Country Is Waiting for Another Innovator." *Life,* June 20, 1960, 114, 116, 122, 125.

————. *Essays in the Public Philosophy.* Boston: Little, Brown, 1955.

————. "The Need for Enlightened Business Leadership." In *Two Timely Talks: Addressed to American Business Leaders.* New York: Association of National Advertisers, 1945.

————. *Public Opinion and Foreign Policy in the United States.* London: Allen & Unwin, 1952.

————. *U.S. Foreign Policy: Shield of the Republic.* Boston: Little, Brown, 1943.

————. *U.S. War Aims.* Boston: Little, Brown, 1944.

Lipset, Seymour Martin. *Political Man: The Social Bases of Politics.* Garden City, N.Y.: Doubleday, 1960.

Lodge, Henry Cabot. *The Storm Has Many Eyes: A Personal Narrative.* New York: Norton, 1973.

Lomperis, Timothy J. *The War Everyone Lost—and Won: America's Intervention in Viet Nam's Twin Struggles.* Baton Rouge: Louisiana State University Press, 1984.

London, Herbert I. *Closing the Circle: A Cultural History of the Rock Revolution.* Chicago: Nelson-Hall, 1984.

Long, George W. "Indochina Faces the Dragon." *National Geographic* 102 (September 1952): 287–328.

Long, Michael E. "Baja California's Rugged Outback." *National Geographic* 142 (October 1972): 542–67.

Look Editors. *Look at America: The Country You Know—and Don't Know.* Boston: Houghton Mifflin, 1946.

Lord, Russell. *The Wallaces of Iowa.* Boston: Houghton Mifflin, 1947.

Lowi, Theodore J. *The End of Liberalism: Ideology, Policy, and the Crisis of Public Authority.* New York: Norton, 1969.

————. *The Politics of Disorder.* New York: Basic Books, 1971.

Luce, Henry R. *The American Century.* New York: Farrar & Rinehart, 1941.

————. "The American Century." *Life,* Feb. 17, 1941, 61–65.

————. "The American Century." *Reader's Digest,* April 1941, 45–49.

————. "Food: We Could Eat Less; Other Men and Women and Children are Starving." *Life,* March 24, 1941, 34.

————. *The Ideas of Henry Luce.* Ed. John K. Jessup. New York: Atheneum, 1969.

Ludington, Townsend. *John Dos Passos: A Twentieth-Century Odyssey.* New York: E. P. Dutton, 1980.

Lundberg, Isabel Cary. "World Revolution, American Plan." *Harper's,* December 1948, 38–46.

Lukacs, John. *A New History of the Cold War.* Garden City, N.Y.: Doubleday, 1966.

Luttwak, Edward N. *The Grand Strategy of the Roman Empire: From the First Century A.D. to the Third.* Baltimore: Johns Hopkins University Press, 1976.

Luttwak, Edward N., and Robert L. Bartley. "Is America on the Way Down?" *Commentary,* March 1992, 15–27.

Lynd, Staughton. *Intellectual Origins of American Radicalism.* New York: Pantheon, 1968.

Lynd, Staughton, and Thomas Hayden. *The Other Side.* New York: New American Library, 1966.

MacArthur, Douglas. *Reminiscences.* New York: McGraw-Hill, 1964.

————. *A Soldier Speaks: Public Papers and Speeches of General of the Army Douglas MacArthur.* Ed. Vorin E. Whan, Jr. New York: Praeger, 1965.

McCarthy, Eugene J. *The Limits of Power: America's Role in the World.* New York: Holt, Rinehart and Winston, 1967.

McCarthy, Joseph R. *America's Retreat from Victory: The Story of George Catlett Marshall.* New York: Devin-Adair, 1951.

McClosky, Herbert. "Consensus and Ideology in American Politics." *American Political Science Review* 58 (June 1964): 361–82.

McCloy, John J. "Western Germany's Progress under Marshall Plan." *Department of State Bulletin,* January 14, 1952, 45–46.

Macdonald, Dwight. "The (American) People's Century." *Partisan Review* 9 (July–August 1942): 294–310.

———. *Henry Wallace: The Man and the Myth.* New York: Vanguard Press, 1948.

McDowell, Bart. "Those Successful Japanese." *National Geographic* 145 (March 1974): 322–59.

McGhee, George. "Role of American Business in Germany." *Atlantic Community Quarterly* 4 (Fall 1966): 408–15.

McKelway, St. Clair. "A Reporter with the B-29s." *New Yorker,* June 23, 1945, 26–39.

Mackinder, Halford J. *Democratic Ideals and Reality: A Study in the Politics of Reconstruction.* New York: Holt, 1942 (orig. 1919).

———. *Democratic Ideals and Reality.* Ed. Anthony J. Pearce. New York: Norton, 1962.

———. "The Geographical Pivot of History." *The Geographical Journal* 23 (April 1904): 421–37.

———. "The Round World and the Winning of the Peace." *Foreign Affairs* 21 (July 1943): 595–605.

MacLeish, Archibald. *Collected Poems, 1917–1952.* Boston: Houghton Mifflin, 1952; enlarged ed., 1985.

———. "Colloquy for the States." *Atlantic Monthly,* October 1939, 484–87.

———. *Freedom Is the Right to Choose: An Inquiry into the Battle for the American Future.* Boston: Beacon Press, 1951.

———. "A Great Power—Or a Great People?" *New York Times,* Nov. 19, 1972, sec. 4, p. 11.

———. "We Have Purpose . . . We All Know It." *Life,* May 30, 1960, 86, 88, 93.

McMurry, Ruth Emily, and Muna Lee. *The Cultural Approach: Another Way in International Relations.* Chapel Hill: University of North Carolina Press, 1947.

McNamara, Robert S. *The Essence of Security: Reflections in Office.* New York: Harper & Row, 1968.

MacNeil, Neil. *An American Peace.* New York: Scribner's, 1944.

McNeill, William Hardy. *America, Britain, & Russia: Their Co-operation and Conflict, 1941–1946.* New York: Oxford University Press, 1953.

———. "Mythistory, or Truth, Myth, History, and Historians." *American Historical Review* 91 (February 1986): 1–10.

———. Review of *The Twentieth Century,* by Caroline F. Ware et al. *American Historical Review* 73 (June 1968): 1479–80.

Maddox, Robert James. *The New Left and the Origins of the Cold War.* Princeton, N.J.: Princeton University Press, 1973.

Magruder, Jeb Stuart. *An American Life: One Man's Road to Watergate.* New York: Atheneum, 1974.

Magruder, William M. "For the SST: Why the U.S. Needs It." *U.S. News & World Report,* March 15, 1971, 68.

Marcuse, Herbert. *Counterrevolution and Revolt.* Boston: Beacon Press, 1972.

———. *An Essay on Liberation.* Boston: Beacon Press, 1969.

———. *One-Dimensional Man: Studies in the Ideology of Advanced Industrial Society.* Boston: Beacon Press, 1964.

Markel, Lester, ed. *Public Opinion and Foreign Policy.* New York: Published for the Council on Foreign Relations by Harper & Brothers, 1949.

Markowitz, Norman D. *The Rise and Fall of the People's Century: Henry A. Wallace and American Liberalism, 1941–1948.* New York: Free Press, 1973.

Martin, Harold H. "Biggest City in the World." *Saturday Evening Post,* Dec. 6, 1958, 24–25, 93–94, 96–97.

Marx, Karl. *Capital: A Critique of Political Economy.* 3 vols. New York: International Publishers, 1967.

Mason, Edward S. *Controlling World Trade: Cartels and Commodity Agreements.* New York: McGraw-Hill, 1946.

Masters, Dexter, and Katharine Way, eds. *One World or None.* N.p.: McGraw-Hill, 1946.

Masur, Gerhard. Review of *Toynbee's Approach to World Politics,* by Henry L. Mason. *American Historical Review* 65 (April 1960): 650–51.

Mather, Kirtley F. *Enough and to Spare: Mother Earth Can Nourish Every Man in Freedom.* New York: Harper & Brothers, 1944.

——. "Petroleum—Today and Tomorrow." *Science,* Dec. 19, 1947, 603–9.

Matusow, Allen J. *The Unraveling of America: A History of Liberalism in the 1960s.* New York: Harper & Row, 1984.

Maurois, André. *From My Journal.* Trans. Joan Charles. New York: Harper & Brothers, 1948.

May, Ernest R. *Imperial Democracy: The Emergence of America as a Great Power.* New York: Harcourt, Brace & World, 1961.

Mead, Margaret. *And Keep Your Powder Dry: An Anthropologist Looks at America.* New York: Morrow, 1942.

Meadows, Donella H., Dennis L., Meadows, Jørgen Randers, and William W. Behrens III. *The Limits to Growth: A Report for the Club of Rome's Project on the Predicament of Mankind.* New York: Universe Books, 1972.

Melman, Seymour. "The Butter That's Traded off for Guns." *New York Times,* April 22, 1985, A19.

——. *Our Depleted Society.* New York: Holt, Rinehart and Winston, 1965.

——. *Pentagon Capitalism: The Political Economy of War.* New York: McGraw-Hill, 1970.

——. *Profits without Production.* New York: Knopf, 1983.

Merk, Frederick. *Manifest Destiny and Mission in American History: A Reinterpretation.* New York: Knopf, 1963.

Merton, Robert K., Leonard Broom, and Leonard S. Cottrell, Jr., eds. *Sociology Today: Problems and Prospects.* New York: Basic Books, 1959.

Mikesell, Raymond F. *Foreign Exchange in the Postwar World.* New York: Twentieth Century Fund, 1954.

Miller, G. William. "Federal Reserve Chief's Blueprint for Prosperity." *U.S. News & World Report,* June 19, 1978, 72.

Miller, Henry. *The Air-Conditioned Nightmare.* 2 vols. New York: New Directions, 1945–47.

Millett, Kate. *Sexual Politics.* Garden City, N.Y.: Doubleday, 1970.

Mills, C. Wright. "Bounteous New Man." Review of *People of Plenty: Economic Abundance and the American Character,* by David M. Potter. *Saturday Review,* July 16, 1955, 19.

——. *The Causes of World War Three.* New York: Simon and Schuster, 1958.

——. "Letter to the New Left." *New Left Review,* no. 5 (September–October 1960): 18–23.

——. *The New Men of Power: America's Labor Leaders.* New York: Harcourt, Brace, 1948.

——. *The Power Elite.* New York: Oxford University Press, 1956.

——. *Power, Politics and People: The Collected Essays of C. Wright Mills.* Ed. Irving Louis Horowitz. New York: Oxford University Press, 1963.

——. *White Collar: The American Middle Classes.* New York: Oxford University Press, 1951.

Mines, Samuel. *The Last Days of Mankind: Ecological Survival or Extinction.* New York: Simon and Schuster, 1971.

Molotov, V. M. *Problems of Foreign Policy: Speeches and Statements, April 1945–November 1948.* Moscow: Foreign Languages Publishing House, 1949.

Moore, W. Robert. "Britain Tackles the East African Bush." *National Geographic* 97 (March 1950): 311–51.

——. "Busy Corner—the Cape of Good Hope." *National Geographic* 82 (August 1942): 197–223.

————. "The Cities That Gold and Diamonds Built." *National Geographic* 82 (December 1942): 735–66.

————. "White Magic in the Belgian Congo." *National Geographic* 101 (March 1952): 321–62.

Morgan, Robin, ed. *Sisterhood Is Powerful: An Anthology of Writings from the Women's Liberation Movement.* New York: Random House, 1970.

Morgenthau, Hans J. "The Decline of American Power." *New Republic,* Dec. 9, 1957, 10–14.

————. *The Impasse of American Foreign Policy.* Chicago: University of Chicago Press, 1962.

————. *In Defense of the National Interest: A Critical Examination of American Foreign Policy.* New York: Knopf, 1952.

————. *A New Foreign Policy for the United States.* New York: Published for the Council on Foreign Relations by Praeger, 1969.

————. "The Pathology of American Power." *International Security* 1 (Winter 1977): 3–20.

————. *Politics among Nations: The Struggle for Power and Peace.* New York: Knopf, 1948; 2d ed., 1954; 3d ed., 1960; 4th ed., 1967; 5th ed., 1973.

————. *The Purpose of American Politics.* New York: Knopf, 1960.

————. *Scientific Man vs. Power Politics.* Chicago: University of Chicago Press, 1946.

————. *Truth and Power: Essays of a Decade, 1960–70.* New York: Praeger, 1970.

Morgenthau, Henry, Jr. "Bretton Woods and International Coöperation." *Foreign Affairs* 23 (January 1945): 182–94.

Morison, Samuel Eliot, and Henry Steele Commager. *The Growth of the American Republic.* 2 vols. New York: Oxford University Press, 1950.

Morita, Akio. "Sometimes a Problem Is Overexaggerated." *U.S. News & World Report,* July 29, 1985, 51–52.

Morley, Felix. "For What Are We Fighting?" *Saturday Evening Post,* April 18, 1942, 9–10, 40–43.

Moss, Norman. *Men Who Play God: The Story of the H-Bomb and How the World Came to Live with It.* New York: Harper & Row, 1968.

Moynihan, Daniel Patrick, and James R. Schlesinger. "Debunking the Myth of Decline." *New York Times Magazine,* June 19, 1988, 34–36, 52–53.

Murphy, Robert. *Diplomat among Warriors.* Garden City, N.Y.: Doubleday, 1964.

Murrow, Edward R. *This Is London.* Ed. Elmer Davis. New York: Simon and Schuster, 1941.

Nagel, Paul C. *This Sacred Trust: American Nationality, 1798–1898.* New York: Oxford University Press, 1971.

Neils, Patricia. *China Images in the Life and Times of Henry Luce.* Savage, Md.: Rowman & Littlefield, 1990.

Neumann, Sigmund. "Fashions in Space." *Foreign Affairs* 21 (January 1943): 276–88.

Neumann, William L. *After Victory: Churchill, Roosevelt, Stalin and the Making of the Peace.* New York: Harper & Row, 1967.

Nevins, Allan. "America in 1947—and After." *Virginia Quarterly Review* 24 (Winter 1948): 140–48.

Niebuhr, Reinhold. "American Pride and Power." *American Scholar* 17 (Autumn 1948): 393–94.

————. *Christian Realism and Political Problems.* New York: Scribner's, 1953.

————. *Christianity and Power Politics.* New York: Scribner's, 1940.

————. *Discerning the Signs of the Times: Sermons for Today and Tomorrow.* New York: Scribner's, 1946.

————. *Does Civilization Need Religion? A Study in the Social Resources and Limitations of Religion in Modern Life.* New York: Macmillan, 1927.

————. *Faith and History: A Comparison of Christian and Modern Views of History.* New York: Scribner's, 1949.

————. "The Illusion of World Government." *Foreign Affairs* 27 (April 1949): 379–88.

————. *The Irony of American History.* New York: Scribner's, 1952.

————. "Is There a Revival of Religion?" *New York Times Magazine,* Nov. 19, 1950, 13, 60–63.

————. "Toward New Intra-Christian Endeavors." *Christian Century,* Dec. 31, 1969, 1662–67.

Ninkovich, Frank A. *The Diplomacy of Ideas: U.S. Foreign Policy and Cultural Relations, 1938–1950.* Cambridge: Cambridge University Press, 1981.

Nishina, Yoshio. "A Japanese Scientist Describes the Destruction of His Cyclotrons." *Bulletin of the Atomic Scientists* 3 (June 1947): 145, 167.

O'Connor, John E., and Martin A. Jackson, eds. *American History/American Film: Interpreting the Hollywood Image.* New York: Frederick Ungar, 1979.

Ogburn, William Fielding, ed. *Technology and International Relations.* Chicago: University of Chicago Press, 1949.

Olcott, Charles S. *The Life of William McKinley.* 2 vols. Boston: Houghton Mifflin, 1916.

Oppenheimer, J. Robert. "International Control of Atomic Energy." *Foreign Affairs* 26 (January 1948): 239–52.

Osgood, Robert E. *Alliances and American Foreign Policy.* Baltimore: Johns Hopkins University Press, 1968.

———. *Ideals and Self-Interest in America's Foreign Relations: The Great Transformation of the Twentieth Century.* Chicago: University of Chicago Press, 1953.

———. *Limited War: The Challenge to American Strategy.* Chicago: University of Chicago Press, 1957.

O'Sullivan, J.L. "Annexation." *United States Magazine, and Democratic Review,* July and August 1845, 5–10.

Packard, George R. "The Coming U.S.-Japan Crisis." *Foreign Affairs* 66 (Winter 1987/88): 348–67.

Padover, Saul K. "The American Century?" *American Scholar* 17 (Winter 1947–48): 85–90.

Palmer, C. B. "The Building of S.S. United States." *New York Times Magazine,* March 30, 1952, 14–15, 28–30.

Pan Am Corporation. *Annual Report,* 1985. New York, n.d.

Pargellis, Stanley, ed. *The Quest for Political Unity in World History.* Washington, D.C.: U.S. Government Printing Office, 1944.

Parkes, Henry Bamford. *The American Experience: An Interpretation of the History and Civilization of the American People.* New York: Knopf, 1947.

Parsons, Talcott. *Sociological Theory and Modern Society.* New York: Free Press, 1967.

Paterson, Thomas G. *On Every Front: The Making of the Cold War.* New York: Norton, 1979.

Paterson, Thomas G., ed. *Kennedy's Quest for Victory: American Foreign Policy, 1961–1963.* New York: Oxford University Press, 1989.

Peale, Norman Vincent. *The Power of Positive Thinking.* New York: Prentice-Hall, 1952.

Pells, Richard H. *The Liberal Mind in a Conservative Age: American Intellectuals in the 1940s and 1950s.* New York: Harper & Row, 1985.

Perry, Ralph Barton. *Characteristically American.* New York: Knopf, 1949.

Peterson, Peter G. "America: Still the Top Producer, But . . .: Interview with Peter G. Peterson, Assistant to the President for International Economic Affairs." *U.S. News & World Report,* July 12, 1971, 34–37.

Pfeffer, Richard M., ed. *No More Vietnams? The War and the Future of American Foreign Policy.* New York: Published for the Adlai Stevenson Institute of International Affairs by Harper & Row, 1968.

Phillips, Thomas R. "The Growing Missile Gap." *Reporter,* Jan. 8, 1959, 10–16.

Pope-Hennessy, James. *America Is an Atmosphere.* London: Home & Van Thal, 1947.

Potter, David M. "Between Two Worlds." Review of *The Affluent Society,* by John Kenneth Galbraith. *Saturday Review,* June 7, 1958, 31–32.

———. *History and American Society: Essays of David M. Potter.* Ed. Don E. Fehrenbacher. New York: Oxford University Press, 1973.

———. *People of Plenty: Economic Abundance and the American Character.* Chicago: University of Chicago Press, 1954.

Powell, Ralph L. "Everyone a Soldier: The Communist Chinese Militia." *Foreign Affairs* 39 (October 1960): 100–111.

Power, Thomas S., with Albert A. Arnhym. *Design for Survival.* New York: Coward-McCann, 1965.

Powers, H. H. "The War as a Suggestion of Manifest Destiny." *Annals of the American Academy of Political and Social Science* 12 (September 1898): 173–92.

Pratt, Julius W. *Expansionists of 1898: The Acquisition of Hawaii and the Spanish Islands.* Baltimore: Johns Hopkins University Press, 1936.

———. "John L. O'Sullivan and Manifest Destiny." *New York History* 14 (July 1933): 213–34.

———. "The 'Large Policy' of 1898." *Mississippi Valley Historical Review* 19 (September 1932): 219–42.

———. "The Origin of 'Manifest Destiny.'" *American Historical Review* 32 (July 1927): 795–98.

Prendergast, Curtis, with Geoffrey Colvin. *The World of Time Inc.: The Intimate History of a Changing Enterprise.* Vol. 3, 1960–1980. New York: Atheneum, 1986.

Prestowitz, Clyde V., Jr. *Trading Places: How We Allowed Japan to Take the Lead.* New York: Basic Books, 1988.

Price, Harry Byard. *The Marshall Plan and Its Meaning.* Ithaca, N.Y.: Cornell University Press, 1955.

Price, Willard. "The Thames Mirrors England's Varied Life." *National Geographic* 114 (July 1958): 45–93.

Prothro, James W., and Charles M. Grigg. "Fundamental Principles of Democracy: Bases of Agreement and Disagreement." *Journal of Politics* 22 (May 1960): 276–94.

Putnam, John J. "Yesterday's Congo, Today's Zaire." *National Geographic* 143 (March 1973): 398–432.

Quester, George H. *American Foreign Policy: The Lost Consensus.* New York: Praeger, 1982.

Radin, Max. "Justice at Nuremberg." *Foreign Affairs* 24 (April 1946): 369–84.

Ramo, Simon. *America's Technology Slip.* New York: John Wiley and Sons, 1980.

Range, Willard. *Franklin D. Roosevelt's World Order.* Athens: University of Georgia Press, 1959.

Ravitch, Diane, and Chester E. Finn, Jr. *What Do Our 17-Year-Olds Know? A Report on the First National Assessment of History and Literature.* New York: Harper & Row, 1987.

Reed, David. "Asia's Four Little Dragons." *Reader's Digest,* September 1986, 131–35.

Reich, Charles A. *The Greening of America.* New York: Random House, 1970.

Reischauer, Edwin O. "The Broken Dialogue with Japan." *Foreign Affairs* 39 (October 1960): 11–26.

Renner, George T. "Maps for a New World." *Collier's,* June 6, 1942, 14–16, 28.

Reston, James B. *Prelude to Victory.* New York: Knopf, 1942.

Reuther, Walter P. "A Sense of National Purpose." *Business Topics,* Spring 1964, 15–20.

Riesman, David. *Abundance for What? And Other Essays.* Garden City, N.Y.: Doubleday, 1964.

Riesman, David, with Reuel Denney and Nathan Glazer. *The Lonely Crowd: A Study of the Changing American Character.* New Haven: Yale University Press, 1950; rev. ed., 1970.

Rienow, Robert, and Leona Train Rienow. *Moment in the Sun: A Report on the Deteriorating Quality of the American Environment.* New York: Dial Press, 1967.

Roberts, Cecil. *And So to America.* Garden City, N.Y.: Doubleday, 1947.

Roberts, Chalmers M. *First Rough Draft: A Journalist's Journal of Our Times.* New York: Praeger, 1973.

Roberts, Henry L., and Paul A. Wilson. *Britain and the United States: Problems in Cooperation.* New York: Published for the Council on Foreign Relations by Harper & Brothers, 1953.

Roche, James M. "American Business Is Plainly in Trouble." *U.S. News & World Report,* April 12, 1971, 91–93.

Rockefeller, Nelson A. "Need for Expanding Use of U.S. Books Overseas." *Department of State Bulletin,* Oct. 17, 1955, 616.

Rockefeller Brothers Fund. *Prospect for America: The Rockefeller Panel Reports.* Garden City, N.Y.: Doubleday, 1961.

Rodnick, David. *Postwar Germans: An Anthropologist's Account.* New Haven: Yale University Press, 1948.

Roelofs, H. Mark. *Ideology and Myth in American Politics: A Critique of a National Political Mind.* Boston: Little, Brown, 1976.

Rose, Sanford. "U.S. Foreign Trade: There's No Need to Panic." *Fortune,* August 1971, 108–11, 186–89.

Rosecrance, Richard, ed. *America as an Ordinary Country: U.S. Foreign Policy and the Future.* Ithaca, N.Y.: Cornell University Press, 1976.

Rosenau, James N., and Ole R. Holsti. "U.S. Leadership in a Shrinking World: The Breakdown of Consensus and the Emergence of Conflicting Belief Systems." *World Politics* 35 (April 1983): 368–92.

Rosenberg, Emily S. *Spreading the American Dream: American Economic and Cultural Expansion, 1890–1945.* New York: Hill and Wang, 1982.

Rossiter, Clinton. *Conservatism in America.* New York: Knopf, 1955.

———. *Seedtime of the Republic: The Origin of the American Tradition of Political Liberty.* New York: Harcourt, Brace, 1953.

———. "We Must Show the Way to Enduring Peace." *Life,* June 13, 1960, 99, 112, 115, 116, 118.

Roskin, Michael. "What 'New Isolationism'?" *Foreign Policy,* no. 6 (Spring 1972): 118–27.

Rostow, Eugene V. "The Great Transition." *Fortune,* January 1945, 142–44, 179–83.

Rostow, W. W. *The Process of Economic Growth.* New York: Norton, 1952.

———. "Book Review Essay: Beware of Historians Bearing False Analogies." *Foreign Affairs* 66 (Spring 1988): 863–68.

———. *The Stages of Economic Growth: A Non-Communist Manifesto.* Cambridge: Cambridge University Press, 1960.

Roszak, Theodore. *The Making of a Counter Culture: Reflections on the Technocratic Society and Its Youthful Opposition.* Garden City, N.Y.: Doubleday, 1969.

Rowe, David Nelson. *China among the Powers.* New York: Harcourt, Brace, 1945.

Rubin, Jerry. *Do It: Scenarios of the Revolution.* New York: Simon and Schuster, 1970.

———. *Growing (up) at Thirty-Seven.* New York: M. Evans, 1976.

Rubin, Ronald I. *The Objectives of the U.S. Information Agency: Controversies and Analysis.* New York: Praeger, 1966.

Russell, Bertrand. *Power: A New Social Analysis.* New York: Norton, 1938.

Russell, Ruth B. *United Nations Experience with Military Forces: Political and Legal Aspects.* Washington, D.C.: Brookings Institution, 1964.

Salisbury, Harrison E. "Stand by for a Billion Iacoccas." *U.S. News & World Report,* Feb. 8, 1988, 30.

Salzman, Mark. *Iron & Silk.* New York: Random House, 1986.

Samuels, Gertrude. "Passage to Freedom in Viet Nam." *National Geographic* 107 (June 1955): 858–74.

Samuelson, Paul A. "At Last, Devaluation." *New York Times,* Aug. 18, 1971, 37.

———. *Economics.* New York: McGraw-Hill, 1948: 2d ed., 1951; 7th ed., 1967; 9th ed., 1973; 10th ed., 1976.

Sanford, Charles L. *The Quest for Paradise: Europe and the American Moral Imagination.* Urbana: University of Illinois Press, 1961.

Sarnoff, David. "Turn the Cold War Tide in America's Favor." *Life,* June 6, 1960, 108, 110, 117, 118.

———. *Program for a Political Offensive against World Communism.* N.p., 1955.

Scherman, Harry. "The Last Best Hope of Earth." *Atlantic Monthly,* November 1941, 567–74.

———. "The Last Best Hope of Earth." *Reader's Digest,* December 1941, 107–11.

Schiller, Herbert I. *Mass Communications and American Empire.* New York: Augustus M. Kelley, 1969.

Schlesinger, Arthur M. *Paths to the Present.* New York: Macmillan, 1949.

Schlesinger, Arthur M., Jr. *The Age of Jackson.* Boston: Little, Brown, 1945.

———. *The Bitter Heritage: Vietnam and American Democracy, 1941–1966.* Boston: Houghton Mifflin, 1967.

———. *The Crisis of Confidence: Ideas, Power and Violence in America.* Boston: Houghton Mifflin, 1969.

———. *The Crisis of the Old Order, 1919–1933*. The Age of Roosevelt. Boston: Houghton Mifflin, 1957.

———. *The Disuniting of America*. New York: Norton, 1992.

———. "Origins of the Cold War." *Foreign Affairs* 46 (October 1967): 22–52.

———. Review of *The American Political Tradition and the Men Who Made It*, by Richard Hoftstadter. *American Historical Review* 54 (April 1949): 612–13.

———. *A Thousand Days: John F. Kennedy in the White House*. Boston: Houghton Mifflin, 1965.

———. *The Vital Center: The Politics of Freedom*. Boston: Houghton Mifflin, 1949.

Schmeisser, Peter. "Is America in Decline?" *New York Times Magazine*, April 17, 1988, 24–27, 66–68, 96.

Scholz, Karl. "Need We Fear Russia's Economic Strength?" *Social Science* 27 (January 1952): 3–7.

Schorske, Carl E. "The Dilemma in Germany." *Virginia Quarterly Review* 24 (Winter 1948): 29–42.

Schriever, Bernard A. "'1960—Best Year We've Had in the Missile Business.'" *U.S. News & World Report*, Jan 23, 1961, 69–71.

Schuman, Frederick L. *The Commonwealth of Man: An Inquiry into Power Politics and World Government*. New York: Knopf, 1952.

———. "International Ideals and the National Interest." *Annals of the American Academy of Political and Social Science* 280 (March 1952): 27–36.

Schurz, Carl. "Manifest Destiny." *Harper's New Monthly Magazine*, October 1893, 737–46.

Schwab, George, ed. *United States Foreign Policy at the Crossroads*. Westport, Conn.: Greenwood Press, 1982.

Schwarz, Solomon M. "How Much Oil Has Russia?" *Foreign Affairs* 24 (July 1946): 736–41.

Seabury, Paul. *The Rise and Decline of the Cold War*. New York: Basic Books, 1967.

Seligman, Ben B. *Economics of Dissent*. Chicago: Quandrangle, 1968.

Servan-Schreiber, J.-J. *The American Challenge*. With a Foreword by Arthur Schlesinger, Jr. New York: Atheneum, 1968.

Sewell, James P. *UNESCO and World Politics: Engaging in International Relations*. Princeton, N.J.: Princeton University Press, 1975.

Sharp, Paul F. "Three Frontiers: Some Comparative Studies of Canadian, American, and Australian Settlement." *Pacific Historical Review* 24 (November 1955): 369–77.

Sherwood, Robert E. "The Front Line Is in Our Hearts." *Ladies' Home Journal*, August 1941, 21, 103–4.

Shor, Franc. "The City They Call Red China's Showcase." *National Geographic* 118 (August 1960): 192–223.

———. "Japan: The Exquisite Enigma." *National Geographic* 118 (December 1960): 733–79.

———. "Life under Shellfire on Quemoy." *National Geographic* 115 (March 1959): 414–38.

Shotwell, James T. "After the War." *International Conciliation*, no. 376 (January 1942): 31–35.

Shreve, Forrest. "The Saguaro, Cactus Camel of Arizona." *National Geographic* 88 (December 1945): 695–704.

Shuster, George N. *UNESCO: Assessment and Promise*. New York: Published for the Council on Foreign Relations by Harper & Row, 1963.

Simpich, Frederick. "Grass Makes Wyoming Fat." *National Geographic* 88 (August 1945): 153–88.

———. "Louisiana Trades with the World." *National Geographic* 92 (December 1947): 705–38.

———. "More Water for California's Great Central Valley." *National Geographic* 90 (November 1946): 645–64.

———. "South Dakota Keeps Its West Wild." *National Geographic* 91 (May 1947): 555–88.

Simpich, Frederick, Jr. "Changing Formosa, Green Island of Refuge." *National Geographic* 111 (March 1957): 327–64.

Sivard, Ruth Leger. *World Military and Social Expenditures, 1978*. Leesburg, Va.: WMSE Publications, 1978.

Slichter, Sumner H. "Foreign Trade and Postwar Stability." *Foreign Affairs* 21 (July 1943): 674–89.

Slomich, Sidney J. *The American Nightmare*. New York: Macmillan, 1971.

Smith, Adam. *The Wealth of Nations.* 2 vols. New York: Everyman's Library, 1910.

Smith, Henry Nash. Review of *The Course of American Democratic Thought,* by Ralph Henry Gabriel. *Mississippi Valley Historical Review* 43 (December 1956): 468–69.

———. *Virgin Land: The American West as Symbol and Myth.* Cambridge: Harvard University Press, 1950.

Smith, Howard K. *The State of Europe.* New York: Knopf, 1949.

Smith, R. Harris. *OSS: The Secret History of America's First Central Intelligence Agency.* Berkeley: University of California Press, 1972.

Smith, Walter Bedell. *My Three Years in Moscow.* Philadelphia: Lippincott, 1950.

Smyser, William Leon. "São Tomé, the Chocolate Island." *National Geographic* 89 (May 1946): 657–80.

Sorensen, Theodore C. *Decision-Making in the White House: The Olive Branch or the Arrows.* New York: Columbia University Press, 1963.

———. *Kennedy.* New York: Harper & Row, 1965.

Spiro, Herbert J. *A New Foreign Policy Consensus?* The Washington Papers, no. 64. Published for the Center for Strategic and International Studies. Georgetown University. Beverly Hills: Sage Publications, 1979.

Sprout, Harold, and Margaret Sprout. "Command of the Atlantic Ocean." *Encyclopaedia Britannica,* 1945 ed. Chicago: Encyclopaedia Britannica, 1945, 2:637.

———. *Toward a New Order of Sea Power: American Naval Policy and the World Scene, 1918–1922.* Princeton, N.J.: Princeton University Press, 1943.

Sprout, Harold, and Margaret Sprout, eds. *Foundations of National Power.* Princeton, N.J.: Princeton University Press, 1945; 2d ed., New York: Van Nostrand, 1951.

Spykman, Nicholas John. *America's Strategy in World Politics: The United States and the Balance of Power.* New York: Harcourt, Brace, 1942.

———. *The Geography of the Peace.* New York: Harcourt, Brace, 1944.

Staley, Eugene. *World Economy in Transition: Technology vs. Politics, Laissez Faire vs. Planning, Power vs. Welfare.* New York: Council on Foreign Relations, 1939.

Stassen, Harold E. "Stalin at Midnight." *Ladies' Home Journal,* July 1947, 36–37, 116–21.

Steel, Ronald. "A Spheres of Influence Policy." *Foreign Policy,* no. 5 (Winter 1971–72): 107–18.

Stein, Gunther. *The World the Dollar Built.* New York: Monthly Review Press, 1953.

Stephens, Oren. *Facts to a Candid World: America's Overseas Information Program.* Stanford, Calif.: Stanford University Press, 1955.

Stevenson, Adlai. "Extend Our Vision . . . to All Mankind." *Life,* May 30, 1960, 87, 94, 97, 99, 100, 102.

Stoddard, Lothrop. "Racial Realities in Europe." *Saturday Evening Post,* March 22, 1924, 14–15, 156–58.

———. *The Rising Tide of Color against White World-Supremacy.* Introduction by Madison Grant. New York: Scribner's, 1927.

Strausz-Hupé, Robert. *Geopolitics: The Struggle for Space and Power.* New York: G. P. Putnam's Sons, 1942.

Streit, Clarence K. *Union Now: A Proposal for a Federal Union of the Democracies of the North Atlantic.* New York: Harper & Brothers, 1939.

———. *Union Now with Britain.* New York: Harper & Brothers, 1941.

Stromberg, Roland N. *Collective Security and American Foreign Policy: From the League of Nations to NATO.* New York: Praeger, 1963.

Strong, Josiah. *Our Country: Its Possible Future and Its Present Crisis.* New York: Baker & Taylor, 1885.

Sumner, William Graham. *Essays of William Graham Sumner.* Ed. Albert Galloway Keller and Maurice R. Davie. 2 vols. New Haven: Yale University Press, 1934.

Swanberg, W. A. *Luce and His Empire.* New York: Scribner's, 1972.

Swerdlow, Amy. *Women Strike for Peace: Traditional Motherhood and Radical Politics in the 1960s.* Chicago: University of Chicago Press, 1993.

Taft, Robert A. *A Foreign Policy for Americans.* Garden City, N.Y.: Doubleday, 1951.

————. "Senator Taft's Peace Program." *New York Times Magazine,* Feb. 6, 1944, 8, 34–35.

Terrill, Ross. "Sichuan: Where China Changes Course." *National Geographic* 168 (September 1985): 280–317.

Textor, Robert B. *Cultural Frontiers of the Peace Corps.* Cambridge: MIT Press, 1966.

Theobald, Robert. *The Challenge of Abundance.* New York: Potter, 1961.

————. *The Economics of Abundance: A Non-Inflationary Future.* New York: Pitman, 1970.

————. *Free Men and Free Markets.* New York: Potter, 1963.

————. *Habit and Habitat.* Englewood Cliffs, N.J.: Prentice-Hall, 1972.

————. *The Rich and the Poor.* New York: Potter, 1960.

Thomas, Norman. "How to Fight for Democracy." *Annals of the American Academy of Political and Social Science* 216 (July 1941): 58–64.

Thomas, Tony. *Hollywood and the American Image.* Westport, Conn.: Arlington House, 1981.

Thompson, Dorothy. "A War for What?" *Ladies' Home Journal,* May 1943, 6, 158–59.

Thompson, Kenneth W. *Political Realism and the Crisis of World Politics: An American Approach to Foreign Policy.* Princeton, N.J.: Princeton University Press, 1960.

Thompson, Kristin. *Exporting Entertainment: America in the World Film Market, 1907–34.* London: BFI, 1985.

Thomson, Charles A. H. *Overseas Information Service of the United States Government.* Washington, D.C.: Brookings Institution, 1948.

Thomson, Charles A. H., and Walter H. C. Laves. *Cultural Relations and U.S. Foreign Policy.* Bloomington: Indiana University Press, 1963.

Tillich, Paul. *The Protestant Era.* Chicago: University of Chicago Press, 1948.

Tocqueville, Alexis de. *Democracy in America.* 2 vols. New York: Knopf, 1945.

Tolchin, Martin, and Susan Tolchin. *Buying into America: How Foreign Money Is Changing the Face of Our Nation.* New York: Times Books, 1988.

Topping, Audrey. "Return to Changing China." *National Geographic* 140 (December 1971): 800–833.

Toynbee, Arnold J. *America and the World Revolution and Other Lectures.* New York: Oxford University Press, 1962.

————. *Civilization on Trial.* New York: Oxford University Press, 1948.

————. "Encounters between Civilizations." *Harper's,* April 1947, 289–94.

————. "Hippie Revolt on War." *San Francisco Chronicle,* May 18, 1967, 1, 18.

————. "The Present Point in History." *Foreign Affairs* 26 (October 1947): 187–95.

————. *A Study of History.* 11 vols. New York: Oxford University Press, 1934–59.

————. *A Study of History.* 2 vols. Abridged by D. C. Somervell. New York: Oxford University Press, 1947 and 1957.

Toynbee, Arnold, and Max Lerner. "Is There an American Civilization, Distinct from Europe's?" *Western World,* December 1958, 29–39.

Toynbee, Arnold, Max Lerner, and others. "Is America a Civilization?" *Shenandoah* 10 (Autumn 1958): 3–45.

Tripp, Brenda M. H. "UNESCO in Perspective." *International Conciliation,* no. 497 (March 1954): 323–83.

Trippe, Juan. *Foreign Trade in the Air Age.* Address delivered in New York City, October 28, 1943. N.p.

————. *Ocean Air Transport.* London: Delivered before the Royal Aeronautical Society, 1941.

Tucker, Robert W. *A New Isolationism: Threat or Promise?* New York: Universe Books, 1972.

————. *The Radical Left and American Foreign Policy.* Baltimore: Johns Hopkins University Press, 1971.

Turner, Frederick Jackson. "The Character and Influence of the Indian Trade in Wisconsin: A Study of the Trading Post as an Institution." *Johns Hopkins University Studies in Historical and Political Science,* 9th ser., 11–12. Baltimore: Johns Hopkins University Press, 1891.

————. *The Early Writings of Frederick Jackson Turner.* Madison: University of Wisconsin Press, 1938.

————. *The Frontier in American History.* New York: Holt, 1921.

Turner, Ralph. "Technology and Geopolitics." *Military Affairs* 7 (Spring 1943): 5–15.

Twining, Nathan F. *Neither Liberty Nor Safety: A Hard Look at U.S. Military Policy and Strategy.* New York: Holt, Rinehart and Winston, 1966.

Udall, Stewart L. *The Quiet Crisis.* New York: Holt, Rinehart and Winston, 1963.

Unger, Irwin. *The Movement: A History of the American New Left, 1959–1972.* New York: Dodd, Mead, 1975.

———. "The 'New Left' and American History: Some Recent Trends in United States Historiography." *American Historical Review* 72 (July 1967): 1237–63.

Unger, Irwin, ed. *Beyond Liberalism: The New Left Views American History.* Waltham, Mass.: Xerox College Publishing, 1971.

University of Chicago. "Death of the Comintern." *University of Chicago Round Table,* no. 272, June 6, 1943. Chicago: University of Chicago, 1943.

———. "Russia's Foreign Policy." *University of Chicago Round Table,* no. 286, Sept. 12, 1943. Chicago: University of Chicago, 1943.

University of Michigan, Surrey Research Center. *Four Americans Discuss Aid to Europe: Illustrative Interviews from National Survey,* Study no. 18. Ann Arbor, Mich.: University of Michigan, 1947.

Van Doren, Carl. *The Great Rehearsal: The Story of the Making and Ratifying of the Constitution of the United States.* New York: Viking, 1948.

Vandenberg, Arthur H. *The Private Papers of Senator Vandenberg.* Ed. Arthur H. Vandenberg, Jr. Boston: Houghton Mifflin, 1952.

Vogel, Ezra F. " 'Copy the Japanese' But 'Do It the American Way.' " *U.S. News & World Report,* Sept. 2, 1985, 45.

———. *Japan as Number One: Lessons for America.* Cambridge: Harvard University Press, 1979.

———. "Pax Nipponica?" *Foreign Affairs* 64 (Spring 1986): 752–67.

Von Karman, Theodore. *Where We Stand: A Report Prepared for the AAF Scientific Advisory Group.* Wright Field, Dayton, Ohio: Headquarters Air Materiel Command, 1946.

Vosburgh, Frederick G. "This Is My Own." *National Geographic* 89 (January 1946): 113–28.

Wagner, Linda W. *Dos Passos: Artist as American.* Austin: University of Texas Press, 1979.

Walker, Howell. "Aroostook County, Maine, Source of Potatoes." *National Geographic* 94 (October 1948): 459–78.

Wallace, Henry. "Beyond the Atlantic Charter." *New Republic,* Nov. 23, 1942, 667–69.

———. *The Century of the Common Man.* Ed. Russell Lord. New York: Reynal & Hitchcock, 1943.

———. *Democracy Reborn.* Ed. Russell Lord. New York: Reynal & Hitchcock, 1944.

———. *Our Job in the Pacific.* New York: American Council, Institute of Pacific Relations, 1944.

———. *The Price of Free World Victory.* New York: L. B. Fischer, 1942.

———. "The Price of Free World Victory." *Free World,* June 1942, 9–13.

———. "The Price of Free World Victory: The Century of the Common Man." *Vital Speeches of the Day,* June 1, 1942, 482–85.

———. *The Price of Vision: The Diary of Henry A. Wallace, 1942–1946.* Ed. John Morton Blum. Boston: Houghton Mifflin, 1973.

———. *Sixty Million Jobs.* New York: Simon and Schuster, 1945.

———. *Soviet Asia Mission.* New York: Reynal & Hitchcock, 1946.

———. *Toward World Peace.* New York: Reynal & Hitchcock, 1948.

———. "Wallace Defines 'American Fascism.' " *New York Times Magazine,* April 9, 1944, 7, 34–35.

———. "The Way to Abundance." Review of *The Tennessee Valley Authority,* by David E. Lilienthal. *New Republic,* March 27, 1944, 414–16.

———. "We Must Save Free Enterprise." *Saturday Evening Post,* Oct. 23, 1943, 12–13, 51–54.

———. "What We Will Get out of the War." *American Magazine,* March 1943, 22–23, 98–104.

———. "Where I Was Wrong." *This Week Magazine,* Sept. 7, 1952, 7, 39, 46.

Walker, J. Samuel. *Henry A. Wallace and American Foreign Policy.* Westport, Conn.: Greenwood Press, 1976.

Walton, Richard J. *Henry Wallace, Harry Truman, and the Cold War.* New York: Viking Press, 1976.

Walzer, Michael. "The Young Radicals: A Symposium." *Dissent* 9 (Spring 1962): 129–63.

Wanger, Walter. "OWI and Motion Pictures." *Public Opinion Quarterly* 7 (Spring 1943): 100–110.

Ward, Barbara. "Britain in the Shadow." *Harper's,* November 1947, 392–401.

Ward, John William. *Andrew Jackson: Symbol for an Age.* New York: Oxford University Press, 1955.

Ware, Caroline F., K. M. Panikkar, and J. M. Romein. *The Twentieth Century.* Vol. 6: *History of Mankind: Cultural and Scientific Development.* New York: Published for the International Commission for a History of the Scientific and Cultural Development of Mankind by Harper & Row, 1966.

Webb, Robert K. "Britain Faces Prosperity." *Foreign Policy Bulletin* 39 (Sept. 1, 1960): 189–91.

Weigert, Hans W. *Generals and Geographers: The Twilight of Geopolitics.* New York: Oxford University Press, 1942.

———. "Haushofer and the Pacific." *Foreign Affairs* 20 (July 1942): 732–42.

Weigert, Hans W., and Vilhjalmur Stefansson, eds. *Compass of the World: A Symposium on Political Geography.* New York: Macmillan, 1944.

Weigert, Hans W., Vilhjalmur Stefansson, and Richard Edes Harrison, eds. *New Compass of the World: A Symposium on Political Geography.* New York: Macmillan, 1949.

Weinberg, Albert K. *Manifest Destiny: A Study of Nationalist Expansionism in American History.* Baltimore: Johns Hopkins University Press, 1935.

Welles, Sumner. *The Time for Decision.* New York: Harper & Brothers, 1944.

White, Donald W. "The 'American Century' in World History." *Journal of World History* 3 (Spring 1992): 105–27.

———. "History and American Internationalism: The Formulation from the Past after World War II." *Pacific Historical Review* 58 (May 1989): 145–72.

———. "'It's a Big Country': A Portrait of the American Landscape after World War II." *Journal of the West* 26 (January 1987): 80–86.

———. "The Nature of World Power in American History: An Evaluation at the End of World War II." *Diplomatic History* 11 (Summer 1987): 181–202.

White, Peter T. "Hanoi: The Capital Today." *National Geographic* 176 (November 1989): 558–93.

———. "Laos." *National Geographic* 171 (June 1987): 772–95.

———. "A Little Humanity Amid the Horrors of War." *National Geographic* 170 (November 1986): 646–79.

———. "Saigon: Fourteen Years After." *National Geographic* 176 (November 1989): 604–21.

White, Theodore H. "The Danger from Japan." *New York Times Magazine,* July 28, 1985, 18–23, 31–43, 57–59.

———. *Fire in the Ashes: Europe in Mid-Century.* New York: William Sloane Associates, 1953.

———. "For President Kennedy: An Epilogue." *Life,* Dec. 6, 1963, 158–59.

———. *In Search of History: A Personal Adventure.* New York: Harper & Row, 1978.

White, Theodore H., and Annalee Jacoby. *Thunder out of China.* New York: William Sloane Associates, 1946.

White, W. L. *Report on the Russians.* New York: Harcourt, Brace, 1945.

Whittlesey, Derwent. *The Earth and the State: A Study of Political Geography.* New York: Holt, 1944 (orig. 1939).

Whitton, John B., ed. *The Second Chance: America and the Peace.* Princeton, N.J.: Princeton University Press, 1944.

Whyte, William H., Jr. *The Organization Man.* New York: Simon and Schuster, 1956.

Wilcox, Clair. *A Charter for World Trade.* New York: Macmillan, 1949.

Williams, John H. "The British Crisis." *Foreign Affairs* 28 (October 1949): 1–17.

———. "Currency Stabilization: American and British Attitudes." *Foreign Affairs* 22 (January 1944): 233–47.

———. "Currency Stabilization: The Keynes and White Plans." *Foreign Affairs* 21 (July 1943): 645–58.

———. "End of the Marshall Plan." *Foreign Affairs* 30 (July 1952): 593–611.

Williams, William Appleman. *America Confronts a Revolutionary World: 1776–1976.* New York: Morrow, 1976.

———. "American Century: 1941–1957." *Nation,* Nov. 2, 1957, 297–301.

———. "The Frontier Thesis and American Foreign Policy." *Pacific Historical Review* 24 (November 1955): 379–95.

———. *The Roots of the Modern American Empire: A Study of the Growth and Shaping of Social Consciousness in a Marketplace Society.* New York: Random House, 1969.

———. *The Tragedy of American Diplomacy.* Cleveland: World, 1959; rev. eds., 1962, 1972.

Willkie, Wendell L. *One World.* New York: Simon and Schuster, 1943.

———. "One World." *Life,* April 26, 1943, 73–81.

———. "Our Reservoir of World Respect and Hope." *Vital Speeches of the Day,* Nov. 1, 1942, 34–39.

———. "We Must Work with Russia—Willkie." *New York Times Magazine,* Jan. 17, 1943, 5, 25.

Winant, John Gilbert. *Letter from Grosvenor Square: An Account of a Stewardship.* Boston: Houghton Mifflin, 1947.

Winfield, Gerald F. "China's Basic Problems." *Foreign Policy Reports* 25 (March 15, 1949): 2–5.

———. "This Is China: Portrait of a Nation." *New York Times Magazine,* Jan. 9, 1949, 8–9, 12–13.

Wirth, Louis. "Consensus and Mass Communication." *American Sociological Review* 13 (February 1948): 1–15.

Wohl, Paul. "Transport in the Development of Soviet Policy." *Foreign Affairs* 24 (April 1946): 466–83.

Wohlstetter, Albert. "The Delicate Balance of Terror." *Foreign Affairs* 37 (January 1959): 211–34.

———. "A Purpose Hammered out of Reflection and Choice." *Life,* June 20, 1960, 115, 126, 128, 131, 133, 134.

Wood, Michael. *America in the Movies, or "Santa Maria, It Had Slipped My Mind."* New York: Basic Books, 1975.

Wriston, Henry M. *Diplomacy in a Democracy.* New York: Harper & Brothers, 1956.

Yank Editors. *The Best from Yank: The Army Weekly.* New York: Dutton, 1945.

Yank Staff, eds. *Yank—The GI Story of the War.* Ed. Debs Myers, Jonathan Kilbourn, and Richard Harritz. New York: Duell, Sloan and Pearce, 1947.

Yergin, Daniel. *Shattered Peace: The Origins of the Cold War and the National Security State.* Boston: Houghton Mifflin, 1977.

York, Herbert F. "In Space, It's Russia; In Weapons, 'U.S. Is Catching up Fast.'" *U.S. News & World Report,* Sept. 28, 1959, 64–66.

Zincke, F. Barham. *Last Winter in the United States: Being Table Talk Collected during a Tour through the Late Southern Confederation, the Far West, the Rocky Mountains, &c.* London: John Murray, 1868.

Zinn, Howard. *SNCC: The New Abolitionists.* Boston: Beacon Press, 1965.

Zurcher, Arnold J., and Richmond Page, eds. *America's Place in the World Economy.* New York: Institute on Postwar Reconstruction, New York University, 1945.

INDEX

Abu Dhabi, 416

Acheson, Dean: on communist expansionism, 105, 254–55; on decline, 422; on democracy, 255; establishes defensive frontier, 19; and foreign aid, 200; on free world unity, 254–55; on hometown America, 128–29; on industrial basis of power, 55; on Korea, 257; McCarthy accuses, 108; on national character, 65; on NATO, 255; on nuclear weapons, 63, 261–62; on popular music, 223; on replacing the European world order, 29, 30; on Soviet-American conflict in Germany, 35; on trade, 184, 185

Adams, Brooks, 113, 114–15

Adams, Herbert Baxter, 113, 117

Adams, John, 22

Aden, 30

Advertising, 136, 145, 236

Affluence. *See* Prosperity

Afghanistan, 208, 219, 408

Africa: American perceptions of, 36–37, 415; and Civil Rights movement, 328, 329, 330, 331–32; Japanese in, 411–12; Marshall Plan, 204; World War II in, 36. *See also* particular countries

African Queen, The, 227

Aid, foreign: and alliances, 255; in American ideologies, 11, 189–90, 196, 330; and American wealth, 189, 190–91; benefits to U.S., 204, 206, 210; as charity, 189–90, 330; consensus for, 190, 193–94, 197, 199, 207, 269, 282–83; cost of, 203, 207–8, 281, 401; to counter communism, 196, 197, 199, 200, 202, 206, 207–8, 219, 254, 288; as enlightened self-interest, 191, 193–94, 201–2, 433; ethnocentric tendencies, 209; food, 190, 193–98, 208; and foreign policy, 191, 200, 209–10; humanitarian, 193, 194, 200, 203, 209, 433; imperialistic, 191, 198; inflationary, 203; international aid organizations, 193–98, 209–10; lend-lease, 82, 166, 168, 176, 191–93, 210; medical, 208; military, 192, 197, 204, 257, 288; New Left criticism, 318; for political stability, 196, 197, 198–99, 200, 201–2, 206; and productivity, 57–58, 193–94, 206, 210; public opinion, 192–94, 203, 283, 433; recipients' attitudes, 209–10, 219; rejection of, 401; repayment of debts, 192–93; technological, 205–8; U.S. insists on unilateral, 195–98, 207, 209–10, 270, 436; during World War II, 191–93; to recover from World War II, 191, 193–205, 210; worldwide, 205–10. *See also* Marshall Plan; Peace Corps; Point Four; United Nations Relief and Rehabilitation Administration (UNRRA)

Air Force, U.S., 58, 60–62, 370

Air travel, 57, 162, 170–71, 233–34, 389, 390

Aksyonov, Vassily, 224, 230

Alaska, 49, 115

Albania, 103

Algeria, 57

All Quiet on the Western Front, 228

Allen, George, 240–41

Alliances: America's world role, 269, 270, 283, 287, 299; continuous commitment, 19–20; danger of war, 247, 248, 256; decline of, 404; of developing nations, 415–16; and foreign aid, 255; public opinion, 249; U.S.-led, 253–57, 299, 404, 434; unstable, 271. *See also* ANZUS pact; Baghdad Pact; Central Treaty Organization (CENTO); North Atlantic Treaty Organization (NATO); Southeast Asia Treaty Organization (SEATO)

531

534 Index

Character, American (*continued*)
377–80; and public policy, 79; technological, 68, 69, 388, 390, 418; "Ugly
American," 281–82; in World War II,
66, 67, 68–70; work ethic, 386–87. *See
also* Morale
Chiang Kai-shek, 40, 41, 42, 247, 289
Childs, Marquis W., 115
Chile, 51, 133, 176
China: aid to, 200, 210; American culture in,
227, 229, 417–18; American images of,
40–42, 286–87, 412–14; American interests in, 200; American support of, 19;
and Century of the Common Man, 10–
11; colonialism in, 41; communist revolution, 19, 41–42, 108, 210, 257, 286,
425; Cultural Revolution, 412; economic growth, 412–15; geographic
expanse, 50; as a great power, 40, 247,
414–15, 419; in historical cycle of
power, 114, 119; investment in, 173;
Korean War, 267; military, 60; nuclear
weapons, 287, 414; Open Door policy,
316; population, 40, 42, 53, 287, 413;
production in, 173, 287; and race, 330;
relations with U.S., 414; standard of living, 57, 173, 413; and Taiwan, 289–90;
threatens Japan, 289; trade, 165, 413; in
United Nations, 249, 414; U.S. troops
in, 257; World War II, 40, 75, 196. *See
also* Taiwan
China, Republic of. *See* Taiwan
Christian Science Monitor, 93
Churchill, Winston, 18, 31, 34, 40, 95, 218,
244–45, 247, 253
Civil Rights movement, 321, 328–32, 334,
354
Civil War, American, 363
Clay, Lucius, 33, 34
Clayton, William L., 195, 200–201
Cliburn, Van, 224
Clough, Shepard B., 56
Cochrane, Edward, 169
Cold War: anticommunist, 89; consensus,
312, 315; end of, 408–9, 428, 434; fear
of "hot war," 105, 321; and foreign aid,
198; militarism, 306, 321; myths of, 8,
14, 427–28; responsibility for, 107, 319.
See also Soviet Union; Soviet-American
relations
Collier's, 263–64
Colonialism: American, 2, 4, 49; America re-
jects, 80, 206; and Anglo-American

union, 246; collapse of European empires, 32, 36; European expansion, 29,
36–37; and racism, 331–32; Vietnam
War, 359. *See also* Empires; Frontier;
Imperialism
Columbia, 133, 208, 259
Comic books, 221, 222
Commager, Henry Steele, 67, 68–70, 122,
377–78
Common Market, 205, 293, 297, 404–7
Communism: American affluence undercuts,
220–21; American tolerance for, 105–6;
European, encouraged by postwar problems, 196, 202; expansionist, 102–5, 109,
258, 283, 286, 296; free world unified
against, 254–55; international conspiracy, 258, 277, 286, 326; public opinion
polls, 98, 99, 103; relatively unproductive, 254–55; religion under, 102; single-
party system, 99; totalitarian, 96, 99,
102, 104–5; and the United Nations,
252; in the U.S., 108, 310; versus fascism, 77, 98, 124. *See also* Anticommunism; Soviet Union
Compton, Arthur, 54
Condliffe, John, 164, 179
Congress of Vienna, 29
Connally, John, 396, 397
Consensus: for American preeminence, 279;
among allies, 255; anticolonial, 243; anticommunism, 89–90, 107, 109–10,
148, 257, 315, 321; class differences,
148; complacent, 332, 380–81; counterconsensus, 362, 365, 423; decline perceived, 341–43, 374–75; definition,
142–43, 155, 157, 461 n2; democratic,
76, 79, 85, 142–43, 245, 315; dissent
from, 151–52, 157, 309, 310, 312–16,
319, 321, 332–35, 339; economics,
143–47; feminist critique of, 327–28;
foreign aid, 190, 193–94, 197, 199, 207,
269, 282–83; foreign policy, 76–77,
253, 307, 313, 333; fragmentation, 324,
335, 356, 367–68, 423–24, 430, 431;
free trade, 167, 168; hardening of, 308,
333, 334, 348, 430; historiography,
122–26, 155, 235, 356–57; imperialism
versus self-determination, 245, 269; for
international cooperation, 234, 248–49;
internationalism, 76–77, 78, 79–80, 85,
89, 93, 110, 143, 279, 308, 421, 429;
Korean War, 258; and the land, 127; loss
of confidence, 276; McCarthy threatens,